PLANT NAMES A·Z

The complete guide to using the correct plant names

Karen Platt
compiler of the Seed Search

Published by Karen Platt

D0100831

This first edition of Plant Names A-Z is dedicated to Bel Amri Mokhtar Ben Hmida, to Joshua and to my Mother.

British Library Cataloguing in publication Data.
A Catalogue record of this book is available from the British Library.

ISBN 0 9528810 3 9

First Edition: January 1999

Written, Edited, Typeset and Published by:
Karen Platt
35 Longfield Rd
Crookes
Sheffield
S10 1QW
www.seedsearch.demon.co.uk

Cover Design:
Alan Coventry Design
Sheffield
Tel: 0114 234 6708
www.ac-design.demon.co.uk

TABLE OF CONTENTS

Preface - First Edition

This is the first edition of Plant Names I have compiled and published. Whilst compiling the Seed Search for the last three years I have found that most plant name changes are being ignored by the people who matter. Seed suppliers list seeds by synonyms and often list the same seed twice under different names. This leads to confusion and is extremely misleading to the consumer.

There does not exist any other book where you can check the correct name for plants including annuals, cacti and vegetables, in an easy to use format where you can see each synonym at a glance with the correct botanical name by its side.

So, I have gathered information on synonyms and also on common names which are used in many seed catalogues and, in my opinion, lead to even greater confusion. There are over 8,000 synonyms in use, that's 8,000 seeds and plants incorrectly labelled.

Plant families have also been included as a necessary part of the book. It is interesting to view plants as a family which share the same characteristics.

I have listed some of the botanical terms and given their meanings. Furthermore, gardening has a language all of its own and there is a horticultural dictionary included too. I recently read an article about a new system of plant classification by DNA 'finger printing'. It has a long way to go and there is talk of it taking twenty years for the system to be adopted. In the meantime, I hope that the people who matter - growers, seed suppliers, nursery staff, garden centre managers will all embrace the existing method of nomenclature and the many changes which occur each year and label seeds and plants correctly. If labels are changed accordingly the names are soon learned. The most annoying thing is when plant names are changed and then change back again as has happened once or twice.

Botanical names are the only universally recognised system.

There is only one correct botanical name for each plant, so please let's use it. I feel it is important for the consumer to know exactly what it is they are buying and that the retailer of seeds and plants has a duty to ensure their stock is labelled correctly.

Nomenclature

Throughout Plant Names, I have endeavoured to follow the Rules of Nomenclature set out in the International Code of Botanical Nomenclature 1994 (ICBN) and the International Code of Nomenclature for Cultivated Plants 1995 (ICNCP).

Some cultivar names are rendered invalid, often with no alternative, most are not listed as yet. This refers to cultivar names which are wholly or partly in Latin, which the code has not allowed since 1959. It also applies to cultivars using a Latin generic name -Viola 'Gazania'.

A cultivar is defined by the Code as 'Distinct, uniform and stable'. This excludes many seed-raised plants which are often included in the cultivar name. These are better known

by cultivar-group names. However, the ICNP has stated that after 1 January 1996 a group name shall only be valid if it has appeared previously in published form with a description or reference to a previously published description. Hybrids appear normally without quotation marks which denote a cultivar.

Where plant names are originated in foreign languages (other than English) they are given in their correct name and they should not be sold under translations. See Article 28 of the 1995 ICNCP. It is considered that many of the German names and English translations of Coreopsis may just be synonyms. The Code sets out that the translations of any name should not be represented in the same font, I have set them in the same font here as I am asking you to totally disregard translations and they are only given to enable you to put the correct name to your plants.

There is also considerable debate still ensuing from the 1994 ICBN on the correct spellings of latinized names, I will include these when the interpretation of these is perfectly clear and not liable to be changed further.

Hyphenation is permitted by the Code to divide separate words such as novi-belgii, but not after a 'compounding form' such as albo.

Other changes will no doubt follow and shall be included in future editions. I am committed to providing an easy-to-use refence for correct names. I am not responsible for any of the name changes and in some degree wish botanists would leave plant naming more stable. However, I shall bring future changes to you when they occur.

Families and Genera

Families and genera used in Plant Names are almost always those given in Brummit's Vascular Plant Families and Genera. You may find other sources which disagree.

Botanical Naming

Family names are a group of genera which share similar characteristics. Botanists differ in opinion on the number of families, there are between 350 and 500 families altogether.

Genera defines a group of plants, which are sub-divided into species.

The ICBN require the rank of each infraspecific botanical epithet to be given. If the genus is mentioned a subsequent time, it is abbreviated to a single letter. This is the practice followed in Plant Names A-Z.

In the binomial system devised by Linnaeus the first half on the name is the genus, the second part being the species. The gender of the species must agree with that of the genus. Furthermore, species can be broken down into subspecies, varietas and forma. Cultivars are designated by the use of single quotation marks. This is one area of plant naming which is widely abused.

Subspecies is a term used to denote a marked difference from the type of a species. A variety less markedly so. Forma is used when the species differs only in one characteristic .

The correct way to write a plant name using the above system is Genus first, beginning with upper case, followed by the species name in lower case e.g. Abies procera.

Cultivar names appear in single quotation marks, beginning with upper case letters as in Abies korena 'Flava'. If the cultivar name consists of more than one word, they both begin with upper case letters.

The exception to this is Japanese names such as Prunus 'Beni-no-dora' where the first part only is in upper case. Some cultivars are correctly named with the species, others without it.

Author citations

In some cases the same species name has been used by two or more authors for quite different plants. These may be entirely different species, and the author name is therefore given separated from the species by a hyphen.

Avoiding the pitfalls

Some of the most common errors are in incorrectly labelling subspecies as cultivars, or varietas as cultivars, so check this carefully.

The use of alba is widespread and many plants labelled as such are labelled incorrectly. The same situation applies to variegata.

The biggest problem I encounter in my work is the widespread use of synonyms which I wholeheartedly discourage. They form the first and for me the most important section of the book.

The use of common names is also still very widespread and confusing.

Another trap is the actual spelling, double check if you are unsure. Watch for caerulea and coerulea, thibetica and tibetica, nepaulensis and napaulensis to mention just a few, as well as suffixes such as -oides and ioides. All are correct, you need to make sure you are using the correct spelling for the species.

NOTES ON SYNONYMS

Synonyms occur mainly because a plant has changed its name. Botanists re-classify plants since we now know more about plants than when Linnaeus originally classified them. There is often more than one synonym in existence for a given plant.

Genus and species can change. Spelling of the species can change as the original genus may have been masculine and the new genus feminine, or vice versa. If we are going to know our plants we have to disregard synonyms and embrace any changes in nomenclature.

I find plants and seeds listed by two different names in catalogues as if they are two different plants. The unsuspecting consumer may purchase these as two different plants. Far better for us to get our plant labelling right . Compiling the Seed Search, I have found seed listed three times in one catalogue, under three different names. Furthermore, I have found catalogues which list the synonym as if it is the botanical name, with the botanical name given in brackets as if it is the synonym. I have never yet found a catalogue with the correct names running all the way through.This leads to a great deal of confusion which I hope Plant Names A-Z will help to solve.

Every supplier has a duty to use the correct name for what is being sold on to the consumer. True, the names change, and it is frustrating, but we have a right to know what we are buying.

I have tried to make the synonym section as comprehensive as possible, and I hope you find it a useful and accurate source. The time to re-label your plants is now.

ON COMMON NAMES

I would like to see these eliminated from catalogues and labelling. There are catalogues which give botanical names for most plants, only to insert the odd common name, such as Marigold and Nasturtium. Why the sudden reversion?

However, I admit to finding common names simply fascinating, but I do believe they should be like nicknames and confined to more or less personal use between friends. The reason for this is that, fascinating though they are, plant names are local. You can use a plant name in Yorkshire and it might mean a totally different plant in Cornwall. Again, they are used world-wide and I have included here some German, South African, American and Australian common names as well as those used here in England

I sometimes feel frustrated when people use common names, as I am not sure we are talking about the same plant.

True, some people would think you were being a snob if you used a botanical name, but it is the only way we can make sure we are talking about the same thing.

In addition, some plants have a myriad of common names, Arum maculatum has been recorded as having 90 common names.

Many common names are disappearing altogether , and I would not like that to happen, they should be kept alive in conversation and recorded locally or in a register.

They reveal aspects which are not found in the botanical names and are therefore an important part of our plant heritage. Common names can tell us about habitat, the flowering time of the plant, scent or a likeness.

I have mainly concentrated on the plants available as seed in the Seed Search, but am now broadening my scope for the next edition, when this section will blossom. There are over 11,000 listed here.

NOTES ON FAMILIES

Knowledge of families will deepen your understanding of the plant kingdom and how plants are related to one another.

They are not often included in books on gardening and are not included in the binomial system of plant naming.

I have included over 300 families with the particular genus given with the family it belongs to.

Those not verified are marked with an asterisk.

NOTES ON VEGETABLES

Vegetables are nearly always given in common name and this is the method I followed in the Seed Search. The botanical name lists given here should prove useful, although I have only ever come across a handful of catalogues which list vegetables by their botanical name. This section also includes herbs and fruit.

NOTES ON LATIN

The majority of botanical names are of latin origin. If you do not know any latin you will find this section useful as it explains the meaning of the species. E.g. scandens means climbing, so it tells us about the habit of any plant with that name.

As with common names, the botanical name can tell us about the habit, the habitat, people or places and a whole host of other things including colour. I often hear people say common names tell you nothing about the plant or , on the other hand, botanical names tell you nothing about the plant, but as you can see, they both do.

DICTIONARY

Last of all, as gardening has its own language I thought it extremely useful to include here a horticultural dictionary. All the terms in common usage are included here, including some specialised terms. I hope you find the definitions of some use. There are also references to botanical names in this section.

HOW TO USE THIS BOOK

The text is arranged alphabetically in each section.

In the synonyms section, the synonym is given first, the correct botanical name in the right hand column. Take note that the name is often more than one line long, in particular with cultivars.

In the common-botanical section, the common name is given first, the botanical name is given in the right hand column. Check with the synonyms first.

In the Family names section, the genus is given first, with the family name in the right hand column.

In the vegetable, herb and fruit section, the common name is given first with the botancal name in the right hand column.

In the explanation of latin terms, the latin is given first, with the meaning in English in the right hand column.

Last of all, in the dictionary, the horticultural term is given first, with the meaning in the right hand column.

Disclaimer

As the compiler and editor of Plant Names I have taken every care, in the time available, to check all the information included in this edition. Sometimes, it is impossible to check a plant name because there is no existing reference. Nevertheless, in a work of this nature, containing many thousands of records, errors and omissions are likely to occur. The compiler and editor of Plant Names cannot be held responsibile for any consequences arising from any such errors.

Please let me know if you do find any errors, so that I may correct them for the next edition.

Abbreviations

h	of gardens
f	forma
n.r.	nomen rejiciendum
	a name to be rejected
ssp	subspecies
sp	species
spp	species plural
v	varietas

If, by my efforts, I can clear up some of the confusion which surrounds plant names, then I will have achieved my aim. I hope you will find Plant Names a comprehensive and accurate source book.

Synonyms

Abelia rupestris h	A. x grandiflora
Abelia rupestris -Lindley	A. chinensis
Abelia x grandiflora 'Aurea'	A. x grandiflora 'Goldsport'
Abelia x grandiflora 'Gold Strike'	A. x grandiflora 'Goldsport'
Abelia x grandiflora 'Variegata'	A. x grandiflora 'Francis Mason'
Abies brachyphylla dwarf	A. homolepis 'Prostrata'
Abies cephalonica 'Nana'	A. cephalonica 'Meyer's Dwarf'
Abies concolor 'Candicans'	A. concolor 'Argentea'
Abies concolor 'Glauca'	A. concolor 'Violacea'
Abies concolor 'Glauca Compacta'	A. concolor 'Compacta'
Abies concolor 'Hillier Broom'	A. concolor 'Hillier's Dwarf'
Abies delavayi v delavayi Fabri Group	A. fabri
Abies delavayi v delavayi 'Nana Headfort'	A. fargesii 'Headfort'
Abies ernesti	A. recurvata v ernestii
Abies forrestii	A. delavayi v smithii
Abies koreana 'Aurea'	A. koreana 'Flava'
Abies koreana 'Prostrata'	A. koreana 'Prostrate Beauty'
Abies marocana	A. pinsapo v marocana
Abies nobilis	A. procera
Abies pectinata	A. alba
Abies procera 'Compacta'	A. procera 'Prostrata'
Abies sutchuenensis	A. fargesii
Abies venusta	A. bracteata
Abromeitiella chlorantha	A. brevifolia
Abutilon globosum	A. x hybridum
Abutilon 'Louise de Marignac'	A. 'Louis Marignac'
Abutilon striatum h	A. pictum
Abutilon x hybridum 'Savitzii'	A. 'Savitzii'
Acacia armata	A. paradoxa
Acacia cyanophylla	A. saligna
Acacia julibrissin	Albizia julibrissin
Acacia juniperina	A. ulicifolia
Acacia polybotrya h	A. glaucocarpa
Acacia sentis	A. victoriae
Acaena adscendens h	A. magellanica ssp magellanica
Acaena adscendens Margery Fish	A. affinis
Acaena adscendens -Vahl	A. magellanica ssp laevigata
Acaena anserinifolia h	A. novae-zelandiae
Acaena caerulea	A. caesiiglauca
Acaena glaucophylla	A. magellanica ssp magellanica
Acaena microphylla Copper Carpet	A. microphylla 'Kupferteppich'
Acaena microphylla 'Glauca'	A. caesiiglauca
Acaena pallida 'Pewter'	A. saccaticupula 'Blue Haze'
Acaena profundeincisa	A. anserinifolia Druce
Acaena 'Purple Carpet'	A. microphylla 'Kupferteppich'
Acaena sanguisorbae -Linnaeus	A. anserinifolia -Druce
Acaena viridior	A. anserinifolia -Druce
Acalypha pendula	A. reptans
Acanthocalycium aurantiacum	Echinopsis thionantha
Acanthocalycium violaceum	Echinopsis spiniflora
Acanthocalyx	Morina

Acantholimon androsaceum	A. ulicinum
Acanthopanax	Eleutherococcus
Acanthopanax ricinifolius	Kalopanax septemlobus
Acanthophoenix crinita	A. rubra
Acanthus balcanicus	A. hungaricus
Acanthus longifolius	A. hungaricus
Acanthus spinosissimus	A. spinosus Spinosissimus Group
Acer buergerianum 'Integrifolium'	A. buergerianum 'Subintegrum'
Acer caesium ssp giraldii	A. giraldii
Acer campbellii ssp sinense	A. sinense
Acer campbellii ssp wilsonii	A. wilsonii
Acer capillipes v morifolium	A. morifolium
Acer cappadocicum v mono	A. mono
Acer catalpifolium	A. longipes ssp catalpifolium
Acer cinnamomifolium	A. coriaceifolium
Acer creticum	A. sempervirens
Acer dasycarpum	A. saccharinum
Acer davidii 'Silver Vein'	A. x conspicuum 'Silver Vein'
Acer 'Dissectum'	A. palmatum v dissectum
Acer flabellatum	A. campbellii ssp flabellatum
Acer fulvescens	A. longipes
Acer ginnala	A. tataricum ssp ginnala
Acer globosum	A. platanoides 'Globosum'
Acer grandidentatum	A. saccharum ssp grandidentatum
Acer japonicum 'Aureum'	A. shirasawanum 'Aureum'
Acer japonicum 'Ezo-no-momiji'	A. shirasawanum 'Ezo-no-momiji'
Acer japonicum f microphyllum	A. shirasawanum 'Microphyllum'
Acer japonicum 'Filicifolium'	A. japonicum 'Aconitifolium'
Acer japonicum 'Laciniatum'	A. japonicum 'Aconitifolium'
Acer japonicum 'Ogurayama'	A. shirasawanum 'Ogurayama'
Acer kawakamii	A. caudatifolium
Acer lobelii -Bunge	A. turkestanicum
Acer mono v tricuspis	A. cappadocicum ssp sinicum v tricaudatum
Acer morrisonense	A. caudatifolium
Acer negundo 'Argenteovariegatum'	A. negundo 'Variegatum'
Acer negundo 'Elegantissimum'	A. negundo 'Elegans'
Acer nikoense	A. maximowiczianum
Acer orientale	A. sempervirens
Acer palmatum 'Akaji-nishiki'	A. truncatum 'Ajaki-nishiki'
Acer palmatum 'Aoshime-no-uchi'	A. palmatum 'Shinobugaoka'
Acer palmatum 'Beni-shigitatsusawa'	A. palmatum 'Aka Shigitatsusawa'
Acer palmatum 'Bonfire'	A. truncatum 'Ajaki-nishiki'
Acer palmatum 'Carminium'	A. palmatum 'Corallinum'
Acer palmatum 'Chishio'	A. palmatum 'Shishio'
Acer palmatum 'Chishio Improved'	A. palmatum 'Shishio'
Acer palmatum 'Effegi'	A. palmatum 'Fireglow'
Acer palmatum 'Ever Red'	A. palmatum v dissectum 'Dissectum Nigrum'

Synonyms

Name	Synonym
Acer palmatum 'Frederici Guglielmi'	A. palmatum v dissectum 'Dissectum Variegatum'
Acer palmatum 'Heptalobum Elegans Purpureum'	A. palmatum 'Hessei'
Acer palmatum 'Junihitoe'	A. shirasawanum 'Junihitoe'
Acer palmatum 'Little Princess'	A. palmatum 'Mapi-no-machihime'
Acer palmatum 'Nomurishidare' misapplied	A. palmatum 'Shojo-shidare'
Acer palmatum 'Pine Bark Maple'	A. palmatum 'Nishiki-gawa'
Acer palmatum 'Reticulatum'	A. palmatum 'Shigitatsu-sawa'
Acer palmatum 'Ribesifolium'	A. palmatum 'Shishigashira'
Acer palmatum 'Roseomarginatum'	A. palmatum 'Kagiri-nishiki'
Acer palmatum 'Rough Bark Maple'	A. palmatum 'Arakawa'
Acer palmatum 'Senkaki'	A. palmatum 'Sango-kaku'
Acer palmatum 'Septemlobum Elegans'	A. palmatum 'Heptalobum Elegans'
Acer palmatum 'Septemlobum Purpureum'	A. palmatum 'Hessei'
Acer palmatum 'Sessilifolium' dwarf	A. palmatum 'Hagoromo'
Acer palmatum 'Sessilifolium' tall	A. palmatum 'Koshimino'
Acer palmatum 'Wou-nishiki'	A. palmatum 'O-nishiki'
Acer papilio	A. caudatum
Acer pectinatum ssp forrestii	A. forrestii
Acer pictum	A. mono
Acer platanoides 'Lorbergii'	A. platanoides 'Palmatifidum'
Acer platanoides 'Parkway'	A. platanoides 'Columnarbroad'
Acer platanoides 'Spaethii' h	A. pseudoplatanus 'Atropurpureum'
Acer regelii	A. pentapotamicum
Acer rubrum 'Scarsen'	A. rubrum 'Scarlet Sentinel'
Acer rufinerve f 'Albolimbatum'	A. rufinerve 'Hatsuyuki'
Acer rufinerve f 'Albomarginatum'	A. rufinerve 'Hatsuyuki'
Acer rufinerve f albolimbatum	A. rufinerve 'Hatsuyuki'
Acer saccharinum 'Elegans'	A. x freemanii 'Elegant'
Acer saccharinum 'Fastigiatum'	A. saccharinum f pyramidale
Acer saccharinum 'Laciniatum Wieri'	A. saccharinum 'Wieri'
Acer saccharum 'Columnare'	A. saccharum 'Newton Sentry'
Acer saccharum 'Monumentale'	A. saccharum 'Temple's Upright'
Acer saccharum ssp barbatum	A. saccharum ssp floridanum
Acer sikkimense ssp metcalfii	A. metcalfii
Acer 'Silver Vein'	A. x conspicuum 'Silver Vein'
Acer stachyophyllum	A. tetramerum
Acer syriacum	A. obtusifolium
Acer tegmentosum ssp glaucorufinerve	A. rufinerve
Acer villosum	A. sterculiaceum
Acer x conspicuum 'Silver Cardinal'	A. 'Silver Cardinal'
Aceriphyllum	Mukdenia
Achillea Appleblossom	A. 'Apfelblute'
Achillea argentea h	A. clavennae
Achillea argentea -Lamark	Tanacetum argenteum
Achillea aurea	A. chrysocoma
Achillea decolorans	A. ageratum
Achillea eupatorium	A. filipendulina
Achillea Flowers of Sulphur	A. 'Schwefelblute'
Achillea 'Great Expectations'	A. 'Hoffnung'
Achillea millefolium 'Lavender Beauty'	A. millefolium 'Lilac Beauty'
Achillea 'Peter Davis'	Hippolytia herderi
Achillea ptarmica 'Innocence'	A. ptarmica 'Unschuld'
Achillea ptarmica 'Schneeball'	A. ptarmica 'Boule de Neige'
Achillea ptarmica 'The Pearl'	A. ptarmica The Pearl Group
Achillea pumila	A. distans ssp tanacetifolia
Achillea 'Salmon Beauty'	A. 'Lachsschonheit'
Achillea 'Sandstone'	A. 'Wesersandstein'
Achillea 'Sulphur Flowers'	A. 'Schwefelblute'
Achillea 'The Beacon'	A. 'Fanal'
Achillea tomentosa 'Maynard's Gold'	A. tomentosa 'Aurea'
Achillea umbellata 'Weston'	A. x kolbiana 'Weston'
Achimenes bella	Eucodonia verticillata
Achimenes coccinea	A. erecta
Achimenes ehrenbergii	Eucodonia ehrenbergii
Achimenes longiflora 'Alba'	A. 'Jaureguia Maxima'
Achimenes pulchella	A. erecta
Achimenes 'Shirley Fireglow'	A. 'Harveyi'
Achimenes Snow White	A. 'Schneewittchen'
Achiote	Bixa orellana
Achnatherum	Stipa
Acidanthera	Gladiolus
Acidanthera bicolor	Gladiolus callianthus
Acidanthera bicolor v murieliae	Gladiolus callianthus
Acidanthera murieliae	Gladiolus callianthus
Aciphylla latifolia	Anisotome latifolia
Acnistus australis	Dunalia australis
Acokanthera spectabilis	A. oblongifolia
Aconitum anglicum	A. napellus ssp napellus Anglicum Group
Aconitum cilicicum	Eranthis hyemalis Cilicica Group
Aconitum compactum	A. napellus ssp vulgare
Aconitum compactum 'Carneum'	A. napellus ssp vulgare 'Carneum'
Aconitum fischeri h	A. carmichaelii
Aconitum hyemale	Eranthis hyemalis
Aconitum lamarckii	A. lycoctonum ssp neapolitanum
Aconitum napellus 'Albiflorus'	A. napellus ssp vulgare 'Albidum'
Aconitum napellus 'Carneum'	A. napellus ssp vulgare 'Carneum'
Aconitum neapolitanum	A. lycoctonum ssp neapolitanum
Aconitum orientale h	A. lycoctonum ssp vulparia
Aconitum pyrenaicum	A. lycoctonum ssp neapolitanum
Aconitum ranunculifolius	A. lycoctonum ssp neapolitanum
Aconitum septentrionale	A. lycoctonum ssp lycoctonum
Aconitum septentrionale 'Ivorine'	A. 'Ivorine'
Aconitum volubile h	A. hemsleyanum
Aconitum vulpuria	A. lycoctonum ssp vulparia
Aconitum x tubergenii	Eranthis hyemalis

Synonyms

	Tubergenii Group
Aconogonon	Persicaria
Acrocladium	Calliergon
Acroclinium	Rhodanthe
Acroclinium roseum	Rhodanthe chlorocephala ssp roseum
Actaea nigra	A. spicata
Actaea pachypoda	A. alba
Actaea rubra alba	A. rubra f neglecta
Actaea spicata v alba	A. spicata
Actaea spicata v rubra	A. erythrocarpa -Fischer
Actinella scaposa	Tetraneuris scaposa
Actinidia chinensis h	A. deliciosa
Actinomeris alternifolia	Verbesina alternifolia
Adelocaryum	Lindelofia
Adenia buchananii	A. digitata
Adenium arabicum	A. obesum
Adenium micranthum	A. obesum
Adenium speciosum	A. obesum
Adenophora latifolia h	A. pereskiifolia
Adenophora liliiflora	A. liliifolia
Adenophora nipponica	A. nikoensis v stenophylla
Adenophora polymorpha	A. nikoensis
Adenophora polymorpha v tashiroi	A. tashiroi
Adenostyles alpina	Cacalia glabra
Adhatoda duvernoia	Justicia adhatoda
Adhatoda vasica	Justicia adhatoda
Adiantum capillus-veneris 'Mairisii'	A. x mairisii
Adiantum cuneatum	A. raddianum
Adiantum pedatum Asiatic form	A. pedatum 'Japonicum'
Adiantum pedatum 'Roseum'	A. pedatum 'Japonicum'
Adiantum pedatum v aleuticum	A. pedatum v subpumilum
Adiantum pedatum v minus	A. pedatum v subpumilum
Adiantum pedatum v subpumilum f minimum -(W.H.Wagner) Lellinger	A. aleuticum
Adiantum raddianum 'Fragrans'	A. raddianum 'Fragrantissimum'
Adiantum raddianum 'Gracilis'	A. raddianum 'Gracillimum'
Adlumia cirrhosa	A. fungosa
Adonidia merrillii	Veitchia merrillii
Adonis amurensis 'Plena'	A. amurensis 'Pleniflora'
Adromischus clavifolius	A. cooperi
Aechmea caerulea	A. lueddemanniana
Aechmea marmorata	Quesnelia marmorata
Aegle sepiaria	Poncirus trifoliata
Aeonium bertoletianum	A. tabuliforme
Aeonium exsul	A. canariense
Aeonium subplanum	A. canariense v subplanum
Aeonium x domesticum	Aichryson x domesticum
Aerides japonica	Sedirea japonica
Aeschynanthus 'Hillbrandii'	A. hildebrandii
Aeschynanthus lobbianus	A. radicans
Aeschynanthus marmoratus	A. longicaulis
Aeschynanthus parvifolius	A. radicans
Aeschynanthus radicans lobbianus	A. radicans
Aeschynanthus splendens	A. speciosus
Aeschynanthus zebrinus	A. longicaulis
Aesculus arguta	A. glabra v arguta
Aesculus georgiana	A. sylvatica
Aesculus hippocastanum 'Flore Pleno'	A. hippocastanum

Aesculus hippocastanum 'Globosa'	A. hippocastanum 'Umbraculifera'
Aesculus octandra	A. flava
Aesculus pavia 'Penduliflora'	A. x mutabilis 'Penduliflora'
Aesculus splendens	A. pavia
Aesculus x mississippiensis	A. x bushii
Aethionema graecum	A. saxatile
Aethionema pulchellum	A. grandiflorum Pulchellum Group
Agapanthus Danube	A. 'Donau'
Agapanthus orientalis	A. praecox ssp orientalis
Agapanthus Palmer's hybrids	A. Headbourne hybrids
Agapanthus umbellatus	A. praecox ssp orientalis
Agapetes macrantha	A. variegata v macrantha
Agapetes rugosa	A. incurvata
Agapetes rugosa x serpens	A. 'Ludgvan Cross'
Agastache anethiodora	A. foeniculum
Agastache anisata	A. foeniculum
Agastache mexicana 'Rosea'	A. cana
Agathaea	Felicia
Agathaea coelestis	Felicia amelloides
Agave affinis	A. sobria
Agave altissima	A. americana
Agave avellanidens	A. sebastiana
Agave cernua	A. attenuata
Agave cerulata	A. sobria
Agave coarctata	A. mitriformis
Agave consideranti	A. victoriae-reginae
Agave dentiens	A. deserti
Agave gigantea	Furcraea foetida
Agave glaucescens	A. attenuata
Agave hartmannii	A. parviflora
Agave huachuensis	A. parryi v huachucensis
Agave hystrix	A. stricta
Agave mitis	A. celsii
Agave nelsonii	A. deserti
Agave parryi v couesii	A. parryi v parryi
Agave pringlei	A. deserti
Agave scaphoidea	A. utahensis
Agave vestita	A. schidigera
Ageratina	Eupatorium
Ageratina adenophera	Eupatorium adenophera
Ageratina altissima	Eupatorium rugosum
Ageratina ligustrina	Eupatorium ligustrinum
Aglaonema 'Pewter'	A. 'Malay Beauty'
Aglaonema roebelinii	A. crispum
Agrimonia odorata -Miller	A. repens
Agropyron glaucum	Elymus hispidus
Agropyron magellanicum	Elymus magellanicus
Agropyron pubiflorum	Elymus magellanicus
Agropyron scabrum	Elymus scabrus
Agrostemma coeli-rosa	Silene coeli-rosa
Agrostemma coronaria	Lychnis coronaria
Agrostemma githago 'Purple Queen'	A. githago 'Milas Cerise'
Agrostemma githago 'Rose Queen'	A. githago 'Milas'
Agrostis calamagrostis	Calamagrostis epigejos
Agrostis karsensis	A. stolonifera
Ailanthus glandulosa	A. altissima
Aira flexuosa	Deschampsia flexuosa
Ajuga metallica	A. pyramidalis
Ajuga reptans 'Argentea'	A. reptans 'Variegata'
Ajuga reptans 'Jumbo'	A. reptans 'Jungle Beauty'
Ajuga reptans 'Macrophylla'	A. reptans 'Catlin's Giant'

	'Baumannii'

Synonyms

Ajuga reptans 'Purpurea'	A. reptans 'Atropurpurea'	Allium violaceum	A. carinatum
Ajuga reptans 'Rainbow'	A. reptans 'Multicolor'	Alnus crispa	A. viridis ssp crispa
Ajuga reptans 'Tricolor'	A. reptans 'Multicolor'	Alnus firma v multinervis	A. pendula
Akebia lobata	A. trifoliata	Alnus firma v sieboldiana	A. sieboldiana
Albizia distachya	Paraserianthes lophantha	Alnus oregona	A. rubra
Albizia lophantha	Paraserianthes lophantha	Alnus serrulata	A. rugosa
Albuca minor	A. canadensis	Alocasia indica v metallica h	A. plumbea
Alchemilla arvensis	Aphanes arvensis	Alocasia lowii v veitchii	A. veitchii
Alchemilla hoppeana h	A. plicatula	Alocasia nigra	A. plumbea 'Nigra'
Alchemilla 'Mr. Polland's Variety'	A. venosa	Alocasia picta	A. veitchii
Alchemilla pedata	A. abyssinica	Alocasia whinkii	A. 'Uhinkii'
Alchemilla splendens	A. x fulgens	Aloe arabica	A. vera
Alchemilla vulgaris h	A. xanthochlora	Aloe atherstonei	A. pluridens
Alisma natans	Luronium natans	Aloe ausana	A. variegata
Alisma ranunculoides	Baldellia ranunculoides	Aloe barbadensis	A. vera
Allamanda neriifolia	A. schottii	Aloe ellenbergeri	A. aristata
Allamanda violacea	A. blanchettii	Aloe galpinii	A. ferox
Allardia glabra	A. tridactylites	Aloe indica	A. vera
Allemanda	Allamanda	Aloe paniculata	A. striata
Allium aflatunense h	A. holllandicum	Aloe perfoliata v arborescens	A. arborescens
Allium albidum	A. denudatum	Aloe platyphylla	A. zebrina
Allium albopilosum	A. cristophii	Aloe prolifera	A. brevifolia
Allium amabile	A. mairei v amabile	Aloe punctata	A. variegata
Allium ambiguum	A. roseum v carneum	Aloe socotrina	A. ferox
Allium azureum	A. caeruleum	Aloe supralaevis	A. ferox
Allium beesianum h	A. cyaneum	Aloe xanthocantha	A. mitriformis
Allium bulgaricum	Nectaroscordum siculum ssp bulgaricum	Aloinella haworthioides	Aloe haworthioides
		Alonsoa albiflora h	A. acutifolia candida
Allium caeruleum azureum	A. caeruleum	Alonsoa caulialata	A. meridionalis
Allium christophii	A. cristophii	Alonsoa grandiflora	A. warscewiczii
Allium cirrhosum	A. carinatum ssp pulchellum	Alonsoa linifolia	A. linearis
		Alonsoa myrtifolia	A. acutifolia
Allium cowanii	A. neapolitanum Cownaii Group	Alonsoa warscewiczii pale form	A. warscewiczii 'Peachy-keen'
Allium elatum	A. macleanii	Alophia lahue	Herbertia lahue
Allium farreri	A. cyathophorum v farreri	Aloysia citriodora	A. triphylla
Allium flavum 'Glaucum'	A. flavum 'Blue Leaf'	Alpinia nutans h	A. zerumbet
Allium glaucum	A. senescens ssp montanum v glaucum	Alpinia sanderae h	A. vittata
		Alpinia speciosa	A. zerumbet
Allium griffithianum	A. rubellum	Alsobia	Episcia
Allium jajlae	A. rotundum ssp jajlae	Alsobia dianthiflora	Episcia dianthiflora
Allium jesdianum 'Michael Hoog'	A. rosenbachianum 'Michael Hoog'	Alsophila	Cyathea
		Alsophila australis h	Cyathea cooperi
Allium kansuense	A. sikkimense	Alstroemeria aurantiaca	A. aurea
Allium multibulbosum	A. nigrum	Alstroemeria gayana	A. pelegrina
Allium murrayanum h	A. unifolium	Alstroemeria 'Orchid'	A. 'Walter Fleming'
Allium narcissiflorum h	A. insubricum	Alstroemeria pulchella -Sims	A. psittacina
Allium neriniflorum	Caloscordum neriniflorum	Alstroemeria 'Regina'	A. 'Victoria'
		Alstroemeria 'Stacova'	A. 'Margaret'
Allium nuttallii	A. drummondii	Alstroemeria 'Stadoran'	A. 'Beatrix'
Allium odorum -Linnaeus	A. ramosum -Linnaeus	Alstroemeria violacea	A. paupercula
Allium ostrowskianum	A. oreophilum	Alternanthera amoena	A. ficoidea v amoena
Allium oviflorum	A. macranthum	Alternanthera versicolor	A. ficoidea 'Versicolor'
Allium pedemontanum	A. narcissiflorum -Villars	Althaea rosea	Alcea rosea
Allium pulchellum	A. carinatum ssp pulchellum	Althaea rugosostellulata	Alcea rugosa
		Alyssum argenteum h	A. murale
Allium pyrenaicum h	A. angulosum	Alyssum corymbosum	Aurinia corymbosa
Allium ramosum -Jacquin	A. obliquum	Alyssum gemonense	Aurinia petraea
Allium roseum 'Grandiflorum'	A. roseum v bulbiferum	Alyssum maritimum	Lobularia maritima
Allium scorodoprasum ssp jajlae	A. rotundum ssp jajlae	Alyssum montanum Mountain Gold	A. montanum 'Berggold'
Allium senescens v calcareum	A. senescens ssp montanum	Alyssum petraeum	Aurinia petraea
		Alyssum saxatile	Aurinia saxatilis
Allium sibthorpianum	A. paniculatum	Alyssum vesicaria	Coluteocarpus vesicarius
Allium siculum	Nectaroscordum siculum	Amana	Tulipa
		Amaryllis belladonna 'Pallida'	A. belladonna 'Elata'
Allium tibeticum	A. sikkimense	Amaryllis belladonna 'Parkeri Alba'	x Amarygia parkeri 'Alba'

Synonyms

Name	Synonym
Amblyopetalum caeruleum	Tweedia caerulea
Amelanchier florida	A. alnifolia v semi-integrifolia
Amelanchier lamarckii 'Rubescens'	A. x grandiflora 'Rubescens'
Amomum cardamomum	A. compactum
Ampelopsis brevipedunculata	A. glandulosa v brevipedunculata
Ampelopsis glandulosa v brevipedunculata 'Tricolor'	A. glandulosa v brevipedunculata 'Elegans'
Ampelopsis henryana	Parthenocissus henryana
Ampelopsis heterophylla	A. brevipedunculata v maximowiczii
Ampelopsis sempervirens h	Cissus striata
Ampelopsis tricuspidata 'Veitchii'	Parthenocissus tricuspidata 'Veitchii'
Amphicome	Incarvillea
Amsonia salicifolia	A. tabernaemontana v salicifolia
Amygdalus	Prunus
Anacampseros intermedia	A. telephiastrum
Anacampseros varians	A. telephiastrum
Anacharis densa	Egeria densa
Anacyclus depressus	A. pyrethrum v depressus
Anagallis collina	A. monellii
Anagallis linifolia	A. monellii ssp linifolia
Anaphalis cinnamomea	A. margaritacea v cinnamomea
Anaphalis margaritacea New Snow	A. margaritacea 'Neuschnee'
Anaphalis nubigena	A. nepalensis v monocephala
Anaphalis triplinervis Summer Snow	A. triplinervis 'Sommerschnee'
Anaphalis triplinervis v intermedia	A. nepalensis
Anaphalis yedoensis	A. margaritacea v yedoensis
Anchusa angustissima	A. leptophylla ssp incana
Anchusa caespitosa	A. cespitosa -Lamarck
Anchusa caespitosa h	A. leptophylla ssp incana
Anchusa italica	A. azurea
Anchusa laxiflora	Borago pygmaea
Anchusa myosotidiflora	Brunnera macrophylla
Anchusa sempervirens	Pentaglottis sempervirens
Ancistrocactus	Sclerocactus
Ancistrocactus crassihamatus	Sclerocactus uncinatus v crassihamatus
Ancistrocactus megarhizus	Sclerocactus scheeri
Ancistrocactus scheeri	Sclerocactus scheeri
Ancistrocactus uncinatus	Sclerocactus uncinatus
Andromeda polifolia 'Compacta Alba'	A. polifolia 'Alba'
Andromeda rosmarinifolia	A. polifolia
Andropogon ischaemum	Bothriochloa ischaemum
Andropogon scoparius	Schizachyrium scoparium
Androsace carnea v halleri	A. carnea ssp rosea
Androsace imbricata	A. vandellii
Androsace jacquemontii	A. villosa v jacquemontii
Androsace laggeri	A. carnea v laggeri
Androsace limprichtii	A. sarmentosa v watkinsii
Androsace microphylla	A. mucronifolia -Watt
Androsace mollis	A. sarmentosa v yunnanensis
Androsace mucronifolia h	A. sempervivoides
Androsace primuloides -Duby	A. studiosorum
Androsace primuloides h	A. sarmentosa
Androsace salicifolia	A. lactiflora
Androsace vitaliana	Vitaliana primuliflora
Androsace watkinsii	A. sarmentosa v watkinsii
Andryala lanata	Hieracium lanatum
Anemone biarmiensis	A. narcissiflora ssp biarmiensis
Anemone 'Bressingham Glow'	A. hupehensis v japonica 'Bressingham Glow'
Anemone coronaria De Caen Group 'His Excellency'	A. coronaria De Caen Group 'Hollandia'
Anemone coronaria De Caen Group 'The Bride'	A. coronaria De Caen Group 'Die Braut'
Anemone fasciculata	A. narcissiflora
Anemone globosa	A. multifida
Anemone hepatica	Hepatica nobilis
Anemone hupehensis Pink Shell	A. hupehensis 'Rosenschale'
Anemone hupehensis v japonica Prince Henry	A. hupehensis v japonica 'Prinz Heinrich'
Anemone japonica	A. x hybrida
Anemone magellanica h	A. multifida
Anemone nemerosa 'Currey's Pink'	A. nemerosa 'Lismore Pink'
Anemone nemerosa 'Plena'	A. nemerosa 'Flore Pleno'
Anemone patens	Pulsatilla patens
Anemone pulsatilla	Pulsatilla vulgaris
Anemone ranunculoides 'Flore Pleno'	A. ranunculoides 'Pleniflora'
Anemone stellata	A. hortensis
Anemone stellata v heldreichii	A. hortensis ssp heldreichii
Anemone sulphurea	Pulsatilla alpina ssp apiifolia
Anemone sylvestris 'Flore Pleno'	A. sylvestris 'Elise Fellmann'
Anemone vernalis	Pulsatilla vernalis
Anemone vitifolia	A. tomentosa
Anemone vitifolia 'Robustissima'	A. tomentosa
Anemone x elegans	A. x hybrida
Anemone x hybrida 'Alba' h UK	A. x hybrida 'Honorine Jobert'
Anemone x hybrida 'Alba' h USA	A. x hybrida 'Lady Ardilaun'
Anemone x hybrida 'Bowles' Pink'	A. hupehensis 'Bowles' Pink'
Anemone x hybrida 'Bressingham Glow'	A. hupehensis v japonica 'Bressingham Glow'
Anemone x hybrida 'Lady Gilmour'	A. x hybrida 'Margarete'
Anemone x hybrida Prince Henry	A. hupehensis v japonica 'Prinz Heinrich'
Anemone x hybrida 'Prinz Heinrich'	A. hupehensis v japonica 'Prinz Heinrich'
Anemone x hybrida Queen Charlotte	A. x hybrida 'Konigin Charlotte'
Anemone x hybrida 'Tourbillon'	A. x hybrida 'Whirlwind'
Anemone x hybrida 'White Giant'	A. x hybrida 'Geante des Blanches'
Anemone x hybrida 'White Queen'	A. x hybrida 'Geante des Blanches'

Synonyms

Name	Synonym
Anemone x hybrida 'Wirbelwind'	A. x hybrida 'Whirlwind'
Anemone x intermedia	A. x lipsiensis
Anemone x seemannii	A. x lipsiensis
Anemonella thalictroides 'Schoaf's Double'	A. thalictroides 'Oscar Schoaf'
Anemonella thalictroides 'Schoaf's Pink'	A. thalictroides 'Oscar Schoaf'
Angelica curtisii	A. triquinata
Angelica montana	A. sylvestris
Angelica officinalis	A. archangelica
Angophora cordifolia	A. hispida
Anhalonium retusum	Ariocarpus retusus
Anhalonium trigonum	Ariocarpus trigonus
Anisodontea huegelii	Alyogyne huegelii
Anisodontea x hypomadara h	A. capensis
Anisodontea x hypomandarum	A. x hypomadara - Sprague (Bates)
Anneliesia candida	Miltonia candida
Anoiganthus	Cyrtanthus
Anoiganthus luteus	Cyrtanthus breviflorus
Anomatheca cruenta	A. laxa
Antennaria aprica	A. parvifolia
Antennaria dioica 'Aprica'	A. parvifolia
Antennaria dioica tomentosa	A. dioica v hyperborea
Antennaria dioica v rosea	A. microphylla
Antennaria macrophylla h	A. microphylla
Antennaria parvifolia v rosea	A. microphylla
Anthemis aizoon	Achillea ageratifolia ssp aizoon
Anthemis biebersteiniana	A. marschalliana
Anthemis biebersteinii	A. marschalliana
Anthemis frutescens	Argyranthemum frutescens
Anthemis montana	A. cretica ssp cretica
Anthemis nobilis	Chamaemelum nobile
Anthemis rudolphiana	A. marschalliana
Anthemis tinctoria 'Grallagh Gold'	A. 'Grallagh Gold'
Anthemis tinctoria 'Pride of Grallagh'	A. 'Pride of Grallagh'
Anthericum algeriense	A. liliago v major
Anthericum liliago 'Major'	A. liliago v major
Anthericum ramosum plumosum	Trichopetalum plumosum
Antholyza	Crocosmia
Antholyza coccinea	Crocosmia paniculata
Antholyza crocosmioides	Crocosmia latifolia
Antholyza paniculata	Crocosmia paniculata
Anthurium andraeanum 'Rose'	A. x ferrierense 'Roseum'
Anthurium cordatum	A. leuconeurum
Anthurium x cultorum	A. x ferrierense
Anthurium x rothschildianum	A. 'Rothschildianum'
Anthyllis hermanniae 'Compacta'	A. hermanniae 'Minor'
Antirrhinum asarina	Asarina procumbens
Antirrhinum glutinosum	A. hispanicum ssp hispanicum
Aphelandra fascinator	A. aurantiaca
Apios tuberosa	A. americana
Aponogeton krausseanus	A. desertorum
Aporocactus conzattii	A. martianus
Aporocactus mallisoniiii	x Aporoheliocereus smithii
Aprica arachnoides	Haworthia arachnoidea
Aquilegia akitensis h	A. flabellata v pumila
Aquilegia alpina 'Hensol Harebell'	A. 'Hensol Harebell'
Aquilegia amaliae	A. ottonis ssp amaliae
Aquilegia aragonensis	A. pyrenaica
Aquilegia baicalensis	A. vulgaris Baicalensis
Aquilegia buergeriana v oxysepala	Group A. oxysepala
Aquilegia cazorlensis	A. pyrenaica ssp cazorlensis
Aquilegia clematiflora	A. vulgaris v stellata
Aquilegia ecalcarata	Semiaquilegia ecalcarata
Aquilegia flabellata 'Nana Alba'	A. flabellata v pumila f alba
Aquilegia glauca	A. fragrans
Aquilegia hinckleyana	A. chrysantha v hinckleyana
Aquilegia hirsutissima	A. viscosa ssp hirsutissima
Aquilegia japonica	A. flabellata v pumila
Aquilegia montana	A. alpina
Aquilegia 'Mrs Scott-Elliot'	A. Mrs Scott-Elliot Hybrids
Aquilegia nevadensis	A. vulgaris ssp nevadensis
Aquilegia nigricans	A. atrata
Aquilegia reuteri	A. bertolonii
Aquilegia Snow Queen	A. 'Schneekonigin'
Aquilegia stellata	A. vulgaris v stellata
Aquilegia Vervaeneana Group 'Woodside'	A. vulgaris Vervaeneana Group
Aquilegia vulgaris 'Aureovariegata'	A. vulgaris Vervaeneana Group
Aquilegia vulgaris 'Blue Star'	A. (Star Series) 'Blue Star'
Aquilegia vulgaris clematiflora	A. vulgaris v stellata
Aquilegia vulgaris 'Dove'	A. (Songbird Series) 'Dove'
Aquilegia vulgaris 'Gold Finch'	A. (Songbird Series) 'Goldfinch'
Aquilegia vulgaris 'Magpie'	A. vulgaris 'William Guiness'
Aquilegia vulgaris Munstead White	A. vulgaris 'Nivea'
Aquilegia vulgaris Olympica Group	A. olympica
Aquilegia vulgaris 'Pink Spurless'	A. vulgaris v stellata pink
Aquilegia vulgaris 'Red Star'	A. (Star Series) 'Red Star'
Aquilegia vulgaris 'Robin'	A. (Songbird Series) 'Robin'
Aquilegia vulgaris variegated foliage	A. vulgaris Vervaeneana Group
Aquilegia vulgaris 'White Spurless'	A. vulgaris v stellata white
Aquilegia vulgaris 'White Star'	A. (Star Series) 'White Star'
Arabis albida	A. alpina ssp caucasica
Arabis alpina ssp caucasica 'Plena'	A. alpina ssp caucasica 'Flore Pleno'
Arabis alpina ssp caucasica Snowcap	A. alpina ssp caucasica 'Schneehaube'
Arabis billardieri	A. caucasica
Arabis blepharophylla Spring Charm	A. blepharophylla 'Fruhlingszauber'
Arabis caucasica	A. alpina ssp caucasica
Arabis caucasica 'Flore Pleno'	A. alpina ssp caucasica 'Flore Pleno'
Arabis caucasica 'Rosabella'	A. x arendsii 'Rosabella'
Arabis ferdinandi-coburgi 'Variegata'	A. procurrens 'Variegata'
Arabis muralis	A. collina
Arabis rosea	A. collina
Arabis Snow Cap	A. alpina ssp caucasica 'Schneehaube'
Arabis soyeri ssp jacquinii	A. soyeri ssp coriacea
Arabis stricta	A. scabra
Aralia chinensis h	A. elata

Synonyms

Name	Synonym
Aralia elata 'Albomarginata'	A. elata 'Variegata'
Aralia elegantissima	Schefflera elegantissima
Aralia japonica	Fatsia japonica
Aralia papyrifer	Tetrapanax payrifer
Aralia sieboldii -de Vriese	Fatsia japonica
Araucaria cookii	A. columnaris
Araucaria excelsa	A. heterophylla
Araucaria imbricata	A. araucana
Araujia sericofera	A. sericifera
Arborvitae	Thuja
Arbutus glandulosa	Arctostaphylos glandulosa
Arcrostaphylos uva-ursi 'Snow Camp'	A. x media 'Snow Camp'
Arcterica	Pieris
Arctotis stoechadifolia	A. venusta
Arctous alpinus	Arctostaphylos alpinus
Ardisia crenulata	Ardisia crenata
Areca lutescens	Chrysalidocarpus lutescens
Arecastrum	Syagrus
Arecastrum romanzoffianum	Syagrus romanzoffiana
Aregelia	Neoregelia
Aregelia carolinae	Neoregelia carolinae
Arenaria alfacarensis	A. lithops
Arenaria caespitosa	Minuartia verna ssp caespitosa
Arenaria magellanica	Colobanthus quitensis
Arenaria obtusiloba	Minuartia obtusiloba
Arenaria pinifolia	Minuartia circassica
Arenaria pulvinata	A. lithops
Arenaria recurva	Minuartia recurva
Arenaria tetraquetra v granatensis	A. tetraquetra ssp amabilis
Arenaria verna	Minuartia verna
Arequipa hempeliana	Oreocereus hempelianus
Argyranthemum 'Apricot Surprise'	A. 'Peach Cheeks'
Argyranthemum Boston Yellow daisy	A. callichrysum
Argyranthemum callichrysum Yellow Star	A. callichrysum 'Etoile d'Or'
Argyranthemum canariense h	A. frutescens ssp canariae
Argyranthemum 'Cheek's Peach'	A. 'Peach Cheeks'
Argyranthemum 'Chelsea Girl'	A. gracile 'Chelsea Girl'
Argyranthemum 'Flamingo'	Rhodanthemum gayanum
Argyranthemum foeniculaceum h pink	A. 'Petite Pink'
Argyranthemum 'Jamaica Snowstorm'	A. 'Snow Storm'
Argyranthemum mawii	Rhodanthemum gayanum
Argyranthemum 'Mini-snowflake'	A. 'Blizzard'
Argyranthemum 'Nevada Cream'	A. 'Qinta White'
Argyranthemum ochroleucum	A. maderense
Argyranthemum 'Pink Delight'	A. 'Petite Pink'
Argyranthemum 'Royal Haze'	A. foeniculaceum 'Royal Haze' -Webb
Argyranthemum 'Silver Queen'	A. foeniculaceum h
Argyreia speciosa	A. nervosa
Argyrocytisus	Cytisus
Argyrocytisus battandieri	Cytisus x beanii
Argyroderma aureum	A. delaetti
Argyroderma blandum	A. delaetti
Argyroderma brevipes	A. fissum
Argyroderma schlechteri	A. pearsonii
Arisaema atrorubens	A. triphyllum
Arisaema helleborifolium	A. tortuosum
Arisaema japonicum	A. serratum
Arisaema ochraceum	A. nepenthoides
Arisaema ringens h	A. robustum
Arisaema sazensoo	A. sikokianum
Arisaema utile	A. verrucosum v utile
Aristea thyrsiflora	A. major
Aristolochia durior	A. macrophylla
Aristolochia elegans	A. littoralis
Aristolochia gigas	A. grandiflora
Aristolochia ringens -Link & Otto	A. labiata
Aristolochia sipho	A. macrophylla
Aristotelia macqui	A. chilensis
Armeria arenaria	A. alliacea
Armeria atrosanguinea	A. pseudarmeria
Armeria caespitosa	A. juniperifolia
Armeria cespitosa	A. juniperifolia
Armeria latifolia	A. pseudarmeria
Armeria maritima Dusseldorf Pride	A. maritima 'Dusseldorfer Stolz'
Armeria maritima ssp alpina	A. alpina
Armeria patagonica	Armeria maritima
Armeria plantaginea	A. alliacea
Armeria setacea	A. girardii
Armeria vulgaris	A. maritima
Arnebia echioides	A. pulchra
Arnebia longiflora	A. pulchra
Aronia arbutifolia 'Brilliant'	A. x prunifolia 'Brilliant'
Aronia melanocarpa 'Brilliant'	A. x prunifolia 'Brilliant'
Arorangi	Olearia macrodonta
Arrabidaea magnifica	Saritaea magnifica
Artemisia arborescens 'Brass Band'	A. 'Powis Castle'
Artemisia assoana	A. caucasica
Artemisia caerulescens	Seriphidium caerulescens
Artemisia camphorata	A. alba
Artemisia cana	Seriphidium canum
Artemisia canariensis	A. thuscula
Artemisia canescens h	A. alba 'Canescens'
Artemisia canescens -Willdenow	A. armeniaca
Artemisia cretacea	Seriphidium nutans
Artemisia discolor	A. ludoviciana v incompta
Artemisia douglasiana 'Valerie Finnis'	A. ludoviciana 'Valerie Finnis'
Artemisia ferganensis	Seriphidium ferganense
Artemisia gnaphalodes	A. ludoviciana
Artemisia gracilis	A. scoparia
Artemisia kitadakensis 'Guizhou'	A. lactiflora Guizhou Group
Artemisia lactiflora dark form	A. lactiflora Guizhou Group
Artemisia lactiflora purpurea	A. lactiflora Guizhou Group
Artemisia lactiflora 'Variegata'	A. vulgaris 'Variegata'
Artemisia lanata -Willdenow	A. caucasica
Artemisia laxa	A. umbelliformis
Artemisia ludoviciana v latifolia	A. ludoviciana v latiloba
Artemisia maritima	Seriphidium maritimum
Artemisia mutellina	A. umbelliformis
Artemisia nova	Seriphidium novum
Artemisia nutans	Seriphidium nutans
Artemisia palmeri -A Gray	Seriphidium palmeri
Artemisia palmeri h	A. ludoviciana
Artemisia pedemontana	A. caucasica
Artemisia procera	A. abrotanum
Artemisia purshiana	A. ludoviciana
Artemisia sieberi sp Guiz 137	A. lactiflora Guizhou Group

Synonyms

Artemisia splendens h	A. alba 'Canescens'	Arundinaria pygmaea	Pleioblastus pygmaeus
Artemisia stelleriana 'Mori'	A. stelleriana 'Boughton Silver'	Arundinaria quadrangularis	Chimonobambusa quadrangularis
Artemisia stelleriana 'Prostrata'	A. stelleriana 'Boughton Silver'	Arundinaria simonii	Pleioblastus simonii
Artemisia stelleriana 'Silver Brocade'	A. stelleriana 'Boughton Silver'	Arundinaria spathiflora	Thamnocalamus spathiflorus
Artemisia tridentata	Seriphidium tridentatum	Arundinaria tessellata	Thamnocalamus tessellatus
Artemisia vallesiaca	Seriphidium vallesiacum	Arundinaria vagans	Sasaella ramosa
Artemisia vulgaris 'Canescens'	A. alba 'Canescens'	Arundinaria variegata	Pleioblastus variegatus
Arthropodium cirrhatum	A. cirratum	Arundinaria veitchii	Sasa veitchii
Arthropodium millefoliatum	A. milleflorum	Arundinaria viridistriata	Pleioblastus auricomus
Arthropodium paniculatum	A. milleflorum	Arundinaria 'Wang Tsai'	Bambusa multiplex 'Fernleaf'
Arthropodium reflexum	A. candidum	Arundo conspicua	Chionochloa conspicua
Arum conophalloides	A. rupicola v rupicola	Arundo donax 'Variegata'	A. donax v versicolor
Arum cornutum	Sauromatum venosum	Asarina antirrhiniflora	Maurandella antirrhiniflora
Arum detruncatum v detruncatum	A. rupicola v rupicola		
Arum dioscoridis v leipoldtii	A. dioscoridis	Asarina barclayana	Maurandya barclayana
Arum dioscoridis v smithii	A. dioscoridis	Asarina erubescens	Lophospermum erubescens
Arum dracunculus	Dracunculus vulgaris		
Arum italicum 'Pictum'	A. italicum ssp italicum 'Marmoratum'	Asarina hispanica	Antirrhinum hispanicum
		Asarina lophantha	Lophospermum erubescens
Arum nickelii	A. concinnatum		
Arum orientale ssp besserianum	A. besserianum	Asarina lophospermum	Lophospermum erubescens
Arum petteri h	A. nigrum		
Arum pictum 'Taff's Form'	A. italicum ssp italicum 'White Winter'	Asarina purpusii	Maurandya purpusii
		Asarina scandens	Maurandya scandens
Aruncus dioicus Child of Two Worlds	A. dioicus 'Zweiweltenkind'	Asarum marmoratum	A. hartwegii
		Asclepias fasciculata	A. fascicularis
Aruncus plumosus	A. dioicus	Asclepias fruticosa	Gomphocarpus fruticosus
Aruncus sylvestris	A. dioicus		
Arundinaria amabilis	Pseudosasa amabilis	Asclepias physocarpa	Gomphocarpus physocarpus
Arundinaria anceps	Yushania anceps	Asparagus meyeri	A. densiflorus 'Meyersii'
Arundinaria angustifolia	Pleioblastus chino f angustifolius	Asparagus meyersii	A. densiflorus 'Meyersii'
		Asparagus 'Myers'	A. densiflorus 'Meyersii'
Arundinaria auricoma	Pleioblastus auricomus	Asparagus plumosus	A. setaceus
Arundinaria chino	Pleioblastus chino	Asparagus sprengeri	A. densiflorus Sprengeri Group
Arundinaria disticha	Pleioblastus pygmaeus v distichus		
Arundinaria falconeri	Himalayacalamus falconeri	Asperula aristata ssp thessala	A. sintenisii
		Asperula athoa h	A. suberosa
Arundinaria fargesii	Bashania fargesii	Asperula azurea	A. orientalis
Arundinaria fastuosa	Semiarundinaria fastuosa	Asperula lilaciflora v caespitosa	A. lilaciflora ssp lilaciflora
		Asperula nitida ssp puberula	A. sintenisii
Arundinaria fortunei	Pleioblastus variegatus	Asperula odorata	Galium odoratum
Arundinaria funghomii	Schizostachyum funghomii	Asphodeline Yellow Candle	A. lutea 'Gelbkerze'
Arundinaria hindsii	Pleioblastus hindsii h	Asphodelus brevicaulis	Asphodeline brevicaulis
Arundinaria hookeriana h	Hiamalayacalamus falconeri 'Damarapa'	Asphodelus cerasiferus	A. ramosus
		Asphodelus lusitanicus	A. ramosus
Arundinaria hookeriana -Munro	Himalayacalamus hookerianus	Asphodelus luteus	Asphodeline lutea
		Asphodelus microcarpus	A. aestivus
Arundinaria humilis	Pleioblastus humilis	Asphodelus tenuifolius	A. fistulosus
Arundinaria japonica	Pseudosasa japonica	Asplenium alternans	A. dalhousieae
Arundinaria jaunsarensis	Yushania anceps	Asplenium furcatum -Thunberg	A. aethiopicum
Arundinaria macrosperma	A. gigantea	Asplenium robinsonii	A. australasicum f robinsonii
Arundinaria maling	Yushania maling		
Arundinaria marmorea	Chimonobambusa marmorea	Astelia chathamica 'Silver Spear'	A. chathamica
		Astelia cunninghamii	A. solandri
Arundinaria murieliae	Fargesia murieliae	Astelia graminifolia	Collospermum microspermum
Arundinaria nitida	Fargesia nitida		
Arundinaria oedogonata	Clavinodum oedogonatum	Astelia nervosa v chathamica	A. chathamica
		Aster acris	A. sedifolius
Arundinaria palmata	Sasa palmata	Aster ageratoides	A. trinervius ssp ageratoides
Arundinaria pumila	Pleioblastus humilis v pumilus		
		Aster alpinus 'Dark Beauty'	A. alpinus 'Dunkle

Synonyms

Name	Synonym
	Schone'
Aster alpinus v himalaicus	A. himalaicus
Aster amelloides	Felicia amelloides
Aster amellus Empress	A. amellus 'Glucksfund'
Aster amellus Pink Zenith	A. amellus 'Rosa Erfullung'
Aster amellus Violet Queen	A. amellus 'Veilchenkonigin'
Aster asper	A. bakerianus
Aster capensis	Felicia amelloides
Aster capensis 'Variegatus'	Felicia amelloides variegated
Aster coelestis	Felicia amelloides
Aster cordifolius 'Little Carlow'	A. 'Little Carlow' (cordifolius hybrid)
Aster cordifolius 'Little Dorrit'	A. 'Little Dorrit' (cordifolius hybrid)
Aster cordifolius 'Photograph'	A. 'Photograph'
Aster corymbosus	A. divaricatus
Aster diffusus	A. lateriflorus
Aster ericoides 'Hon. Vicary Gibbs'	A. 'Hon. Vicary Gibbs' (ericoides hybrid)
Aster ericoides 'Monte Cassino'	A. pringlei 'Monte Cassino'
Aster hybridus luteus	x Solidaster luteus
Aster likiangensis	A. asteroides
Aster linosyris 'Goldilocks'	A. linosyris
Aster mongolicus	Kalimeris mongolica
Aster natalensis	Felicia rosulata
Aster novae-angliae 'Alma Potschke'	A. novae-angliae 'Andenken an Alma Potschke'
Aster novae-angliae Autumn Snow	A. novae-angliae 'Herbstschnee'
Aster novae-angliae September Ruby	A. novae-angliae 'Septemberrubin'
Aster novi-belgii Antwerp Pearl	A. novi-belgii 'Antwerpse Parel'
Aster novi-belgii 'Christina'	A. novi-belgii 'Kristina'
Aster novi-belgii 'Climax Albus'	A. 'White Climax'
Aster novi-belgii 'Rector'	A. novi-belgii 'The Rector'
Aster novi-belgii Snow Cushion	A. novi-belgii 'Schneekissen'
Aster pappei	Felicia amoena
Aster petiolatus	Felicia petiolata
Aster rotundifolius 'Variegatus'	Felicia amelloides variegated
Aster scandens	A. carolinianus
Aster tibeticus	A. flaccidus
Aster tongolensis Summer Greeting	A. tongolensis 'Sommergruss'
Aster tradescantii h	A. pilosus v demotus
Aster vimineus 'Delight'	A. lateriflorus 'Delight'
Aster vimineus -Lamarck	A. lateriflorus
Aster vimineus 'Ptarmicoides'	A. ptarmicoides
Aster x frikartii Wonder of Stafa	A. x frikartii 'Wunder von Stafa'
Asteriscus 'Gold Coin'	A. maritimus
Asteromoea mongolica	Kalimerus mongolica
Astilbe 'Bronze Elegans'	A. 'Bronce Elegans' (simplicifolia hybrid)
Astilbe chinensis v taquetii Purple Lance	A. chinensis taquetii 'Purpurlanze'
Astilbe Cologne	A. 'Koln' (japonica hybrid)
Astilbe davidii	A. chinensis v davidii
Astilbe glaberrima saxosa	A. 'Saxosa'
Astilbe 'Gnom'	A. x crispa 'Gnom'
Astilbe japonica v terrestris	A. glaberrima v saxatilis
Astilbe Ostrich Plume	A. 'Straussenfeder' (thunbergii hybrid)
Astilbe 'Perkeo'	A. x crispa 'Perkeo'
Astilbe pumila	A. chinensis v pumila
Astilbe simplicifolia Bronze Elegance	A. 'Bronce Elegans' (simplicifolia hybrid)
Astilbe simplicifolia 'Gnome'	A. x crispa 'Gnom'
Astilbe 'Supeba'	A. chinensis v taquetii 'Superba'
Astilbe x arendsii Bridal Veil	A. x arendsii 'Brautschleier'
Astilbe x arendsii 'Cherry Ripe'	A. x arendsii 'Feuer'
Astilbe x arendsii Diamond	A. x arendsii 'Diamant'
Astilbe x arendsii 'Drayton Glory'	A. x rosea 'Peach Blossom'
Astilbe x arendsii Fire	A. x arendsii 'Feuer'
Astilbe x arendsii Glow	A. x arendsii 'Glut'
Astilbe x arendsii Hyacinth	A. x arendsii 'Hyazinth'
Astilbe x arendsii Pink Pearl	A. x arendsii 'Rosa Perle'
Astilbe x arendsii Red Light	A. x arendsii 'Rotlicht'
Astilbe x arendsii Salmon Queen	A. x arendsii 'Lachskonigin'
Astilbe x arendsii White Gloria	A. x arendsii 'Weisse Gloria'
Astragalus tragacantha h	A. massiliensis
Astrantia carniolica major	A. major
Astrantia carniolica v rubra	A. major rubra
Astrantia carniolica 'Variegata'	A. major 'Sunningdale Variegated'
Astrantia helleborifolia h	A. maxima
Astrantia major carinthiaca	A. major ssp involucrata
Astrantia major ssp involucrata 'Margery Fish'	A. major ssp involucrata 'Shaggy'
Astrantia major 'Variegata'	A. major 'Sunningdale Variegated'
Astrantia rubra	A. major rubra
Asystasia bella	Mackaya bella
Asystasia violacea	A. gangetica
Athyrium filix-femina Victoriae Group	A. filix-femina Cruciatum Group
Athyrium goeringianum	A. niponicum
Athyrium goeringianum 'Pictum'	A. niponicum v pictum
Athyrium niponicum f metallicum	A. niponicum v pictum
Athyrium niponicum 'Pictum'	A. niponicum v pictum
Athyrium nipponicum	A. niponicum
Athyrium proliferum	Diplazium proliferum
Atragene	Clematis
Atriplex portulacoides	Halimione portulacoides
Atropa mandragora	Mandragora officinarum
Aubrieta albomarginata	A. 'Argenteovariegata'
Aubrieta Blaue Schonheit	A. 'Blue Beauty'
Aubrieta 'Carnival'	A. 'Hartswood Purple'
Aubrieta 'Golden King'	A. 'Aureovariegata'
Aubrieta libanotica	A. columnae macrostyla
Aubrieta scardica ssp scardica	A. gracilis ssp scardica
Aubrieta 'Schofield's Double'	A. 'Bob Saunders'
Aubrieta Spring Charm	A. 'Fruhlingszauber'
Aubrieta x cultorum 'Albomarginata'	A. 'Argenteovariegata'
Aucuba japonica 'Maculata'	A. japonica 'Variegata'
Aurinia Gold Ball	A. saxatilis 'Goldkugel'
Avena candida	Helictotrichon sempervirens
Avena sempervirens	Helictotrichon

Name	Synonym
Avenula	sempervirens Helictotrichon
Ayapana	Eupatorium
Azolla caroliniana	A. mexicana
Azolla caroliniana -Willdenow	A. filiculoides
Azorella glebaria -A Gray	Bolax gummifera
Azorella glebaria h	A. trifurcata
Azorella gummifera	Bolax gummifera
Azorella nivalis	A. trifurcata
Azureocereus	Browningia
Azureocereus hertlingianus	Browningia hertlingiana
Babiana disticha	B. plicata
Bahia lanata	Eriophyllum lanatum
Ballota nigra 'Variegata'	B. nigra 'Archer's Variegated'
Balsamita	Tanacetum
Bambusa glaucescens	B. multiplex
Bambusa multiplex 'Chinese Goddess'	B. multiplex v riviereorum
Bambusa multiplex 'Wang Tsai'	B. multiplex 'Fernleaf'
Bambusa pubescens	Dendrocalamus strictus
Baptisia leucantha	B. lactea
Baptisia leucophaea	B. bracteata
Barbacenia elegans	Talbotia elegans
Barbarea praecox	B. verna
Barleria suberecta	Dicliptera suberecta
Barosma pulchella	Agathosma pulchella
Bartlettina	Eupatorium
Bartlettina sordida	Eupatorium sordidum
Bartonia aurea	Mentzelia lindleyi
Bauhinia alba	B. variegata
Bauhinia punctata	B. galpinii
Bauhinia purpurea h	B. variegata
Beauverdia	Leucocoryne
Begonia acerifolia	B. vitifolia
Begonia angularis	B. stipulacea
Begonia 'Can-can'	B. 'Herzog von Sagan'
Begonia compta	B. stipulacea
Begonia 'Corallina de Lucerna'	B. 'Lucerna'
Begonia dietrichiana	B. echinosepala 'Dietrichiana'
Begonia discolor	B. grandis ssp evansiana
Begonia disticha	B. stipulacea
Begonia 'Elaine's Baby'	B. 'Elaine Wilkerson'
Begonia 'Feastii'	B. 'Erythrophylla'
Begonia feastii 'Helix'	B. x erythrophylla 'Helix'
Begonia 'Fire Flush'	B. 'Bettina Rothschild'
Begonia 'Flaming Queen'	B. 'Feuerkonigin'
Begonia fuchsioides 'Rosea'	B. foliosa v miniata 'Rosea'
Begonia glaucophylla	B. radicans
Begonia griffithii	B. annulata
Begonia haageana	B. scharffii
Begonia incana	B. peltata
Begonia 'Iron Cross'	B. masoniana
Begonia limmingheana	B. radicans
Begonia 'Lucerna'	B. x corallina 'Lucerna'
Begonia martiana	B. gracilis v martiana
Begonia nigramarga	B. bowerae v nigramarga
Begonia procumbens	B. radicans
Begonia 'Ruhrtal'	B. 'Merry Christmas'
Begonia sceptrum	B. aconitifolia
Begonia semperflorens h	B. x carrierei
Begonia 'Silver'	B. pustulata 'Argentea'
Begonia zebrina	B. stipulacea
Bellevalia pycnantha h	B. paradoxa
Bellis Hen and Chicken	B. perennis 'Prolifera'

Name	Synonym
Bellis perennis 'Lipstick'	B. perennis 'Habanera White with Red Tips' (Habanera Series)
Bellis perennis 'Single Blue'	B. rotundifolia 'Caerulescens'
Beloperone	Justicia
Beloperone guttata	Justicia brandegeeana
Berberis aquifolium	Mahonia aquifolium
Berberis aquifolium 'Fascicularis'	Mahonia x wagneri 'Pinnacle'
Berberis bealei	Mahonia japonica Bealei Group
Berberis brevipedunculata -Bean	B. prattii
Berberis buxifolia 'Nana' h	B. buxifolia 'Pygmaea'
Berberis buxifolia v nana h	Berberis buxifolia 'Pygmaea'
Berberis candidula 'Jytte'	B. 'Jytte'
Berberis 'Chenault'	B. x hybridogagnepainii 'Chenaultii'
Berberis 'Chenaultii'	B. x hybridogagnepainii 'Chenaultii'
Berberis coryi	B. wilsoniae v subcaulialata
Berberis dulcis 'Nana'	B. buxifolia 'Pygmaea'
Berberis erythroclada	B. concinna
Berberis gagnepainii h	B. gagnepainii v lanceifolia
Berberis gagnepainii 'Purpure'	B. x interposita 'Wallich's Purple'
Berberis hookeri v latifolia	B. manipurana
Berberis knightii	B. manipurana
Berberis 'Little Favourite'	B. thunbergii 'Atropurpurea Nana'
Berberis Park Jewel	B. x media 'Parkjuweel'
Berberis polyantha h	B. prattii
Berberis sanguinea h	B. panlanensis
Berberis thunbergii 'Atropurpurea Superba'	B. x ottawensis 'Superba'
Berberis thunbergii 'Crimsom Pygmy'	B. thunbergii 'Atropurpurea Nana'
Berberis thunbergii 'Green Mantle'	B. thunbergii 'Kelleriis'
Berberis thunbergii 'Green Marble'	B. thunbergii 'Kelleriis'
Berberis thunbergii 'Silver Mile'	B. x ottawensis 'Silver Mile'
Berberis wilsoniae 'Marianne'	B. wilsoniae 'Graciella'
Berberis x media Park Jewel	B. x media 'Parkjuweel'
Berberis x media Park Juwel	B. x media 'Parkjuweel'
Berberis x ottawensis 'Purpurea'	B. x ottawensis f purpurea
Berberis x rubrostilla	B. 'Rubrostilla'
Berberis x stenophylla 'Cornish Cream'	B. x stenophylla 'Lemon Queen'
Berberis x stenophylla 'Cream Showers'	B. x stenophylla 'Lemon Queen'
Bergenia acanthifolia	B. x spathulata
Bergenia beesiana	B. purpurascens
Bergenia Bell Tower	B. 'Glockenturm'
Bergenia ciliata x crassifolia	B. x schmidtii
Bergenia crassifolia 'Orbicularis'	B. x schmidtii
Bergenia delavayi	B. purpurascens v delavayi
Bergenia 'Delbees'	B. purpurascens 'Ballawley'
Bergenia Evening Glow	B. 'Abendglut'
Bergenia 'Lambrook'	B. 'Margery Fish'
Bergenia milesii	B. stracheyi
Bergenia Morning Red	B. 'Morgenrote'

Name	Synonym
Bergenia purpurascens 'Ballawley'	B. 'Ballawley'
Bergenia Silverlight	B. 'Silberlicht'
Bergenia Snow Queen	B. 'Schneekonigin'
Bergenia stracheyi 'Alba'	B. stracheyi Alba Group
Bergenia stracheyi f alba	B. stracheyi Alba Group
Bergenia Winter Fairy Tale	B. 'Wintermarchen'
Betonica	Stachys
Betula alba -Linnaeus	B. pendula
Betula caerulea-grandis	B. x caerulea
Betula celtiberica	B. pubescens ssp celtiberica
Betula costata h	B. ermanii 'Grayswood Hill'
Betula fruticosa	B. humilis
Betula 'Inverleith'	B. utilis v jacquemontii 'Inverleith'
Betula jacquemontii	B. utilis v jacquemontii
Betula lutea	B. alleghaniensis
Betula occidentalis	B. fontinalis
Betula pendula 'Dalecarlica' h	B. pendula 'Laciniata'
Betula pendula f crispa	B. pendula 'Laciniata'
Betula platyphylla v szechuanica	B. szechuanica
Betula resinifera -Britton	B. neoalaskana
Betula tatewakiana	B. ovalifolia
Betula verrucosa	B. pendula
Bidens atrosanguinea	Cosmos atrosanguineus
Bidens humilis	B. triplinervia v macrantha
Bignonia capensis	Tecoma capensis
Bignonia grandiflora	Campsis grandiflora
Bignonia jasminoides	Pandorea jasminoides
Bignonia lindleyana	Clytostoma callistegioides
Bignonia pandorana	Pandorea pandorana
Bignonia radicans	Campsis radicans
Bignonia stans	Tecoma stans
Bignonia unguis-cati	Macfadyena unguis-cati
Bilderdyckia aubertii	Fallopia aubertii
Bilderdyckia baldschuanica	Fallopia baldschuanica
Bilderdykia	Fallopia
Billbergia rhodocyanea	Aechmea fasciata
Billbergia saundersii	B. chlorosticta
Biota orientalis	Thuja orientalis
Bistorta	Persicaria
Bistorta affine	Persicaria affinis
Bistorta amplexicaulis	Persicaria amplexicaulis
Bistorta macrophylla	Persicaria macrophylla
Bistorta major	Persicaria bistorta
Bistorta milletii	Persicaria milletii
Bistorta vacciniifolia	Persicaria vacciniifolia
Blechnum alpinum	B. penna-marina ssp alpinum
Blechnum cordatum	B. chilense
Blechnum magellanicum misapplied	B. chilense
Blechnum occidentale nanum	B. glandulosum
Blechnum spicant incisum	B. spicant 'Rickard's Serrate'
Blechnum tabulare misapplied	B. chilense
Bletilla hyacinthina	B. striata
Bletilla striata alba	B. striata v japonica f gebina
Bocconia	Macleaya
Bocconia cordata	Macleaya cordata
Bocconia microcarpa	Macleaya microcarpa
Bolax glebaria	Azorella trifurcata
Boltonia incisa	Kalimeris incisa
Boltonia latisquama	B. asteroides v latisquama
Bomarea kalbreyeri h	B. caldasii
Bomarea pubigera h	B. andimarcana
Bonifazia quezalteca	Disocactus quezaltecus
Borago laxiflora	B. pygmaea
Boronia elatior	B. molloyae
Borzicactus	Oreocereus
Borzicactus leucotrichus	Oreocereus hempelianus
Bothriochilus	Coelia
Bothriochilus bellus	Coelia bella
Bothriochloa caucasica	B. bladhii
Botryostege	Elliottia
Bougainvillea 'Ailsa Lambe'	B. 'Mary Palmer' (Spectoperuviana Group)
Bougainvillea 'Apple Blossom'	B. x buttiana 'Audrey Grey'
Bougainvillea 'Audrey Grey'	B. x buttiana 'Audrey Grey'
Bougainvillea 'Aussie Gold'	B. 'Carson's Gold'
Bougainvillea 'Brasiliensis'	B. spectabilis 'Lateritia'
Bougainvillea 'Bridal Bouquet'	B. x buttiana 'Mahara Off-White'
Bougainvillea 'Brilliant'	B. 'Raspberry Ice'
Bougainvillea 'California Gold'	B. x buttiana 'Golden Glow'
Bougainvillea 'Cherry Blossom'	B. x buttiana 'Mahara Off-white'
Bougainvillea 'Crimson Lake'	B. x buttiana 'Mrs. Butt'
Bougainvillea 'Dauphine'	B. x buttiana 'Mahara Pink'
Bougainvillea 'Delicate'	B. 'Blondie'
Bougainvillea 'Doctor David Barry'	B. glabra 'Doctor David Barry'
Bougainvillea 'Double Yellow'	B. 'Carson's Gold'
Bougainvillea 'Durban'	B. glabra 'Jane Snook'
Bougainvillea 'Elizabeth Angus'	B. glabra 'Elizabeth Angus'
Bougainvillea 'Enchantment'	B. 'Mary Palmer's Enchantment'
Bougainvillea 'Fair Lady'	B. 'Blondie'
Bougainvillea 'Flamingo Pink'	B. 'Chiang Mai Beauty'
Bougainvillea glabra 'Variegata'	B. glabra 'Harrissii'
Bougainvillea 'Golden Dubloon'	B. x buttiana 'Mahara Orange'
Bougainvillea 'Golden Glow'	B. x buttiana 'Golden Glow'
Bougainvillea 'Golden Maclean'	B. x buttiana 'Golden Maclean'
Bougainvillea 'Harlequin'	B. 'Thimma' (Spectoperuviana Group)
Bougainvillea 'Harrissii'	B. glabra 'Harrissii'
Bougainvillea 'Hawaiian Gold'	B. x buttiana 'Golden Glow'
Bougainvillea 'Hawaiian Scarlet'	B. 'Scarlet O'Hara'
Bougainvillea 'Helen Johnson'	B. 'Temple Fire'
Bougainvillea 'Hugh Evans'	B. 'Blondie'
Bougainvillea 'Indian Flame'	B. 'Partha'
Bougainvillea 'Jamaica Red'	B. x buttiana 'Jamaica Red'
Bougainvillea 'Jane Snook'	B. glabra 'Jane Snook'
Bougainvillea 'Jennifer Fernie'	B. glabra 'Jennifer Fernie'
Bougainvillea 'Kauai Royal'	B. glabra 'Elizabeth Angus'
Bougainvillea 'Klong Fire'	B. x buttiana 'Mahara Double Red'

Name	Synonym
Bougainvillea 'Lady Mary Baring'	B. x buttiana 'Lady Mary Baring'
Bougainvillea 'Lemmer's Special'	B. 'Partha'
Bougainvillea 'Limberlost Beauty'	B. x buttiana 'Mahara Off-White'
Bougainvillea 'Los Banos Beauty'	B. x buttiana 'Mahara Pink'
Bougainvillea 'Magnifica'	B. glabra 'Magnifica'
Bougainvillea 'Magnifica Traillii'	B. glabra 'Magnifica'
Bougainvillea 'Mahara Double Red'	B. x buttiana 'Mahara Double Red'
Bougainvillea 'Mahara Off-white'	B. x buttiana 'Mahara Off-white'
Bougainvillea 'Mahara Orange'	B. x buttiana 'Mahara Orange'
Bougainvillea 'Mahara Pink'	B. x buttiana 'Mahara Pink'
Bougainvillea 'Mahara White'	B. x buttiana 'Mahara Off-white'
Bougainvillea 'Mahatma Gandhi'	B. 'Mrs H.C.Buck' (Spectoperuviana Group)
Bougainvillea 'Mardi Gras'	B. x buttiana 'Mardi Gras'
Bougainvillea 'Mini-Thai'	B. 'Lord Willingdon'
Bougainvillea 'Mrs Butt'	B. x buttiana 'Mrs Butt'
Bougainvillea 'Mrs Butt Variegated'	B. x buttiana 'Mrs Butt Variegated'
Bougainvillea 'Mrs Helen McLean'	B. x buttiana 'Mrs Helen McLean'
Bougainvillea 'Mrs McLean'	B. x buttiana 'Mrs McLean'
Bougainvillea 'Orange Glow'	B. Camarillo Fiesta (spectabilis hybrid)
Bougainvillea 'Orange King'	B. 'Louis Wathen'
Bougainvillea 'Pagoda Pink'	B. x buttiana 'Mahara Pink'
Bougainvillea 'Penelope'	B. 'Mary Palmer's Enchantment'
Bougainvillea 'Pink Champagne'	B. x buttiana 'Mahara Pink'
Bougainvillea 'Pink Pixie'	B. 'Lord Willingdon'
Bougainvillea 'Poultonii'	B. x buttiana 'Poultonii'
Bougainvillea 'Poultonii Special'	B. x buttiana 'Poulton's Special'
Bougainvillea 'Pride of Singapore'	B. glabra 'Pride of Singapore'
Bougainvillea 'Princess Mahara'	B. x buttiana 'Mahara Double Red'
Bougainvillea 'Purple King'	B. x buttiana 'Texas Dawn'
Bougainvillea 'Rainbow Gold'	B. x buttiana 'Rainbow Gold'
Bougainvillea 'Robyn's Glory'	B. x buttiana 'Texas Dawn'
Bougainvillea 'Rosenka'	B. x buttiana 'Rosenka'
Bougainvillea 'San Diego Red'	B. 'Scarlett O'Hara'
Bougainvillea 'Sanderiana'	B. glabra 'Sanderiana'
Bougainvillea 'Sanderiana Variegated'	B. glabra 'Harrisii'
Bougainvillea 'Singapore Pink'	B. glabra 'Doctor David Barry'
Bougainvillea 'Smartipants'	B. 'Lord Willingdon'
Bougainvillea 'Snow Cap'	B. 'Mary Palmer' (Spectoperuviana Group)
Bougainvillea Surprise	B. 'Mary Palmer' (Spectoperuviana Group)
Bougainvillea 'Tango'	B. 'Miss Manila'
Bougainvillea 'Thai Gold'	B. x buttiana 'Mahara Orange'

Name	Synonym
Bougainvillea 'Tom Thumb'	B. 'Temple Fire'
Bougainvillea 'Tropical Rainbow'	B. 'Raspberry Ice'
Bougainvillea 'Variegata' (glabra)	B. glabra 'Harrisii'
Bougainvillea 'Variegata' (spectabilis)	B. spectabilis 'Variegata'
Bougainvillea 'Vicky'	B. 'Thimma' (Spectoperuviana Group)
Boussingaultia	Anredera
Boussingaultia baselloides -Hook	Anredera cordifolia
Bouteloua oligostachys	B. gracilis
Bouvardia humboldtii	B. longiflora
Bouvardia triphylla	B. ternifolia
Boykinia elata	B. occidentalis
Boykinia heucheriformis	B. jamesii
Boykinia tellimoides	Peltoboykinia tellimoides
Brachychilum	Hedychium
Brachycome	Brachyscome
Brachyglottis 'Sunshine Variegated'	B. 'Moira Reid' Dunedin Group
Brachyscome nivalis v alpina	B. tadgellii
Brachysema acuminatum	B. celsianum
Brachysema lanceolatum	B. celsianum
Bracteantha acuminata -De Candolle	B. subundulata
Brassaia	Schefflera
Brassica japonica	B. juncea v crispifolia
Bravoa geminiflora	Polianthes geminiflora
Brevoortia	Dichelostemma
Breynia nivosa	B. disticha
Bridgesia spicata	Ercilla volubilis
Brittonastrum	Agastache
Brittonastrum mexicanum	Agastache mexicana
Brodiaea capitata	Dichelostemma pulchellum
Brodiaea congesta	Dichelostemma congestum
Brodiaea 'Corrina'	Triteleia 'Corrina'
Brodiaea grandiflora	B. coronaria
Brodiaea hyacinthina	Triteleia hyacintha
Brodiaea ida-maia	Dichelostemma ida-maia
Brodiaea ixioides	Triteleia ixioides
Brodiaea laxa	Triteleia laxa
Brodiaea lutea	Triteleia lixioides
Brodiaea peduncularis	Triteleia peduncularis
Brodiaea pulchella	Dichelostemma pulchellum
Brodiaea purdyi	B. minor
Brodiaea volubilis	Dichelostemma volubile
Bromus catharticus	B. unioloides
Bromus macrostachys	B. lanceolatus
Browallia elata	B. americana
Brownea grandiceps	B. ariza
Brownea princeps	B. ariza
Brugmansia bicolor	B. sanguinea
Brugmansia cornigera	B. arborea
Brugmansia meteloides	Datura inoxia
Brugmansia rosei	B. sanguinea ssp sanguinea 'Flava'
Brugmansia sanguinea 'Rosea'	B. x insignis pink
Brugmansia suaveolens rosea	B. x insignis pink
Brugmansia suaveolens x versicolor	B. x insignis
Brugmansia versicolor h	B. arborea
Brugmansia x candida 'Plena'	B. x candida 'Knightii'
Brunfelsia calycina	B. pauciflora
Brunfelsia eximia	B. pauciflora
Brunnera macrophylla 'Alba'	B. macrophylla 'Betty Bowring'

Synonyms

Name	Synonym
Brunnera macrophylla 'Variegata'	B. macrophylla 'Dawson's White'
Brunsvigia multiflora	B. orientalis
Brunsvigia rosea 'Minor'	Amaryllis belladonna
Bryophyllum	Kalanchoe
Bryophyllum daigremontianum	Kalanchoe daigremontiana
Bryophyllum tubiflorum	Kalanchoe delagoensis
Bryophyllum uniflorum	Kalanchoe uniflora
Buddleja brevifolia	B. abbreviata
Buddleja davidii 'Glasnevin Blue'	B. davidii 'Glasnevin'
Buddleja davidii 'Nanho Petite Indigo'	B. davidii 'Nanho Blue'
Buddleja davidii 'Nanho Petite Purple'	B. davidii 'Nanho Purple'
Buddleja davidii 'Petite Indigo'	B. davidii 'Nanho Blue'
Buddleja davidii 'Petite Plum'	B. davidii 'Nanho Purple'
Buddleja davidii 'Pink Charming'	B. davidii 'Charming'
Buddleja heliophila	B. delavayi
Buddleja nicodemia	B. madagascariensis
Buddleja sterniana	B. crispa
Buddleja tibetica	B. crispa
Bulbine caulescens	B. frutescens
Bulbinella setosa	B. cauda-felis
Bulbinopsis	Bulbine
Buphthalmum salicifolium 'Golden Beauty'	B. salicifolium 'Golden Wonder'
Buphthalmum speciosum	Telekia speciosa
Bupleurum angulosum copper	B. longifolium
Bupleurum rotundifolium 'Leprechaun Green Gold'	B. rotundifolium 'Green Gold'
Burchellia capensis	B. bubalina
Butea frondosa	B. momosperma
Buxus aurea 'Marginata'	B. sempervirens 'Marginata'
Buxus japonica 'Nana'	B. microphylla
Buxus microphylla 'Asiatic Winter'	B. microphylla 'Winter Gem'
Buxus microphylla v insularis	B. sinica v insularis
Buxus microphylla v koreana	B. sinica v insularis
Buxus microphylla v riparia	B. riparia
Buxus microphylla v sinica	B. sinica
Buxus 'Newport Blue'	B. sempervirens 'Newport Blue'
Buxus sempervirens 'Argentea'	B. sempervirens 'Argenteovariegata'
Buxus sempervirens 'Aurea'	B. sempervirens 'Argenteovariegata'
Buxus sempervirens 'Aurea Maculata'	B. sempervirens 'Argenteovariegata'
Buxus sempervirens 'Aurea Marginata'	B. sempervirens 'Marginata'
Buxus sempervirens 'Aureomarginata'	B. sempervirens 'Marginata'
Buxus sempervirens 'Blue Spire'	B. sempervirens 'Blue Cone'
Buxus sempervirens 'Gold Tip'	B. sempervirens 'Notata'
Buxus sempervirens 'Japonica Aurea'	B. sempervirens 'Latifolia Maculata'
Buxus sempervirens 'Kingsville'	B. microphylla 'Compacta'
Buxus sempervirens 'Langley Pendula'	B. sempervirens 'Langley Beauty'
Buxus sempervirens 'Latifolia'	B. sempervirens 'Bullata'
Buxus sempervirens 'Longifolia'	B. sempervirens 'Angustifolia'
Buxus sempervirens 'Silver Variegated'	B. sempervirens 'Elegantisima'
Cacalia coccinea	Emilia coccinea
Cacalia sagittata	Emilia coccinea
Cacalia sonchifolia	Emilia sonchifolia
Caladium x hortulanum	C. bicolor
Calamintha alpina	Acinos alpinus
Calamintha clinopodium	Clinopodium vulgare
Calamintha corsica	Acinos corsicus
Calamintha nepetoides	C. nepeta ssp nepeta
Calamintha vulgaris	Clinopodium vulgare
Calandrinia megarhiza	Claytonia megarhiza
Calandrinia megarhiza v nivalis	Claytonia megarhiza v nivalis
Calandrinia sibirica	Claytonia sibirica
Calanthe bicolor	C. discolor v flava
Calanthe striata	C. sieboldii
Calathea albicans	C. micans
Calathea discolor	C. lutea
Calathea insignis	C. lancifolia
Calathea kegeljanii	C. bella
Calathea oppenheimiana	Ctenanthe oppenheimiana
Calathea orbiculata	C. truncata
Calathea ornata	C. majestica
Calceolaria acutifolia	C. polyrhiza
Calceolaria plantaginea	C. biflora
Calceolaria rugosa	C. integrifolia
Calceolaria scabiosifolia	C. tripartita
Calla aethiopica	Zantedeschia aethiopica
Calliandra brevipes	C. selloi
Calliandra inaequilatera	C. haematocephala
Callianthemum rutifolium	C. coriandrifolium
Calliopsis tinctoria	Coreopsis tinctoria
Callistemon citrinus 'Albus'	C. citrinus 'White Anzac'
Callistemon glaucus	C. speciosus
Callistemon pallidus 'Austraflora Candleglow'	C. pallidus 'Candle Glow'
Callistemon paludosus	C. sieberi
Callitriche autumnalis	C. hermaphroditica
Callitriche verna	C. palustris
Callitris cupressiformis	C. rhomboidea
Callitris tasmanica	C. rhomboidea
Calluna vulgaris 'Alba Elongata'	C. vulgaris 'Mair's Variety'
Calluna vulgaris 'Aureifolia'	C. vulgaris 'Hammondii Aureifolia'
Calluna vulgaris 'Doctor Murray's White'	C. vulgaris 'Mullardoch'
Calluna vulgaris 'Elegantissima Walter Ingwersen'	C. vulgaris 'Walter Ingwersen'
Calluna vulgaris 'Elongata'	C. vulgaris 'Mair's Variety'
Calluna vulgaris 'Foxii Lett's Form'	C. vulgaris 'Velvet Dome'
Calluna vulgaris 'Hammondii Aurea'	C. vulgaris 'Hammondii Aureifolia'
Calluna vulgaris 'Hiemalis Southcote'	C. vulgaris 'Durfordii'
Calluna vulgaris 'J.F.Letts'	C. vulgaris 'John F.Letts'
Calluna vulgaris 'Marinka'	C. vulgaris 'Red Carpet'
Calluna vulgaris 'Mousehole Compact'	C. vulgaris 'Mousehole'
Calluna vulgaris 'Pepper and Salt'	C. vulgaris 'Hugh Nicholson'
Calluna vulgaris 'Pink Beale'	C. vulgaris 'H.E.Beale'
Calluna vulgaris Red October	C. vulgaris 'Rote Oktober'
Calluna vulgaris 'Rigida Prostrata'	C. vulgaris 'Alba Rigida'
Calluna vulgaris 'Rowland Haagen'	C. vulgaris 'Roland Haagen'
Calluna vulgaris 'Snowball'	C. vulgaris 'My Dream'
Calluna vulgaris 'Spring Charm'	C. vulgaris 'Spring Torch'

Name	Synonym
Calluna vulgaris 'Sunningdale'	C. vulgaris 'Finale'
Calluna vulgaris 'White Princess'	C. vulgaris 'White Queen'
Calocedrus decurrens 'Nana'	C. decurrens 'Depressa'
Calocephalus brownii	Leucophyta brownii
Calochortus eurycarpus	C. nitidus
Calonyction	Ipomoea
Calonyction aculeatum	Ipomoea alba
Caltha laeta	C. palustris v palustris
Caltha polypetala h	C. palustris v palustris
Calycanthus chinensis	Sinocalycanthus chinensis
Calycanthus floridus v laevigatus	C. floridus v glaucus
Calydorea speciosa	C. xiphioides
Calyptridium umbellatum	Spraguea umbellata
Calystegia japonica 'Flore Pleno'	C. hederacea 'Flore Pleno'
Camassia esculenta	C. quamash
Camassia fraseri	C. scilloides
Camassia leichtlinii 'Alba' h	C. leichtlinii ssp leichtlinii
Camassia leichtlinii 'Blauwe Donau'	C. leichtlinii sspsuksdorfii 'Blauwe Donau'
Camassia leichtlinii Blue Danube	C. leichtlinii ssp suksdorfii 'Blauwe Donau'
Camassia suksdorfii Blue Danube	C. leichtlinii sspsuksdorfii 'Blauwe Donau'
Camellia 'Auburn White'	C. japonica 'Mrs Bertha A.Harms'
Camellia 'Baby Face'	C. reticulata 'Tongzimian'
Camellia 'Barchi'	C. japonica 'Contessa Samailoff'
Camellia 'Bertha Harms Blush'	C. japonica 'Mrs Bertha A.Harms'
Camellia 'Chandler's Elegans'	C. japonica 'Elegans'
Camellia chrysantha	C. nitidissima v nitidissima
Camellia 'Contessa Lavinia Maggi'	C. japonica 'Lavinia Maggi'
Camellia 'Czar'	C. japonica 'The Czar'
Camellia 'Dawn'	C. x vernalis 'Ginryu'
Camellia 'Delia Williams'	C. x williamsii 'Citation'
Camellia 'Donckelaeri'	C. japonica 'Masayoshi'
Camellia 'Eclipsis'	C. japonica 'Press's Eclipse'
Camellia 'Faustina Lechi'	C. japonica 'Faustina'
Camellia 'Frau Minna Seidel'	C. japonica 'Otome'
Camellia 'Hiemalis Hiryu'	C. hiemalis 'Kanjiro'
Camellia 'Imbricata Rubra'	C. japonica 'Imbricata'
Camellia japonica 'Baron Gomer'	C. japonica 'Comte de Gomer'
Camellia japonica 'Blackburnia'	C. japonica 'Althaeiflora'
Camellia japonica 'Bush Hill Beauty'	C. japonica 'Lady de Saumarez'
Camellia japonica 'Chandleri Elegans'	C. japonica 'Elegans'
Camellia japonica 'Charming Betty'	C. japonica 'Funny Face Betty'
Camellia japonica 'Colonel Firey'	C. japonica 'C.M.Hovey'
Camellia japonica 'Compton's Brow'	C. japonica 'Gauntlettii'
Camellia japonica 'Daitairin'	C. japonica 'Dewatairin'
Camellia japonica 'Effendee'	C. sasanqua 'Rosea Plena'
Camellia japonica 'Fimbriata Alba'	C. japonica 'Fimbriata'
Camellia japonica 'Glen 40'	C. japonica 'Coquettii'
Camellia japonica 'Hassaku'	C. japonica 'Hassaku-shibori'
Camellia japonica 'Hatsuzakura'	C. japonica 'Dewatairin'
Camellia japonica Herme	C. japonica 'Hikarugenji'
Camellia japonica 'Joy Sander'	C. japonica 'Apple Blossom'
Camellia japonica 'Kellingtoniana'	C. japonica 'Gigantea'
Camellia japonica 'Kouron-jura'	C. japonica 'Konronkoku'
Camellia japonica Lady Clare	C. japonica 'Akashigata'
Camellia japonica 'Lady Marion'	C. japonica 'Kumasaka'
Camellia japonica 'Lady Vansittart Red'	C. japonica 'Lady Vansittart Pink'
Camellia japonica 'Lotus'	C. japonica 'Gauntlettii'
Camellia japonica 'Magellan'	C. japonica 'Dona Herzilia de Frietas Magalhaes'
Camellia japonica 'Magnoliiflora'	C. japonica 'Hagoromo'
Camellia japonica 'Magnoliiflora Alba'	C. japonica 'Miyakodori'
Camellia japonica 'Mathotiana Purple King'	C. japonica 'Julia Drayton'
Camellia japonica 'Mathotiana Rubra'	C. japonica 'Julia Drayton'
Camellia japonica 'Monstruosa Rubra'	C. japonica 'Gigantea Red'
Camellia japonica 'Nagasaki'	C. japonica 'Mikenjaku'
Camellia japonica 'Nigra'	C. japonica 'Konronkoku'
Camellia japonica 'Paul's Apollo'	C. japonica 'Apollo'
Camellia japonica 'Paul's Jupiter'	C. japonica 'Jupiter'
Camellia japonica 'Peachblossom'	C. japonica 'Fleur Dipater'
Camellia japonica 'Pink Perfection'	C. japonica 'Otome'
Camellia japonica 'Pope Pius IX'	C. japonica 'Prince Eugene Napoleon'
Camellia japonica 'Pride of Descanso'	C. japonica 'Yukibotan'
Camellia japonica 'Purity'	C. japonica 'Shiragiku'
Camellia japonica 'Purple Emperor'	C. japonica 'Julia Drayton'
Camellia japonica 'Rainbow'	C. japonica 'O-niji'
Camellia japonica 'Shin-akebono'	C. japonica 'Akebono'
Camellia japonica 'Sieboldii'	C. japonica 'Tricolor'
Camellia japonica ssp rusticana	C. rusticana
Camellia japonica 'Tinsie'	C. japonica 'Bokuhan'
Camellia japonica 'Tricolor Red'	C. japonica 'Lady de Saumarez'
Camellia japonica 'Victor de Bisschop'	C. japonica 'Le Lys'
Camellia japonica 'Victor Emmanuel'	C. japonica 'Blood of China'
Camellia japonica 'Yoibijin'	C. japonica 'Suibijin'
Camellia 'Jury's Charity'	C. x williamsii 'Charity'
Camellia 'Madame Victor de Bisschop'	C. japonica 'Le Leys'
Camellia 'Magnolia Queen'	C. japonica 'Priscilla Brooks'
Camellia maliiflora	C. maliflora
Camellia 'Pink Spangles'	C. japonica 'Mathotiana Rosea'
Camellia 'Portuense'	C. 'Japonica Variegata'
Camellia reticulata 'Flore Pleno'	C. reticulata 'Songzilin'
Camellia 'Robert Fortune'	C. reticulata 'Songzilin'
Camellia 'Salonica'	C. x williamsii 'Shimna'
Camellia saluenensis 'Apple Blossom'	C. 'Showa-wabisuke'
Camellia saluenensis x japonica	C. x williamsii
Camellia sasanqua 'Flamingo'	C. sasanqua 'Fukuzutsumi'
Camellia sasanqua 'Flore Pleno'	C. maliflora
Camellia 'Splendens'	C. japonica 'Coccinea'
Camellia 'Stella Polare'	C. japonica 'Etoile Polaire'
Camellia thea	C. sinensis
Camellia 'Tinsie'	C. japonica 'Bokuhan'
Camellia 'Toko'	C. sasanqua 'Azuma-beni'
Camellia 'Tomorrow Supreme'	C. japonica 'Tomorrow Variegated'
Camellia 'Tricolor Sieboldii'	C. japonica 'Tricolor'
Camellia 'Usu-otome'	C. japonica 'Otome'
Camellia vernalis 'Dawn'	C. vernalis 'Ginryu'

Synonyms

Camellia 'Waterloo'	C. japonica 'Etherington White'	Campanula x haylodgensis	C. x haylodgensis 'Plena'
		Campanula x innesii	C. 'John Innes'
Camellia 'Yukihaki'	C. japonica 'Yukishiro'	Campanula x wockei	C. x wockei 'Puck'
Campanula acutangula	C. arvatica	Campanumoea	Codonopsis
Campanula alaskana	C. rotundifolia v alaskana	Campelia zanonia	Tradescantia zanonia
Campanula alliarifolia 'Ivory Bells'	C. alliarifolia	Campsis chinensis	Campsis grandiflora
Campanula allionii	C. alpestris	Campsis radicans 'Yellow Trumpet'	Campsis radicans f flava
Campanula alpina ssp orbelica	C. orbelica	Camptosorus	Asplenium
Campanula amabilis 'Planiflora'	C. persicifolia v planiflora	Camptosorus rhizophyllus	Asplenium rhizophyllum
Campanula bellardii	C. cochleariifolia	Canarina campanula	C. canariensis
Campanula betulaefolia	C. betulifolia	Candollea	Hibbertia
Campanula carpatica Blue Clips	C. carpatica 'Blaue Clips'	Canna Assault	C. 'Assaut'
Campanula carpatica 'Turbinata'	C. carpatica v turbinata	Canna edulis	C. indica
Campanula carpatica White Clips	C. carpatica 'Weisse Clips'	Canna Firebird	C. 'Oiseau de Feu'
		Canna King Humbert orange-red	C. 'Roi Humbert'
Campanula cephallenica	C. garganica ssp cephallenica	Canna 'Malawiensis Variegata'	C. 'Striata'
		Canna malawiensis 'Variegata'	C. 'Striata'
Campanula cochleariifolia 'Warleyensis'	C. x haylodgensis 'Warley White'	Canna 'Pretoria'	C. 'Striata'
		Cantua dependens	C. buxifolia
Campanula dasyantha	C. chamissonis	Capsicum annuum v acuminatum	C. annuum
Campanula denticulata	C. betulifolia	Caralluma albocastanea	Orbeopsis albocastanea
Campanula elatines v garganica	C. garganica	Caralluma dummeri	Pachycymbium dummeri
Campanula eriocarpa	C. latifolia 'Eriocarpa'		
Campanula finitima	C. betulifolia	Caralluma lutea	Orbeopsis lutea
Campanula garganica 'Aurea'	C. garganica 'Dickson's Gold'	Caralluma pillansii	Quaqua pillansii
		Cardamine asarifolia h	Pachyphragma macrophyllum
Campanula glomerata Crown of Snow	C. glomerata 'Schneekrone'		
		Cardamine latifolia -Vahl	C. raphanifolia
Campanula isophylla 'Variegata'	C. 'Balchiniana'	Carduus benedictus	Cnicus benedictus
Campanula lactiflora alba	C. lactiflora white	Carex conica 'Hime-kan-suge'	C. conica 'Snowline'
Campanula linifolia	C. carnica	Carex elata 'Bowles' Golden'	C. elata 'Aurea'
Campanula medium v calycanthema	C. medium 'Calycanthema'	Carex 'Evergold'	C. oshimensis 'Evergold'
		Carex forsteri	C. pseudocyperus
Campanula muralis	C. portenschlagiana	Carex fortunei 'Variegata'	C. morrowii 'Variegata'
Campanula nitida	C. persicifolia v planiflora	Carex glauca	C. flacca ssp flacca
Campanula nitida v planiflora	C. persicifolia v planiflora	Carex glauca -Scopoli	C. flacca
Campanula olympica h	C. rotundifolia 'Olympica'	Carex 'Hime-kan-suge'	C. conica
Campanula ossetica	Symphyandra ossetica	Carex morrowii 'Evergold'	C. oshimensis 'Evergold'
Campanula pallida ssp tibetica	C. cashmeriana	Carex morrowii h	C. oshimensis
Campanula persicifolia 'Alba Plena'	C. persicifolia 'Alba Coronata'	Carex ornithopoda 'Aurea'	C. ornithopoda 'Variegata'
Campanula persicifolia 'Caerulea Coronata'	C. persicifolia 'Coronata'	Carex riparia 'Bowles' Golden'	C. elata 'Aurea'
Campanula persicifolia 'George Chiswell'	C. persicifolia 'Chettle Charm'	Carex stricta 'Aurea'	C. elata 'Aurea'
		Carex stricta 'Bowles' Golden'	C. elata 'Aurea'
Campanula persicifolia 'Hetty'	C. persicifolia 'Hampstead White'	Carex stricta -Goodenough	C. elata
		Carissa grandiflora	C. macrocarpa
Campanula persicifolia ssp sessiliflora	C. latifolia	Carissa spectabilis	Acokanthera oblongifolia
Campanula persicifolia v nitida	C. persicifolia v planiflora	Carlina acaulis caulescens	C. acaulis ssp simplex
Campanula pilosa	C. chamissonis	Carmichaelia australis	C. arborea
Campanula pilosa v dasyantha	C. chamissonis	Carpinus betulus 'Pyramidalis'	C. betulus 'Fastigiata'
Campanula planiflora	C. persicifolia v planiflora	Carpinus fargesii	C. laxiflora v macrostachya
Campanula poscharskyana 'Glandore'	C. 'Glandore'		
Campanula pusilla	C. cochleariifolia	Carum petroselinum	Petroselinum crispum
Campanula recurva	C. incurva	Caryopteris mastacanthus	C. incana
Campanula rhomboidalis -Gorter	C. rapunculoides	Cassandra	Chamaedaphne
Campanula rotundifolia 'Caerulea Plena'	C. rotundifolia 'Flore Pleno'	Cassia alata	Senna alata
		Cassia artemisoides	Senna artemisoides
Campanula takesimana 'Elizabeth'	C. 'Elizabeth'	Cassia corymbosa -Lam.	Senna corymbosa - (Lam.) Irwin & Barneby
Campanula tubulosa	C. buseri		
Campanula turbinata	C. carpatica v turbinata	Cassia corymbosa v plurijuga	Senna x floribunda
Campanula vidalii	Azorina vidalii	Cassia didymobotrya	Senna didymobotrya
Campanula wanneri	Symphyandra wanneri	Cassia obtusifolia	Senna obtusifolia
Campanula 'Warley White'	C. x haylodgensis 'Warley White'	Cassia siamea	Senna siamea
		Cassia x floribunda	Senna x floribunda
Campanula 'Warleyensis'	C. x haylodgensis 'Warley White'	Cassinia fulvida	C. leptophylla ssp fulvida
		Cassinia vauvilliersii	C. leptophylla ssp

Synonyms

Name	Synonym
Castanea sativa 'Argenteovariegata'	vauvilliersii
Castanea sativa 'Aureomarginata'	C. sativa 'Albomarginata'
Castanopsis chrysophylla	C. sativa 'Variegata'
Casuarina littoralis	Chrysolepis chrysophylla
Casuarina stricta	Allocasuarina littoralis
Catalpa bignonioides 'Purpurea'	Allocasuarina verticillata
	C. x erubescens 'Purpurea'
Cathcartia villosa	Meconopsis villosa
Cattleya Mother's Favourite	Cattleya 'Jose Marti'
Cautleya lutea	C. gracilis
Cayratia thomsonii	Parthenocissus thomsonii
Ceanothus azureus	C. coeruleus
Ceanothus 'Comtesse de Paris'	C. x delileanus 'Comtesse de Paris'
Ceanothus dentatus h	C. x lobbianus
Ceanothus repens	C. thyrsiflorus v repens
Ceanothus x regius 'Cynthia Postan'	C. 'Cynthia Postan'
Cedrela sinensis	Toona sinensis
Cedronella mexicana	Agastache mexicana
Cedronella triphylla	C. canariensis
Cedrus atlantica	C. libani ssp atlantica
Cedrus brevifolia	C. libani ssp brevifolia
Celastrus articulatus	C. orbiculatus
Celastrus punctatus	C. orbiculatus v punctatus
Celmisia webbiana	C. walkeri
Celsia	Verbascum
Celsia acaulis	Verbascum acaule
Celsioverbascum	Verbascum
Centaurea cana	C. triumfettii ssp cana
Centaurea candidissima h	C. cineraria
Centaurea candidissima -Lamarck	C. rutifolia
Centaurea cynaroides	Leuzea centauroides
Centaurea fischeri	C. cheiranthifolia v purpurascens
Centaurea gymnocarpa	C. cineraria
Centaurea montana rosea	C. montana carnea
Centaurea moschata	Amberboa moschata
Centaurea nervosa	C. uniflora ssp nervosa
Centaurea 'Pulchra Major'	Leuzea centauroides
Centaurea rhapontica	Leuzea rhapontica
Centaurium chloodes	C. confertum
Centaurium portense	C. scilloides
Centradenia rosea	C. inaequilateralis
Cephalaria tatarica	C. gigantea
Cephalocereus euphorbioides	Neobuxbaumia euphorbioides
Cercidophyllum japonicum 'Pendulum'	C. japonicum f pendulum
Cercis siliquastrum 'Alba'	C. siliquastrum f albida
Cercocarpus breviflorus	C. montanus v paucidentatus
Cereus emoryi	Bergerocactus emoryi
Cereus flagelliformis	Aporocactus flagelliformis
Cereus forbesii	C. validus
Cereus peruvianus h	C. uruguayanus
Ceriman	Monstera deliciosa
Ceropegia disticha ssp haygarthii	C. haygarthii
Ceropegia lanceolata	C. longifolia
Ceropegia purpureum	C. elegans
Ceropegia sandersoniae	C. sandersonii
Ceropegia woodii	C. linearis ssp woodii
Cestrum purpureum	C. elegans
Ceterach	Asplenium
Ceterach officinarum	A. ceterach
Chaenomeles lagenaria	C. speciosa
Chaenomeles maulei	C. japonica
Chaenomeles sinensis	Pseudocydonia sinensis
Chaenomeles speciosa 'Apple Blossom'	C. speciosa 'Moerloosei'
Chaenomeles speciosa 'Choshan'	C. x superba 'Yaegaki'
Chaerophyllum hirsutum 'Rubrifolium'	C. hirutum 'Roseum'
Chamaecereus silvestrii	Echinopsis chamaecereus
Chamaecyparis funebris	Cupressus funebris
Chamaecyparis lawsoniana 'Albospica Nana'	C. lawsoniana 'Nana Albospica'
Chamaecyparis lawsoniana 'Allumii Aurea'	C. lawsoniana 'Alumigold'
Chamaecyparis lawsoniana 'Argentea'	C. lawsoniana 'Argenteovariegata'
Chamaecyparis lawsoniana 'Blue Nantais'	C. lawsoniana 'Bleu Nantais'
Chamaecyparis lawsoniana 'Columnaris Aurea'	C. lawsoniana 'Golden Spire'
Chamaecyparis lawsoniana 'Dwarf Blue'	C. lawsoniana 'Pick's Dwarf Blue'
Chamaecyparis lawsoniana 'Ellwood's Variegata'	C. lawsoniana 'Ellwood's White'
Chamaecyparis lawsoniana 'Fletcheri Aurea'	C. lawsoniana 'Yellow Transparent'
Chamaecyparis lawsoniana 'Glauca Spek'	C. lawsoniana 'Spek'
Chamaecyparis lawsoniana 'Globus'	C. lawsoniana 'Barabits Globe'
Chamaecyparis lawsoniana 'Green Spire'	C. lawsoniana 'Green Pillar'
Chamaecyparis lawsoniana 'Hogger's Blue Gown'	C. lawsoniana 'Blue Gown'
Chamaecyparis lawsoniana 'Jackman's Green Hedger'	C. lawsoniana 'Green Hedger'
Chamaecyparis lawsoniana 'Jackman's Variety'	C. lawsoniana 'Green Pillar'
Chamaecyparis lawsoniana 'Lanei'	C. lawsoniana 'Lane'
Chamaecyparis lawsoniana 'Lanei Aurea'	C. lawsoniana 'Lane'
Chamaecyparis lawsoniana 'Milford Blue Jacket'	C. lawsoniana 'Blue Jacket'
Chamaecyparis lawsoniana 'Minima Densa'	C. lawsoniana 'Minima'
Chamaecyparis lawsoniana 'Nana Lutea'	C. lawsoniana 'Lutea Nana'
Chamaecyparis lawsoniana 'Nyewoods Silver'	C. lawsoniana 'Chilworth Silver'
Chamaecyparis lawsoniana 'Nymph'	C. lawsoniana 'Ellwood's Nymph'
Chamaecyparis lawsoniana Pot of Gold	C. lawsoniana 'Golden Pot'
Chamaecyparis lawsoniana 'Rogersii'	C. lawsoniana 'Nana Rogersii'
Chamaecyparis lawsoniana 'Smithii' - Dallim.&Jackson	C. lawsoniana 'Lutea Smithii'
Chamaecyparis lawsoniana 'Van Pelt's Blue'	C. lawsoniana 'Pelt's Blue'

Synonyms

Chamaecyparis lawsoniana 'Yellow Queen' C. lawsoniana 'Golden Queen'
Chamaecyparis lawsoniana 'Yellow Success' C. lawsoniana 'Golden Queen'
Chamaecyparis leylandii x Cupressocyparis leylandii
Chamaecyparis obtusa 'Aureovariegata' C. obtusa 'Opaal'
Chamaecyparis obtusa 'Chima-anihiba' C. obtusa 'Pygmaea Densa'
Chamaecyparis obtusa 'Crippsii Aurea' C. obtusa 'Crippsii'
Chamaecyparis obtusa 'Densa' C. obtusa 'Nana Densa'
Chamaecyparis obtusa 'Graciosa' C. obtusa 'Loenik'
Chamaecyparis obtusa 'Nana Rigida' C. obtusa 'Rigid Dwarf'
Chamaecyparis obtusa 'Nana Variegata' C. obtusa 'Mariesii'
Chamaecyparis pisifera 'Aurea Nana' C. pisifera 'Strathmore'
Chamaecyparis pisifera 'Filifera Sungold' C. pisifera 'Sungold'
Chamaecyparis pisifera 'Gold Dust' C. pisifera 'Plumosa Aurea'
Chamaecyparis pisifera 'Nana Aurea' C. pisifera 'Strathmore'
Chamaecyparis pisifera 'Plumosa Densa' C. pisifera 'Plumosa Compressa'
Chamaecyparis pisifera 'Plumosa Purple Dome' C. pisifera 'Purple Dome'
Chamaecyparis pisifera 'Rogersii' C. pisifera 'Plumosa Rogersii'
Chamaecyparis pisifera 'Squarrosa Veitchii' C. pisifera 'Squarrosa'
Chamaecyparis thyoides 'Kewensis' C. thyoides 'Glauca'
Chamaecyparis thyoides 'Red Star' C. thyoides 'Rubicon'
Chamaecytisus hirsutus v demissus C. demissus
Chamaecytisus purpureus 'Incarnatus' C. purpureus 'Atropurpureus'
Chamaedorea erumpens C. seifrizii
Chamaedorea metallica h C. microspadix
Chamaenerion Epilobium
Chamaepericlymenum Cornus
Chamaepericlymenum canadense Cornus canadensis
Chamaerops excelsa h Trachycarpus fortunei
Chamaerops excelsa -Thunberg Rhapis excelsa
Chamaespartium Genista
Chamaespartium sagittale Genista sagittalis
Chamaespartium sagittale ssp delphinense Genista delphinensis
Cheiranthus Erysimum
Cheiridopsis candidissima C. denticulata
Cheiridopsis purpurata C. purpurea
Chelidonium japonicum Hylomecon japonica
Chelone barbata Penstemon barbatus
Chelone obliqua v alba C. glabra
Chiapasia nelsonii Disocactus nelsonii
Chiastophyllum oppositifolium 'Frosted Jade' C. oppositifolium 'Jim's Pride'
Chiastophyllum simplicifolium C. oppositifolium
Chiliotrichum amelloides C. diffusum
Chimonanthus fragrans C. praecox
Chimonanthus praecox 'Concolor' C. praecox v luteus
Chimonanthus praecox 'Luteus' C. praecox v luteus
Chimonobambusa falcata Drepanostachyum falcatum
Chimonobambusa hookeriana h Himalayacalamus falconeri 'Damarapa'
Chiogenes Gaultheria
Chionocloa conspicua 'Rubra' C. rubra
Chionodoxa cretica C. nana
Chionodoxa gigantea C. luciliae Gigantea Group
Chionodoxa luciliae h C. forbesii

Chionodoxa siehei C. forbesii Siehei Group
Chionodoxa tmolusi C. forbesii 'Tmoli'
Chlorophytum capense h C. comosum
Chlorophytum laxum 'Variegatum' C. laxum 'Bichetii'
Chondrosum gracile Bouteloua gracilis
Chrysalidocarpus lutescens Dypsis lutescens
Chrysanthemopsis Rhodanthemum
Chrysanthemum alpinum Leucanthemopsis alpina
Chrysanthemum arcticum -Linnaeus Arctanthemum arcticum
Chrysanthemum argenteum Tanacetum argenteum
Chrysanthemum balsamita Tanacetum balsamita
Chrysanthemum 'Bronze Mei-kyo' C. 'Bronze Elegance'
Chrysanthemum 'Bronze Pamela' C. 'Pamela'
Chrysanthemum catananche Rhodanthemum catananche
Chrysanthemum cinerariifolium Tanacetum cinerariifolium
Chrysanthemum clusii Tanacetum corymbosum ssp clusii
Chrysanthemum coccineum Tanacetum coccineum
Chrysanthemum corymbosum Tanacetum corymbosum
Chrysanthemum 'Cottage Pink' C. 'Emperor of China'
Chrysanthemum densum Tanacetum densum ssp amani
Chrysanthemum foeniculaceum Argyranthemum foeniculaceum -(Willd) Webb & Sch.Bip.
Chrysanthemum frutescens Argyranthemum frutescens
Chrysanthemum gayanum Rhodanthemum gayanum
Chrysanthemum 'Gold Margaret' C. 'Golden Margaret'
Chrysanthemum haradjanii Tanacetum haradjanii
Chrysanthemum hosmariense Rhodanthemum hosmariense
Chrysanthemum 'Jessie Cooper' C. 'Mrs Jessie Cooper'
Chrysanthemum leucanthemum Leucanthemum vulgare
Chrysanthemum macrophyllum Tanacetum macrophyllum
Chrysanthemum maresii Rhodanthemum hosmariense
Chrysanthemum mawii Rhodanthemum gayanum
Chrysanthemum maximum h Leucanthemum x superbum
Chrysanthemum maximum -Ramond Leucanthemum maximum (Ramond)
Chrysanthemum naktongense Chrysanthemum zawadskii v latilobum
Chrysanthemum nipponicum Nipponanthemum nipponicum
Chrysanthemum 'Orange Margaret' C. 'Fleet Margaret'
Chrysanthemum pacificum Ajania pacifica
Chrysanthemum parthenium Tanacetum parthenium
Chrysanthemum 'Peach Margaret' C. 'Salmon Margaret'
Chrysanthemum pectinata Leucanthemopsis pectinata
Chrysanthemum praeteritium Tanacetum praeteritum
Chrysanthemum 'Primrose Courtier' C. 'Yellow Courtier'
Chrysanthemum 'Primrose Margaret' C. 'Buff Margaret'
Chrysanthemum ptarmiciflorum Tanacetum ptarmiciflorum
Chrysanthemum 'Red Glory' C. 'Red Woolman's Glory'
Chrysanthemum roseum Tanacetum coccineum
Chrysanthemum rubellum Chrysanthemum zawadskii

Synonyms

Chrysanthemum serotinum — Leucanthemella serotina
Chrysanthemum 'Tom Parr' — C. 'Doctor Tom Parr'
Chrysanthemum tricolor — C. carinatum
Chrysanthemum uliginosum — Leucanthemella serotina
Chrysanthemum welwitschii — C. segetum
Chrysanthemum x koreanum — Dendranthema grandiflorum

Chrysanthemum x superbum — Leucanthemum x superbum
Chrysopsis — Heterotheca
Chusquea culeou 'Breviglumis' — C. culeou 'Tenuis'
Cimicifuga acerina — C. japonica
Cimicifuga cordifolia -Pursh — C. americana
Cimicifuga cordifolia -Torrey & A Gray — C. rubifolia
Cimicifuga racemosa 'Purpurea' — C. simplex v simplex Atropurpurea Group

Cimicifuga racemosa v cordifolia — C. rubifolia
Cimicifuga ramosa — C. simplex v simplex 'Pritchard's Giant'
Cineraria cruentus h — Pericallis x hybrida
Cineraria florists' — Pericallis x hybrida
Cineraria maritima — Senecio cineraria
Cineraria x hybrida — Pericallis x hybrida
Cirrhopetalum guttulatum — Bulbophyllum guttulatum

Cirrhopetalum medusae — Bulbophyllum medusae
Cirsium diacantha — Ptilostemon diacantha
Cirsium helenioides — C. heterophyllum
Cissus bainesii — Cyphostemma bainesii
Cissus capensis — Rhoicissus capensis
Cissus juttae — Cyphostemma juttae
Cissus voinieriana — Tetrastigma voinierianum
Cistus albanicus — C. sintenisii
Cistus algarvensis — Halimium ocymoides
Cistus atriplicifolius — Halimium atriplicifolium
Cistus 'Barnsley Pink' — C. 'Grayswood Pink'
Cistus 'Chelsea Pink' — C. 'Grayswood Pink'
Cistus coeris — C. x hybridus
Cistus crispus h — C. x pulverulentus
Cistus crispus 'Prostratus' — C. crispus -Linnaeus
Cistus crispus 'Sunset' — C. x pulverulentus 'Sunset'

Cistus formosus — Halimium lasianthum
Cistus halimifolius — Halimium halimifolium
Cistus incanus — C. creticus ssp incanus
Cistus incanus ssp creticus — C. creticus ssp creticus
Cistus incanus ssp incanus — C. creticus ssp incanus
Cistus ingwerseniana — x Halimiocistus 'Ingwersenii'

Cistus ladanifer h — C. x cyprius
Cistus ladanifer Palhinhae Group — C. ladanifer v sulcatus
Cistus ladaniferus — C. ladanifer -Linnaeus
Cistus lasianthus — Halimium lasianthum
Cistus 'Merrist Wood Cream' — x Halimiocistus wintonensis 'Merrist Wood Cream'

Cistus ochreatus — C. symphytifolius ssp leucophyllus
Cistus palhinae — C. ladanifer v sulcatus
Cistus parviflorus h — C. 'Grayswood Pink'
Cistus populifolius v lasiocalyx — C. populifolius ssp major
Cistus psilosepalus — C. hirsutus v psilosepalus
Cistus revolii h — x Halimiocistus sahucii
Cistus rosmarinifolius — C. clusii
Cistus sahucii — x Halimiocistus sahucii
Cistus salvifolius x monspeliensis — C. x florentinus

Cistus 'Snowflake' — C. 'Snow Fire'
Cistus 'Tania Compton' — C. x cyprius 'Tania Compton'
Cistus tomentosus — Helianthemum nummularium ssp tomentosum
Cistus villosus — C. incanus
Cistus wintonensis — x Halimiocistus wintonensis
Cistus x corbariensis — C. x hybridus
Cistus x florentinus h — x Halimiocistus 'Ingwersenii'
Cistus x laxus 'Snow Queen' — C. x laxus 'Snow White'
Cistus x longifolius — C. x nigricans
Cistus x loretii h — C. x dansereaui
Cistus x loretii -Rouy/Foue — C. x stenophyllus
Cistus x lusitanicus -Maund — C. x dansereaui
Cistus x obtusifolius h — C. x nigricans
Cistus x pulverulentus 'Warley Rose' — C. x crispatus 'Warley Rose'
Cistus x purpureus 'Betty Taudevin' — C. x purpureus
Cistus x verguinii v albiflorus — C. x dansereaui unblotched
Citharexylum quadrangulare -Jacquin — C. spinosum
Citronella mucronata — C. gongonha
Citrus Calamondin — x Citrofortunella microcarpa
Citrus deliciosa — C. x nobilis
Citrus japonica — Fortunella japonica
Citrus Kumquat — Fortunella margarita
Citrus limon 'Quatre Saisons' — C. limon 'Garey's Eureka'
Citrus limon x sinensis — C. x meyeri
Citrus madurensis — Fortunella japonica
Citrus medica 'Cidro Digitado' — C. medica v sarcodactylis
Citrus microcarpa Philippine Lime — x Citrofortunella microcarpa
Citrus mitis — x Citrofortunella microcarpa
Citrus reticulata Satsuma Group — C. unshiu
Citrus reticulata 'Suntina' — C. reticulata 'Nova'
Citrus reticulata x paradisi — C. x tangelo
Citrus sinensis 'Jaffa' — C. sinensis 'Shamouti'
Clarkia elegans — C. unguiculata
Claytonia alsinoides — C. sibirica
Claytonia australasica — Neopaxia australasica
Claytonia parvifolia — Naiocrene parvifolia
Cleistocactus jujuyensis — C. hyalacanthus
Cleistocactus wendlandiorum — C. brookei
Clematis alpina 'Columbine White' — C. alpina 'White Columbine'
Clematis alpina 'Jan Lindmark' — C. macropetala 'Jan Lindmark'
Clematis alpina 'Tage Lundell' — C. 'Tage Lundell'
Clematis 'Andre Devillers' — C. 'Directeur Andre Devillers'
Clematis barbellata 'Pruinina' — C. 'Pruinina'
Clematis Blue Angel — C. 'Blekitny Aniol'
Clematis 'Blue Boy' — C. 'Elsa Spath'
Clematis 'Blue Boy' — C. x eriostemon 'Blue Boy'
Clematis buchananiana -Finet & Gagnep. — C. rehderiana
Clematis calycina — C. cirrhosa
Clematis 'Capitaine Thuilleaux' — C. 'Souvenir du Capitaine Thuilleaux'
Clematis 'Cardinal Wyszynski' — C. 'Kardynal Wyszynski'
Clematis chinensis h — C. terniflora

Synonyms

Name	Synonym
Clematis chrysantha v paucidentata	C. hilariae
Clematis chrysocoma h	C. montana v sericea
Clematis crispa 'Rosea'	C. crispa 'Cylindrica'
Clematis cunninghamii	C. parviflora
Clematis dioscoreifolia	C. terniflora
Clematis douglasii	C. hirsutissima
Clematis fargesii	C. potaninii
Clematis finetiana h	C. indivisa
Clematis flammula 'Rubra Marginata'	C. x triternata 'Rubromarginata'
Clematis florida 'Bicolor'	C. florida 'Sieboldii'
Clematis florida v bicolor	C. florida 'Sieboldii'
Clematis forrestii	C. napaulensis
Clematis fusca h	C. japonica
Clematis fusca koreana	C. koreana
Clematis fusca v kamtschatica	C. fusca -Turczaninow ssp fusca
Clematis glauca h	C. intricata
Clematis 'Grandiflora Sanguinea' -Johnson	C. 'Sodertalje'
Clematis grata h	C. x jouiniana
Clematis hendersonii -Koch	C. x eriostemon 'Hendersonii'
Clematis hendersonii -Standley	C. x eriostemon 'Hendersonii'
Clematis hexapetala -De Candolle	C. forsteri
Clematis hexapetala h	C. recta ssp recta v lasiosepala
Clematis ianthina	C. fusca v violacea -Turczaninow
Clematis integrifolia 'Hendersonii' -Koch	C. x eriostemon 'Hendersonii'
Clematis integrifolia white	C. integrifolia v albiflora
Clematis ispahanica	C. orientalis -Linnaeus
Clematis japonica v obvallata	C. obvallata
Clematis John Paul II	C. 'Jan Pawel II'
Clematis koreana 'Brunette'	C. 'Brunette'
Clematis macropetala 'Blue Lagoon'	C. macropetala 'Lagoon'
Clematis macropetala 'Floralia'	C. 'Floralia'
Clematis macropetala 'Harry Smith'	C. macropetala 'Chili'
Clematis macropetala 'White Moth'	C. alpina ssp sibirica 'White Moth'
Clematis macropetala 'White Swan'	C. 'White Swan'
Clematis 'Madame le Coultre'	C. 'Marie Boisselot'
Clematis Masquerade	C. 'Maskarad'
Clematis maximowicziana	C. terniflora
Clematis montana alba	C. montana
Clematis montana 'Grandiflora'	C. montana f grandiflora
Clematis montana 'Rubens Superba'	C. montana 'Superba'
Clematis montana 'Spooneri'	C. montana v sericea
Clematis 'Mother Theresa'	C. 'Matka Teresa'
Clematis 'Mrs Oud'	C. 'Mevrouv Oud'
Clematis 'Mrs Robert Brydon'	C. x jouiniana 'Mrs Robert Brydon'
Clematis 'North Star'	C. 'Pohjanael'
Clematis orientalis 'Bill MacKenzie'	C. 'Bill MacKenzie'
Clematis orientalis h	C. tibetana ssp vernayi
Clematis orientalis 'Orange Peel'	C. tibetana ssp vernayi 'Orange Peel'
Clematis orientalis 'Sherriffii'	C. tibetana ssp vernayi LS&E 13342
Clematis 'Pamela Jackman'	C. alpina 'Pamela Jackman'
Clematis paniculata -Gmelin	C. indivisa
Clematis paniculata -Thunberg	C. terniflora
Clematis 'Pink Champagne'	C. 'Kakio'
Clematis potaninii v souliei	C. potaninii v potaninii
Clematis 'Purpurea Plena Elegans'	C. viticella 'Purpurea Plena Elegans'
Clematis 'Ramona'	C. 'Hybrida Sieboldii'
Clematis sibirica	C. alpina ssp sibirica
Clematis simsii -Britt./A.Br.	C. pitcheri
Clematis simsii -Sweet	C. crispa
Clematis spooneri	C. montana v sericea
Clematis spooneri 'Rosea'	C. x vedrariensis 'Rosea'
Clematis Summer Snow	C. 'Paul Farges'
Clematis tangutica 'Aureolin'	C. 'Aureolin'
Clematis tangutica 'Bill MacKenzie'	C. 'Bill MacKenzie'
Clematis terniflora v mandschurica	C. mandschurica
Clematis terniflora v robusta	C. terniflora v terniflora
Clematis texensis 'Duchess of Albany'	C. 'Duchess of Albany'
Clematis texensis 'Etoile Rose'	C. 'Etoile Rose'
Clematis texensis 'Gravetye Beauty'	C. 'Gravetye Beauty'
Clematis 'The Princess of Wales'	C. 'Princess Diana'
Clematis thunbergii h	C. terniflora
Clematis thunbergii -Steudel	C. hirsuta
Clematis vernayi	C. tibetana ssp vernayi
Clematis verticillaris	C. occidentalis
Clematis virginiana h	C. vitalba
Clematis virginiana -Hooker	C. ligusticifolia
Clematis viticella 'Abundance'	C. 'Abundance'
Clematis viticella 'Alba Luxurians'	C. 'Alba Luxurians'
Clematis viticella 'Betty Corning'	C. 'Betty Corning'
Clematis viticella 'Etoile Violette'	C. 'Etoile Violette'
Clematis viticella 'Minuet'	C. 'Minuet'
Clematis viticella 'Polish Spirit'	C. 'Polish Spirit'
Clematis viticella 'Venosa Violacea'	C. 'Venosa Violacea'
Clematis x fargesioides	C. 'Paul Farges'
Clematis 'Xerxes'	C. 'Elsa Spath'
Clematis 'Yellow Queen'	C. 'Moonlight'
Clementsia	Rhodiola
Cleome pungens h	C. hassleriana
Cleome spinosa h	C. hassleriana
Clerodendrum fallax	C. speciosissimum
Clerodendrum fragrans v pleniflorum	C. chinense 'Pleniflorum'
Clerodendrum philippinum	C. chinense 'Pleniflorum'
Clethra paniculata	C. alnifolia 'Paniculata'
Cleyera fortunei	C. japonica 'Fortunei'
Cleyera fortunei 'Variegata'	C. japonica 'Fortunei'
Clianthus dampieri	C. formosus
Clianthus puniceus 'Flamingo'	C. puniceus 'Roseus'
Clianthus 'Red Admiral'	C. puniceus
Clianthus 'Red Cardinal'	C. puniceus
Clianthus 'White Heron'	C. puniceus 'Albus'
Clinopodium acinos	Acinos arvensis
Clinopodium ascendens	Calamintha syvatica
Clinopodium calamintha	Calamintha nepeta
Clinopodium grandiflorum	Calamintha grandiflora
Clintonia alpina	C. udensis
Clusia rosea	C. major
Cocculus trilobus	C. orbiculatus
Cochlearia armoracia	Armoracia rusticana
Cocos capitata	Butia capitata
Cocos plumosa	Syagrus romanzoffiana
Cocos weddelliana	Lytocaryum weddellianum
Codonopsis convolvulacea 'Alba'	C. grey-wilsonii 'Himal Snow'
Codonopsis convolvulacea Forrest's form	C. forrestii -Diels
Codonopsis forrestii h	C. grey-wilsonii
Codonopsis handeliana	C. tubulosa
Codonopsis nepalensis -Grey Wilson	C. grey-wilsonii
Codonopsis ussuriensis	C. lanceolata
Coeloglossom x Dactylorhiza	x Dactyloglossom

Synonyms

Coelogyne ochracea	C. nitida
Colchicum autumnale 'Major'	C. byzantinum
Colchicum autumnale minor album plenum	C. autumnale 'Alboplenum'
Colchicum autumnale 'Plenum'	C. autumnale 'Pleniflorum'
Colchicum autumnale 'Roseum Plenum'	C. autumnale 'Pleniflorum'
Colchicum autumnale v major	C. byzantinum
Colchicum autumnale v minor	C. autumnale
Colchicum bornmuelleri h	C. speciosum v bornmuelleri h
Colchicum bowlesianum	C. bivonae
Colchicum 'Conquest'	C. 'Glory of Heemstede'
Colchicum crociflorum	C. kesselringii
Colchicum doerfleri	C. hungaricum
Colchicum illyricum	C. giganteum
Colchicum laetum h	C. parnassicum
Colchicum minor album plenum	C. autumnale 'Alboplenum'
Colchicum neapolitanum	C. longiflorum
Colchicum procurrens	C. boissieri
Colchicum sibthorpii	C. bivonae
Colchicum speciosum v illyricum	C. giganteum
Coleus	Plectranthus
Coleus	Solenostemon
Coleus blumei v verschaffeltii	Solenostemon scutellarioides
Coleus thyrsoideus	Plectranthus thyrsoideus
Colletia armata	C. hystrix
Colletia cruciata	C. paradoxa
Collinsia bicolor -Benth	C. heterophylla
Collomia cavanillesii	C. biflora
Colocasia antiquorum	C. esculenta
Colquhounia coccinea v mollis	C. coccinea v vestita
Columnea hirta 'Variegata'	C. 'Light Prince'
Columnea 'Stavanger Variegated'	C. 'Broget Stavanger'
Coluteocarpus reticulatus	C. vesicarius
Comarostaphylis	Arctostaphylos
Comarum	Potentilla
Comarum palustre	Potentilla palustris
Commelina coelestis	C. tuberosa Coelestis Group
Commelina virginica h	C. erecta
Conophytum longum	Ophthalmophyllum longum
Consolea falcata	Opuntia falcata
Consolida ambigua	C. ajacis
Convallaria japonica	Ophiopogon jaburan
Convolvulus elegantissimus	C. althaeoides ssp tenuissimus
Convolvulus mauritanicus	C. sabatius
Convolvulus minor	C. tricolor
Convolvulus nitidus	C. boissieri
Convolvulus purpureus	Ipomoea purpurea
Cooperanthes	Zephyranthes
Cooperia	Zephyranthes
Copiapoa barquitensis	C. hypogaea
Copiapoa haseltoniana	C. cinerea v gigantea
Coprosma acerosa	C. brunnea
Coprosma acerosa f brunnea	C. brunnea
Coprosma baueri	C. repens
Coprosma baueriana	C. repens
Coprosma billardierei	C. quadrifida
Coprosma robusta 'Williamsii'	C. robusta 'Williamsii
Variegata'	C. fruticosa 'Firebrand'
Cordyline fruticosa 'Red Draceana'	
Cordyline terminalis	C. fruticosa
Coreopsis auriculata Cutting Gold	C. auriculata 'Schnittgold'
Coreopsis Baby Sun	C. 'Sonnenkind'
Coreopsis grandiflora Ruby Throat	C. grandiflora 'Rotkehlchen'
Coreopsis maximilianii	Helianthus maximilianii
Coreopsis Sun Child	C. 'Sonnenkind'
Coreopsis verticillata 'Golden Shower'	C. verticillata 'Grandiflora'
Coriaria thymifolia	C. microphylla
Cornus alba 'Argenteovariegata'	C. alba 'Variegata'
Cornus alba 'Westonbirt'	C. alba 'Sibirica'
Cornus alternifolia 'Variegata'	C. alternifolia 'Argentea'
Cornus angustifolia	C. linifolia
Cornus baileyi	C. stolonifera 'Baileyi'
Cornus candidissima	C. racemosa
Cornus florida 'Tricolor'	C. florida 'Welchii'
Cornus foemina	C. stricta
Cornus 'Kelsey's Dwarf'	C. stolonifera 'Kelseyi'
Cornus mas 'Elegantissima'	C. mas 'Aureoelegantissima'
Cornus nuttallii 'Ascona'	C. 'Ascona'
Cornus pubescens	C. occidentalis
Cornus sanguinea 'Compressa'	C. hessei
Cornus sanguinea 'Winter Flame'	C. sanguinea 'Winter Beauty'
Cornus sericea	C. stolonifera
Cornus stolonifera 'Kelsey's Dwarf'	C. stolonifera 'Kelseyi'
Cornus stolonifera 'Nana'	C. stolonifera 'Kelseyi'
Cornus stolonifera 'White Spot'	C. stolonifera 'White Gold'
Coronilla cappadocica	C. orientalis
Coronilla comosa	Hippocrepis comosa
Coronilla emerus	Hippocrepis emerus
Coronilla glauca	C. valentina ssp glauca
Correa 'Carmine Bells'	C. 'Dusky Bells'
Correa 'Harrisii'	C. 'Mannii'
Correa 'Pink Bells'	C. 'Dusky Bells'
Correa 'Rubra'	C. 'Dusky Bells'
Correa speciosa	C. reflexa
Cortaderia argentea	C. selloana
Cortaderia conspicua	Chionochloa conspicua
Cortaderia richardii h	C. fulvida
Cortaderia selloana 'Gold Band'	C. selloana 'Aureolineata'
Cortaderia selloana 'Silver Stripe'	C. selloana 'Albolineata'
Cortaderia Tot Toe	C. richardii -(Endlicher) Zotor
Corydalis alexeenkoana ssp vittae	C. vittae
Corydalis ambigua h	C. fumariifolia
Corydalis 'Blue Panda'	C. flexuosa 'Blue Panda'
Corydalis bulbosa	C. cava
Corydalis bulbosa -De Candolle	C.solida
Corydalis caucasica v alba misapplied	C. malkensis
Corydalis decipiens	C. solida ssp incisa
Corydalis glauca	C. sempervirens
Corydalis halleri	C. solida
Corydalis pseudofumaria alba	C. ochroleuca
Corydalis scandens	Dicentra scandens
Corydalis solida ssp densiflora	C. solida ssp incisa
Corydalis thalictrifolia -Franchet	C. saxicola
Corydalis transsylvanica h	C. solida f transsylvanica
Corylopsis platypetala	C. sinensis v calvescens
Corylopsis platypetala v laevis	C. sinensis v calvescens
Corylopsis veitchiana	C. sinensis v calvescens f veitchiana

Synonyms

Corylopsis willmottiae	C. sinensis v sinensis
Corylus avellana 'Bollwylle'	C. maxima 'Halle'sche Riesennuss'
Corylus avellana 'Laciniata'	C. avellana 'Heterophylla'
Corylus avellana 'Merveille de Bollwyller'	C. maxima 'Halle'sche Riesennuss'
Corylus avellana 'Nottingham Prolific'	C. avellana 'Pearson's Prolific'
Corylus avellana 'Purpurea'	C. avellana 'Fuscorubra'
Corylus colurna x avellana	C. x colurnoides
Corylus maxima 'Fertile de Coutard'	C. maxima 'White Filbert'
Corylus maxima 'Fruhe van Frauendorf'	C. maxima 'Red Filbert'
Corylus maxima 'Grote Lambertsnoot'	C. maxima 'Kentish Cob'
Corylus maxima Halle Giant	C. maxima 'Halle'sche Riesennuss'
Corylus maxima 'Lambert's Filbert'	C. maxima 'Kentish Cob'
Corylus maxima 'Longue d'Espagne'	C. maxima 'Kentish Cob'
Corylus maxima 'Monsiuer de Bouweller'	C. maxima 'Halle'sche Riesennuss'
Corylus maxima New Giant	C. maxima 'Neue Riesennuss'
Corylus maxima 'Purple Filbert'	C. maxima 'Purpurea'
Corylus maxima 'Red Zellernut'	C. maxima 'Red Filbert'
Corylus maxima 'Spanish White'	C. maxima 'White Filbert'
Corylus maxima 'White Spanish Filbert'	C. maxima 'White Filbert'
Corylus maxima 'Witpit Lambertsnoot'	C. maxima 'White Filbert'
Coryphantha calochlora	C. nickelsiae
Coryphantha conoidea	Neolloydia conoidea
Coryphantha radians	C. cornifera
Coryphantha vivipara	Escobaria vivipara
Cosmos sulphureus 'Lemon Queen'	C. sulphureus 'Butterkist'
Cosmos sulphureus 'Yellow Garden'	C. sulphureus 'Butterkist'
Costus igneus	C. cuspidatus
Cotinus americanus	C. obovatus
Cotinus coggygria 'Flame'	C. 'Flame'
Cotinus coggygria 'Foliis Purpureis'	C. coggygria Rubrifolius Group
Cotoneaster acutifolius v laetevirens	C. laetevirens
Cotoneaster adpressus 'Tom Thumb'	C. adpressus 'Little Gem'
Cotoneaster adpressus v praecox	C. nanshan
Cotoneaster 'Autumn Fire'	C. 'Herbstfeuer'
Cotoneaster bullatus f floribundus	C. bullatus
Cotoneaster bullatus v macrophyllus	C. rehderi
Cotoneaster buxifolius blue-leaved	C. lidjiangensis
Cotoneaster buxifolius f vellaeus	C. astrophorus
Cotoneaster conspicuus v decorus	C. conspicuus 'Decorus'
Cotoneaster dammeri 'Oakwood'	C. radicans 'Eichholz'
Cotoneaster dammeri 'Streibs Findling'	C. procumbens
Cotoneaster dammeri v radicans - Schneider	C. radicans
Cotoneaster distichus	C. nitidus
Cotoneaster distichus v tongolensis	C. splendens
Cotoneaster 'Erlinda'	C. x suecicus 'Erlinda'
Cotoneaster franchetii v sternianus	C. sternianus
Cotoneaster hjelmqvistii 'Robustus'	C. hjelmqvistii
Cotoneaster hjelmqvistii 'Rotundifolius'	C. hjelmqvistii
Cotoneaster horizontalis v perpusillus	C. perpusillus
Cotoneaster horizontalis v wilsonii	C. ascendens
Cotoneaster horizontalis 'Variegatus'	C. atropurpureus 'Variegatus'
Cotoneaster humifusus	C. dammeri
Cotoneaster 'Hybridus Pendulus'	C. salicifolius 'Pendulus'
Cotoneaster melanotrichus	C. cochleatus
Cotoneaster melanotrichus 'Donard Gem'	C. astrophorus
Cotoneaster microphyllus h	C. purpurascens
Cotoneaster microphyllus 'Teulon Porter'	C. astrophorus
Cotoneaster microphyllus v cochleatus - (Franch) Rehd.&Wils	C. cochleatus
Cotoneaster microphyllus v cochleatus misapplied	C. cashmiriensis
Cotoneaster microphyllus v thymifolius h	C. linearifolius
Cotoneaster microphyllus v thymifolius - (Lindley) Koehne	C. integrifolius
Cotoneaster multiflorus h	C. purpurascens
Cotoneaster nitidifolius	C. glomerulatus
Cotoneaster praecox 'Boer'	C. duthieanus 'Boer'
Cotoneaster pyrenaicus	C. congestus
Cotoneaster 'Rothschilianus'	C. salicifolius 'Rothschildianus'
Cotoneaster 'Royal Beauty'	C. x suecicus 'Coral Beauty'
Cotoneaster salicifolius Autumn Fire	C. 'Herbstfeuer'
Cotoneaster salicifolius 'Gnome'	C. salicifolius 'Gnom'
Cotoneaster salicifolius Park Carpet	C. salicifolius 'Parkteppich'
Cotoneaster salicifolius v rugosus h	C. hylmoei
Cotoneaster serotinus misapplied	C. meiophyllus
Cotoneaster splendens 'Sabrina'	C. splendens
Cotoneaster thymifolius	C. integrifolius
Cotoneaster wardii h	C. mairei
Cotoneaster x suecicus 'Skogsholmen'	C. x suecicus 'Skogholm'
Cotoneaster x watereri 'Avonbank'	C. salicifolius 'Avonbank'
Cotoneaster x watereri 'Cornubia'	C. frigidus 'Cornubia'
Cotoneaster x watereri 'Pendulus'	C. salicifolius 'Pendulus'
Cotula atrata	Leptinella atrata
Cotula atrata v dendyi	Leptinella dendyi
Cotula goyenii	Leptinella goyenii
Cotula minor	Leptinella minor
Cotula pectinata	Leptinella pectinata
Cotula perpusilla	Leptinella pusilla
Cotula potentilloides	Leptinella potentillina
Cotula pyrethrifolia	Leptinella pyrethrifolia
Cotula reptans	Leptinella scariosa
Cotula rotundata	Leptinella rotundata
Cotula scariosa	Leptinella scariosa
Cotula sericea	Leptinella albida
Cotula serrulata	Leptinella serrulata
Cotula squalida	Leptinella squalida
Cotyledon alternans	Adromischus maculatus
Cotyledon chrysantha	Rosularia chrysantha
Cotyledon cooperi	Adromischus cooperi
Cotyledon gibbiflora v metallica	Echeveria gibbiflora v metallica
Cotyledon gibbiflora v metallica	Echeveria gibbiflora v metallica
Cotyledon maculata	Adromischus maculatus
Cotyledon oblonga	C. orbiculata v oblonga
Cotyledon oppositifolia	Chiastophyllum oppositifolium
Cotyledon paniculata	Tylecodon paniculatus
Cotyledon reticulata	Tylecodon reticulatus
Cotyledon simplicifolia	Chiastophyllum oppositifolium
Cotyledon tomentosa v ladismithensis	C. ladismithensis
Cotyledon wallichii	Tylecodon papillaris ssp wallichii
Cotyledon zeyheri	Adromischus cristatus v zeyheri
Craspedia richea	C. glauca
Crassula argentea	C. ovata
Crassula corymbosula	C. capitella ssp thyrsiflora
Crassula deceptrix	C. deceptor

Synonyms

Crassula lycopodioides	C. muscosa
Crassula maculata h	Adromischus maculatus
Crassula portulacea	C. ovata
Crassula recurva	C. helmsii
Crassula rosularis	C. orbicularis
Crassula sedifolia	C. milfordiae
Crassula sediformis	C. milfordiae
Crassula thyrsiflora	C. capitella ssp thyrsiflora
Crataegus cordata	C. phaenopyrum
Crataegus crus-galli h	C. persimilis 'Prunifolia'
Crataegus laevigata 'Coccinea Plena'	C. laevigata 'Paul's Scarlet'
Crataegus laevigata 'Flore Pleno'	C. laevigata 'Plena'
Crataegus mexicana	C. pubescens f stipulacea
Crataegus orientalis	C. laciniata
Crataegus oxyacantha	C. laevigata
Crataegus prunifolia	C. persimilis 'Prunifolia'
Crawfurdia speciosa	Gentiana speciosa
Crenularia	Aethionema
Crinitaria	Aster
Crinum aquaticum	C. campanulatum
Crinum capense	C. bulbispermum
Crinum longifolium	C. bulbispermum
Crinum x powellii 'Longifolium'	C. bulbispermum
Criogenes	Cypripedium
Crocosmia aurea h	C. x crocosmiiflora 'George Davison' - Davison
Crocosmia aurea 'Lady MacKenzie'	C. x crocosmiiflora 'Emily MacKenzie'
Crocosmia aurea 'Mrs Morrison'	C. x crocosmiiflora 'Mrs Geoffrey Howard'
Crocosmia aurea Newry seedling	C. x crocosmiiflora 'Prometheus'
Crocosmia aurea 'Princess'	C. x crocosmiiflora 'Red Knight'
Crocosmia aurea 'Rheingold'	C. x crocosmiiflora 'Golden Glory'
Crocosmia aurea 'Solfaterre Coleton Fishacre'	C. x crocosmiiflora 'Gerbe d'Or'
Crocosmia 'Citronella' h	C. 'Golden Fleece'
Crocosmia 'Darkleaf Apricot'	C. x crocosmiiflora 'Gerbe d'Or'
Crocosmia 'Eldorado'	C. x crocosmiiflora 'E.A.Bowles'
Crocosmia 'Fire King' h	C. x crocosmiiflora 'Jackanapes'
Crocosmia 'George Davison' h	C. x crocosmiiflora 'Golden Glory'
Crocosmia 'George Davison' h	C. x crocosmiiflora 'Sulphurea'
Crocosmia 'Golden Fleece' -Lemoine	C. x crocosmiiflora 'Gerbe d'Or'
Crocosmia 'Lady Wilson' h	C. x crocosmiiflora 'Norwich Canary'
Crocosmia 'Late Cornish'	C. x crocosmiiflora 'QueenAlexandra' - J.E.Fitt
Crocosmia 'Mount Stewart'	C. x crocosmiiflora 'Jessie'
Crocosmia 'Mr Bedford'	C. x crocosmiiflora 'Croesus'
Crocosmia rosea	Tritonia disticha ssp rubrolucens
Crocosmia 'Rowden Bronze'	C. x crocosmiiflora
Crocosmia 'Rowden Chrome'	C. x crocosmiiflora 'GeorgeDavison'- Davison
Crocosmia 'Saturn'	C. 'Jupiter'
Crocus albiflorus	C. vernus ssp albiflorus
Crocus asturicus	C. serotinus ssp salzmannii
Crocus aureus	C. flavus ssp flavus
Crocus biflorus v parkinsonii	C. biflorus ssp biflorus
Crocus biliottii	C. aerius
Crocus cancellatus v ciliatus	C. cancellatus ssp cancellatus
Crocus candidus v subflavus	C. olivieri ssp olivieri
Crocus 'Cloth of Gold'	C. angustifolius
Crocus clusii	C. serotinus ssp clusii
Crocus 'Dutch Yellow'	C. x luteus 'Golden Yellow'
Crocus flavus	C. flavus ssp flavus
Crocus 'Golden Mammoth'	C. x luteus 'Golden Yellow'
Crocus goulimyi 'Albus'	C. goulimyi 'Mani White'
Crocus hadriaticus v chrysobelonicus	C. hadriaticus
Crocus iridiflorus	C. banaticus
Crocus 'Large Yellow'	C. x luteus 'Golden Yellow'
Crocus lazicus	C. scharojanii
Crocus 'Mammoth Yellow'	C. x luteus 'Golden Yellow'
Crocus 'Princess Beatrix'	C. chrysanthus 'Prinses Beatrix'
Crocus pulchellus 'Zephyr'	C. 'Zephyr'
Crocus 'Purpureus'	C. vernus 'Purpureus Grandiflorus'
Crocus salzmannii	C. serotinus ssp salzmannii
Crocus sativus v cartwrightianus	C. cartwrightianus
Crocus scepusiensis	C. vernus ssp vernus v scepusiensis
Crocus sibiricus	C. sieberi
Crocus sieberi 'Bowles' White'	C. sieberi 'Albus'
Crocus speciosus f albus	C. speciosus 'Albus'
Crocus susianus	C. angustifolius
Crocus suterianus	C. olivieri ssp olivieri
Crocus vernus 'Joan of Arc'	C. vernus 'Jeanne d'Arc'
Crocus vernus ssp vernus 'Grandiflorus'	C. vernus 'Purpureus Grandiflorus'
Crocus x stellaris	C. x luteus 'Stellaris'
Crocus 'Yellow Mammoth'	C. x luteus 'Golden Yellow'
Crocus zonatus	C. kotschyanus ssp kotschyanus
Crossandra undulifolia	C. infundibuliformis
Crucianella stylosa	Phuopsis stylosa
Cryptanthopsis navioides	Orthophytum navioides
Cryptanthus acaulis v ruber	C. acaulis 'Rubra'
Cryptanthus bromelioides v tricolor	C. bromeliodes 'Tricolor'
Cryptocereus anthonyanus	Selenicereus anthonyanus
Cryptomeria fortunei	C. japonica v sinensis
Cryptomeria japonica 'Enko-sugi'	C. japonica 'Araucarioides'
Cryptomeria japonica 'Littleworth Dwarf'	C. japonica 'Littleworth Gnom'
Cryptomeria japonica 'Lobbii Nana'	C. japonica 'Nana'
Cryptomeria japonica 'Midare-sugi'	C. japonica 'Viridis'

Synonyms

Cryptomeria japonica 'Monstrosa Nana'	C. japonica 'Mankichi-sugi'
Cryptomeria japonica 'Sekka-sugi'	C. japonica 'Cristata'
Cryptomeria japonica 'Wogon'	C. japonica 'Aurea'
Cryptomeria japonica 'Yatsubusa'	C. japonica 'Tansu'
Cryptomeria japonica 'Yore-sugi'	C. japonica 'Spiralis'
Cryptomeria sinensis	C. japonica v sinensis
Cryptostemma calendulaceum	Arctotheca calendula
Cudrania	Maclura
Cudrania tricuspidata	Maclura tricuspidata
Cunninghamia lanceolata 'Compacta'	C. lanceolata 'Bano'
Cunninghamia sinensis	C. lanceolata
Cunninghamia unicaniculata	C. lanceolata
Cuphea llavea	C. x purpurea
Cuphea llavea v miniata h	C. x purpurea
Cuphea miniata h	C. x purpurea
Cuphea platycentra	C. ignea
Cupressus arizonica v bonita	C. arizonica v arizonica
Cupressus cashmeriana	C. torulosa 'Cashmeriana'
Cupressus glabra	C. arizonica v glabra
Cupressus glabra 'Arctic'	C. arizonica v arizonica 'Arctic'
Cupressus lawsoniana	Chamaecyparis lawsoniana
Cupressus leylandii	x Cupressocyparis leylandii
Cupressus lindleyi	C. lusitanica
Cupressus macrocarpa 'Sulphurea'	C. macrocarpa 'Crippsii'
Cupressus nootkatensis	Chamaecyparis nootkatensis
Cupressus obtusa	Chamaecyparis obtusa
Cupressus pisifera	Chamaecyparis pisifera
Cupressus sempervirens 'Green Pencil'	C. sempervirens 'Green Spire'
Cupressus sempervirens 'Pyrimidalis'	C. sempervirens 'Stricta'
Cupressus sempervirens v sempervirens	C. sempervirens 'Stricta'
Cupressus thyoides	Chamaecyparis thyoides
Curtonus	Crocosmia
Curtonus paniculatus	Crocosmia paniculata
Cyananthus integer h	C. microphyllus
Cyananthus zhongdienensis	C. chungdienensis
Cyanella capensis	C. hyacinthoides
Cyathodes fasciculata	Leucopogon fasciculatus
Cyathodes fraseri	Leucopogon fraseri
Cycas kennedyana	C. papuana
Cycas thouarsii	C. rumphii
Cyclamen alpinum	C. trochopteranthum
Cyclamen coum 'Album'	C. coum f albissimum
Cyclamen coum v abchasicum	C. coum ssp caucasicum
Cyclamen creticum x repandum	C. x meiklei
Cyclamen europaeum	C. purpurascens
Cyclamen fatrense	C. purpurascens ssp purpurascens
Cyclamen ibericum	C. coum ssp caucasicum
Cyclamen ibericum album	C. coum ssp caucasicum
Cyclamen latifolium	C. persicum
Cyclamen neapolitanum	C. hederifolium
Cyclamen orbiculatum	C. coum
Cyclamen peloponnesiacum	C. repandum ssp peloponnesiacum
Cyclamen purpurascens v fatrense	C. purpurascens ssp purpurascens
Cyclamen repandum 'Pelops' misapplied	C. repandum ssp peloponnesiacum f peloponnesiacum
Cyclobothra lutea	Calochortus barbatus
Cydonia japonica	Chaenomeles speciosa
Cydonia oblonga 'Bereczcki'	C. oblonga 'Vranja'
Cydonia oblonga 'Portugal'	C. oblonga 'Lusitanica'
Cydonia sinensis	Pseudocydonia sinensis
Cydonia speciosa	Chaenomeles speciosa
Cymbalaria muralis 'Albiflora'	C. muralis 'Pallidor'
Cymbidium grandiflorum	C. hookerianum
Cymbidium pendulum	C. aloifolium
Cynara hystrix	C. baetica ssp maroccana
Cynoglossom imeritinum	C. glochidiatum
Cynoglossom longiflorum	Lindelofia longiflora
Cypella plumbea	C. coelestis
Cyperorchis elegans	Cymbidium elegans
Cyperus alternifolius h	C. involucratus
Cyperus diffusus h	C. albostriatus
Cyperus elegans h	C. albostriatus
Cyperus flabelliformis	C. involucratus
Cyperus haspan h	C. papyrus 'Nanus'
Cyperus isocladus h	C. papyrus 'Nanus'
Cyperus sumula h	C. cyperoides
Cyperus vegetus	C. eragrostis
Cyphomandra crassicaulis	C. betacea
Cypripedium guttatum v yatabeanum	C. yatabeanum
Cypripedium japonicum v formosanum	C. formosanum
Cypripedium japonicum v japonicum	C. japonicum
Cyrtanthus parviflorus	C. brachyscyphus
Cyrtanthus purpureus	C. elatus
Cyrtanthus speciosus	C. elatus
Cyrtochilum macranthum	Oncidium macranthum
Cyrtomium falcatum 'Mayi'	C. falcatum 'Cristatum'
Cytisus albus h	C. multiflorus
Cytisus albus Hacq	Chamaecytisus albus
Cytisus 'Andreanus'	C. scoparius f andreanus
Cytisus canariensis	Genista canariensis
Cytisus demissus	Chamaecytisus hirsutus demissus
Cytisus hirsutus	Chamaecytisus hirsutus
Cytisus leucanthus	Chamaecytisus albus
Cytisus maderensis	Genista maderensis
Cytisus monspessulanus	Genista monspessulana
Cytisus nigrescens	C. nigricans
Cytisus nubigenus	C. supranubius
Cytisus purpureus	Chamaecytisus purpureus
Cytisus racemosus h	Genista x spachiana
Cytisus Red Favourite	C. 'Roter Favorit'
Cytisus scoparius v prostratus	C. scoparius ssp maritimus
Cytisus sessilifolius	Cytisophyllum sessilifolium
Cytisus supinus	Chamaecytisus supinus
Cytisus x praecox	C. x praecox 'Warminster'
Cytisus x praecox 'Canary Bird'	C. x praecox 'Goldspeer'
Cytisus x spachianus	Genista x spachiana
Daboecia cantabrica 'Donard Pink'	D. cantabrica 'Pink'
Daboecia cantabrica 'William Buchanan'	D. cantabrica ssp scotica 'William Buchanan'
Daboecia polifolia	D. cantabrica
Daboecia x scotica cultivars	D. cantabrica ssp scotica cultivars
Dacrydium bidwillii	Halocarpus bidwillii
Dacrydium franklinii	Lagarostrobos franklinii
Dacrydium laxifolium	Lepidothamnus laxifolius
Dactylorhiza fuchsii x purpurella	D. x venusta
Dactylorhiza maculata ssp fuchsii	D. fuchsii
Dactylorhiza maderensis	D. foliosa

Synonyms

Dactylorhiza majalis ssp praetermissa — Dactylorhiza majalis praetermissa — D. praetermissa
Dactylorhiza majalis x sambucina — D. 'Madonna'
Dactylorhiza mascula — Orchis mascula
Dahlia 'Dandy' — D. 'Harvest Dandy'
Dahlia Firebird — D. 'Vuurvogel'
Dahlia 'Imp' — D. 'Harvest Imp'
Dahlia 'Inflammation' — D. 'Harvest Inflammation'
Dahlia Pride of Berlin — D. 'Stolze von Berlin'
Dahlia 'Red Dwarf' — D. 'Harvest Red Dwarf'
Dahlia 'Samantha' — D. 'Harvest Samantha'
Dahlia 'Tiny Tot' — D. 'Harvest Tiny Tot'
Dahlia 'Unwins Dwarf' — D. Unwins Dwarf Group
Daiswa — Paris
Dammara — Agathis
Daphne collina — D. sericea Collina Group
Daphne glandulosa — D. oleoides
Daphne japonica 'Striata' — D.odora 'Aureomarginata'
Daphne mezereum 'Bowles' White' — D. mezereum 'Bowles' Variety'
Daphne mezereum 'Grandiflora' — D. mezereum v autumnalis
Daphne neapolitana — D. x napolitana
Daphne odora 'Marginata' — D. odora 'Aureomarginata'
Daphne odora v leucantha — D. odora f alba
Daphne petraea 'Alba' — D. petraea 'Tremalzo'
Daphne retusa — D. tangutica Retusa Group
Daphne x burkwoodii 'Variegata' broad cream edge — D. x burkwoodii 'Somerset Variegated'
Daphne x burkwoodii 'Variegata' broad gold edge — D. x burkwoodii 'Somerset Gold Edge'
Daphne x burkwoodii 'Variegata' narrow gold edge — D. x burkwoodii 'Carol Mackie'
Dasylirion gracile -Planchon — D. acrotrichum
Dasylirion hartwegianum — Calibanus hookeri
Datura arborea — Brugmansia arborea
Datura aurea — Brugmansia aurea
Datura chlorantha — Brugmansia chlorantha
Datura cornigera — Brugmansia arborea
Datura meteloides — D. inoxia
Datura rosea — Brugmansia x insignis pink
Datura rosei — Brugmansia sanguinea
Datura sanguinea — Brugmansia sanguinea
Datura suaveolens — Brugmansia suaveolens
Datura versicolor — Brugmansia versicolor - Lagerheim
Datura versicolor 'Grand Marnier' — Brugmansia x candida 'Grand Marnier'
Datura x candida — Brugmansia x candida
Daubentonia — Sesbania
Davallia bullata — D. mariesii
Davallia fejeenis — D. solida v fejeenis
Davallia pyxidata — D. solida v pyxidata
Delosperma 'Basutoland' — D. nubigenum
Delphinium ambiguum — Consolida ajacis
Delphinium beesianum 'Andenken an August Koeneman' — D. (Belladonna Group) 'Wendy'
Delphinium beesianum 'Pink Sensation' — D. x ruysii 'Pink Sensation'

Delphinium 'Blue Butterfly' — D. grandiflorum 'Blue Butterfly'
Delphinium caucasicum — D. speciosum
Delphinium chinense — D. grandiflorum
Delphinium consolida — Consolida ajacis
Delphinium grandiflorum Blue Dwarf — D. grandiflorum 'Blauer Zwerg'
Delphinium 'Lady Hambleden' — D. 'Patricia, Lady Hambleden'
Delphinium nudicaule v luteum — D. luteum
Delphinium 'Royal Flush' — D. 'Langdon's Royal Flush'
Delphinium zalil — D. semibarbatum
Dendranthema cultivars — Chrysanthemum
Dendranthema nankingense — Chrysanthemum nankingense
Dendranthema pacificum — Ajania pacifica
Dendriopoterium — Sanguisorba
Dendrobenthamia — Cornus
Dendrobium aggregatum — D. lindleyi
Dendrobium phalaenopsis — D. biggibum v phalaenopsis
Dendrobium pierardii — D. aphyllum
Dentaria digitata — Cardamine pentaphyllos
Dentaria enneaphylla — Cardamine enneaphyllos
Dentaria microphylla — Cardamine microphyllos
Dentaria pentaphylla — Cardamine pentaphyllos
Dentaria pinnata — Cardamine heptaphylla
Dentaria polyphylla — Cardamine kitaibelii
Deparia petersenii — Lunathyrium japonicum
Derwentia — Parahebe
Deschampsia cespitosa Bronze Veil — D. cespitosa 'Bronzeschleier'
Deschampsia cespitosa 'Fairy's Joke' — D. cespitosa v vivipara
Deschampsia cespitosa Gold Dust — D. cespitosa 'Goldstaub'
Deschampsia cespitosa Golden Dew — D. cespitosa 'Goldtau'
Deschampsia cespitosa Golden Pendant — D. cespitosa 'Goldgehange'
Deschampsia cespitosa Golden Veil — D. cespitosa 'Goldschleier'
Deschampsia flexuosa 'Aurea' — D. flexuosa 'Tatra Gold'
Desfontainia spinosa hookeri — D. spinosa
Desmazeria — Catapodium rigidum
Desmodium praestans — D. yunnanense
Desmodium tiliifolium — D. elegans
Deutzia chunii — D. ningpoensis
Deutzia crenata 'Flore Pleno' — D. scabra 'Plena'
Deutzia gracilis 'Carminea' — D. x rosea 'Carminea'
Deutzia gracilis 'Variegata' — D. gracilis 'Marmorata'
Deutzia 'Pink Pompon' — D. 'Rosea Plena'
Deutzia x magnifica 'Rubra' — D. 'Strawberry Fields'
Deutzia x wellsii — D. scabra 'Candidissima'
Dianella caerulea 'Variegata' — D. tasmanica 'Variegata'
Dianthus 'A.J.Macself' — D. 'Dad's Favourite'
Dianthus atrorubens — D. carthusianorum Atrorubens Group
Dianthus 'Auvergne' — D. x arvernensis
Dianthus 'Blush' — D. 'Souvenir de la Malmaison'
Dianthus 'Bourboule' — D. 'La Bourboule'
Dianthus 'Brilliant' — D. deltoides 'Brilliant'
Dianthus caesius — D. gratianopolitanus
Dianthus caesius 'Compactus' — D. gratianopolitanus 'Compactus Eydangeri'
Dianthus 'Candy' — D. 'Sway Candy'
Dianthus 'Catherine's Choice' — D. 'Rhian's Choice'

Synonyms

Name	Synonym
Dianthus 'Charles Musgrave'	D. 'Musgrave's Pink'
Dianthus Cheddar pink	D. gratianopolitanus
Dianthus 'Cheryl'	D. 'Houndspool Cheryl'
Dianthus cinnabarinus	D. biflorus
Dianthus 'Constance Finnis'	D. 'Fair Folly'
Dianthus deltoides Flashing Light	D. deltoides 'Leuchtfunk'
Dianthus 'Doris Ruby'	D. 'Houndspool Ruby'
Dianthus 'Double Irish'	D. 'Irish Pink'
Dianthus 'Ember Rose'	D. 'Le Reve'
Dianthus 'Emperor'	D. 'Bat's Double Red'
Dianthus Fringed pink	D. superbus
Dianthus 'Green Eyes'	D. 'Musgrave's Pink'
Dianthus haematocalyx 'Alpinus'	D. haematocalyx ssp pindicola
Dianthus 'Haytor'	D. 'Haytor White'
Dianthus hispanicus	D. pungens
Dianthus 'Huntsman'	D. 'Allen's Huntsman'
Dianthus 'Joan's Blood'	D. alpinus 'Joan's Blood'
Dianthus kitaibelii	D. petraeus ssp petraeus
Dianthus 'La Bourbille'	D. 'La Bourboule'
Dianthus 'Laced Prudence'	D. 'Prudence'
Dianthus 'Little Old Lady'	D. 'Chelsea Pink'
Dianthus 'Madame Dubarry'	D. 'Dubarry'
Dianthus 'Manningtree Pink'	D. 'Cedric's Oldest'
Dianthus 'Maria'	D. 'Allen's Maria'
Dianthus 'Mida'	D. 'Melody'
Dianthus 'Montrose Pink'	D. 'Cockenzie Pink'
Dianthus 'Mrs N.Clark'	D. 'Nellie Clark'
Dianthus 'Musgrave's White'	D. 'Musgrave's Pink'
Dianthus neglectus	D. pavonius
Dianthus noeanus	D. petraeus ssp noeanus
Dianthus 'Oakington Rose'	D. 'Oakington'
Dianthus 'Old Blush'	D. 'Souvenir de la Malmaison'
Dianthus 'Patricia Bell'	D. turkestanicus 'Patricia Bell'
Dianthus pavonius roysii	D. 'Roysii'
Dianthus pindicola	D. haematocalyx ssp pindicola
Dianthus 'Pink Calypso'	D. 'Truly Yours'
Dianthus 'Princess Charming'	D. gratianopolitanus 'Princess Charming'
Dianthus 'Raby Castle'	D. 'Lord Chatham'
Dianthus 'Reine de Henri'	D. 'Quuen of Henri'
Dianthus 'Revell's Lady Wharncliffe'	D. 'Lady Wharncliffe'
Dianthus 'Ruby'	D. 'Houndspool Ruby'
Dianthus 'Ruby Doris'	D. 'Houndspool Ruby'
Dianthus 'Russling Robin'	D. 'Fair Maid of Kent'
Dianthus 'Sir Cedric Morris'	D. 'Cedric's Oldest'
Dianthus 'Square Eyes'	D. 'Old Square Eyes'
Dianthus strictus v brachyanthus	D. integer ssp minutiflorus
Dianthus suendermannii	D. petraeus
Dianthus The Bloodie pink	D. 'Caesar's Mantle'
Dianthus 'Tiny Rubies'	D. gratianopolitanus 'Tiny Rubies'
Dianthus 'W.A.Musgrave'	D. 'Musgrave's Pink'
Dianthus 'White Sim'	D. 'White William Sim'
Diascia 'Apricot' h	D. barberae 'Hopley's Apricot'
Diascia 'Blush'	D. integerrima 'Blush'
Diascia cordata h	D. barberae 'Fisher's Flora'
Diascia cordifolia	D. barberae 'Fisher's Flora'
Diascia elegans	D. fetcaniensis
Diascia elegans	D. vigilis
Diascia felthamii	D. fetcaniensis
Diascia flanaganii	D. stachyoides
Diascia flanaganii	D. vigilis
Diascia 'Hector Harrison'	D. 'Salmon Supreme'
Diascia integerrima 'Alba'	D. integerrima 'Blush'
Diascia integerrima 'Ivory Angel'	D. integerrima 'Blush'
Diascia integrifolia	D. integerrima
Diascia rigescens pale form	D. rigescens 'Anne Rennie'
Diascia 'Ruby Field'	D. barberae 'Ruby Field'
Diascia x Linaria	Nemesia caerulea
Dicentra 'Boothman's Variety'	D. 'Stuart Boothman'
Dicentra eximia 'Alba'	D. eximia 'Snowdrift'
Dicentra eximia h	D. formosa
Dicentra oregona	D. formosa ssp oregona
Dicentra thalictrifolia	D. scandens
Dictamnus fraxinella	D. albus v purpureus
Didiscus coeruleus	Trachymene coerulea
Didymochlaena lunulata	D. truncatula
Didymosperma caudatum	Arenga caudata
Dieffenbachia amoena h	D. seguine 'Amoena'
Dieffenbachia maculata	D. seguine
Dieffenbachia maculata	D. seguine 'Maculata'
Dieffenbachia maculata 'Hi-colour'	D. seguine 'Tropic Snow'
Dieffenbachia maculata 'Rudolph Roehrs'	D. seguine 'Rudolph Roehrs'
Dieffenbachia maculata 'Snow Queen'	D. seguine 'Tropic Snow'
Dieffenbachia maculata 'Tropic Topaz'	D. seguine 'Tropic Snow'
Dieffenbachia 'Memoria'	D. seguine 'Memoria Corsii'
Dieffenbachia 'Pia'	D. seguine 'Pia'
Dieffenbachia picta	D. seguine
Dieffenbachia 'Roehrsii'	D. seguine 'Rudolph Roehrs'
Dieffenbachia 'Rudolph Roehrs'	D. seguine 'Rudolph Roehrs'
Dieffenbachia seguine 'Amoena'	D. 'Amoena'
Dieffenbachia x memoria-corsii	D. seguine 'Memoria Corsii'
Dierama ensifolium	D. pendulum
Dierama pumilum -(Baker) N.E.Br.	D. pendulum v pumilum
Dierama pumilum h	D. dracomontanum
Diervilla middendorffiana	Weigela middendorffiana
Dietes vegeta h	D. iridioides
Digitalis ambigua	D. grandiflora
Digitalis apricot hybrids	D. purpurea 'Sutton's Apricot'
Digitalis canariensis	Isoplexis canariensis
Digitalis eriostachya	D. lutea
Digitalis heywoodii	D. purpurea ssp heywoodii
Digitalis kishinskyi	D. parviflora
Digitalis lamarckii h	D. lanata
Digitalis micrantha	D. lutea ssp australis
Digitalis orientalis	D. grandiflora
Dimorphotheca annua	D. pluvialis
Dimorphotheca aurantiaca h	D. sinuata
Dimorphotheca barberiae h	Osteospermum jucundum
Dimorphotheca ecklonis	Osteospermum ecklonis
Diosphaera asperuloides	Trachelium asperuloides
Dipidax	Onixotis
Diplacus	Mimulus
Diplacus glutinosus	Mimulus aurantiacus
Dipladenia	Mandevilla

Synonyms

Diplarrhena moraea West Coast form	D. latifolia
Diplazium japonicum	Lunathyrium japonicum
Diplocyathus ciliata	Orbea ciliata
Dipsacus sylvestris	D. fullonum
Dipteracanthus	Ruellia
Disa grandiflora	D. uniflora
Discocactus tricornis	D. placentiformis
Diuranthera	Chlorophytum
Dizygotheca elegantissima	Schefflera elegantissima
Dodecatheon amethystinum	D. pulchellum
Dodecatheon cusickii	D. pulchellum ssp cusickii
Dodecatheon integrifolium	D. hendersonii
Dodecatheon latifolium	D. hendersonii
Dodecatheon pauciflorum -(Dur) E.Greene	D. meadia
Dodecatheon pauciflorum h	D. pulchellum
Dodecatheon pulchellum radicatum	D. pulchellum
Dodecatheon radicatum	D. pulchellum
Dodecatheon tetrandrum	D. jeffreyi
Dolichos lablab	Lablab purpureus
Dolichos lignosus	Dipogon lignosus
Dolichos niger	Lablab purpureus
Dolichos purpureus	Lablab purpureus
Dolichothele baumii	Mammillaria baumii
Dolichothele camptotricha	Mammillaria camptotricha
Dombeya mastersii	D. burgessiae
Dondia	Hacquetia
Doodia squarrosa	D. caudata
Doronicum caucasicum	D. orientale
Doronicum cordatum	D. columnae
Doronicum orientale 'Fruhlingspracht'	D 'Fruhlingspracht'
Doronicum plantagineum 'Excelsum'	D x excelsum 'Harpur Crewe'
Doronicum plantagineum 'Harpur Crewe'	D x excelsum 'Harpur Crewe'
Doronicum Spring Beauty	D 'Fruhlingspracht'
Dorotheanthus littlewoodii	D. bellidiformis
Dorycnium	Lotus
Dorycnium hirsutum	Lotus hirsutus
Doryopteris elegans	Hemionitis elegans
Doryopteris pedata v palmata	D. palmata
Douglasia laevigata	Androsace laevigata
Douglasia montana	Androsace montana
Douglasia nivalis	Androsace nivalis
Douglasia vitaliana	Vitaliana primuliflora
Doxantha capreolata	Bignonia capreolata
Doxantha unguis-cati	Macfadyena unguis-cati
Draba aizoon	D. lasiocarpa
Draba bertolonii -Boissier	D. loeseleurii
Draba bertolonii -Nyman	D. aspera
Draba bertolonii -Thell.	D. brachystemon
Draba bryoides	D. rigida v bryoides
Draba compacta	D. lasiocarpa Compacta Group
Draba daurica	D. glabella
Draba imbricata	D. rigida v imbricata
Draba repens	D. sibirica
Draba rupestris	D. norvegica
Draba scardica	D. lasiocarpa
Draba stylaris	D. incana Stylaris Group
Dracaena australis	Cordyline australis
Dracaena cinta 'Tricolor'	D. marginata 'Tricolor'
Dracaena congesta	Cordyline stricta
Dracaena deremensis	D. fragrans Deremensis Group
Dracaena deremensis 'Souvenir de Schrijver'	D. fragrans Deremensis Group 'Warneckei'
Dracaena deremensis 'Warneckei'	D. fragrans Deremensis Group 'Warneckei'
Dracaena indivisa	Cordyline indivisa
Dracaena stricta	Cordyline stricta
Dracocephalum altaiense	D. imberbe
Dracocephalum canescens	Lallemantia canescens
Dracocephalum govaniana	Nepeta govaniana
Dracocephalum mairei	D. renatii
Dracocephalum moldavicum	D. moldavica
Dracocephalum prattii	Nepeta prattii
Dracocephalum ruyschianum v speciosum	D. arguense
Dracocephalum sibiricum	Nepeta sibirica
Dracocephalum speciosum	D. arguense
Dracocephalum virginicum	Physostegia virginiana
Dregea corrugata	D. sinensis
Drejerella guttata	Justicia brandegeeana
Drepanostachyum falconeri h	Himalayacalamus falconeri 'Damarapa'
Drepanostachyum hookerianum	Himalayacalamus hookerianus
Drimys aromatica	D. lanceolata
Drimys axillaris	Pseudowintera axillaris
Drimys colorata	Pseudowintera colorata
Drimys lanceolata Latifolia Group	D. winteri v chilensis
Drosera dichotoma	D. binata ssp dichotoma
Drosera intermedia x rotundifolia	D. x beleziana
Dryas lanata	D. octopetala v argentea
Dryas tenella	D. integrifolia
Dryopteris affinis 'Crispa Congesta'	D. affinis 'Crispa Gracilis'
Dryopteris affinis 'Cristata The King'	D. affinis 'Cristata'
Dryopteris atrata h	D. cycadina
Dryopteris austriaca h	D. dilatata
Dryopteris borreri	D. affinis ssp borreri
Dryopteris filix-mas 'Crispa Congesta'	D. affinis 'Crispa Congesta'
Dryopteris hexagonoptera	Phegopteris hexagonoptera
Dryopteris hirtipes	D. cycadina
Dryopteris odontoloma	D. nigropaleacea
Dryopteris pseudomas	D. affinis
Duchesnea chrysantha	D. indica
Duchesnea indica 'Variegata'	D. indica 'Harlequin'
Duranta plumieri	D. erecta
Duranta repens	D. erecta
Duvernoia	Justicia
Dyckia argentea	Hechtia argentea
Eccremocactus bradei	Weberocereus bradei
Eccremocarpus ruber	E. scaber f carmineus
Eccremocarpus 'Ruber'	E. scaber f carmineus
Echeveria cooperi	Adromischus cooperi
Echeveria glauca -Bak.	E. secunda v glauca
Echeveria x fruticosa	Pachyveria glauca
Echidnopsis chrysantha	E. scutellata ssp planiflora
Echinacea purpurea 'Bright Star'	E. purpurea 'Leuchtstern'
Echinocactus asterias	Astrophytum asterias
Echinocactus capricornis	Astrophytum capricorne
Echinocactus chilensis	Neoporteria chilensis
Echinocactus hartmannii	Discocactus hartmannii
Echinocactus ingens	E. platyacanthus
Echinocactus myriostigma	Astrophytum myriostigma
Echinocactus ornatus	Astrophytum ornatum
Echinocactus ritteri	Aztekium ritteri

Synonyms

Echinocactus scheeri	Sclerocactus scheeri
Echinocactus uncinatus	Sclerocactus uncinatus
Echinocereus baileyi	E. reichenbachii v baileyi
Echinocereus procumbens	E. pentalophus
Echinodorus ranunculoides	Baldellia ranunculoides
Echinofossulocactus	Stenocactus
Echinofossulocactus lamellosus	Stenocactus crispatus
Echinofossulocactus pentacanthus	Stenocactus obvallatus
Echinofossulocactus violaciflorus	Stenocactus obvallatus
Echinomastus macdowellii	Thelocactus macdowellii
Echinops albus	E. 'Nivalis'
Echinops ritro h	E. bannaticus
Echinopsis multiplex	E. oxygona
Echinospartum	Genista
Echioides longiflorum	Arnebia pulchra
Echium bourgaeanum	E. wildprettii
Echium fastuosum	E. candicans
Echium pinnifolium	E. pininana
Edgeworthia papyrifera	E. chrysantha
Edraianthus graminifolius albus	E. graminifolius ssp niveus
Edwardsia microphylla	Sophora microphylla
Ehretia ovalifolia	E. acuminata v obovata
Ehretia thyrsiflora	E. acuminata v obovata
Eichhornia speciosa	E. crassipes
Elaeagnus angustifolia Caspica Group	E. 'Quicksilver'
Elaeagnus argentea	E. commutata
Elaeagnus glabra 'Reflexa'	E. x reflexa
Elaeagnus pungens 'Argenteovariegata'	E. pungens 'Variegata'
Elaeagnus pungens 'Aureovariegata'	E. pungens 'Maculata'
Elatostema daveauanum	E. repens v repens
Eleutherococcus pictus	Kalopanax septemlobus
Eleutherococcus septemlobus	Kalopanax septemlobus
Elisena longipetala	Hymenocallis longipetala
Elliottia bracteata	Tripetaleia bracteata
Elliottia paniculata	Tripetaleia paniculata
Elliottia pyroliflorus	Cladothamnus pyroliflorus
Elodea crispa	Lagarosiphon major
Elodea densa	Egeria densa
Elymus arenarius	Leymus arenarius
Elymus giganteus	Leymus racemosus
Elymus glaucus h	E. hispidus
Embothrium coccineum v lanceolatum	E. coccineum Lanceolatum Group
Emilia flammea	E. coccinea
Emilia javanica h	E. coccinea
Endymion	Hyacinthoides
Endymion hispanicus	Hyacinthoides hispanica
Endymion non-scriptus	Hyacinthoides non-scripta
Ephedra nebrodensis	E. major
Epidendrum radicans	E. ibaguense
Epilobium angustifolium f leucanthum	E. angustifolium v album
Epilobium californicum h	Zauschneria californica
Epilobium californicum -Haussknecht	Zauschneria californica ssp angustifolia
Epilobium canum	Zauschneria californica ssp cana
Epilobium chlorifolium v kaikourense	Zauschneria chlorifolium
Epilobium garrettii	Zauschneria californica ssp garrettii
Epilobium microphyllum	Zauschneria californica ssp cana
Epilobium rosmarinifolium	Zauschneria dodonaei
Epilobium septentrionale	Zauschneria

	septentrionalis
Epilobium villosum	Zauschneria californica ssp mexicana
Epilobium wilsonii h	Zauschneria chlorifolium
Epimedium cremeum	E. grandiflorum ssp koreanum
Epimedium grandiflorum 'Violaceum'	E. grandiflorum f violaceum
Epimedium koreanum	E. grandiflorum ssp koreanum
Epimedium macranthum	E. grandiflorum
Epimedium pinnatum ssp elegans	E. pinnatum ssp colchicum
Epimedium x youngianum 'Lilacinum'	E. x youngianum 'Roseum'
Epiphyllanthus obovatus	Schlumbergera opuntioides
Epiphyllum ackermannii	Nopalxochia ackermannii
Epiphyllum 'Gloria'	Epicactus 'Gloria'
Epiphyllum 'Jennifer Ann'	Epicactus 'Jennifer Ann'
Epiphyllum 'M.A.Jeans'	Epicactus 'M.A.Jeans'
Epiphyllum macdougallii	Nopalxochia macdougallii
Epiphyllum strictum	Nopalxochia hookeri
Epipremnum pictum 'Argyraeus'	Scindapsus pictus 'Argyraeus'
Equisetum hyemale v robustum	E. hyemale v affine
Eragrostis abyssinica	E. tef
Eranthemum atropurpureum	Pseuderanthemum atropurpureum
Eranthemum nervosum	E. pulchellum
Eranthis keiskei	E. pinnatifida
Ercilla spicata	E. volubilis
Erdisia	Corryocactus
Erdisia erecta	Corryocactus erectus
Erdisia squarrosa	Corryocactus squarrosus
Eremurus aurantiacus	E. stenophyllus ssp aurantiacus
Eremurus bungei	E. stenophyllus ssp stenophyllus
Eremurus elwesii	E. aitchisonii
Eremurus x isabellinus Fire Torch	E. x isabellinus 'Feuerfackel'
Eremurus x isabellinus Snow Lance	E. x isabellinus 'Schneelanze'
Erianthus	Saccharum
Erica arborea 'Arbora Gold'	E. arborea 'Albert's Gold'
Erica arborea 'Arnold's Gold'	E. arborea 'Albert's Gold'
Erica carnea 'Amy Doncaster'	E. carnea 'Treasure Trove'
Erica carnea 'Mr. Reeves'	E. x darleyensis 'Darley Dale'
Erica carnea 'Myreton Ruby'	E. carnea 'Myretoun Ruby'
Erica carnea 'Pink Beauty'	E. carnea 'Pink Pearl'
Erica carnea 'Sherwoodii'	E. carnea 'Sherwood Creeping'
Erica carnea 'Urville'	E. carnea 'Vivellii'
Erica carnea 'White Glow'	E. x darleyensis 'White Glow'
Erica carnea 'White Perfection'	E. x darleyensis 'White Perfection'
Erica cinerea 'Graham Thomas'	E. cinerea 'C.G.Best'
Erica cinerea 'Pink Lace'	E. cinerea 'Pink Ice'
Erica codonodes	E. lusitanica
Erica corsica	E. terminalis
Erica crawfurdii	E. mackayana

Synonyms

Name	Valid name
Erica erigena 'Irish Lemon'	E. x stuartii 'Irish Lemon'
Erica 'Heaven Scent'	E. x griffithsii 'Heaven Scent'
Erica herbacea	E. carnea
Erica hibernica	E. erigena
Erica hybrida 'Irish Lemon'	E. x stuartii 'Irish Lemon'
Erica manipuliflora 'Waterfall'	E. manipuliflora 'Cascade'
Erica manipuliflora x vagans 'Valerie Griffiths'	E. x griffithsii 'Valerie Griffiths'
Erica mediterranea	E. erigena
Erica scoparia ssp scoparia 'Pumila'	E. scoparia ssp scoparia 'Minima'
Erica terminalis stricta	E. terminalis
Erica tetralix 'Dr. Ronald Gray'	E. mackayana 'Doctor Ronald Gray'
Erica tetralix 'Morning Glow'	E. x watsonii 'F.White'
Erica tetralix 'Plena'	E. mackayana 'Plena'
Erica tetralix 'Ruby's Velvet'	E. tetralix 'Ruby's Variety'
Erica vagans 'Alba Nana'	E. vagans 'Nana'
Erica vulgaris	Calluna vulgaris
Erica x darleyensis 'Alba'	E. x darleyensis 'Silberschmelze'
Erica x darleyensis 'Cherry Stevens'	E. x darleyensis 'Furzey'
Erica x darleyensis 'Darleyensis'	E. x darleyensis 'Darley Dale'
Erica x darleyensis 'Dunwood Splendour'	E. x darleyensis 'Arthur Johnson'
Erica x darleyensis 'J.H.Brummage'	E. x darleyensis 'Jack H.Brummage'
Erica x darleyensis 'Mediterranea Superba'	E. x darleyensis 'Superba'
Erica x darleyensis Molten Silver	E. x darleyensis 'Silberschmelze'
Erica x darleyensis 'Pink Perfection'	E. x darleyensis 'Darley Dale'
Erica x praegeri	E. x stuartii
Erica x stuartii 'Charles Stuart'	E. x stuartii 'Stuartii'
Erica x veitchii 'Albert's Gold'	E. arborea 'Albert's Gold'
Erica x williamsiana	E. williamsii
Erigeron Azure Fairy	E. 'Azurfee'
Erigeron Black Sea	E. 'Schwarzes Meer'
Erigeron Darkest of All	E. 'Dunkelste Aller'
Erigeron mucronatus	E. karvinskianus
Erigeron Pink Jewel	E. 'Rosa Juwel'
Erigeron Pink Triumph	E. 'Rosa Triumph'
Erigeron pyrenaicus h	E. alpinus
Erigeron pyrenaicus -Rouy	Aster pyrenaeus
Erigeron Red Sea	E. 'Rotes Meer'
Erigeron rotundifolius 'Caerulescens'	Bellis rotundifolia 'Caerulescens'
Erigeron Snow White	Bellis 'Schneewittchen'
Erigeron trifidus	E. compositus v discoideus
Erinacea pungens	E. anthyllis
Eriocactus	Parodia
Eriocactus apricus	Parodia concinna
Eriocapitella	Anemone
Eriocereus jusbertii	Harrisia jusbertii
Eriocereus martianus	Aporocactus martianus
Eriocereus pomanensis	Harrisia bonplandii
Eriogonum douglasii	E. caespitosum ssp douglasii
Eriogonum torreyanum	E. umbellatum v torreyanum
Eriophorum vaginatum	Scirpus fauriei v vaginatus
Eriophyllum lutescens	E. lanatum v monoense
Eritrichium rupestre	E. canum
Fritrichium sericeum	E. canum
Eritrichium strictum	E. canum
Erodium balearicum	E. x variabile 'Album'
Erodium chamaedryoides	E. reichardii
Erodium chamaedryoides 'Roseum'	E. x variabile 'Roseum'
Erodium 'County Park'	E. foetidum 'County Park'
Erodium daucoides h	E. castellanum
Erodium heteradenum	E. petraeum
Erodium hymenodes h	E. trifolium
Erodium macradenum	E. glandulosum
Erodium manescavii	E. manescaui
Erodium 'Merstham Pink'	E. foetidum 'County Park'
Erodium petraeum ssp crispum	E. cheilanthifolium
Erodium petraeum ssp crispum -(Gowan) Willd.	E. foetidum
Erodium petraeum ssp glandulosum	E. glandulosum
Erodium reichardii cultivars	E. x variabile
Erodium romanum	E. acaule
Erodium salzmannii	E. cicutarium ssp cicutarium
Erodium supracanum	E. rupestre
Erodium trichomanifolium h	E. cheilanthifolium
Erodium trichomanifolium h	E. valentinum
Erodium x hybridum h	E. 'Sara Francesca'
Erpetion	Viola
Erpetion hederaceum	Viola hederacea
Erpetion reniforme	Viola hederacea
Ervatamia coronaria	Tabernaemontana divaricata
Eryngium biebersteinianum -Nevski	E. caucasicum
Eryngium bromeliifolium h	E. agavifolium
Eryngium decaisneanum	E. pandanifolium
Eryngium decaisneanum -Delaroux	E. proteiflorum
Eryngium Miss Wilmott's Ghost	E. giganteum
Eryngium paniculatum	E. erburneum
Eryngium planum Blue Dwarf	E. planum 'Blauer Zwerg'
Erysimum alpinum h	E. hieraciifolium
Erysimum arenicola v torulosum	E. torulosum
Erysimum arkansanum	E. helveticum
Erysimum concinnum	E. suffrutescens
Erysimum 'Devon Gold'	E. 'Plant World Gold'
Erysimum 'Dorothy Elmhirst'	E. 'Mrs L.K.Elmhirst'
Erysimum 'E.A.Bowles'	E. 'Bowles' Mauve'
Erysimum 'Harpur Crewe'	E. cheiri 'Harpur Crewe'
Erysimum pumilum -De Candolle	E. helveticum
Erysimum rupestre	E. pulchellum
Erysimum sintenisianum	E. alpestre
Erysimum 'Sissinghurst Variegated'	E. linifolium 'Variegatum'
Erysimum x kewensis 'Harpur Crewe'	E. cheiri 'Harpur Crewe'
Erythraea	Centaurium
Erythrina indica	E. variegata
Erythrina princeps	E. humeana
Erythronium cliftonii	E. multiscapoideum Cliftonii Group
Erythronium grandiflorum ssp chrysandrum	E. grandiflorum
Erythronium hartwegii	E. multiscapoideum
Erythronium purdyi	E. multiscapoideum
Erythronium revolutum 'White Beauty'	E. californicum 'White Beauty'
Erythronium 'White Beauty'	E. californicum 'White Beauty'
Escallonia fonkii	E. alpina

Synonyms

Name	Synonym
Escallonia 'Hopley's Gold'	E. laevis 'Gold Brian'
Escallonia montevidensis	E. bifida
Escallonia organensis	E. laevis
Escallonia punctata	E. rubra
Escallonia rubra 'Pygmaea'	E. rubra 'Woodside'
Esmeralda sanderiana	Euanthe sanderiana
Eucalyptus debeuzevillei	E. pauciflora ssp debeuzevillei
Eucalyptus divaricata	E. gunnii divaricata
Eucalyptus niphophila	E. pauciflora ssp niphophila
Eucalyptus pauciflora v nana	E. gregsoniana
Eucalyptus simmondsii	E. nitida
Eucalyptus stuartiana	E. bridgesiana
Eucharidium	Clarkia
Eucharis grandiflora h	E. amazonica
Eucodonia 'Cornell Gem'	x Achicodonia 'Cornell Gem'
Eucomis punctata	E. comosa
Eucomis undulata	E. autumnalis
Eugenia aromatica	Syzygium aromaticum
Eugenia australis h	Syzygium paniculatum
Eugenia paniculata	Syzygium paniculatum
Eugenia smithii	Acmena smithii
Eugenia ugni	Ugni molinae
Eunomia	Aethionema
Eunomia oppositifolia	Aethionema oppositifolium
Euodia daniellii	Tetradium daniellii
Euodia hupehensis	Tetradium daniellii Hupehense Group
Euonymus alatus 'Ciliodentatus'	E. alatus 'Compactus'
Euonymus farreri	E. nanus
Euonymus fortunei 'Gold Spot'	E. fortunei 'Sunspot'
Euonymus fortunei 'Gold Tip'	E. fortunei Golden Prince
Euonymus fortunei 'Silver Gem'	E. fortunei 'Variegatus'
Euonymus hamiltonianus ssp hians	E. hamiltonianus ssp sieboldianus
Euonymus hamiltonianus v yedoensis	E. hamiltonianus ssp sieboldianus
Euonymus japonicus 'Aureopictus'	E. japonicus 'Aureus'
Euonymus japonicus 'Aureovariegatus'	E. japonicus 'Ovatus Aureus'
Euonymus japonicus 'Duc d'Anjou' h	E. japonicus 'Viridivariegatus'
Euonymus japonicus 'Luna'	E. japonicus 'Aureus'
Euonymus japonicus 'Macrophyllus Albus'	E. japonicus 'Latifolius Albomarginatus'
Euonymus japonicus 'Marieke'	E. japonicus 'Ovatus Aureus'
Euonymus 'Microphyllus Aureus'	E. japonicus 'Microphyllus Pulchellus'
Euonymus 'Microphyllus Variegatus'	E. japonicus 'Microphyllus Albovariegatus'
Euonymus radicans	E. fortunei radicans
Euonymus rosmarinifolius	E. nanus
Euonymus sachalinensis h	E. planipes
Euonymus yedoensis	E. hamiltonianus ssp sieboldianus
Eupatorium ageratoides	E. rugosum
Eupatorium ianthinum	E. sordidum
Eupatorium maculatum	E. purpureum ssp maculatum
Eupatorium micranthum	E. ligustrinum
Eupatorium rugosum album	E. album
Eupatorium urticifolium	E. rugosum
Eupatorium weinmannianum	E. ligustrinum
Euphorbia amygdaloides 'Rubra'	E. amygdaloides 'Purpurea'
Euphorbia biglandulosa	E. rigida
Euphorbia characias ssp wulfenii Kew form	E. characias ssp wulfenii 'John Tomlinson'
Euphorbia characias ssp wulfenii 'Purpurea'	E. characias ssp wulfenii 'Purple and Gold'
Euphorbia cyparissias 'Betten'	E. x gayeri 'Betten'
Euphorbia cyparissias 'Purpurea'	E. cyparissias 'Clarice Howard'
Euphorbia epithymoides	E. polychroma
Euphorbia 'Golden Foam'	E. stricta
Euphorbia heterophylla h	E. cyathophora
Euphorbia longifolia -D Don	E. donii
Euphorbia longifolia h	E. cornigera
Euphorbia longifolia -Lamarck	E. mellifera
Euphorbia pilosa 'Major'	E. polychroma 'Major'
Euphorbia polychroma 'Purpurea'	E. polychroma 'Candy'
Euphorbia reflexa	E. seguieriana ssp niciciana
Euphorbia robbiae	E. amygdaloides v robbiae
Euphorbia serrulata	E. stricta
Euphorbia splendens	E. milii v splendens
Euphorbia uralensis	E. x pseudovirgata
Euphorbia variegata	E. marginata
Euphorbia veneta	E. characias ssp wulfenii
Euphorbia wallichii -Kohli	E. cornigera
Euphorbia wallichii misap.	E. donii
Euphorbia wulfenii	E. characias ssp wulfenii
Euphorbia x waldsteinii	E. virgata
Euptelea franchetii	E. pleiosperma
Eurya japonica 'Variegata'	Cleyera japonica 'Fortunei'
Euryops evansii	E. acraeus
Euryops sericeus	Ursinia sericeus
Eustoma russellianum	E. grandiflorum
Evodia	Tetradium
Evolvulus glomeratus 'Blue Daze'	E. pilosus 'Blue Daze'
Evolvulus glomeratus h	E. pilosus
Exochorda alberti	E. korolkowii
Fagopyrum cymosum	F. dibotrys
Fagus americana	F. grandifolia
Fagus sylvatica 'Albovariegata'	F. sylvatica 'Albomarginata'
Fagus sylvatica 'Fastigiata'	F. sylvatica 'Dawyck'
Fagus sylvatica Purple-leaved Group	F. sylvatica Atropurpurea Group
Fagus sylvatica 'Roseomarginata'	F. sylvatica 'Purpurea Tricolor'
Fagus sylvatica 'Tricolor' h	F. sylvatica 'Purpurea Tricolor'
Fallopia aubertii	F. baldschuanica
Farfugium japonicum 'Albovariegatum'	F. japonicum 'Argenteum'
Farfugium tussilagineum	F. japonicum
Fargesia spathacea h	F. murieliae
Farsetia clypeata	Fibigia clypeata
Fascicularia andina	F. bicolor
Fascicularia kirchhoffiana	F. bicolor ssp canaliculata
Fascicularia pitcairniifolia h	F. bicolor ssp bicolor
Fatsia papyrifera	Tetrapanax papyrifer
Fauria	Nephrophyllidium
Feijoa	Acca
Felicia amethystina	F. 'Snowman'

Synonyms

Name	Synonym
Felicia capensis	F. amelloides
Felicia capensis 'Variegata'	F. amelloides variegated
Felicia coelestis	F. amelloides
Felicia natalensis	F. rosulata
Felicia pappei	F. amoena
Fenestraria rhopalophylla	F. aurantiaca f rhopalophylla
Ferocactus acanthodes h	F. cylandraceus
Ferocactus bicolor	Thelocactus bicolor
Ferocactus crassihamatus	Sclerocactus uncinatus v crassihamatus
Ferocactus setispinus	Thelocactus setispinus
Ferraria undulata	F. crispa
Ferula chiliantha	F. communis ssp glauca
Ferula communis 'Gigantea'	F. communis
Ferula 'Giant Bronze'	Foeniculum vulgare 'Giant Bronze'
Festuca glauca Blue Fox	F. glauca 'Blaufuchs'
Festuca glauca Blue Glow	F. glauca 'Blauglut'
Festuca glauca 'Pallens'	F. longifolia
Festuca glauca Sea Blue	F. glauca 'Meerblau'
Festuca glauca Sea Urchin	F. glauca 'Seeigel'
Festuca glauca 'Seven Seas'	F. valesiaca 'Silbersee'
Festuca scoparia	F. gautieri
Festuca valesiaca 'Silver Sea'	F. valesiaca 'Silbersee'
Ficus australis h	F. rubiginosa 'Australis'
Ficus carica 'Noir de Provence'	F. carica 'Reculver'
Ficus carica 'White Genoa'	F. carica 'White Marseilles'
Ficus diversifolia	F. deltoidea v diversifolia
Ficus foveolata -Wallich	F. sarmentosa
Ficus radicans	F. sagittata
Ficus repens	F. pumila
Ficus retusa h	F. microcarpa
Ficus triangularis	F. natalensis ssp leprieurii
Filipendula alnifolia 'Variegata'	F. ulmaria 'Variegata'
Filipendula digitata 'Nana'	F. palmata 'Nana'
Filipendula hexapetala	F. vulgaris
Filipendula hexapetala 'Flore Pleno'	F. vulgaris 'Multiplex'
Filipendula palmata 'Digitata Nana'	F. palmata 'Nana'
Filipendula palmata purpurea	F. purpurea
Filipendula purpurea f alba	F. purpurea f albiflora
Filipendula 'Queen of the Prairies'	F. rubra
Filipendula rubra 'Magnifica'	F. rubra 'Venusta'
Filipendula rubra 'Venusta Magnifica'	F. rubra 'Venusta'
Filipendula vulgaris 'Flore Pleno'	F. vulgaris 'Multiplex'
Filipendula vulgaris 'Plena'	F. vulgaris 'Multiplex'
Firmiana platanifolia	F. simplex
Fitroya patagonica	F. cupressoides
Fittonia argyroneura	F. albivensis Argyroneura Group
Fittonia verschaffeltii	F. albivensis Verschaffeltii Group
Fitzroya patagonica	F. cupressoides
Fockea capensis	F. crispa
Foeniculum vulgare 'Bronze'	F. vulgare 'Purpureum'
Forsythia 'Goldcluster'	F. 'Melee d'Or'
Forsythia suspensa 'Variegata'	F. suspensa 'Taff's Arnold'
Fothergilla monticola	F. major Monticola Group
Fragaria alpina	F. vesca 'Semperflorens'
Fragaria alpina 'Alba'	F. vesca 'Semperflorens Alba'
Fragaria alpina 'Fraise des Bois'	F. vesca
Fragaria 'Bowles' Double'	F. vesca 'Multiplex'
Fragaria indica	Duchesnea indica
Fragaria 'Variegata'	F. x ananassa 'Variegata'
Fragaria vesca 'Flore Pleno'	F. vesca 'Multiplex'
Fragaria vesca 'Plymouth Strawberry'	F. vesca 'Muricata'
Frailea asterioides	F. castanea
Frailea pulcherrima	F. pygmaea
Francoa glabrata	F. ramosa
Francoa 'Purple Spike'	F. sonchifolia Rogerson's form
Francoa ramosa alba	F. ramosa
Fraxinus angustifolia 'Flame'	F. angustifolia 'Raywood'
Fraxinus excelsior 'Diversifolia Pendula'	F. excelsior 'Heterophylla Pendula'
Fraxinus mariesii	F. sieboldiana
Fraxinus oregona	F. latifolia
Fraxinus oxycarpa	F. angustifolia
Fraxinus pennsylvanica v lanceolata	F. pennsylvanica v subintegerrima
Fraxinus spaethiana 'Veltheimii'	F. angustifolia 'Monophylla'
Freesia alba -Foster	F. lactea
Freesia armstrongii	F. corymbosa
Freesia refracta v alba	F. lactea
Fremontia	Fremontodendron
Frerea	Caralluma
Frerea indica	C. frerei
Freylinia cestroides	F. lanceolata
Fritillaria arabica	F. persica
Fritillaria assyriaca	F. uva-vulpis
Fritillaria carduchorum	F. minuta
Fritillaria citrina	F. bithynica
Fritillaria delphinensis	F. tubiformis
Fritillaria graeca ssp ionica	F. graeca ssp thessala
Fritillaria hispanica	F. lusitanica
Fritillaria imperialis 'Crown upon Crown'	F. imperialis 'Prolifera'
Fritillaria imperialis 'Lutea Maxima'	F. imperialis 'Maxima Lutea'
Fritillaria imperialis 'Maxima'	F. imperialis 'Rubra Maxima'
Fritillaria ionica	F. graeca sspthessala
Fritillaria karadaghensis	F. crassifolia ssp kurdica
Fritillaria lanceolata	F. affinis
Fritillaria latifolia v nobilis	F. latifolia
Fritillaria lutea	F. collina
Fritillaria neglecta	F. messanensis ssp gracilis
Fritillaria nigra h	F. pyrenaica
Fritillaria oranensis	F. messanensis
Fritillaria phaeanthera	F. affinis v gracilis
Fritillaria roderickii	F. grayana
Fritillaria rubra major	F. imperialis 'Rubra Maxima'
Fritillaria sphaciotica	F. messanensis
Fritillaria tenella	F. orientalis
Fritillaria verticillata v thunbergii	F. thunbergii
Fuchsia aprica h	F. x bacillaris
Fuchsia aprica -Lundell	F. microphylla ssp aprica
Fuchsia arborea	F. arborescens
Fuchsia boliviana 'Alba'	F. boliviana v alba -Carriere
Fuchsia boliviana -Britton	F. sanctae-rosae
Fuchsia boliviana f puberulenta	F. boliviana -Carriere
Fuchsia boliviana v luxurians	F. boliviana v alba -Carriere
Fuchsia 'Burning Bush'	F. 'Autumnale'
Fuchsia canescens -Munz	F. ampliata
Fuchsia cordifolia h	F. splendens
Fuchsia corymbiflora alba	F. boliviana v alba -

Synonyms

	Carriere	Gagea arvensis	G. villosa
Fuchsia 'Cottinghamii'	F. x bacillaris 'Cottinghamii'	Gaillardia aristata h	G. x grandiflora
		Gaillardia Burgundy	G. 'Burgunder'
Fuchsia dependens	F. corymbiflora	Gaillardia Goblin	G. 'Kobold'
Fuchsia 'Doctor'	F. 'The Doctor'	Gaillardia Golden Goblin	G. 'Goldkobold'
Fuchsia 'Earl of Beaconsfield'	F. 'Laing's Hybrid'	Gaillardia Torchlight	G. 'Fackelschein'
Fuchsia 'Enstone'	F. magellanica v molinae 'Enstone'	Gaillardia Yellow Goblin	G. 'Goldkobold'
		Galanthus 'Arnott's Seedling'	G. 'S.Arnott'
Fuchsia 'Fascination'	F. 'Emile de Wildeman'	Galanthus byzantinus	G. plicatus ssp byzantinus
Fuchsia Filigree	F. 'Filigraan'		
Fuchsia fulgens 'Gesneriana'	F. 'Gesneriana'	Galanthus cabardensis	G. transcaucasicus
Fuchsia fulgens 'Rubra Grandiflora'	F. 'Rubra Grandiflora'	Galanthus caucasicus h double	G. 'Lady Beatrix Stanley'
Fuchsia 'Geertien'	F. 'Dutch Geertien'	Galanthus corcyrensis spring flowering	G. reginae-olgae ssp vernalis
Fuchsia gracilis	F. magellanica v gracilis		
Fuchsia 'Heidi Weiss'	F. 'White Ann'	Galanthus corcyrensis winter flowering	G. reginae-olgae ssp reginae-olgae Winter-flowering group
Fuchsia 'Heinrich Henkel'	F. 'Andenken an Heinrich Henkel'		
Fuchsia 'Hemsleyana'	F. microphylla ssp hemsleyana	Galanthus elwesii v minor	G. gracilis
		Galanthus graecus -Boiss.	G. elwesii
Fuchsia hidalgensis	F. microphylla ssp hidalgensis	Galanthus graecus h	G. gracilis
		Galanthus kemulariae	G. transcaucasicus
Fuchsia 'Koralle'	F. 'Coralle'	Galanthus ketskovelii	G. transcaucasicus
Fuchsia 'Leverhulme'	F. 'Leverkusen'	Galanthus lagodechianus	G. transcaucasicus
Fuchsia 'Logan Garden'	F. magellanica 'Logan Woods'	Galanthus latifolius	G. ikariae Latifolius Group
		Galanthus lutescens	G. nivalis 'Sandersii'
Fuchsia lycioides h	F. 'Lycioides'	Galanthus nivalis 'Howick Yellow'	G. nivalis 'Sandersii'
Fuchsia magellanica 'Alba'	F. magellanica v molinae	Galanthus nivalis 'Lutescens'	G. nivalis 'Sandersii'
Fuchsia magellanica 'Globosa'	F. 'Globosa'	Galanthus platyphyllus	G. ikariae Latifolius Group
Fuchsia magellanica 'Riccartonii'	F. 'Riccartonii'	Galanthus 'Sam Arnott'	G. 'S.Arnott'
Fuchsia minimiflora	F. microphylla ssp hidalgensis	Galanthus 'Scharlockii'	G. nivalis Scharlockii Group
Fuchsia 'Oosje'	F. x bacillaris 'Oosje'	Galax aphylla	G. urceolata
Fuchsia 'Overbecks'	F. magellanica v molinae 'Sharpitor'	Galega 'Her Majesty'	G. 'His Majesty'
		Galeobdolon	Lamium
Fuchsia parviflora h	F. x bacillaris	Galeobdolon argentatum	Lamium galeobdolon 'Florentinum'
Fuchsia 'Princess Dollar'	F. 'Dollar Princess'		
Fuchsia 'Prodigy'	F. 'Enfant Prodigue'	Galium aureum	G. firmum
Fuchsia 'Reflexa'	F. x bacillaris 'Reflexa'	Galium cruciata	Cruciata laevipes
Fuchsia 'Reverend Elliott'	F. 'President Elliott'	Galium perpusillum	Asperula perpusilla
Fuchsia rosea h	F. 'Globosa'	Gamolepis	Steirodiscus
Fuchsia rosea -Ruiz & Pav.	F. lycioides -Andrews	Gardenia augusta 'Hadley'	G. augusta 'Belmont'
Fuchsia 'Rufus The Red'	F. 'Rufus'	Gardenia augusta 'Prostrata Variegata'	G. augusta 'Radicans Variegata'
Fuchsia scandens	F. decussata		
Fuchsia serratifolia -Hooker	F. austromontana	Gardenia capensis	Rothmannia capensis
Fuchsia serratifolia -Ruiz & Pav.	F. denticulata	Gardenia florida	G. augusta
Fuchsia 'Sharpitor'	F. magellanica v molinae 'Sharpitor'	Gardenia globosa	Rothmannia globosa
		Gardenia grandiflora	G. augusta
Fuchsia Sugarbush	F. 'Suikerbossie'	Gardenia jasminoides	G. augusta
Fuchsia sylvatica -Munz	F. nigricans	Gardenia rothmannia	Rothmannia capensis
Fuchsia tetradactyla	F. encliandra ssp tetardactyla	Gasteria liliputana	G. bicolor v liliputana
		Gasteria pulchra	G. obliqua
Fuchsia 'Thompsonii'	F. magellanica 'Thompsonii'	Gasteria verrucosa	G. carinata v verrucosa
		Gaultheria furiens	G. insana
Fuchsia 'Tricolor'	F. magellanica v gracilis 'Tricolor'	Gaultheria mucronata Mother of Pearl	G. mucronata 'Parelmoer'
Fuchsia 'Variegated Procumbens'	F. procumbens 'Argentea'	Gaultheria mucronata Signal	G. mucronata 'Signaal'
Fuchsia 'Versicolor'	F. magellanica 'Versicolor'	Gaultheria mucronata Snow White	G. mucronata 'Sneeuwwitje'
Fuchsia vulcanica -Andre	F. ampliata		
Fuchsia 'Wendy'	F. 'Snowcap'	Gaultheria nana -Colenso	G. parvula
Fuchsia 'Whiteknights Goblin'	F. denticulata 'Whiteknights Goblin'	Gaultheria nummularioides 'Minuta'	G. nummularioides v elliptica
		Gaultheria ovalifolia	G. fragrantissima
Fumaria lutea	Corydalis lutea	Gaultheria prostrata	G. myrsinoides
Furcraea foetida v mediopicta 'Variegata'	F. foetida v mediopicta	Gaultheria prostrata purpurea	G. myrsinoides
Furcraea foetida 'Variegata'	F. foetida v mediopicta	Gaultheria willisiana	G. eriophylla
Furcraea gigantea	F. foetida	Gazania double yellow	G. 'Yellow Buttons'
Furcraea gigantea 'Mediopicta'	F. foetida v mediopicta		

Synonyms

Gazania splendens	G. rigens
Gazania uniflora	G. rigens v uniflora
Geissorhiza rochensis	G. radians
Gelasine azurea	G. coerulea
Gelidocalamus fangianus	Chimonobambusa microphylla
Genista decumbens	Cytisus decumbens
Genista delphinensis	G. sagittalis ssp delphinensis
Genista 'Emerald Spreader'	G. pilosa 'Yellow Spreader'
Genista fragrans	G. canariensis
Genista humifusa	G. pulchella
Genista monosperma	Retama monosperma
Genista pilosa 'Lemon Spreader'	G. pilosa 'Yellow Spreader'
Genista sagittalis minor	G. sagittalis ssp delphinensis
Genista striata	Cytisus striatus
Genista tinctoria 'Plena'	G. tinctoria 'Flore Pleno'
Genista villarsii	G. pulchella
Gentiana acaulis 'Dinarica'	G. dinarica
Gentiana acaulis occidentalis	G. occidentalis
Gentiana 'Alpha'	G. x hexafarreri 'Alpha'
Gentiana cashmeriana	Gentiana cachemirica
Gentiana crinita	Gentianopsis crinita
Gentiana excisa	G. acaulis
Gentiana gracilipes 'Yuatensis'	G. wutaiensis
Gentiana kesselringii	G. walujewii
Gentiana kochiana	G. acaulis
Gentiana kurroo v brevidens	G. dahurica
Gentiana lagodechiana	G. septemfida v lagodechiana
Gentiana macrophylla	G. burseri v villarsii
Gentiana menziesii	G. sceptrum
Gentiana ochroleuca	G. villosa
Gentiana phlogifolia	G. cruciata
Gentiana purdomii	G. gracilipes
Gentiana scabra v saxatilis	G. scabra v buergeri
Gentiana sino-ornata 'Praecox'	G. x macaulayi 'Praecox'
Gentiana stylophora	Megacodon stylophorus
Gentiana verna ssp angulosa	G. verna ssp balcanica
Gentiana verna ssp pontica	G. verna ssp balcanica
Gentiana verna ssp tergestina	G. verna ssp balcanica
Gentiana wellsii	G. x macaulayi 'Wells' Variety'
Gentiana 'Wellsii'	G. x macaulayi 'Wells' Variety'
Gentiana x bernardii	G. x stevenagensis 'Bernardii'
Gentiana x hascombensis	G. septemfida v lagodechiana 'Hascombensis'
Geogenanthus undatus	G. poepigii
Geranium aconitifolium -L'Heritier	G. rivulare
Geranium anemonifolium	G. palmatum
Geranium argenteum 'Purpureum'	G. x lindavicum 'Alanah'
Geranium armenum	G. psilostemon
Geranium atlanticum h	G. malviflorum
Geranium atlanticum -Hooker	G. malviflorum
Geranium 'Buxton's Blue'	G. wallichianum 'Buxton's Variety'
	G. lambertii
Geranium candicans h	G. x lindavicum 'Apple Blossom'
Geranium cinereum 'Apple Blossom'	
Geranium 'Claridge Druce'	G. x oxonianum 'Claridge Druce'
Geranium clarkei 'Kashmir Blue'	G. 'Kashmir Blue'
Geranium dalmaticum x macrorrhizum	G. x cantabrigiense
Geranium dclavayi h	G. sinense
Geranium endressii 'Prestbury White'	G. 'Prestbury Blush'
Geranium endressii 'Wargrave Pink'	G. x oxonianum 'Wargrave Pink'
Geranium eriostemon -Fischer	G. platyanthum
Geranium grandiflorum	G. himalayense
Geranium grandiflorum v alpinum	G. himalayense 'Gravetye'
Geranium grevilleanum	G. lambertii
Geranium h	Pelargonium
Geranium himalayense alpinum	G. himalayense 'Gravetye'
Geranium himalayense 'Birch Double'	G. himalayense 'Plenum'
Geranium himalayense meeboldii	G. himalayense
Geranium ibericum misapplied	G. x magnificum
Geranium ibericum ssp jubatum	G. x magnificum
Geranium ibericum v platyphyllum	G. platyphyllum -Fisch & Meyer
Geranium 'Kate Folkard'	G. 'Kate'
Geranium libanoticum	G. libani
Geranium 'Little Devil'	G. 'Little David'
Geranium macrorrhizum roseum	G. macrorrhizum
Geranium meeboldii	G. himalayense
Geranium 'Mourning Widow'	G. phaeum
Geranium napuligerum h	G. farreri
Geranium nodosum dark form	G. nodosum 'Swiss Purple'
Geranium nodosum pale form	G. nodosum 'Svelte Lilac'
Geranium phaeum black	G. phaeum 'Mourning Widow'
Geranium platypetalum -Franchet	G. sinense
Geranium platypetalum misapplied	G. x magnificum
Geranium pratense 'Bicolor'	G. pratense 'Striatum'
Geranium pratense 'Flore Pleno'	G. pratense 'Plenum Violaceum'
Geranium pratense 'Kashmir Purple'	G. clarkei 'Kashmir Purple'
Geranium pratense 'Kashmir White'	G. clarkei 'Kashmir White'
Geranium pratense 'Plenum Purpureum'	G. pratense 'Plenum Violaceum'
Geranium pratense 'Rectum Album'	G. clarkei 'Kashmir White'
Geranium punctatum h	G. x monacense 'Muldoon'
Geranium punctatum variegatum	G. x monacense 'Variegatum'
Geranium pyrenaicum 'Bill Wallace'	G. pyrenaicum 'Bill Wallis'
Geranium rectum 'Album'	G. clarkei 'Kashmir White'
Geranium renardii blue	G. renardii 'Whiteknights'
Geranium robertianum f bernettii	G. robertianum 'Album'
Geranium sanguineum 'Splendens'	G. sanguineum v striatum 'Splendens'
Geranium sanguineum v lancastrense	G. sanguineum v striatum
Geranium sanguineum v prostratum	G. sanguineum v striatum
Geranium sessiliflorum ssp novae-zelandiae 'Nigrescens'	G. sessiliflorum ssp novae-zelandiae 'Nigricans'
Geranium sessiliflorum ssp novae-zelandiae red-leaved	G. sessiliflorum ssp novae- zelandiae

	'Porter's Pass'
Geranium 'Southcombe Star'	G. x oxonianum 'Southcombe Star'
Geranium stapfianum v roseum	G. orientalitibeticum
Geranium striatum	G. versicolor
Geranium subcaulescens	G. cinereum v subcaulescens
Geranium thurstonianum	G. x oxonianum 'Thurstonianum'
Geranium tuberosum v charlesii	G. kotschyi v charlesii
Geranium violareum	Pelargonium 'Splendide'
Geranium wilfordii h	G. thunbergii
Geranium x lindavicum 'Purpureum'	G. x lindavicum 'Alanah'
Geranium x oxonianum 'Prestbury White'	G. 'Prestbury Blush'
Geranium yunnanense mis.	G. pogonanthum
Gesneria cardinalis	Sinningia cardinalis
Gesneria x cardosa	Sinningia x cardosa
Gesneria zebrina	Smithiantha zebrina
Geum alpinum	G. montanum
Geum borisii	G. 'Borisii'
Geum chiloense 'Lady Stratheden'	G. 'Lady Stratheden'
Geum chiloense 'Mrs Bradshaw'	G. 'Mrs J.Bradshaw'
Geum coccineum h	G. chiloense
Geum 'Feuerball'	G. 'Mrs J.Bradshaw'
Geum 'Goldball'	G. 'Lady Stratheden'
Geum magellanicum	G. parviflorum
Geum 'Princess Juliana'	G. 'Prinses Juliana'
Geum quellyon	G. chiloense
Geum reptans	Sieversia reptans
Geum rivale 'Leonardii'	G. rivale 'Leonard's Variety'
Gilia aggregata	Ipomopsis aggregata
Gilia californica	Leptodactylon californicum
Gilia stenothyrsa	Ipomopsis stenothyrsa
Gladiolus blandus	G. carneus
Gladiolus blandus v carneus	G. carneus
Gladiolus byzantinus	G. communis ssp byzantinus
Gladiolus grandis	G. liliaceus
Gladiolus hirsutus	G. caryophyllaceus
Gladiolus 'Murieliae'	G. callianthus 'Murieliae'
Gladiolus nanus	G. colvillei
Gladiolus primulinus	G. natalensis
Gladiolus psittacinus	G. dalenii
Gladiolus purpureoauratus	G. papilio Purpureoauratus Group
Gladiolus quartinianus	G. dalenii
Gladiolus segetum	G. italicus
Gladiolus x colvilei 'The Bride'	G. 'The Bride'
Glandularia bipinnatifida	Verbena bipinnatifida
Glandularia pulchella	Verbena tenera
Glandulicactus crassihamatus	Sclerocactus uncinatus v crassihamatus
Glandulicactus uncinatus	Sclerocactus uncinatus
Glaucidium palmatum 'Album'	G. palmatum v leucanthum
Glaucium flavum aurantiacum	G. flavum f fulvum
Glaucium flavum orange	G. flavum f fulvum
Glaucium flavum red	G. corniculatum
Glaucium phoenicum	G. corniculatum
Globularia bellidifolia	G. meridionalis
Globularia cordifolia ssp bellidifolia	G. meridionalis
Globularia cordifolia ssp meridionalis	G. meridionalis
Globularia nana	G. repens
Globularia pygmaea	G. meridionalis

Gloriosa carsonii	G. superba 'Carsonii'
Gloriosa lutea	G. superba 'Lutea'
Gloriosa minor	G. superba
Gloriosa rothschildiana	G. superba 'Rothschildiana'
Gloriosa simplex	G. superba
Gloxinia speciosa	Sinningia speciosa
Glyceria aquatica	G. maxima
Glyceria aquatica variegata	G. maxima v variegata
Glyceria plicata	G. notata
Glyceria spectabilis 'Variegata'	G. maxima v variegata
Glycyrrhiza glandulifera	G. glabra
Glyptostrobus lineatus	G. pensilis
Gnaphalium 'Fairy Gold'	Helichrysum thianschanicum 'Goldkind'
Gnaphalium keriense	Anaphalis keriensis
Gnaphalium subrigidum	Anaphalis subrigida
Gnaphalium trinerve	Anaphalis trinervis
Godetia	Clarkia
Godetia amoena	Clarkia amoena
Godetia grandiflora	Clarkia amoena
Grevillea alpestris	G. alpina
Grevillea 'Kentlyn'	G. 'Mason's Hybrid'
Grevillea lanigera 'Mt. Taboritha'	G. lanigera 'Compacta'
Grevillea lanigera 'Prostrate'	G. lanigera 'Compacta'
Grevillea 'Ned Kelly'	G. 'Mason's Hybrid'
Grevillea sulphurea	G. juniperina f sulphurea
Grewia parviflora	G. biloba
Grindelia speciosa	G. chiloensis
Guillauminia albiflora	Aloe albiflora
Gunnera brasiliensis	G. manicata
Gunnera chilensis	G. tinctoria
Gunnera scabra	G. tinctoria
Guzmania 'Claret'	Neoregelia Claret Group
Guzmania tricolor	G. monostachya
Gymnocalycium mihanovichii 'Hibotan'	G. mihanovichii 'Red Head'
Gymnocalycium mihanovichii 'Red Cap'	G. mihanovichii 'Red Head'
Gymnogramma	Gymnopteris
Gymnogramma triangularis	Pityrogramma triangularis
Gynerium argenteum	Cortaderia selloana
Gynura sarmentosa h	G. aurantiaca 'Purple Passion'
Gypsophila aretioides 'Compacta'	G. aretioides 'Caucasica'
Gypsophila dubia	G. repens 'Dubia'
Gypsophila gracilescens	G. tenuifolia
Gypsophila paniculata Snowflake	G. paniculata 'Schneeflocke'
Gypsophila repens Pink Beauty	G. repens 'Rosa Schonheit'
Gypsophila 'Rosy Veil'	G. 'Rosenschleier'
Gypsophila transylvanica	G. petraea
Gypsophila Veil of Roses	G. 'Rosenschleier'
Haageocereus acranthus	H. limensis
Haageocereus australis	H. decumbens
Habenaria radiata	Pecteilis radiata
Haberlea rhodopensis v ferdinandi-coburgii	H. ferdinandi-coburgii
Habranthus andersonii	H. tubispathus
Haemanthus kalbreyeri	Scadoxus multiflorus ssp multiflorus
Haemanthus katherinae	Scadoxus multiflorus ssp katherinae
Haemanthus magnificus	Scadoxus puniceus

Synonyms

Haemanthus multiflorus — Scadoxus multiflorus
Haemanthus natalensis — Scadoxus puniceus
Haemanthus puniceus — Scadoxus puniceus
Hakea saligna — H. salicifolia
Hakea sericea h — H. lissosperma
Hakonechloa macra 'Variegata' — H. macra 'Alboaurea'
Halesia tetraptera — H. carolina
Halimium commutatum — H. calycinum
Halimium formosum — H. lasianthum
Halimium libanotis — H. calycinum
Halimium wintonense — x Halimiocistus wintonensis

Hamamelis 'Magic Fire' — H. x intermedia 'Feuerzauber'
Hamamelis mollis 'Brevipetala' — H. 'Brevipetala'
Hamamelis mollis 'Pallida' — H. x intermedia 'Pallida'
Hamamelis mollis 'Select' — H. x intermedia 'Westerstede'
Hamamelis x intermedia 'Copper Beauty' — H. x intermedia 'Jelena'
Hamatocactus crassihamatus — Sclerocactus uncinatus v crassihamatus
Hamatocactus hamatacanthus — Ferocactus hamatacanthus
Hamatocactus setispinus — Thelocactus setispinus
Hamatocactus uncinatus — Sclerocactus uncinatus
Haplopappus acaulis — Stenotus acaulis
Haplopappus brandegeei — Erigeron aureus
Haplopappus coronopifolius — H. glutinosus
Haplopappus lyallii — Tonestus lyallii
Hardenbergia monophylla — H. violacea
Hardenbergia violacea 'Alba' — H. violacea 'White Crystal'
Harrimanella — Cassiope
Harrisia pomanensis — H. bonplandii
Haworthia margaritifera — H. pumila
Haworthia planifolia — H. cymbiformis
Haworthia setata — H. arachnoidea
Haworthia venosa ssp tessellata — H. tessellata
Haynaldia — Dasypyrum
Hebe albicans 'Pewter Dome' — H. 'Pewter Dome'
Hebe albicans prostrate form — H. albicans 'Snow Cover'
Hebe albicans 'Red Edge' — H. 'Red Edge'
Hebe allanii — H. amplexicaulis v hirta
Hebe anomala h — H. 'Imposter'
Hebe anomala -(J.B.Armstrong) Ckn. — H. odora
Hebe 'Aoira' — H. recurva 'Aoira'
Hebe 'Azurea' — H. venustula
Hebe 'Azurens' — H. 'Maori Gem'
Hebe 'Bowles' Variety' — H. 'Bowles' Hybrid'
Hebe brachysiphon 'White Gem' — H. 'White Gem' (Brachysiphon hybrid)
Hebe buchananii 'Nana' — H. buchananii 'Minor'
Hebe buxifolia 'Champagne' — H. x bishopiana
Hebe buxifolia h — H. odora
Hebe 'Carl Teschner' — H. 'Youngii'
Hebe catarractae — Parahebe catarractae
Hebe colensoi 'Glauca' — H. 'Leonard Cockayne'
Hebe 'Cookiana' — H. stricta macroura 'Cookiana'
Hebe darwiniana — H. glaucophylla
Hebe 'Dorothy Peach' — H. 'Watson's Pink'
Hebe 'E.B.Anderson' — H. 'Caledonia'
Hebe elliptica 'Variegata' — H. x franciscana 'Variegata'
Hebe 'Emerald Gem' — H. 'Emerald Green'
Hebe 'Eversley Seedling' — H. 'Bowles' Hybrid'
Hebe 'Gauntlettii' — H. 'Eveline'

Hebe 'Godefroyana' — H. pinguifolia 'Godefroyana'
Hebe 'Green Globe' — H. 'Emerald Green'
Hebe hookeriana — Parahebe hookeriana
Hebe 'James Stirling' — H. ochracea 'James Stirling'
Hebe 'Knightshayes' — H. 'Caledonia'
Hebe 'La Seduisante' — H. speciosa 'La Seduisante'
Hebe 'Lady Ardilaun' — H. 'Amy'
Hebe laevis — H. venustula
Hebe lapidosa — H. rupicola
Hebe latifolia — H. x franciscana 'Blue Gem'
Hebe 'Lavender Spray' — H. 'Hartii'
Hebe lyallii — Parahebe lyallii
Hebe lycopodioides 'Aurea' — H. armstrongii
Hebe mackenii — H. 'Emerald Green'
Hebe 'Margery Fish' — H. 'Primley Gem'
Hebe 'McEwanii' — H. 'Macewanii'
Hebe 'Mercury' — H. pimeleoides 'Mercury'
Hebe 'Milmont Emerald' — H. 'Emerald Green'
Hebe parviflora h — H. 'Bowles' Hybrid'
Hebe pauciflora h — H. 'Christensenii'
Hebe perfoliata — Parahebe perfoliata
Hebe 'Pink Payne' — H. 'Eveline'
Hebe 'Pink Pearl' — H. 'Gloriosa'
Hebe 'Porlock Purple' — Parahebe catarractae 'Delight'
Hebe 'Purple Queen' — H. 'Amy'
Hebe 'Purple Tips' h — H. speciosa 'Tricolor'
Hebe 'Red Ruth' — H. 'Eveline'
Hebe 'Royal Purple' — H. 'Alicia Amherst'
Hebe salicifolia 'Snow Wreath' — H. 'Snow Wreath'
Hebe salicornioides 'Aurea' — H. propinqua 'Aurea'
Hebe selaginoides h — H. 'Loganioides'
Hebe speciosa 'Johny Day' — H. 'Johny Day'
Hebe speciosa 'Purple Queen' — H. 'Amy'
Hebe speciosa 'Ruddigore' — H. speciosa 'La Seduisante'
Hebe 'Spender's Seedling' h — H. parviflora v angustifolia - (Vahl) Ckn & Allan
Hebe 'Sussex Carpet' — H. albicans 'Sussex Carpet'
Hebe 'Tom Marshall' — H. canterburiensis
Hebe 'Tricolor' — H. speciosa 'Tricolor'
Hebe 'Veitchii' — H. 'Alicia Amherst'
Hebe 'Waikiki' — H. 'Mrs Winder'
Hebe 'Wardiensis' — H. pinguifolia 'Wardiensis'
Hebe 'Warleyensis' — H. 'Mrs. Winder'
Hebe 'Willcoxii' — H. buchananii 'Sir George Fenwick'
Hebe x andersonii 'Argenteovariegata' — H. x andersonii 'Variegata'
Hebe x andersonii 'Aureovariegata' — H. x andersonii 'Aurea'
Hebe x bishopiana 'Champagne' — H. x bishopiana
Hebe x franciscana 'Purple Tips' — H. speciosa 'Variegata'
Hedera algeriensis — H. canariensis h
Hedera azorica typica — H. azorica 'Sao Miguel'
Hedera canariensis 'Algeriensis' — H. canariensis h
Hedera canariensis 'Cantabrian' — H. maroccana 'Spanish Canary'
Hedera canariensis v azorica — H. azorica
Hedera canariensis 'Variegata' h — H. canariensis 'Gloire de

Synonyms

Hedera caucasigena	H. helix f caucasigena
Hedera chinensis	H. nepalensis v sinensis
Hedera chinensis typica	H. nepalensis v sinensis
Hedera cinerea	H. nepalensis
Hedera colchica 'Arborescens'	H. colchica 'Dendroides' Arborescent
Hedera colchica 'Dentata Aurea'	H. colchica 'Dentata Variegata'
Hedera colchica 'My Heart'	H. colchica
Hedera colchica 'Paddy's Pride'	H. colchica 'Sulphur Heart'
Hedera colchica 'Variegata'	H. colchica 'Dentata Variegata'
Hedera cristata	H. helix 'Parsley Crested'
Hedera helix 'Abundance'	H. helix 'California'
Hedera helix 'Albany'	H. hibernica 'Albany'
Hedera helix 'Anne Borch'	H. hibernica 'Anne Marie'
Hedera helix 'Anne Marie'	H. hibernica 'Anne Marie'
Hedera helix 'Annette'	H. helix 'California'
Hedera helix 'Aran' mis.	H. helix 'Rutherford's Arran'
Hedera helix 'Arran'	H. hibernica 'Arran'
Hedera helix 'Aurea Densa'	H. helix 'Aureovariegata'
Hedera helix 'Bird's Foot'	H. helix 'Pedata'
Hedera helix 'Brigette'	H. helix 'California'
Hedera helix 'Caenwoodiana'	H. helix 'Pedata'
Hedera helix 'Calico'	H. helix 'Schafer Three'
Hedera helix 'Chicago Variegated'	H. helix 'Harald'
Hedera helix 'Christian'	H. helix 'Direktor Badke'
Hedera helix 'Clotted Cream'	H. helix 'Caecilia'
Hedera helix 'Cristata'	H. helix 'Parsley Crested'
Hedera helix 'Cristata Melanie'	H. helix 'Melanie'
Hedera helix 'Curley-Q'	H. helix 'Dragon Claw'
Hedera helix 'Curleylocks'	H. helix 'Manda's Crested'
Hedera helix 'Curly Locks'	H. helix 'Manda's Crested'
Hedera helix 'Cuspidata Major'	H. hibernica 'Cuspidata Major'
Hedera helix 'Cuspidata Minor'	H. hibernica 'Cuspidata Minor'
Hedera helix 'Cyprus'	H. cypria
Hedera helix 'Deltoidea'	H. hibernica 'Deltoidea'
Hedera helix 'Discolor'	H. helix 'Minor Marmorata'
Hedera helix 'Emerald Gem'	H. helix 'Angularis'
Hedera helix 'Emerald Jewel'	H. helix 'Pittsburgh'
Hedera helix 'Erin'	H. helix 'Pin Oak'
Hedera helix 'Ester'	H. helix 'Harald'
Hedera helix 'Fringette'	H. helix 'Manda's Fringette'
Hedera helix 'Gold Harald'	H. helix 'Goldchild'
Hedera helix 'Golden Ann'	H. helix 'Ceridwen'
Hedera helix 'Golden Ester'	H. helix 'Ceridwen'
Hedera helix 'Golden Kolibri'	H. helix 'Midas Touch'
Hedera helix 'Golden Shamrock'	H. helix 'Golden Envoy'
Hedera helix 'Goldfinger'	H. helix 'Goldstern'
Hedera helix 'Goldheart'	H. helix 'Oro di Bogliasco'
Hedera helix 'Gracilis'	H. hibernica 'Gracilis'
Hedera helix 'Green Feather'	H. helix 'Triton'
Hedera helix 'Green Finger'	H. helix 'Tres Coupe'
Hedera helix 'Green Spear'	H. helix 'Spear Point'
Hedera helix 'Hahn's Green Ripple'	H. helix 'Green Ripple'
Hedera helix 'Hahn's Self-Branching'	H. helix 'Pittsburgh'
Hedera helix 'Hamilton'	H. hibernica 'Hamilton'
Hedera helix 'Harry Wood'	H. helix 'Modern Times'
Hedera helix 'Helvig'	H. helix 'White Knight'
Hedera helix 'Hispanica'	H. maderensis ssp iberica
Hedera helix 'Hite's Miniature'	H. helix 'Merion Beauty'
Hedera helix 'Holly'	H. helix 'Parsley Crested'
Hedera helix 'Ideal'	H. helix 'California'
Hedera helix 'Imp'	H. helix 'Brokamp'
Hedera helix 'Ingelise'	H. helix 'Sagittifolia Variegata'
Hedera helix 'Ingrid'	H. helix 'Harald'
Hedera helix 'Itsy Bitsy'	H. helix 'Pin Oak'
Hedera helix 'Jerusalem'	H. helix 'Schafer Three'
Hedera helix 'Jubilaum Goldherz'	H. helix 'Goldheart'
Hedera helix 'Jubilee Goldheart'	H. helix 'Goldheart'
Hedera helix 'Liz'	H. helix 'Eva'
Hedera helix 'Lucy Kay'	H. helix 'Lady Kay'
Hedera helix 'Maculata'	H. helix 'Minor Marmorata'
Hedera helix 'Marginata Elegantissima'	H. helix 'Tricolor'
Hedera helix 'Marginata Minor'	H. helix 'Cavendishii'
Hedera helix 'Marmorata'	H. helix 'Luzii'
Hedera helix 'Meagheri'	H. helix 'Green Feather'
Hedera helix 'Mini Green'	H. helix 'Ivalace'
Hedera helix 'Minima'	H. helix 'Donerailensis'
Hedera helix 'Miss Maroc'	H. helix 'Manda Fringette'
Hedera helix 'Oro di Bogliasco'	H. helix 'Goldheart'
Hedera helix 'Pallida'	H. hibernica 'Hibernica Variegata'
Hedera helix 'Parsley Crested'	H. hibernica 'Cristata'
Hedera helix 'Poetica'	H. helix f poetarum
Hedera helix 'Poetica Arborea'	H. helix f poetarum
Hedera helix 'Purpurea'	H. helix 'Atropurpurea'
Hedera helix 'Ray's Supreme'	H. helix 'Pittsburgh'
Hedera helix 'Rottingdean'	H. hibernica 'Rottingdean'
Hedera helix 'Salt and Pepper'	H. helix 'Minor Marmorata'
Hedera helix 'Scutifolia'	H. helix 'Glymii'
Hedera helix 'Silver Queen'	H. helix 'Tricolor'
Hedera helix ssp hibernica	H. hibernica
Hedera helix 'Suzanne'	H. nepalensis v nepalensis 'Suzanne'
Hedera helix 'Woodsii'	H. helix 'Modern Times'
Hedera himalaica	H. nepalensis
Hedera pastuchovii -form Troodos, Cyprus	H. cypria
Hedera rhombea 'Japonica'	H. rhombea
Hedychium coronarium v flavescens	H. flavescens
Heeria	Heterocentron
Heimerliodendron	Pisonia
Heimerliodendron brunonianum	Pisonia umbellifera
Helenium Copper Spray	H. 'Kupfersprudel'
Helenium Dark Beauty	H. 'Dunkelpracht'
Helenium Golden Youth	H. 'Goldene Jugend'
Helenium 'Mahogany'	H. 'Goldlackzwerg'
Helenium Red and Gold	H. 'Rotgold'
Helianthemum alpestre serpyllifolium	H. nummularium ssp glabrum
Helianthemum chamaecistus	H. nummularium
Helianthemum 'Fireball'	H. 'Mrs C. W. Earle'
Helianthemum globularifolium	Tuberaria globulariifolia
Helianthemum guttatum	Tuberaria guttata
Helianthemum 'Mrs Clay'	H. 'Fire Dragon'
Helianthemum ovatum	H. nummularium ssp obscurum
Helianthemum 'Red Orient'	H. 'Supreme'
Helianthemum Rose Queen	H. 'Rosa Konigin'
Helianthemum serpyllifolium	H. nummularium ssp

Synonyms

Helianthemum 'Snow Queen'	glabrum
Helianthemum tomentosum	H. 'The Bride'
Helianthemum tuberaria	H. nummularium
Helianthemum umbellatum	Tuberaria lignosa
Helianthemum 'Wisley Pink'	Halimium umbellatum
Helianthemum 'Yellow Queen'	H. 'Rhodanthe Carneum'
Helianthus cucumerifolius	H. 'Golden Queen'
	H. debilis ssp cucumerifolius
Helianthus orgyalis	H. salicifolius
Helianthus quinquenervis	Helianthella quinquenervis
Helianthus rigidus	H. x laetiflorus
Helianthus scaberrimus	H. x laetiflorus
Helianthus sparsifolius	H. atrorubens
Helichrysum acuminatum	Bracteantha subundulata
Helichrysum alveolatum	H. splendidum
Helichrysum angustifolium	H. italicum
Helichrysum angustifolium -Cretan form	H. italicum ssp microphyllum
Helichrysum asperum	Ozothamnus purpurascens
Helichrysum bracteatum	Bracteantha bracteata
Helichrysum 'Coco'	Bracteantha 'Coco'
Helichrysum coralloides	Ozothamnus coralloides
Helichrysum 'County Park Silver'	Ozothamnus 'County Park Silver'
Helichrysum diosmifolium	Ozothamnus diosmifolius
Helichrysum 'Elmstead'	H. stoechas 'White Barn'
Helichrysum ericifolium	Ozothamnus purpurascens
Helichrysum ericoides	Dolichothrix ericoides
Helichrysum glomeratum	H. aggregatum
Helichrysum hookeri	Ozothamnus hookeri
Helichrysum italicum 'Nanum'	H. italicum ssp microphyllum
Helichrysum lanatum	H. thianschanicum
Helichrysum ledifolium	Ozothamnus ledifolius
Helichrysum marginatum	H. milfordiae
Helichrysum microphyllum -Bentham & Hooker	Ozothamnus microphyllus
Helichrysum microphyllum -Cambessedes	H. italicum
Helichrysum microphyllum h	Plecostachys serpyllifolia
Helichrysum 'Mo's Gold'	H. argyrophyllum
Helichrysum petiolare 'Aureum'	H. petiolare 'Limelight'
Helichrysum petiolatum	H. petiolare
Helichrysum purpurascens	Ozothamnus purpurascens
Helichrysum rosmarinifolium	Ozothamnus rosmarinifolius
Helichrysum selaginoides	Ozothamnus selaginoides
Helichrysum selago	Ozothamnus selago
Helichrysum serotinum	H. italicum ssp serotinum
Helichrysum serypllifolium	Plecostachys serpyllifolia
Helichrysum sessile	H. sessilioides
Helichrysum siculum	H. stoechas ssp barrelieri
Helichrysum Sulphur Light	H. 'Schwefellicht'
Helichrysum thianschanicum Golden Baby	H. thianschanicum 'Goldkind'
Helichrysum thysoideum	Ozothamnus thyrsoideus
Helichrysum trilineatum	H. splendidum
Helichrysum tumidum	Ozothamnus selago v tumidus
Helichrysum virgineum	H. sibthorpii
Helichrysum woodii	H. arwae
Heliconia 'Guyana Red'	H. 'Bucky'
Heliconia humilis	H. bihai
Heliconia humilis h	H. stricta 'Dwarf Jamaican'
Heliophila longifolia	H. coronopifolia
Heliopsis Golden Plume	H. helianthoides v scabra 'Goldgefieder'
Heliopsis helianthoides 'Limelight'	Helianthus 'Lemon Queen'
Heliopsis helianthoides v scabra Golden Plume	Helianthus helianthoides v scabra 'Goldgefieder'
Heliopsis helianthoides v scabra Goldgreenheart	Helianthus helianthoides v scabra 'Goldgrunherz'
Heliopsis helianthoides v scabra Summer Sum	H. helianthoides v scabra 'Sommersonne'
Heliopsis scabra	Helianthus helianthoides v scabra
Heliosperma alpestris	Silene alpestris
Heliotropium anchusifolium	H. amplexicaule
Heliotropium peruvianum	H. arborescens
Helipterum albicans	Leucochrysum albicans
Helipterum anthemoides	Rhodanthe anthemoides
Helipterum humboldtianum	Pteropogon humboldtianus
Helipterum manglesii	Rhodanthe manglesii
Helipterum roseum	Rhodanthe chlorocephala ssp rosea
Helleborus argutifolius mottle-leaved	H. argutifolius 'Pacific Mist'
Helleborus atrorubens h	H. orientalis ssp abchasicus Early Purple Group -Lamarck
Helleborus bocconei ssp bocconei	H. multifidus ssp bocconei
Helleborus colchicus	H. orientalis ssp abchasicus -Lamarck
Helleborus corsicus	H. argutifolius
Helleborus lividus ssp corsicus	H. argutifolius
Helleborus niger major	H. niger ssp macranthus
Helleborus orientalis olympicus -	H. orientalis ssp orientalis Lamarck
Helleborus x nigristern	H. x ericsmithii
Heloniopsis breviscapa	H. orientalis v breviscapa
Heloniopsis grandiflora	H. orientalis v breviscapa
Heloniopsis japonica	H. orientalis
Heloniopsis orientalis v yakusimensis	H. orientalis v kawanoi
Helxine soleirolii	Soleirolia soleirolii
Hemerocallis flava	H. lilioasphodelus
Hemerocallis 'Golden Orchid'	H. 'Dubloon'
Hemerocallis 'Kwanso Flore Pleno'	H. fulva 'Green Kwanso'
Hemerocallis 'Kwanso Flore Pleno Variegata'	H. fulva 'Kwanso Variegata'
Hemerocallis 'Puddin'	H. 'Brass Buckles'
Hemerocallis vespertina	H. thunbergii
Hemigraphis colorata	H. alternata
Hepatica angulosa	H. transsilvanica
Hepatica nobilis double pink	H. nobilis 'Rubra Plena'
Hepatica triloba	H. nobilis
Heptapleurum	Schefflera
Heracleum antasiaticum	H. stevenii

Synonyms

Hermannia candicans — H. incana
Hermannia erodioides — H. depressa
Hermannia verticillata — H. pinnata
Hertia — Othonna
Hesperantha buhrii — H. cucullata 'Rubra'
Hesperantha inflexa — H. vaginata
Hesperantha lutea — H. falcata
Hesperantha mossii — H. baurii
Hesperis lutea — Sisymbrium luteum
Hesperis matronalis alba — H. matronalis v albiflora
Hesperoyucca — Yucca
Heteromeles — Photinia
Heterotropa — Asarum
Heuchera Coral Bells — H. sanguinea
Heuchera 'Dennis Davidson' — H. 'Huntsman'
Heuchera Feuerregen — H. 'Pluie de Feu'
Heuchera Firefly — H. 'Leuchtkafer'
Heuchera glauca — H. americana
Heuchera Rain of Fire — H. 'Pluie de Feu'
Hexastylis — Asarum
Heyderia decurrens — Calocedrus decurrens
Hibbertia tetrandra — H. cuneiformis
Hibbertia volubilis — H. scandens
Hibiscus abelmoschus — Abelmoschus moschatus
Hibiscus eetveldeanus — H. acetosella
Hibiscus huegelii — Alyogyne huegelii
Hibiscus manihot — Abelmoschus manihot
Hibiscus 'Red Shield' — H.acetosella 'Coppertone'
Hibiscus rosa-sinensis 'Dainty Pink' — H. rosa-sinensis 'Fantasia'
Hibiscus rosa-sinensis 'Full Moon' — H. rosa-sinensis 'Mrs. James E. Hendry'
Hibiscus rosa-sinensis 'La France' — H. rosa-sinensis 'Fantasia'
Hibiscus rosa-sinensis 'Pink La France' — H. rosa-sinensis 'Fantasia'
Hibiscus rosa-sinensis 'Swan Lake' — H. rosa-sinensis 'Dainty White'
Hibiscus rosa-sinensis 'White La France' — H. rosa-sinensis 'Dainty White'
Hibiscus syriacus Blue Bird — H. syriacus 'Oiseau Bleu'
Hibiscus syriacus 'Elegantissimus' — H. syriacus 'Lady Stanley'
Hibiscus syriacus 'Variegatus' — H. syriacus 'Meehanii'
Hieracium aurantiacum — Pilosella aurantiaca
Hieracium bombycinum — H. mixtum
Hieracium brunneocroceum — Pilosella aurantiaca ssp carpathicola
Hieracium pilosella — Pilosella officinarum
Hieracium praecox — H. glaucum
Hieracium variegatum — Hypochaeris variegata
Hieracium welwitschii — H. lanatum
Hieracium x stoloniflorum — Pilosella stoloniflora
Hippeastrum advenum h — Rhodophiala advena
Hippeastrum bifidum — Rhodophiala bifida
Hippeastrum morelianum — H. aulicum
Hippeastrum pratense — Rhodophiala pratensis
Hippeastrum procerum — Worsleya raineri
Hippeastrum roseum — Rhodophiala rosea
Hippeastrum rutilum — H. striatum
Hippobroma — Laurentia
Hoheria microphylla — H. angustifolia
Hoheria populnea v lanceolata — H. sexstylosa
Holcus mollis 'Variegatus' — H. mollis 'Albovariegatus'
Homalocephala texensis — Echinocactus texensis
Homeria breyniana

Homeria breyniana v aurantiaca — H. flaccida
Homoglossum — Gladiolus
Hosta 'Alba' (sieboldiana) — H. 'Elegans Alba' (sieboldiana)
Hosta albomarginata — H. 'Paxton's Original' (sieboldii)
Hosta 'Argentea Variegata' (undulata) — H. undulata v undulata
Hosta 'Aurea' (sieboldii) — H. sieboldii f subcrocea
Hosta aureafolia — H. 'Starker Yellow Leaf'
Hosta 'Aureoalba' (fortunei) — H. 'Spinners'
Hosta 'Aureomaculata' (fortunei) — H. fortunei v albopicta
Hosta 'Aureostriata' (tardiva) — H. 'Inaho'
Hosta bella — H. fortunei v obscura
Hosta caput-avis — H. kikutii v caput-avis
Hosta 'Cream Delight' (undulata) — H. undulata v undulata
Hosta 'Cream Edge' — H. 'Fisher Cream Edge' (fortunei)
Hosta 'Crispula' — H. crispula
Hosta 'Decorata' — H. decorata
Hosta 'Eldorado' — H. 'Frances Williams' (sieboldiana)
Hosta 'Elegans' — H. sieboldiana v elegans
Hosta 'Fortis' — H. undulata v erromena
Hosta fortunei f aurea — H. fortunei v albopicta f aurea
Hosta fortunei v albopicta variegated — H. 'Crowned Imperial' (fortunei)
Hosta fortunei v albopicta variegated — H. 'Hyacinthina Variegata'
Hosta fortunei v gigantea — H. montana
Hosta 'Gigantea' (sieboldiana) — H. elata
Hosta glauca — H. sieboldiana v elegans
Hosta 'Golden' — H. 'Birchwood Parky's Gold'
Hosta 'Golden Age' — H. 'Gold Haze' (fortunei)
Hosta 'Golden Circles' — H. 'Frances Williams' (sieboldiana)
Hosta 'Golden' (nakaiana) — H. 'Birchwood Parky's Gold'
Hosta 'Golden Nakaiana' — H. 'Birchwood Parky's Gold'
Hosta helonioides f albopicta — H. rohdeifolia
Hosta 'Holstein' — H. 'Halcyon' (Tardiana Group)
Hosta 'Japan Boy' — H. 'Montreal'
Hosta 'Japan Girl' — H. 'Mount Royal'
Hosta 'Kabitan' — H. sieboldii f kabitan
Hosta lancifolia v fortis — H. lancifolia
Hosta 'Mediovariegata' (undulata) — H. undulata v undulata
Hosta minor f alba h — H. sieboldii v alba
Hosta 'Minor' (ventricosa) — H. minor
Hosta 'Mount Kirishima' (sieboldii) — H. 'Kirishima'
Hosta 'Nana' (ventricosa) — H. minor
Hosta 'Obscura Marginata' (fortunei) — H. fortunei v aureomarginata
Hosta 'Opipara' — H. opipara
Hosta 'Phyllis Campbell' (fortunei) — H. 'Sharmon' (fortunei)
Hosta 'Picta' (fortunei) — H. fortunei v albopicta
Hosta plantaginea v grandiflora — H. plantaginea v japonica
Hosta 'Robusta' (fortunei) — H. sieboldiana v elegans
Hosta 'Rohdeifolia' — H. rohdeifolia
Hosta 'Sazanami' (crispula) — H. crispula
Hosta sieboldiana 'Elegans' — H. sieboldii v elegans
Hosta sieboldiana 'Frances Williams' — H. 'Frances Williams' (sieboldiana)
Hosta sieboldiana v thunbergiana — H. sieboldii f spathulata
Hosta 'Silver Crown' — H. 'Albomarginata'

Synonyms

Hosta 'Thomas Hogg' — H. undulata v albomarginata
Hosta 'Tokudama' — H. tokudama
Hosta 'Tokudama Aureonebulosa' — H. tokudama f aureonebulosa
Hosta 'Tokudama Flavocircinalis' — H. tokudama f flavocircinalis
Hosta 'Undulata' — H. undulata v undulata
Hosta 'Undulata Albomarginata' — H. undulata v albomarginata
Hosta 'Undulata Erromena' — H. undulata v erromena
Hosta 'Undulata Univittata' — H. undulata v univittata
Hosta 'Variegata' (gracillima) — H. 'Vera Verde'
Hosta 'Variegata' (tokudama) — H. tokudama f aureonebulosa
Hosta 'Variegata' (undulata) — H. undulata v undulata
Hosta 'Variegata' (ventricosa) — H. 'Aureomarginata' (ventricosa)
Hosta 'Variegated' (fluctuans) — H. 'Sagae'
Hosta 'Ventricosa' — H. ventricosa
Hosta 'Ventricosa Aureomaculata' — H. ventricosa v aureomaculata
Hosta 'Ventricosa Variegata' — H. 'Aureomarginata' (ventricosa)
Hosta venusta yakusimensis — H. kikutii v yakusimensis
Hosta 'Verte' (sieboldii) — H. sieboldii f spathulata
Hosta 'Viridis Marginata' (Tardiana Group) — H. sieboldii f kabitan
Hosta 'Wayside Perfection' — H. 'Royal Standard'
Hosta 'Windsor Gold' — H. 'Nancy Lindsay' (fortunei)
Hosta 'Wogon Giboshi' — H. 'Wogon' (sieboldii)
Hosta 'Yellow Edge' (fortunei) — H. fortunei v aureomarginata
Hosta 'Yellow Edge' (sieboldiana) — H. 'Frances Williams' (sieboldiana)
Houstonia caerulea h — H. michauxii
Houstonia serpyllifolia — H. michauxii
Houttuynia cordata 'Plena' — H. cordata 'Flore Pleno'
Houttuynia cordata 'Tricolor' — H. cordata 'Chameleon'
Hovea celsii — H. elliptica
Hovea longifolia v montana — H. montana
Hovea purpurea v montana — H. montana
Howeia — Howea
Hoya bella — H. lanceolata ssp bella
Hoya darwinii h — H. australis
Hoya fuscomarginata — H. pottsii
Hoya nepalensis — H. polyneura
Huernia primulina — H. thuretii v primulina
Hugueninia alpina — H. tanacetifolia
Humata pyxidata — Davallia solida v pyxidata - (Hook.) Noot.
Humea elegans — Calomeria amaranthoides
Huntleya burtii — H. meleagris
Hutchinsia — Thlaspi
Hyacinthella dalmatica — H. pallens
Hyacinthoides hispanica Donau — H. hispanica 'Danube'
Hyacinthus amethystinus — Brimeura amethystina
Hyacinthus azureus — Muscari azureum
Hyacinthus comosus 'Plumosus' — Muscari comosum 'Plumosum'
Hyacinthus fastigiatus — Brimeura fastigiata
Hyacinthus orientalis 'Salmonetta' — H. orientalis 'Oranje Boven'
Hyacinthus orientalis Snow White — H. orientalis 'Sneeuwwitje'
Hyacinthus romanus — Bellevalia romana

Hydrangea anomala ssp petiolaris dwarf form — H. anomala ssp petiolaris cordifolia
Hydrangea aspera 'Rosthornii' — H. aspera ssp robusta
Hydrangea 'Blue Tit' — H. macrophylla 'Blaumeise'
Hydrangea cinerea — H. arborescens ssp discolor
Hydrangea cinerea 'Sterilis' — H. arborescens ssp discolor 'Sterilis'
Hydrangea integerrima — H. serratifolia
Hydrangea macrophylla Alpen Glow — H. macrophylla 'Alpengluhen'
Hydrangea macrophylla Blue Prince — H. macrophylla 'Blauer Prinz'
Hydrangea macrophylla 'Blue Sky' — H. macrophylla 'Blaumeise'
Hydrangea macrophylla 'Blue Wave' — H. macrophylla 'Mariesii Perfecta'
Hydrangea macrophylla 'Cordata' — H. arborescens
Hydrangea macrophylla 'Firelight' — H. macrophylla 'Leuchtfeuer'
Hydrangea macrophylla Gentian Dome — H. macrophylla 'Enziandom'
Hydrangea macrophylla 'James Grant' — H. macrophylla 'Grant's Choice'
Hydrangea macrophylla 'Mini Hornli' — H. macrophylla 'Hornli'
Hydrangea macrophylla Morning Red — H. macrophylla 'Morgenrot'
Hydrangea macrophylla 'Pax' — H. macrophylla 'Nymphe'
Hydrangea macrophylla Pheasant — H. macrophylla 'Fasan'
Hydrangea macrophylla Pink Elf — H. macrophylla 'Pia'
Hydrangea macrophylla 'Preziosa' — H. 'Preziosa'
Hydrangea macrophylla Queen Wilhelmina — H. macrophylla 'Koningin Wilhelmina'
Hydrangea macrophylla Redbreast — H. macrophylla 'Rotkehlchen'
Hydrangea macrophylla Sister Therese — H. macrophylla 'Soeur Therese'
Hydrangea macrophylla ssp serrata — H. serrata
Hydrangea macrophylla 'Teller Variegated' — H. macrophylla 'Tricolor'
Hydrangea macrophylla Teller Weiss — H. macrophylla 'Libelle'
Hydrangea macrophylla 'Variegata' — H. macrophylla 'Maculata'
Hydrangea macrophylla 'Vicomte de Vibraye' — H. macrophylla 'Generale Vicomtesse de Vibraye'
Hydrangea macrophylla Vulcan — H. macrophylla 'Vulcain'
Hydrangea macrophylla 'White Swan' — H. macrophylla 'Le Cygne'
Hydrangea quercifolia 'Flore Pleno' — H. quercifolia Snow Flake
Hydrangea sargentiana — H. aspera ssp sargentiana
Hydrangea serrata 'Acuminata' — H. serrata 'Bluebird'
Hydrangea serrata 'Belle Deckle' — H. serrata 'Blue Deckle'
Hydrangea serrata 'Preziosa' — H. 'Preziosa'
Hydrangea sinensis — H. scandens ssp chinensis
Hydrangea 'Sterilis' — H. arborescens ssp discolor 'Sterilis'
Hydrangea tiliifolia — H. anomala ssp petiolaris
Hydrangea umbellata — H. scandens ssp chinensis
Hydrangea villosa — H. aspera Villosa Group
Hydrocleis — Hydrocleys
Hydrocotyle asiatica — Centella asiatica

Synonyms

Hydrocotyle ranunculoides — H. americana
Hylotelephium — Sedum
Hylotelephium roseum — Sedum alboroseum
Hylotelephium sieboldii 'Variegatum' — Sedum spathulifolium 'Cape Blanco'

Hymenanthera — Melicytus
Hymenanthera crassifolia — Melicytus crassifolius
Hymenanthera dentata — Melicytus dentatus
Hymenocallis calathina — H. narcissiflora
Hymenocallis occidentalis — H. caroliniana
Hymenoxys acaulis — Tetraneuris acaulis
Hymenoxys grandiflora — Tetraneuris grandiflora
Hypericum androsaemum 'Orange Flair' — H. x inodorum 'Orange Flair'

Hypericum androsaemum 'Variegatum' — H. androsaemum 'Gladys Brabazon'

Hypericum beanii 'Gold Cup' — H. x cyathiflorum 'Gold Cup'

Hypericum 'Citrinum' — H. olympicum f uniflorum 'Citrinum'

Hypericum cuneatum — H. pallens
Hypericum elatum — H. x inodorum
Hypericum empetrifolium 'Prostatum' — H. empetrifolium ssp tortuosum

Hypericum fragile h — H. olympicum f minus
Hypericum 'Gold Penny' — H. androsaemum 'Dart's Golden Penny'

Hypericum grandiflorum — H. kouytchense
Hypericum leschenaultii h — H. 'Rowallane'
Hypericum 'Mrs Brabazon' — H. androsaemum 'Gladys Brabazon'

Hypericum olympicum 'Grandiflorum' — H. olympicum f uniflorum

Hypericum patulum v forrestii — H. forrestii
Hypericum patulum v grandiflorum — H. kouytchense
Hypericum patulum v henryi - Rehder et hort — H. pseudohenryi
Hypericum patulum v henryi -Veitch ex Bean — H. beanii
Hypericum polyphyllum — H. olympicum f minus
Hypericum polyphyllum 'Citrinum' — H. olympicum f minus 'Sulphureum'

Hypericum polyphyllum 'Grandiflorum' — H. olympicum f uniflorum

Hypericum polyphyllum 'Sulphureum' — H. olympicum f minus 'Sulphureum'

Hypericum polyphyllum 'Variegatum' — H. olympicum f minus 'Variegatum'

Hypericum pseudopetiolatum v yakusimense — H. kiusianum v yakusimense

Hypericum quadrangulum -Linnaeus — H. tetrapterum
Hypericum reptans h — H. olympicum f minus
Hypericum rhodoppeum — H. cerastioides ssp mueselianum
Hypericum 'Sungold' — H. kouytchense
Hypericum 'Variegatum' — H. x moserianum 'Tricolor'

Hypericum x inodorum 'Albury Purple' — H. androsaceum 'Albury Purple'

Hypericum x moserianum 'Variegatum' — H. x moserianum 'Tricolor'

Hypericum yakusimense — H. kiusianum v yakusimense

Hypocyrta — Nematanthus
Hypocyrta radicans — Nematanthus gregarius

Hypocyrta strigillosa — Nematanthus strigillosus
Hypoestes sanguinolenta misapplied — H. phyllostachya
Hypoxis rooperi — H. hemerocallidea
Hypoxis stellata — H. capensis
Hypsela longiflora — H. reniformis
Hyssopus aristatus — H. officinalis ssp aristatus
Hyssopus officinalis ssp angustifolius — H. officinalis officinalis
Iberis candolleana — I. pruitii Candolleana Group

Iberis commutata — I. sempervirens
Iberis jordanii — I. pruitii
Iberis saxatilis candolleana — I. pruitii Candolleana Group

Iberis sempervirens Little Gem — I. sempervirens 'Weisser Zwerg'

Iberis sempervirens Snowdrift — I. sempervirens 'Zwergschneeflocke'

Iberis sempervirens Snowflake — I. sempervirens 'Schneeflocke'

Idria columnaris — Fouquieria columnaris
Ilex altaclarensis — I. x altaclerensis
Ilex aquifolium 'Argentea Pendula' — I. aquifolium 'Argentea Marginata Pendula'

Ilex aquifolium 'Argentea Variegata' — I. aquifolium 'Argentea Marginata'

Ilex aquifolium 'Aurea Ovata' — I. aquifolium 'Ovata Aurea'

Ilex aquifolium 'Aurea Regina' — I. aquifolium 'Golden Queen'

Ilex aquifolium 'Aureovariegata Pendula' — I. aquifolium 'Weeping Golden Milkmaid'

Ilex aquifolium 'Crispa Aureomaculata' — I. aquifolium 'Crispa Aureopicta'

Ilex aquifolium 'Fructu Luteo' — I. aquifolium 'Bacciflava'
Ilex aquifolium Moonlight holly — I. aquifolium 'Flavescens'
Ilex aquifolium 'Myrtifolia Aureovariegata' — I. aquifolium 'Myrtifolia Aurea Maculata'

Ilex aquifolium 'Pendula Mediopicta' — I. aquifolium 'Weeping Golden Milkmaid'

Ilex aquifolium 'Silver King' — I. aquifolium 'Silver Queen'

Ilex aquifolium 'Silver Sentinel' — I. x altaclerensis 'Belgica Aurea'

Ilex aquifolium 'Waterer's Gold' — I. aquifolium 'Watereriana'

Ilex chinensis misapplied — I. purpurea
Ilex crenata 'Aureovariegata' — I. crenata 'Variegata'
Ilex crenata 'Bullata' — I. crenata 'Convexa'
Ilex crenata 'Compacta' — I. crenata 'Bennett's Compact'

Ilex crenata f latifolia — I. latifolia
Ilex crenata 'Fukarin' — I. crenata 'Shiro-fukarin'
Ilex crenata 'Luteovariegata' — I. crenata 'Variegata'
Ilex crenata 'Snowflake' — I. crenata 'Shiro-fukarin'
Ilex crenata v nummularioides — I. crenata 'Mariesii'
Ilex 'Dazzler' — I. cornuta 'Dazzler'
Ilex hascombensis — I. aquifolium 'Hascombensis'

Ilex insignis — I. kingiana
Ilex mariesii — I. crenata 'Mariesii'
Ilex perado 'Aurea' — I. x altaclerensis 'Belgica Aurea'

Ilex perado latifolia — I. perado ssp platyphylla
Ilex pernyi v veitchii — I. bioritsensis
Ilex platyphylla — I. perado ssp platyphylla
Ilex poneantha — I. kusanoi

Synonyms

Ilex 'Pyramidalis' — I. aquifolium 'Pyramidalis'

Ilex verticillata 'Compacta' — I. verticillata 'Nana'

Ilex verticillata 'Red Sprite' — I. verticillata 'Nana'

Ilex x altaclerensis 'Maderensis Variegata' — I. aquifolium 'Maderensis Variegata'

Ilex x altaclerensis 'Silver Sentinel' — I. x altaclerensis 'Belgica Aurea'

Iliamna — Sphaeralcea

Illicium religiosum — I. anisatum

Impatiens oliveri — I. sodenii

Impatiens roylei — I. glandulifera

Impatiens sultani — I. walleriana

Imperata cylindrica 'Red Baron' — I. cylindrica 'Rubra'

Incarvillea brevipes — I. mairei

Incarvillea mairei v mairei f multifoliata — I. zhongdianensis

Incarvillea mairei v mairei f multifoliata ACE 64 — I. zhongdianensis ACE 2201

Indigofera gerardiana — I. heterantha

Inula afghanica h — I. magnifica

Inula dysenterica — Pulicaria dysenterica

Inula glandulosa — I. orientalis

Inula 'Golden Beauty' — Buphthalmum salicifolium 'Golden Wonder'

Inula macrocephala h — I. royleana

Iochroma tubulosa — I. cyanea

Iochroma violacea — Cestrum violaceum

Ipomoea acuminata — I. indica

Ipomoea bona-nox — I. alba

Ipomoea coccinea v hederifolia -(L.) A.Gray — I. hederifolia

Ipomoea imperialis — I. nil

Ipomoea learii — I. indica

Ipomoea palmata — I. cairica

Ipomoea rubrocaerulea — I. tricolor

Ipomoea rubrocaerulea 'Heavenly Blue' — I. tricolor 'Heavenly Blue'

Ipomoea tuberosa — Merremia tuberosa

Ipomoea versicolor — I. lobata

Ipomoea violacea h — I. tricolor

Ipomoea x sloteri — I. x multifida

Iris 'Angel's Tears' — I. histrioides 'Angel's Eye'

Iris anglica — I. latifolia

Iris arenaria — I. humilis

Iris aurea — I. crocea

Iris barnumae polakii — I. polakii

Iris biglumis — I. lactea

Iris brandzae — I. sintenisii ssp brandzae

Iris bucharica h — I. orchioides

Iris caerulea — I. albomarginata

Iris 'Cambridge Blue' — I. 'Monspur Cambridge Blue'

Iris 'Campbellii' — I. lutescens 'Campbellii'

Iris canadensis — I. hookeri

Iris 'Chain White' — I. 'Chain Wine'

Iris chamaeiris — I. lutescens

Iris chrysographes 'Rubra' — I. chrysographes v rubella

Iris colchica — I. graminea

Iris cretensis — I. unguicularis ssp cretensis

Iris cuprea — I. fulva

Iris 'Die Braut' — I. 'Bride'

Iris 'Elegant' — I. laevigata 'Weymouth Elegant'

Iris elegantissima — I. iberica ssp elegantissima

Iris ewbankiana — I. acutiloba ssp lineolata

Iris extremorientalis — I. sanguinea

Iris flavissima — I. humilis

Iris foetidissima chinensis — I. foetidissima v citrina

Iris foliosa — I. brevicaulis

Iris 'Galathea' — I. ensata 'Galathea'

Iris 'Gerald Derby' — I. x robusta 'Gerald Derby'

Iris gormanii — I. tenax

Iris graminifolia — I. kerneriana

Iris halophila — I. spuria ssp halophila

Iris histrioides 'Angel's Tears' — I. histrioides 'Angel's Eye'

Iris 'Hokkaido' — I. ensata 'Perry's Hokkaido'

Iris illyrica — I. pallida

Iris jordana — I. atrofusca

Iris kaempferi — I. ensata

Iris klattii — I. spuria ssp musulmanica

Iris laevigata 'Elegant' — Iris laevigata 'Weymouth Elegant'

Iris laevigata 'Midnight' — I. laevigata 'Weymouth Midnight'

Iris laevigata 'Purity' — I. laevigata 'Weymouth Purity'

Iris laevigata 'Rose Queen' — I. ensata 'Rose Queen'

Iris laevigata 'Surprise' — I. laevigata 'Weymouth Surprise'

Iris laevigata 'Weymouth' — I. laevigata 'Weymouth Blue'

Iris 'Martyn Rix' — I. confusa 'Martyn Rix'

Iris mellita — I. suaveolens

Iris mellita v rubromarginata — I. suaveolens

Iris 'Moonlight Waves' — I. ensata 'Moonlight Waves'

Iris 'Nancy Lindsay' — I. lutescens 'Nancy Lindsay'

Iris nepalensis — I. decora

Iris nertschinskia — I. sanguinea

Iris ochroleuca — I. orientalis

Iris orientalis 'Alba' — I. sanguinea 'Alba'

Iris 'Pacific Coast Hybrids' — I. Californian Hybrids

Iris pallida 'Aurea' — I. pallida 'Variegata'

Iris pallida 'Aurea Variegata' — I. pallida 'Variegata'

Iris pallida v dalmatica — I. pallida ssp pallida

Iris 'Princess Beatrice' — I. pallida ssp pallida

Iris pumila ssp attica — I. attica

Iris purpurea — I. galatica

Iris 'Reginae' — I. variegata v reginae

Iris 'Rose Queen' — I. ensata 'Rose Queen'

Iris rudskyi — I. variegata

Iris serbica — I. reichenbachii

Iris setosa dwarf form — I. hookeri

Iris setosa 'Hookeri' — I. hookeri

Iris setosa 'Kirigamini' — I. setosa 'Hondoensis'

Iris setosa ssp canadensis — I. hookeri

Iris setosa v nana — I. hookeri

Iris shrevei — I. virginica v shrevei

Iris sibirica 'Alba' — I. 'Sibirica Alba'

Iris sibirica 'Baxteri' — I. 'Sibirica Baxteri'

Iris sibirica 'Clouded Moon' — I. sibirica 'Forncett Moon'

Iris sibirica cream — I. sibirica 'Primrose Cream'

Iris sibirica 'Redflare' — I. sibirica 'Melton Red Flare'

Iris sibirica 'Snow Queen' — I. sanguinea 'Snow

Synonyms

Synonyms

Juniperus virginiana 'Helle'
Juniperus virginiana 'Skyrocket' — Spray' / J. chinensis 'Spartan'

Juniperus x gracilis 'Blaauw' — J. scopulorum 'Skyrocket'
Juniperus x media — J. chinensis 'Blaauw'
Juniperus x media 'Hetzii' — J. x pfitzeriana
Juniperus x pfitzeriana 'Blaauw' — J. virginiana 'Hetz'
Juniperus x pfitzeriana 'Blue Cloud' — J. chinensis 'Blaauw'
Juniperus x pfitzeriana 'Old Gold Carbery' — J. virginiana 'Blue Cloud'
Juniperus x pfitzeriana 'Carbery Gold'

Juniperus x pfitzeriana 'Sea Green' — J. x pfitzeriana 'Mint Julep'

Jurinea ceratocarpa — Saussurea ceratocarpa
Jurinella — Jurinea
Jussiaea — Ludwigia
Justicia brandegeeana 'Lutea' — J. brandegeeana 'Yellow Queen'

Justicia coccinea — Pachystachys coccinea
Justicia floribunda — J. rizzinii
Justicia ghiesbreghtiana h — J. spicigera
Justicia guttata — J. brandegeeana
Justicia pauciflora — J. rizzinii
Justicia pohliana — J. carnea
Justicia suberecta — Dicliptera suberecta
Kaempferia ovalifolia — K. parishii
Kalanchoe schweinfurthii — K. laciniata
Kalanchoe somaliensis — K. marmorata
Kalanchoe tubiflora — K. delagoensis
Kalanchoe zimbabwensis — K. lateritia
Kalimeris yomena 'Variegata' — K. yomena 'Shogun'
Kalmia polifolia 'Glauca' — K. microphylla
Kalmia polifolia v microphylla — K. microphylla
Kalopanax pictus — K. septemlobus
Kalopanax ricinifolius — K. septemlobus
Kennedya — Kennedia
Kentia acuminata — Carpentaria acuminata
Kentia belmoreana — Howea belmoreana
Kentia canterburyana — Hedyscepe canterburyana

Kentia forsteriana — Howea forsteriana
Kentia joannis — Veitchia joannis
Kentranthus — Centranthus
Kerria japonica (single) — K. japonica 'Simplex'
Kerria japonica 'Variegata' — K. japonica 'Picta'
Kigelia pinnata — K. africana
Kitaibelia — Kitaibela
Kitchingia — Kalanchoe
Kleinia articulata — Senecio articulatus
Kleinia repens — Senecio serpens
Kleinia rowleyanus — Senecio rowleyanus
Kniphofia 'C.M.Pritchard' h — K. rooperi
Kniphofia elegans — K. schimperi
Kniphofia galpinii h — K. triangularis ssp triangularis
Kniphofia macowanii — K. triangularis ssp triangularis
Kniphofia nelsonii — K. triangularis ssp triangularis
Kniphofia 'Nobilis' — K. uvaria 'Nobilis'
Kniphofia snowdenii h — K. thomsonii v snowdenii
Kniphofia tuckii -Baker — K. ensifolia
Kochia — Bassia
Kochia trichophylla — Bassia scoparia f trichophylla

Koeleria cristata — K. macrantha

Kohleria digitaliflora — K. warscewiezii
Korolkowia sewerzowii — Fritillaria sewerzowii
Laburnum vulgare — L. anagyroides
Lachenalia angustifolia — L. contaminata
Lachenalia glaucina — L. orchioides v glaucina
Lachenalia pendula — L. bulbifera
Lachenalia tricolor — L. aloides
Lachenalia 'Tricolor' — L. aloides
Lachnanthes tinctoria — L. caroliana
Lactuca alpina — Cicerbita alpina
Lactuca bourgaei — Cicerbita bourgaei
Lactuca plumieri — Cicerbita plumieri
Laelia majalis — L. speciosa
Lamiastrum — Lamium
Lamium album 'Aureovariegatum' — L. album 'Goldflake'
Lamium galeobdolon Silver Carpet — L. galeobdolon 'Silberteppich'
Lamium galeobdolon 'Variegatum' — L. galeobdolon 'Florentinum'
Lamium garganicum ssp pictum — L. garganicum ssp striatum
Lamium garganicum ssp reniforme — L. garganicum ssp striatum
Lamium luteum — L. galeobdolon
Lamium maculatum 'Gold Leaf' — L. maculatum 'Aureum'
Lamium maculatum 'Shell Pink' — L. maculatum 'Roseum'
Lampranthus aberdeenensis — Delosperma aberdeenense
Lampranthus edulis — Carpobrotus edulis
Lampranthus lehmannii — Delosperma lehmannii
Lampranthus oscularis — L. deltoides
Lampranthus pallidus — Delosperma pallidum
Lantana aculeata f varia — L. camara f varia
Lantana camara Cloth of Gold — L. camara 'Drap d'Or'
Lantana camara Goldmine — L. camara 'Mine d'Or'
Lantana delicatissima — L. montevidensis
Lantana sellowiana — L. montevidensis
Lapeirousia cruenta — Anomatheca laxa
Lapeirousia laxa — Anomatheca laxa
Larix europaea — L. decidua
Larix leptolepis — L. kaempferi
Larix russica — L. sibirica
Larix sukaczevii — L. sibirica
Larix x eurolepis — L. x marschlinsii
Lasiagrostis — Stipa
Lathyrus azureus h — L. sativus
Lathyrus clymenum articulatus — L. articulatus
Lathyrus cyaneus h — L. vernus
Lathyrus fremontii h — L. laxiflorus
Lathyrus gmelinii 'Aureus' — L. aureus
Lathyrus inermis — L. laxiflorus
Lathyrus laetiflorus v vestitus — L. vestitus
Lathyrus latifolius Pink Pearl — L. latifolius 'Rose Perle'
Lathyrus latifolius Weisse Perle — L. latifolius 'White Pearl'
Lathyrus luteus — L. gmelinii
Lathyrus luteus 'Aureus' — L. aureus
Lathyrus luteus h — L. aureus
Lathyrus magellanicus — L. nervosus
Lathyrus montanus — L. linifolius v montanus
Lathyrus sativus v azureus — L. sativus
Lathyrus vernus aurantiacus — L. aureus
Laurelia serrata — L. sempervirens
Laurus canariensis — L. azorica
Laurustinus — Viburnum tinus
Lavandula angustifolia 'Alba Nana' — L. angustifolia 'Nana Alba'
Lavandula angustifolia 'Bowles' Grey — L. angustifolia 'Bowles'

Synonyms

Lavandula angustifolia 'Bowles' Variety — L. angustifolia 'Bowles' Early'
Lavandula 'Cornard Blue' — L. 'Sawyers'
Lavandula dentata silver — L. dentata v candicans
Lavandula 'Hidcote Blue' — L. angustifolia 'Hidcote'
Lavandula 'Jean Davis' — L. angustifolia 'Jean Davis'
Lavandula 'Loddon Pink' — L. angustifolia 'Loddon Pink'
Lavandula officinalis — L. angustifolia
Lavandula pterostoechas pinnata — L. pinnata
Lavandula 'Rosea' — L. angustifolia 'Rosea'
Lavandula spica 'Hidcote Purple' — L. angustifolia 'Hidcote'
Lavandula spica -n. r. — L. angustifolia
Lavandula spica -n. r. — L. latifolia
Lavandula spica -n. r. — L. x intermedia
Lavandula stoechas 'Papillon' — L. stoechas ssp pedunculata
Lavandula stoechas v albiflora — L. stoechas f leucantha
Lavandula vera -De Cand. — L. angustifolia
Lavandula vera h — L. x intermedia Dutch Group
Lavatera arborea 'Rosea' — L. 'Rosea'
Lavatera bicolor — L. maritima
Lavatera cachemirica — L. cachemiriana
Lavatera maritima bicolor — L. maritima
Lavatera olbia 'Rosea' — L. 'Rosea'
Lavatera 'Peppermint Ice' — L. thuringiaca 'Ice Cool'
Lavatera 'Variegata' — L. 'Wembdon Variegated'
Lawsonia alba — L. inermis
Layia elegans — L. platyglossa
Lechenaultia — Leschenaultia
Ledebouria adlamii — L. cooperi
Ledebouria violacea — L. socialis
Ledum hypoleucum — L. palustre f dilatatum
Leea coccinea — L. guineensis
Lemaireocereus euphorbioides — Neobuxbaumia euphorbioides
Lemaireocereus thurberi — Stenocereus thurberi
Lembotropis — Cytisus
Lemna polyrhiza — Spirodela polyrhiza
Leonotis leonurus — L. ocymifolia
Leontice albertii — Gymnospermium albertii
Leontopodium aloysiodorum — L. haplophylloides
Leontopodium nivale — L. alpinum ssp nivale
Leontopodium palibinianum — L. ochroleucum v campestre
Leontopodium sibiricum — L. leontopodioides
Leontopodium tataricum — L. discolor
Leopoldia comosa — Muscari comosum
Leopoldia spreitzenhoferi — Muscari spreitzenhoferi
Leopoldia tenuiflora — Muscari tenuiflorum
Lepachys columnifera — Ratibida columnifera
Lepachys pinnata — Ratibida pinnata
Leptinella pectinata v sericea — L. albida
Leptinella reptans — L. scariosa
Leptospermum citratum — L. petersonii
Leptospermum cunninghamii — L. myrtifolium
Leptospermum ericoides — Kunzea ericoides
Leptospermum flavescens misapplied — L. glaucescens
Leptospermum flavescens -Sm. — L. polygalifolium
Leptospermum humifusum — L. rupestre
Leptospermum lanigerum 'Cunninghamii' — L. myrtifolium
Leptospermum lanigerum 'Silver Sheen' — L. myrtifolium 'Silver Sheen'

Leptospermum phylicoides — Kunzea ericoides
Leptospermum prostratum — L. rupestre
Leptospermum pubescens — L. lanigerum
Leptospermum rodwayanum — L. grandiflorum
Leptospermum scoparium v prostratum h — L. rupestre
Lespedeza hedysaroides — L. juncea
Lespedeza tiliifolia — Desmodium elegans
Leucaena leucocephala — L. latisiliqua
Leucanthemopsis hosmariensis — Rhodanthemum hosmariense
Leucanthemopsis radicans — L. pectinata
Leucanthemum atlanticum — Pyrethropsis atlantica
Leucanthemum catananche — Pyrethropsis catananche
Leucanthemum hosmariensis — Rhodanthemum hosmariense
Leucanthemum mawii — Rhodanthemum gayanum
Leucanthemum maximum uliginosum — Leucanthemella serotina
Leucanthemum nipponicum — Nipponanthemum nipponicum
Leucanthemum vulgare May Queen — L. vulgare 'Maikonigin'
Leucanthemum x superbum 'Everest' — L. x superbum 'Mount Everest'
Leucanthemum x superbum 'Little Princess' — L. x superbum 'Silberprinzesschen'
Leucanthemum x superbum Sunshine — L. x superbum 'Sonnenschein'
Leucanthemum x superbum 'Tizi-n-Test' — Rhodanthemum gayanum 'Tizi-n-Test'
Leucojum hiemale — L. nicaeense
Leucopogon colensoi — Cyathodes colensoi
Leucopogon parviflorus — Cyathodes parviflora
Leucospermum nutans — L. cordifolium
Leucothoe fontanesiana — L. walteri
Leucothoe populifolia — Agarista populifolia
Lewisia longifolia — L. cotyledon v cotyledon
Lewisia nevadensis bernardina — L. nevadensis
Lewisia pygmaea ssp longipetala — L. longipetala
Leymus giganteus — L. racemosus
Leymus hispidus — Elymus hispidus
Lhotzkya — Calytrix
Liatris callilepis — L. spicata
Liatris spicata callilepis — L. spicata
Liatris spicata Goblin — L. spicata 'Kobold'
Libertia chilensis — L. formosa
Libocedrus chilensis — Austrocedrus chilensis
Libocedrus decurrens — Calocedrus decurrens
Libonia — Justicia
Libonia floribunda — Justicia rizzinii
Licuala muelleri — L. ramsayi
Ligularia clivorum — L. dentata
Ligularia oblongata — Cremanthodium oblongatum
Ligularia reniformis — Cremanthodium reniforme
Ligularia smithii — Senecio smithii
Ligularia tangutica — Sinacalia tangutica
Ligularia tussilaginea — Farfugium japonicum
Ligustrum chenaultii — L. compactum
Ligustrum japonicum 'Coriaceum' — L. japonicum 'Rotundifolium'
Ligustrum ovalifolium 'Aureomarginatum' — L. ovalifolium 'Aureum'
Ligustrum ovalifolium 'Variegatum' — L. ovalifolium 'Argenteum'
Ligustrum texanum — L. japonicum 'Texanum'

Name	Synonym
Ligustrum x vicaryi	L. 'Vicaryi'
Lilium albanicum	L. pyrenaicum ssp carniolicum v albanicum
Lilium 'Aristo'	L. 'Orange Aristo'
Lilium auratum 'Gold Band'	L. auratum v platyphyllum
Lilium canadense v flavum	L. canadense
Lilium canadense v rubrum	L. canadense v coccineum
Lilium carniolicum	L. pyrenaicum ssp carniolicum
Lilium cordatum	Cardiocrinum cordatum
Lilium 'Delta'	L. leichtlinii 'Delta'
Lilium 'Elite'	L. 'Gibraltar'
Lilium giganteum	Cardiocrinum giganteum
Lilium heldreichii	L. chalcedonicum
Lilium 'Le Reve'	L. 'Joy'
Lilium maculatum v davuricum	L. dauricum
Lilium 'Marhan'	L. x dalhansonii 'Marhan'
Lilium martagon v dalmaticum	L. martagon v cattaniae
Lilium 'Mr.Ed'	L. 'Ed'
Lilium 'Mr.Ruud'	L. 'Ruud'
Lilium ponticum	L. pyrenaicum ssp ponticum
Lilium 'Prominence'	L. 'Firebrand'
Lilium pyrenaicum v aureum	L. pyrenaicum v pyrenaicum
Lilium pyrenaicum yellow	L. pyrenaicum v pyrenaicum
Lilium Red Knight (Red Night RHS encycl, PF lists this separately)	L. 'Roter Cardinal'
Lilium 'Royal Gold'	L. regale 'Royal Gold'
Lilium shastense	L. kelleyanum
Lilium szovitsianum	L. monadelphum
Lilium tenuifolium	L. pumilum
Lilium thunbergianum	L. maculatum
Lilium tigrinum	L. lancifolium
Lilium 'Uchida Kanoka'	L. speciosum 'Uchida'
Lilium willmottiae	L. davidii v willmottiae
Lilium x marhan 'J.S.Dijt'	L. 'Jacques S.Dijt'
Lilium 'Yellow Giant'	L. 'Joanna'
Limnanthemum nymphoides	Nymphoides peltata
Limnanthemum peltatum	Nymphoides peltata
Limonium dumosum	Goniolimon tataricum v angustifolium
Limonium globulariifolium	L. ramosissimum
Limonium latifolium	L. platyphyllum
Limonium reticulata	L. bellidifolium
Limonium spicata	Psylliostachys spicata
Limonium suworowii	Psylliostachys suwororii
Limonium tataricum	Goniolimon tataricum
Limonium tetragonum	L. dregeanum
Linanthastrum	Linanthus
Linaria cymbalaria	Cymbalaria muralis
Linaria glareosum	Chaenorhinum glareosum
Linaria 'Globosa Alba'	Cymbalaria muralis 'Globosa Alba'
Linaria glutinosa	L. bipunctata
Linaria hepaticifolia	Cymbalaria hepaticifolia
Linaria origanifolia	Chaenorhinum origanifolium
Linaria pallida	Cymbalaria pallida
Linaria pilosa	Cymbalaria pilosa
Linaria purpurea 'Alba'	L. purpurea 'Springside White'
Linaria purpurea 'Radcliffe Innocence'	L. purpurea 'Springside White'
Lindelofia anchusiflora h	L. longiflora
Lindelofia anchusoides h	L. longiflora
Lindelofia spectabilis	L. longiflora
Linum bulgaricum	L. tauricum
Linum monogynum 'Nelson'	L. monogynum v diffusum
Linum perenne Blue Sapphire	L. perenne 'Blau Saphir'
Linum salsoloides	L. suffruticosum ssp salsoloides
Linum sibiricum	L. perenne
Lippia canescens	Phyla canescens
Lippia chamaedrifolia	Verbena peruviana
Lippia citriodora	Aloysia triphylla
Lippia nodiflora	Phyla nodiflora
Lippia repens	Phyla nodiflora
Liquidambar formosana v monticola	L. formosana Monticola Group
Liriope exiliflora Silvery Sunproof	L. exiliflora 'Ariaka-janshige'
Liriope graminifolia h	L. muscari
Liriope graminifolia v densiflora	L. muscari
Liriope hyacinthifolia	Reineckea carnea
Liriope muscari 'Alba'	L. muscari 'Monroe White'
Liriope platyphylla	L. muscari
Lisianthus russelianus	Eustoma grandiflorum
Lithodora graminifolia	Moltkia suffruticosa
Lithodora x intermedia	Moltkia x intermedia
Lithophragma bulbiferum	L. glabrum
Lithops bella	L. karasmontana ssp bella
Lithops hookeri	L. turbiniformis
Lithops kuibisensis	L. schwantesii
Lithops schwantesii v kuibisensis	L. schwantesii
Lithospermum diffusum	Lithodora diffusa
Lithospermum doerfleri	Moltkia doerfleri
Lithospermum graminifolium	Moltkia suffruticosa
Lithospermum oleifolium	Lithodora oleifolia
Lithospermum purpureocaeruleum	Buglossoides purpurocaerulea
Lithospermum rosmarinifolium	Lithodora rosmarinifolia
Lithospermum zahnii	Lithodora zahnii
Litocarpus cordifolia	Aptenia cordifolia
Litsea glauca	Neolitsea sericea
Lloydia graeca	Gagea graeca
Loasa lateritia	Caiophora lateritia
Lobeira macdougallii	Nopalxochia macdougallii
Lobelia angulata	Pratia angulata
Lobelia 'Cinnabar Deep Red'	L. 'Fan Tiefrot'
Lobelia 'Cinnabar Rose'	L. 'Fan Zinnoberrosa'
Lobelia Compliment Blue	L. 'Kompliment Blau'
Lobelia Compliment Deep Red	L. 'Kompliment Tiefrot'
Lobelia Compliment Purple	L. 'Kompliment Purpur'
Lobelia Compliment Scarlet	L. 'Kompliment Scharlach'
Lobelia erinus 'Richardii'	L. richardsonii
Lobelia Fan Deep Red	L. 'Fan Tiefrot'
Lobelia 'Flamingo'	L. 'Pink Flamingo'
Lobelia pedunculata	Pratia pedunculata
Lobelia perpusilla	Pratia perpusilla
Lobelia physaloides	Pratia physaloides
Lobelia repens	Pratia repens
Lobelia treadwellii	Pratia angulata

Synonyms

Lobelia vedrariensis — L. x gerardii 'Vedrariensis'
Lobelia 'Zinnoberrosa' — L. 'Fan Zinnoberrosa'
Lobivia aurea — Echinopsis aurea
Lobivia backebergii — Echinopsis backebergii
Lobivia caespitosa — Echinopsis maximiliana
Lobivia cinnabarina — Echinopsis cinnabarina
Lobivia ferox — Echinopsis ferox
Lobivia pentlandii — Echinopsis pentlandii
Lobivia pygmaea — Rebutia pygmaea
Lobivia silvestrii — Echinopsis chamaecereus

Lomaria — Blechnum
Lomaria gibba — Blechnum gibbum
Lomatia longifolia — L. myricoides
Lomatophyllum citreum — L. occidentale v citreum
Lonicera caprifolium f pauciflora — L. x italica
Lonicera 'Early Cream' — L. caprifolium
Lonicera flexuosa — L. japonica v repens
Lonicera giraldii h — L. acuminata
Lonicera glaucohirta — L. periclymenum v glaucohirta
Lonicera 'Gold Flame' — L. x heckrottii 'Gold Flame'
Lonicera grata — L. x americana -(Miller) K.Koch
Lonicera henryi v subcoriacea — L. henryi
Lonicera japonica 'Peter Adams' — L. japonica 'Horwood Gem'
Lonicera japonica v repens 'Red Coral' — L. japonica 'Superba'
Lonicera japonica 'Variegata' — L. japonica 'Aureoreticulata'
Lonicera nitida Maygreen — L. nitida 'Maigrun'
Lonicera nitida 'Silver Lining' — L. pileata 'Silver Lining'
Lonicera periclymenum 'Belgica' misapplied —
Lonicera periclymenum 'Belgica' misapplied — L. pileata 'Silver Lining'
Lonicera periclymenum 'Florida' — L. periclymenum 'Serotina'
Lonicera pilosa -Maxim. — L. strophiophora
Lonicera sempervirens 'Dropmore Scarlet' — L. x brownii 'Dropmore Scarlet'
Lonicera syringantha — L. rupicola v syringantha
Lonicera x americana h — L. x italica
Lophocereus schottii — Pachycereus schottii
Lophomyrtus x ralphii 'Gloriosa' — L. x ralphii 'Variegata'
Lophomyrtus x ralphii 'Tricolor' — L. x ralphii 'Sundae'
Lophophora echinata — L. williamsii
Lophophora lutea — L. williamsii
Loropetalum chinense 'Burgundy' — L. chinense f rubrum
Lotus mascaensis h — L. sessilifolius
Lotus pedunculatus — L. uliginosus
Lotus suffruticosus — L. pentaphyllus ssp pentaphyllus
Lunaria biennis — L. annua
Lupinus cruckshankii — L. mutabilis cruckshankii
Lupinus 'Dwarf Lulu' — L. 'Lulu'
Lupinus lyallii — L. lepidus v lobbii
Lupinus pilosus — L. varius ssp orientalis
Luzula maxima — L. sylvatica
Luzula maxima 'Aurea' — L. sylvatica 'Aurea'
Luzula sylvatica 'A.Rutherford' — L. sylvatica 'Taggart's Cream'
Luzula sylvatica 'Aureomarginata' — L. sylvatica 'Marginata'
Lycaste candida — L. brevispatha

'Treadwellii'

Lycaste gigantea — L. longipetala
Lycaste virginalis — L. skinneri
Lychnis coeli-rosi — Silene coeli-rosi
Lychnis coronaria 'Abbotswood Rose' — L. x walkeri 'Abbotswood Rose'
Lychnis dioica — Silene dioica
Lychnis flos-jovis 'Minor' — L. flos-jovis 'Nana'
Lychnis kubotae — x Lycene kubotae
Lychnis lagascae — Petrocoptis pyrenaica ssp glaucifolia
Lychnis viscaria alpina — L. viscaria
Lychnis viscaria 'Flore Pleno' — L. viscaria 'Splendens Plena'
Lychnis yunnanensis alba — L. yunnanensis
Lycianthes rantonnetii — Solanum rantonnetii
Lycium halimifolium — L. barbarum
Lycopsis — Anchusa
Lysimachia ciliata 'Purpurea' — L. ciliata 'Firecracker'
Lysimachia lyssii — L. congestiflora
Lysimachia punctata verticillata — L. verticillaris
Lythrum salicaria Firecandle — L. salicaria 'Feuerkerze'
Machaeranthera pattersonii — M. bigelovii
Machaerocereus eruca — Stenocereus eruca
Maclura aurantiaca — M. pomifera
Macrodiervilla — Weigela
Macropiper crocatum — Piper ornatum
Macrotomia echioides — Arnebia pulchra
Macrozamia corallipes — M. spiralis
Macrozamia dyeri — M. riedlei
Magnolia acuminata 'Miss Honeybee' — M. cordata 'Miss Honeybee'
Magnolia cordata — M. acuminata v subcordata
Magnolia denudata v purpurascens — M. sprengeri v diva
Magnolia glauca — M. virginiana
Magnolia heptapeta — M. denudata
Magnolia insignis — Manglietia insignis
Magnolia kobus 'Norman Gould' — M. stellata 'Norman Gould'
Magnolia macrophylla ssp ashei — M. ashei
Magnolia obovata -Diels — M. officinalis
Magnolia obovata -Thunb. — M. hypoleuca
Magnolia parviflora — M. sieboldii
Magnolia 'Pickard's Sundew' — M. 'Sundew'
Magnolia quinquepeta — M. liliiflora
Magnolia salicifolia 'W.B.Clarke' — M. 'W.B.Clarke'
Magnolia 'Schmetterling' — M. 'Pickard's Schmetterling'
Magnolia sinensis — M. sieboldii ssp sinensis
Magnolia x kewensis 'Kewensis' — M. x kewensis 'Kew Clone'
Magnolia x soulangeana 'Alba Superba' — M. x soulangeana 'Alba'
Magnolia x soulangeana 'Nigra' — M. liliiflora 'Nigra'
Magnolia x soulangeana 'Rubra' misapplied — M. x soulangeana 'Rustica Rubra'
Magnolia x watsonii — M. x weisneri
Mahonia acanthifolia — M. napaulensis
Mahonia aquifolium 'Fascicularis' — M. x wagneri 'Pinnacle'
Mahonia bealei — M. japonica Bealei Group
Mahonia japonica 'Hiemalis' — M. japonica 'Hivernant'
Mahonia pinnata h — M. x wagneri 'Pinnacle'
Mahonia 'Undulata' — M. x wagneri 'Undulata'
Maianthemum dilatatum — M. bifolium v kamtschaticum
Maianthemum racemosum — Smilacina racemosa

Synonyms

Synonym	Accepted name
Majorana onites	Origanum onites
Malus 'Aldenhamensis'	M. x purpurea 'Aldenhamensis'
Malus domestica 'American Mother'	M. domestica 'Mother'
Malus domestica 'Balsam'	M. domestica 'Green Balsam'
Malus domestica 'Bewley Down Pippin'	M. domestica 'Crimson King'
Malus domestica 'Blenheim Red'	M. domestica 'Red Blenheim'
Malus domestica 'Boston Russet'	M. domestica 'Roxbury Russet'
Malus domestica Crispin	M. domestica 'Mutsu'
Malus domestica Delbards	M. domestica Jubilee (Delbards)
Malus domestica 'Early Victoria'	M. domestica 'Emneth Early'
Malus domestica 'Early Worcester'	M. domestica 'Tydeman's Early Worcester'
Malus domestica 'Echtermeyer'	M. x gloriosa 'Oekonomierat Echtermeyer'
Malus domestica 'Emperor Alexander'	M. domestica 'Alexander'
Malus domestica 'Forfar'	M. domestica 'Dutch Mignonne'
Malus domestica 'Gala Royal'	M. domestica 'Royal Gala'
Malus domestica 'Green Roland'	M. domestica 'Greenup's Pippin'
Malus domestica 'Isaac Newton's Tree'	M. domestica 'Flower of Kent'
Malus domestica 'John Toucher's'	M. domestica 'Crimson King'
Malus domestica 'Jonagold Crowngold'	M. domestica 'Crowngold'
Malus domestica 'Jubilee'	M. domestica 'Royal Jubilee'
Malus domestica Katy	M. domestica 'Katja'
Malus domestica 'Laxton's Epicure'	M. domestica 'Epicure'
Malus domestica 'Laxton's Fortune'	M. domestica 'Fortune'
Malus domestica Miel d'Or	M. domestica 'Honeygold'
Malus domestica 'Mondial Gala'	M. domestica 'Gala Mondial'
Malus domestica 'Port Wine'	M. domestica 'Harry Master's Jersey'
Malus domestica 'Reine des Reinettes'	M. domestica 'King of the Pippins'
Malus domestica 'Saint Edmund's Russet'	M. domestica 'Saint Edmund's Pippin'
Malus domestica 'Sir Isaac Newton's'	M. domestica 'Flower of Kent'
Malus domestica 'Snell's Glass Apple'	M. domestica 'Glass Apple'
Malus domestica 'Sour Natural'	M. domestica 'Langworthy'
Malus domestica 'Stone's'	M. domestica 'Loddington'
Malus domestica 'Superb'	M. domestica 'Laxton's Superb'
Malus domestica Swiss Orange	M. domestica 'Schweizer Orange'
Malus domestica 'Wellington'	M. domestica 'Dumeller's Seedling'
Malus domestica 'Wyatt's Seedling'	M. domestica 'Langworthy'
Malus 'Echtermeyer'	M. x gloriosa 'Oekonomierat Echtermeyer'
Malus 'Golden Hornet'	M. x zumi 'Golden Hornet'
Malus 'Hillieri'	M. x schiedeckeri 'Hillieri'
Malus 'Kaido'	M. x micromalus
Malus Perpetu	M. 'Evereste'
Malus 'Profusion'	M. x moerlandsii 'Profusion'
Malus pumila v niedzwetskyana	M. pumila 'Niedzwetskyana'
Malus 'Red Jade'	M. x schiedeckeri 'Red Jade'
Malus 'Red Siberian'	M. x robusta 'Red Siberian'
Malus sargentii	M. toringo ssp sargentii
Malus sieboldii	M. toringo
Malus sieboldii 'Calocarpa'	M. x zumi v calocarpa
Malus x purpurea 'Pendula'	M. x gloriosa 'Oekonomierat Echtermeyer'
Malus x zumi 'Calocarpa'	M. x zumi v calocarpa
Malus 'Yellow Siberian'	M. x robusta 'Yellow Siberian'
Malva bicolor	Lavatera maritima
Malva crispa	M. verticillata
Malva moschata 'Romney Marsh'	Althaea officinalis 'Romney Marsh'
Malvastrum capensis	Anisodontea capensis
Malvastrum coccineum	Sphaeralcea coccinea
Malvastrum hypomadarumh	Anisodontea capensis
Malvastrum peruvianum	Modiolastrum peruvianum
Malvastrum x hypomadarum	Anisodontea x hypomadara - (Sprague) Bates
Malvaviscus conzattii	M. arboreus v drummondii
Malvaviscus grandiflorus	M. arboreus v drummondii
Malvaviscus mollis	M. arboreus
Mamillopsis senilis	Mammillaria senilis
Mammillaria centricirrha	M. magnimamma
Mammillaria conoidea	Neolloydia conoidea
Mammillaria dealbata	M. haageana
Mammillaria shurliana	M. blossfeldiana
Mandevilla suaveolens	M. laxa
Mandevilla tweediana	M. laxa
Mandevilla x amabilis 'Alice du Pont'	M. x amoena 'Alice du Pont'
Manettia bicolor	M. luteorubra
Manettia inflata	M. luteorubra
Maranta leuconeura 'Erythroneura'	M. leuconeura v erythroneura
Maranta leuconeura 'Kerchoveana'	M. leuconeura v kerchoveana
Maranta leuconeura 'Massangeana'	M. leuconeura v massangeana
Maranta makoyana	Calathea makoyana
Marginatocereus marginatus	Stenocereus marginatus
Margyricarpus setosus	M. pinnatus
Mariscus	Cyperus
Markhamia platycalyx	M. lutea
Marniera chrysocardium	Epiphyllum chrysocardium

Marrubium candidissimum	M. incanum
Marsdenia erecta	Cionura erecta
Martynia	Proboscidea
Mascarena	Hyophorbe
Masdevallia elephantipes v pachysepala	M. mooreana
Masdevallia ignea	M. militaris
Matricaria chamomilla	M. recutita
Matricaria maritima	Tripleurospermum maritimum
Matricaria parthenium	Tanacetum parthenium
Matthiola bicornis	M. longipetala ssp bicornis
Matthiola thessala	M. fruticulosa
Matucana aurantiaca	Oreocereus aurantiacus
Matucana haynei	Oreocereus haynei
Matucana intertexta	Oreocereus intertexta
Maurandia	Maurandya
Maurandya erubescens	Lophospermum erubescens
Maurandya lophantha	Lophospermum scandens
Maurandya lophospermum	Lophospermum scandens
Maxillaria meleagris	M. cucullata
Meconopsis baileyi	M. betonicifolia
Meconopsis cambrica 'Rubra'	M. cambrica 'Frances Perry'
Meconopsis 'James Cobb'	M. integrifolia ssp integrifolia 'Wolong'
Meconopsis nudicaulis	Papaver nudicaule
Meconopsis wallichii	M. napaulensis
Medicago echinus	M. intertexta
Megalonium	Aeonium
Megasea	Bergenia
Melaleuca erubescens	M. diosmatifolia
Melaleuca nesophylla	M. nesophila
Melaleuca pauciflora	M. biconvexa
Melaleuca quinquenervia	M. viridiflora v rubriflora
Melandrium	Vaccaria
Melandrium elisabethae	Silene elisabethae
Melasphaerula graminea	M. ramosa
Melia azedarach v japonica	M. azedarach
Meliosma oldhamii	M. pinnata v oldhamii
Meliosma pendens	M. dilleniifolia ssp flexuosa
Melissa officinalis 'Variegata' h	M. officinalis 'Aurea'
Melocactus actinacanthus	M. matanzanus
Melocactus communis	M. intortus
Melocactus macrodiscus	M. zehntneri
Melocactus oaxacensis	M. curvispinus
Mentha citrata	M. x piperata f citrata
Mentha cordifolia	M. x villosa
Mentha corsica	M. requienii
Mentha 'Eau de Cologne'	M. x piperta f citrata
Mentha odorata	M. x piperta f citrata
Mentha piperata v citriodora	M. x piperta f citrata
Mentha rotundifolia 'Bowles'	M. x villosa f alopecuroides Bowles' Mint
Mentha rotundifolia h	M. suaveolens
Mentha rubra v raripila	M. x smithiana
Mentha sylvestris	M. longifolia
Mentha viridis	M. spicata
Mentha x gentilis	M. x gracilis
Mentha x gentilis 'Aurea'	M. x gracilis 'Variegata'
Mentha x gentilis 'Variegata'	M. x gracilis 'Variegata'
Mentha x gracilis 'Aurea'	M. x gracilis 'Variegata'
Menziesia alba	Daboecia cantabrica f alba
Menziesia ciliicalyx lasiophylla	M. ciliicalyx v purpurea
Menziesia polifolia	Daboecia cantabrica
Merendera bulbocodium	M. montana
Merendera caucasica	M. trigyna
Merendera eichleri	M. trigyna
Merendera pyrenaica	M. montana
Merendera raddeana	M. trigyna
Mertensia asiatica	M. simplicissima
Mertensia maritima ssp asiatica	M. simplicissima
Mertensia pterocarpa	M. sibirica
Mertensia virginica	M. pulmonarioides
Merxmuellera	Rytidosperma
Meryta sinclairii 'Variegata'	M. sinclairii 'Moonlight'
Mesembryanthemum 'Basutoland'	Delosperma nubigenum
Mesembryanthemum brownii	Lampranthus brownii
Mesembryanthemum cordifolium	Aptenia cordifolia
Mesembryanthemum criniflorum	Dorotheanthus bellidiformis
Mesembryanthemum derenbergianum	Ebracteola derenbergiana
Mesembryanthemum multiradiatum	Lampranthus roseus
Mesembryanthemum ornatulum	Delosperma ornatulum
Mesembryanthemum putterillii	Ruschia putterillii
Mesembryanthemum tricolor	Dorotheanthus gramineus
Metapanax	Pseudopanax
Metasequoia glyptostroboides 'Fastigiata'	M. glyptostroboides 'National'
Metrosideros lucidus	M. umbellatus
Metrosideros tomentosus	M. excelsus
Michelia wilsonii	M. sinensis
Microcoelum	Lytocaryum
Microglossa albescens	Aster albescens
Micromeria corsica	Acinos corsicus
Micromeria rupestris	M. thymifolia
Mikania ternata	M. dentata
Miltonia phalaenopsis	Miltoniopsis phalaenopsis
Miltonia roezlii	Miltoniopsis roezlii
Mimetes lyrigera	M. cucullatus
Mimulus aurantiacus orange	M. aurantiacus v puniceus
Mimulus glutinosus	M. aurantiacus
Mimulus glutinosus atrosanguineus	M. aurantiacus v puniceus
Mimulus glutinosus luteus	M. aurantiacus
Mimulus guttatus variegated	M. guttatus 'Richard Bish'
Mimulus langsdorffii	M. guttatus
Mimulus Red Emperor	M. 'Roter Kaiser'
Mimulus sp -Mac&W 5257	M. 'Andean Nymph' - Mac&W 5257
Mina	Ipomoea
Minuartia caucasica	M. circassica
Minuartia parnassica	M. stellata
Minuartia verna ssp caespitosa 'Aurea'	Sagina subulata 'Aurea'
Minuartia verna ssp gerardii	M. verna ssp verna
Miscanthus sinensis 'Giganteus'	M. floridulus
Miscanthus sinensis Silver feather	M. 'Silberfeder'
Miscanthus tinctorius 'Nanus Variegatus'	M. oligostachyus 'Nanus Variegatus'
Mnium	Plagiomnium
Molinia altissima	M. caerulea ssp

Synonyms

Molinia litoralis — arundinacea
M. caerulea ssp arundinacea

Moltkia graminifolia — M. suffruticosa
Monarda Blue Stocking — M. 'Blaustrumpf'
Monarda Bowman — M. 'Sagittarius'
Monarda Firecrown — M. 'Feuerschopf'
Monarda 'Libra' — M. 'Balance'
Monarda 'Pisces' — M. 'Fishes'
Monarda Prairie Night — M. 'Prarienacht'
Monarda 'Scorpio' — M. 'Scorpion'
Monarda 'Snow Maiden' — M. 'Schneewittchen'
Monarda 'Snow White' — M. 'Schneewittchen'
Monarda 'Snow Witch' — M. 'Schneewittchen'
Monopsis lutea — Lobelia lutea
Montbretia — Crocosmia
Montia australasica — Neopaxia australasica
Montia californica — Claytonia nevadensis
Montia parvifolia — Naiocrene parvifolia
Montia perfoliata — Claytonia perfoliata
Montia sibirica — Claytonia sibirica
Moraea glaucopsis — M. aristata
Moraea iridioides — Dietes iridioides
Moraea longifolia — Hexaglottis longifolia
Moraea longifolia -Sweet — M. fugax
Moraea pavonia v lutea — M. bellendenii
Moraea spathacea — M. spathulata
Morisia hypogaea — M. monanthos
Morus alba 'Globosa' — M. alba 'Nana'
Morus bombycis — M. alba
Morus nigra 'King James' — M. nigra 'Chelsea'
Mucuna deeringiana — M. pruriens v utilis
Muehlenbeckia axillaris h — M. complexa
Muehlenbeckia complexa 'Nana' — M. axillaris -Walpers
Muehlenbeckia platyclados — Homalocladium platycladum

Mulgedium — Cicerbita
Mulgedium alpinum — Cicerbita alpina
Mulgedium plumieri — Cicerbita plumieri
Murraya exotica — M. paniculata
Musa arnoldiana — Ensete ventricosum
Musa cavendishii — M. acuminata 'Dwarf Cavendish'

Musa coccinea — M. uranoscopus
Musa ensete — Ensete ventricosum
Musa japonica — M. basjoo
Musa nana — Ensete acuminata
Musa x paradisiaca 'Dwarf Cavendish' — Ensete acuminata 'Dwarf Cavendish'

Muscari ambrosiacum — M. muscarimi
Muscari chalusicum — M. pseudomuscari
Muscari comosum 'Monstrosum' — M. comosum 'Plumosum'

Muscari lingulatum — M. aucheri
Muscari moschatum — M. muscarimi
Muscari moschatum v flavum — M. macrocarpum
Muscari muscarimi v flavum — M. macrocarpum
Muscari paradoxum — Bellevalia paradoxa
Muscari pycnantha — Bellevalia paradoxa
Muscari racemosum — M. neglectum
Muscari tubergenianum — M. aucheri
Muscarimia ambrosiacum — Muscari muscarimi
Muscarimia macrocarpum — Muscari macrocarpum
Mussaenda phillippica 'Aurorae' — M. 'Aurorae'
Mutisia retusa — M. spinosa v pulchella
Myoporum acuminatum — M. tenuifolium

Myosotidium nobile — M. hortensia
Myosotis palustris — M. scorpioides
Myosotis rupicola — M. alpestris
Myosotis sylvatica alba — M. sylvatica f lactea
Myrceugenia apiculata — Luma apiculata
Myriophyllum brasiliense — M. aquaticum
Myriophyllum proserpinacoides — M. aquaticum
Myrmecophila tibicinis — Schomburgkia tibicinis
Myrtus apiculata — Luma apiculata
Myrtus bullata — Lophomyrtus bullata
Myrtus bullata 'Gloriosa' — Lophomyrtus x ralphii 'Variegata'
Myrtus chequen — Luma chequen
Myrtus communis 'Jenny Reitenbach' — M. communis ssp tarentina
Myrtus communis 'Microphylla' — M. communis ssp tarentina
Myrtus communis 'Nana' — M. communis ssp tarentina
Myrtus communis 'Tricolor' — M. communis 'Variegata'
Myrtus 'Glanleam Gold' — Luma apiculata 'Glanleam Gold'
Myrtus lechleriana — Amomyrtus luma
Myrtus luma — Luma apiculata
Myrtus nummularia — Myrteola nummularia
Myrtus obcordata — Lophomyrtus obcordata
Myrtus 'Traversii' — Lophomyrtus x ralphii
Myrtus ugni — Ugni molinae
Myrtus x ralphii — Lophomyrtus x ralphii
Naegelia cinnabarina — Smithiantha cinnabarina
Naegelia zebrina — Smithiantha zebrina
Nananthus rubrolineata — Aloinopsis rubrolineata
Nananthus schooneesii — Aloinopsis schooneesii
Nandina domestica 'Nana' — N. domestica 'Pygmaea'
Narcissus 'Albus Plenus Odoratus' — N. poeticus 'Plenus'
Narcissus alpestris — N. pseudonarcissus ssp moschatus
Narcissus Angel's Tears — N. triandrus v triandrus
Narcissus baeticus — N. assoanus v praelongus MS 656
Narcissus bulbocodium tananicus — N. tananicus
Narcissus bulbocodium v mesatlanticus — N. romieuxii ssp romieuxii v mesatlanticus
Narcissus campernellii — N. x odorus
Narcissus 'Campernellii Plenus' — N. x odorus 'Double Campernelle'
Narcissus canaliculatus -Guzonne — N. tazetta ssp lacticolor
Narcissus 'Capax Plenus' — N. 'Eystettensis'
Narcissus compressus — N. x intermedius
Narcissus 'Double Campernelle' — N. odorus 'Double Campernelle'
Narcissus gracilis — N. x tenuior
Narcissus graellsii — N. bulbocodium ssp bulbocodium v graellsii
Narcissus henriquesii — N. jonquilla v henriquesii
Narcissus 'Joy' — Narcissus 'Jolity'
Narcissus 'Joy Bishop' — Narcissus romieuxii 'Joy Bishop'
Narcissus 'Julia Jane' — N. romieuxii 'Julia Jane'
Narcissus juncifolius — N. assoanus
Narcissus 'L'Amour' — N. 'Madelaine'
Narcissus lobularis — N. pseudonarcissus 'Lobularis'
Narcissus marvieri — N. rupicola ssp marvieri
Narcissus minimus — N. asturiensis
Narcissus minor v pumilus 'Plenus' — N. 'Rip van Winkle'

Synonyms

Narcissus nanus	N. minor	Nepenthes rafflesiana x ampullaria	N. x hookeriana
Narcissus Old Pheasant's Eye	N. poeticus v recurvus	Nepeta argolica	N. sibthorpii
Narcissus 'Paper White'	N. papyraceus	Nepeta 'Blue Beauty'	N. sibirica 'Souvenir d'Andre Chaudron'
Narcissus 'Paper White Grandiflorus'	N. papyraceus		
Narcissus poeticus Old Pheasant's Eye	N. poeticus v recurvus	Nepeta glechoma 'Variegata'	Glechoma hederacea 'Variegata'
Narcissus pseudonarcissus ssp obvallaris	N. obvallaris	Nepeta hederacea 'Variegata'	Glechoma hederacea 'Variegata'
Narcissus pseudonarcissus ssp pallidiflorus	N. pallidiflorus	Nepeta lanceolata	N. nepetella
Narcissus pumilus	N. minor v pumilus	Nepeta macrantha	N. sibirica
Narcissus 'Queen Anne's Double'	N. 'Eystettensis'	Nepeta mussinii	N. racemosa
Narcissus requienii	N. assoanus	Nepeta pannonica	N. nuda
Narcissus rifanus	N. romieuxii ssp romieuxii v rifanus	Nepeta reichenbachiana	N. racemosa
Narcissus 'Royal Command'	N. 'Royal Decree'	Nepeta 'Souvenir d'Andre Chaudron'	N. sibirica 'Souvenir d'Andre Chaudron'
Narcissus tazetta aureus	N. aureus		
Narcissus tazetta papyraceus	N. papyraceus	Nephrolepis exaltata 'Aurea'	N. exaltata 'Golden Boston'
Narcissus tenuifolius	N. bulbocodium ssp bulbocodium v tenuifolius	Nephthytis triphylla h	Syngonium podophyllum
Narcissus triandrus v albus	N. triandrus v triandrus	Nerine bowdenii 'Fenwick's Variety'	N. bowdenii 'Mark Fenwick'
Narcissus triandrus v concolor	N. concolor	Nerine corusca 'Major'	N. sarniensis v corusca
Narcissus 'Urchin'	N. 'Pzaz'	Nerine crispa	N. undulata
Narcissus v plenus odoratus	N. poeticus 'Plenus'	Nerium obesum	Adenium obesum
Narcissus 'Van Sion'	N. 'Telamonius Plenus'	Nerium oleander 'Monca'	N. oleander 'Casablanca'
Narcissus zaianicus lutescens S&F 374	N. romieuxii ssp albidus v zaianicus f lutescens SF 374	Nerium oleander 'Monta'	N. oleander 'Tangier'
		Nerium oleander 'Monvis'	N. oleander 'Ruby Lace'
Narcissus zaianicus v albus MS 168	N. romieuxii ssp albidus v zaianicus f albus MS 168	Nerium oleander 'Mrs Roeding'	N. oleander 'Carneum Plenum'
Nautilocalyx tessellatus	N. bullatus	Nicodemia madagascariensis	Buddleja madagascariensis
Neanthe bella	Chamaedorea elegans	Nicolaia elatior	Etlingera elatior
Nectaroscordum dioscoridis	N. siculum ssp bulgaricum	Nicotiana affinis	N. alata
Neillia longiracemosa	N. thibetica	Nidularium carolinae	Neoregelia carolinae
Nematanthus gregarius 'Variegatus'	N. gregarius 'Golden West'	Nidularium flandria	Neoregelia carolinae 'Flandria' (Meyendorffii Group)
Nematanthus radicans	N. gregarius	Nierembergia frutescens	N. scoparia
Nemesia caerulea 'Joan Wilder'	N. caerulea lilac/blue	Nierembergia hippomanica	N. caerulea
Nemesia denticulata 'Confetti'	N. denticulata	Nierembergia rivularis	N. repens
Nemesia foetens	N. caerulea	Noccaea	Thlaspi
Nemesia fruticans misapp.	N. caerulea	Nolana atriplicifolia	N. paradoxa
Nemesia umbonata h	N. caerulea lilac/blue	Nolana grandiflora	N. paradoxa
Nemophila insignis	N. menziesii	Nomocharis mairei	N. pardanthina
Neobesseya asperispina	Escobaria asperispina	Nomocharis nana	Lilium nanum
Neobesseya macdougallii	Ortegocactus macdougallii	Nomocharis oxypetala	Lilium oxypetalum
		Nopalea cochenillifera	Opuntia cochenillifera
Neochilena chilensis	Neoporteria chilensis	Nothofagus antarctica 'Prostrata'	N. antarctica 'Benmore'
Neochilena mitis h	Neoporteria napina	Nothofagus procera	N. alpina
Neodypsis decaryi	Dypsis decaryi	Notholaena	Cheilanthes
Neodypsis leptocheilos	Dypsis leptocheilos	Nothopanax	Polyscias
Neolitsea glauca	N. sericea	Nothoscordum fragrnas	N. gracile
Neolloydia mcdowellii	Thelocactus mcdowellii	Nothoscordum neriniflorum	Caloscordum neriniflorum
Neopanax	Pseudopanax		
Neopanax arboreum	Pseudopanax arboreus	Notocactus apricus	Parodia concinna
Neopaxia australasica blue-leaved	N. australasica 'Kosciusko'	Notocactus brevihamatus	Parodia brevihamatus
		Notocactus claviceps	Parodia claviceps
Neopaxia australasica bronze-leaved	N. australasica 'Ohau'	Notocactus conncinnus	Parodia concinna
Neopaxia australasica green-leaved	N. australasica 'Great Lake'	Notocactus graessneri	Parodia graessneri
		Notocactus haselbergii	Parodia haselbergii
Neopaxia australasica grey	N. australasica 'Kosciusko'	Notocactus leninghausii	Parodia leninghausii
		Notocactus magnifica	Parodia magnifica
Neoporteria litoralis	N. subgibbosa	Notocactus mammulosus	Parodia mammulosa
Neoporteria mitis	N. napina	Notocactus mutabilis	Parodia mutabilis
Neoregelia carolinae 'Tricolor'	N. carolinae f tricolor	Notocactus ottonis	Parodia ottonis
Neoregelia concentrica 'Plutonis'	N. concentrica v plutonis	Notocactus penicillata	Parodia penicillata

Synonyms

Name	Synonym
Notocactus rutilans	Parodia rutilans
Notocactus scopa	Parodia scopa
Notocactus submammulosus	Parodia submammulosa
Nuphar lutea ssp variegata	N. variegata
Nuphar luteum	N. lutea
Nuttallia	Oemleria
Nyctocereus serpentinus	Peniocereus serpentinus
Nymphaea 'Albatross' h	N. 'Hermine'
Nymphaea 'Apple Blossom Pink'	N. 'Marliacea Carnea'
Nymphaea 'Exquisita'	N. 'Odorata Exquisita'
Nymphaea 'Hollandia' h	N. 'Darwin'
Nymphaea 'Laydekeri Rosea' h	N. 'Laydekeri Rosea Prolifera'
Nymphaea 'Luciana'	N. 'Odorata Luciana'
Nymphaea 'Mrs Richmond'	N. 'Fabiola'
Nymphaea 'Occidentalis'	N. alba ssp occidentalis
Nymphaea 'Odorata Alba'	N. odorata
Nymphaea odorata 'Pumila'	N. odorata v minor
Nymphaea 'Odorata William B.Shaw'	N. 'W.B.Shaw'
Nymphaea pygmaea	N. tetragona
Nymphaea 'Pygmaea Alba'	N. tetragona
Nymphaea 'Rembrandt' h	N. 'Meteor'
Nymphaea 'Sunrise'	N. 'Odorata Sulphurea Grandiflora'
Nymphaea tetragona 'Alba'	N. tetragona
Nymphaea 'Tuberosa Flavescens'	N. 'Marliacea Chromatella'
Nymphaea tuberosa 'Rosea'	N. 'Rosea'
Nymphaea x helvola	N. 'Pygmaea Helvola'
Oakesiella	Uvularia
Ochagavia lindleyana	O. carnea
Ochna multiflora	O. serrulata
Ochna serratifolia h	O. serrulata
Ocimum americanum 'Meng Luk'	O. americanum
Ocimum basilicum 'Anise'	O. basilicum 'Horapha'
Ocimum basilicum 'Glycyrrhiza'	O. basilicum 'Horapha'
Ocimum basilicum 'Holy'	O. tenuiflorum
Ocimum basilicum 'Thai'	O. basilicum 'Horapha'
Ocimum canum	O. americanum
Ocimum sanctum	O. tenuiflorum
Odontoglossum bictoniense	Lemboglossum bictoniense
Odontoglossum cervantessii	Lemboglossum cervantessii
Odontoglossum cordatum	Lemboglossum cordatum
Odontoglossum grande	Rossioglossum grande
Odontoglossum rossii	Lemboglossum rossii
Odontoglossum stellatum	Lemboglossum stellatum
Odontoglossum triumphans	Lemboglossum spectatissimum
Oenanthe japonica	O. javanica
Oenothera acaulis 'Lutea' h	O. acaulis 'Aurea'
Oenothera berlandieri	O. speciosa 'Rosea'
Oenothera berlandieri 'Childsii'	O. speciosa 'Rosea'
Oenothera childsii	Oenothera speciosa 'Rosea'
Oenothera cinaeus	O. fruticosa ssp glauca
Oenothera erythrosepala	O. glaziouana
Oenothera Fireworks	O. fruticosa 'Fyrverkeri'
Oenothera fraseri	O. fruticosa ssp glauca
Oenothera fruticosa Fireworks	O. fruticosa 'Fyrverkeri'
Oenothera fruticosa Highlight	O. fruticosa 'Hoheslicht'
Oenothera fruticosa ssp glauca Solstice	O. fruticosa ssp glauca 'Sonnenwende'
Oenothera glabra -Miller	O. biennis
Oenothera glauca	O. fruticosa ssp glauca
Oenothera hookeri	O. elata ssp hookeri
Oenothera lamarckiana	O. glaziouana
Oenothera linearis	O. fruticosa
Oenothera mexicana	O. laciniata
Oenothera missouriensis	O. macrocarpa
Oenothera odorata h	O. glaziouana
Oenothera odorata -Hook. & Arn.	O. biennis
Oenothera odorata 'Sulphurea'	O. stricta 'Sulphurea'
Oenothera pumila	O. perennis
Oenothera speciosa v childsii	O. speciosa 'Rosea'
Oenothera taraxacifolia	O. acaulis
Oenothera tetragona	O. fruticosa ssp glauca
Oenothera tetragona 'Sonnenwende'	O. fruticosa ssp glauca 'Sonnenwende'
Oenothera tetragona v fraseri	O. fruticosa ssp glauca
Olea europaea v europaea 'Pyramidalis'	O. europaea v europaea 'Cipressino'
Olearia albida h	O. 'Talbot de Malahide'
Olearia gunniana	O. phlogopappa
Olearia oleifolia	O. 'Waikariensis'
Olearia phlogopappa 'Rosea'	O. phlogopappa 'Comber's Pink'
Olearia rani h	O. cheesemanii
Olearia semidentata	O. 'Henry Travers'
Olearia stellulata h	O. phlogopappa
Olearia traversii 'Variegata'	O. traversii 'Tweedledum'
Olearia x mollis h	O. ilicifolia
Olearia x scilloniensis h	O. stelluta -De Candolle
Olearia 'Zennorencis'	O. x mollis 'Zennorencis'
Oligostachyum lubricum	Semiarundinaria lubrica
Oliveranthus elegans	Echeveria harmsii
Omphalodes linifolia alba	O. linifolia
Oncidium papilio	Psychopsis papilio
Ononis cenisia	O. cristata
Onoportion	Onopordum
Onopordum arabicum	O. nervosum
Operculina tuberosa	Merremia tuberosa
Ophiopogon 'Black Dragon'	O. planiscapus 'Nigrescens'
Ophiopogon graminifolius	Liriope muscari
Ophiopogon intermedius 'Variegatus'	O. intermedius 'Argenteomarginatus'
Ophiopogon jaburan 'Argenteovittatus'	O. jaburan 'Vittatus'
Ophiopogon jaburan 'Javanensis'	O. jaburan 'Vittatus'
Ophiopogon jaburan 'Variegatus'	O. jaburan 'Vittatus'
Ophiopogon planiscapus 'Arabicus'	O. planiscapus 'Nigrescens'
Ophiopogon planiscapus 'Ebony Knight'	O. planiscapus 'Nigrescens'
Ophiopogon spicatus	Liriope spicata
Ophrys aranifera	O. sphegodes
Ophrys fuciflora	O. holoserica
Ophrys speculum	O. vernixia
Oplismenus africanus 'Variegatus'	O. 'Variegatus'
Oplismenus hirtellus	O. africanus
Opuntia engelmannii	O. ficus-indica
Opuntia engelmannii h	O. phaeacantha
Opuntia humifusa	O. compressa
Opuntia hystricina	O. erinacea
Opuntia linguiformis	O. lindheimeri
Opuntia megacantha	O. ficus-indica
Opuntia rufida	O. microdasys v rufida
Orchis elata	Dactylorhiza elata
Orchis foliosa	Dactylorhiza foliosa

Synonyms

Orchis fuchsii	Dactylorhiza fuchsii	Othonnopsis	Othonna
Orchis maculata	Dactylorhiza maculata	Ourisia elegans	O. coccinea
Orchis maderensis	Dactylorhiza foliosa	Oxalis deppei	O. tetraphylla
Orchis majalis	Dactylorhiza majalis	Oxalis enneaphylla x adenophylla	O. 'Matthew Forrest'
Oreocereus peruviana	Oroya peruviana	Oxalis floribunda	O. articulata
Origanum caespitosum	O. vulgare 'Nanum'	Oxalis inops	O. depressa
Origanum creticum	O. vulgare ssp hirtum	Oxalis lactea double form	O. magellanica 'Nelson'
Origanum heracleoticum h	O. x applei	Oxalis magellanica 'Flore Pleno'	O. magellanica 'Nelson'
Origanum heracleoticum -Linnaeus	O. vulgare ssp hirtum	Oxalis perdicaria	O. lobata
Origanum kopatdaghense	O. vulgare ssp gracile	Oxalis purpurea v bowiei	O. bowiei
Origanum pulchellum	O. x hybridinum	Oxalis regnellii	O. triangularis ssp papilionacea
Origanum sipyleum sp Mac.&W 5882	Nepeta phyllochlamys		
Origanum tournefortii	O. calcaratum	Oxalis rosea h	O. rubra
Origanum villosum	Thymus villosus	Oxalis rosea -Jacquin	O. articulata
Origanum vulgare 'Curly Gold'	O. vulgare 'Aureum Crispum'	Oxalis speciosa	O. purpurea
		Oxalis squamosoradicosa	O. laciniata
Origanum vulgare 'Variegatum'	O. vulgare 'Gold Tip'	Oxalis vespertilionis -Torrey & A.Gray	O. drummondii
Ornithogalum balansae	O. oligophyllum	Oxalis vespertilionis -Zuccarini	O. latifolia
Ornithogalum caudatum	O. longibracteatum	Oxycoccus	Vaccinum
Ornithogalum nanum	O. sigmoideum	Oxypetalum caeruleum	Tweedia caerulea
Ornithogalum sibthorpii	O. sigmoideum	Pachistema	Paxistima
Orobus aureus	Lathyrus aureus	Pachystachys cardinalis	P. coccinea
Orobus vernus	Lathyrus vernus	Pachystegia	Olearia
Orostachys malacophylla	O. aggregata	Pachystema	Paxistima
Oroya neoperuviana	O. peruviana	Pachystima	Paxistima
Orphanidesia gaultherioides	Epigaea gaultherioides	Paeonia albiflora	P. lactiflora
Oscularia deltoides	Lampranthus deltoides	Paeonia arietina	P. mascula ssp arietina
Osmanthus forrestii	O. yunnanensis	Paeonia banatica	P. officinalis ssp banatica
Osmanthus heterophyllus 'Argenteomarginatus'		Paeonia Bird of Rimpo	P. suffruticosa 'Rimpo'
	O. heterophyllus 'Variegatus'	Paeonia caucasica	P. mascula ssp mascula
		Paeonia corallina	P. mascula ssp mascula
Osmanthus heterophyllus 'Aureus' misapplied		Paeonia daurica	P. mascula ssp triternata
Osmanthus heterophyllus 'Aureus' -Rehd.	O. heterophyllus all gold	Paeonia decora	P. peregrina
	O. heterophyllus 'Aureomarginatus'	Paeonia 'Flight of Cranes'	P. suffruticosa 'Renkaku'
Osmanthus heterophyllus Tricolor	O. heterophyllus 'Goshiki'	Paeonia 'Floral Rivalry'	P. suffruticosa 'Hana-kisoi'
Osmanthus ilicifolius	O. heterophyllus	Paeonia 'General MacMahon'	P. lactiflora 'Augustin d'Hour'
Osmanthus x fortunei 'Variegatus'	O. heterophyllus 'Latifolius Variegatus'	Paeonia humilis	P. officinalis ssp microcarpa
Osmaronia	Oemleria	Paeonia 'Isani Gidui'	P. lactiflora 'Isami-jishi'
Osmunda regalis Undulata Group	O. regalis Cristata Group	Paeonia japonica h	P. lactiflora
Osteospermum 'African Queen'	O. 'Nairobi Purple'	Paeonia kevachensis	P. mascula ssp mascula
Osteospermum barberae h	O. jucundum	Paeonia 'Kinkaku'	P. x lemoinei 'Souvenir de Maxime Cornu'
Osteospermum 'Blackthorn Seedling'	O. jucundum 'Blackthorn Seedling'	Paeonia 'Kinko'	P. x lemoinei 'Alice Harding'
Osteospermum 'Bloemhoff Belle'	O. 'Nairobi Purple'	Paeonia 'Kinshi'	P. x lemoinei 'Chromatella'
Osteospermum 'Brickell's Hybrid'	O. 'Chris Brickell'	Paeonia 'Kintei'	P. x lemoinei 'L'Esperance'
Osteospermum caulescens h	O. 'Prostratum'	Paeonia lactiflora 'President Taft'	P. lactiflora 'Reine Hortense'
Osteospermum 'Coconut Ice'	O. 'Croftway Coconut Ice'		
Osteospermum ecklonis v prostratum	O. 'Prostratum'	Paeonia lithophila	P. tenuifolia ssp lithophila
Osteospermum 'Killerton Pink'	O. jucundum 'Killerton Pink'	Paeonia lobata 'Fire King'	P. peregrina
		Paeonia lutea	P. delavayi v lutea
Osteospermum 'Langtrees'	O. jucundum 'Langtrees'	Paeonia lutea v ludlowii	P. delavayi v ludlowii
Osteospermum 'Merriments Joy'	O. jucundum 'Merriments Joy'	Paeonia 'Magnificent Flower'	P. suffruticosa 'Hana-daijin'
Osteospermum 'Pale Face'	O. 'Lady Leitrim'	Paeonia mollis	P. officinalis ssp villosa
Osteospermum 'Peggyi'	O. 'Nairobi Purple'	Paeonia 'Mrs Gwyn Lewis'	P. 'Duchesse de Nemours'
Osteospermum 'Port Wine'	O. 'Nairobi Purple'		
Osteospermum 'Prostratum'	O. 'White Pim'	Paeonia officinalis ssp humilis	P. officinalis ssp microcarpa
Osteospermum 'Silver Spoons'	O. 'Croftway Silverspoons'		
Osteospermum 'Starshine'	O. ecklonis 'Starshine'	Paeonia paradoxa	P. officinalis ssp microcarpa
Osteospermum 'Tauranga'	O. 'Whirligig'		
Osteospermum 'Tresco Peggy'	O. 'Nairobi Purple'		
Osteospermum 'Tresco Purple'	O. 'Nairobi Purple'		
Osteospermum 'Wine Purple'	O. 'Nairobi Purple'		

Paeonia peregrina 'Sunshine' — P. peregrina 'Otto Froebel'
Paeonia potaninii — P. delavayi Potaninii Group
Paeonia rockii — P. suffruticosa ssp rockii
Paeonia romanica — P. peregrina
Paeonia russoi — P. mascula ssp russoi
Paeonia sinensis — P. lactiflora
Paeonia suffruticosa Bird of Rimpo — P. suffruticosa 'Rimpo'
Paeonia suffruticosa Black Dragon Brocade — P. suffruticosa 'Kokuryu-nishiki'
Paeonia suffruticosa Brocade of the Naniwa — P. suffruticosa 'Naniwa-nishiki'
Paeonia suffruticosa Charming Age — P. suffruticosa 'Howki'
Paeonia suffruticosa Cherries of Imperial Palace — P. suffruticosa 'Gosho-zakura'
Paeonia suffruticosa Double Cherry — P. suffruticosa 'Yae-zakura'
Paeonia suffruticosa Eternal Camellias — P. suffruticosa 'Yachiyo-tsubaki'
Paeonia suffruticosa Five Continents — P. suffruticosa 'Godaishu'
Paeonia suffruticosa Flight of Cranes — P. suffruticosa 'Renkaku'
Paeonia suffruticosa Floral Rivalry — P. suffruticosa 'Hana-kisoi'
Paeonia suffruticosa 'Joseph Rock' — P. suffruticosa ssp rockii
Paeonia suffruticosa Kamada Brocade — P. suffruticosa 'Kamada-nishiki'
Paeonia suffruticosa King of Flowers — P. suffruticosa 'Kaow'
Paeonia suffruticosa King of White Lions — P. suffruticosa 'Hakuojisi'
Paeonia suffruticosa 'Kinkaku' — P. x lemoinei 'Souvenir de Maxime Cornu'
Paeonia suffruticosa 'Kinshi' — P. x lemoinei 'Alice Harding'
Paeonia suffruticosa Knight's Dance — P. suffruticosa 'No-kagura'
Paeonia suffruticosa Magnificent Flower — P. suffruticosa 'Hana-daijin'
Paeonia suffruticosa Moon World — P. suffruticosa 'Gessekai'
Paeonia suffruticosa Palace of Gems — P. suffruticosa 'Shugyo-kuden'
Paeonia suffruticosa Pride of Taisho — P. suffruticosa 'Taisho-no-hokori'
Paeonia suffruticosa 'Rock's Variety' — P. suffruticosa ssp rockii
Paeonia suffruticosa Seven Gods of Fortune — P. suffruticosa 'Sitifukujin'
Paeonia suffruticosa 'Sunshine' — P. peregrina 'Otto Froebel'
Paeonia suffruticosa The Sun — P. suffruticosa 'Taiyo'
Paeonia suffruticosa Twilight — P. suffruticosa 'Higurashi'
Paeonia suffruticosa Wisteria at Kamada — P. suffruticosa 'Kamada-fuji'
Paeonia 'Victor Hugo' — P. lactiflora 'Felix Crousse'
Pallenis spinosus — Asteriscus spinosus
Pandanus odoratissimus — P. tectorius
Pandanus tectorius 'Veitchii' — P. veitchii
Pandorea jasminoides 'Alba' — P. jasminoides 'Lady Di'
Pandorea jasminoides 'Variegata' — P. jasminoides 'Charisma'
Pandorea lindleyana — Clytostoma callistegioides
Pandorea ricasoliana — Podranea ricasoliana
Panicum violaceum — P. miliaceum 'Violaceum'
Panicum virgatum 'Haense Herms' — P. virgatum 'Hanse Herms'
Papaver alpinum ssp burseri — P. burseri
Papaver alpinum ssp rhaeticum — P. rhaeticum
Papaver bracteatum — P. orientale v bracteatum
Papaver commutatum 'Ladybird' — P. commutatum

Papaver heldreichii — P. spicatum
Papaver miyabeanumtatewakii — P. miyabeanum
Papaver nanum 'Flore Pleno' — P. 'Fireball'
Papaver nudicaule Garden Gnome Group — P. nudicaule Gartenzwerg Group
Papaver orientale 'Mrs Marrow's Plum' — P. orientale 'Patty's Plum'
Papaver orientale 'Nanum Flore Pleno' — P. 'Fireball'
Papaver orientale Princess Victoria Louise — P. orientale 'Prinzessin Victoria Louise'
Papaver orientale Stormtorch — P. orientale 'Sturmfackel'
Papaver rhoeas Fairy Wings — P. rhoeas 'Mother of Pearl'
Parabenzoin — Lindera
Parahebe catarractae 'Porlock Purple' — P. catarractae 'Delight'
Parahebe 'Greencourt' — P. catarractae 'Delight'
Paraquilegia adoxoides — Semiaquilegia adoxoides
Paraquilegia grandiflora — P. anemonoides
Paraserianthes distachya — P. lophantha
Parasyringa — Ligustrum
Parietaria officinalis — P. judaica
Parodia liliputana — Blossfeldia liliputana
Parodia sanguiniflora — P. microsperma
Paronychia nivea — P. capitata
Paronychia serpyllifolia — P. kapela
Parrya menziesii — Phoenicaulis cheiranthoides
Parthenocissus himalayana 'Purpurea' — P. himalayana v rubrifolia
Parthenocissus striata — Cissus striata
Parthenocissus thomsonii — Cayratia thomsonii
Passiflora banksii — P. aurantia
Passiflora chinensis — P. caerulea
Passiflora 'Empress Eugenie' — P. x belotii
Passiflora fulgens — P. coccinea
Passiflora incana — P. seemannii
Passiflora 'Lavender Lady' — P. 'Amethyst'
Passiflora 'Lilac Lady' — P. x violacea 'Tresederi'
Passiflora lowei — P. ligularis
Passiflora 'Mavis Mastics' — P. x violacea 'Tresederi'
Passiflora mayana — P. caerulea
Passiflora menispermifolia — P. pilosa
Passiflora obtusifolia — P. coriacea
Passiflora onychina — P. amethystina
Passiflora 'Purple Passion' — P. edulis f edulis
Passiflora retipetala — P. cyanea
Passiflora sanguinea — P. vitifolia
Passiflora serrata — P. serratodigitata
Passiflora velutina — P. coccinea
Passiflora x alatocaerulea — P. x belotii
Passiflora x belotii 'Imperatrice Eugenie' — P. x belotii
Passiflora x caerulea racemosa — P. x violacea
Passiflora x caeruleoracemosa — P. x violacea
Passiflora x innesii — P. x decaisneana 'Innesii'
Passiflora x tresederi — P. x violacea 'Tresederi'
Passiflora x violacea 'Lilac Lady' — P. x violacea 'Tresederi'
Paulownia fargesii -Osborn — P. tomentosa 'Lilacina'
Paulownia imperialis — P. tomentosa
Paurotis wrightii — Acoelorraphe wrightii
Pavetta caffra — Pavetta capensis
Pavonia multiflora h — P. x gledhillii
Pavonia x intermedia — P. x gledhillii
Paxistima myrinites — P. myrtifolia
Pectinaria pillansii — Stapeliopsis pillansii
Pelargonium 'A Happy Thought' — P. 'Happy Thought'
Pelargonium acerifolium h — P. vitifolium
Pelargonium acerifolium -L'Heritier — P. cucullatum ssp strigifolium

Synonyms

Pelargonium asperum -Ehr. ex Willd.
P. 'Graveolens'
Pelargonium 'Aurore'
P. 'Unique Aurore'
Pelargonium Balcon Imperial
P. 'Roi des Balcons Imperial'
Pelargonium 'Balcon Lilas'
P. 'Roi des Balcons Lilas'
Pelargonium 'Balcon Rose'
P. 'Hederinum'
Pelargonium 'Balcon Rouge'
P. 'Roi des Balcons Imperial'
Pelargonium 'Balcon Royale'
P. 'Roi des Balcons Imperial'
Pelargonium 'Ballerina'
P. 'Carisbrooke'
Pelargonium 'Beauty of Eastbourne'
P. 'Lachskonigin'
Pelargonium 'Berryl Bodey'
P. 'Mrs L.R.Bodey'
Pelargonium 'Black Butterfly'
P. 'Brown's Butterfly'
Pelargonium 'Black Vesuvius'
P. 'Red Black Vesuvius'
Pelargonium 'Blue Beard'
P. 'Barbe Bleu'
Pelargonium 'Blue Spring'
P. 'Blauer Fruhling'
Pelargonium 'Brook's Purple'
P. 'Royal Purple'
Pelargonium 'Cal'
P. 'Salmon Irene'
Pelargonium canescens
P. 'Blandfordianum'
Pelargonium 'Cardinal'
P. 'Kardinal'
Pelargonium 'Carnival' (Regal)
P. 'Marie Vogel'
Pelargonium 'Cerise Carnation'
P. 'Mrs H.J.Jones'
Pelargonium 'Chocolate Tomentosum'
P. 'Chocolate Peppermint'
Pelargonium 'Clorinda Variegated'
P. 'Variegated Clorinda'
Pelargonium coriandrifolium
P. myrrhifolium
Pelargonium 'Countess Mariza'
P. 'Grafin Mariza'
Pelargonium 'Countess of Scarborough'
P. 'Lady Scarborough'
Pelargonium 'Crocodile'
P. 'The Crocodile'
Pelargonium 'Dark Presidio'
P. 'Dark Mabel'
Pelargonium 'Deacon Finito'
P. 'Finito'
Pelargonium 'Deacon Golden Mist'
P. 'Golden Mist'
Pelargonium 'Decora Mauve'
P. 'Decora Lilas'
Pelargonium 'Double Henry Jacoby'
P. 'Double Jacoby'
Pelargonium 'Duke of Edinburgh'
P. 'Hederinum Variegatum'
Pelargonium 'Dwarf Miriam Read'
P. 'Dwarf Miriam Baisey'
Pelargonium 'Easter Greeting'
P. 'Ostergruss'
Pelargonium echinatum 'Miss Stapleton'
P. 'Miss Stapleton'
Pelargonium 'Emma Hossle'
P. 'Frau Emma Hossle'
Pelargonium 'Filicifolium'
P. 'Filicifoium' (Denticulatum Group)
Pelargonium fissifolium 'Creamy Nutmeg'
P. 'Creamy Nutmeg'
Pelargonium fissifolium 'Snowy Nutmeg'
P. 'Fragrans Variegatum' (Fragrans Group)
Pelargonium 'Fragrans'
P. Fragrans Group
Pelargonium 'Frosty'
P. 'Variegated Kleine Liebling'
Pelargonium 'Frosty Petit Pierre'
P. 'Variegated Kleine Liebling'
Pelargonium glaucum
P. lanceolatum
Pelargonium 'Gooseberry Leaf'
P. grossularioides
Pelargonium 'Grandma Fischer'
P. 'Grossmutter Fischer'
Pelargonium 'Greengold Petit Pierre'
P. 'Greengold Kleine Liebling'
Pelargonium 'H. Guinier'
P. 'Charles Gounod'
Pelargonium 'Hillscheider Amethyst'
P. 'Amethyst'
Pelargonium 'Jackie Gall'
P. 'Jackie'
Pelargonium 'Joan of Arc'
P. 'Jeanne d'Arc'
Pelargonium karrooense 'Graham Rice'
P. 'Grollie's Cream'
Pelargonium 'King of Balcon'
P. 'Hederinum'
Pelargonium 'L'Enfer'
P. 'Mephistopheles'
Pelargonium 'Lady Alice of Valencia'
P. 'Grenadier'
Pelargonium 'Lavender Mini Cascade'
P. 'Lila Mini Cascade'
Pelargonium Lila Compakt-Cascade
P. 'Decora Lilas'
Pelargonium 'Lilac Cascade'
P. 'Roi des Balcons Lilas'

Pelargonium 'Lilac Domino'
P. 'Telston's Prima'
Pelargonium 'Liverbird'
P. 'Harlequin Miss Liver Bird'
Pelargonium 'Lord Baden-Powell'
P. 'Colonel Baden-Powell'
Pelargonium 'Lord de Ramsay'
P. 'Tip Top Duet'
Pelargonium 'Madame Guinier'
P. 'Charles Gounod'
Pelargonium 'Madame Margot'
P. 'Hederinum Variegatum'
Pelargonium 'Marble Sunset'
P. 'Wood's Surprise'
Pelargonium 'Meshed Pink Gay Baby'
P. 'Laced Sugar Baby'
Pelargonium 'Mexicanerin'
P. 'Rouletta'
Pelargonium 'Miriam Basey'
P. 'Dwarf Miriam Baisey'
Pelargonium 'Monsieur Ninon' h
P. 'Madame Auguste Nonin'
Pelargonium 'Mrs Henry Cox'
P. 'Mr Henry Cox'
Pelargonium Pearl Necklace
P. 'Perlenkette'
Pelargonium 'Petit Pierre'
P. 'Kleine Liebling'
Pelargonium 'Pink Capitatum'
P. 'Pink Capricorn'
Pelargonium 'Pink Cascade'
P. 'Hederinum'
Pelargonium 'Pink Gay Baby'
P. 'Sugar Baby'
Pelargonium 'Pink Mini Cascade'
P. 'Rose Mini Cascade'
Pelargonium Pinto Series
P. Pulsar Series
Pelargonium 'Princess of Balcon'
P. 'Roi des Balcons Lilas'
Pelargonium 'Purple Light'
P. 'Purple Gem'
Pelargonium quercifolium 'Fair Ellen'
P. 'Fair Ellen'
Pelargonium 'Red Mini Cascade'
P. 'Rote Mini Cascade'
Pelargonium rogersianum
P. worcesterae
Pelargonium 'Roi des Balcons'
P. 'Hederinum'
Pelargonium 'Roi des Balcons Rose'
P. 'Hederinum'
Pelargonium 'Salmon Queen'
P. 'Lachskonigin'
Pelargonium Snow Queen
P. 'Schneekonigin'
Pelargonium 'Sofie'
P. 'Decora Rose'
Pelargonium 'Stellar Arctic Star'
P. 'Arctic Star'
Pelargonium 'Stellar Grenadier'
P. 'Grenadier'
Pelargonium 'Stellar Hannaford Star'
P. 'Hannaford Star'
Pelargonium 'Susan Baldwin'
P. 'Salmon Kovalevski'
Pelargonium 'Sussex Lace'
P. 'White Mesh'
Pelargonium 'The Culm'
P. 'Culm'
Pelargonium 'The Czar'
P. 'Czar'
Pelargonium 'The Dart'
P. 'Dart'
Pelargonium tomentosum 'Chocolate'
P. 'Chocolate Peppermint'
Pelargonium tricolor h
P. 'Splendide'
Pelargonium 'Variegated Fragrans'
P. 'Fragrans Variegatum' (Fragrans Group)
Pelargonium 'Variegated Petit Pierre'
P. 'Variegated Kleine Liebling'
Pelargonium 'Ville de Paris'
P. 'Hederinum'
Pelargonium violareum h
P. 'Splendide'
Pelargonium viscosum
P. glutinosum
Pelargonium x fragrans
P. Fragrans Group
Pelargonium x schottii
P. x sanguineum
Pelargonium x stapletoniae
P. 'Miss Stapleton'
Pellaea hastata
P. calomelanos
Pellionia
Elatostema
Pellionia daveauana
Elatostema repens
Pellionia pulchra
Elatostema pulchra
Pellionia repens
Elatostema repens
Peltandra alba
P. saggitifolia
Peltandra virginica -Schott
P. undulata
Peltiphyllum
Darmera
Peltiphyllum peltatum
Darmera peltata
Pennisetum compressum
P. alopecuroides
Pennisetum longistylum
P. villosum
Pennisetum rueppellii
P. setaceum
Penstemon alpinus ssp brandegeei
P. brandegeei
Penstemon antirrhinoides
Keckiella antirrhinoides

Synonyms

Penstemon 'Apple Blossom' h	P. 'Thorn'	Peperomia verschaffeltii	A. marmorata
Penstemon arizonicus	P. whippleanus	Pereskia amapola	A. nemerosa
Penstemon 'Barbara Barker'	P. 'Beech Park'	Pereskia grandiflorus	A. grandifolia
Penstemon 'Bisham Seedling'	P. 'White Bedder'	Pereskia sacharosa h	A. nemerosa
Penstemon 'Blue Spring'	P. heterophylla 'Blue Springs'	Pereskiopsis spathulata	A. diguetii
		Perilla frutescens v nankinensis	A. frutescens v crispa
Penstemon bridgesii	P. rostriflorus	Pernettya	Gaultheria
Penstemon 'Burford Purple'	P. 'Burgundy'	Pernettya prostrata	Gaultheria myrsinoides
Penstemon 'Burford Seedling'	P. 'Burgundy'	Pernettya prostrata	Gaultheria mysinoides
Penstemon 'Burford White'	P. 'White Bedder'	Persicaria affinis 'Dimity'	P. affinis 'Superba'
Penstemon caeruleus	P. angustifolius	Persicaria amplexicaulis 'Arun Gem'	P. amplexicaulis v pendula
Penstemon californicus	P. linarioides ssp californicus	Persicaria filiformis	P. virginiana
		Persicaria scoparia	Polygonum scoparium
Penstemon campanulatus pulchellus	P. campanulatus	Persicaria sphaerostachya -Meissner	P. macrophylla
Penstemon cordifolius	Keckiella cordifolia	Petalostemon	Dalea
Penstemon 'Cottage Garden Red'	P. 'Windsor Red'	Petamenes	Gladiolus
Penstemon cristatus	P. eriantherus	Petrocallis lagascae	P. pyrenaica
Penstemon diffusus	P. serrulatus	Petrophyton	Petrophytum
Penstemon digitalis 'Purpureus'	P. digitalis 'Husker's Red'	Petroselinum crispum 'Italian'	P. crispum v neapolitanum
Penstemon 'Drinkwater Red'	P. 'Drinkstone'		
Penstemon 'Firebird'	P. 'Schoenholzeri'	Petroselinum hortense	P. crispum
Penstemon 'Garden Red'	P. 'Windsor Red'	Petroselinum tuberosum	P. crispum v tuberosum
Penstemon 'Garnet'	P. 'Andenken an Friedrich Hahn'	Peucedanum graveolens	Anethum graveolens
		Phaedranthus	Distictis
Penstemon heterophyllus ssp australis	P. australis	Phaedranthus buccinatorius	Distictis buccinatoria
Penstemon heterophyllus 'True Blue'	P. heterophyllus	Phaiophleps biflora	Olsynium biflorum
Penstemon 'John Nash' h	P. 'Alice Hindley'	Phaiophleps nigricans	Sisyrinchium striatum
Penstemon 'June'	P. 'Hidcote Pink'	Phaius maculatus	Phaius flavus
Penstemon kunthii	P. campanulatus	Phalaris arundinacea 'Elegantissima'	P. arundinacea v picta 'Picta'
Penstemon 'Lord Home'	P. 'George Home'		
Penstemon menziesii	P. davidsonii v menziesii	Phalaris arundinacea 'Picta'	P. arundinacea v picta 'Picta'
Penstemon 'Mrs Morse'	P. 'Chester Scarlet'		
Penstemon newberryi ssp berryi	P. berryi	Phalaris arundinacea 'Tricolor'	P. arundinacea v picta 'Picta'
Penstemon 'Phyllis'	P. 'Evelyn'		
Penstemon pubescens	P. hirsutus	Phalaris arundinacea v picta 'Mervyn Feesey'	
Penstemon pulchellus -Lindley	P. campanulatus		P. arundinacea v picta 'Feesey'
Penstemon 'Purple and White'	P. 'Countess of Dalkeith'		
Penstemon 'Purpureus Albus'	P. 'Countess of Dalkeith'	Phalaris tuberosa stenoptera	P. aquatica
Penstemon roezlii -Regel	P. laetus v roezlii	Phanera	Bauhinia corymbosa
Penstemon 'Royal White'	P. 'White Bedder'	Phanerophlebia caryotidea	Cyrtomium caryotideum
Penstemon 'Ruby'	P. 'Schoenholzeri'	Phanerophlebia falcata	Cyrtomium falcatum
Penstemon scouleri	P. fruticosus v scouleri	Phanerophlebia fortunei	Cyrtomium fortunei
Penstemon 'Sissinghurst Pink'	P. 'Evelyn'	Pharbitis	Ipomoea
Penstemon 'Snow Storm'	P. 'White Bedder'	Phaseolus caracalla	Vigna caracalla
Penstemon 'Snowflake'	P. 'White Bedder'	Philadelphus coronarius 'Bowles' Variety'	P. coronarius 'Variegatus'
Penstemon sonomensis	P. newberryi v sonomensis	Philadelphus delavayi v calvescens	P. purpureus
		Philadelphus 'Innocence Variegatus'	P. 'Innocence'
Penstemon 'Sour Grapes' h	P. 'Stapleford Gem'	Philadelphus Silver Showers	P. 'Silberregen'
Penstemon 'Souvenir d'Andre Torres' misapplied	P. 'Chester Scarlet'	Philadelphus 'Souvenir de Billiard'	P. insignis
Penstemon taosensis	P. crandallii ssp taosensis	Philadelphus x lemoinei 'Erectus'	P. 'Erectus'
Penstemon ternatus	Keckiella ternata	Philesia buxifolia	P.magellanica
Penstemon 'Threave Pink'	P. 'Pink Endurance'	Phillyrea decora	Osmanthus decorus
Penstemon 'True Sour Grapes'	P. 'Sour Grapes' -M.Fish	Phillyrea media	P. latifolia
Penstemon tusharensis	P. caespitosus ssp suffruticosus	Philodendron andraeanum	P. melanochrysum
		Philodendron auritum h	Syngonium auritum
Pentapterygium	Agapetes	Philodendron elegans	P. angustisectum
Pentas carnea	P. lanceolata	Philodendron epipremnum	Epipremnum pinnatum
Peperomia hederifolia	A. griseoargentea	Philodendron hastatum h	P. domesticum
Peperomia magnoliifolia	A. obtusifolia Magnoliifolia Group	Philodendron laciniatum	P. pedatum
		Philodendron micans	P. scandens f micans
Peperomia nummulariifolia	A. rotundifolia	Philodendron oxycardium	P. scandens f oxycardium
Peperomia 'Princess Astrid'	A. orba	Philodendron panduriforme	P. bipennifolium
Peperomia pulchella	A. verticillata	Philodendron sellowianum	P. imbe
Peperomia resediflora	A. fraseri	Philodendron sodiroi	P. ornatum
Peperomia sandersii	A. argyreia	Philodendron trifoliatum	Syngonium auritum

Name	Synonym
Phlebodium	Polypodium
Phlomis samia -Boissier	P. russeliana
Phlomis samia ssp maroccana	P. bovei ssp maroccana
Phlomis viscosa h	P. russeliana
Phlox amoena h	P. x procumbens
Phlox amoena 'Variegata'	P. x procumbens 'Variegata'
Phlox canadensis	P. divaricata
Phlox 'Chattahoochee'	P. divaricata ssp laphamii
Phlox 'Daniel's Cushion'	P. subulata 'McDaniel's Cushion'
Phlox depressa	P. multiflora ssp depressa
Phlox douglasii Lilac Queen	P. douglasii 'Lilakonigin'
Phlox douglasii 'Tycoon'	P. subulata 'Tamaongalei'
Phlox drummondii 'Twinkle'	P. drummondii 'Sternenzauber'
Phlox maculata 'Avalanche'	P. maculata 'Schneelawine'
Phlox mesoleuca	P. nana ssp ensifolia
Phlox Mexican Hybrids	P. nana
Phlox 'Millstream'	P. x procumbens 'Millstream'
Phlox 'Mrs Campbell'	P. paniculata 'Elizabeth Campbell'
Phlox paniculata 'Count Zeppelin'	P. paniculata 'Graf Zeppelin'
Phlox paniculata July Glow	P. paniculata 'Juliglut'
Phlox paniculata 'Latest Red'	P. paniculata 'Spatrot'
Phlox paniculata Lavender Cloud	P. paniculata 'Lavendelwolke'
Phlox paniculata 'Mount Fujiyama'	P. paniculata 'Fujiyama'
Phlox paniculata 'Spitfire'	P. paniculata 'Frau A. von Mauthner'
Phlox subulata 'Beauty of Ronsdorf'	P. subulata 'Ronsdorfer Schone'
Phlox subulata 'Blue Eyes'	P. subulata 'Oakington Blue Eyes'
Phlox subulata 'Bressingham Blue Eyes'	P. subulata 'Oakington Blue Eyes'
Phlox subulata 'Drumm'	P. subulata 'Tamaongalei'
Phlox subulata 'Kimono'	P. subulata 'Tamaongalei'
Phlox subulata 'Mikado'	P. subulata 'Tamaongalei'
Phlox subulata 'Snow Queen'	P. subulata 'Maischnee'
Phodina	Callisia
Phoenix humilis	P. loureirii
Phormium colensoi	P. cookianum
Phormium cookianum 'Alpinum Purpureum'	P. tenax 'Nanum Purpureum'
Phormium 'Rainbow Chief'	P. 'Maori Chief'
Phormium 'Rainbow Maiden'	P. 'Maori Maiden'
Phormium 'Rainbow Queen'	P. 'Maori Queen'
Phormium 'Rainbow Sunrise'	P. 'Maori Sunrise'
Phormium tenax 'Rainbow Queen'	P. 'Maori Queen'
Phormium tenax 'Rainbow Sunrise'	P. 'Maori Sunrise'
Photinia glabra 'Pink Lady'	P. glabra 'Parfait'
Photinia glabra 'Rubens'	P. x fraseri 'Rubens'
Photinia glabra 'Variegata'	P. glabra 'Parfait'
Photinia serrulata	P. serratifolia
Phragmites australis giganteus	P. australis ssp altissimus
Phragmites communis	P. australis
Phygelius aequalis albus	P. aequalis 'Yellow Trumpet'
Phygelius aequalis 'Aureus'	P. aequalis 'Yellow Trumpet'
Phygelius aequalis 'Cream Trumpet'	P. aequalis 'Yellow Trumpet'
Phygelius aequalis 'Indian Chief'	P. x rectus 'African Queen'
Phygelius capensis coccineus	P. capensis
Phygelius capensis x aequalis	P. x rectus
Phygelius 'Golden Gate'	P. aequalis 'Yellow Trumpet'
Phygelius x rectus 'Winton Fanfare'	P. x rectus 'Winchester Fanfare'
Phylica pubescens	P. plumosa
Phyllanthus nivosus	Breynia disticha
Phyllitus	Asplenium
Phyllocactus biformis	Disocactus biformis
Phyllocactus eichlamii	Disocactus eichlamii
Phyllodoce aleutica ssp glanduliflora white	P. aleutica ssp glanduliflora 'Flora Slack'
Phyllodoce caerulea japonica	P. nipponica
Phyllodoce glanduliflora	P. aleutica ssp glanduliflora
Phyllodoce taxifolia	P. caerulea
Phyllostachys aurea 'Violascens'	P. violascens
Phyllostachys bambusoides Holochrysa	P. bambusoides 'Allgold'
Phyllostachys bambusoides 'Sulphurea'	P. bambusoides 'Allgold'
Phyllostachys bambusoides 'Violascens'	P. violascens
Phyllostachys congesta h	P. atrovaginata
Phyllostachys edulis f pubescens	P. edulis
Phyllostachys edulis subconvexa	P. viridiglaucescens
Phyllostachys f pubescens	P. edulis
Phyllostachys 'Henonis'	P. nigra v henonis
Phyllostachys heteroclada 'Solid Stem' misapplied	P. heteroclada 'Straight Stem'
Phyllostachys heterocycla	P. edulis v heterocycla
Phyllostachys heterocycla f pubescens	P. edulis
Phyllostachys purpurata	P. heteroclada
Phyllostachys sulphurea 'Sulphurea'	P. bambusoides 'Allgold'
Phyllostachys sulphurea v viridis 'Mitis'	P. suphurea v viridis
Phyllostachys viridis	P. suphurea v viridis
Phyodina	Callisia
Physocarpus ribesifolius 'Aureus'	P. opulifolius 'Luteus'
Physostegia Schneekrone	P. virginiana 'Crown of Snow'
Physostegia 'Snow Queen'	P. virginiana 'Summer Snow'
Physostegia speciosa	P. virginiana ssp speciosa
Physostegia virginiana ssp speciosa 'Rose Bouquet'	P. virginiana ssp speciosa 'Bouquet Rose'
Phyteuma balbisii	P. cordatum
Phyteuma comosum	Physoplexis comosa
Phyteuma halleri	P. ovatum
Phytolacca clavigera	P. polyandra
Phytolacca decandra	P. americana
Picea abies 'Excelsa'	P. abies
Picea abies 'Veitchii'	P. abies 'Gregoryana Veitchii'
Picea abies 'Will's Dwarf'	P. abies 'Wills Zwerg'
Picea glauca 'Albertiana Conica'	P. abies v albertiana 'Conica'
Picea glauca 'J.W.Daisy's White'	P. abies 'J.W.Daisy's White'
Picea kosteri 'Glauca'	P. pungens 'Koster'
Picea likiangensis v balfouriana	P. balfouriana
Picea likiangensis v purpurea	P. purpurea
Picea omorika 'Gnom'	P. x mariorika 'Gnom'
Picea pungens 'Glauca Globosa'	P. pungens 'Globosa'
Picea pungens 'Prostrata'	P. pungens 'Glauca

Synonyms

Picea sitchensis 'Papoose' — P. sitchensis 'Tenas'
Picrasma ailanthoides — P. quassioides
Pieris japonica 'Don' — P. japonica 'Pygmaea'
Pieris japonica 'Variegata' h — P. japonica 'White Rim'
Pieris japonica 'Wada's Pink' — P. japonica 'Christmas Cheer'

Pilea mollis — P. involucrata
Pilocereus senilis — Cephalocereus senilis
Pilosocereus leucocephalus — P. palmeri
Pimelea coarctata — P. prostrata
Pinellia pinnatisecta — P. tripartita
Pinguicula caudata — P. moranensis v caudata
Pinus albicaulis 'Nana' — P. albicaulis 'Noble's Dwarf'

Pinus austriaca — P. nigra ssp nigra
Pinus brutia — P. halepensis ssp brutia
Pinus cembra 'Aurea' — P. cembra 'Aureovariegata'

Pinus cembra 'Nana' — P. pumila 'Nana'
Pinus chylla — P. wallichiana
Pinus densiflora 'Ja-nome' — P. densiflora 'Oculus Draconis'

Pinus densiflora 'Tagyosho' — P. densiflora 'Umbraculifera'

Pinus excelsa — P. wallichiana
Pinus griffithii — P. wallichiana
Pinus insignis — P. radiata
Pinus leucodermis — P. heldreichii v leucodermis

Pinus magnifica — P. montezumae
Pinus monticola 'Pygmy' — P. monticola 'Raraflora'
Pinus mugo 'Carsten's Winter Gold' — P. mugo 'Winter Gold'
Pinus mugo v mughus — P. mugo v mugo
Pinus mugo v rostrata — P. mugo ssp uncinata
Pinus nigra ssp maritima — P. nigra ssp laricio
Pinus nigra v austriaca — P. nigra ssp nigra
Pinus nigra v corsicana — P. nigra ssp laricio
Pinus pumila 'Dwarf Blue' — P. pumila 'Glauca'
Pinus pumila 'Saphir' — P. parviflora 'Saphir'
Pinus sibirica — P. cembra ssp sibirica
Pinus strobus f nana — P. strobus 'Radiata'
Pinus strobus 'Nana' — P. strobus 'Radiata'
Pinus strobus 'Nivea' — P. strobus 'Alba'
Pinus sylvestris 'Edwin Hillier' — P. sylvestris 'Argentea'
Pinus sylvestris 'Jade' — P. sylvestris 'Iceni'
Pinus sylvestris 'Nana' — P. sylvestris 'Watereri'
Pinus sylvestris 'Scott's Dwarf' — P. sylvestris 'Nisbet's Gem'

Pinus thunbergiana — P. thunbergii
Pinus thunbergii 'Yatsubusa' — P. thunbergii 'Sayonara'
Pinus uncinata — P. mugo ssp uncinata
Piper excelsum — Macropiper excelsum
Piptanthus forrestii — P. nepalensis
Piptanthus laburnifolius — P. nepalensis
Pisonia brunoniana — P. umbellifera
Pittosporum 'Nanum Variegatum' — P. tobira 'Variegatum'
Pittosporum tenuifolium 'John Flanagan' — P. 'Margaret Turnbull'
Pittosporum tenuifolium 'Sunburst' — P. tenuifolium 'Eila Keightley'

Plagianthus betulinus — P. regius
Plagianthus lyallii — Hoheria lyallii
Plagiorhegma — Jeffersonia
Plantago major 'Atropurpurea' — P. major 'Rubrifolia'
Plantago major 'Bowles' Variety — P. major 'Rosularis'
Plantago rosea — P. major 'Rosularis'

Plantago uniflora — Littorella uniflora
Platanus orientalis 'Laciniata' — P. orientalis f digitata
Platanus x acerifolia — P. x hispanica
Platycerium alcicorne h — P. bifurcatum
Platycerium grande h — P. superbum
Platycladus orientalis — Thuja orientalis
Platycodon grandiflorus Mother of Pearl — P. grandiflorus 'Perlmutterschale'

Platycodon grandiflorus 'Shell Pink' — P. grandiflorus 'Perlmutterschale'

Plectranthus behrii — P. fruticosus
Plectranthus coleoides 'Marginatus' — P. forsteri 'Marginatus'
Plectranthus coleoides 'Variegatus' — P. madagascariensis 'Variegated Mintleaf'

Plectranthus Swedish ivy — P. australis
Pleioblastus chino chrysanthus — Sasa chrysantha
Pleioblastus fortunei — P. variegatus
Pleioblastus 'Gauntlettii' — P. humilus v pumilus
Pleioblastus glaber 'Albostriatus' — Sasaella masamuneana f albostriata

Pleioblastus simonii v heterophyllus — P. simonii f variegatus
Pleioblastus viridistriatus — P. auricomus
Pleione bulbocodioides Pricei Group — P. formosana Pricei Group

Pleione chunii — P. aurita
Pleione pinkepankii — P. albiflora
Pleione pogonioides h — P. speciosa
Pleione pogonioides -Rolfe — P. bulbocodioides
Pleione yunnanensis h — P. bulbocodioides 'Yunnan'

Pleomele — Dracaena
Pleroma macrantha — Tibouchina urvilleana
Plumbago capensis — P. auriculata
Plumbago indica rosea — P. indica
Plumbago larpentiae — Ceratostigma plumbaginoides

Plumbago rosea — P. indica
Plumeria acuminata — P. rubra v acuminata
Plumeria 'Singapore' — P. obtusa
Pneumatopteris — Cyclosorus
Podocarpus andinus — Prumnopitys andina
Podocarpus chilinus — P. salignus
Podocarpus cunninghamii — P. hallii
Podocarpus dacrydioides — Dacrycarpus dacrydioides

Podocarpus ferrugineus — Prumnopitys ferruginea
Podocarpus 'Golden Dwarf' — Prumnopitys ferruginea 'Golden Dwarf'

Podocarpus spicatus — Prumnopitys taxifolia
Podophyllum emodi — P. hexandrum
Podophyllum emodi v chinense — P. hexandrum v chinense
Podophyllum japonicum — Ranzania japonica
Pogonatherum paniceum — P. saccharoideum
Pogostemon patchouly — P. cablin
Poinciana gilliesii — Caesalpinia gilliesii
Poinciana pulcherrima — Caesalpinia pulcherrima
Poinciana regia — Delonix regia
Polemonium acutifolium v nipponicum — P. caeruleum v nipponicum

Polemonium 'Apricot Beauty' — P. carneum 'Apricot Delight'

Polemonium caeruleum Himalayan misapplied — P. cashmerianum
Polemonium caeruleum 'Humile' — P. 'Northern Lights'
Polemonium caeruleum v album — P. caeruleum ssp caeruleum f album

Synonyms

Polemonium caeruleum v grandiflorum	P. caeruleum ssp himalayanum
Polemonium confertum	P. viscosum
Polemonium flavum	P. foliosissimum v flavum
Polemonium foliosissimum h	P. archibaldiae
Polemonium foliosissimum v albiflorum	P. foliosissimum v alpinum
Polemonium occidentale	P. caeruleum ssp amygdalinum
Polemonium pulchellum -Salisbury	P. reptans
Polemonium pulchellum -Turczaninow	P. caeruleum
Polemonium pulcherrimum h	P. boreale
Polemonium pulcherrimum 'Tricolor' h	P. boreale
Polemonium reptans 'Album'	P. reptans 'Virginia White'
Polemonium reptans 'Dawn Flight'	P. 'Dawn Flight'
Polemonium reptans 'Lambrook Manor'	P. 'Lambrook Mauve'
Polemonium reptans 'Pink Beauty'	P. 'Pink Beauty'
Polemonium richardsonii -Graham	P. boreale
Polemonium richardsonii h	P. 'Northern Lights'
Polemonium viscosum v eximium	P. eximium
Polygala chamaebuxus 'Purpurea'	P. chamaebuxus v grandiflora
Polygala chamaebuxus 'Rhodoptera'	P. chamaebuxus v grandiflora
Polygala chamaebuxus v rhodoptera	P. chamaebuxus v grandiflora
Polygala myrtifolia 'Grandiflora'	P. x dalmaisiana
Polygonatum canaliculatum	P. biflorum
Polygonatum commutatum	P. biflorum
Polygonatum cyrtonema h	Disporopsis pernyi
Polygonatum 'Falcon'	P. humile
Polygonatum giganteum	P. biflorum
Polygonatum latifolium	P. hirtum
Polygonatum multiflorum giganteum h	P. biflorum
Polygonatum multiflorum h	P. x hybridum
Polygonatum odoratum 'Grace Barker'	P. x hybridum 'Striatum'
Polygonatum odoratum v pluriflorum 'Variegatum' misapplied	P. falcatum 'Variegatum'
Polygonatum officinale	P. odoratum
Polygonatum pluriflorum	P. graminifolium
Polygonatum pumilum	P. falcatum
Polygonatum x hybridum 'Variegatum'	P. x hybridum 'Striatum'
Polygonum affine	Persicaria affinis
Polygonum amplexicaule	Persicaria amplexicaulis
Polygonum aubertii	Fallopia baldschuanica
Polygonum baldschuanicum	Fallopia baldschuanica
Polygonum bistorta	Persicaria bistorta
Polygonum campanulatum	Persicaria campanulatus
Polygonum capitatum	Persicaria capitata
Polygonum carneum	Persicaria bistorta ssp carnea
Polygonum compactum	Fallopia japonica v compacta
Polygonum cuspidatum	Fallopia japonica
Polygonum equisetiforme h	P. scoparium
Polygonum macrophyllum	Persicaria macrophylla
Polygonum milletii	Persicaria milletii
Polygonum molle	Persicaria mollis
Polygonum multiflorum	Fallopia multiflora
Polygonum odoratum	Persicaria odorata
Polygonum orientale	Persicaria orientalis
Polygonum polystachyum	Persicaria wallichii
Polygonum reynoutria	Fallopia japonica v compacta
Polygonum runciforme	Persicaria runcinata
Polygonum sphaerostachyum	Persicaria macrophylla

Polygonum tenuicaule	Persicaria tenuicaulis
Polygonum vaccinifolium	Persicaria vaccinifolia
Polygonum virginianum	Persicaria virginiana
Polypodium australe	P. cambricum
Polypodium vulgare 'Crispum Cristatum'	P. vulgare 'Congestum Cristatum'
Polypodium vulgare 'Jean Taylor'	P. vulgare 'Congestum Cristatum'
Polypodium vulgare 'Longicaudatum'	P. glycyrrhiza 'Longicaudatum'
Polystichum aculeatum 'Pulcherrimum'	P. setiferum 'Pulcherrimum Bevis'
Polystichum caryotideum	Cyrtomium caryotideum
Polystichum falcatum	Cyrtomium falcatum
Polystichum fortunei	Cyrtomium fortunei
Polystichum proliferum h	P. setiferum Acutilobum Group
Polystichum setiferum angulare	P. setiferum
Polystichum setiferum Percristatum Group	P. setiferum 'Cristatogracile'
Polystichum setiferum 'Plumosodensum'	P. setiferum 'Plumosomultilobum'
Polystichum setiferum Proliferum Group	P. setiferum Acutilobum Group
Polyxena pygmaea	P. ensifolia
Pontederia lanceolata	P. cordata v lancifolia
Populus alba 'Bolleana'	P. alba f pyramidalis
Populus alba Rocket	P. alba 'Raket'
Populus gileadensis	P. x candicans
Populus glauca	P. jacquemontii v glauca
Populus nigra 'Afghanica'	P. nigra 'Thevestina'
Populus nigra 'Italica Aurea'	P. nigra 'Lombardy Gold'
Populus nigra 'Pyramidalis'	P. nigra v italica
Populus tacamahaca	P. balsamifera
Populus 'Tacatricho 32'	P. 'Balsam Spire'
Populus tremula 'Fastigiata'	P. tremula 'Erecta'
Populus 'TT 32'	P. 'Balsam Spire'
Populus violascens	P. lasiocarpa v tibetica
Populus x canadensis 'Serotina Aurea'	P. x canadensis 'Aurea'
Populus x euroamericana	P. x canadensis
Populus x jackii	P. x candicans
Populus x jackii 'Gileadensis'	P. x candicans
Potentilla ambigua	P. cuneata
Potentilla arbuscula -D Don	P. fruticosa v arbuscula - (D Don) Maxim.
Potentilla arbuscula h	P. fruticosa 'Elizabeth'
Potentilla argyrophylla	P. atrosanguinea v argyrophylla
Potentilla atrosanguinea v leucochroa	P. atrosanguinea v argyrophylla
Potentilla crantzii 'Nana'	P. crantzii 'Pygmaea'
Potentilla davurica v mandschurica h	P. fruticosa 'Manchu'
Potentilla davurica 'Veitchii'	P. fruticosa v veitchii
Potentilla 'Everest'	P. fruticosa 'Mount Everest'
Potentilla fragiformis	P. megalantha
Potentilla fruticosa 'Argentea Nana'	P. fruticosa 'Beesii'
Potentilla fruticosa 'Blink'	P. fruticosa 'Princess'
Potentilla fruticosa 'Donard Orange'	P. fruticosa 'Donard Gold'
Potentilla fruticosa 'Farreri'	P. fruticosa 'Gold Drop'
Potentilla fruticosa 'Farreri Prostrata'	P. fruticosa v pyrenaica
Potentilla fruticosa Goldkugel	P. fruticosa 'Gold Drop'
Potentilla fruticosa 'Knap Hill Buttercup'	P. fruticosa 'Knap Hill'
Potentilla fruticosa Moonlight	P. fruticosa 'Maanelys'
Potentilla fruticosa 'Nana Argentea'	P. fruticosa 'Beesii'
Potentilla fruticosa 'Nugget'	P. fruticosa 'Dart's

Synonyms

Potentilla fruticosa v arbuscula h

Potentilla fruticosa v dahurica 'Hersii'
Potentilla fulgens
Potentilla Glory of Nancy
Potentilla 'Gold Clogs'
Potentilla gracilis ssp nuttallii
Potentilla 'Mandschurica'
Potentilla 'Monarch's Velvet'

Potentilla nepalensis 'Craigieburn Cochineal'
Potentilla parvifolia 'Gold Drop'
Potentilla 'Pyrenaica'
Potentilla recta 'Citrina'
Potentilla recta 'Macrantha'
Potentilla tabernaemontani
Potentilla ternata

Potentilla thurberi 'White Queen'
Potentilla tommasiniana
Potentilla tormentilla
Potentilla tridentata
Potentilla verna
Potentilla villosa
Potentilla willmottiae

Poterium
Pothos celatocaulis

Pratia treadwellii

Preslia cervina
Primula acaulis
Primula allionii 'Aire Waves'
Primula allionii 'Clarence Elliott'

Primula allionii 'Elliott's Large'
Primula allionii 'Elliott's Variety'
Primula allionii 'Guiseppi's Form'
Primula allionii Hartside 383/12

Primula allionii 'Hemswell Blush'
Primula allionii 'Hemswell Ember'
Primula allionii -JCA 4161/21

Primula allionii -JCA 4161/22

Primula allionii -KRW
Primula allionii 'Pink Aire'
Primula allionii x pedemontana
Primula alpicola v luna
Primula 'Altaica'
Primula altaica grandiflora
Primula amoena
Primula anisodora
Primula auricula 'Guildersome Green'

Primula auricula 'Kath Dryden'
Primula auricula ssp balbisii
Primula Barnhaven Gold-laced Group

Primula Barnhaven Reds
Primula beluensis
Primula 'Bewerley White'

Nugget'
P. fruticosa 'Elizabeth'
P. fruticosa 'Snowflake'
P. lineata
P. recta 'Gloire de Nancy'
P. aurea 'Goldklumpen'
P. gracilis v glabrata
P. fruticosa 'Manchu'
P. thurberi 'Monarch's Velvet'

P. 'Craigieburn Cochineal'
P. fruticosa 'Gold Drop'
P. fruticosa v pyrenaica
P. recta pallida
P. recta 'Warrenii'
P. neumanniana
P. aurea ssp chrysocraspeda
P. 'White Queen'
P. cinerea
P. erecta
Sibbaldiopsis tridentata
P. neumanniana
P. crantzii
P. nepalensis 'Miss Willmott'
Sanguisorba
Rhaphidophora celatocaulis
Pratia angulata 'Treadwellii'
Mentha cervina
P. vulgaris
P. 'Aire Waves'
P. 'Clarence Elliott' (allionii hybrid)
P. allionii 'Edinburgh'
P. allionii 'Edinburgh'
P. allionii 'Mrs Dyas'
P. allionii 'Gilderdale Glow'
P. 'Hemswell Blush'
P. 'Hemswell Ember'
P. allionii 'Travellers' -JCA 4161/21
P. allionii 'Jenny' -JCA 4161/22
P. allionii 'Ken's Seedling'
P. 'Pink Aire'
P. x sendtneri
P. alpicola v alpicola
P. elatior ssp meyeri
P. elatior ssp meyeri
P. elatior ssp meyeri
P. wilsonii v anisodora
P. auricula 'Geldersome Green'
P. allionii 'Kath Dryden'
P. auricula ssp ciliata
P. Gold-laced Group - Barnhaven
P. Tartan Reds Group
P. x pubescens 'Freedom'
P. x pubescens 'Bewerley White'

Primula bhutanica

Primula bileckii
Primula 'Boothman's Ruby'

Primula bulleyana ssp beesiana
Primula crispa
Primula 'Dianne'
Primula 'Double Lilac'
Primula edgeworthii
Primula 'Freedom'
Primula 'Garryard Guinevere'
Primula glaucescens ssp calycina

Primula glutinosa Allioni
Primula gracilipes 'Major'
Primula gracilipes 'Minor'
Primula halleri 'Longiflora'
Primula helodoxa
Primula hyacinthina

Primula ianthina
Primula littoniana
Primula longiflora
Primula marginata 'Holden Clough'

Primula marginata 'Hyacinthia'
Primula melanops

Primula minima
Primula minima
Primula minima
Primula minima x glutinosa
Primula mistassinica v macropoda
Primula nepalensis
Primula nivalis -Pallas
Primula nutans -Delavay
Primula obconica 'Apricot Brandy'

Primula petiolaris -LS&H 19856
Primula praenitens
Primula 'Quaker's Bonnet'
Primula 'Ravenglass Vermilion'
Primula rosea 'Delight'

Primula rotundifolia
Primula sibirica
Primula sibthorpii
Primula sinoplantaginea

Primula sinopurpurea

Primula smithiana
Primula 'Snow Carpet'
Primula 'Snow Cushion'
Primula sorachiana
Primula uralensis
Primula vernalis
Primula villosa v cottica
Primula viscosa Allioni
Primula vulgaris double white
Primula vulgaris green-flowered
Primula wardii
Primula warshenewskiana

P. whitei 'Sherriff's Variety'
P. x forsteri 'Bileckii'
P. x pubescens 'Boothman's Variety'
P. beesiana
P. glomerata
P. x forsteri 'Dianne'
P. vulgaris 'Lilacina Plena'
P. nana
P. x pubescens 'Freedom'
P. 'Guinevere'
P. glaucescens ssp glaucescens
P. allionii
P. bracteata
P. petiolaris
P. halleri
P. prolifera
P. bellidifolia ssp hyacinthina
P. prolifera
P. vialii
P. halleri
P. marginata 'Holden Variety'
P. 'Hyacinthia'
P. chionantha ssp melanops
P. x forsteri
P. x truncata
P. x vochinensis
P. x floerkeana
P. laurentiana
P. tanneri ssp nepalensis
P. chionantha
P. flaccida
P. obconica 'Appleblossom'
P. 'Redpoll'
P. sinensis
P. vulgaris 'Lilacina Plena'
P. 'Inverewe'
P. rosea 'Micia Visser de Geer'
P. roxburghii
P. erythra
P. nutans -Georgi
P. vulgaris ssp sibthorpii
P. chionantha ssp sinoplantaginea
P. chionantha ssp sinopurpurea
P. prolifera
P. 'Schneekissen'
P. 'Schneekissen'
P. yuparensis
P. veris ssp macrocalyx
P. vulgaris
P. villosa
P. latifolia
P. vulgaris 'Alba Plena'
P. vulgaris 'Viridis'
P. involucrata
P. involucrata ssp yargonensis

Synonyms

Primula 'Wedgwood'	P. x pubescens 'Wedgwood'
Primula 'Windrush'	P. x berninae 'Windrush'
Primula 'Winter White'	P. 'Gigha'
Primula 'Wisley Crimson'	P. 'Wisley Red'
Primula x arctotis	P. x pubescens
Primula x chunglenta	P. x chungensis x pulverulenta
Primula x deschmannii	P. x vochinensis
Primula x flagellicaulis	P. x polyantha
Primula x juliana	P. x pruhonicensis
Primula x pubescens 'Carmen'	P. x pubescens 'Boothman's Variety'
Primula x serrata	P. x vochinensis
Primula x steinii	P. x forsteri
Primula x variabilis	P. x polyantha
Primula yargonensis	P. involucrata ssp yargonensis
Proboscidea jussieui	P. louisianica
Proboscidea proboscidea	P. louisianica
Prosartes	Disporum
Prosopis chilensis	P. glandulosa
Prostanthera rotundifolia 'Chelsea Girl'	P. rotundifolia rosea
Protea barbata	P. speciosa
Protea barbigera	P. magnifica
Protea mellifera	P. repens
Protea minor	P. longifolia
Prumnopitys elegans	P. andina
Prunella grandiflora 'Little Red Riding Hood'	P. grandiflora 'Rotkappchen'
Prunella incisa	P. vulgaris
Prunella x webbiana	P. grandiflora
Prunus amygdalus	P. dulcis
Prunus armeniaca 'De Nancy'	P. armeniaca 'Gros Peche'
Prunus 'Asano'	P. 'Geraldinae'
Prunus avium 'Birchenhayes'	P. avium 'Early Birchenhayes'
Prunus avium 'Bottlers'	P. avium 'Preserving'
Prunus avium 'Cherokee'	P. avium 'Lapins'
Prunus avium 'Grandiflora'	P. avium 'Plena'
Prunus avium 'May Duke'	P. x gondouinii 'May Duke'
Prunus avium 'Merton Reward'	P. x gondouinii 'Merton Reward'
Prunus avium 'Napoleon'	P. avium 'Bigarreau Napoleon'
Prunus 'Blaze'	P. cerasifera 'Nigra'
Prunus 'Blushing Bride'	P. 'Shogetsu'
Prunus capuli	P. salicifolia
Prunus 'Cheals' Weeping'	P. 'Kiku-shidare-zakura'
Prunus conradinae	P. hirtipes
Prunus domestica 'Cropper'	P. domestica 'Laxton's Cropper'
Prunus domestica 'Delicious'	P. domestica 'Laxton's Delicious'
Prunus domestica 'Denniston's Superb'	P. domestica 'Imperial Gage'
Prunus domestica 'Early Orleans'	P. domestica 'Monsieur Hatif'
Prunus domestica 'Early Prolific'	P. domestica 'Rivers' Early Prolific'
Prunus domestica 'Early Rivers'	P. domestica 'Rivers' Early Prolific'
Prunus domestica 'Laxton's Bountiful'	P. domestica 'Bountiful'
Prunus domestica 'Quetsche d'Alsace'	P. domestica German Prune Group
Prunus domestica 'Reine Claude Doree'	P. domestica Greengage Group
Prunus domestica ssp insititia	P. insititia
Prunus domestica 'Willingham'	P. domestica 'Willingham Gage'(Greengage Group)
Prunus glandulosa 'Rosea Plena'	P. glandulosa 'Sinensis'
Prunus 'Hillieri Spire'	P. 'Spire'
Prunus 'Hisakura'	P. 'Choshu hizakura'
Prunus Hollywood	P. 'Trailblazer'
Prunus insititia 'Golden Bullace'	P. insititia 'White Bullace'
Prunus insititia 'King of Damsons'	P. insititia 'Bradley's King Damson'
Prunus insititia 'Mirabelle Petite'	P. insititia 'Mirabelle de Metz'
Prunus insititia 'Shropshire Damson'	P. insititia 'Prune Damson'
Prunus Korean Hill Cherry	P. x verecunda
Prunus kurilensis	P. nipponica v kurilensis
Prunus laurocerasus 'Aureovariegata'	P. laurocerasus 'Taff's Golden Gleam'
Prunus laurocerasus Green Carpet	P. laurocerasus 'Grunerteppich'
Prunus laurocerasus 'Magnoliifolia'	P. laurocerasus 'Latifolia'
Prunus laurocerasus 'Marbled White'	P. laurocerasus 'Castlewellan'
Prunus 'Mount Fuji'	P. 'Shirotae'
Prunus mume 'Beni-shidori'	P. mume 'Beni-chidori'
Prunus mume 'Omoi-no-wac'	P. mume 'Omoi-no-mama'
Prunus myrobalana	P. cerasifera Myrobalan Group
Prunus padus 'Grandiflora'	P. padus 'Watereri'
Prunus 'Pink Star'	P. pendula 'Stellata'
Prunus pissardii	P. cerasifera 'Pissardii'
Prunus 'Pissardii Nigra'	P. cerasifera 'Nigra'
Prunus 'Sekiyama'	P. 'Kanzan'
Prunus serrula v tibetica	P. serrula
Prunus serrulata 'Erecta'	P. 'Amanogawa'
Prunus serrulata 'Grandiflora'	P. 'Ukon'
Prunus serrulata 'Longipes'	P. 'Okumiyako'
Prunus serrulata 'Miyak'	P. 'Okumiyako'
Prunus serrulata 'Rosea'	P. 'Kiku-shidare-zakura'
Prunus serrulata v pubescens	P. x verecunda
Prunus serrulata v spontanea	P. jamasakura
Prunus 'Shidare-zakura'	P. 'Kiku-shidare-zakura'
Prunus 'Shimidsu'	P. 'Shogetsu'
Prunus 'Shimizu-zakura'	P. 'Okumiyako'
Prunus 'Takasago'	P. x sieboldii 'Caespitosa'
Prunus tibetica	P. serrula
Prunus 'Wood's Variety'	P. cerasifera 'Woodsii'
Prunus x cistena 'Crimson Dwarf'	P. x cistena
Prunus x hillieri 'Spire'	P. 'Spire'
Prunus x subhirtella 'Pendula' h	P. pendula 'Pendula Rosea'
Prunus x subhirtella'Pendula Rubra'	P. pendula 'Pendula Rubra'
Prunus x subhirtella 'Stellata'	P. pendula 'Stellata'
Prunus x subhirtella v ascendens	P. pendula v ascendens
Prunus x yedoensis 'Pendula'	P. x yedoensis 'Shidare-yoshino'
Prunus x yedoensis 'Perpendens'	P. x yedoensis 'Shidare-yoshino'
Prunus yamadae	P. incisa f yamadae
Prunus 'Yoshino'	P. x yedoensis

Synonyms

Prunus 'Yoshino Pendula' — P. x yedoensis 'Shidare-yoshino'

Pseuderanthemum atropurpureum 'Tricolor' — P. atropurpureum 'Variegatum'

Pseudofumaria alba — Corydalis ochroleuca
Pseudofumaria lutea — Corydalis lutea
Pseudofumaria ochroleuca — Corydalis ochroleuca
Pseudogynoxis chenopodiodes — Senecio confusus
Pseudolarix kaempferi — P. amabilis
Pseudomuscari — Muscari
Pseudorhipsalis alata — Disocactus alatus
Pseudorhipsalis macrantha — Disocactus macranthus
Pseudosasa amabilis h — Arundinaria tecta
Pseudosasa japonica 'Variegata' — P. japonica 'Akebonosuji'
Pseudotsuga taxifolia — P. menziesii
Pseudozygocactus epiphylloides — Hatiora epiphylloides
Psidium cattleyanum — P. littorale v longipes
Psygmorchis pusilla — Oncidium pusillum
Pteracanthus — Strobilanthes
Pterocactus kuntzei — P. tuberosus
Pterocephalus parnassi — P. perennis
Ptilotrichum spinosum — Alyssum spinosum
Ptilotrichum spinosum 'Roseum' — Alyssum spinosum 'Roseum'

Ptychosperma alexandrae — Archontophoenix alexandrae

Pueraria hirsuta — P. lobata
Pueraria thunbergiana — P. lobata
Pulmonaria angustifolia 'Beth's Pink' — P. 'Beth's Pink'
Pulmonaria angustifolia 'Rubra' — P. rubra
Pulmonaria azurea — P. angustifolia ssp azurea
Pulmonaria 'Highdown' — P. 'Lewis Palmer'
Pulmonaria longifolia 'Coen Jansen' — P. longifolia 'Ankum'
Pulmonaria longifolia 'Lewis Palmer' — P. 'Lewis Palmer'
Pulmonaria 'Mawson's Variety' — P. 'Mawson's Blue'
Pulmonaria montana — P. mollis
Pulmonaria officinalis rubra — P. rubra
Pulmonaria rubra v alba — P. rubra v albocorollata
Pulmonaria saccharata 'Blauhimmel' — P. 'Blauhimmel'
Pulmonaria saccharata 'Picta' — P. saccharata
Pulmonaria saccharata 'Sissinghurst White' — P. officinalis 'Sissinghurst White'

Pulmonaria vallarsae 'Margery Fish' — P. 'Margery Fish'
Pulsatilla alpina ssp sulphurea — P. alpina ssp apiifolia
Pulsatilla vulgaris 'Red Clock' — P. vulgaris 'Rode Klokke'
Pulsatilla vulgaris Rote Glokke — P. vulgaris 'Rode Klokke'
Pulsatilla vulgaris WhiteSwan — P. vulgaris 'Weisse Schwan'

Puschkinia libanotica — P. scilloides v libanotica
Puya caerulea — P. coerulea
Puya violacea — P. coerulea v violacea
Pygmaea — Chionohebe
Pyracantha gibbsii — P. atalantioides
Pyracantha gibbsii 'Flava' — P. atalantioides 'Aurea'
Pyracantha 'Golden Sun' — P. 'Soleil d'Or'
Pyracantha 'John Stedman' — P. 'Stedman's'
Pyracantha 'Monrovia' — P. coccinea 'Lalandei'
Pyracantha 'Orange Giant' — P. coccinea 'Kasan'
Pyracantha 'Waterer's Orange' — P. 'Watereri'
Pyracantha x watereri — P. 'Watereri'
Pyracantha 'Yellow Sun' — P. 'Soleil d'Or'
Pyrethropsis atlantica — Rhodanthemum atlanticum

Pyrethropsis gayana — Rhodanthemum gayanum

Pyrethropsis hosmariense — Rhodanthemum hosmariense
Pyrethrum 'Brenda' — Tanacetum coccineum 'Brenda'
Pyrethrum coccineum — Tanacetum coccineum
Pyrethrum parthenium — Tanacetum parthenium
Pyrethrum ptarmiciforum — Tanacetum ptarmiciflorum
Pyrethrum radicans — Leucanthemopsis pectinata
Pyrethrum roseum — Tanacetum coccineum
Pyrostegia ignea — P. venusta
Pyrrhocactus crispus — Neoporteria crispa
Pyrus communis 'Chalk' — P. communis 'Crawford'
Pyrus communis 'Fertility Improved' — P. communis 'Improved Fertility'
Pyrus communis 'Sweet Huffcap' — P. communis 'Hellen's Early'
Pyrus communis 'Triumph' — P. communis 'Packham's Triumph'
Pyrus japonica — Chaenomeles speciosa
Pyrus pyrifolia '20th Century' — P. pyrifolia 'Nijisseiki'
Quamoclit coccinea — Ipomoea coccinea
Quamoclit lobata — Ipomoea lobata
Quamoclit pennata — Ipomoea quamoclit
Quercus aegilops — Q. macrolepis
Quercus borealis — Q. rubra
Quercus cerris 'Variegata' — Q. cerris 'Argenteovariegata'
Quercus conferta — Q. frainetto
Quercus fruticosa — Q. lusitanica -Lamarck
Quercus glabra — Lithocarpus glaber
Quercus incana -Roxburgh — Q. leucotrichophora
Quercus pedunculata — Q. robur
Quercus petraea 'Laciniata' — Q. petraea 'Insecata'
Quercus prinus -Engelm. — Q. montana
Quercus pumila -Michaux — Q. prinus -Linnaeus
Quercus pumila -Walt. — Q. phellos
Quercus serrata — Q. acutissima
Quercus sessiliflora — Q. petraea
Quercus x hispanica — Q. x lucombeana
Quercus x hispanica 'Lucombeana' — Q. x lucombeana 'William Lucombe'

Quiongzhuea tumidinoda — Chimonobambusa tumidissinoda

Racosperma — Acacia
Ramonda pyrenaica — R. myconi
Ranunculus bulbosus farreri — R. bulbosus 'F.M.Burton'
Ranunculus bulbosus 'Speciosus Plenus' — R. constantinopolitanus 'Plenus'
Ranunculus ficaria anemone centred — R. ficaria 'Collarette'
Ranunculus ficaria 'Bowles Double' — R. ficaria 'Double Bronze'
Ranunculus ficaria 'Bowles Double' — R. ficaria 'Picton's Double'
Ranunculus ficaria 'Cupreus' — R. ficaria v aurantiacus
Ranunculus ficaria double cream — R. ficaria 'Double Mud'
Ranunculus ficaria double yellow — R. ficaria flore-pleno
Ranunculus ficaria 'E.A.Bowles' — R. ficaria 'Collarette'
Ranunculus ficaria 'Holly' — R. ficaria 'Holly Green'
Ranunculus ficaria ssp major — R. ficaria ssp chrysocephalus
Ranunculus gouanii 'Plenus' — R. constantinopolitanus 'Plenus'
Ranunculus rupestris — R. spicatus
Ranunculus speciosus 'Flore Pleno' — R. constantinopolitanus

Synonyms

Ranunculus speciosus 'Plenus' — R. constantinopolitanus 'Plenus'
Raoulia australis h — R. hookeri
Raoulia leontopodium — Leucogenes leontopodium
Raoulia lutescens — R. australis Lutescens Group -Hooker
Raoulia x Leucogenes — x Leucoraoulia
Raoulia x loganii — x Leucoraoulia loganii
Raphidophora — Rhaphidophora
Rebutia muscula — R. fiebrigii
Rebutia pulchra — R. rauschii
Rebutia violaciflora — R. minuscula
Rechsteineria — Sinningia
Rechsteineria leucotricha — Sinningia canescens
Rehmannia angulata — R. elata
Reinwardtia tetragyna — R. indica
Reinwardtia trigyna — R. indica
Restio subverticillatus — Ischyrolepis subverticillata
Reynoutria — Fallopia
Rhamnus alaternus 'Variegata' — R. alaternus 'Argenteovariegata'
Rhaphidophora pinnata — R. celatocaulis
Rhaphiolepis japonica — R. umbellata
Rhaphiolepis ovata — R. umbellata
Rhaphithamnus cyanocarpus — R. spinosus
Rhapis flabelliformis — R. excelsa
Rhazya orientalis — Amsonia orientalis
Rhektophyllum — Cercestis
Rheum 'Ace of Spades' — R. 'Ace of Hearts'
Rheum emodi — R. australe
Rheum palmatum 'Atropurpureum' — R. palmatum 'Atrosanguineum'
Rheum x cultorum — R. x hybridum
Rhipsalidopsis gaertneri — Hatiora gaertneri
Rhipsalidopsis rosea — Hatiora rosea
Rhipsalis cassytha — R. baccifera
Rhipsalis tucumanensis — R. floccosa
Rhodanthemum gayanum 'Flamingo' — R. gayanum
Rhodiola crassipes — R. wallichiana
Rhodiola himalensis — R. 'Keston'
Rhodiola pachyclados — Sedum pachyclados
Rhodocactus grandifolius — Pereskia grandifolia
Rhodochiton volubilis — R. atrosanguineus
Rhododendron 'A.Bedford' — R. 'Arthur Bedford'
Rhododendron 'A.J.Ivens' — R. 'Arthur J.Ivens'
Rhododendron adenophorum — R. adenogynum Adenophorum Group
Rhododendron adroserum USDAPI 52910 — R. lukiangense R11275
Rhododendron aeruginosum — R. campanulatum ssp aeruginosum
Rhododendron agapetum — R. kyawii Agapetum Group
Rhododendron 'Analin' — R. 'Anuschka'
Rhododendron apodectum — R. dichroanthum ssp apodectum
Rhododendron 'Appleblossom' — R. 'Ho-o'
Rhododendron 'Arctic Tern' — x Ledodendron 'Arctic Tern'
Rhododendron bakeri — R. cumberlandense
Rhododendron 'Balsaminiflorum' — R. indicum 'Balsaminiflorum'
Rhododendron bauhiniiflorum — R. triflorum v bauhiniiflorum

Rhododendron beanianum compact form — R. piercei
Rhododendron bergii — R. augustinii ssp rubrum
Rhododendron Blaue Donau — R. 'Blue Danube'
Rhododendron 'Blue Steel' — R. impeditum 'Blue Steel'
Rhododendron brachyanthum -L&S 2764 — R. glaucophyllum v glaucophyllum L&S 2764
Rhododendron brachysiphon — R. maddenii ssp maddenii
Rhododendron bullatum — R. edgeworthii
Rhododendron calostrotum ssp riparium Rock's form R 178 — R. saluense ssp r riparioides R 178
Rhododendron calostrotum ssp riparium USDAPQ 03954/R 18453 — R. saluense ssp riparioides USDAPQ 03954/R 18453
Rhododendron caloxanthum — R. campylocarpum ssp caloxanthum
Rhododendron campylogynum 'Album' — R. 'Leucanthemum'
Rhododendron campylogynum 'Beryl Taylor' — R. 'Beryl Taylor'
Rhododendron campylogynum v leucanthemum — R. 'Leucanthemum'
Rhododendron cardiobasis — R. orbiculare ssp cardiobasis
Rhododendron carolinianum — R. minus v minus Carolinianum Group
Rhododendron 'Centennial' — R. 'Washington State Centennial'
Rhododendron chaetomallum — R. haematodes ssp chaetomallum
Rhododendron chameunum — R. saluense ssp chameunum
Rhododendron chapaense — R. maddenii ssp crassum
Rhododendron chasmanthum — R. augustinii ssp chasmanthum
Rhododendron 'Checkmate' — R. 'Checkmate' (PJM Group)
Rhododendron 'Christmas Cheer' — R. 'Ima-shojo'
Rhododendron chrysanthum — R. aureum
Rhododendron chryseum — R. rupicola v chryseum
Rhododendron chrysomanicum — R. Chrysomanicum Group
Rhododendron ciliatum 'Multiflorum' — R. 'Multiflorum'
Rhododendron ciliicalyx ssp lyi — R. lyi
Rhododendron coelicum F 21830 — R. pocophorum v pocophorum F 21830
Rhododendron concatenans — R. cinnabarinum ssp xanthocodon Concatenans Group
Rhododendron 'Congo' — R. 'Robin Hill Congo'
Rhododendron 'Conroy' — R. cinnabarinum 'Conroy'
Rhododendron cookeanum — R. sikangense Cookeanum Group
Rhododendron Cornish Early Red Group — R. Smithii Group
Rhododendron 'Cornish Red' — R. Smithii Group
Rhododendron 'Cottage Garden's Pride' — R. 'Mrs G W Leak'
Rhododendron 'County of York' — R. 'Catalode'
Rhododendron crassum — R. maddenii ssp crassum
Rhododendron cremastum — R. campylogynum Cremastum Group
Rhododendron 'Crest' (Hawk Group) — R. 'Crest'
Rhododendron 'Crimson Glory' — R. 'Natalie Coe Vitetti'
Rhododendron 'Crimson Glory' — R. 'Natalie Coe Vitetti'
Rhododendron cubittii — R. veitchianum Cubittii

Synonyms

Rhododendron cucullatum — R. roxieanum v cucullatum Group

Rhododendron 'Cunningham's Sulphur' — R. caucasicum 'Cunningham's Sulphur'

Rhododendron 'Damaris Logan' — R. 'Logan Damaris'

Rhododendron dasycladum — R. selense ssp dasycladum

Rhododendron dauricum 'Album' — R. dauricum 'Hokkaido'

Rhododendron 'Daybreak' — R. 'Kirin'

Rhododendron degronianum 'Metternianum' — R. degronianum ssp heptamerum v kyomaruense

Rhododendron delavayi — R. arboreum ssp delavayi

Rhododendron desquamatum — R. rubiginosum Desquamatum Group

Rhododendron 'Diamant Purpur' — R. Diamant Group purple

Rhododendron 'Diamant Rot' — R. Diamant Group red

Rhododendron diaprepes — R. decorum ssp diaprepes

Rhododendron dictyotum — R. traillianum v dictyotum

Rhododendron didymum — R. sanguineum v didymum

Rhododendron discolor — R. fortunei ssp discolor

Rhododendron doshongense — R. agganiphum v agganiphum Doshongense Group

Rhododendron drumonium — R. telmateium

Rhododendron dryophyllum -Balfour & Forrest — R. phaeochrysum v phaeochrysum

Rhododendron dryophyllum h — R. phaeochrysum v levistratum

Rhododendron 'Eastern Fire' — R. kaempferi 'Eastern Fire'

Rhododendron Electra Group — R. augustinii Electra Group

Rhododendron 'Elizabeth Jenny' — R. 'Creeping Jenny'

Rhododendron eriogynum — R. facetum

Rhododendron eritimum — R. anthosphaerum

Rhododendron erubescens — R. oreodoxa v fargesii Erubescens Group

Rhododendron euchaites — R. neriifolium ssp neriifolium Euchaites Group

Rhododendron eudoxum v eudoxum R10950 — R. temenium v mesopolium R10950

Rhododendron eximium — R. falconeri ssp eximium

Rhododendron exquisitum — R. oreotrephes Exquisitum Group

Rhododendron faberi ssp prattii — R. prattii

Rhododendron 'Falcon' — R. 'Hawk Falcon' (Hawk Group)

Rhododendron 'Fanny' — R. 'Pucella'

Rhododendron fargesii — R. oreodoxa v fargesii

Rhododendron fauriei — R. brachycarpum ssp fauriei

Rhododendron fictolacteum — R. rex ssp fictolacteum

Rhododendron fimbriatum — R. hippophaeoides v hippophaeoides Fimbriatum Group

Rhododendron 'Firefly' — R. 'Hexe'

Rhododendron forrestii ssp forrestii — R. chamaethomsonii v chamaethomsonii F

Rhododendron fortunei 'Mrs Butler' — R. fortunei 'Sir Charles Butler'

Rhododendron 'Fred Wynniatt Stanway' — R. 'Stanway'

Rhododendron giganteum — R. protistum v giganteum

Rhododendron 'Glenn Dale Adorable' — R. 'Adorable'

Rhododendron globigerum — R. alutaceum v alutaceum Globigerum Group

Rhododendron glomerulatum — R. yungningense Glomerulatum Group

Rhododendron 'Gold Crown' — R. 'Gold Krone'

Rhododendron 'Goldball' — R. 'Christopher Wren'

Rhododendron 'Golden Bouquet' — R. 'Goldbukett'

Rhododendron 'Golden Horn Persimmon' — R. 'Persimmon'

Rhododendron 'Golden Sunlight' — R. 'Directeur Moerlands'

Rhododendron gratum — R. basilicum

Rhododendron gymnocarpum — R. microgynum Gymnocarpum Group

Rhododendron haematodes ssp chaetomallum KW21077 — R. coelicum KWW 21077

Rhododendron 'Hardijzer's Beauty' — R. 'Hardijzer Beauty'

Rhododendron hardingii — R. annae Hardingii Group

Rhododendron hardyi — R. augustinii ssp hardyi

Rhododendron headfortianum — R. taggianum Headfortianum Group

Rhododendron heliolepis v fumidum — R. heliolepis v heliolepis

Rhododendron hemidartum — R. pocophorum v hemidartum

Rhododendron heptamerum — R. degronianum ssp heptamerum

Rhododendron 'Hino-scarlet' — R. 'Campfire'

Rhododendron hippophaeoides 'Bei-ma-shan' — R. hippophaeoides 'Haba-shan'

Rhododendron 'Hot Shot' — R. 'Girard's Hot Shot'

Rhododendron houlstonii — R. fortunei ssp discolor Houlstonii Group

Rhododendron hylaeum -KW 6401 — R. faucium -KW 6401

Rhododendron hypenanthum — R. anthopogon ssp hypenanthum

Rhododendron hypoglaucum — R. argyrophyllum ssp hypoglaucum

Rhododendron hypoglaucum 'Heane Wood' — R. argyrophyllum ssp hypoglaucum 'Heane Wood'

Rhododendron 'I.M.S' — R. 'Irene Stead'

Rhododendron 'Iceberg' — R. 'Lodauric Iceberg'

Rhododendron 'Icecrean Flavour' — R. 'Flavour'

Rhododendron 'Icecrean Vanilla' — R. 'Vanilla'

Rhododendron impeditum 'Blue Steel' — R. fastigiatum 'Blue Steel'

Rhododendron impeditum 'Moerheim' — R. 'Moerheim'

Rhododendron imperator — R. uniflorum v imperator

Rhododendron indicum v eriocarpum — R. 'Gumpo'

Rhododendron 'Indigo Diamant' — R. Diamant Group indigo

Rhododendron iodes — R. alutaceum v iodes

Rhododendron irroratum -R 72 — R. lukiangense -R 72

Rhododendron iteaphyllum — R. formosum v formosum Iteaphyllum Group

Rhododendron 'J.M. de Montague' — R. 'The Hon. Jean Marie de Montague'

Rhododendron japonicum (A.Gray) Valcken

Rhododendron japonicum v japonicum - 21723 — R. molle ssp japonicum

Synonyms

Schneider

Rhododendron japonicum v pentamerum

Rhododendron 'Jean Mary Montague'

Rhododendron 'Jenny'
Rhododendron 'Jervis Bay' (Hawk Group)
Rhododendron kaempferi 'Damio'
Rhododendron kaempferi 'Firefly'
Rhododendron keleticum

Rhododendron Kewense Group
Rhododendron 'King George' -Loder
Rhododendron kingianum

Rhododendron kiusianum'Amoenum'
Rhododendron 'Koichiro Wada'

Rhododendron kotschyi
Rhododendron 'Lady Bessborough Roberte'
Rhododendron 'Lady Chamberlain Exbury'

Rhododendron 'Lady Chamberlain Golden Queen'
Rhododendron 'Lady Chamberlain Salmon Trout'
Rhododendron 'Lady Roseberry Pink Delight'
Rhododendron lanatum Flinckii Group
Rhododendron 'Ledifolium'

Rhododendron 'Ledifolium Album'

Rhododendron ledifolium 'Bulstrode'
Rhododendron ledifolium 'Magnificum'
Rhododendron ledifolium 'Ripense'
Rhododendron lepidotum 'Reuthe's Purple'
Rhododendron 'Linearifolium'

Rhododendron litiense

Rhododendron lopsangianum

Rhododendron macranthum
Rhododendron macrosmithii
Rhododendron 'Macrostemon'

Rhododendron maculiferum ssp anwheiense
Rhododendron manipurense

Rhododendron mekongense v mekongense Rubroluteum Group

Rhododendron mekongense v mekongense Viridescens Group
Rhododendron 'Melford Lemon'
Rhododendron melinanthum

Rhododendron 'Merlin'

Rhododendron metternichii

Rhododendron microleucum

R. degronianum ssp heptamerum
R. degronianum ssp degronianum
R. 'The Hon. Jean Marie de Montague'
R. 'Creeping Jenny'
R. 'Jervis Bay'
R. kaempferi 'Mikado'
R. 'Hexe'
R. calostrotum ssp keleticum
R. Loderi Group
R. 'Loderi King George'
R. arboreum ssp zeylanicum
R. 'Amoenum'
R. yakushimanum 'Koichiro Wada'
R. myrtifolium

R. 'Roberte'
R. 'Exbury Lady Chamberlain'

R. 'Golden Queen'

R. 'Salmon Trout'

R. 'Pink Lady Roseberry'
R. flinckii
R. mucronatum v mucronatum
R. mucronatum v mucronatum
R. 'Bulstrode'
R. 'Magnificum'
R. ripense
R. 'Reuthe's Purple'
R. macrosepalum 'Linearifolium'
R. wardii v wardii Litiense Group
R. thomsonii ssp lopsangianum
R. indicum
R. argipeplum
R. 'Macrostemum' (Obtusum Group)

R. anwheiense
R. maddenii ssp crassum Otusifolium Group

R. viridescens Rubroluteum Group

R. viridescens
R. 'Ilam Melford Lemon'
R. mekongense v melinanthum
R. 'Hawk Merlin' (Hawk Group)
R. degronianum ssp heptamerum
R. orthocladum v

---

microleucum
Rhododendron micromeres
Rhododendron 'Mikado'
Rhododendron 'Ming'
Rhododendron mollicomum -F30940

Rhododendron monosematum

Rhododendron Morning Red
Rhododendron 'Mucronatum'

Rhododendron 'Mucronatum Amethystinum'
Rhododendron mucronatum v ripense
Rhododendron mucronulatum v chejuense

Rhododendron myiagrum

Rhododendron 'Nakahari Orange'
Rhododendron 'Nakahari-mariko'
Rhododendron nigropunctatum

Rhododendron nilagiricum

Rhododendron nitens

Rhododendron nobleanum
Rhododendron nudiflorum
Rhododendron obtusum f amoenum (Obtusum Group)
Rhododendron 'P.J.Mezitt'
Rhododendron 'Palma'
Rhododendron panteumorphum

Rhododendron 'Paris' (Naomi Group)
Rhododendron patulum

Rhododendron 'Peach Blossom'
Rhododendron pennivenium

Rhododendron peramoenum

Rhododendron phaedropum

Rhododendron phoenicodum

Rhododendron pholidotum

Rhododendron pleistanthum -R 11288
Rhododendron pocophorum -KW 21075
Rhododendron pogonostylum

Rhododendron polyandrum

Rhododendron 'Ponticum'
Rhododendron 'Ponticum' -(A)
Rhododendron poukhanense

Rhododendron praecox
Rhododendron praecox 'Emasculum'
Rhododendron prostigiatum
Rhododendron prostratum

R. leptocarpum
R. kaempferi 'Mikado'
R. 'Ilam Ming'
R. hemitrichotum -F 30940
R. pachytrichum v monosematum
R. 'Morgenrot'
R. mucronatum v mucronatum

R. 'Amethystinum'
R. ripense

R. mucronulatum v taquetii
R. callimorphum v myiagrum
R. nakaharae orange
R. nakaharae 'Mariko'
R. nivale ssp boreale Nigropunctatum Group
R. arboreum ssp nilagiricum
R. calostrotum ssp riparium Nitens Group
R. Nobleanum Group
R. periclymenoides

R. 'Amoenum'
R. 'Peter John Mezitt'
R. parmulatum 'Palma'
R. x erythrocalyx Panteumorphum Group
R. 'Paris'
R. pemakoense Patulum Group
R. 'Saotome'
R. tanastylum v pennivenium
R. arboreum ssp delavayi v peramoenum
R. neriifolium ssp phaedropum
R. neriiflorum ssp neriiflorum Phoenicodum Group
R. heliolepis v brevistylum Pholidotum Group
R. rigidum -R 11288
R. coelicum -KW 21075
R. irroratum ssp pogonostylum
R. maddenii ssp maddenii Polyandrum Group
R. ponticum
R. luteum
R. yedoense v poukhanense
R. 'Praecox'
R. 'Emasculum'
R. 'Prostigiatum'
R. saluense ssp

Synonyms

Rhododendron pruniflorum -KW 7038 — R. brachyanthum ssp hypolepidotum -KW 7038

Rhododendron Psyche Group — R. Wega Group

Rhododendron punctatum — R. minus v minus Punctatum Group

Rhododendron 'Purple Diamond' — R. Diamant Group purple

Rhododendron Queen Emma — R. 'Koningin Emma'

Rhododendron 'Queen Mother' — R. 'The Queen Mother'

Rhododendron Queen Wilhelmina — R. 'Koningin Wilhelmina'

Rhododendron radicans — R. calostrotum ssp keleticum Radicans Group

Rhododendron ravum — R. cuneatum Ravum Group

Rhododendron recurvum — R. roxieanum v roxieanum

Rhododendron 'Red Diamond' — R. Diamant Group red

Rhododendron 'Red Velvet' — R. 'Ilam Red Velvet'

Rhododendron rhabdotum — R. dalhousieae v rhabdotum

Rhododendron ririei -Guiz 75 — R. haofui -Guiz 75

Rhododendron 'Rokoko' — R. 'Hachmann's Rokoko'

Rhododendron roseotinctum — R. sanguineum ssp sanguineum v didymoides Roseotinctum Group

Rhododendron roseum — R. prinophyllum

Rhododendron 'Rosiflorum' — R. indicum 'Balsaminiflorum'

Rhododendron 'Roza Harrison' — R. 'Rosa Stevenson'

Rhododendron rubroluteum — R. viridescens Rubroluteum Group

Rhododendron rude — R. glischrum sso rude

Rhododendron russotinctum — R. alutaceum v russotinctum

Rhododendron scintillans — R. polycladum

Rhododendron scottianum — R. pachypodum

Rhododendron scyphocalyx — R. dichroanthum ssp scyphocalyx

Rhododendron setiferum — R. selense ssp setiferum

Rhododendron shepherdii — R. kendrickii

Rhododendron sidereum -KW 13649 — R. aff grande -KR 13649

Rhododendron Silver Cloud — R. 'Silberwolke'

Rhododendron simulans — R. mimetes v simulans

Rhododendron smithii — R. argipeplum

Rhododendron smithii Argipeplum Group — R. argipeplum

Rhododendron 'Snowflake' — R. 'Kure-no-yuki'

Rhododendron 'Solent Queen' — R. 'Solent Queen' (Angelo Group)

Rhododendron speciosum — R. flammeum

Rhododendron sphaeranthum — R. trichostomum

Rhododendron spiciferum — R. scabrifolium v spiciferum

Rhododendron 'Spring Dream' — R. 'Fruhlingstraum'

Rhododendron 'Spring Pearl' — R. 'Moerheim's Pink'

Rhododendron stenaulum — R. moulmainense

Rhododendron stictophyllum — R. nivale ssp boreale Stictophyllum Group

Rhododendron suberosum — R. yunnanense Suberosum Group

Rhododendron 'Sugi-no-ito' — R. 'Kumo-no-ito'

Rhododendron 'Sunbeam' — R. 'Benifude'

Rhododendron sutchuense v geraldii — R. x geraldii

chameunum ProstratumGroup

Rhododendron 'Talavera' — R. 'Talavera' (Golden Oriole Group)

Rhododendron taliense -SBEC 350 — R. roxieanum v cucullatum -SBEC 350

Rhododendron tamaense — R. cinnabarinum ssp tamaense

Rhododendron 'Tangerine' — R. 'Fabia Tangerine'

Rhododendron telopeum — R. campylocarpum ssp caloxanthum Telopeum Group

Rhododendron tephropeplum Deleiense Group — R. tephropeplum

Rhododendron thomsonii v candelabrum — R. x candelabrum

Rhododendron 'Thousand Butterflies' — R. 'One Thousand Butterflies'

Rhododendron 'Tortoiseshell Champagne' — R. 'Champagne'

Rhododendron triplonaevium — R. alutaceum v russotinctum Triplonaevium Group

Rhododendron tritifolium — R. alutaceum v russotinctum Tritifolium Group

Rhododendron tsangpoense — R. charitopes ssp tsangpoense

Rhododendron tsangpoense Poluninii Group — R. poluninii

Rhododendron tubiforme — R. glaucophyllum v tubiforme

Rhododendron vellereum — R. principis Vellereum Group

Rhododendron viridescens -KW 5829 — R. mekongense v mekongense -KW 5829

Rhododendron viscosum 'Antilope' — R. 'Antilope'

Rhododendron viscosum 'Arpege' — R. 'Arpege'

Rhododendron Volker Gr. — R. Flava Group

Rhododendron wilsoniae — R. latoucheae

Rhododendron x arbutifolium — R. Arbutifolium Group

Rhododendron x hodconeri -LS&H 21296 — R. hodgsonii -LS&H 21296

Rhododendron x hodconeri -TSS 9 — R. hodgsonii -TSS 9

Rhododendron xanthocodon — R. cinnabarinum ssp xanthocodon

Rhododendron yakushimanum ssp makinoi — R. makinoi

Rhododendron yakushimanum ssp yakushimanum — R. 'Ken Janeck'

Rhododendron yungningense -F 29268 — R. impeditum -F 29268

Rhododendron zeylanicum — R. arboreum ssp zeylanicum

Rhodohypoxis 'Tetra White' — R. 'Helen'

Rhodora — Rhododendron

Rhodotypos kerrioides — R. scandens

Rhoeo — Tradescantia

Rhoeo discolor — Tradescantia spathacea

Rhoeo spathacea — Tradescantia spathacea

Rhoicissus rhombifolia — Cissus rhombifolia

Rhus cotinoides — Cotinus obovatus

Rhus cotinus — Cotinus coggygria

Rhus glabra 'Laciniata' h — R. x pulvinata Autumn Lace Group

Rhus hirta — R. typhina

Rhus toxicodendron — R. radicans

Rhus typhina 'Laciniata' h — R. typhina 'Dissecta'

Rhynchelytrum — Melinis

Rhynchelytrum roseum — Melinis repens

Ribes atrosanguineum — R. sanguineum

Synonyms

Ribes aureum h	'Atrorubens' R. odoratum	Rosa Burnet, double white	pink R. pimpinellifolia double white
Ribes glutinosum	R. sanguineum v glutinosum	Rosa 'C.F.Meyer'	R. 'Conrad Ferdinand Meyer'
Ribes rubrum White Versailles	R. rubrum 'Versailles Blanche' (White Currant Group)	Rosa californica 'Plena' Rosa 'Canary Bird'	R. nutkana 'Plena' R. xanthina 'Canary Bird'
Ribes sanguineum double	R. sanguineum 'Plenum'	Rosa canina 'Abbotswood'	R. 'Abbotswood' (canina hybrid)
Ribes sanguineum 'Flore Pleno' Ribes sanguineum 'Roseum'	R. sanguineum 'Plenum' R. sanguineum 'Carneum'	Rosa canina 'Andersonii'	R. 'Andersonii' (canina hybrid)
Ribes uva-crispa v reclinatum 'Aston Red'	R. uva-crispa v reclinatum 'Warrington'	Rosa 'Carol' Rosa 'Caroline Testout'	R. 'Carol Amling' R. 'Madame Caroline Testout'
Ribes uva-crispa v reclinatum 'Green Gascoigne'	R. uva-crispa v reclinatum 'Early Green Hairy'	Rosa 'Cecile Brunner,White' Rosa 'Celestial' Rosa Chapeau de Napoleon	R. 'White Cecile Brunner' R. 'Celeste' R. x centifolia 'Cristata'
Robinia luxurians Robinia pseudoacacia 'Fastigiata'	R. neomexicana R. pseudoacacia 'Pyramidalis'	Rosa chinensis 'Minima' Rosa chinensis 'Mutabilis' Rosa chinensis 'Old Blush'	R. 'Rouletii' R. x odorata 'Mutabilis' R. x odorata 'Pallida'
Robinia pseudoacacia 'Inermis' h	R. pseudoacacia 'Umbraculifera'	Rosa cinnamomea Rosa 'Climbing Little White Pet'	R. majalis R. 'Felicite Perpetue'
Robinia x margaretta Casque Rouge	R. x margaretta 'Pink Cascade'	Rosa 'Climbing Mrs G.A. van Rossem'	R. 'Climbing Mevrouw G.A. van Rossem'
Rochea Rochea falcata	Crassula Crassula perfoliata v minor	Rosa 'Cloth of Gold' Rosa Colibre '80 Rosa Colonial White	R. 'Chromatella' R. Colibre '79 R. 'Climbing Sombreuil'
Rodgersia japonica Rodgersia tabularis Romanzoffia suksdorfii -Green Romanzoffia suksdorfii h Romneya x hybrida Romulea grandiflora Romulea longituba Rondelettia speciosa Rooksbya euphorbioides	R. podophylla Astilboides tabularis R. sitchensis R. californica R. coulteri 'White Cloud' R. bulbocodium R. macowanii R. odorata Neobuxbaumia euphorbioides	Rosa 'Columbian' Rosa Common Moss Rosa 'Comte de Chambord' Rosa 'Comtesse de Lacepede' Rosa 'Comtesse de Murinais' Rosa Cooper's Burmese Rosa 'Corylus' Rosa Cottage Maid Rosa Crested Moss Rosa Crimson Damask	R. 'Climbing Columbia' R. x centifolia 'Muscosa' R. 'Madame Knorr' R. 'Du Maitre d'Ecole' R. 'Shailer's White Moss' R. laevigata 'Cooperi' R. 'Hazel le Rougetel' R. 'Centifolia Variegata' R. x centifolia 'Cristata' R. gallica v officinalis
Rosa 'Abbandonata' Rosa 'Alba Semiplena' Rosa 'Alfred de Dalmas' misapplied Rosa alpina Rosa altaica h	R. 'Laure Davoust' R. x alba 'Alba Semiplena' R. 'Mousseline' R. pendulina R. pimpinellifolia 'Grandiflora'	Rosa 'Cristata' Rosa Cuisse de Nymphe Rosa 'Daily Mail' Rosa 'De Meaux, White' Rosa 'Devoniensis'	R. x centifolia 'Cristata' R. 'Great Maiden's Blush' R. 'Climbing Madame Edouard Herriot' R. 'White de Meaux' R. 'Climbing Devoniensis'
Rosa 'Amelia' Rosa anemoniflora Rosa anemonoides Rosa anemonoides 'Ramona' Rosa apothecary's rose Rosa 'Apricot Garnet' Rosa 'Archiduc Joseph' misapplied Rosa Austrian copper Rosa Austrian yellow Rosa 'Autumn Fire' Rosa 'Autumnalis' Rosa 'Ayrshire Splendens' Rosa banksiae alba Rosa banksiae 'Purezza' Rosa 'Baronne de Rothschild'	R. 'Celsiana' R. x beanii R. 'Anemone' R. 'Ramona' R. gallica v officinalis R. 'Garnette Apricot' R. 'General Schablikine' R. foetida 'Bicolor' R. foetida R. 'Herbstfeuer' R. 'Princesse de Nassau' R. 'Splendens' R. banksiae v banksiae R. 'Purezza' R. 'Baronne Adolph de Rothschild'	Rosa 'Duchess of Portland' Rosa Dwarf King Rosa 'E.H.Morse' Rosa ecae 'Helen Knight' Rosa eglanteria Rosa 'Empress Josephine' Rosa 'F.E.Lester' Rosa 'Fabvier' Rosa 'Fairy Rose' Rosa fargesii h Rosa farreri Rosa farreri v persetosa Rosa filipes 'Brenda Colvin' Rosa Fortune's Double Yellow	R. 'Portlandica' R. 'Zwergkonig' R. 'Ernest H.Morse' R. 'Helen Knight' (ecae hybrid) R. rubiginosa R. x francofurtana R. 'Francis E.Lester' R. 'Colonel Fabvier' R. 'The Fairy' R. moyesii v fargesii R. elegantula R. elegantula 'Persetosa' R. Brenda Colvin' R. x odorata 'Pseudindica'
Rosa 'Belle des Jardins' Rosa 'Black Jack' Rosa 'Blush Noisette' Rosa 'Bouquet Tout Fait' misapplied Rosa 'Bullata' Rosa Burgundian rose Rosa Burnet, double pink	R. 'Centifolia Variegata' R. 'Tour de Malakoff' R. 'Noisette Carnee' R. 'Nastarana' R. x centifolia 'Bullata' R. 'Burgundiaca' R. pimpinellifolia double	Rosa gallica 'Complicata' Rosa gallica 'Conditorum' Rosa 'Garnette Carol' Rosa 'Garnette Golden' Rosa 'Garnette Pink' Rosa 'Garnette Red' Rosa gigantea 'Cooperi'	R. 'Complicata' R. 'Conditorum' R. 'Carol Amling' R. 'Golden Garnette' R. 'Carol Amling' R. 'Garnette' R. 'Cooperi'

Synonyms

Rosa Gipsy Boy	R. 'Zigeunerknabe'
Rosa glutinosa	R. pulverulenta
Rosa Gold Crown	R. 'Goldkrone'
Rosa 'Golden Rambler'	R. 'Alister Stella Gray'
Rosa 'Golden Sunblaze'	R. 'Rise n' Shine'
Rosa 'Grootendorst'	R. 'F.J.Grootendorst'
Rosa Gypsy Boy	R. 'Zigeunerknabe'
Rosa holodonta	R. moyesii f rosea
Rosa Holy Rose	R. x richardii
Rosa Honeymoon	R. 'Honigmond'
Rosa horrida	R. biebersteinii
Rosa hugonis	R. xanthina f hugonis
Rosa Hume's Blush	R. x odorata 'Odorata'
Rosa Jacobite Rose	R. x alba 'Alba Maxima'
Rosa Jacques Cartier	R. 'Marchesa Boccella'
Rosa 'Jenny Duval' misapp.	R. 'President de Seze'
Rosa 'Josephine Wheatcroft'	R. 'Rosina'
Rosa 'Kazanlik' misapplied	R. 'Professeur Emile Perrot'
Rosa 'Kiftsgate'	R. filipes 'Kiftsgate'
Rosa 'Kitchener of Khartoum'	R. 'K of K'
Rosa 'L'Ouche' misapplied	R. 'Louise Odier'
Rosa 'La Belle Sultane'	R. 'Violacea'
Rosa 'La Mortola'	R. brunonii 'La Mortola'
Rosa 'La Reine Victoria'	R. 'Reine Victoria'
Rosa 'La Rubanee'	R. 'Centifolia Variegata'
Rosa 'Lady Hillingdon'(CIT)	R. 'Climbing Lady Hillingdon' (CIT)
Rosa laevigata 'Anemonoides'	R. 'Anemone'
Rosa laevigata 'Cooperi'	R. 'Cooperi'
Rosa 'Lemon Pillar'	R. 'Paul's Lemon Pillar'
Rosa 'Little White Pet'	R. 'White Pet'
Rosa longicuspis h	R. mulliganii
Rosa 'Lubeck'	R. 'Hansestadt Lubeck'
Rosa 'Lutea Maxima'	R. x harisonii 'Lutea Maxima'
Rosa Macartney Rose	R. bracteata
Rosa macrophylla 'Doncasteri'	R. 'Doncasteri'
Rosa 'Madame Eugene Resal' h	R. 'Comtesse du Cayla'
Rosa 'Maiden's Blush,Great'	R. 'Great Maiden's Blush'
Rosa Maltese Rose	R. 'Cecile Brunner'
Rosa 'Master Hugh'	R. macrophylla 'Master Hugh'
Rosa 'Max Graf'	R. x jacksonii 'Max Graf'
Rosa 'Maxima'	R. x alba 'Alba Maxima'
Rosa mirifica stellata	R. stellata v mirifica
Rosa moschata 'Autumnalis'	R. 'Princesse de Nassau'
Rosa moschata v nastarana	R. 'Nastarana'
Rosa moschata v nepalensis	R. brunonii
Rosa 'Mousseuse du Japon'	R. 'Japonica'
Rosa moyesii 'Geranium'	R. 'Geranium' (moyesii hybrid)
Rosa moyesii 'Highdownensis'	R. 'Highdownensis' (moyesii hybrid)
Rosa moyesii 'Hillieri'	R. 'Hillieri'
Rosa moyesii holodonta	R. moyesii f rosea
Rosa moyesii 'Sealing Wax'	R. 'Sealing wax' (moyesii hybrid)
Rosa multiflora 'Platyphylla'	R. multiflora 'Grevillei'
Rosa multiflora v watsoniana	R. watsoniana
Rosa mundi	R. gallica 'Versicolor'
Rosa mundi 'Versicolor'	R. gallica 'Versicolor'
Rosa 'Mutabilis'	R. x odorata 'Mutabilis'
Rosa 'Nathalie Nypels'	R. 'Mevrouw Nathalie Nypels'
Rosa Park's Yellow China	R. x odorata 'Ochroleuca'
Rosa Parson's Pink China	R. x odorata 'Pallida'
Rosa parvifolia	R. 'Burgundiaca'
Rosa 'Paul Lede'	R. 'Climbing Paul Lede'
Rosa Persian Yellow	R. foetida 'Persiana'
Rosa pimpinellifolia 'Altaica' h	R. pimpinellifolia 'Grandiflora'
Rosa pimpinellifolia double yellow	R. x harisonii 'Williams' Double Yellow'
Rosa pimpinellifolia 'Harisonii'	R. x harisonii 'Harison's Yellow'
Rosa pimpinellifolia 'Lutea'	R. x harisonii 'Lutea Maxima'
Rosa pimpinellifolia 'Stanwell Perpetual'	R. 'Stanwell Perpetual'
Rosa pimpinellifolia x pendulina	R. x reversa
Rosa 'Pink Garnette'	R. 'Carol Amling'
Rosa Pink Moss	R. x centifolia 'Muscosa'
Rosa polyantha grandiflora	R. gentiliana
Rosa pomifera	R. villosa
Rosa pomifera 'Duplex'	R. 'Wolley-Dod'
Rosa 'Pompon de Bourgogne'	R. 'Burgundiaca'
Rosa 'Pompon de Paris'	R. 'Climbing Pompon de Paris'
Rosa Portland Rose	R. 'Portlandica'
Rosa Prairie Rose	R. setigera
Rosa 'Prolifera de Redoute' h	R. 'Duchesse de Montebello'
Rosa Quatre Saisons	R. x damascena v semperflorens
Rosa Queen Elizabeth	R. 'The Queen Elizabeth'
Rosa Queen of Denmark	R. 'Konigin von Danemark'
Rosa 'Queen of Hearts'	R. 'Dame de Coeur'
Rosa Queen of the Belgians	R. 'Reine des Belges'
Rosa 'Red Garnette'	R. 'Garnette'
Rosa 'Red Grootendorst'	R. 'F.J.Grootendorst'
Rosa Red Moss	R. 'Henri Martin'
Rosa Red New Dawn	R. 'Etendard'
Rosa Red Rose of Lancaster	R. gallica v officinalis
Rosa 'Red Wing'	R. 'Red Wing' (hugonis hybrid)
Rosa 'Rescht'	R. 'De Rescht'
Rosa 'Rose de Meaux'	R. 'De Meaux'
Rosa 'Rose de Meaux White'	R. 'De Meaux, White'
Rosa 'Rose de Rescht'	R. 'De Rescht'
Rosa 'Rose des Maures'	R. 'Sissinghurst Castle'
Rosa 'Rose du Maitre d'Ecole'	R. 'Du Maitre d'Ecole'
Rosa roxburghii 'Plena'	R. roxburghii f roxburghii
Rosa rubra	R. gallica
Rosa rubrifolia	R. glauca
Rosa rubrifolia 'Carmenetta'	R. 'Carmenetta'
Rosa 'Rubrotincta'	R. 'Hebe's Lip'
Rosa rugosa 'Scabrosa'	R. 'Scabrosa'
Rosa rugosa v kamtschatica	R. rugosa v ventenatiana
Rosa Saint John's Rose	R. x richardii
Rosa Saint Mark's Rose	R. 'Rose d'Amour'
Rosa sancta	R. x richardii
Rosa 'Sanguinea'	R. x odorata Sanguinea Group
Rosa Scarlet Fire	R. 'Scharlachglut'
Rosa 'Scarlet Glow'	R. 'Scharlachglut'
Rosa Scotch Rose	R. pimpinellifolia
Rosa Scotch Yellow	R. x harisonii 'Williams' Double Yellow'
Rosa 'Semiplena'	R. x alba 'Alba Semiplena'
Rosa sericea 'Heather Muir'	R. 'Heather Muir' (sericea hybrid)

Synonyms

Rosa Seven Sisters Rose	R. multiflora 'Grevillei'	Rosmarinus officinalis 'Collingwood	
Rosa sinowilsonii	R. longicuspis	Ingram'	R. officinalis 'Benenden
	sinowilsonii		Blue'
Rosa 'Snow Dwarf'	R. 'Schneezwerg'	Rosmarinus officinalis f pyramidalis	R. officinalis 'Miss
Rosa 'Snow Queen'	R. 'Frau Karl Druschki'		Jessopp's Upright'
Rosa 'Souvenir de Brod'	R. 'Erinnerung an Brod'	Rosmarinus officinalis 'Fastigiatus'	R. officinalis 'Miss
Rosa 'Souvenir de la Malmaison' (ClBb)	R. 'Climbing Souvenir de		Jessopp's Upright'
	la Malmaison' (ClBb)	Rosmarinus officinalis 'Frimley Blue'	R. officinalis 'Primley
Rosa spaldingii	R. nutkana v hispida		Blue'
Rosa 'Spanish Beauty'	R. 'Madame Gregoire	Rosmarinus officinalis 'Gilded'	R. officinalis 'Aureus'
	Staechelin'	Rosmarinus officinalis lavandulaceus	R. officinalis Prostratus
Rosa 'Spencer' misapplied	R. 'Enfant de France'		Group
Rosa spinosissima	R. pimpinellifolia	Rosmarinus officinalis 'Prostratus'	R. officinalis Prostratus
Rosa suffulta	R. arkansana v suffulta		Group
Rosa 'The New Dawn'	R. 'New Dawn'	Rosmarinus officinalis repens	R. officinalis Prostratus
Rosa Thousand Beauties	R. 'Tausendschon'		Group
Rosa Threepenny Bit Rose	R. elegantula 'Persetosa'	Rosmarinus officinalis 'Variegatus'	R. officinalis 'Aureus'
Rosa 'Trigintipetala' misap.	R. 'Professeur Emile	Rosmarinus repens	R. officinalis Prostratus
	Perrot'		Group
Rosa triphylla	R. x beanii	Rosmarinus x lavandulaceus h	R. officinalis Prostratus
Rosa versicolor	R. gallica 'Versicolor'		Group
Rosa 'Village Maid'	R. 'Centifolia Variegata'	Rosmarinus x lavandulaceus -Noe	R. eriocalyx
Rosa villosa -Auct.	R. mollis	Rosularia acuminata	R. alpestris ssp alpestris
Rosa villosa 'Duplex'	R. 'Wolley-Dod'	Rosularia alba	R. sedoides
Rosa virginiana 'Plena'	R. 'Rose d'Amour'	Rosularia crassipes	Rhodiola wallichiana
Rosa 'Viridiflora'	R. x odorata 'Viridiflora'	Rosularia pallida -A.Berger	R. chrysantha
Rosa vosagiaca	R. caesia ssp glauca	Rosularia pallida -Stapf	R. aizoon
Rosa 'White Bath'	R. 'Shailer's White Moss'	Rosularia platyphylla h	R. muratdaghensis
Rosa White Moss	R. 'Comtesse de	Rosularia spatulata h	R. sempervivum ssp
	Murinais'		glaucophylla
Rosa White Moss	R. 'Shailer's White Moss'	Roystonea caribaea	R. borinquena
Rosa White Provence	R. 'Unique Blanche'	Rubus calycinoides -Hay.	R. pentalobus
Rosa White Rose of York	R. x alba 'Alba Semiplena'	Rubus fockeanus h	R. pentalobus
Rosa 'Williams' Double Yellow'	R. x harisonii 'Williams'	Rubus nutans	R. nepalensis
	Double Yellow'	Rubus spectabilis 'Flore Pleno'	R. spectabilis 'Olympic
Rosa willmottiae	R. gymnocarpa v		Double'
	willmottiae	Rubus thibetanus 'Silver Fern'	R. thibetanus
Rosa woodsii v fendleri	R. woodsii	Rubus 'Tridel'	R. 'Benenden'
Rosa 'Woolverstone Church Rose'	R. 'Surpassing Beauty of	Rudbeckia Autumn Sun	R. 'Herbstonne'
	Woolverstone'	Rudbeckia columnifera	Ratibida columnifera
Rosa x alba Celestial	R. 'Celeste'	Rudbeckia deamii	R. fulgida v deamii
Rosa x alba 'Maxima'	R. x alba 'Alba Maxima'	Rudbeckia echinacea purpurea	Echinacea purpurea
Rosa x centifolia 'Parvifolia'	R. 'Burgundiaca'	Rudbeckia gloriosa	R. hirta
Rosa x damascena 'Trigintipetala'		Rudbeckia hirta 'Green Eyes'	R. hirta 'Irish Eyes'
misapplied	R. 'Professeur Emile	Rudbeckia July Gold	R. 'Juligold'
	Perrot'	Rudbeckia laciniata 'Golden Fountain'	R. 'Goldquelle'
Rosa x damascena v bifera	R. x damascena v	Rudbeckia laciniata 'Golden Glow'	R. laciniata 'Hortensia'
	semperflorens	Rudbeckia newmannii	R. fulgida v speciosa
Rosa x macrantha 'Raubritter'	R. 'Raubritter'	Rudbeckia purpurea	Echinacea purpurea
	('Macrantha' hybrid)	Rudbeckia speciosa	R. fulgida v speciosa
Rosa x penzanceana	R. 'Lady Penzance'	Rudbeckia sullivantii	R. fulgida v sullivantii
Rosa Yellow Scotch	R. x harisonii 'Williams'	Ruellia amoena	R. graecizans
	Double Yellow'	Rumex acetosa 'Redleaf'	R. acetosa ssp vineatus
Rosa York and Lancaster	R. x damascena v	Rumex montanus 'Ruber'	R. alpestris 'Ruber'
	versicolor	Ruschia derenbergiana	Ebracteola derenbergiana
Roscoea capitata h	R. scillifolia	Ruscus racemosus	Danae racemosa
Roscoea procera	R. purpurea	Russelia juncea	R. equisetiformis
Roscoea purpurea v procera	R. purpurea	Ruta chalepensis prostrate form	R. chalepensis
Roseocactus fissuratus	Ariocarpus fissuratus		'Dimension Two'
Rosmarinus corsicus 'Prostratus'	R. officinalis Prostratus	Ruta prostrata	R. chalepensis
	Group		'Dimension Two'
Rosmarinus eriocalyx h	R. officinalis Prostratus	Sabal glabra	S. minor
	Group	Sabal guatemalensis	S. mexicana
Rosmarinus lavandulaceus h	R. officinalis Prostratus	Sabal minima	S. minor
	Group	Sabal princeps	S. bermudana
Rosmarinus officinalis 'Aureovariegatus'	R. officinalis 'Aureus'	Sabal pumila	S. minor

Synonyms

Sabal texana — S. mexicana
Sabina — Juniperus
Sageretia theezans — S. thea
Sagina glabra 'Aurca' — S. subulata 'Aurea'
Sagittaria japonica — S. sagittifolia
Saintpaulia 'Granger's Wonderland' — S. 'Wonderland'
Saintpaulia 'Optimara Colorado' — S. 'Colorado'
Saintpaulia 'Rococo Pink' — S. 'Rococo Anna'
Salix adenophylla -Hooker — S. cordata
Salix alba 'Chermesina' h — S. alba ssp vitellina 'Britzensis'

Salix alba f argentea — S. alba v sericea
Salix alba 'Sericea' — S. alba v sericea
Salix alba 'Splendens' — S. alba v sericea
Salix alba 'Vitellina Pendula' — S. alba 'Tristis'
Salix alba 'Vitellina Tristis' — S. alba 'Tristis'
Salix arenaria — S. repens v argentea
Salix babylonica 'Annularis' — S. babylonica 'Crispa'
Salix babylonica 'Tortuosa' — S. babylonica v pekinensis 'Tortuosa'

Salix caprea v pendula (f) — S. caprea 'Weeping Sally'
Salix caprea v pendula (m) — S. caprea 'Kilmarnock'
Salix 'Chrysocoma' — S. x sepulcralis v chrysocoma

Salix 'E.A.Bowles' — S. 'Bowles' Hybrid'
Salix 'Elegantissima' — S. pendula v elegantissima

Salix formosa — S. arbuscula
Salix 'Fuiri-koriyanagi' — S. integra 'Hakuro-nishiki'

Salix furcata — S. fruticulosa
Salix 'Golden Curls' — S. 'Erythroflexuosa'
Salix 'Hagensis' — S. 'The Hague'
Salix hibernica — S. phylicifolia
Salix hylematica — S. fruticulosa
Salix incana — S. elaeagnos
Salix integra 'Albomaculata' — S. integra 'Hakuro-nishiki'

Salix 'Jacquinii' — S. alpina
Salix japonica h — S. babylonica 'Lavelleei'
Salix 'Kuro-me' — S. gracilistyla 'Melanostachys'

Salix lanata 'Mark Postill' — S. 'Mark Postill'
Salix lanata 'Stuartii' — S. 'Stuartii'
Salix matsudana — S. babylonica v pekinensis

Salix matsudana 'Tortuosa' — S. babylonica v pekinensis 'Tortuosa'
Salix matsudana 'Tortuosa Aureopendula' — S. 'Erythroflexuosa'
Salix medemii — S. aegyptiaca
Salix 'Melanostachys' — S. gracilistyla 'Melanostachys'

Salix myrsinites v jacquiniana — S. alpina
Salix myrtilloides x repens — S. x finnmarchica
Salix nepalensis — S. lindleyana
Salix nigricans — S. myrsinifolia
Salix occidentalis — S. humilis
Salix procumbens — S. myrsinites
Salix prunifolia — S. arbuscula
Salix purpurea f gracilis — S. purpurea 'Nana'
Salix purpurea 'Helix' — S. purpurea
Salix repens pendula — S. 'Boyd's Pendulous'
Salix rosmarinifolia h — S. elaeagnos ssp angustifolia

Salix sachalinensis — S. udensis
Salix schraderiana -Will. — S. bicolor -Willdenow

Salix serpyllum — S. fruticulosa
Salix 'Setsuka' — S. udensis 'Sekka'
Salix syrticola — S. cordata
Salix tristis — S. humilis
Salix viminalis 'Bowles' Hybrid' — S. 'Bowles' Hybrid'
Salix vitellina 'Pendula' — S. alba 'Tristis'
Salix x myricoides — S. x bebbii
Salix x smithiana — S. x stipularis
Salvia acetabulosa — S. multicaulis
Salvia ambigens — S. guaranitica 'Blue Enigma'
Salvia angustifolia -Cavan. — S. reptans
Salvia angustifolia -Mich. — S. azurea
Salvia aurea — S. africana-lutea
Salvia bacheriana — S. buchananii
Salvia bertolonii — S. pratensis Bertolonii Group
Salvia bicolor -Desfont. — S. barrelieri
Salvia caerulea h — S. guaranitica 'Black and Blue'
Salvia caerulea -Linnaeus — S. africana-caerulea
Salvia cardinalis — S. fulgens
Salvia chinensis — S. japonica
Salvia concolor h — S. guaranitica
Salvia deserta — S. x sylvestris
Salvia flava v megalantha — S. bulleyana
Salvia forskaohlei — S. forsskaolii
Salvia grahamii — S. microphylla v microphylla
Salvia grandiflora -Etl. HH&K 210 — S. tomentosa Etl. HH&K 210
Salvia greggii 'Blush Pink' — S. microphylla 'Pink Blush'
Salvia greggii 'Peach' misapplied — S. x jamensis 'Pat Vlasto'
Salvia greggii 'Raspberry Royal' — S. 'Raspberry Royale'
Salvia haematodes — S. pratensis Haematodes Group
Salvia hispanica h — S. lavandulifolia
Salvia horminum — S. viridis
Salvia involucrata 'Mrs.Pope' — S. involucrata 'Hadspen'
Salvia lanceolata — S. reflexa
Salvia lemmonii — S. microphylla v wislizenii
Salvia leptophylla — S. reptans
Salvia lycioides h — S. greggi x lycioides
Salvia microphylla v neurepia — S. microphylla v microphylla
Salvia microphylla 'Variegata' splashed — S. microphylla 'Ruth Stungo'
Salvia nemerosa East Friesland — S. nemerosa 'Ostfriesland'
Salvia neurepia — S. microphylla v microphylla
Salvia officinalis 'Alba' — S. officinalis 'Albiflora'
Salvia officinalis latifolia — S. officinalis broad-leaved
Salvia officinalis narrow-leaved — S. lavandulifolia
Salvia officinalis 'Variegata' — S. officinalis 'Icterina'
Salvia patens 'Alba' misap. — S. patens 'White Trophy'
Salvia puberula — S. involucrata v puberula
Salvia regeliana h — S. virgata -Jacq.
Salvia rutilans — S. elegans 'Scarlet Pineapple'
Salvia semiatrata h — S. chamaedryoides
Salvia souliei — S. brevilabra
Salvia splendens Fireball — S. splendens 'Blaze of Fire'

Synonyms

Synonym	Accepted name
Salvia splendens Ryco	S. splendens 'Red Riches'
Salvia tesquicola	S. nemerosa ssp tesquicola
Salvia transcaucasica	S. staminea
Salvia triloba	S. fruticosa
Salvia 'Vatican City'	S. sclarea 'Vatican White'
Salvia villicaulis	S. amplexicaulis
Salvia viridis 'Monarch Bouquet'	S. viridis 'Bouquet'
Salvia viscosa -Sesse &Moc.	S. riparia
Salvia x sylvestris Blue Mound	S. x sylvestris 'Blauhugel'
Salvia x sylvestris Blue Queen	S. x sylvestris 'Blaukonigin'
Salvia x sylvestris May Night	S. x sylvestris 'Mainacht'
Sambucus coraensis	S. sieboldiana v coreana
Sambucus nigra 'Albomarginata'	S. nigra 'Marginata'
Sambucus nigra 'Heterophylla'	S. nigra 'Linearis'
Sambucus nigra 'Purpurea'	S. nigra 'Guincho Purple'
Sambucus nigra 'Variegata'	S. nigra 'Marginata'
Sambucus sieboldiana	S. racemosa v sieboldiana
Sambucus wightiana	S. javanica
Sanchezia glaucophylla	S. speciosa
Sanchezia nobilis h	S. speciosa
Sanchezia spectabilis	S. speciosa
Sanguisorba magnifica alba	S. albiflora
Sanguisorba obtusa v albiflora	S. albiflora
Sanguisorba pimpinella	S. minor
Sanguisorba sitchensis	S. stipulata
Santolina chamaecyparissus ssp tomentosa	S. pinnata
Santolina chamaecyparissus v corsica	S. chamaecyparissus v nana
Santolina incana	S. chamaecyparissus
Santolina neapolitana	S. pinnata ssp neapolitana
Santolina pectinata	S. rosmarinifolia ssp canescens
Santolina pinnata ssp neapolitana cream	S. pinnata ssp neapolitana 'Edward Bowles'
Santolina tomentosa	S. pinnata ssp neapolitana
Santolina virens	S. rosmarinifolia ssp rosmarinifolia
Santolina viridis	S. rosmarinifolia ssp rosmarinifolia
Saponaria 'Bressingham Hybrid'	S. 'Bressingham'
Saponaria officinalis 'Taff's Dazzler'	S. officinalis 'Dazzler'
Saponaria officinalis 'Variegata'	S. officinalis 'Dazzler'
Saponaria pulvinaris	S. pumilio
Saponaria zawadskii	Silene zawadskii
Sarcococca 'Roy Lancaster'	S. ruscifolia 'Dragon Gate'
Sarmienta scandens	S. repens
Sarracenia drummondii	S. leucophylla
Sarracenia x farnhamii	S. x readii 'Farnhamii'
Sasa albomarginata	S. veitchii
Sasa borealis	Sasamorpha borealis
Sasa chrysantha h	Pleiobastus chino
Sasa disticha 'Mirrezuzume'	Pleiobastus pygmaeus 'Mirrezuzume'
Sasa glabra f albostriata	Sasaella masamuneana f albostriata
Sasa humilis	Pleioblastus humilis
Sasa nana	S. veitchii f minor
Sasa ruscifolia	Shibataea kumasasa
Sasa tessellata	Indocalamus tessellatus
Sasaella glabra	S. masamuneana
Satureja montana 'Coerulea'	S. coerulea
Satureja montana subspicata	S. montana ssp illyrica
Satureja repanda	S. spicigera
Satureja reptans	S. spicigera
Sauromatum guttatum	S. venosum
Saxifraga aizoon	S. paniculata
Saxifraga 'Alba' (sempervivum)	S. 'Zita'
Saxifraga 'Alba' (x arco-valleyi)	S. 'Ophelia' (x arco-valleyi)
Saxifraga 'Balcana'	S. paniculata v orientalis
Saxifraga 'Baldensis'	S. paniculata v baldensis
Saxifraga 'Birch Yellow'	S. 'Pseudoborisii' (x borisii)
Saxifraga brunoniana	S. brunonis
Saxifraga callosa lingulata	S. callosa
Saxifraga callosa v bellardii	S. callosa
Saxifraga callosa v lantoscana	S. callosa v australis
Saxifraga 'Carmen'	S. 'Carmen' (x elisabethae)
Saxifraga catalaunica	S. callosa ssp catalaunica
Saxifraga 'Chambers' Pink Pride'	S. 'Miss Chambers' (x urbium)
Saxifraga chrysospleniifolia	S. rotundifolia ssp chrysospleniifolia
Saxifraga corbariensis	S. fragilis
Saxifraga cortusifolia v fortunei	S. fortunei
Saxifraga crustata v vochinensis	S. crustata
Saxifraga cuneifolia v capillipes	S. cuneifolia ssp cuneifolia
Saxifraga densa	S. cherlerioides
Saxifraga 'Dentata' (x urbium)	S. 'Dentata' (x polita)
Saxifraga 'Elizabethae'	S. 'Carmen' (x elisabethae)
Saxifraga exarata pyrenaica	S. androsacea
Saxifraga Fair Maids of France	S. 'Flore Pleno' (granulata)
Saxifraga federici-augusti	S. frederici-augusti
Saxifraga ferdinandi-coburgi v pravislavii	S. ferdinandi-coburgi v rhodopea
Saxifraga ferdinandi-coburgi v radoslavoffii	S. ferdinandi-coburgi v rhodopea
Saxifraga 'Flowers of Sulphur'	S. 'Schwefelblute'
Saxifraga 'Geoides'	S. hirsuta ssp paucicrenata
Saxifraga 'Gertie Pritchard' (x megaseiflora)	S. 'Mrs Gertie Pritchard' (x megaseiflora)
Saxifraga 'Gloriosa' (x gloriana)	S. 'Godiva' (x gloriana)
Saxifraga Golden Prague (x pragensis)	S. 'Zlata Praha' (x pragensis)
Saxifraga 'Gracilis' (x geum)	S. 'Gracilis' (x polita)
Saxifraga grisebachii	S. frederici-augusta ssp grisebachii
Saxifraga grisebachii montenegrina	S. frederici-augusta
Saxifraga 'Hirsuta' (x geum)	S. x geum
Saxifraga 'Irvingii'	S. 'Walter Irving' (x irvingii)
Saxifraga 'Joy'	S. 'Kaspar Maria Sternberg' (x petraschii)
Saxifraga 'Juliet'	S. 'Riverslea' (x hornibrookii)
Saxifraga juniperifolia ssp sancta	S. sancta
Saxifraga juniperifolia v macedonica	S. juniperifolia

Synonyms

Saxifraga 'Kingii'

Saxifraga 'Labradorica' (paniculata)
Saxifraga 'Lady Beatrix Stanley'

Saxifraga lingulata
Saxifraga longifolia 'Tumbling Waters'
Saxifraga Love Me

Saxifraga 'Lutea' (marginata)
Saxifraga luteoviridis
Saxifraga 'Major Lutea'
Saxifraga marginata v balcanica
Saxifraga 'Minor Glauca' (paniculata)

Saxifraga 'Minor' (paniculata)
Saxifraga 'Moonlight'
Saxifraga 'Moonlight Sonata' (x boydii)

Saxifraga moschata
Saxifraga oppositifolia x biflora
Saxifraga paniculata ssp kolenatiana

Saxifraga 'Pixie Alba'
Saxifraga 'Plena' (granulata)

Saxifraga porophylla v thessalica

Saxifraga 'Primulaize'
Saxifraga primuloides

Saxifraga punctata
Saxifraga 'Purpurea' (fortunei)
Saxifraga sancta ssp pseudosancta v macedonica
Saxifraga sarmentosa
Saxifraga sarmentosa 'Tricolor'
Saxifraga 'Sartorii'
Saxifraga scardica v dalmatica
Saxifraga scardica v obtusa
Saxifraga 'Schelleri' (x petraschii)

Saxifraga 'Schleicheri' (x kellereri)

Saxifraga 'Silver Mound'
Saxifraga 'Stormonth's Variety'
Saxifraga 'Unique'

Saxifraga urbium primuloides

Saxifraga 'Valborg'

Saxifraga 'Valentine'

Saxifraga 'Valerie Finnis'
Saxifraga 'Variegata' (umbrosa)

Saxifraga 'Winter Fire'
Saxifraga 'Wisley Primrose'
Saxifraga x apiculata

Saxifraga x arco-valleyi
Saxifraga x biasolettoi

Saxifraga x elisabethae h

S. hypnoides v egmmulosa
S. paniculata neogaea
S. 'Beatrix Stanley' (x anglica)
S. callosa
S. 'Tumbling Waters'
S. 'Miluj Mne' (x poluanglica)
S. 'Faust' (x borisii)
S. corymbosa
S. 'Luteola' (x boydii)
S. marginata v rocheliana
S. paniculata v brevifolia 'Glauca'
S. paniculata v brevifolia
S. 'Sulphurea' (x boydii)
S. 'Mondscheinsonate' (x boydii)
S. exarata ssp moschata
S. x kochii
S. paniculata ssp cartilaginea
S. 'White Pixie'
S. 'Flore Pleno' (granulata)
S. sempervivum f stenophylla
S. x primulaize
S. umbrosa v primuloides
S. nelsoniana
S. 'Rubrifolia' (fortunei)

S. juniperifolia
S. stolonifera
S. 'Tricolor' (stolonifera)
S. 'Pygmalion' (x webrii)
S. obtusa
S. obtusa
S. 'White Star' (x petraschii)
S. 'Schleicheri' (x landaueri)
S. 'Silver Cushion'
S. 'Stella' (x stormonthii)
S. 'Bodensee' (x hofmannii)
S. umbrosa v primuloides
S. 'Cranbourne' (x anglica)
S. 'Cranbourne' (x anglica)
S. 'Aretiastrum' (x boydii)
S. 'Aureopunctata' (x urbium)
S. 'Winterfeuer' (callosa)
S. 'Kolbiana' (x paulinae)
S. 'Gregor Mendel' (x apiculata)
S. 'Arco' (x arco-valleyi)
S. 'Phoenix' (x biasolettoi)
S. 'Carmen' (x elisabethae)

Saxifraga x geuderi

Saxifraga x irvingii

Saxifraga x kellereri

Saxifraga x landaueri
Saxifraga x megaseiflora

Saxifraga x pectinata
Saxifraga x prossenii
Saxifraga x pseudokotschyi

Saxifraga x semmleri
Saxifraga Your Day

Saxifraga Your Friend

Saxifraga Your Good Fortune

Saxifraga Your Kiss

Saxifraga Your Smile

Saxifraga Your Song

Saxifraga Your Success

Scabiosa alpina -L.
Scabiosa arvensis
Scabiosa banatica
Scabiosa 'Butterfly Pink'
Scabiosa gigantea
Scabiosa ochroleuca

Scabiosa parnassi
Scabiosa pterocephala
Scabiosa rumelica
Scabiosa succisa
Scabiosa tatarica
Scadoxus 'Konig Albert'

Scadoxus natalensis
Scaevola 'Blue Wonder'
Scaevola suaveolens
Schefflera octophylla
Schima argentea

Schima khasiana

Schisandra grandiflora rubriflora
Schisandra grandiflora v cathayensis
Schizocentron
Schizocodon
Schizophragma viburnoides
Schizostylis coccinea 'Gigantea'
Schizostylis coccinea 'Grandiflora'
Schizostylis coccinea 'Sunset'
Schlumbergera bridgesii
Scilla adlamii
Scilla amethystina
Scilla campanulata
Scilla chinensis
Scilla cooperi
Scilla hispanica
Scilla italica

S. 'Eulenspiegel' (x geuderi)
S. 'Walter Irving' (x irvingii)
S. 'Johann Kellerer' (x kellereri)
S. 'Leonore' (x landaueri)
S. 'Robin Hood' (x megaseiflora)
S. x fritschiana
S. 'Regina' (x prossenii)
S. 'Denisa' (x pseudokotschyi)
S. 'Martha' (x semmleri)
S. 'Tvuj Den' (x poluanglica)
S. 'Tvuj Pritel' (x poluanglica)
S. 'Tvuj Uspech' (x poluanglica)
S. 'Tvuj Polibek' (x poluanglica)
S. 'Tvuj Usmev' (x poluanglica)
S. 'Tvuj Pisen' (x poluanglica)
S. 'Tvuj Usbech' (x poluanglica)
Cephalaria alpina
Knautia arvensis
S. columbaria
S. 'Pink Mist'
Cephalaria gigantea
S. columbaria v ochroleuca
Pterocephalus perennis
Pterocephalus perennis
Knautia macedonica
Succisa pratensis
Cephalaria gigantea
Haemanthus 'Konig Albert'
S. puniceus
S. aemula 'Blue Wonder'
S. calendulacea
S. heptaphylla
S. wallichii ssp noronhae v superba
S. wallichii ssp wallichii v khasiana
S. rubriflora
S. sphaerandra
Heterocentron
Shortia
Pileostegia viburnoides
S. coccinea 'Major'
S. coccinea 'Major'
S. coccinea 'Sunrise'
S. x buckleyi
Ledebouria cooperi
S. litardierei
Hyacinthoides hispanica
S. scilloides
Ledebouria cooperi
Hyacinthoides hispanica
Hyacinthoides italica

Synonyms

Scilla japonica — S. scilloides
Scilla non-scripta — Hyacinthoides non-scripta
Scilla nutans — Hyacinthoides non-scripta
Scilla ovalifolia — Ledebouria ovalifolia
Scilla pratensis — S. litardierei
Scilla siberica 'Atrocoerulea' — S. siberica 'Spring Beauty'
Scilla socialis — Ledebouria socialis
Scilla tubergeniana — S. mischtschenkoana
Scilla vicentina — Hyacinthoides italica vicentina
Scilla violacea — Ledebouria socialis
Scilla x allenii — x Chionoscilla allenii
Scindapsus aureus — Epipremnum aureum
Scindapsus pictus — Epipremnum pictum
Scindapsus pictus 'Argyraeus' — Epipremnum pictum 'Argyraeum'
Scirpus cernuus — Isolepis cernua
Scirpus cespitosus — Trichophorum cespitosum
Scirpus holoschoenus — Scirpoides holoschoenus
Scirpus lacustris — Schoenoplectus lacustris
Scirpus lacustris 'Spiralis' — Juncus effusus 'Spiralis'
Scirpus tabernaemontani — Schoenoplectus lacustris ssp tabernaemontani
Scoliopus bigelovii — S. bigelowii
Scolopendrium — Asplenium
Scolopendrium vulgare — Asplenium scolopendrium
Scolymus — Cynara
Scopiola sinensis — Atropanthe sinensis
Scrophularia aquatica — S. auriculata
Scrophularia nodosa variegata — S. auriculata 'Variegata'
Scutellaria canescens — S. incana
Scutellaria hastata — S. hastifolia
Scutellaria indica v japonica — S. indica v parvifolia
Scutellaria supina — S. alpina
Seaforthia elegans — Ptychosperma elegans
Securigera — Coronilla
Securigera varia — Coronilla varia
Sedastrum — Sedum
Sedirea japonica — Aerides japonica
Sedum aggregatum — Orostachys aggregata
Sedum aizoon 'Aurantiacum' — S. aizoon 'Euphorbioides'
Sedum albescens — S. forsterianum f purpureum
Sedum album ssp clusianum — S. gypsicola glanduliferum
Sedum album v macranthum — S. album 'Chloriticum'
Sedum algidum — S. alsium
Sedum altissimum — S. sediforme
Sedum amplexicaule — S. tenuifolium
Sedum anopetalum — S. ochroleucum
Sedum anopetalum alpine form — S. ochroleucum ssp montanum
Sedum athoum — S. album
Sedum atlanticum — S. dasyphyllum ssp dasyphyllum v mesatlanticum
Sedum Autumn Joy — S. 'Herbstfreude'
Sedum batesii — S. hemsleyanum
Sedum beyrichianum h — S. glaucophyllum
Sedum bithynicum 'Aureum' — S. hispanicum v minus 'Aureum'

Sedum 'Bronze Queen' — S. lydium
Sedum clusianum — S. gypsicola glanduliferum
Sedum crassipes — Rhodiola wallichiana
Sedum crassularia — Crassula milfordiae
Sedum cyaneum h — S. ewersii v homophyllum
Sedum dasyphyllum mucronatis — S. dasyphyllum ssp dasyphyllum v mesatalanticum
Sedum douglasii — S. stenopetalum 'Douglasii'
Sedum 'Eleanor Fisher' — S. telephium ssp ruprechtii
Sedum ellacombeanum — S. kamtschaticum v ellacombianum
Sedum erythrostichum — S. alboroseum
Sedum fastigiatum — Rhodiola fastigiata
Sedum floriferum — S. kamtschaticum
Sedum heterodontum — Rhodiola heterodonta
Sedum hillebrandtii — S. urvillei Hillebrandtii Group
Sedum himalense — Rhodiola 'Keston'
Sedum hispanicum glaucum — S. hispanicum v minus
Sedum integrifolium — Rhodiola rosea ssp integrifolia
Sedum ishidae — Rhodiola ishidae
Sedum jaeschkei — S. oreades
Sedum kamtschaticum v middendorffianum — S. middendorffianum
Sedum kirilovii — Rhodiola kirilovii
Sedum kostovii — S. grisebachii ssp kostovii
Sedum lydium 'Aureum' — S. hispanicum v minus 'Aureum'
Sedum lydium 'Bronze Queen' — S. lydium
Sedum 'Matrona' — S. telephium 'Matrona'
Sedum maweanum — S. acre v majus
Sedum maximowiczii — S. aizoon
Sedum murale — S. album ssp teretifolium 'Murale'
Sedum nicaeense — S. sediforme
Sedum oppositifolium — S. spurium v album
Sedum oreganum 'Procumbens' — S. oreganum ssp tenue
Sedum pluricaule Rose Carpet — S. pluricaule 'Rosenteppich'
Sedum polytrichoides — Rhodiola komarovii
Sedum primuloides — Rhodiola primuloides
Sedum pruinosum — S. spathulifolium ssp pruinosum
Sedum quadrifidum — Rhodiola quadrifida
Sedum quinquefarium — S. brevifolium quinquefarium
Sedum ramosissimum — Villadia ramosissima
Sedum reflexum -L. — S. rupestre -L.
Sedum retusum — S. obtusatum ssp retusum
Sedum rhodiola — Rhodiola rosea
Sedum rosea — Rhodiola rosea
Sedum rosea v heterodontum — Rhodiola heterodonta
Sedum rubroglaucum h — S. oregonense
Sedum rubroglaucum -Praeger — S. obtusatum
Sedum ruprechtii — S. telephium ssp ruprechtii
Sedum sarocaule — Crassula sarocaulis
Sedum sediforme nicaeense — S. sediforme

Synonyms

Sedum sieboldii 'Foliis Mediovariegatis' — S. sieboldii 'Mediovariegatum'

Sedum sieboldii 'Variegatum' — S. sieboldii 'Mediovariegatum'

Sedum spectabile September Glow — S. spectabile 'Septemberglut'

Sedum spectabile 'Variegatum' — S. alboroseum 'Mediovariegatum'

Sedum spinosum — Orostachys spinosa

Sedum spurium Dragon's Blood — S. spurium 'Schorbuser Blut'

Sedum spurium Purple Carpet — S. spurium 'Purpurteppich'

Sedum spurium 'Tricolor' — S. spurium 'Variegatum'

Sedum stephanii — Rhodiola crassipes v stephanii

Sedum stribrnyi — S. urvillei Stribrnyi Group

Sedum telephium ssp fabaria — S. fabaria

Sedum trollii — Rhodiola trollii

Sedum wallichianum — Rhodiola wallichiana

Sedum 'Weihenstephaner Gold' — S. kamtschaticum v floriferum 'Weihenstephaner Gold'

Sedum weinbergii — Graptopetalum paraguayense

Sedum yezoense — S. pluricaule

Sedum yunnanense — Rhodiola yunnanensis

Seemannia — Gloxinia

Selaginella emmeliana — S. pallescens

Selenicereus chrysocardium — Epiphyllum chrysocardium

Selinum tenuifolium — S. wallichianum

Semiaquilegia simulatrix — S. ecalcarata

Semiarundinaria nitida — Fargesia nitida

Semiarundinaria villosa — S. okuboi

Sempervivella — Rosularia

Sempervivum acuminatum — S. tectorum v glaucum

Sempervivum allionii — Jovibarba allionii

Sempervivum arachnoideum 'Kappa' — S. 'kappa'

Sempervivum arachnoideum 'Laggeri' — S. arachnoideum ssp tomentosum

Sempervivum arachnoideum ssp doellianum — S. arachnoideum v glabrescens

Sempervivum arachnoideum ssp tomentosum misapplied — S. x barbulatum 'Hookeri'

Sempervivum arboreum — Aeonium arboreum

Sempervivum arenarium — Jovibarba arenaria

Sempervivum arvernense — S. tectorum

Sempervivum 'Aureum' — Greenovia aurea

Sempervivum balsamiferum — Aeonium balsamiferum

Sempervivum 'Boisseri' — S. tectorum ssp tectorum 'Boisseri'

Sempervivum borisii — S. ciliosum v borisii

Sempervivum calcareum 'Monstrosum' — S. calcareum 'Grigg's Surprise'

Sempervivum complanatum — Aeonium tabuliforme

Sempervivum 'Correvons' — S. 'Aymon Correvon'

Sempervivum densum — S. tectorum

Sempervivum fimbriatum — S. x barbulatum

Sempervivum haworthii — Aeonium haworthii

Sempervivum helveticum — S. montanum

Sempervivum hirtum — Jovibarba hirta

Sempervivum 'Hookeri' — S. x barbulatum 'Hookeri'

Sempervivum imbricatum — S. x barbulatum

Sempervivum 'Lennick's Glory' — S. 'Cripsyn'

Sempervivum 'Lloyd Praeger' —

Sempervivum 'Malby's Hybrid' — S. 'Reginald Malby'

Sempervivum masferreri — Aeonium sedifolium

Sempervivum montanum 'Rubrum' — S. 'Red Mountain'

Sempervivum 'Nigrum' — S. tectorum 'Nigrum'

Sempervivum nobile — Aeonium nobile

Sempervivum patens — Jovibarba heuffelii

Sempervivum 'Queen Amalia' — S. reginae-amaliae

Sempervivum reginae — S. reginae-amaliae

Sempervivum 'Rubrifolium' — S. marmoreum ssp marmoreum 'Rubrifolium'

Sempervivum schlehanii — S. marmoreum

Sempervivum 'Silberkarneol' — S. 'Silver Jubilee'

Sempervivum 'Simonkaianum' — Jovibarba hirta

Sempervivum soboliferum — Jovibarba sobolifera

Sempervivum stansfieldii — S. arachnoideum ssp tomentosum 'Stansfieldii'

Sempervivum webbianum — S. arachnoideum ssp tomentosum

Senecio abrotanifolius v tiroliensis — S. abrotanifolius

Senecio aureus — Packera aurea

Senecio bicolor ssp cineraria — S. cineraria

Senecio bidwillii — Brachyglottis bidwillii

Senecio buchananii — Brachyglottis buchananii

Senecio candicans — S. cineraria

Senecio chrysanthemoides — Euryops chrysanthemoides

Senecio clivorum — Ligularia dentata

Senecio compactus — Brachyglottis compacta

Senecio cruentus — Pericallis x hybrida

Senecio Dunedin Hybrids — Brachyglottis Dunedin Group

Senecio elaeagnifolius — Brachyglottis elaeagnifolia

Senecio 'Gregynog Gold' — Ligularia 'Gregynog Gold'

Senecio greyi h — Brachyglottis 'Sunshine' (Dunedin Group)

Senecio greyi -Hooker — Brachyglottis greyi

Senecio hectoris — Brachyglottis hectoris

Senecio heritieri — Pericallis lanata

Senecio huntii — Brachyglottis huntii

Senecio kirkii — Brachyglottis kirkii

Senecio laxifolius - Buch. — Brachyglottis laxifolia

Senecio laxifolius h — Brachyglottis 'Sunshine' (Dunedin Group)

Senecio 'Leonard Cockayne' — Brachyglottis 'Leonard Cockayne'

Senecio leucostachys — S. viravira

Senecio maritimus — S. cineraria

Senecio mikanioides — Delairea odorata

Senecio 'Moira Reid' — Brachyglottis 'Moira Reid' (Dunedin Group)

Senecio monroi — Brachyglottis monroi

Senecio populifolius — Pericallis appendiculata

Senecio przewalskii — Ligularia przewalskii

Senecio reinholdii — Brachyglottis rotundifolia

Senecio rotundifolia — Brachyglottis rotundifolia

Senecio spedenii — Brachyglottis spedenii

Senecio 'Sunshine' — Brachyglottis 'Sunshine' (Dunedin Group)

Senecio takedanus — Tephroseris takedanus

Senecio tanguticus — Sinacalia tangutica

Senecio werneriifolius — Packera werneriifolius

Senecio x hybridus — Pericallis x hybridus

Synonyms

Senna obtusa -Clos
Senna tomentosa
Serissa foetida
Serratula shawii
Sesleria caerulea ssp calcarea
Sesleria cylindrica
Setcreasea
Setcreasea purpurea
Setcreasea striata
Sibiraea altaiensis
Sideritis taurica
Sigmatostalix radicans
Silene acaulis 'Pedunculata'
Silene acaulis ssp elongata
Silene acaulis ssp exscapa
Silene alba
Silene dioica 'Compacta'
Silene dioica 'Rubra Plena'
Silene dioica 'Variegata'

Silene maritima
Silene maritima 'Flore Pleno'

Silene multifida
Silene orientalis
Silene rubra 'Flore Pleno'
Silene schafta 'Abbotswood'

Silene sieboldii

Silene uniflora 'Alba Plena'

Silene uniflora 'Flore Pleno'

Silene uniflora 'Variegata'

Silene uniflora Weisskehlchen

Silene vulgaris ssp alpina
Silene vulgaris ssp maritima
Silene vulgaris ssp maritima 'Flore Pleno'

Silene wallichiana
Silene x arkwrightii
Sinarundinaria anceps
Sinarundinaria jaunsarensis
Sinarundinaria maling
Sinarundinaria murieliae
Sinarundinaria nitida
Sinningia leucotricha
Sinobambusa tootsik 'Variegata'
Sinocalamus giganteus

Siphonosmanthus delavayi
Sisyrinchium 'Ball's Mauve'
Sisyrinchium bellum h
Sisyrinchium bermudianum 'Album'
Sisyrinchium bermudianum -Linnaeus
Sisyrinchium birameun
Sisyrinchium boreale
Sisyrinchium brachypus

Sisyrinchium coeruleum
Sisyrinchium cuspidatum
Sisyrinchium douglasii
Sisyrinchium filifolium

S. candolleana
S. multiglandulosa
S. japonica
S. seoanaei
S. albicans
S. argentea
Tradescantia
Tradescantia pallida
Callisia elegans
S. laevigata
S. syriaca
Ornithophora radicans
S. acaulis ssp acaulis
S. acaulis ssp acaulis
S. acaulis ssp bryoides
S. latifolia
S. dioica 'Minikin'
S. dioica 'Flore Pleno'
S. dioica 'Graham's Delight'
S. uniflora
S. uniflora 'Robin Whitebreast'
S. fimbriata
S. compacta
S. dioica 'Flore Pleno'
Lychnis x walkeri 'Abbotswood Rose'
Lychnis coronata v sieboldii
S. uniflora 'Robin Whitebreast'
S. uniflora 'Robin Whitebreast'
S. uniflora 'Druett's Variegated'
S. uniflora 'Robin Whitebreast'
S. uniflora ssp prostrata
S. uniflora
S. uniflora 'Robin Whitebreast'
S. vulgaris
Lychnis x arkwrightii
Yushania anceps
Yushania anceps
Yushania maling
Fargesia murieliae
Fargesia nitida
S. canescens
S. tootsik f albostriata
Dendrocalamus giganteus
Osmanthus delavayi
S. 'E.K.Balls'
S. idahoense v bellum
S. graminoides 'Album'
S. angustifolium -Miller
S. graminoides
S. californicum
S. californicum Brachypus Group
Gelasine coerulea
S. arenarium
Olsynium douglasii
Olsynium filifolium

Sisyrinchium grandiflorum
Sisyrinchium idahoense 'May Snow'
Sisyrinchium iridifolium
Sisyrinchium junceum
Sisyrinchium macounii
Sisyrinchium 'May Snow'
Sisyrinchium 'North Star'
Sisyrinchium scabrum
Sisyrinchium striatum 'Variegatum'
Sisyrinchium x anceps
Skimmia japonica 'Alba'

Skimmia japonica 'Foremannii'
Skimmia japonica 'Fructu Albo'

Skimmia laureola 'Fragrant Cloud'
Skimmia reevesiana

Skimmia rogersii

Skimmia x foremannii h
Smilax asparagoides 'Nanus'

Solandra hartwegii
Solandra nitida
Solanum crispum 'Autumnale'
Soleirolia soleirolii 'Argentea'
Soleirolia soleirolii 'Golden Queen'
Soleirolia soleirolii 'Silver Queen'
Solenomelus chilensis
Solenopsis axillaris
Solenostemon thyrsoideus
Solidago altissima
Solidago Babygold
Solidago brachystachys
Solidago Golden Baby
Solidago 'Golden Fleece'

Solidago 'Golden Rays'
Solidago 'Golden Thumb'
Solidago Goldzwerg
Solidago hybrida
Solidago latifolia
Solidago 'Lemore'

Solidago Strahlenkrone
Solidago virgaurea v cambrica
Solidago vulgaris 'Variegata'
Sollya fusiformis
Sophora prostrata misap.
Sophora viciifolia
Sophronitis grandiflora
Sorbaria aitchisonii

Sorbaria arborea
Sorbaria lindleyana
Sorbus americana erecta
Sorbus aria 'Decaisneana'
Sorbus aria 'Mitchellii'

Sorbus aria v salicifolia
Sorbus aucuparia pluripinnata
Sorbus aucuparia 'Rossica'

Sorbus aucuparia 'Xanthocarpa'

Olsynium douglasii
S. idahoense 'Album'
S. micranthum
Olsynium junceum
S. idahoense
S. idahoense 'Album'
S. 'Pole Star'
S. chilense
S. striatum 'Aunt May'
S. angustifolium -Miller
S. japonica 'Wakehurst White'
S. japonica 'Veitchii'
S. japonica 'Wakehurst White'
S. japonica 'Fragrans'
S. japonica ssp reevesiana
S. japonica Rogersii Group
S. japonica 'Veitchii'
Asparagus asparagoides 'Myrtifolius'
S. maxima
S. maxima
S. crispum 'Glasnevin'
S. soleirolii 'Variegata'
S. soleirolii 'Aurea'
S. soleirolii 'Variegata'
S. pedunculatus
Laurentia axillaris
Plectranthus thyrsoideus
S. canadensis v scabra
S. 'Goldkind'
S. cutleri
S. 'Goldkind'
S. sphacelata 'Golden Fleece'
S. 'Goldstrahl'
S. 'Queenie'
S. 'Golden Dwarf'
x Solidaster luteus
S. flexicaulis
x Solidaster luteus 'Lemore'
S. 'Crown of Rays'
S. virgaurea v minuta
S. virgaurea 'Variegata'
S. heterophylla
S. 'Little Baby'
S. davidii
S. coccinea
S. tomentosa v angustifolia
S. kirilowii
S. tomentosa
S. decora
S. aria 'Majestica'
S. thibetica 'John Mitchell'
S. rupicola
S. scalaris
S. aucuparia 'Rossica Major'
S. aucuparia 'Fructo Luteo'

Synonyms

Sorbus conradinae h

Sorbus conradinae -Koeh.
Sorbus cuspidata
Sorbus decora v nana
Sorbus discolor h
Sorbus domestica 'Maliformis'
Sorbus domestica 'Pyriformis'
Sorbus glabrescens
Sorbus hupehensis 'Rosea'
Sorbus hybrida h
Sorbus koehneana h
Sorbus lanata h
Sorbus matsumurana h
Sorbus 'Mitchellii'

Sorbus moravica 'Laciniata'
Sorbus pekinensis

Sorbus pohuashanensis h
Sorbus prattii v tatsienensis
Sorbus reflexipetala
Sorbus scopulina h
Sorbus umbellata v cretica
Sorbus zahlbruckneri h
Sorghastrum nutans
Sparaxis grandiflora

Sparganium minimum
Sparganium ramosum
Sparmannia
Sparmannia africana 'Plena'

Sparrmannia palmata
Spartina pectinata 'Aureovariegata'

Spartocytisus
Spathipapppus
Specularia speculum-veneris

Speirantha gardenii
Sphacele
Sphaeralcea umbellata
Sphaeromeria argentea
Sphaeropteris
Spiloxene capensis
Spiraea aitchchisonii

Spiraea albiflora
Spiraea arborea
Spiraea aruncus
Spiraea callosa 'Alba'
Spiraea cantoniensis 'Lanceata'

Spiraea crispifolia
Spiraea hendersonii

Spiraea japonica 'Alba'
Spiraea japonica 'Alpina'
Spiraea japonica 'Nyewoods'
Spiraea japonica 'Shiburi'
Spiraea menziesii
Spiraea nipponica v tosaensis h

Spiraea opulifolius

S. pohuashanensis -
(Hance) Hedlund
S. esserteauana
S. vestita
S. aucuparia 'Fastigiata'
S. commixta
S. domestica v pomifera
S. domestica v pyrifera
S. hupehensis
S. hupehensis v obtusa
S. x thuringiaca
S. fruticosa
S. vestita
S. commixta
S. thibetica 'John
Mitchell'
S. aucuparia 'Beissneri'
S. reticulata ssp
pekinensis
S. x kewensis
S. prattii
S. commixta
S. aucuparia 'Fastigiata'
S. graeca
S. alnifolia
S. avenaceum
S. fragrans ssp
grandiflora
S. natans
S. erectum
Sparrmannia
Sparrmannia africana
'Flore Pleno'
S. ricinocarpa
S. pectinata
'Aureomarginata'
Cytisus
Tanacetum
Legousia speculum-
veneris
S. convallarioides
Lepechinia
Phymosia umbellata
Tanacetum nuttallii
Cyathea
Hypoxis capensis
Sorbaria tomentosa v
angustifolia
S. japonica v albiflora
Sorbaria kirilowii
Aruncus dioicus
S. japonica v albiflora
S. cantoniensis 'Flore
Pleno'
S. japonica 'Bullata'
Petrophytum
hendersonii
S. japonica v albiflora
S. japonica 'Nana'
S. japonica 'Nana'
S. japonica 'Shirobana'
S. douglasii ssp menziesii
S. nipponica
'Snowmound'
S. physocarpus
opulifolius

Spiraea palmata
Spiraea palmata elegans

Spiraca prunifolia 'Plena'
Spiraea sorbifolia
Spiraea trichicarpa 'Snow White'
Spiraea ulmaria
Spiraea venusta 'Magnifica'

Spiraea x arguta 'Bridal Wreath'
Spiraea x arguta 'Compacta'
Spiraea x arguta 'Nana'
Spiraea x bumalda
Spiraea x bumalda 'Wulfenii'
Spironema fragrans
Stachys betonica
Stachys byzantina 'Countess Helen von
Stein'
Stachys byzantina gold-leaved

Stachys byzantina large-leaved
Stachys byzantina 'Sheila McQueen'
Stachys byzantina 'Variegata'

Stachys densiflora
Stachys grandiflora
Stachys lanata
Stachys nivea
Stachys olympica
Stachys 'Primrose Heron'

Stachys 'Silver Carpet'

Stachys spicata
Stachys tuberifera
Stachys x ambigua
Stapelia europaea
Stapelia flavirostris
Stapelia nobilis
Stapelia variegata
Statice
Statice bellidifolia
Statice minuta
Statice spicata
Statice suworowii
Steironema ciliata
Stenanthium angustifolium
Stenolobium stans
Stenomesson incarnatum
Stephanandra incisa 'Prostrata'
Stephanotis jasminoides
Sterculia acerifolia

Sterculia diversifolia
Sterculia platanifolia
Sternbergia macrantha
Stewartia 'Korean Splendor'

Stewartia koreana

Stewartia pseudocamellia v koreana

Stipa brachytricha

Stipa lasiagrostis
Stokesia cyanea

Filipendula palmata
Filipendula palmata
'Elegantissima'
S. prunifolia
Sorbaria sorbifolia
S. 'Snow White'
Filipendula ulmaria
Filipendula rubra
'Venusta'
S. 'Arguta'
S. x cinerea
S. x cinerea
S. japonica 'Bumalda'
S. japonica 'Walluf'
Callisia fragrans
S. officinalis

S. byzantina 'Big Ears'
S. byzantina 'Primrose
Heron'
S. byzantina 'Big Ears'
S. byzantina 'Cotton Boll'
S. byzantina 'Striped
Phantom'
S. monieri
S. macrantha
S. byzantina
S. discolor
S. byzantina
S. byzantina 'Primrose
Heron'
S. byzantina 'Silver
Carpet'
S. macrantha
S. affinis
S. officinalis
Caralluma europaea
S. grandiflora
S. gigantea
Orbea variegata
Limonium
Limonium bellidifolium
Limonium minutum
Psylliostachys spicata
Psylliostachys suworowii
Lysimachia ciliata
S. gramineum
Tecoma stans
S. variegatum
S. incisa 'Crispa'
S. floribunda
Brachychiton
acericifolius
Brachychiton populneus
Firmiana simplex
S. clusiana
S. pseudocamellia
Koreana Group
S. pseudocamellia
Koreana Group
S. pseudocamellia
Koreana Group
Calamagrostis
brachytricha
S. calamagrostis
S. laevis

Synonyms

Stransvaesia	Photinia
Strelitzia reginae 'Pygmaea'	S. reginae 'Humilis'
Strelitzia reginae v juncea	S. juncea
Streptanthera cuprea	Sparaxis elegans
Streptanthera elegans	Sparaxis elegans
Streptocarpella	Streptocarpus
Stromanthe amabilis	Ctenanthe amabilis
Stromanthe lutea	S. jacquinii
Struthiopteris niponica	Blechnum niponicum
Stuartia	Stewartia
Styphelia colensoi	Cyathodes colensoi
Styrax japonicus 'Roseus'	S. japonicus Benibana Group
Submatucana aurantiaca	Cleistocactus aurantiacus
Sulcorebutia	Rebutia
Sulcorebutia arenacea	Rebutia arenacea
Sulcorebutia rauschii	Rebutia rauschii
Sulcorebutia tiraquensis	Rebutia tiraquensis
Swainsonia	Swainsona
Swida alba	Cornus alba
Swida alternifolia	Cornus alternifolia
Swida amomum	Cornus amomum
Swida controversa	Cornus controversa
Syagrus weddelliana	Lytocaryum weddelianum
Sycopsis orbiculatus 'Variegatus'	S. orbiculatus 'Foliis Variegatus'
Sycopsis rivularis	S. albus v laevigatus
Sycopsis tutcheri	Distylium racemosum tutcheri
Symphoricarpos albus 'Variegatus'	S. albus 'Taff's White'
Symphoricarpos orbiculatus 'Albovariegatus'	S. orbiculatus 'Taff's Silver Edge'
Symphoricarpos orbiculatus 'Argenteovariegatus'	S. orbiculatus 'Taff's Silver Edge'
Symphoricarpos orbiculatus 'Bowles' Golden Variegated'	S. orbiculatus 'Foliis Variegatis'
Symphoricarpos orbiculatus 'Variegatus'	S. orbiculatus 'Foliis Variegatis'
Symphoricarpos rivularis	S. albus v laevigatus
Symphyandra pendula alba	S. pendula
Symphytum grandiflorum	S. ibericum
Symphytum ibericum 'Jubilee'	S. 'Goldsmith'
Symphytum ibericum 'Variegatum'	S. 'Goldsmith'
Symphytum 'Jubilee'	S. 'Goldsmith'
Symphytum peregrinum	S. x uplandicum
Symphytum 'Roseum'	S. 'Hidcote Pink'
Synadenium grantii 'Rubrum'	S. compactum v rubrum
Synadenium grantii v rubrum	S. compactum v rubrum
Synnotia	Sparaxis
Syringa afghanica	S. protolaciniata
Syringa amurensis	S. reticulata v amurensis
Syringa 'Isabella'	S. x prestoniae 'Isabella'
Syringa julianae	S. pubescens ssp julianae
Syringa microphylla	S. pubescens ssp microphylla
Syringa microphylla 'Superba'	S. pubescens ssp microphylla 'Superba'
Syringa palibiniana	S. meyeri 'Palibin'
Syringa patula h	S. meyeri 'Palibin'
Syringa patula -(Palibin) Nakai	S. pubescens ssp patula
Syringa pekinensis	S. reticulata ssp pekinensis
Syringa reflexa	S. komarorii ssp reflexa
Syringa reticulata v mandschurica	S. reticulata v amurensis
Syringa velutina	S. patula -(Palibin) Nakai
Syringa vulgaris 'Christopher Columbus'	S. vulgaris 'Christophe Colomb'
Syringa vulgaris 'Glory of Horstenstein'	S. vulgaris 'Ruhm von Horstenstein'
Syringa vulgaris 'Souvenir de Louis Spaeth'	S. vulgaris 'Andenken an Ludwig Spath'
Syringa x persica v laciniata	S. x laciniata -Miller
Tabebuia donnell-smithii	Cybistax donnell-smithii
Tabebuia pentaphylla h	T. rosea
Tabernaemontana coronaria	T. divaricata
Tacitus	Graptopetalum
Tacitus bellus	Graptopetalum bellum
Tacsonia mollissima	Passiflora mollissima
Tacsonia van-volxemii	Passiflora antioquiensis
Tacsonia x exoniensis	Passiflora x exoniensis
Tamarix germanica	Myricaria germanica
Tamarix pentandra	T. ramosissima
Tamarix ramosissima 'Summer Glow'	T. ramosissima 'Rubra'
Tamarix tetrandra v purpurea	T. parviflora
Tanacetum balsamita tomentosum	T. balsamita ssp balsametoides
Tanacetum balsamita v tanacetoides	T. balsamita ssp balsamita
Tanacetum capitatum	Sphaeromeria capitata
Tanacetum herderi	Hippolytia herderi
Tanacetum pallidum	Leucanthemopsis pallida
Tanacetum parthenium 'Sissinghurst White'	T. parthenium 'Rowallane'
Tanakea	Tanakea
Tasmannia	Drimys
Taxodium ascendens	T. distichum v imbricatum
Taxus baccata 'Argentea Minor'	T. baccata 'Dwarf White'
Taxus baccata 'Hibernica'	T. baccata 'Fastigiata'
Taxus baccata 'Variegata'	T. baccata Aurea Group
Tecoma australis	Pandorea pandorana
Tecoma grandiflora	Campsis grandiflora
Tecoma radicans	Campsis radicans
Tecoma ricasoliana	Podranea ricasoliana
Tecomaria	Tecoma
Tecomaria petersii	Tecoma capensis
Tecophilaea cyanocrocus 'Purpurea'	T. cyanocrocus 'Violacea'
Telesonix	Boykinia
Teline	Genista
Tellima grandiflora 'Purpurea'	T. grandiflora Rubra Group
Ternstroemia gymnanthera	T. japonica
Testudinaria elephantipes	Dioscorea elephantipes
Tetragonolobus	Lotus
Tetranema mexicanum	T. roseum
Tetrapanax papyriferus	T. payrifer
Tetrapathaea	Passiflora
Teucrium aroanum	T. aroanium
Teucrium chamaedrys h	T. x lucidrys
Teucrium majoricum	T. polium f pii-fontii
Teucrium massiliense h	T. x lucidrys
Teucrium pulverulentum	T. cossonii
Teucrium rosmarinifolium	T. creticum
Thalictrum adiantifolium	T. minus adiantifolium
Thalictrum angustifolium	T. lucidum

Synonyms

Thalictrum aquilegiifolium Purple Cloud	T. aquilegiifolium 'Thundercloud'	Thymus minus	Calamintha nepeta
Thalictrum coreanum	T. ichangense	Thymus montanus -Waldstein & Kitaibel	T. pulegioides
Thalictrum dipterocarpum h	T. delavayi	Thymus odoratissimus	T. pallasianus ssp pallasianus
Thalictrum flavum 'Chollerton'	T. sp Afghanistan	Thymus praecox	T. polytrichus
Thalictrum flexuosum	T. minus ssp minus	Thymus praecox 'Coccineus'	T. serpyllum v coccineus
Thalictrum koreanum	T. ichangense	Thymus praecox ssp arcticus	T. polytrichus ssp britannicus
Thalictrum minus ssp saxatile	T. minus ssp olympicum		
Thalictrum speciosissimum	T. flavum ssp glaucum	Thymus praecox ssp arcticus v albus	T. polytrichus ssp britannicus v albus
Thamnocalamus falcatus	Drepanostachyum falcatum		
Thamnocalamus falconeri	Himalayacalamus falconeri	Thymus richardii ssp nitidus 'Compactus Albus'	T. richardii ssp nitidus 'Snow White'
Thamnocalamus funghomii	Schizostachyum funghomii	Thymus serpyllum 'Albus Variegatus'	T. 'Hartington Silver'
Thamnocalamus khasianus	Drepanostachyum khasianum	Thymus serpyllum 'Lavender Sea'	T. 'Lavender Sea'
Thamnocalamus maling	Yushania maling	Thymus serpyllum 'Minus'	T. serpyllum 'Minor'
Thamnocalamus spathaceus h	Fargesia murieliae	Thymus serpyllum 'Pink Ripple'	T. 'Pink Ripple'
Thapsia decipiens	Melanoselinum decipiens	Thymus serpyllum 'Ruby Glow'	T. 'Ruby Glow'
		Thymus serpyllum ssp lanuginosus	T. pseudolanuginosus
Thea	Camellia	Thymus serpyllum 'Variegatus'	T. 'Hartington Silver'
Thelycrania	Cornus	Thymus 'Silver Posie'	T. vulgaris 'Silver Posie'
Thelypteris hexagonoptera	Phegopteris hexagonoptera	Thymus x citriodorus 'Anderson's Gold'	T. vulgaris 'Bertram Anderson'
Thelypteris limbosperma	Oreopteris limbosperma		
Thelypteris oreopteris	Oreopteris limbosperma	Thymus x citriodorus 'Silver Posie'	T. vulgaris 'Silver Posie'
Thelypteris phegopteris	Phegopteris connectilis	Thymus x citriodorus 'Variegatus' misapplied	T. x citriodorus 'Golden King'
Thermopsis caroliniana	T. villosa	Tiarella collina	T. wherryi
Thermopsis fabacea	T. lupinoides	Tiarella cordifolia v collina	T. wherryi
Thevetia neriifolia	T. peruviana	Tibouchina semidecandra h	T. urvilleana
Thlaspi alpestre	T. alpinum	Tibouchina semidecandra ssp floribunda h	T. organensis
Thlaspi biebersteinii	Pachyphragma macrophyllum	Tilia argentea	T. tomentosa
		Tilia begoniifolia	T. dasystyla
Thlaspi macrophyllum	Pachyphragma macrophyllum	Tilia 'Euchlora'	T. x euchlora
		Tilia 'Hillieri'	T. 'Harold Hillier'
Thrinax bahamensis	T. morrisii	Tilia intermedia	T. x europaea
Thrinax ponceana	T. morrisii	Tilia monticola	T. heterophylla
Thuja occidentalis 'Emerald'	T. occidentalis 'Smaragd'	Tilia petiolaris	T. 'Petiolaris'
Thuja occidentalis 'Orientalis Semperaurescens'		Tilia platyphyllos 'Corallina'	T. platyphyllos 'Rubra'
	T. orientalis 'Semperaurea'	Tilia platyphyllos 'Erecta'	T. platyphyllos 'Fastigiata'
Thuja occidentalis 'Wareana Aurea'	T. occidentalis 'Wareana Lutescens'	Tilia x euchlora 'Redmond'	T. americana 'Redmond'
		Tilia x vulgaris	T. x europaea
Thuja orientalis 'Miller's Gold'	T. orientalis 'Aurea Nana'	Tillaea	Crassula
Thuja plicata 'Stolwijk's Gold'	T. occidentalis 'Stolwijk'	Tillandsia benthamiana	T. erubescens
Thujopsis dolabrata 'Laetevirens'	T. dolabrata 'Nana'	Tillandsia dianthoidea	T. aeranthos
Thujopsis koraiensis	Thuja koraiensis	Tillandsia ionantha v scaposa	T. kolbii
Thunbergia gibsonii	T. gregorii	Tillandsia tenuifolia v surinamensis	T. tenuifolia v tenuifolia
Thymus 'Anderson's Gold'	T. x citriodorus 'Bertram Anderson'	Tillandsia valenzueliana	T. variabilis
		Tillandsia velickiana	T. matudae
Thymus azoricus	T. caespititius	Tipuana speciosa	T. rotundifolia
Thymus carnosus misap.	T. vulgaris 'Erectus'	Tipuana speciosa	T. tipu
Thymus drucei	T. polytrichus ssp britannicus	Tolmiea 'Goldsplash'	T. menziesii 'Taff's Gold'
		Tolmiea menziesii 'Maculata'	T. menziesii 'Taff's Gold'
Thymus 'E.B.Anderson'	T. x citriodorus 'Bertram Anderson'	Tolmiea menziesii 'Variegata'	T. menziesii 'Taff's Gold'
		Tovara	Persicaria
Thymus erectus	T. vulgaris 'Erectus'	Townsendia wilcoxiana h	T. rothrockii
Thymus herba-barona citrata	T. herba-barona 'Lemon-scented'	Toxicodendron	Rhus
		Toxicodendron succedaneum	Rhus succedanea
Thymus 'Highland Cream'	T. 'Hartington Silver'	Toxicodendron vernicifluum	Rhus verniciflua
Thymus lanuginosus h	T. pseudolanuginosus	Trachelospermum majus h	T. jasminoides 'Japonicum'
Thymus 'Lemon Caraway'	T. herba-barona 'Lemon-scented'		
		Trachelospermum majus -Nakai	T. asiaticum
Thymus marschallianus	T. pannonicus	Tradescantia albiflora	T. fluminensis
Thymus micans	T. caespititius	Tradescantia blossfeldiana	T. cerinthoides
		Tradescantia canaliculata	T. ohiensis
		Tradescantia multiflora	Tripogandra multiflora

Synonyms

Tradescantia navicularis	Callisia navicularis
Tradescantia pendula	T. zebrina
Tradescantia pexata	T. sillamontana
Tradescantia tricolor	T. zebrina
Tradescantia velutina	T. sillamontana
Tradescantia x andersoniana 'Caerulea Plena'	T. virginiana 'Caerulea Plena'
Tradescantia x andersoniana Carmine Glow	T. x andersoniana 'Karminglut'
Tradescantia zebrina pendula	T. zebrina
Tragopogon roseus	T. ruber
Trichocereus bridgesii	Echinopsis bridgesii
Trichocereus candicans	Echinopsis candicans
Trichocereus grandiflorus	Echinopsis huascha
Trichocereus huascha	Echinopsis huascha
Trichocereus shaferi	Echinopsis schickendantzii
Trichocereus spachianus	Echinopsis spachianus
Trichosanthes anguina	T. cucumerina v anguina
Tricuspidaria	Crinodendron
Tricuspidaria lanceolata	Crinodendron hookerianum
Tricyrtis bakeri	T. latifolia
Tricyrtis dilatata	T. macropoda
Tricyrtis flava ssp ohsumiensis	T. ohsumiensis
Tricyrtis japonica	T. hirta
Tricyrtis stolonifera	T. formosana Stolonifera Group
Trifolium pratense 'Chocolate'	T. pratense 'Purple Velvet'
Trifolium pratense 'Dolly North'	T. pratense 'Susan Smith'
Trifolium pratense 'Ice Cool'	T. repens 'Green Ice'
Trifolium repens 'Gold Net'	T. pratense 'Susan Smith'
Trifolium repens 'Pentaphyllum'	T. repens 'Quinquefolium'
Trifolium repens 'Tetraphyllum Purpureum'	T. repens ' Purpurascens Quadrifolium'
Trillium sessile v luteum	T. luteum
Trillium stylosum	T. catesbyi
Tristagma 'Rolf Fiedler'	Ipheion 'Rolf Fiedler'
Tristagma uniflorum	Ipheion uniflorum
Tristania conferta	Lophostemon confertus
Tristania laurina	Tristaniopsis laurina
Triteleia californica	Brodiaea californica
Triteleia laxa Queen Fabiola	T. laxa 'Koningin Fabiola'
Triteleia uniflora	Ipheion uniflorum
Tritoma	Kniphofia
Tritonia fenestrata	T. crocata
Tritonia hyalina	T. crocata hyalina
Tritonia longiflora	Ixia paniculata
Tritonia rosea	T. disticha ssp rubrolucens
Tritonia rubrolucens	T. disticha ssp rubrolucens
Trollius europaeus 'Superbus'	T. x cultorum 'Superbus'
Trollius ledebourii h	T. chinensis
Trollius x cultorum Fireglobe	T. x cultorum 'Feuertroll'
Trollius x cultorum Gold Fountain	T. x cultorum 'Goldquelle'
Tropaeolum aduncum	T. peregrinum
Tropaeolum canariense	T. peregrinum
Tropaeolum tricolor	T. tricolorum
Tsuga canadensis 'Coles'	T. canadensis 'Cole's Prostrate'
Tsuga canadensis f pendula	T. canadensis 'Pendula'
Tsuga canadensis 'Nana Gracilis'	T. canadensis 'Gracilis'
Tsuga canadensis 'Prostrata'	T. canadensis 'Branklyn'
Tsuga canadensis 'Pygmaea'	T. canadensis 'Abbott's Pygmy'
Tsuga menziesii	Pseudotsuga menziesii
Tsusiophyllum tanakae	Rhododendron tsusiophyllum
Tulbaghia fragrans	T. simmleri
Tulbaghia maritima	T. cepacea v maritima
Tulbaghia pulchella	T. simmleri
Tulbaghia violacea 'Variegata'	T. violacea 'Silver Lace'
Tulipa aitchisonii	T. clusiana
Tulipa amabilis PF 8955	T. hoogiana PF 8955
Tulipa 'Apricot Jewel'	T. linifolia 'Apricot Jewel' (Batalinii Group)
Tulipa 'Aurea'	T. greigii 'Aurea'
Tulipa bakeri	T. saxatilis Bakeri Group
Tulipa batalinii	T. linifolia Batalinii Group
Tulipa 'Bird of Paradise'	T. 'Mrs Keightley'
Tulipa chrysantha -Boissier	T. montana
Tulipa chrysantha -Boissier ex Baker	T. clusiana v chrysantha
Tulipa didieri	T. passeriniana
Tulipa eichleri	T. undulatifolia
Tulipa 'Fireside'	T. 'Vlammenspel'
Tulipa 'Gay Presto'	T. 'Estella Rijnveld'
Tulipa 'General de Wet'	T. 'Generaal de Wet'
Tulipa 'Grand Duc'	T. 'Keizerskroon'
Tulipa 'Greenland'	T. 'Groenland'
Tulipa 'Lilac Wonder'	T. saxatilis 'Lilac Wonder' (Bakeri Group)
Tulipa 'Lilliput'	T. humilis 'Lilliput'
Tulipa Magician	T. 'Magier'
Tulipa marjoletii	T. marjolletii
Tulipa maximowiczii	T. linifolia Maximowiczii Group
Tulipa Merry Widow	T. 'Lustige Witwe'
Tulipa 'Orange Sun'	T. 'Oranjezon'
Tulipa persica	T. celsiana
Tulipa polychroma	T. biflora
Tulipa pulchella	T. humilis v pulchella Albocaerulea Oculata Group
Tulipa pulchella humilis	T. humilis
Tulipa 'Queen Wilhelmina'	T. 'Koningin Wilhelmina'
Tulipa 'Red Emperor'	T. 'Madame Lefeber'
Tulipa rhodopea	T. urumoffii
Tulipa 'Ringo'	T. 'Kees Nelis'
Tulipa 'Spectacular Gold'	T.'Goldenes Deutschland'
Tulipa stellata	T. clusiana v stellata
Tulipa stellata v chrysantha	T. clusiana v chrysantha
Tulipa 'Sweetheart'	T. 'Princess Juliana'
Tulipa 'Topic'	T. 'Golden Oxford'
Tulipa violacea	T. humilis Violacea Group
Tulipa 'White Emperor'	T. 'Purissima'
Tulipa whittallii	T. orphanidea Whittallii Group
Tulipa wilsoniana	T. montana
Tunica	Petrorhagia
Turbinicarpus schmiedickeanus	Neolloydia schmiedickeana
Tylecodon wallichii	T. papillaris ssp wallichii
Typha stenophylla	T. laxmannii
Ulex europaeus 'Plenus'	U. europaeus 'Flore Pleno'
Ulex nanus	U. minor
Ulmus angustifolia	U. minor ssp angustifolia
Ulmus angustifolia v cornubiensis	U. minor 'Cornubiensis'
Ulmus 'Camperdownii'	U. glabra 'Camperdownii'
Ulmus carpinifolia	U. minor

Synonyms

Ulmus carpinifolia v cornubiensis	U. minor 'Cornubiensis'
Ulmus carpinifolia v sarniensis	U. minor 'Sarniensis'
Ulmus 'Commelin'	U. x hollandica 'Commelin'
Ulmus 'Dicksonii'	U. minor 'Dicksonii'
Ulmus glabra 'Horizontalis'	U. glabra 'Pendula'
Ulmus montana	U. glabra
Ulmus parvifolia 'Pygmaea'	U. parvifolia 'Hokkaido'
Ulmus 'Vegeta'	U. x hollandica 'Vegeta'
Ulmus 'Wheatleyi Aurea'	U. minor 'Dicksonii'
Ulmus x elegantissima 'Jacqueline Hillier'	U. x hollandica 'Jacqueline Hillier'
Ulmus x hollandica 'Wredei'	U. minor 'Dampieri Aurea'
Uniola latifolia	Chasmanthium latifolium
Urceolina miniata	Stenomesson miniatum
Urceolina pendula	Stenomesson miniatum
Urceolina peruviana	Stenomesson miniatum
Urechites	Pentalinon
Ursinia geyeri	U. chrysanthemoides v geyeri
Utricularia exoleta	U. gibba
Uvularia pudica	U. caroliniana
Vaccaria segetalis	V. hispanica
Vaccinum donianum	V. sprengelii
Vaccinum mortinia	V. floribundum
Vaccinum palustre	V. oxycoccus
Valeriana 'Alba'	Centranthus ruber albus
Valeriana 'Coccinea'	Centranthus ruber
Valerianella olitoria	V. locusta
Vallota speciosa	Cyrtanthus elatus
Vanda sanderiana	Euanthe sanderiana
Vellozia elegans	Talbotia elegans
Veltheimia glauca	V. capensis
Veltheimia roodiae	V. capensis
Veltheimia undulata	V. bracteata
Veltheimia viridifolia h	V. capensis
Veltheimia viridifolia -Jacquin	V. bracteata
Venidium	Arctotis
Verbascum 'Arctic Summer'	V. bombyciferum 'Polarsommer'
Verbascum 'Broussa'	V. bombyciferum
Verbascum longifolium v pannosum	V. olympicum
Verbascum thapsiforme	V. densiflorum
Verbena alpina h	V. x maonettii
Verbena chamaedrifolia	V. peruviana
Verbena chamaedrioides	V. peruviana
Verbena 'Mahonettii'	V. x maonettii
Verbena patagonica	V. bonariensis
Verbena 'Pink Bouquet'	V. 'Silver Anne'
Verbena pulchella	V. tenera
Verbena 'Tenerife'	V. 'Sissinghurst'
Verbena venosa	V. rigida
Veronica amethystina	V. spuria
Veronica austriaca ssp teucrium 'Shirley Blue'	V. 'Shirley Blue'
Veronica austriaca v dubia	V. prostrata
Veronica Blue Bouquet	V. longifolia 'Blaubundel'
Veronica bonarota	Paederota bonarota
Veronica candida	V. spicata ssp incana
Veronica chamaedrys 'Variegata'	V. chamaedrys 'Miffy Brute'
Veronica formosa	Hebe formosa
Veronica hendersonii	V. subsessilis hendersonii
Veronica incana	V. spicata ssp incana
Veronica kellereri	V. spicata
Veronica longifolia Blue Giantess	V. longifolia 'Blauriesin'
Veronica longifolia 'Foerster's Blue'	V. longifolia 'Blauriesin'
Veronica lyallii	Parahebe lyallii
Veronica peduncularis 'Oxford Blue'	V. peduncularis 'Georgia Blue'
Veronica perfoliata	Parahebe perfoliata
Veronica prenja	V. austriaca
Veronica prostrata Blue Mirror	V. prostrata 'Blauspiegel'
Veronica prostrata 'Miss Willmott'	V. prostrata 'Warley Blue'
Veronica repens	V. reptans
Veronica rupestris	V. prostrata
Veronica saxatilis	V. fruticans
Veronica selleri	V. wormskjoldii
Veronica spicata Blue Fox	V. spicata 'Blaufuchs'
Veronica spicata Red Fox	V. spicata 'Rotfuchs'
Veronica spicata rosea	V. spicata 'Erika'
Veronica stelleri	V. wormskjoldii
Veronica teucrium	V. austriaca ssp teucrium
Veronica virginica	Veronicastrum virginicum
Veronica 'White Icicle'	V. spicata 'Icicle'
Veronicastrum virginicum roseum	V. virginicum v incarnatum
Vestia lycioides	V. foetida
Viburnum alnifolium	V. lantanoides
Viburnum farreri 'Album'	V. farreri 'Candidissimum'
Viburnum fragrans -Bunge	V. farreri
Viburnum 'Fulbrook'	V. x burkwoodii 'Fulbrook'
Viburnum mariesii	V. plicatum 'Mariesii'
Viburnum opulus 'Sterile'	V. opulus 'Roseum'
Viburnum opulus 'Watanabe'	V. plicatum 'Nanum Semperflorens'
Viburnum plicatum 'Nanum'	V. plicatum 'Nanum Semperflorens'
Viburnum pubescens	V. dentatum v pubescens
Viburnum semperflorens	V. plicatum 'Nanum Semperflorens'
Viburnum theiferum	V. setigerum
Viburnum tinus 'Pyramidale'	V. tinus 'Strictum'
Viburnum tomentosum	V. plicatum
Viburnum watanabei	V. plicatum 'Nanum Semperflorens'
Viburnum x pragense	V. 'Pragense'
Vicia angustifolia	V. sativa ssp nigra
Victoria regia	V. amazonica
Victoria trickeri	V. cruziana
Villadia hemsleyana	Sedum hemsleyanum
Villaresia	Citronella
Villarsia bennettii	Nymphoides peltata 'Bennettii'
Villarsia nymphoides	Nymphoides peltata 'Bennettii'
Vinca herbacea 'Hidcote Purple'	V. major v oxyloba
Vinca 'Hidcote Purple'	V. major v oxyloba
Vinca hirsuta h	V. major v oxyloba
Vinca major 'Dartington Star'	V. major v oxyloba
Vinca major 'Elegantissima'	V. major 'Variegata'
Vinca major hirsuta h	V. major v oxyloba
Vinca major 'Surrey Marble'	V. major 'Maculata'
Vinca major v pubescens	V. major ssp hirsuta -(Boiss.) Stearn
Vinca minor 'Alba Aureavariegata'	V. minor 'Alba Variegata'
Vinca minor 'Bowles' Blue'	V. minor 'La Grave'
Vinca minor 'Bowles' Variety'	V. minor 'La Grave'

Synonyms

Vinca minor 'Caerulea Plena'	V. minor 'Azurea Flore Pleno'	Viscaria vulgaris	Lychnis viscaria
Vinca minor 'Dartington Star'	V. major v oxyloba	Vitex negundo cannabifolia	V. incisa
Vinca minor 'Double Burgundy'	V. minor 'Multiplex'	Vitis aconitifolia	Ampelopsis aconitifolia
Vinca minor Green Carpet	V. minor 'Gruner Teppich'	Vitis Black Hamburgh	V. vinifera 'Schiava Grossa'
Vinca minor 'Purpurea'	V. minor 'Atropurpurea'	Vitis capensis	Rhoicissus capensis
Vinca minor 'Rubra'	V. minor 'Atropurpurea'	Vitis ficifolia	V. thunbergii
Vinca minor 'Variegata'	V. minor 'Argenteovariegata'	Vitis henryana	Parthenocissus henryana
Vinca minor 'Variegata Aurea'	V. minor 'Aureovariegata'	Vitis heterophylla	Ampelopsis glandulosa v maximowiczii
Vinca rosea	Catharanthus roseus	Vitis inconstans	Parthenocissus tricuspidata
Vincetoxicum officinale	V. hirundinaria	Vitis quinquefolia	Parthenocissus quinquefolia
Viola 'Admiral Avellan'	V. 'Amiral Avellan'	Vitis Seibel 13053	V. 'Cascade'
Viola adunca v minor	V. labradorica	Vitis Seibel 5455	V. 'Plantet'
Viola albanica	V. magellensis	Vitis Seyve Villard 12.375	V. 'Villard Blanc'
Viola arenaria	V. rupestris	Vitis Seyve Villard 5276	V. 'Seyval Blanc'
Viola bosniaca	V. elegantula bosniaca	Vitis striata	Cissus striata
Viola 'Boughton Blue'	V. 'Belmont Blue'	Vitis thomsonii	Parthenocissus thomsonii
Viola chaerophylloides	V. dissecta v chaerophyloides	Vitis 'Trollinger'	V. vinifera 'Schiava Grossa'
Viola cornuta 'Minor Alba'	V. cornuta 'Alba Minor'	Vitis vinifera 'Apiifolia'	V. vinifera 'Ciotat'
Viola curtisii	V. tricolor v curtisii	Vitis vinifera 'Black Alicante'	V. vinifera 'Alicante'
Viola 'E.A.Bowles'	V. 'Bowles' Black'	Vitis vinifera 'Black Hamburgh'	V. vinifera 'Schiava Grossa'
Viola eizanensis	V. dissecta v chaerophylloides f eizanensis	Vitis vinifera 'Blue Portuguese'	V. vinifera 'Portugieser'
Viola erecta	V. elatior	Vitis vinifera 'Chasselas d'Or'	V. vinifera 'Chasselas'
Viola 'Freckles'	V. soraria 'Freckles'	Vitis vinifera 'Glory of Boskoop'	V. 'Boskoop Glory'
Viola 'Haslemere'	V. 'Nellie Britton'	Vitis vinifera 'Golden Chasselas'	V. vinifera 'Chasselas'
Viola hederacea v sieberi	V. sieberiana	Vitis vinifera 'Malbec'	V. vinifera 'Cot'
Viola heterophylla ssp epirota	V. bertolonii	Vitis vinifera 'Muscadet'	V. vinifera 'Melon de Bourgogne'
Viola koreana	V. grypoceraas	Vitis vinifera Riesling-Silvaner	V. vinifera 'Muller-Thurgau'
Viola labradorica h	V. riviniana Purpurea Group	Vitis vinifera 'Royal Muscadine'	V. vinifera 'Chasselas'
Viola labradorica purpurea h	V. riviniana Purpurea Group	Vitis vinifera Strawberry Grape	V. 'Fragola'
Viola 'Lady Saville'	V. 'Sissinghurst'	Vitis vinifera 'Thompson Seedless'	V. vinifera 'Sultana'
Viola lutea ssp elegans	V. lutea	Vitis voinieriana	Tetrastigma voinierianum
Viola macedonica	V. tricolor ssp macedonica	Vittadinia cuneata	V. australis
Viola 'Neapolitan'	V. 'Pallida Plena'	Wahlenbergia pumilio	Edraianthus pumilio
Viola 'Netta Statham'	V. 'Belmont Blue'	Wahlenbergia serpyllifolia	Edraianthus serpyllifolius
Viola obliqua	V. cucullata	Wahlenbergia tasmanica	W. saxicola
Viola odorata apricot	V. 'Sulphurea'	Waldheimia	Allardia
Viola odorata dumetorum	V. alba	Waldsteinia trifolia	W. ternata
Viola odorata 'Sulphurea'	V. 'Sulphurea'	Washingtonia filamentosa	W. filifera
Viola papilionacea	V. sororia	Watsonia ardernei	W. borbonica ssp ardernei
Viola pensylvanica	V. pubescens v eriocarpa	Watsonia beatricis	W. pillansii
Viola 'Princess of Wales'	V. 'Princesse de Galles'	Watsonia brevifolia	W. laccata
Viola purpurea misapplied	V. riviniana Purpurea Group	Watsonia bulbillifera	W. meriana
Viola 'Queen Victoria'	V. 'Victoria Regina'	Watsonia coccinea -Baker	W. spectabilis
Viola reniforme	V. hederacea	Watsonia pyrimadata	W. borbonica
Viola rugulosa	V. canadensis v rugulosa	Watsonia roseoalba	W. humilis
Viola saxatilis	V. tricolor ssp subalpina	Wattakaka	Dregea
Viola 'Swanley White'	V. 'Comte de Brazza'	Weigela 'Avalanche' h	W. 'Candida'
Viola 'The Czar'	V. 'Czar'	Weigela 'Avalanche' -Lemoine	W. praecox 'Avalanche'
Viola velutina	V. gracilis	Weigela 'Bristol Snowflake'	W. 'Snowflake'
Viola 'Victoria'	V. 'Czar Bleu'	Weigela florida 'Variegata Aurea'	W. florida 'Aureovariegata'
Viola 'White Ladies'	V. cucullata 'Alba'	Weingartia neocumingii	Rebutia neocumingii
Viola yakusimana	V. verecunda v yakusimana	Welwitschia bainesii	W. mirabilis
Viola zoysii	V. calcarata ssp zoysii	Werckleocereus glaber	Weberocereus glaber
Virgilia capensis	V. oroboides	Westringia rosmariniformis	W. fruticosa
Viscaria alpina	Lychnis alpina	Widdringtonia cupressoides	W. nodiflora
Viscaria elegans	Silene coeli-rosa		

Synonyms

Widdringtonia whytei	W. nodiflora
Wigandia macrophylla	W. caracasana
Wigginsia	Parodia
Wigginsia vorwerkiana	Parodia vorwerkiana
Wilcoxia albiflora	Echinocereus leucanthus
Wilcoxia schmollii	Echinocereus schmollii
Wisteria brachybotrys 'Alba'	W. brachybotrys 'Shiro Kapitan'
Wisteria brachybotrys 'Alba Plena'	W. brachybotrys 'Shiro Kapitan'
Wisteria brachybotrys f alba	W. brachybotrys 'Shiro Kapitan'
Wisteria brachybotrys f plena	W. brachybotrys 'Shiro Kapitan'
Wisteria chinensis	W. sinensis
Wisteria floribunda 'Double Black Dragon'	W. floribunda 'Violacea Plena'
Wisteria floribunda 'Honbeni'	W. floribunda 'Rosea'
Wisteria floribunda 'Honko'	W. floribunda 'Rosea'
Wisteria floribunda Jakohn-fuji	W. floribunda 'Reindeer'
Wisteria floribunda 'Lipstick'	W. floribunda 'Kuchi-beni'
Wisteria floribunda 'Macrobotrys'	W. floribunda 'Multijuga'
Wisteria floribunda Murasaki-naga	W. floribunda 'Purple Patches'
Wisteria floribunda 'Peaches and Cream'	W. floribunda 'Kuchi-beni'
Wisteria floribunda 'Pink Ice'	W. floribunda 'Rosea'
Wisteria floribunda Shiro-nagi	W. floribunda 'Snow Showers'
Wisteria floribunda 'Shiro-noda'	W. floribunda 'Alba'
Wisteria floribunda 'Yae Kokuryu'	W. floribunda 'Violacea Plena'
Wisteria multijuga 'Alba'	W. floribunda 'Alba'
Wisteria sinensis Shiro-capital	W. sinensis 'Alba'
Wisteria venusta 'Alba'	W. brachybotrys 'Shiro Kapitan'
Wisteria venusta 'Alba Plena'	W. brachybotrys 'Shiro Kapitan'
Wisteria venusta purpurea	W. venusta v violacea
Wisteria x formosa Black Dragon	W. x formosa 'Kokuryu'
Wisteria x formosa Domino	W. x formosa 'Issai'
Wittia amazonica	Disocactus amazonicus
Wittiocactus amazonicus	Disocactus amazonicus
Worsleya procera	W. rayneri
x Achimenantha 'Cerulean Mink'	x Smithicodonia 'Cerulean Mink'
x Amarcrinum howardii	x A. memoria-corsii 'Howardii'
x Aporoheliocereus mallisonii	x Aporoheliocereus smithii
x Brunsdonna	x Amarygia
x Carmispartium astens	x C. hutchinsii
x Citrofortunella Limequat	C. x floridana
x Citrofortunella microcarpa 'Variegata'	C. microcarpa 'Tiger'
x Citrofortunella mitis	C. microcarpa
x Crinodonna	x Amarcrinum
x Crinodonna corsii	x Amarcrinum memoria-corsii
x Cupressocyparis 'Galway Gold'	x C. leylandii 'Castlewellan'
x Cupressocyparis 'Variegata'	x C. leylandii 'Harlequin'
x Fatshedera lizei 'Aureopicta'	x F. lizei 'Aurea'
x Fatshedera lizei 'Lemon and Lime'	x F. lizei 'Annemieke'
x Fatshedera lizei 'Maculata'	x F. lizei 'Annemieke'
x Gaulnettya	Gaultheria

x Halimiocistus algarvensis	Halimium ocymoides
x Halimiocistus revolii h	x H. sahucii
x Halimiocistus 'Susan'	Halimium 'Susan'
x Osmarea burkwoodii	Osmanthus x burkwoodii
x Solidaster hybridus	x S. luteus
x Stravinia	Photinia
x Venidioarctotis	Arctotis
Xanthorhiza apiifolia	X. simpliciissima
Xanthosoma lindenii	Caladium lindenii
Xylorhiza	Machaeranthera
Yucca angustifolia	Y. glauca
Yucca filifera 'Ivory'	Y. flaccida 'Ivory'
Yucca gloriosa 'Aureovariegata'	Y. gloriosa 'Variegata'
Yucca guatemalensis	Y. elephantipes
Yucca parviflora	Hesperaloe parviflora
Zantedeschia melanoleuca	Z. albomaculata
Zantedeschia pentlandii	Z. angustiloba
Zanthorhiza	Xanthorhiza
Zauschneria arizonica	Z. californica ssp latifolia
Zauschneria californica 'Glasnevin'	Z. californica 'Dublin'
Zauschneria cana villosa	Z. californica ssp mexicana
Zebrina pendula	Tradescantia zebrina
Zelkova cretana	Z. carpinifolia
Zelkova cretica	Z. abelicea
Zelkova keaki	Z. serrata
Zephyranthes andersonii	Habranthus tubispathus
Zephyranthes carinata	Z. grandiflora
Zephyranthes robusta	Habranthus robustus
Zinnia angustifolia h	Z. haageana
Zinnia haageana 'Classic'	Z. haageana 'Orange Star'
Zinnia mexicana	Z. haageana
Zizania caducifolia	Z. latifolia
Ziziphus sativa	Z. jujuba
Zygocactus truncatus	Schlumbergera truncata
Zygopetalum mackayi	Z. mackaii

Common-
Botanical Names

Common-Botanical Names

Aambeibossie	Aerva leucera	Agave, McKelvey	Agave mckelveyana
Aardroos	Mystropetalon	Agave, New Mexico	Agave neomexicana
Aaron's beard	Hypericum calycinum	Agave, Parry's	Agave parryi
Aaron's rod	Solidago	Agave, Royal	Agave victoriae-reginae
Aaron's rod	Verbascum thapsus	Agave, Schott's	Agave schottii
Aasblom	Orbea variegata	Agave, small-flowered	Agave parviflora
	(Stapelia)	Agave, thread	Agave filifera
Aasbossie	Coleonema album	Agave, threadleaf	Agave filifera
Abele	Populus alba	Agave, Utah	Agave utahensis
Absinth	Artemisia absinthium	Agdaegeneesbos	Otholobium decumbens
Abutilon, trailing	Abutilon	Ageratum, wild	Eupatorium coelestinum
	megapotamicum	Agrimony	Agrimonia eupatoria
Acacia, cat-claw	Acacia gregii	Agrimony, Chinese	Agrimonia pilosa
Acacia, common	Robinia pseudoacacia	Agrimony, common	Agrimonia eupatoria
Acacia, desert sweet	Acacia smallii	Agrimony, hemp	Eupatorium cannabinum
Acacia, everblooming	Acacia floribunda	Agrimony, water	Bidens vulgata
Acacia, false	Robinia pseudoacacia	Agtdaegeneesbos	Lobostemon fruticosus
Acacia, flaky	Acacia exuvialis	Air plant	Tillandsia
Acacia, large-leaved	Acacia macrothyrsa	Air plant , South American	Kalanchoe fedtschenkoi
Acacia, mop-head	Robinia pseudoacacia	Ajmud (Ajmund)	Carum roxburgianum
	'Umbraculifera'	Ajowan	Carum copticum
Acacia, mountain	Brachystegia	Akeake	Dodonaea viscosa
	glaucescens		'Purpurea'
Acacia, pearl	Acacia podalyriifolia	Akebia five-leaf	Akebia quinata
Acacia, prairie	Acacia angustissima	Albizia, bitter	Albizia amara
Acacia, prairie	Desmanthus illinoensis	Albizia, forest long-podded	Albizia schimperana
Acacia, rose	Robinia hispida	Albizia, paperbark	Albizia tanganikensis
Acacia, sand	Acacia arenaria	Albizia, plum	Paraserianthes lophantha
Acacia, thorn white	Acacia constricta	Albizia, sickle-leaved	Albizia harveyi
Acacia, three thorned	Acacia senegal v rostrata	Alder	Alnus
Achiote	Bixa orellana	Alder, African red	Cunonia capensis
Aconite	Aconitum	Alder, black	Alnus glutinosa
Aconite, winter	Eranthis hyemalis	Alder, black	Ilex verticillata
Adam's needle	Yucca filamentosa	Alder, buckthorn	Rhamnus frangula
Adam's tree	Fouquieria diguetii	Alder, common	Alnus glutinosa
Adder's meat	Stellaria holostea	Alder, common eastern	Alnus rugosa
Adder's tongue	Ophioglossum vulgatum	Alder, evergreen	Alnus jorullensis
Adder's tongue, footed	Scoliopus bigelowii	Alder, green	Alnus viridis
Adder's tongue, yellow	Erythronium	Alder, green European	Alnus viridis
	americanum	Alder, grey	Alnus incana
Adonis	Adonis aestivalis	Alder, Indian	Alnus nepalensis
Aeroplane propeller	Crassula perfoliata v	Alder, Italian	Alnus cordata
	falcata	Alder, Japanese	Alnus japonica
African blue lily	Agapanthus	Alder, Manchurian	Alnus hirsuta
African daisy	Arctotis	Alder, Mountain	Alnus tenuifolia
African daisy	Dimorphotheca	Alder, Oregon	Alnus rubra
African daisy, blue-eyed	Arctotis venusta	Alder, red	Alnus rubra
African fountain grass	Pennisetum setaceum	Alder, rock	Canthium mundianum
African hemp	Sparrmannia africana	Alder, Sitka	Alnus sinuata
African lily	Agapanthus africanus	Alder, thin-leaved	Alnus incana
African marigold	Tagetes erecta	Alder, thinleaf	Alnus tenuifolia
African milkbush	Synadenium grantii	Alder, water white	Brachylaena neriifolia
African red alder	Cunonia capensis	Alder, white	Alnus incana
African tulip tree	Spathodea campanulata	Alder, white	Clethra
African violet	Saintpaulia	Alder, white California	Alnus rhombifolia
African violet, false	Streptocarpus saxorum	Alder, witch	Fothergilla gardenii
African walnut	Schotia brachypetala	Alecost	Tanacetum balsamita
Afrikaner, blue	Gladiolus carinatus	Alehoof	Glechoma hederacea
Afrikaner, brown	Gladiolus liliaceus	Alexander palm	Archontophoenix
Afrikaner, bruin	Gladiolus maculatus		alexandrae
Afrikaner, red	Gladiolus priorii	Alexanders	Smyrnium perfoliatum
Afrikaner, red	Gladiolus watsonioides	Alexanders, golden	Zizia aurea
Afrikaner, small brown	Gladiolus hyalinus	Alexanders, golden heart-leaf	Zizia aptera
Agati, white	Sesbania grandiflora	Alexandrian laurel	Danae racemosa
Agave, Havard	Agave havardiana	Alfalfa	Medicago sativa
Agave, hedgehog	Agave stricta	Algarrobo	Prosopis juliflora

Common-Botanical Names

Algerian iris	Iris unguicularis	Anemone, false rue	Isopyrum
Algerian iris, winter	Iris unguicularis	Anemone, Japanese	Anemone hupehensis v japonica
Algerian oak	Quercus canariensis		
Alkanet	Anchusa	Anemone, Japanese	Anemone x hybrida
Alkanet, green	Pentaglottis	Anemone, Lesser's	Anemone x lesseri
Alkanet, green	Pentaglottis sempervirens	Anemone, long-headed	Anemone cylindrica
		Anemone, Monte Baldo	Anemone baldensis
All heal	Prunella vulgaris	Anemone, Narcissus-flowered	Anemone narcissiflora
All heal	Valerianella officinalis	Anemone, poppy	Anemone coronaria
Alleghe(a)ny vine	Adlumia fungosa	Anemone, rue	Anemonella thalictroides
Alligator tree	Liquidamber styraciflua	Anemone, snowdrop	Anemone sylvestris
Allium, drumstick	Allium sphaerocephalon	Anemone, wood	Anemone nemerosa
Allophyllus, dune	Allophylus natalensis	Anemone, yellow	Anemone ranunculoides
Allspice	Calycanthus	Angel wings	Caladium bicolor
Allspice	Chimonanthus praecox	Angel's eyes	Veronica chamaedrys
Allspice	Pimenta dioica	Angel's fishing rod	Dierama
Allspice, Californian	Calycanthus occidentalis	Angel's tears	Billbergia x windii
Allspice, Carolina	Calycanthus floridus	Angel's tears	Narcissus triandrus
Almond, common	Prunus dulcis	Angel's trumpet	Datura inoxia
Almond, desert	Prunus emarginata	Angel's trumpet	Datura stramonium
Almond, dwarf Russian	Prunus tenella	Angel's trumpets	Brugmansia
Almond, flowering	Prunus triloba	Angel's trumpets	Brugmansia x candida
Almond, Indian	Terminalia catappa	Angel's trumpets, common	Brugmansia arborea
Almond, native (AU)	Terminalia canescens	Angel's trumpets, red	Brugmansia sanguinea
Almond, pink	Alphitonia petriei	Angelica	Angelica archangelica
Almond, tropical	Terminalia catappa	Angelica	Angelica atropurpurea
Almond, wild	Brabejum stellatifolium	Angelica, bear's	Angelica ursina
Aloe, American	Manfreda virginica	Angelica, Korean	Angelica gigas
Aloe, bitter	Aloe ferox	Angelica, mountain	Angelica arguta
Aloe, lace	Aloe aristata	Angelica tree, American	Aralia spinosa
Aloe, partridge	Aloe variegata	Angelica tree, Chinese	Aralia chinensis
Aloe, partridge breasted	Aloe variegata	Angelica tree, Japanese	Aralia elata
Aloe, soap	Aloe maculata	Angelica, wild	Angelica sylvestris
Aloe, tiger	Aloe variegata	Anisatum, Chinese	Illicium anisatum
Aloe vera	Aloe vera	Anise	Pimpinella anisum
Aloe, Zimbabwe	Aloe excelsa	Anise, Chinese	Illicium anisatum
Alpenrose	Rhododendron ferrugineum	Anise hyssop	Agastache foeniculum
		Anise, purple	Illicium floridanum
Alpenrose, hairy	Rhododendron hirsutum	Anise root	Osmorhiza occidentalis
Alpine azalea	Loiseleuria procumbens	Anise, star	Illicium parviflorum
Alpine calamint	Acinos alpinus	Anise, star	Illicium verum
Aluminium plant	Pilea cadierei	Aniseed	Pimpinella anisum
Alumroot	Heuchera americana	Annatto	Bixa orellana
Alumroot	Heuchera cylindrica	Annatto tree	Bixa orellana
Alumroot	Heuchera richardsonii	Anthurium, crystal	Anthurium crystallinum
Alumroot, long-flowered	Heuchera longiflora	Anthurium, King	Anthurium veitchii
Alumroot, prairie	Heuchera richardsonii	Anysboegoe	Agathosma crenulata
Alumroot, small-flowered	Heuchera micrantha	Aotus, pointed	Aotus lanigera
Alyssum, sweet	Lobularia maritima	Apache plume	Fallugia paradoxa
Amaranth, cereal grain	Amaranthus hypochondriacus	Aparota	Enterolobium cyclocarpum
Amaranth, globe	Gomphrena globosa	Apiespeul	Senna petersiana
Amaranth, Mexican grain	Amaranthus cruentus	Apple	Malus
Amaranth, purple	Amaranthus cruentus	Apple, Balsam	Clusia major
Amaranth, red	Amaranthus cruentus	Apple berry, common	Billardiera scandens
Amaryllis	Hippeastrum hybrids	Apple berry, purple	Billardiera longiflora
Amaryllis, blue	Worsleya	Apple berry, sweet	Billardiera cymosa
Amatungulu	Carissa macrocarpa	Apple, bitter	Cucumis myriocarpus
Ambrosia	Chenopodium botrys	Apple, Chinese	Malus spectabilis
Amsonia, Arkansas	Amsonia hubrectii	Apple, Chinese May	Podophyllum pleianthum
Amsonia, narrow-leaved	Amsonia hubrectii	Apple, crab	Malus
Amulla	Eremophila debilis	Apple, kangaroo	Solanum aviculare
Anemome, Apennine	Anemone apennina	Apple, kangaroo	Solanum laciniatum
Anemone, alpine	Pulsatilla alpina	Apple, Kari (Kei)	Dovyalis caffra
Anemone, Canada	Anemone canadensis	Apple leaf	Lonchocarpus cappassa
Anemone, false	Anemonopsis	Apple, love	Mandragora officinarum

Common-Botanical Names

Apple, love	Solanum aculeatissum	Arum lily	Zantedeschia aethiopica
Apple, May	Podophyllum peltatum	Arum lily, white	Zantedeschia aethiopica
Apple of Peru	Nicandra	Arum, pink	Zantedeschia rehmannii
Apple of Peru	Nicandra physalodes	Arum, umbrella	Amorphophallus konjac
Apple, oval kei	Dovyalis zeyheri	Asafoetida	Ferula assa-foetida
Apple, plum-leaved	Malus prunifolia	Asarabacca	Asarum europaeum
Apple, red	Acmena ingens	Ash	Fraxinus
Apple, rose	Syzygium jambos	Ash, alpine	Eucalyptus delegatensis
Apple, Sargent	Malus toringo ssp	Ash, American mountain	Sorbus americana
	sargentii	Ash, Arizona	Fraxinus velutina
Apple, star	Diospyros simii	Ash, Bennett's	Flindersia bennettiana
Apple, white	Syzygium forte ssp forte	Ash, black	Fraxinus nigra
Apricot	Prunus armeniaca	Ash, Blue Mountain	Eucalyptus oreades
Apricot, hardy	Prunus armeniaca	Ash, Cape	Ekebergia capensis
Apricot, Japanese	Prunus mume	Ash, claret	Fraxinus angustifolia
Apricot, Manchurian	Prunus mandshurica		'Raywood'
Apricot, sweet kernel	Prunus armeniaca	Ash, coast	Eucalyptus sieberi
Aquiboquil	Lardizabala biternata	Ash, common	Fraxinus excelsior
Arabian tea	Catha edulis	Ash, crow's	Flindersia australis
Aralia, false	Schefflera elegantissima	Ash, desert	Fraxinus angustifolia
Aralia, fern-leaf	Polyscias filicifolia	Ash, English	Fraxinus excelsior
Aralia, Japanese	Fatsia japonica	Ash, European	Fraxinus excelsior
Arbor-vitae, American	Thuja occidentalis	Ash, flowering	Fraxinus ornus
Arbor-vitae, Chinese	Thuja orientalis	Ash, glossy white	Bersama lucens
Arbor-vitae, western	Thuja plicata	Ash, green	Fraxinus pennsylvanica
Arborvitae	Thuja	Ash, Korean mountain	Sorbus alnifolia
Arbutus, trailing	Epigaea repens	Ash, Mallee Blue Mountain	Eucalyptus stricta
Archangel	Angelica archangelica	Ash, Mallee Kangaroo Island	Eucalyptus remota
Archangel, yellow	Lamium galeobdolon	Ash, Manna	Fraxinus ornus
Argyle apple	Eucalyptus cinerea	Ash, Moreton Bay	Eucalyptus tessellaris
Arnica, American	Arnica chamissonis	Ash, mountain	Eucalyptus regnans
Arnica, Cordilleran	Arnica mollis	Ash, mountain	Sorbus aucuparia
Arnica, European	Arnica montana	Ash, mountain white	Eucalyptus fraxinoides
Arnica, heartleaf	Arnica cordifolia	Ash, mountain whte	Eucalyptus stricta
Arnica, meadow	Arnica chamissonis	Ash, narrow-leaved	Fraxinus angustifolia
Arnica, mountain	Arnica latifolia	Ash, one-leaved	Fraxinus excelsior f
Arnica, nodding	Arnica parryi		diversifolia
Aroena	Quaqua	Ash, Oregon	Fraxinus latifolia
Arorangi	Olearia macrodonta	Ash, pigeon house	Eucalyptus triflora
Arrow arum	Peltandra	Ash, prickly	Zanthoxylum clava-
Arrow arum, green	Peltandra virginica		herculis
Arrow arum, white	Peltandra sagittifolia	Ash, red	Alphitonia excelsa
Arrow-wood, downy	Viburnum	Ash, red	Fraxinus pennsylvanica
	rafinesquianum	Ash, rock	Ekebergia pterophylla
Arrow-wood, Southern	Viburnum dentatum	Ash, Shamel	Fraxinus uhdei
Arrowhead	Sagittaria	Ash, silver top	Eucalyptus sieberi
Arrowhead, American	Sagittaria latifolia	Ash, velvet	Fraxinus velutina
Arrowhead, common	Sagittaria latifolia	Ash, wafer	Ptelea trifoliata
Arrowhead, Japanese	Sagittaria sagittifolia	Ash, weeping	Fraxinus excelsior
Arrowhead vine	Syngonium		'Pendula'
	podophyllum	Ash, white	Alphitonia petriei
Arrowroot, East Indian	Pueraria lobata	Ash, white	Eucalyptus fraxinoides
Arrowroot, Florida	Zamia furfuracea	Ash, white	Eucalyptus oreades
Arrowroot, Florida	Zamia pumila	Ash, white	Fraxinus americana
Arrowroot, Japanese	Pueraria lobata	Ashwaganda	Withania somnifera
Arrowroot, South sea	Tacca leontopetaloides	Asoka	Saraca indica
Arsenic bush	Senna planitiicola	Asparagus, Bath	Ornithogalum
Artichoke, globe	Cynara cardunculus		pyrenaicum
	Scolymus Group	Asparagus, Chinese	Asparagus
Artillery plant	Pilea microphylla		cochinchinensis
Arugula	Eruca	Asparagus fern	Asparagus densiflorus
Arum, bog	Calla palustris	Asparagus, Prussian	Ornithogalum
Arum, Cretan	Arum creticum		pyrenaicum
Arum, dragon	Dracunculus vulgaris		Populus
Arum, golden	Zantedeschia elliottiana	Aspen	Populus tremuloides
Arum lily	Zantedeschia	Aspen, American	Populus grandidentata
		Aspen, bigtooth	

92

Common-Botanical Names

Common	Botanical	Common	Botanical
Aspen, common	Populus tremula	Autograph tree	Clusia major
Aspen, quaking	Populus tremuloides	Autumn joy	Sedum spectabile
Aspen, weeping	Populus tremula 'Pendula'	Autumn starwort	Callitriche hermaphroditica
Asphodel	Asphodelus		Geum
Asphodel, alpine	Tofieldia calyculata	Avens	Geum montanum
Asphodel, bog	Narthecium ossifragum	Avens, alpine	Sieversia reptans
Asphodel, white	Asphodelus albus	Avens, creeping	Geum triflorum
Asphodel, yellow	Asphodeline lutea	Avens, long-plumed	Dryas
Aster, alpine	Aster alpinus	Avens, mountain	Dryas octopetala
Aster, annual	Callistephus	Avens, mountain	Geum rivale
Aster, aromatic	Aster oblongifolius	Avens, water	Geum urbanum
Aster, beach	Erigeron glaucus	Avens, wood	Geum aleppicum
Aster, big-leaved	Aster macrophyllus	Avens, yellow	Geum macrophyllum
Aster, blue	Aster anomalus	Avens, yellow	Banisteriopsis caapi
Aster, blue fall	Aster oblongifolius	Ayahuasca	Polygonum hydropiper 'Fastigiatum'
Aster, calico	Aster lateriflorus	Azabu-tade	
Aster, Chinese	Callistephus	Azalea	Rhododendron
Aster, climbing	Aster carolinianus	Azalea, alpine	Loiseleuria
Aster, crooked-stemmed	Aster prenanthoides	Azalea, trailing	Loiseleuria procumbens
Aster, Curtis'	Aster curtisii	Azorole	Crataegus azarolus
Aster, Douglas'	Aster subspicatus	Aztec dream herb	Calea zacatechichi
Aster, Drummond's	Aster drummondii	Aztec sweet herb	Lippia dulcis
Aster, false	Boltonia asteroides	Babantsi	Jatropha curcas
Aster, flat-topped	Aster umbellatus	Baby blue eyes	Nemophila menziesii
Aster, flax-leaved	Aster linariifolius	Baby's breath	Gypsophila paniculata
Aster, frost	Aster pilosus	Baby's breath, creeping	Gypsophila repens
Aster, golden	Chrysopsis camporum	Baby's breath, Manchurian	Gypsophila oldhamiana
Aster, golden Maryland	Chrysopsis mariana	Baby's tears	Soleirolia soleirolii
Aster, hairy golden	Heterotheca villosa	Baby's toes	Fenestraria aurantiaca f rhopalophylla
Aster, heart-leaved	Aster cordifolius		Craspedia
Aster, heath	Aster ericoides	Bachelor's buttons	Craspedia globosa
Aster, later purple	Aster patens	Bachelor's buttons	Craspedia uniflora
Aster, Mohave	Machaeranthera tortifolia	Bachelor's buttons	Gomphrena canescens
Aster, New England	Aster novae-angliae	Bachelor's buttons	Ranunculus aconitifolius
Aster, New York	Aster novi-belgii	Bachelor's buttons	Ranunculus acris 'Flore Pleno'
Aster, panicled	Aster simplex		
Aster, prairie	Aster tanacetifolius	Bachelor's buttons, perennial	Centaurea montana
Aster, prairie	Aster x frikartii	Bachelor's buttons, white	Ranunculus aconitifolius 'Flore Pleno'
Aster, showy	Aster conspicuus		
Aster, side-flowered	Aster lateriflorus		Lotus corniculatus
Aster, silky	Aster sericeus	Bacon and eggs	Bacopa caroliniana
Aster, sky blue	Aster azureus	Bacopa, lemon	Baeckia virgata
Aster, smooth	Aster laevis	Baeckea, tall	Baeckia virgata
Aster, smooth blue	Aster laevis	Baeckea, twiggy	Baeckia linifolia
Aster, stiff	Aster linariifolius	Baeckea, weeping	Aegle marmelos
Aster, Stokes	Stokesia	Bael	Angelica dahurica
Aster, swamp	Aster puniceus	Bai zhi	Imperata cylindrica
Aster, Tartarian	Aster tataricus	Bai-mao-gen	Meum athamanticum
Aster, turbinate	Aster turbinellus	Baldmoney	Dipogon lignosus
Aster, upland white	Aster ptarmicoides	Ballar	Exocarpos sparteus
Aster, wavy	Aster undulatus	Ballart, broom	Platycodon
Aster, white	Aster ptarmicoides	Balloon flower	Cardiospermum halicacabum
Aster, wild	Felicia aethiopica	Balloon vine	
Aster, willow	Aster praealtus		Melissa
Aster, wood blue	Aster cordifolius	Balm	Melittis
Aster, wood white	Aster divaricatus	Balm, bastard	Melissa officinalis
Astilbe, native (US)	Astilbe biternata	Balm, bee	Monarda didyma
Aubretia	Aubrieta	Balm, bee	Monarda punctata
Auricula	Primula auricula	Balm, bee spotted	Monarda clinopodia
Australian fuchsia	Correa	Balm, bee white	Melissa officinalis
Australian mint bush	Prostanthera	Balm, lemon	Melissa officinalis 'Aurea'
Australian pea	Dipogon lignosus	Balm, lemon variegated	Dracocephalum moldavica
Australian pine	Casuarina	Balm, Moldavian	
Australian vine	Mukia maderspermata		Cedronella canariensis
Austrian briar	Rosa foetida	Balm of Gilead	

Common-Botanical Names

Common	Botanical	Common	Botanical
Balm of Gilead	Populus x candicans	Banjine, silky yellow	Pimelea suaveolens
Balm of Gilead, false	Cedronella canariensis	Banjines	Pimelea
Balm, Vietnamese	Elsholtzia ciliata	Banksia, acorn	Banksia prionotes
Balsam	Impatiens	Banksia, Albany	Banksia coccinea
Balsam	Impatiens balsamina	Banksia, Ashbyi's	Banksia ashbyi
Balsam, Himalayan	Impatiens glandulifera	Banksia, Baxter's	Banksia baxteri
Balsam, Indian	Impatiens glandulifera	Banksia, bird's nest	Banksia baxteri
Balsam root	Balsamorhiza	Banksia, Brown's	Banksia brownii
Balsam root, arrowleaf	Balsamorhiza sagittata	Banksia, bull	Banksia grandis
Balsam root, Hooker's	Balsamorhiza hookeri	Banksia, Burdett's	Banksia burdettii
Balsam, star	Zaluzianskya	Banksia, Caley's	Banksia caleyi
Balsam, wild	Impatiens hochstetteri ssp hochstetteri	Banksia, coast	Banksia attenuata
		Banksia, coast	Banksia integrifolia
Balsamita	Tanacetum	Banksia, coastline	Banksia praemorsa
Bamboo	Bambusa	Banksia, creeping	Banksia repens
Bamboo, anceps	Yushania	Banksia, cut-leaf	Banksia praemorsa
Bamboo, anceps	Yushania anceps	Banksia, dainty	Banksia pulchella
Bamboo, arrow	Pseudosasa japonica	Banksia, desert	Banksia ornata
Bamboo, black	Phyllostachys nigra	Banksia, Dryandra-leaved	Banksia dryandroides
Bamboo, Buddha's belly	Bambusa ventricosa	Banksia, Echidna	Banksia lindleyana
Bamboo, dwarf white-stripe	Pleioblastus variegatus	Banksia, Eneabba	Banksia hookeriana
Bamboo fern	Coniogramme	Banksia, feather-leaved	Banksia brownii
Bamboo, fishpole	Phyllostachys aurea	Banksia, fern-leaved	Banksia oblongifolia
Bamboo, fountain	Fargesia nitida	Banksia, firewood	Banksia menziesii
Bamboo, giant	Dendrocalamus giganteus	Banksia, giant	Banksia grandis
Bamboo, giant timber	Phyllostachys bambusoides	Banksia, glasshouse mountain	Banksia conferta v conferta
Bamboo, golden	Phyllostachys aurea	Banksia, golden	Banksia ashbyi
Bamboo, golden-groove	Phyllostachys aureosulcata	Banksia, golden stalk	Banksia media
Bamboo, heavenly	Nandina domestica	Banksia, golden-ball	Banksia laevigata v fuscolutea
Bamboo, hedge	Bambusa mutiplex	Banksia, granite Albany	Banksia verticillata
Bamboo, Muriel	Fargesia murieliae	Banksia, hair-pin	Banksia spinulosa
Bamboo, Narihira	Semiarundinaria fastuosa	Banksia, hair-pin	Banksia spinulosa v collina
Bamboo, noble	Himalayacalamus falconeri	Banksia, hair-pin	Banksia spinulosa v spinulosa
Bamboo, sacred	Nandina domestica	Banksia, heath-leaved	Banksia ericifolia
Bamboo, umbrella	Fargesia murieliae	Banksia, heath-leaved	Banksia ericifolia v ericifolia
Bamboo, yellow-groove	Phyllostachys aureosulcata	Banksia, heath-leaved	Banksia ericifolia v macrantha
Bamboo, zigzag	Phyllostachys flexuosa	Banksia, hill	Banksia collina
Ban Xia	Pinellia ternata	Banksia, hill	Banksia spinulosa v collina
Banana	Musa	Banksia, holly-leaved	Banksia ilicifolia
Banana, Abyssinian	Ensete ventricosum	Banksia, Hooker's	Banksia hookeriana
Banana, Assam	Musa velutina	Banksia, lantern red	Banksia caleyi
Banana bush	Ervatamia angustisepala	Banksia, lantern yellow	Banksia lemanniana
Banana, edible	Musa acuminata 'Dwarf Cavendish'	Banksia, Lehmann's	Banksia lemanniana
Banana, Ethiopian	Ensete ventricosum	Banksia, Lesueur	Banksia tricuspis
Banana, flowering	Musa ornata	Banksia, Lullfitz's	Banksia lullfitzii
Banana, Japanese	Musa basjoo	Banksia, marsh	Banksia paludosa
Banana, scarlet	Musa uranoscopus	Banksia, Menzies	Banksia menziesii
Banana, wild	Ensete ventricosum	Banksia, mountain	Banksia canei
Banana, wild Natal	Strelitzia nicolai	Banksia, mountain	Banksia oreophila
Banana, wooden	Entandrophragma caudatum	Banksia, native (AU)	Banksia dentata
Baneberry	Actaea	Banksia, nodding	Banksia nutans v nutans
Baneberry, red	Actaea rubra	Banksia, oak-leaf	Banksia solandri
Baneberry, white	Actaea alba	Banksia, oak-leaved	Banksia quercifolia
Bangalay	Eucalyptus botryoides	Banksia, orange	Banksia prionotes
Bangalow palm	Archontophoenix cunninghamiana	Banksia, palm	Banksia elderana
		Banksia, pine	Banksia tricuspis
Banjine, coastal	Pimelea ferruginea	Banksia, porcupine	Banksia lindleyana
Banjine, showy	Pimelea spectabilis	Banksia, propeller	Banksia candolleana
		Banksia, prostate	Banksia petiolaris

Common-Botanical Names

Banksia, prostrate

Banksia, river
Banksia, rose-fruited
Banksia, round-fruited

Banksia, sand
Banksia, sandplain

Banksia, saw
Banksia, scarlet
Banksia, sceptre
Banksia, showy
Banksia, silver
Banksia, slender
Banksia, Solander's
Banksia, southern plains
Banksia, Stirling Ranges
Banksia, swamp
Banksia, swamp
Banksia, swamp red
Banksia, swordfish
Banksia, teasel
Banksia, teddy bear
Banksia, tennis-ball

Banksia, violet
Banksia, Wallum
Banksia, Wallum
Banksia, water bush
Banksia, woolly orange
Banksia, woolly-spiked
Banksia, yellow
Banyan
Banyan
Banyan, Australian
Banyan, Malay
Baobab tree
Barbados pride
Barbara's buttons
Barbed-wire plant
Barbel palm
Barberry
Barberry, creeping
Barberry, Darwin's
Barley
Barley, meadow

Barley, wall
Barrel, brown
Barrenwort
Bartsia, alpine
Basboom
Basil
Basil
Basil, anise

Basil, camphor

Basil, East Indian
Basil, greek bush

Basil, green
Basil, holy
Basil, lemon
Basil, lime

Banksia gardneri ssp
gardneri
Banksia seminuda
Banksia laricina
Banksia sphaerocarpa v
sphaerocarpa
Banksia attenuata
Banksia attenuata dwarf
form
Banksia serrata
Banksia coccinea
Banksia sceptrum
Banksia speciosa
Banksia marginata
Banksia attenuata
Banksia solandri
Banksia media
Banksia solandri
Banksia littoralis
Banksia robur
Banksia occidentalis
Banksia elderana
Banksia pulchella
Banksia baueri
Banksia laevigata v
laevigata
Banksia violacea
Banksia aemula
Banksia serratifolia
Banksia occidentalis
Banksia victoriae
Banksia baueri
Rosa banksiae 'Lutea'
Ficus benghalensis
Ficus virens
Ficus macrophylla
Ficus microcarpa
Adansonia digitata
Caesalpinia pulcherrima
Marshallia grandiflora
Tylecodon reticulatus
Acanthophoenix
Berberis
Mahonia repens
Berberis darwinii
Hordeum
Hordeum
brachyantherum
Hordeum murinu
Eucalyptus fastigiata
Epimedium
Bartsia alpina
Dais cotinifolia
Ocimum
Ocimum basilicum
Ocimum basilicum
'Horapha'
Ocimum
kilimandscharicum
Ocimum gratissimum
Ocimum basilicum v
minimum
Ocimum viride
Ocimum sanctum
Ocimum americanum
Ocimum americanum

Basil, Peruvian
Basil, sacred
Basil, sweet
Basil thyme
Basil thyme
Basil, tree
Basil, West African
Basil, wild
Basswood
Basswood, Carolina
Basterkiepersol
Bat flower
Bat flower
Bat tree
Batchelor's buttons
Bath Asparagus

Bats-in-the-belfrey
Bauhinia
Bauhinia, bush

Bauhinia, Natal
Bauhinia, red
Bauhinia, small-leaved

Bauhinia tree, yellow
Bauhinia, white
Baviaanskloofseder
Bay, bull
Bay, California
Bay, laurel
Bay, loblolly
Bay, sweet
Bay, sweet
Bay, tree
Bayberry
Bayberry, Northern
Bayberry, Pacific
Bayonet plant
Bayonet, Spanish
Bayonet, Spanish
Bayonet tree
Beach Naupaka

Bead plant
Bead tree
Bead-tree
Bean, black
Bean, Egyptian
Bean, flat climbing
Bean, Hottentot
Bean, ice cream
Bean, Indian
Bean, Kaffir
Bean, lucky creeper
Bean, ordeal
Bean, Queensland
Bean, red
Bean, snail
Bean tree
Bean tree
Bean tree, black

Bean tree, golden
Bean tree, Indian
Bean tree, lucky

Ocimum micranthum
Ocimum tenuiflorum
Ocimum basilicum
Acinos alpinus
Acinos arvensis
Ocimum gratissimum
Ocimum viride
Clinopodium vulgare
Tilia americana
Tilia caroliniana
Schefflera umbellifera
Tacca chantrierei
Tacca integrifolia
Oroxylum indicum
Arctium sp
Ornithogalum
pyrenaicum
Campanula trachelium
Lysiphyllum gilvum
Lysiphyllum
cunninghamii
Bauhinia natalensis
Bauhinia galpinii
Lysiphyllum
cunninghamii
Bauhinia purpurea
Bauhinia petersiana
Widdringtonia schwarzii
Magnolia grandiflora
Umbellularia californica
Laurus nobilis
Gordonia lasianthus
Laurus nobilis
Magnolia virginiana
Laurus
Myrica pensylvanica
Myrica pensylvanica
Myrica californica
Aciphylla
Yucca aloifolia
Yucca baccata
Yucca aloifolia
Scaevola frutescens v
sericea
Nertera granadensis
Adenanthera pavonina
Melia azedarach
Kennedia nigricans
Lablab purpureus
Dalbergia obovata
Schotia brachypetala
Inga edulis
Lablab purpureus
Erythrina lysistemon
Abrus precatorius
Dissotis canescens
Bauhinia cattonii
Dysoxylum muelleri
Vigna caracalla
Lysiphyllum gilvum
Markhamia zanzibarica
Castanospermum
australe
Markhamia obtusifolia
Catalpa bignonioides
Erythrina caffra

Common-Botanical Names

Common	Botanical
Bean tree, lucky	Erythrina lysistemon
Bean, wild	Hakea cyclocarpa
Bean, wild	Strophostyles eiosperma
Bean, wild Jack	Canavalia maritima
Bear's breeches	Acanthus
Bear's ear	Arctotis
Bear's ear	Primula auricula
Bear's foot	Helleborus foetidus
Bear's paw fern	Aglaomorpha meyeniana
Bearberry	Arctostaphylos
Bearberry, alpine	Artostaphylos alpina
Bearberry, common	Arctostaphylos uva-ursi
Beardstongue, desert	Penstemon pseudospectabilis
Beardstongue, foxglove	Penstemon digitalis
Beardstongue, large flowered	Penstemon grandiflorus
Beardstongue, pale	Penstemon pallidus
Beardstongue, scarlet	Penstemon barbatus
Beardstongue, slender	Penstemon gracilis
Beardstongue, slender	Penstemon procerus
Beautiful fir	Abies amabilis
Beauty berry	Callicarpa
Beauty bush	Kolkwitzia
Bedstraw	Galium
Bedstraw, northern	Galium boreale
Bedstraw, yellow	Galium verum
Bee-bums	Impatiens glandulifera
Beebee tree	Tetradium daniellii
Beech	Fagus
Beech, American	Fagus grandifolia
Beech, Antarctic	Nothofagus antarctica
Beech, Australian white	Gmelina leichardtii
Beech, black	Nothofagus solandri
Beech, brown	Cryptocarya glaucescens
Beech, Cape	Rapanea melanophloeos
Beech, common	Fagus sylvatica
Beech, copper	Fagus sylvatica Atropurpurea Group
Beech, European	Fagus sylvatica
Beech, fern-leaved	Fagus sylvatica 'Aspleniifolia'
Beech, Indian	Pongamia pinnata
Beech, Japanese	Fagus crenata
Beech, mountain	Nothofagus solandri v cliffortioides
Beech, myrtle	Nothofagus cunninghamii
Beech, oriental	Fagus orientalis
Beech, purple	Fagus sylvatica Atropurpurea Group
Beech, silver	Nothofagus menzesii
Beech, southern	Nothofagus
Beech, weeping	Fagus sylvatica 'Pendula'
Beechwood, broad-leaved	Faurea speciosa
Beefsteak plant	Iresine herbstii
Beefsteak plant	Perilla frutescens
Beefwood	Grevillea striata
Beefwood, coast	Allocasuarina verticillata
Beefwood, horsetail	Casuarina equisetifolia
Beet	Beta
Beetberry	Chenopodium foliosum
Beggar's buttons	Arctium sp
Beggarweed	Desmodium tortuosum
Begonia, angelwing	Begonia coccinea
Begonia, Christmas	Begonia x cheimantha
	'Gloire de Lorraine'
Begonia, crazy-leaf	Begonia 'Phyllomanica'
Begonia, Evans	Begonia grandis ssp evansiana
Begonia, eyelash	Begonia bowerae
Begonia, Fuchsia	Begonia fuchsioides
Begonia, Guinea-wing	Begonia albopicta
Begonia, hardy	Begonia grandis ssp evansiana
Begonia, Hollyhock	Begonia gracilis v martiana
Begonia, iron-cross	Begonia masoniana
Begonia, King	Begonia rex
Begonia, leopard	Begonia manicata
Begonia, lettuce leaf	Begonia 'Crestabruchii'
Begonia, maple-leaf	Begonia dregei
Begonia, maple-leaf	Begonia x weltoniensis
Begonia, metal-leaf	Begonia metallica
Begonia, metallic leaf	Begonia metallica
Begonia, painted-leaf	Begonia rex
Begonia, palm-leaf	Begonia luxurians
Begonia, shrimp	Begonia radicans
Begonia, stitched leaf	Begonia mazae f viridis
Begonia, strawberry	Saxifraga stolonifera
Begonia, trout-leaved	Begonia x argenteoguttata
Begonia, watermelon	Elatotstema repens
Begonia, wild	Begonia sutherlandii
Begonia, wild	Rumex venosus
Belah	Casuarina cristata
Bell bush, forest	Mackaya bella
Bell heather	Erica cinerea
Bell pepper	Capsicum annuum Grossum Group
Bell tree, Asian	Radermachera sinica
Bell, yellow	Fritillaria pudica
Bell-flower, Tibetan	Codonopsis clematidea
Bell-fruit, corky	Gyrosyemon ramulosus
Bell-fruit tree	Codonocarpus cotinifolius
Bella sombra	Phytolacca dioica
Belladonna	Atropa belladonna
Bellflower	Campanula
Bellflower, Adriatic	Campanula garganica
Bellflower, alpine	Campanula alpina
Bellflower, bearded	Campanula barbata
Bellflower, Canary Island	Canarina canariensis
Bellflower, Carpathian	Campanula carpatica
Bellflower, Chilean	Lapageria rosea
Bellflower, chimney	Campanula pyramidalis
Bellflower, Chinese	Platycodon
Bellflower, clustered	Campanula glomerata
Bellflower, creeping	Campanula rapunculoides
Bellflower, dalmatian	Campanula portenschlagiana
Bellflower, fairy	Wahlenbergia krebsii ssp krebsii
Bellflower, giant	Campanula latifolia
Bellflower, giant	Ostrowskia
Bellflower, gland	Adenophora
Bellflower, greater	Campanula latifolia
Bellflower, Italian	Campanula isophylla
Bellflower, milky	Campanula lactifora
Bellflower, Mount Cenis	Campanula cenisia
Bellflower, nettle-leaved	Campanula trachelium

Common-Botanical Names

Bellflower, peach-leaved	Campanula persicifolia	Billardiera, red	Billardiera erubescens
Bellflower, perforate	Campanula excisa	Billardiera, white	Billardiera candida
Bellflower, Pyrenean	Campanula speciosa	Billy buttons	Craspedia
Bellflower, spreading	Campanula patula	Billy buttons, pink	Gomphrena canescens
Bellflower, tall	Campanula americana	Bilsted	Liquidamber styraciflua
Bellflower, yellow	Campanula thyrsoides	Bindii, grey	Sclerolaena diacantha
Bellida, rosy	Bellida graminea	Bindweed	Calystegia
Bells of Ireland	Moluccella laevis	Bindweed	Convolvulus
Bellwort	Uvularia	Bindweed, blushing	Convolvulus erubescens
Bellwort	Uvularia grandiflora	Biota	Thuja orientalis
Belvedere	Bassia scoparia f	Birch	Betula
	trichophylla	Birch, Arctic	Betula nana
Benjamin	Lindera benzoin	Birch, black	Betula nigra
Benzoin	Styrax benzoin	Birch, bog	Betula pumila
Bergamot	Monarda	Birch, canoe	Betula papyrifera
Bergamot	Monarda didyma	Birch, cherry	Betula lenta
Bergamot, lemon	Monarda citriodora	Birch, Chinese red	Betula albosinensis
Bergamot, wild	Monarda fistulosa	Birch, Chinese white	Betula albosinensis
Bergboegoe	Empleureum	Birch, downy	Betula pubescens
	unicapsularis	Birch, dwarf	Betula nana
Bergcaalbos	Brachylaena rotundata	Birch, Erman's	Betula ermanii
Berghardepeer	Olinia emarginata	Birch, grey	Betula populifolia
Bergkambroo	Fockea edulis	Birch, Himalayan	Betula utilis
Bergkankerbossie	Sutherlandia montana	Birch, Japanese cherry	Betula grossa
Bergkatjietee	Tritonia lineata	Birch, Japanese white	Betula japonica
Bergkiepersol	Cussonia paniculata	Birch, Manchurian	Betula platyphylla
Bergklapperbos	Montinia		japonica
Bergmagriet	Ursinia anthemoides	Birch, monarch	Betula maximowicziana
Bergplakkie	Crassula nudicaulis	Birch, paper	Betula papyrifera
Bergpypie	Gladiolus carneus	Birch, river	Betula fontinalis
Bergsipres	Widdringtonia nodiflora	Birch, river	Betula nigra
Berrigan	Eremophila longifolia	Birch, Russian rock	Betula ermanii
Besemriet	Elegia capensis	Birch, silver	Betula pendula
Besemtrosvy	Ficus sur	Birch, Swedish	Betula pendula
Besenkaree	Rhus erosa		'Dalecarlica'
Bessieheide	Erica baccans	Birch, sweet	Betula lenta
Betel leaf	Piper betel	Birch, Szechuan	Betula szechuanica
Betel nut palm	Areca catechu	Birch, Transcaucasian	Betula medwedewii
Betonica	Stachys	Birch, weeping	Betula pendula
Betony	Stachys	Birch, white	Betula pendula
Betony, marsh	Pedicularis lanceolata	Birch, white Japanese	Betula platyphylla
Betony, water	Scrophularia auriculata		japonica
Betony, wood	Pedicularis canadensis	Birch, yellow	Betula alleghaniensis
Betony, wood	Stachys officinalis	Bird catcher tree	Pisonia umbellifera
Betony, wood swamp	Pedicularis lanceolata	Bird flower	Crotalaria cunninghamii
Betony, woolly	Stachys byzantina	Bird flower, green	Crotalaria cunninghamii
Bhringaraj	Eclipta alba	Bird flower, regal	Crotalaria cunninghamii
Bian Xu	Polygonum aviculare	Bird of Paradise	Caesalpinia mexicana
Bible leaf	Tanacetum balsamita	Bird of Paradise	Strelitzia
Bicacaro	Canarina canariensis	Bird of Paradise	Strelitzia reginae
Bidi-bidi	Acaena	Bird of Paradise shrub	Caesalpinia gilliesii
Bidi-bidi, Blue mountain	Acaena inermis	Bird of Paradise tree	Strelitzia nicolai
Bidi-bidi, red	Acaena novae-zealandiae	Bird tree, Carnarvon	Crotalaria cunninghamii
Bidi-bidi, scarlet	Acaena microphylla	Bird's eye	Gilia tricolor
Biesroei	Bobartia aphylla	Bird's eye bush	Ochna
Bietou	Chrysanthemoides	Bird's eyes	Gilia tricolor
	monilifera	Bird's nest	Sansevieria trifasciata
Big tree	Sequoiadendron		'Hahnii'
	giganteum	Bird's nest fern	Asplenium australasicum
Bilberry	Vaccinum	Bird's nest fern	Asplenium nidus
Bilberry	Vaccinum myrtillus	Bird-bush, Canary	Crotalaria agatiflora
Bilberry, dwarf	Vaccinum caespitosum	Birdplum	Berchemia discolor
Billardiera, beautiful	Billardiera floribunda	Birth root	Trillium erectum
Billardiera, blue-spotted	Billardiera caerulea-	Birthwort	Aristolochia clematitis
	punctata	Bishop's cap	Astrophytum
Billardiera, painted	Billardiera bicolor		myriostigma

Common-Botanical Names

Common	Botanical
Bishop's cap	Mitella diphylla
Bishop's flower	Ammi majus
Bishop's mitre	Astrophytum myriostigma
Bishop's mitre	Epimedium
Bishop's wort	Stachys officinalis
Bishopsweed	Aegopodium
Bishopsweed	Ammi majus
Bistort	Persicaria amplexicaulis
Bistort	Persicaria bistorta
Bistort, alpine	Persicaria vivipara
Bitter cress	Cardamine
Bitter-pea	Daviesia latifolia
Bitter-pea, blunt-leaf	Daviesia mimosioides
Bitter-pea, gorse	Daviesia ulicifolia
Bitter-pea, sandplain	Daviesia acicularis
Bitteraalwyn	Aloe ferox
Bitterappelliefie	Withania somnifera
Bitterbessie	Chironia baccifera
Bitterbos	Chrysocoma ciliata
Bitterbush, Antelope	Purshia tridentata
Bittercress	Cardamine
Bittercress, trifoliate	Cardamine trifolia
Bittergousblom	Arctotis fastuosa
Bitternut	Carya cordiformis
Bitterroot	Lewisia rediviva
Bittersweet	Celastrus
Bittersweet, American	Celastrus scandens
Bittersweet, climbing	Celastrus scandens
Bittersweet, false	Celastrus scandens
Bittersweet, oriental	Celastrus orbiculatus
Bittersweet, shrubby	Celastrus scandens
Bitterwort	Gentiana lutea
Black bean tree	Castanospermum australe
Black Jacks	Plantago lanceolata
Black kangaroo paw	Macropidia fuliginosa
Black pine, European	Pinus nigra
Black pine, Japanese	Pinus thunbergii
Black root	Veronicastrum virginicum
Black Sally	Eucalyptus stellulata
Black sarana	Fritillaria camschatcensis
Black snake root	Cimicifuga racemosa
Black-eyed Susan	Gazania
Black-eyed Susan	Rudbeckia fulgida
Black-eyed Susan	Rudbeckia hirta
Black-eyed Susan	Thunbergia alata
Black-eyed Susan, sweet	Rudbeckia subtomentosa
Black-eyed Suzy	Abrus precatorius
Blackberry	Rubus fruticosus
Blackberry	Rubus villosus
Blackberry lily	Belamcanda chinensis
Blackberry, native (US)	Rubus ursinus
Blackberry, trailing	Rubus ursinus
Blackberry, wild	Rubus discolor
Blackboy, Cundeelee	Xanthorrhoea thorntonii
Blackboy, slender	Xanthorrhoea gracilis
Blackboy, western	Xanthorrhoea preissii
Blackbuff	Eucalyptus todtiana
Blackbutt	Eucalyptus pilularis
Blackbutt, Albany	Eucalyptus staeri
Blackbutt, Cleland's	Eucalyptus clelandii
Blackbutt, coastal	Eucalyptus todtiana
Blackbutt, Dundas	Eucalyptus dundasii
Blackbutt, Fraser range	Eucalyptus fraseri
Blackbutt, Goldfields	Eucalyptus le-soueffii
Blackbutt, Kondinin	Eucalyptus kondinensis
Blackbutt, New England	Eucalyptus andrewsii
Blackbutt, pear-fruited	Eucalyptus pyrocarpa
Blackbutt, stocking	Eucalyptus kondinensis
Blackbutt, Swan River	Eucalyptus patens
Blackbutt, Woodward's	Eucalyptus woodwardii
Blackbutt, yellow-flowered	Eucalyptus stricklandii
Blackcurrant	Ribes nigrum
Blackfoot daisy	Melampodium leucanthum
Blackhaw, rusty	Viburnum rufidulum
Blackthorn	Bursaria spinosa
Blackthorn	Prunus spinosa
Blackwood	Acacia melanoxylon
Blackwood, frosted	Eucalyptus collina
Blackwood, silver-leaved	Eucalyptus collina
Bladder fern	Cystopteris
Bladder fern, brittle	Cystopteris fragilis
Bladder nut	Diospyros whyteana
Bladder senna	Colutea arborescens
Bladdernut	Staphylea
Bladdernut	Staphylea pinnata
Bladdernut	Staphylea trifolia
Bladderpod	Physaria
Bladderwort	Utricularia
Blade thorn	Acacia fleckii
Blaeberry	Vaccinum myrtillus
Blanket flower	Gaillardia
Blanket flower	Gaillardia pulchella
Blanket flower, large-blossomed	Gaillardia grandiflora
Blanket, Indian	Gaillardia pulchella
Blazing star	Liatris
Blazing star	Mentzelia laevicaulis
Blazing star	Mentzelia lindleyi
Blazing star, button	Liatris aspera
Blazing star, dense	Liatris spicata
Blazing star, dotted	Liatris punctata
Blazing star, dwarf	Liatris cylindracea
Blazing star, dwarf	Liatris microcephala
Blazing star, marsh	Liatris spicata
Blazing star, meadow	Liatris ligulistylis
Blazing star, prairie	Liatris pycnostachya
Blazing star, rough	Liatris aspera
Blazing star, Savanna	Liatris scariosa newlandii
Blazing star, scaly	Liatris squarrosa
Blazing star, ten-petals	Mentzelia decapetala
Bledo	Celosia floribunda
Bleeding heart	Dicentra eximia
Bleeding heart	Dicentra spectabilis
Bleeding heart tree	Omalanthus populifolius
Bleeding heart, wild	Dicentra formosa
Blinkbaarwitessenhout	Bersama lucens
Blinkblaar	Rhamnus prinoides
Blinkblaarmispel	Vangueria esculenta
Blister bush	Grevillea pyramidalis
Blombiesie	Elegia cuspidata
Blombiesie	Menodora juncea
Blombos	Metalasia muricata
Blompeperbossie	Heliophila carnosa
Blood flower	Asclepias curassavica
Blood flower	Scadoxus multiflorus ssp katherinae
Blood leaf	Iresine
Blood leaf	Iresine lindenii

Common-Botanical Names

Common Name	Botanical Name
Blood lily	Haemanthus
Blood-drop	Stylomecon heterophylla
Blood-drop emlets	Mimulus aurantiacus
Blood-wort, human	Stylophorum lasiocarpum
Bloodroot	Sanguinaria canadensis
Bloodwood	Eucalyptus ptychocarpa
Bloodwood	Eucalyptus terminalis
Bloodwood, brown	Eucalyptus trachyphloia
Bloodwood, Clarkson's	Eucalyptus clarksoniana
Bloodwood, desert	Eucalyptus setosa
Bloodwood, dwarf yellow	Eucalyptus eximia nana
Bloodwood, grey	Eucalyptus porrecta
Bloodwood, gum-topped	Eucalyptus dichromophloia
Bloodwood, inland	Eucalyptus terminalis
Bloodwood, long-fruited	Eucalyptus polycarpa
Bloodwood, pink	Eucalyptus intermedia
Bloodwood, red	Eucalyptus gummifera
Bloodwood, rough-leaved	Eucalyptus sessilis
Bloodwood, rough-leaved	Eucalyptus setosa
Bloodwood, rusty	Eucalyptus ferruginea
Bloodwood, sandhill	Eucalyptus centralis
Bloodwood, small-flowered	Eucalyptus polycarpa
Bloodwood, small-fruited	Eucalyptus dichromophloia
Bloodwood, smooth-stemmed	Eucalyptus bleeseri
Bloodwood, spring	Eucalyptus ptychocarpa
Bloodwood, swamp	Eucalyptus ptychocarpa
Bloodwood, twin-leaved	Eucalyptus perfoliata
Bloodwood, yellow	Eucalyptus eximia
Bloodwort	Rumex sanguineus
Bloodwort	Sanguinaria
Blossom pea, water	Podalyria calyptrata
Blossom tree	Virgilia capensis
Blossom tree	Virgilia oroboides
Blossom tree, gold	Barklya syringifolia
Blossom tree, pink	Virgilia divaricata
Blou-aalwyn	Aloe glauca
Blou-ooguintjie	Moraea aristata
Blouberglelie	Scilla natalensis
Bloublommetjie	Felicia echinata
Bloubos	Diospyros pallens
Bloukeur	Psoralea oligophyllaa
Bloukeur	Psoralea pinnata
Blouklokkie	Gladiolus rogersii
Blouklokkiesbos	Mackaya bella
Bloukoolhout	Leucospermum muirii
Blousuikerbos	Protea neriifolia
Blousuurkanol	Aristea major
Bloutulp	Moraea bipartita
Blue beauty	Cheiranthera filifolia
Blue bells	Campanula
Blue bells	Mertensia pulmonarioides
Blue bugle	Ajuga genevensis
Blue bush	Acacia convenyi
Blue bush	Eucalyptus macrocarpa
Blue candle	Myrtillocactus geometrizans
Blue cohosh	Caulophyllum thalictroides
Blue cupidone	Catananche
Blue curls	Phacelia congesta
Blue hesper palm	Brahea armata
Blue stars	Aristea ecklonii

Common Name	Botanical Name
Blue stars	Chamaescilla corymbosa
Blue-bell, New Zealand	Wahlenbergia pygmaea
Blue-bottle	Centaurea cyanus
Blue-eyed Mary	Collinsia verna
Blue-eyed Mary	Omphalodes verna
Blue-eyed Mary	Sisyrinchium angustifolium
Blue-fan palm	Brahea armata
Blue-flowered torch	Tillandsia lindenii
Bluebell	Hyacinthoides
Bluebell	Hyacinthoides non-scripta
Bluebell , Australian	Sollya heterophylla
Bluebell, Californian	Nemophila menziesii
Bluebell, Californian	Phacelia campanularia
Bluebell ,climbing	Sollya heterophylla
Bluebell creeper	Sollya heterophylla
Bluebell, English	Hyacinthoides non-scripta
Bluebell, New Zealand	Wahlenbergia albomarginata
Bluebell, northern	Trichodesma zeylanicum
Bluebell, riversdale	Gladiolus rogersii
Bluebell, Scottish	Campanula rotundifolia
Bluebell, Spanish	Hyacinthoides hispanica
Bluebell, Texan	Eustoma grandiflorum
Bluebells, desert	Phacelia campanularia
Bluebells, Virginia	Mertensia pulmonarioides
Blueberry	Vaccinum corymbosum
Blueberry Ash	Elaeocarpus reticulatus
Blueberry, box	Vaccinum ovatum
Blueberry, climbing	Billardiera longiflora
Blueberry, creeping	Vaccinum crassifolium
Blueberry, highbush	Vaccinum corymbosum
Blueberry, lowbush	Vaccinum angustifolium v laevifolium
Blueberry, red	Vaccinum parvifolium
Blueberry, swamp	Vaccinum corymbosum
Blueberry, thin-leaved	Vaccinum membranaceum
Blueblossom	Ceanothus thyrsiflorus
Blueblossom, creeping	Ceanothus thyrsiflorus v repens
Bluebonnet, Texas	Lupinus texensis
Blueboy, yellow	Stirlingia latifolia
Bluebush	Maireana brevifolia
Bluebush, ball-leaf	Maireana glomerifolia
Bluebush, black	Maireana pyramidata
Bluebush, cottony	Maireana carnosa
Bluebush, felty	Maireana tomentosa
Bluebush, flat-leaved	Maireana planifolia
Bluebush, Gascoyne	Maireana polypterygia
Bluebush, golden	Maireana georgei
Bluebush, low	Maireana astrotricha
Bluebush, Mallee erect	Maireana pentatropis
Bluebush, Mulga	Maireana convexa
Bluebush, pussy	Maireana melanocoma
Bluebush, sage-leaved	Diospyros lycioides ssp geurkei
Bluebush, Sago	Maireana pyramidata
Bluebush, satiny	Maireana georgei
Bluebush, shy	Maireana platycarpa
Bluebush, spiny	Maireana aphylla
Bluebush, three-winged	Maireana triptera
Bluebush, woolly	Maireana eriantha

Common-Botanical Names

Common	Botanical
Bluestem, big	Andropogon gerardii
Bluestem, little	Schizachyrium scoparium
Bluestem, sand	Andropogon hallii
Bluestem, yellow	Bothriochloa ischaemum
Bluets	Hedyotis
Bluets, creeping	Hedyotis michauxii
Bluets, longleaf	Hostonia longifolia
Blueweed	Echium vulgare
Blushing bride	Serruria florida
Bo tree	Ficus religiosa
Bo-he	Mentha haplocalyx
Boab tree	Adansonia gregorii
Boat Lily	Tradescantia spathacea
Bobbejaan komkommer	Coccinea quinqueloba
Bobbejaandruif	Rhoicissus digitata
Bobbejaantou	Rhoicissus tridentata
Bobbjaanklou	Leucospermum cordifolium
Bobble nut	Macadamia ternifolia
Bobby buttons	Galium aparine
Bobie-bobie	Phebalium squameum
Boekaalwyn	Aloe suprafoliata
Boerboon (bean), bush	Schotia latifolia
Boerboon (bean), karoo	Schotia afra
Boerboon (bean), weeping	Schotia brachypetala
Bog pimpernel	Anagallis tenella
Bog rosemary	Andromeda
Bog star	Parnassia
Bogbean	Menyanthes trifoliata
Bokbaaivygie	Dorotheanthus bellidiformis ssp bellidiformis
Bokbaaivygie, narrow-leaved	Dorotheanthus gramineus
Bokbaaivygie, smalblaar	Dorotheanthus gramineus
Bokbaaivygies	Cleretum papulosum ssp schlechteri
Bokdrol	Canthium inerme
Bold beauty	Gompholobium ovatum
Boldo	Peumus boldus
Bollywood, brown	Litsea leefeana
Bombweed	Epilobium angustifolium
Bone-apple, small	Coddia rudis
Boneset	Eupatorium perfoliatum
Boneset, false	Brickellia eupatorioides
Boneset, false	Kuhnia eupatorioides
Boneset, purple	Eupatorium purpureum
Boneset, tall	Eupatorium altissimum
Bontbessie	Gasteria bicolor
Bontkalkoentjie	Gladiolus speciosus
Bontrokpypie	Hesperantha radiata
Boobialla	Myoporum insulare
Boojum tree	Fouquieria columnaris
Boomeralla	Myoporum tenuifolium
Boomlelie	Cyrtanthus epiphyticus
Boonaree	Heterodendron oleifolium
Boongul	Eucalyptus transcontinentalis
Borage	Borago officinalis
Boree	Acacia pendula
Boronia, blue	Boronia ramosa
Boronia, brown	Boronia megastigma
Boronia, brown perfumed	Boronia megastigma
Boronia, bushy	Boronia fastigiata
Boronia, desert	Boronia inornata
Boronia, false	Phyllanthus calycinus
Boronia, forest	Boronia rosmarinifolia
Boronia, granite	Boronia cymosa
Boronia, mauve	Boronia denticulata
Boronia, pinnate	Boronia pinnata
Boronia, red	Boronia heterophylla
Boronia, rosemary pink	Boronia rosmarinifolia
Boronia, scented	Boronia megastigma
Boronia, showy	Boronia ledifolia
Boronia, Snowy River	Boronia ledifolia
Boronia, tall	Boronia molloyae
Boronia, Wallum	Boronia falcifolia
Bosdrolpeer	Dombeya tiliacea
Bosdruif	Rhoicissus tomentosa
Boskoorsbessie	Codiaeum sylvaticum
Boslelie	Clivia miniata
Bossiaea, baby	Bossiaea preissii
Bossiaea, beautiful	Bossiaea pulchella
Bossiaea, elegant	Bossiaea dentata
Bossiaea, large-flowered	Bossiaea ornata
Bossiaea, leafy	Bossiaea foliosa
Bossiaea, sword	Bossiaea ensata
Bossiaea, variable	Bossiaea heterophylla
Bostaaibos	Rhus chirindensis
Boston ivy	Parthenocissus tricuspidata
Bosui	Ornithogalum tenuifolium ssp tenuifolium
Bosvaderlandswilg	Combretum krausii
Bosverfbos	Indigofera natalensis
Bosvlier	Nuxia floribunda
Botterblom	Arctotis acaulis
Botterblom	Ranunculus multifidus
Botterblom	Sparaxis fragrans
Botterblom	Tylecodon paniculatus
Bottle palm	Baeucarnea recurvata
Bottle plant	Hatiora salicornioides
Bottle tree	Brachychiton populneus
Bottle tree, Australian	Adansonia gregorii
Bottle tree, broad-leaf	Brachychiton australis
Bottle tree, Chinese	Firmiana simplex
Bottle tree, Queensland	Brachychiton rupestris
Bottle tree, scrub	Brachychiton discolor
Bottlebrush	Callistemon
Bottlebrush, Albany	Callistemon speciosus
Bottlebrush, alpine	Callistemon pityoides
Bottlebrush, alpine	Callistemon sieberi
Bottlebrush, bonsai	Beaufortia heterophylla
Bottlebrush, compact	Beaufortia schaueri
Bottlebrush, crimson	Callistemon citrinus
Bottlebrush, Dubarda	Callistemon phoeniceus
Bottlebrush, fiery	Callistemon phoeniceus
Bottlebrush, Goldfield	Melaleuca coccinea
Bottlebrush, granite	Melaleuca elliptica
Bottlebrush, gravel	Beaufortia sparsa
Bottlebrush, green	Callistemon flavovirens
Bottlebrush, green	Callistemon viridiflorus
Bottlebrush, Kei	Greyia flanaganii
Bottlebrush, lemon	Callistemon pallidus
Bottlebrush, little	Beaufortia micrantha
Bottlebrush, narrow-leaved	Callistemon linearis
Bottlebrush, Natal	Greyia sutherlandii
Bottlebrush, one-sided	Calothamnus quadrifidus

Common-Botanical Names

Common Name	Botanical Name
Bottlebrush, pine	Callistemon pinifolius
Bottlebrush, pink	Beaufortia schaueri
Bottlebrush, pink-tipped	Callistemon salignus
Bottlebrush, Ravensthorpe	Beaufortia orbifolia
Bottlebrush, red	Callistemon citrinus
Bottlebrush, red	Callistemon polandii
Bottlebrush, red	Mimetes cucullatus
Bottlebrush, river	Callistemon sieberi
Bottlebrush, sand plain	Beaufortia squarrosa
Bottlebrush, scarlet	Callistemon macropunctatus
Bottlebrush, scarlet	Callistemon rugulosus
Bottlebrush, silver	Beaufortia incana
Bottlebrush, stiff	Callistemon rigidus
Bottlebrush, swamp	Beaufortia sparsa
Bottlebrush, thick-leaved	Callistemon pachyphyllus
Bottlebrush, Tonghi	Callistemon subulatus
Bottlebrush, Transvaal	Greyia radlkoferi
Bottlebrush, Wallum	Callistemon pachyphyllus
Bottlebrush, weeping	Callistemon viminalis
Bottlebrush, white	Callistemon salignus
Bottlebrush, white weeping	Callistemon salignus
Bottlebrush, willow	Callistemon salignus
Bottletree	Brachychiton
Bouncing Bet	Saponaria officinalis
Bourtree	Sambuca nigra
Bowen green	Terminalia sp
Bower of beauty	Pandorea jasminoides
Bower plant	Pandorea jasminoides
Bower vine	Pandorea jasminoides
Bowgada	Acacia linophylla
Bowman's root	Gillenia trifoliata
Bowman's root	Veronicastrum
Box	Buxus
Box, apple	Eucalyptus bridgesiana
Box, apple Creswick	Eucalyptus aromaphloia
Box, Balearic	Buxus balearica
Box, Bimble	Eucalyptus populnea
Box, black	Eucalyptus largiflorens
Box, blue	Eucalyptus baueriana
Box, Brisbane	Lophostemin confertus
Box, broad-leaved	Eucalyptus behriana
Box, brush	Lophostemon confertus
Box, brush tree	Lophostemon confertus
Box, Christmas	Sarcococca
Box, coastal grey	Eucalyptus moluccana
Box, common	Buxus sempervirens
Box, Coowarra	Eucalyptus cambageana
Box, creeping	Mitchella repens
Box elder	Acer negundo
Box, flood	Eucalyptus microtheca
Box, fuzzy	Eucalyptus conica
Box, granite-rock	Eucalyptus petraea
Box, grey	Eucalyptus microcarpa
Box, grey coast	Eucalyptus bosistoana
Box, grey Gippsland	Eucalyptus bosistoana
Box, grey northern	Eucalyptus argillacea
Box, gum-topped	Eucalyptus miniata
Box, Himalayan	Buxus wallichiana
Box, inland grey	Eucalyptus woollsiana
Box, large-leaved	Eucalyptus nortonii
Box, long-leaved	Eucalyptus goniocalyx
Box, narrow-leaved grey	Eucalyptus petraea
Box, peppermint	Eucalyptus odorata
Box, poplar	Eucalyptus populnea
Box, prickly	Bursaria spinosa
Box, Queensland	Lophostemon confertus
Box, red	Eucalyptus polyanthemos
Box, red western	Eucalyptus intertexta
Box, red white	Eucalyptus polyanthemos
Box, river Reid	Eucalyptus brownii
Box, sea	Alyxia buxifolia
Box, silver	Eucalyptus pruinosa
Box, slaty	Eucalyptus dawsonii
Box, small-leaved	Buxus microphylla
Box, steel	Eucalyptus rummeryi
Box, sweet	Sarcococca
Box thorn, Chinese	Lycium barbarum
Box, Victorian	Pittosporum undulatum
Box, white	Eucalyptus albens
Box, white-topped	Eucalyptus quadrangulata
Box, yellow	Eucalyptus melliodora
Boxwood	Buxus
Boxwood, African	Myrsine africana
Brachysema, creeping	Brachysema latifolium
Bracken	Pteridium aquilinum
Brahmi	Centella asiatica
Brake	Pteris
Brake, Cretan	Pteris cretica
Brake, jungle	Pteris umbrosa
Brake, painted	Pteris tricolor
Brake, shaking	Pteris tremula
Brake, silver	Pteris argyraea
Brake, spider	Pteris multifida
Brake, sword	Pteris ensiformis
Brake, tender	Pteris tremula
Bramble	Rubus fruticosus
Bramble	Rubus ulmifolius 'Bellidiflorus'
Bramble, rock	Rubus saxatilis
Brandy bottle	Nuphar lutea
Brass buttons	Cotula coronopifolia
Bread fruit, scrub	Pandanus monticola
Bread fruit tree	Pandanus pedunculatus
Breadfruit, Mexican	Monstera deliciosa
Breath of heaven	Diosma ericoides
Bredasdorpsuikerbos	Protea neriifolia
Breeblaarboekenhout	Faurea speciosa
Breeblaarsuikerbos	Protea eximia
Breekhout	Alberta magna
Breelya	Gastrolobium laytonii
Breeriviergeelhout	Podocarpus elongatus
Brewer spruce	Picea breweriana
Briar, sensitive	Schrankia nuttallii
Briar, sensitive	Schrankia uncinata
Briar, sweet	Rosa rubiginosa
Bridal bouquet	Porana paniculata
Bridal wreath	Francoa
Bridal wreath	Francoa sonchifolia
Bridal wreath	Spiraea 'Arguta'
Bridal wreath	Spiraea x vanhouttei
Bridal wreath	Stephanotis floribunda
Bride's bonnet	Clintonia uniflora
Bride's bush, common	Pavetta gardenifolia
Bride's bush, forest	Pavetta lanceolata
Bride's bush, small-leaved	Pavetta zeyheri
Brigalow	Acacia harpophylla

Common-Botanical Names

Common	Botanical	Common	Botanical
Bristle cone fir	Abies bracteata	Buckeye, red	Aesculus pavia
Brittle bush	Encelia farinosa	Buckeye, sweet	Aesculus flava
Broad-leaved kindling bark	Eucalyptus dalrympleana	Buckeye, yellow	Aesculus flava
Broadleaf	Griselinia littoralis	Buckler fern	Dryopteris
Brobs (gorse branches)	Ulex europaeus	Buckler fern, broad	Dryopteris dilatata
Brodiaea, harest	Brodiaea coronaria	Buckler fern, common	Dryopteris dilatata
Bromeliad, bird's nest	Nidularium	Buckler fern, narrow	Dryopteris carthusiana
Bromeliad, blushing	Neoregelia carolinae	Buckthorn	Rhamnus
Bromeliad, blushing	Nidularium fulgens	Buckthorn, alder	Rhamnus alnifola
Bromeliads,King of the	Vriesea hieroglyphica	Buckthorn, alder	Rhamnus frangula
Brooklime	Veronica beccabunga	Buckthorn, common	Rhamnus cathartica
Broom	Cytisus	Buckthorn, Italian	Rhamnus alaternus
Broom	Genista	Buckthorn, sea	Hippophae rhamnoides
Broom	Ruscus	Buckwheat	Fagopyrum esculentum
Broom	Spartium	Buckwheat, California	Eriogonum fasciculatum
Broom, blue	Psoralea pinnata	Buckwheat , Medawaska	Fagopyrum tartaricum
Broom bush	Templetonia eugena	Buckwheat, saffron	Eriogonum crocatum
Broom bush, desert	Templetonia eugena	Buckwheat, sulphur	Eriogonum umbellatum
Broom, butcher's	Ruscus aculeatus	Buckwheat, umbrella desert	Eriogonum umbellatum
Broom, climbing butcher's	Semele androgyna	Buckwheat, wild	Eriogonum
Broom, common	Cytisus scoparius	Buffalo berry	Shepherdia argentea
Broom corn	Sorghum vulgare	Buffalo berry, russet	Shepherdia canadensis
Broom, dyer's	Genista tinctoria	Buffalo grass	Buchloe dactyloides
Broom, fragrant	Cytisus racemosus	Buffalo pea	Thermopsis montana
Broom, hedgehog	Erinacea anthyllis	Buffalo-thorn	Ziziphus mucronata
Broom, Moroccan	Cytisus battandieri	Buffalo-wood	Burchellia
Broom, Mount Etna	Genista aetnenis	Bugbane	Cimicifuga
Broom, pineapple	Cytisus battandieri	Bugbane, American	Cimicifuga americana
Broom, pink	Notospartium carmichaeliae	Bugbane, Asian	Cimicifuga simplex
		Bugle	Ajuga
Broom, Portuguese	Cytisus multiflorus	Bugle, bronze	Ajuga reptans 'Atropurpurea'
Broom, purple	Chamaecytisus purpureus		
		Bugle, red	Blancoa canescens
Broom, purple	Polygala virgata	Bugler, Arizona	Penstemon pseudospectabilis
Broom, Scotch	Cytisus scoparius		
Broom, Spanish	Spartium	Bugler, Royal red	Aeschynanthus pulcher
Broom, Spanish white	Cytisus multiflorus	Bugler, Utah	Penstemon utahensis
Broom, Warminster	Cytisus x praecox 'Warminster'	Bugleweed	Lycopus
		Bugleweed	Lycopus virginicus
Broom, weeping	Chordospartium stevensonii	Bugloss	Anchusa
		Bugloss	Anchusa officinalis
Broom, weeping white	Retama monosperma	Bugloss, Siberian	Brunnera macrophylla
Broom-corn	Sorghum	Bugloss, viper's	Echium
Broombush	Melaleuca uncinata	Bugloss, viper's	Echium vulgare
Broomweed	Gutierrezia	Builbos	Peltophorum africanum
Broomweed	Gutierrezia sarothrae	Bull-oak	Allocasuarina luehmannii
Brother berry	Chrysanthemoides monilifera	Bull-oak, bushy	Allocasuarina trichodon
		Bullace	Prunus insititia
Brother-Brother	Gastrolobium tetragonophyllum	Bullock bush	Templetonia retusa
		Bullock's heart	Annona reticulata
Brown-eyed Susan	Rudbeckia triloba	Bulrush	Typha
Browntop, silky	Eulalia aurea	Bulrush	Typha latifolia
Bruce bush	Acacia maslinii	Bulrush, dark green	Scirpus atrovirens
Bruinsalie	Salvia africana-lutea	Bulrush, dark green	Scirpus atrovirens v georgianus
Brush box	Lophostemon confertus		
Brushes and combs	Dipsacus fullonum	Bulrush, great	Scirpus validus
Bryony, black	Tamus communis	Bulrush, hardstem	Scirpus acutus
Bryony, white	Bryonia dioica	Bulrush, lesser	Typha angustifolia
Buchu	Agathosma betulina	Bulrush, reddish	Scirpus pendulus
Buchu, oval	Agathosma crenulata	Bunch berry	Cornus canadensis
Buckbean	Menyanthes trifoliata	Bunch flower	Melanthium virginicum
Buckeye	Aesculus	Bundle flower, Illinois	Desmanthus illinoensis
Buckeye, bottlebrush	Aesculus parviflora	Bundy	Eucalyptus goniocalyx
Buckeye, California	Aesculus californica	Bunnies' ears	Stachys byzantina
Buckeye, dwarf	Aesculus pavia	Bunny ears	Opuntia microdasys v pallida
Buckeye, Ohio	Aesculus glabra		

Common-Botanical Names

Common	Botanical	Common	Botanical
Bunny tails	Ptilotus latifolius	Butterfly plant	Monopsis decipiens
Bunny's tail	Lagurus ovatus	Butterfly tree	Bauhinia purpurea
Bunya-bunya	Araucaria bidwillii	Butterfly tree	Melicope elleryana
Bur Marigold	Bidens pilosa	Butterfly weed	Asclepias tuberosa
Bur Marigold, nodding	Bidens cernua	Butternut	Juglans cinerea
Bur reed, branched	Sparganium erectum	Butternut, rose	Blepharocarya involucrigera
Bur-reed	Sparganium		
Bur-reed, great	Sparganium eurycarpum	Butterwort	Pinguicula
Bur-reed, least	Sparganium minimus	Butterwort, large-flowered	Pinguicula grandiflora
Burdock	Arctium	Button sourees	Arctium sp
Burdock, great(er)	Arctium lappa	Button-willow	Cephalanthus occidentalis
Burdock, lesser	Arctium minus		
Burdock, woolly	Arctium tomentosum	Buttonbush	Cephalanthus occidentalis
Burgan	Kunzea ericoides		
Buri	Corypha elata	Buttons, blue	Succisa pratensis
Buri	Melaleuca sheathiana	Buttons, yellow	Helichrysum semipapposum
Burnet	Sanguisorba		
Burnet, American	Sanguisorba canadensis	Buttonwood	Platanus occidentalis
Burnet, Canadian	Sanguisorba canadensis	Byfield fern northern	Bowenia spectabilis
Burnet, greater	Sanguisorba officinalis	Cabbage, flowering	Brassica
Burnet, saxifrage	Pimpinella saxifraga	Cabbage, ornamental	Brassica oleracea
Burnet, small	Sanguisorba minor	Cabbage palm	Cordyline
Burning bush	Bassia scoparia	Cabbage palm, New Zealand	Cordyline australis
Burning bush	Bassia scoparia f trichophylla	Cabbage palm, saw	Acoelorraphe wrightii
		Cabbage tree	Cordyline
Burning Bush	Dictamnus albus	Cabbage tree	Cussonia paniculata
Burning bush	Euonymus alatus	Cabbage tree, common	Cussonia spicata
Burrawang	Macrozamia communis	Cabbage tree, High Veldt	Cussonia paniculata
Burrawang	Macrozamia spiralis	Cabbage tree, Low Veldt	Cussonia spicata
Burrawong	Macrozamia communis	Cabbage tree, mock	Cussonia natalensis
Burro's tail	Sedum morganianum	Cabbage tree, mountain	Cussonia paniculata
Burweed	Zanthium strumarium	Cabbage tree palm	Livistona australis
Bush groundsel	Baccharis halimifolia	Cabbage tree, spiked	Cussonia spicata
Bush honeysuckle	Diervilla	Cactus, ball golden	Parodia
Bush nut	Stylobasium spathulatum	Cactus, barrel	Ferocactus
		Cactus, barrel blue Texas	Echinocactus horizontalonius
Bush tea	Aspalanthus linearis		
Bush violet	Browallia	Cactus, barrel golden	Echinocactus grusonii
Bushman's clothes pegs	Grevillea glauca	Cactus, chain	Rhipsalis paradoxa
Bushpea, Carolina	Thermopsis villosa	Cactus, Christmas	Schlumbergera
Busy Lizzie	Impatiens	Cactus, Christmas	Schlumbergera x buckleyi
Busy Lizzie	Impatiens walleriana		
Butter and eggs	Linaria vulgaris	Cactus, Christmas desert	Opuntia ficus-indica
Butter tree	Tylecodon paniculatus	Cactus, Colombian ball	Parodia vorwerkiana
Butterbur	Petasites hybridus	Cactus, cotton-pole	Opuntia vestita
Buttercup	Ranunculus	Cactus, crab	Schlumbergera truncata
Buttercup, alpine	Ranunculus alpestris	Cactus, dumpling	Lophophora williamsii
Buttercup, bristly	Ranunculus pensylvanicus	Cactus, Easter	Hatiora rosea
		Cactus, Easter	Rhipsalidopsis gaertneri
Buttercup, bulbous	Ranunculus bulbosus	Cactus, fishbone	Epiphyllum anguliger
Buttercup, double creeping	Ranunculus repens v pleniflorus	Cactus, gold lace	Mammillaria elongata
		Cactus, grizzly bear	Opuntia erinacea v ursina
Buttercup, double meadow	Ranunculus acris 'Flore Pleno'	Cactus, hedgehog	Echinocereus fendleri v rectispinus
Buttercup, giant	Ranunculus lyallii	Cactus, hedgehog claret cup	Echinocereus triglochidiatus
Buttercup, meadow	Ranunculus acris		
Buttercup, northern	Corchorus walcottii	Cactus, hedgehog red-flowered	Echinocereus coccineus
Buttercup, Persian	Ranunculus asiaticus	Cactus, hedgehog strawberry	Echinocereus enneacanthus
Buttercup, prairie	Ranunculus rhomboideus		
Buttercup, Pyrenean	Ranunculus pyrenaeus	Cactus, lamb's tail	Echinocereus schmollii
Buttercups, yellow	Hibbertia scandens	Cactus, lobster	Schlumbergera truncata
Butterfly bush	Buddleja davidii	Cactus, melon	Melocactus intortus
Butterfly flower	Bauhinia monandra	Cactus, mistletoe	Rhipsalis baccifera
Butterfly flower	Schizanthus	Cactus, old lady	Mammillaria hahniana
Butterfly pea	Centrosema virginiana	Cactus, old man	Cephalocereus senilis
		Cactus, old man	Oreocereus celsianus

Common-Botanical Names

Common Name	Botanical Name
Cactus, old man Peruvian	Espostoa lanata
Cactus, old-woman	Mammillaria hahniana
Cactus, orchid	Epiphyllum
Cactus, organ-pipe	Stenocereus thurberi
Cactus pea	Bossiaea walkeri
Cactus, peanut	Echinopsis chamaecereus
Cactus, pincushion	Escobaria vivipara
Cactus, pincushion	Mammillaria
Cactus, powder-puff	Mammillaria bocasana
Cactus, prickly pear brown-spined	Opuntia phaeacantha
Cactus, prickly pear large-rooted	Opuntia macrorhizia
Cactus, prickly pear Santa Rita	Opuntia violacea v santa rita
Cactus, rainbow	Echinocereus pectinatus
Cactus, rainbow green-flowered	Echinocereus viridiflorus
Cactus, rose	Pereskia grandifolia
Cactus, saguaro	Carnegiea gigantea
Cactus, scarlet ball	Parodia haselbergii
Cactus, silver ball	Parodia scopa
Cactus, silver dollar	Astrophytum asterias
Cactus, snowball	Mammillaria bocasana
Cactus, snowball cushion	Mammillaria candida
Cactus, spine barrel red	Ferocactus gracilis
Cactus, starfish	Orbea variegata
Cactus, strap	Epiphyllum
Cactus, strawberry	Mammillaria prolifera
Cactus, toad	Orbea variegata
Cactus, torch	Trichocereus
Cactus, torch Peruvian	Echinopsis spachianus
Cactus, Turk's cap	Melocactus
Cactus, walking stick	Opuntia imbricata v arborescens
Cadaga (Cadaghi)	Eucalyptus torelliana
Cadjeput, silver	Melaleuca argentea
Calabash, sweet	Passiflora maliformis
Calabazilla	Cucurbita foetidisima
Calamint	Acinos
Calamint	Calamintha officinalis
Calamint, cushion	Clinopodium vulgare
Calamint, lesser	Calamintha nepeta
Calamint, showy	Calamintha grandiflora
Calamus	Acorus calamus americanus
Calico bush	Kalmia latifolia
Calico flower	Aristolochia littoralis
Calico plant	Alternanthera bettzichiana
California lilac	Ceanothus
California red fir	Abies magnifica
California rose-bay	Rhododendron californicum
Calla lily, white	Zantedeschia aethiopica
Calliopsis	Coreopsis tinctoria
Calomondin	x Citrofortunella microcarpa
Caltrop	Tribulus terrestris
Camas, blue	Camassia quamash
Camas, Cusick's	Camassia cusickii
Camas, Leichtlin's	Camassia leichtlinii
Camash	Camassia
Camass, white	Zigadenus elegans
Camassia common	Camassia quamash
Camdeboo	Celtis africana
Camel bush	Acacia inaequilatera
Camel grass	Angianthus tomentosus
Camel thorn	Acacia erioloba
Camel thorn	Acacia giraffae
Camel thorn, grey	Acacia haematoxylon
Camel's foot	Piliostigma thonningii
Camellia common	Camellia japonica
Camomile	Chamaemelum nobile
Camphor bush	Tarchonanthus camphoratus
Camphor laurel	Cinnamomum camphora
Camphor tree	Cinnamomum camphora
Campion	Lychnis
Campion	Silene
Campion, alpine	Lychnis alpina
Campion, double sea	Silene uniflora 'Robin Whitebreast'
Campion, moss	Silene acaulis
Campion, night-flowering	Silene noctiflora
Campion, red	Silene dioica
Campion, rose	Lychnis coronaria
Campion, snowy	Silene nivea
Campion, starry	Silene stellata
Camwood, sand	Baphia massaiensis
Canary bird bush	Crotalaria agatiflora
Canary creeper	Senecio tamoides
Canary creeper	Tropaeolum peregrinum
Cancer bush	Sutherlandia frutescens
Cancer bush	Sutherlandia microphylla
Cancer weed	Salvia lyrata
Candle bush	Senna alata
Candle nut tree	Aleurites moluccana
Candle plant	Plectranthus oertendahlii
Candle plant	Senecio articulatus
Candle plant, Empress	Senna alata
Candle thorn	Acacia hebeclada ssp tristis
Candle tree	Parmentiera cerifera
Candlebark	Eucalyptus rubida
Candlebark, red	Eucalyptus rubida
Candlemas bells	Galanthus nivalis
Candlestick, golden	Banksia spinulosa v collina
Candlestick shrub	Senna alata
Candlewood	Rothmannia capensis
Candytuft	Iberis
Candytuft, common	Iberis amara
Candytuft, common	Iberis umbellata
Candytuft, evergreen	Iberis sempervirens
Candytuft, florist's	Iberis amara
Cane, dwarf	Chamaedorea seifrizii
Cane, Lawyer	Calamus australis
Cane, Lawyer fishtail	Calamus caryotoides
Cane, Lawyer yellow	Calamus moti
Canna, edible	Canna edulis
Canterbury bells	Campanula medium
Canterbury bells	Campanula medium 'Calycanthema'
Capa de oro	Solandra maxima
Cape Arid climber	Kennedia beckxiana
Cape dandelion	Arctotheca calendula
Cape figwort	Phygelius capensis
Cape gooseberry	Physalis edulis
Cape gooseberry	Physalis peruviana
Cape kaffirboom	Erythrina caffra
Cape Leeuwinclimber	Kennedia macrophylla
Cape marigold	Dimorphotheca
Cape may	Coleonema album

Common-Botanical Names

Common	Botanical	Common	Botanical
Cape pondweed	Aponogeton distachyos	Cassia, smooth	Senna pleurocarpa ssp
Cape Tulip	Haemanthus coccineus		pleurocarpa
Caper bush	Capparis spinosa inermis	Cassia, sprawling	Senna aciphylla
Caper bush	Capparis spinosa v	Cassia, spring pod	Senna artemisioides ssp
	nummularia		circinnata
Caper bush, wild	Capparis sepiaria	Cassia, sticky	Senna glutinosa ssp
Caraway	Carum		glutinosa
Caraway	Carum carvi	Cassia, straight leaf	Senna artemisioides ssp
Caraway, false	Ridolfia seetum		sturtii
Caraway, thyme	Thymus herba-barona	Cassia, variable	Senna artemisioides ssp
Caraway, tuberous	Bunium bulbocastanum		sturtii
Carbeen	Eucalyptus tessellaris	Cassia, velvet	Senna renigera
Cardamom	Elettaria cardamomum	Cassia, white	Senna glutinosa ssp
Cardboard plant	Zamia furfuracea		pruinosa
Cardinal climber	Ipomoea x multifida	Cassie	Acacia formesiana
Cardinal climber	Lobelia cardinalis	Cassinia, drooping	Cassinia arcuata
Cardinal flower	Lobelia cardinalis	Cassinia, inland	Cassinia laevis
Cardinal flower	Sinningia cardinalis	Cassinia, sticky	Cassinia uncata
Cardinal flower, blue	Lobelia siphilitica	Cassinopsis, spiny	Cassinopsis ilicifolia
Cardinal's guard	Pachystachys coccinea	Cast iron plant	Aspidistra
Cardoon	Cynara cardunculus	Castor bean	Ricinus communis
Caricature plant	Graptophyllum pictum	Castor oil plant	Ricinus communis
Carl doddies	Plantago lanceolata	Cat thorn	Scutia myrtina
Carline thistle	Carlina	Cat thyme	Teucrium marum
Carline thistle, stemless	Carlina acaulis	Cat's claw creeper	Macfadyena unguis-cati
Carnation	Dianthus	Cat's claw vine	Macfadyena
Carnation, wild	Dianthus caryophyllus	Cat's claw vine, common	Macfadyena unguis-cati
Carnival bush	Ochna	Cat's ear	Hypochaeris radicata
Carob	Ceratonia siliqua	Cat's ears	Antennaria
Carob bean	Ceratonia siliqua	Cat's ears	Calochortus
Carolina water shield	Cabomba caroliniana	Cat's foot	Antennaria dioica
Carpet plant	Episcia	Cat's paw	Anigozanthus
Carrion flower	Orbea variegata	Cat's paw	Anigozanthus humilis
	(Stapelia)	Cat's paw	Antennaria neglecta
Carrion flower	Stapelia	Cat's paw, Albany	Anigozanthus preissii
Carrot tree	Steganotaenia araliacea	Cat's paw, common	Anigozanthus humilis
Carrotwood tree	Cupaniopsis	Cat's tail	Phleum pratense ssp
	anacardioides		bertolonii
Cartwheel plant	Heracleum	Cat's tail	Typha
	mantegazzianum	Cat's tail (Cattail)	Typha latifolia
Casabanana	Sicana odorifera	Cat's tail, miniature	Typha minima
Cascara	Rhamnus purshia	Cat's tail, red hot	Acalypha hispida
Cascara sagrada	Rhamnus purshiana	Cat's whiskers	Becium grandiflorum v
Cashew nut	Anacardium occidentale		obovatum
Caspian locust	Gleditsia caspica	Cat's whiskers	Tacca chantrieri
Cassava	Manihot esculenta	Catalpa, Chinese	Catalpa ovata
Cassia, apple blossom	Cassia javanica	Catalpa, northern	Catalpa speciosa
Cassia, candlestick	Senna venusta	Catalpa, southern	Catalpa bignonioides
Cassia, cigar	Cassia brewsteri	Catalpa, western	Catalpa speciosa
Cassia, clay	Senna artemisioides ssp	Catchfly	Lychnis
	hamersleyensis	Catchfly	Silene
Cassia, crinkled	Senna artemisioides ssp	Catchfly, alpine	Lychnis alpina
	helmsii	Catchfly, German	Lychnis viscaria
Cassia, desert	Senna artemisioides ssp	Catchfly, nodding	Silene pendula
	filifolia	Catchfly, Royal	Silene regia
Cassia, desert	Senna eremophila	Catchfly, Sweet-William	Silene armeria
Cassia, green	Senna glutinosa ssp	Caterpillar pod, small	Ormocarpum kirkii
	chatelainiana	Cathedral bell	Cobaea scandens
Cassia, grey	Senna artemisioides ssp	Cathedral windows	Calathea makoyana
	helmsii	Catherine wheel	Leucospermum
Cassia, Java	Cassia javanica		catherinae
Cassia, limestone	Senna artemisioides ssp	Catmint	Nepeta
	oligophylla	Catmint, giant	Nepeta grandiflora
Cassia, pepper leaf	Senna barclayana	Catmint, wild	Ballota africana
Cassia, purging	Cassia fistula	Catnip	Nepeta cataria
Cassia, silver	Senna artemisioides	Catnip, camphor	Nepeta camphorata

Common-Botanical Names

Common	Botanical	Common	Botanical
Catnip, Greek	Nepeta parnassica	Centaury, American wild	Centaurium muhlenbergii
Catnip, Japanese	Nepeta tenuiflora		
Catnip, lemon	Nepeta cataria 'Citriodora'	Centaury, common	Centaurium erythraea
Catnip, Syrian	Nepeta curvifolia	Centaury, Monterrey	Centaurium muhlenbergii
Cattail, narrow-leaved	Typha angustifolia		
Caucasian fir	Abies nordmanniana	Centaury, perennial	Centaurium scilloides
Caudex vine, South African	Triaspis nelsonii	Century plant	Agave
Cauliflower bush	Verticordia eriocephala	Century plant, Mexican	Agave americana
Cauliflower, wild	Verticordia eriocephala	Cereus, giant Mexican	Pachycereus pringlei
Caustic bush	Grevillea pyramidalis	Cereus, night-blooming	Cereus uruguayanus
Cayenne pepper	Capsicum annuum Longum Group	Cereus, night-blooming	Hylocereus undatus
		Cereus, powder-blue	Stenocereus pruinosus
Ceanothus, Carmel	Ceanothus griseus	Ceriman	Monstera deliciosa
Ceanothus, feltleaf	Ceanothus arboreus	Cha-Phloo	Piper sarmentosum
Ceanothus, hollyleaf	Ceanothus purpureus	Chagrilla roja	Bomarea lobbiana
Ceanothus, Lemmon's	Ceanothus lemmonii	Chain fern	Woodwardia
Ceanothus, Monterey	Ceanothus rigidus	Chain fern, Asian	Woodwardia unigemmata
Ceanothus, red-stem	Ceanothus sanguineus		
Ceanothus, Santa Barbara	Ceanothus impressus	Chain fern, European	Woodwardia radicans
Ceanothus, wedgeleaf	Ceanothus cuneatus	Chain plant	Callisia fragrans
Cedar	Cedrus	Chain plant	Callisia navicularis
Cedar, American white	Thuja occidentalis	Chalice vine	Solandra
Cedar, Atlas	Cedrus libani ssp atlantica	Chalta	Dillenia indica
		Chamal	Dioon edule
Cedar, Australian	Toona australis	Chamomile	Chamaemelum
Cedar, blue Atlas	Cedrus libani Glauca Group	Chamomile, dyer's	Anthemis tinctoria
		Chamomile, English	Chamaemelum nobile
Cedar, Chilean incense	Austrocedrus chilensis	Chamomile, false	Tripleurospermum
Cedar, Chinese	Toona sinensis	Chamomile, German	Matricaria recutita
Cedar, Clanwilliam	Widdringtonia cedarbergensis	Chamomile, glacier	Achillea nana
		Chamomile, lawn	Chamaemelum nobile
Cedar, Cyprus	Cedrus libani ssp brevifolia	Chamomile, oil	Chamaemelum nobile
		Chamomile, ox-eye	Anthemis tinctoria
Cedar, deodar	Cedrus deodora	Chamomile, Roman	Chamaemelum nobile
Cedar, eastern red	Juniperus virginiana	Chamomile, St.John's	Anthemis sancti-johannis
Cedar, eastern white	Thuja occidentalis	Chamomile, wild	Matricaria recutita
Cedar, incense	Calocedrus decurrens	Chaparral	Larrea tridentata
Cedar, Indian	Cedrus deodora	Chaparro	Castela emoryi
Cedar, Japanese	Cryptomeria japonica	Chapman River climber	Billardiera ringens
Cedar, mountain	Widdringtonia nodiflora	Chaste tree	Vitex agnus-castus
Cedar, northern white	Thuja occidentalis	Chastity tree	Vitex agnus-castus
Cedar of Goa	Cupressus lusitanica	Checkerberry	Gaultheria procumbens
Cedar of Lebanon	Cedrus libani	Checkerbloom	Sidalcea malviflora
Cedar, pencil	Juniperus virginiana	Checkerbloom, Swale	Sidalcea campestris
Cedar, pencil	Polyscias murrayi	Cheddar pink	Dianthus gratianopolitanus
Cedar, pink	Acrocarpus fraxinifolius		
Cedar, red	Juniperus virginiana	Cheese tree	Glochidion
Cedar, red	Toona australis	Cheeseberry	Cyathodes glauca
Cedar, summit	Athrotaxis x laxifolia	Cheesewood	Pittosporum bicolor
Cedar, Tasmanian	Arthrotaxis x laxifolia	Cheesewood	Pittosporum undulatum
Cedar, western red	Thuja plicata	Cheggies (fruit)	Aesculus hippocastanum
Cedar, white	Melia azedarach	Chequer tree	Sorbus torminalis
Cedar, white	Melia azedarach ssp australasica	Chequers (fruit)	Sorbus torminalis
		Cherimoya	Annona cherimola
Cedar, white	Thuja occidentalis	Cherry, Acerola	Malpighia punicifolia
Cedar, Willowmore	Widdringtonia schwartzii	Cherry, Barbados	Malpighia glabra
Celandine, greater	Chelidonium majus	Cherry, bell-flowered	Prunus campanulatus
Celandine, lesser	Ranunculus ficaria	Cherry, bird	Prunus padus
Celandine poppy	Stylophorum diphyllum	Cherry, bitter	Prunus emarginata
Celery	Apium graveolens	Cherry, black	Prunus serotinus
Celery leaf	Apium graveolens secalinum	Cherry, bladder	Physalis alkekengi
		Cherry, Brazilian	Acmena uniflora
Celery pine	Phyllocladus	Cherry, Brazilian	Eugenia uniflora
Celery wood	Polyscias 'Elegans'	Cherry, brush	Eugenia australis
Cenizo	Leucophyllum frutescens	Cherry, brush	Eugenia paniculatum
Centaury	Centaurium	Cherry, brush Australian	Syzygium paniculatum

Common-Botanical Names

Cherry, bush — Maerua caffra
Cherry, Carolina — Prunus caroliniana
Cherry, Catalina — Prunus lyonii
Cherry, choke — Prunus virginiana
Cherry, Christmas — Solanum pseudocapsicum

Cherry, Cornelian — Cornus mas
Cherry, downy — Prunus tomentosa
Cherry, false Jerusalem — Solanum capsicastrum
Cherry, Fuji — Prunus incisa
Cherry, great white — Prunus 'Taihaku'
Cherry, ground — Physalis
Cherry, Higan — Prunus x subhirtella
Cherry, Hill — Prunus jamasakura
Cherry, holly-leaved — Prunus ilicifolia
Cherry, Jerusalem — Solanum pseudocapsicum

Cherry, Korean — Prunus japonica
Cherry laurel — Prunus laurocerasus
Cherry, magenta — Eugenia paniculatum
Cherry, Mahaleb — Prunus mahaleb
Cherry, Manchurian — Prunus maackii
Cherry, Mexican — Prunus salicifolia
Cherry, Nanking — Prunus tomentosa
Cherry, ornamental — Prunus
Cherry pepper — Capsicum annuum Cerasiforme Group

Cherry pie — Heliotropium arborescens

Cherry, pin — Prunus pensylvanica
Cherry, rosebud — Prunus x subhirtella
Cherry, Saint Lucie — Prunus mahaleb
Cherry, sargent — Prunus sargentii
Cherry, scrub — Acmena myrtifolia
Cherry, scrub — Eugenia australis
Cherry, Spanish — Mimusops elengi
Cherry, Surinan — Eugenia uniflora
Cherry, Taiwan — Prunus campanulata
Cherry, Virginian bird — Prunus virginiana
Cherry, weeping — Exocarpos sparteus
Cherry, wild — Prunus avium
Cherry, wild rum — Prunus serotina
Cherry, winter — Cardiospermum halicacabum
Cherry, winter — Physalis alkekengi
Cherry, winter — Solanum capsicastrum
Cherry, winter — Solanum pseudocapsicum
Cherry, Yoshino — Prunus x yedoensis
Chervil, common — Anthriscus cerefolium
Chervil, golden — Chaerophyllum aureum
Chestnut — Castanea
Chestnut, American — Castanea dentata
Chestnut, Cape — Calodendron capense
Chestnut, Chinese — Castanea mollissima
Chestnut, horse Chinese — Aesculus chinensis
Chestnut, Moreton Bay — Castanospermum australe

Chestnut, Spanish — Castanea sativa
Chestnut, sweet — Castanea sativa
Chestnut vine — Tetrastigma voinierianum
Chestnut, water — Trapa
Chestnut, water — Trapa nutans
Chia — Salvia hispanica
Chia, Tarahumara — Salvia tiliifolia
Chickling pea — Lathyrus sativus

Chickweed — Cerastium
Chickweed — Stellaria media
Chickweed, sea — Honkenya peploides
Chickweed wintergreen — Trientalis europaea
Chicory — Cichorium
Chicory — Cichorium intybus
Chihuahua flower — Graptopetalum
Chile nut — Gevuina avellana
Chilean bamboo — Chusquea culeou
Chilean bellflower — Lapageria
Chilean fire bush — Embothrium
Chilean fire bush — Embothrium coccineum
Chilean glory flower — Eccremocarpus scaber
Chilean incense cedar — Austrocedrus chilensis
Chilean pine — Araucaria araucana
Chilli pepper — Capsicum annuum
China aster — Callistephus
China doll — Radermachera sinica
China fir — Cunninghamia
China fir — Cunninghamia lanceolata
Chinaberry — Melia azederach
Chinaberry — Melia composita
Chinaman's breeches — Dicentra spectabilis
Chincherinchee — Ornithogalum thyrsoides

Chinese artichoke — Stachys affinis
Chinese astragalus — Astragalus membranaceus

Chinese evergreen — Aglaonema
Chinese fir — Cunninghamia lanceolata

Chinese fire berry — Ardisia crispa
Chinese forget-me-not — Cynoglossum amabile
Chinese gooseberry — Actinidia deliciosa
Chinese hat plant — Holmskioldia sanguinea
Chinese houses — Collinsia bicolor
Chinese lanterns — Nymania capensis
Chinese lanterns — Physalis alkekengi
Chinese lanterns — Physalis alkekengi v franchetii
Chinese silkworm — Cudrania tricuspidata
Chinese spinach — Amaranthus tricolor cultivars
Chinese-lantern — Abutilon grandiflorum
Chinese-lantern, desert — Abutilon otocarpum
Chnkapin, golden — Chrysilepis chrysophylla
Chinkerinchee — Ornithogalum pruinosum
Chinquapin, bush — Castaniopsis sempervirens
Chinquapin, water — Nelumbo lutea
Chittamwood — Cotinus obovatus
Chittick — Lambertia inermis
Chives — Allium schoenoprasum
Chives, Chinese — Allium tuberosum
Chives, garlic — Allium tuberosum
Chocolate berry — Vitex payos
Chocolate cosmos — Cosmos atrosanguineus
Chocolate flower — Berlandiera lyrata
Chocolate vine — Akebia
Chokeberry — Aronia
Chokeberry, black — Aronia melanocarpa
Chokeberry, purple — Arnebia x prunifolia
Chokeberry, red — Arnebia arbutifolia
Chokeberry, red — Aronia arbutifolia

Common-Botanical Names

Chokers (fruit)
Cholla, buckthorn

Cholla, jumping
Cholla, tree

Chorizema, climbing
Chorizema, painted
Chotito
Christ's tears
Christ's thorn

Christ's thorn
Christmas bells
Christmas bells
Christmas bells, giant
Christmas bells, small
Christmas bells, Tasmanian
Christmas berry
Christmas berry
Christmas berry tree
Christmas box
Christmas bush

Christmas bush, New Zealand
Christmas bush, Victorian
Christmas fern

Christmas horns
Christmas pride
Christmas rose
Christmas tree
Christmas tree
Christmas tree, Kalahari
Christmas tree, New South Wales

Christmas tree, New Zealand
Christmas tree, New Zealand
Christmas tree, W. Australia
Chrysanthemum, alpine
Chrysanthemum, Bedouin

Chrysanthemum, edible

Chulupa
Chusan palm
Cicely, sweet
Cigar flower
Cigar plant, Mexican
Cilician fir
Cinderella slippers
Cineraria, wild
Cineraria, wild giant
Cinnamon

Cinnamon vine
Cinnamon vine
Cinquefoil
Cinquefoil, alpine
Cinquefoil, bush
Cinquefoil, golden
Cinquefoil, Himalayan
Cinquefoil, hoary
Cinquefoil, marsh
Cinquefoil, Nepal
Cinquefoil, prairie

Sorbus torminalis
Cylindropuntia
acanthocarpa
Cylindropuntia fulgida
Opuntia imbricata v
arborescens
Chorizema diversifolium
Chorizema aciculare
Polyscias filicifolia
Coix lacryma-jobi
Euphorbia milii v
splendens
Paliurus spina-chrsiti
Blandfordia
Sandersonia aurantiaca
Blandfordia grandiflora
Blandfordia nobilis
Blandfordia punicea
Chironia baccifera
Photinia arbutifolia
Schinus terebinthifolius
Sarcococca
Ceratopetalum
gummiferum
Metrosideros excelsus
Prostanthera lasianthos
Polystichum
acrostichoides
Delphinium nudicaule
Ruellia macrantha
Helleborus niger
Metrosideros excelsus
Picea abies
Dichrostachys cinerea
Ceratopetalum
gummiferum
Metrosideros robusta
Metrosideros tomentosa
Nuytsia floribunda
Leucanthemopsis alpina
Chrysanthemum
coronarium
Chrysanthemum
coronarium
Passiflora maliformis
Trachycarpus fortunei
Myrris
Cuphea ignea
Cuphea ignea
Abies cilicica
Sinningia regina
Senecio elegans
Senecio glastifolius
Cinnamomum
zeylanicum
Dioscorea
Dioscorea batatas
Potentilla
Potentilla crantzii
Potentilla fruticosa
Potentilla aurea
Potentilla atrosanguinea
Potentilla argentea
Potentilla palustris
Potentilla nepalensis
Potentilla arguta

Cinquefoil, rock
Cinquefoil, slender
Cinquefoil, Texan
Circle flower
Cistus, common gum
Cistus, narrow-leaved
Citron
Citronella grass
Citronella plant
Claggy Meggies
Clammyweed
Clanwilliamseder

Clarkia, elegant
Clary, annual
Clary, biennial
Clary, meadow
Clary, Turkish

Clary, Vatican

Clary, wild
Claw flower

Claw flower
Claw flower, Barrens
Claw flower, dense
Claw flower, dwarf
Claw flower, Murchison

Claw flower, pink
Clear eye
Cleavers
Cleavers
Clematis, alpine
Clematis, blue-flowered
Clematis, fine-leaved
Clematis, forest
Clematis, golden
Clematis, ground
Clematis, mountain

Clematis, purple

Clematis, western
Clematis, western
Clematis, western white
Clementine
Cleome, sticky
Clerodendrum, woolly

Clethra, cinnamon
Clethra, summersweet
Cliff brake, purple-stemmed
Cliff rose
Cliffbush
Cliffrose
Climbing fumitory
Clivers
Clock vine, Bengal
Clock vine, bush
Cloud tree, white
Clove
Clove root
Clover
Clover

Potentilla rupestris
Potentilla gracilis
Potentilla simplex
Lysimachia punctata
Cistus x cyprius
Cistus monspeliensis
Citrus medica
Cymbopogon nardus
Cedronella canariensis
Galium aparine
Polanisia uniglandulosa
Widdringtonia
cedarbergensis
Clarkia unguiculata
Salvia viridis
Salvia sclarea
Salvia pratensis
Salvia sclarea
turkestanica
Salvia sclarea
turkestanica
Salvia verbenaca
Calothamnus
chrysantherus
Melaleuca pulchella
Calothamnus validus
Calothamnus pinifolius
Calothamnus lehmannii
Calothamnus
homallophyllus
Melaleuca pulchella
Salvia sclarea
Arctium sp
Galium aparine
Clematis alpina
Clematis columbiana
Clematis microphylla
Clematis glycinoides
Clematis tangutica
Clematis recta
Clematis occidentalis v
grosseserrata
Clematis occidentalis v
grosseserrata
Clematis microphylla
Clematis pubescens
Clematis ligusticifolia
Citrus reticulata
Cleome viscosa
Clerodendrum
tomentosum
Clethra acuminata
Clethra alnifolia
Pellaea atropurpurea
Cowania mexicana
Jamesia americana
Cowania stansburiana
Adlumia fungosa
Galium aparine
Thunbergia grandiflora
Thunbergia erecta
Melaleuca bracteata
Syzygium aromaticum
Geum urbanum
Trifolium
Trifolium africanum

Common-Botanical Names

Common	Botanical
Clover, alpine	Trifolium alpinum
Clover, bush	Lespedeza
Clover, bush Japanese	Lespedeza bicolor
Clover, bush prairie	Lespedeza leptostachya
Clover, bush round-headed	Lespedeza capitata
Clover, bush shrub	Lespedeza bicolor
Clover, bush slender	Lespedeza virginica
Clover, bushland	Goodia lotifolia
Clover carpet	Kennedia carinata
Clover, crimson	Trifolium incarnatum
Clover, desert grassland	Dalea exile
Clover, Dutch	Trifolium repens
Clover, elk	Aralia californica
Clover, giant headed	Trifolium macrocephalum
Clover, hairy canary	Lotus hirsutus
Clover, Italian	Trifolium incarnatum
Clover, lucky	Oxalis tetraphylla
Clover, O' Conner's strawberry	Trifolium fragiferum
Clover, prairie leafy	Dalea foliosum
Clover, prairie purple	Dalea purpureum
Clover, red	Trifolium pratense
Clover, rose	Trifolium hirtum
Clover, Spanish	Gomphrena globosa
Clover, sweet	Melilotus officinalis
Clover, tom-cat	Trifolium tridentatum
Clover tree	Goodia lotifolia
Clover, water	Marsilea
Clover, water	Marsilea quadrifolia
Clover, white	Trifolium repens
Clover, white wild	Trifolium repens
Club foot	Pachypodium lamerei
Club, golden	Orontium
Club moss	Lycopodium
Club-rush	Schoenoplectus lacustris ssp tabernaemontana 'Zebrinus'
Club-rush, round-headed	Scirpoides holoschoenus
Clusterleaf, Lebombo	Terminalia phanerophlebia
Clyders (Clydon)	Galium aparine
Coachwhip	Fouquieria splendens
Coachwood	Ceratopetalum apetalum
Coal wood	Lachnostylis hirta
Cobnut	Corylus avellana
Cock's comb	Erythrina crista-galli
Cock's foot	Dactylis glomerata
Cockies' tongues	Templetonia retusa
Cocklebur	Zanthium strumarium
Cocklebur, Siberian	Zanthium sibiricum
Cockroach berry	Solanum aculeatissimum
Cockroach bush	Senna notabilis
Cockroach bush	Senna petersiana
Cockscomb	Celosia
Cockscomb	Celosia argentea v cristata
Cockspur flower, Zulu	Plectranthus zuluensis
Cockspur thorn	Crataegus crus-galli
Coco de plata	Calamus discolor
Coco-de-mer	Lodoicea
Coco-yam	Colocasia esculenta
Coconut	Cocos
Coconut, double	Lodoicea
Coffee	Coffea arabica
Coffee berry	Coprosma hirtella
Coffee, dwarf	Coffea arabica nana
Coffee shrub	Cassia occidentalis
Coffee tree	Polyscias guilfoylei
Coffee tree, Kentucky	Gymnocladus dioica
Coffee, wild	Polyscias guilfoylei
Coffeeberry	Rhamnus californica
Cohosh	Cimicifuga
Cohosh, black	Cimicifuga racemosa
Cohosh, blue	Caulophyllum thalictroides
Cola de pescado (fishtail)	Chamaedorea ernesti-augusti
Colane	Owenia acidula
Coleus	Solenostemon scutellarioides
Coleus, prostrate	Plectranthus oertendahlii
Colewort	Crambe
Coltsfoot	Tussilago farfara
Coltsfoot, alpine	Homogyne alpina
Coltsfoot, sweet	Petasites frigidus
Coltsfoot, sweet	Petasites frigidus v palmatus
Columbine	Aquilegia
Columbine	Aquilegia vulgaris
Columbine, alpine	Aquilegia alpina
Columbine, Canadian	Aquilegia canadensis
Columbine, dark	Aquilegia atrata
Columbine, fragrant	Aquilegia fragrans
Columbine, Japanese fan	Aquilegia flabellata
Columbine, Moorcroft's	Aquilegia moorcroftiana
Columbine, Rocky Mountain	Aquilegia caerulea
Columbine, Rocky mountain	Aquilegia saximontana
Columbine, Sitka	Aquilegia formosa
Columbine, small-flowered	Aquilegia brevistyla
Columbine, wild	Aquilegia canadensis
Combretum, spiny	Combretum obovatum
Comfrey	Symphytum
Comfrey, common	Symphytum officinale
Comfrey, creeping	Symphytum ibericum
Comfrey, Russian	Symphytum x uplandicum
Comfrey, tuberous	Symphytum tuberosum
Comfrey, yellow	Symphytum ibericum
Commiphora, sweet-root	Commiphora neglecta
Commiphora, velvet	Commiphora mollis
Common apple berry	Billardiera scandens
Common bog rosemary	Andromeda polifolia
Common rasp fern	Doodia media
Compass plant	Silphium laciniatum
Cone bush	Isopogon
Cone bush, tall	Isopogon anemonifolius
Cone pepper	Capsicum annuum Conioides Group
Cone pepper, red	Capsicum annuum Fasciculatum Group
Conebush, acacialeaf	Leucadendron macowanii
Conebush, bredasdorp	Leucadendron laxum
Conebush, broadleaf	Leucadendron gandogeri
Conebush, dune	Leucadendron coniferum
Conebush, gardenrout	Leucadendron conicum
Conebush, green-flowered	Leucadendron l oranthifolium
Conebush, gumleaf	Leucadendron eucalyptifolium
Conebush, laurel leaf	Leucadendron laureolum

Conebush, Outeniqua	Leucadendron uliginosum ssp uliginosum
Conebush, Pondoland	Leucadendron pondoense
Conebush, rock	Leucadendron strobilinium
Conebush, rough-leaf	Leucadendron modestum
Conebush, sickleleaf	Leucadendron xanthoconus
Conebush, spear-leaf fragrant	Leucadendron spissifolium ssp fragrans
Conebush, spear-leaf Kareedouwvlakte	Leucadendron spissifolium ssp phillipsii
Conebush, spear-leaf Natal	Leucadendron spissifolium ssp natalense
Conebush, spicy	Leucadendron tinctum
Conebush, spinning top	Leucadendron rubrum
Conebush, star	Leucadendron stellare
Conebush, stream common	Leucadendron salicifolium
Conebush, sun	Leucadendron sessile
Conebush, sunshine common	Leucadendron salignum
Conebush, Witsenberg	Leucadendron chamelea
Conebush, Worcester	Leucadendron flexuosum
Coneflower	Echinacea
Coneflower	Echinacea angustifolia
Coneflower	Rudbeckia
Coneflower, barrel	Isopogon trilobus
Coneflower, Bush's	Echinacea paradoxa
Coneflower, clasp-leaved	Dracopis amplexicaulis
Coneflower, clustered	Isopogon polycephalus
Coneflower, cut-leaf	Rudbeckia laciniata
Coneflower, drooping	Ratibida pinnata
Coneflower, eastern	Rudbeckia triloba
Coneflower, green-headed	Rudbeckia laciniata
Coneflower, grey-head	Ratibida pinnata
Coneflower, long-headed	Ratibida columnifera
Coneflower, Missouri	Rudbeckia missouriensis
Coneflower, narrow-leaved	Echinacea angustifolia
Coneflower, nodding	Isopogon teretifolius
Coneflower, orange	Rudbeckia fulgida
Coneflower, pale	Echinacea pallida
Coneflower, pin-cushion	Isopogon dubius
Coneflower, prairie	Ratibida
Coneflower, purple	Echinacea purpurea
Coneflower, rose	Isopogon dubius
Coneflower, rose	Isopogon formosus
Coneflower, spreading	Isopogon divergens
Coneflower, Stirling Range	Isopogon baxteri
Coneflower, Stirling Range	Isopogon latifolius
Coneflower, sweet	Rudbeckia subtomentosa
Coneflower, Tennessee	Echinacea tennesseensis
Coneflower, thin-leaved	Rudbeckia triloba
Coneflower, three-lobed	Rudbeckia triloba
Coneflower, yellow	Ratibida columnifera
Coneflower, yellow	Ratibida pinnata
Coneflower, yellow purple	Echinacea paradoxa
Conesticks	Petrophile
Conesticks, prickly	Petrophile sessilis
Confederate jasmine	Trachelospermum jasminoides

Confederate, rose	Hibiscus mutabilis
Confederate vine	Antigonon leptopus
Conkers (fruit)	Aesculus hippocastanum
Coobah	Acacia salicina
Coobah, river	Acacia stenophylla
Coobah, small	Acacia ligulata
Coogara	Arytera divaricata
Cook pine	Araucaria columnaris
Coolamon	Syzygium moorei
Coolibah	Eucalyptus coolabah
Coolibah	Eucalyptus microtheca
Coolibah, gum barked	Eucalyptus intertexta
Coolibah, mountain	Eucalyptus orgadophila
Coolibah, powder bark	Eucalyptus victrix
Coontie	Zamia floridania
Coontie	Zamia pumila
Copey	Clusia major
Copihue	Lapageria rosea
Copper beech	Fagus sylvatica Atropurpurea Group
Copper cups	Pileanthus peduncularis
Copper pod	Peltophorum pterocarpum
Copperleaf	Acalypha wilkesiana
Coprosma, rough	Coprosma hirtella
Coprosma, shining	Coprosma nitida
Coquito	Jubaea chilensis
Coral bean	Erythrina herbacea
Coral bean, south-west	Erythrina flabelliformis
Coral bells	Heuchera sanguinea
Coral berry	Aechmea fulgens
Coral bush	Templetonia retusa
Coral cactus	Rhipsalis cereuscula
Coral creeper	Kennedia coccinea
Coral drops	Bessera
Coral drops	Bessera elegans
Coral flower	Heuchera
Coral gem	Lotus berthelotii
Coral honeysuckle	Lonicera sempervirens
Coral pea	Hardenbergia
Coral pea	Kennedia
Coral pea	Kennedia coccinea
Coral pea, black	Kennedia nigricans
Coral pea, dusky	Kennedia rubicunda
Coral pea, purple	Hardenbergia violacea
Coral pea, white	Hardenbergia violacea alba
Coral plant	Berberidopsis corallina
Coral plant	Jatropha multifida
Coral plant	Russelia equisetiformis
Coral tree	Erythrina
Coral tree	Erythrina abyssinica
Coral tree, bat's wing	Erythrina vespertilio
Coral tree, cockspur	Erythrina crista-galli
Coral tree, common	Erythrina crista-galli
Coral tree, crybaby	Erythrina lysistemon
Coral tree, naked	Erythrina americana
Coral vine	Antigonon
Coral vine, common	Kennedia coccinea
Coral vine, Mexican	Antigonon leptopus
Coral-wort	Dentaria bulbifera
Coralberry	Ardisia crenata
Coralberry	Ardisia crispa
Coralberry	Symphoricarpos orbiculatus
Corallita	Antigonon

Common-Botanical Names

Common	Botanical	Common	Botanical
Corallita, white	Porana paniculata	Cotton, tree	Gossypium arboreum
Coralroot	Corallorhiza	Cotton tree	Hibiscus tiliaceus
Cordao	Leonotis nepetifolia	Cotton tree, silk	Ceiba pentandra
Coreopsis	Coreopsis grandiflora	Cotton, wild	Asclepias rostrata
Coreopsis, eared	Coreopsis auriculata	Cotton, wild	Cochlospermum
Coreopsis, garden	Coreopsis tinctoria		vitifolium
Coreopsis, lanceleaf	Coreopsis lanceolata	Cotton, wild	Gossypium davidsonii
Coreopsis, pink	Coreopsis rosea	Cotton, wild	Gossypium herbaceum
Coreopsis, plains	Coreopsis tinctoria		ssp africanum
Coreopsis, prairie	Coreopsis palmata	Cotton, wild	Hibiscus diversifolius
Coreopsis, sand	Coreopsis lanceolata	Cotton, wild	Hibiscus moscheutos
Coreopsis, tall	Coreopsis tripteris	Cotton, wild	Ipomoea albivenia
Coreopsis, thread-leaved	Coreopsis verticillata	Cottonbush	Maireana aphylla
Coriander	Coriandrum	Cottonheads, gold	Conostylis candicans
Coriander, Mexican	Eryngium foetidum	Cottonweed	Froelichia floridana
Coriander, Roman	Nigella sativa	Cottonwood	Hibiscus tiliaceus
Coriander, thorny	Eryngium foetidum	Cottonwood	Populus deltoides
Coriander, Vietnamese	Persicaria odorata	Cottonwood, black	Populus trichocarpa
Cork tree,Amur	Phellodendron amurense	Cottonwood, Eastern	Populus deltoides
Corkbark	Hakea suberea	Cottonwood, mountain	Cassinia leptophylla ssp
Corkbark fir	Abies lasiocarpa v		vauvilliersii
	arizonica	Couch, common	Elytrigia repens
Corkbark, straggly	Hakea eyreana	Couch, hairy	Elymus hispidus
Corkscrew flower	Vigna caracalla	Couch, rat's tail	Sporobolus mitchellii
Corkwood, pink-flowered	Melicope elleryana	Cough root	Lomatium dissectum
Corkwood, swamp	Sesbania formosa	Council tree	Ficus altissima
Corn	Zea mays	Council weed	Artemisia vulgaris
Corn cockle	Agrostemma	Coventry bells	Campanula trachelium
Corn, Indian	Zea	Cow itch tree	Lagunaria patersonii
Corn lily	Clintonia borealis	Cow paigle	Primula veris
Corn, ornamental	Zea japonica	Cow soap	Vaccaria
Corn plant	Dracaena fragrans	Cow strupple	Primula veris
Corn poppy	Papaver rhoeas	Cow's tongue	Opuntia linguiformis
Cornel	Cornus	Cow-wheat, crested	Melampyrum cristatum
Cornel, Bentham's	Cornus capitata	Cow-wheat, field	Melampyrum arvense
Cornel, dwarf	Cornus canadensis	Cowberry	Vaccinum vitis-idaea
Cornel, dwarf	Cornus suecia	Cows and bulls	Arum maculatum
Cornel, Japanese	Cornus officinalis	Cowslip	Primula veris
Cornelian cherry	Cornus mas	Cowslip, American	Dodecatheon
Cornflower	Centaurea cyanus	Cowslip, blue	Pulmonaria angustifolia
Cornflower, globe	Centaurea macrocephala	Cowslip, Cape	Lachenalia
Cornflower, mountain	Centaurea montana	Cowslip, giant	Primula florindae
Cornflower, native (AU)	Brunonia australis	Cowslip, Himalayan	Primula sikkimensis
Cornflower, Persian	Centaurea dealbata	Cowslip, Jerusalem	Pulmonaria officinalis
Corydalis, cold water	Corydalis aquae-gelidae	Cowslip, Tibetan yellow	Primula florindae
Corydalis, golden	Corydalis aurea	Cowslip, Virginia	Mertensia
Corydalis, pale	Corydalis sempervirens		pulmonarioides
Costmary	Tanacetum balsamita	Cowtail pine	Cephalotaxus
Cotoneaster, creeping	Cotoneaster nanshan		harringtoniana
Cotoneaster, Diel's	Cotoneaster dielsianus	Coyote bush	Baccharis pilularis
Cotoneaster, tree	Cotoneaster frigidus	Crab apple	Schizomeria ovata
Cotoneaster, willow-leaf	Cotoneaster salicifolius	Crab apple, common	Malus sylvestris
Cotton	Gossypium herbaceum	Crab apple, flowering	Malus
Cotton, American upland	Gossypium hirsutum	Crab apple, Japanese flowering	Malus floribunda
Cotton ball	Espostoa lanata	Crab apple, Manchurian	Malus baccata v
Cotton bush	Ptilotus obovatus		mandschurica
Cotton, false	Asclepias burchellii	Crab apple, Oriental	Malus brevipes
Cotton grass	Eriophorum	Crab apple, Siberian	Malus baccata
Cotton grass, broad-leaved	Eriophorum latifolium	Crab apple, tea	Malus hupehensis
Cotton grass, comon	Eriophorum	Crab apple, wild	Malus sylvestris
	angustifolium	Crab apple, wild sweet	Malus coronaria
Cotton lavender	Santolina	Crab claws	Stylomecon heterophylla
	chamaecyparissus	Crab, Hupeh	Malus hupehensis
Cotton rose	Hibiscus mutabilis	Crab, purple	Malus x purpurea
Cotton thistle	Onopordum acanthium	Crab's eye plant	Abrus precatorius
Cotton top, Arizona	Trichachne californica	Crabapple, western	Pyrus fusca

Common-Botanical Names

Common	Botanical	Common	Botanical
Cradle Orchid	Anguloa clowesii	Crocus, saffron	Crocus sativus
Cramp bark	Viburnum opulus	Crocus, spring	Crocus vernus
Cranberry	Vaccinum	Cross vine	Bignonia
Cranberry	Vaccinum macrocarpon	Cross vine	Bignonia capreolata
Cranberry, American	Viburnum trilobum	Cross-berry, Karoo	Grewia robusta
Cranberry bush, European	Viburnum opulus	Cross-berry, large-flowered white	Grewia pachycalyx
Cranberry, Chilean	Ugni molinae	Cross-leaved heath	Erica tetralix
Crane flower	Strelitzia reginae	Crosswort	Phuopsis stylosa
Cranesbill	Geranium	Croton	Codiaeum
Cranesbill, Armenian	Geranium psilostemon	Crowberry	Empetum nigrum
Cranesbill, bloody	Geranium sanguineum	Crowberry, common	Rhus pentheri
Cranesbill, cut-leaved	Geranium dissectum	Crowfoot	Ranunculus
Cranesbill, dusky	Geranium phaeum	Crowfoot, glacier	Ranunculus gracilis
Cranesbill, French	Geranium endressii	Crowfoot, water	Ranunculus aquatilis
Cranesbill, meadow	Geranium pratense	Crown fern	Blechnum discolor
Cranesbill, Pyrenean	Geranium pyrenaicum	Crown Imperial	Fritillaria imperialis
Cranesbill, Stewart's	Geranium pratense ssp stewartianum	Crown of gold	Barklya syringifolia
		Crown of thorns	Euphorbia milii
Cranesbill, veined	Geranium versicolor	Crown vetch	Coronilla varia
Cranesbill, wood	Geranium sylvaticum	Crownbeard, yellow	Verbesina helianthoides
Crassula, red	Crassula perfoliata v minor	Cruel plant	Araujia sericifera
		Crusader's spears	Urginea maritima
Creamcups	Platystemon	Cuckoo flower	Arum maculatum
Creamcups	Platystemon californicus	Cuckoo flower	Cardamine pratensis
Creek wiga	Eremophila bignoniiflora	Cuckoo pint	Arum maculatum
Creeper, coral	Kennedia coccinea	Cucumber, horny	Cucumis metuliferus
Creeper, fine red	Kennedia eximia	Cucumber, serpent	Trichosanthes cucumerina v anguina
Creeper, miniature	Kennedia microphylla		
Creeping beauty	Protea venusta	Cucumber, squiring	Ecballium
Creeping buttons	Peperomia rotundifloia	Cucumber tree	Magnolia acuminata
Creeping Charlie	Pilea nummulariifolia	Cucumber tree, large-leaved	Magnolia macrophylla
Creeping devil	Stenocereus eruca	Cucumber, wild	Echinocystis lobata
Creeping Jenny	Lysimachia nummularia	Cudgerie	Flindersia schottiana
Creeping Jenny, golden	Lysimachia nummalaria 'Aurea'	Cudweed	Artemisia ludoviciana
		Culantro	Eryngium foetidum
Creosote bush	Larrea tridentata	Culver's root	Veronicastrum virginicum
Crepe flower	Lagerstroemeria indica		
Crepe ginger	Costus speciosus	Cumin	Cuminum
Crepe myrtle	Lagerstroemeria floribunda	Cumin	Cuminum cyminum
		Cumin, black	Nigella sativa
Crepe myrtle	Lagerstroemeria indica	Cup and saucer plant	Cobaea scandens
Crepe myrtle, Cape	Lagerstroemeria speciosa	Cup flower	Nierembergia
		Cup of gold	Solandra maxima
Crepe myrtle, giant	Lagerstroemeria speciosa	Cup plant	Silphium perfoliatum
		Cup plant, Indian	Silphium perfoliatum
Crepe myrtle, native (AU)	Lagerstroemeria archerana	Cupa de desierto	Thevetia thevetioides
		Cupania, cashew-leaf	Cupaniopsis anacardioides
Crepe myrtle, Queen's	Lagerstroemeria flos reginae	Cupid's bower	Achimenes
Crepe myrtle, Queen's	Lagerstroemeria speciosa	Cupid's dart	Catananche
		Cups-and-saucers	Karomia speciosa
Crepe myrtle, Queen's	Lagerstroemeria speciosa	Curd herb	Trigonella caerulea
		Curracabah	Acacia concurrens
Cress	Lepidium	Currant	Ribes
Cress, chamois	Hutchinsia alpina	Currant, alpine	Ribes alpinum
Cress, Indian	Tropaeolum majus	Currant, Buffalo	Ribes odoratum
Cress, violet	Ionopsidium acaule	Currant bush	Scaevola spinescens
Cress, winter	Barbarea vulgaris	Currant bush, mountain	Coprosma nitida
Crinkle bush	Lomatia silaifolia	Currant bush, prickly	Coprosma quadrifida
Crocus, Autumn	Colchicum	Currant, flowering	Ribes
Crocus, Autumn	Crocus nudiflorus	Currant, flowering red	Ribes sanguineum
Crocus, celandine	Crocus korolkowii	Currant, fuchsia-flowered	Ribes speciosum
Crocus, Chilean	Conanthera bifolia	Currant, golden	Ribes odoratum
Crocus, Chilean blue	Tecophilaea cyanocrocus	Currant, Indian	Symphoricarpos orbiculatus
Crocus, cloth of gold	Crocus angustifolius		
Crocus, Dutch	Crocus vernus	Currant, squaw	Ribes cereum

Common-Botanical Names

Currant, sticky — Ribes viscosissimum
Currawong (Curawang) — Acacia doratoxylon
Curry bush — Cassinia laevis
Curry bush — Hypericum revolutum
Curry flower — Lysinema ciliatum
Curry plant — Helichrysum italicum
Curry plant — Helichrysum italicum ssp serotinum

Curuba — Sicana odorifera
Curuba di indio — Passiflora
Cushag — Senecio jacobaea
Cushion bush — Leucophyta brownii
Cushion bush, Suurberg — Oldenburgia arbuscula
Custard apple — Annona squamosa
Custard apple, wild — Annona senagalensis
Cut tail — Eucalyptus fastigiata
Cycad, ferocious blue — Encephalartos horridus
Cycad, Lebombo — Encephalartos lebomboensis

Cycad, Modjadji — Encephalartos transvenosus

Cycad, prickly — Encephalartos altensteinii
Cycad, Suurberg — Encephalartos longifolius
Cyperus, crowfoot — Cyperus schweinitzii
Cyperus, Schweinitz's — Cyperus schweinitzii
Cyperus, slender — Cyperus filiculmis
Cypress — Chamaecyparis
Cypress — Cupressus
Cypress, Arizona — Cupressus arizonica
Cypress, Baker — Cupressus bakeri
Cypress, bald — Taxodium distichum
Cypress Bay — Callitris rhomboidea
Cypress, Bhutan — Cupressus torulosa
Cypress, book leaf — Thuja orientalis
Cypress, broom — Bassia scoparia f trichophylla

Cypress, deciduous — Taxodium distichum
Cypress, dwarf — Actinostrobus acuminatus

Cypress, dwarf — Thuja orientalis nanus
Cypress, false — Chamaecyparis
Cypress, Guadalupe — Cupressus guadalupensis
Cypress, Hinoki — Chamaecyparis obtusa
Cypress, Italian — Cupressus sempervirens
Cypress, Italian — Cupressus sempervirens horizontalis

Cypress, Italian — Cupressus sempervirens 'Stricta'
Cypress, Japanese false — Chamaecyparis obtusa
Cypress, Kashmir — Cupressus torulosa 'Cashmeriana'

Cypress, Lawson — Chamaecyparis lawsoniana

Cypress, Lawson false — Chamaecyparis lawsoniana

Cypress, Mediterranean — Cupressus sempervirens
Cypress, Mexican — Cupressus lusitanica
Cypress, mock — Bassia scoparia f trichophylla

Cypress, Monterey — Cupressus macrocarpa
Cypress, Montezuma — Taxodium mucronatum
Cypress, mountain — Widdringtonia nodiflora
Cypress, mourning — Cupressus funebris
Cypress, native (AU) — Actinostrobus pyramidalis

Cypress, Nootka — Chamaecyparis nootkanensis

Cypress, outeniqua — Widdringtonia nodiflora
Cypress, Patagonian — Fitzroya cupressoides
Cypress, pine — Callitris
Cypress pine — Callitris rhomboidea
Cypress, pine black — Callitris endlicheri
Cypress, pine coastal — Callitris columellaris
Cypress, pine dwarf — Callitris monticola
Cypress, pine northern — Callitris intratropica
Cypress, pine small — Callitris drummondii
Cypress, pine southern — Callitris preissii
Cypress, pine white — Callitris columellaris
Cypress, pine white — Callitris glaucophylla
Cypress, Port Orford — Chamaecyparis lawsoniana

Cypress, sandplain — Actinostrobus arenarius
Cypress, Sawara — Chamaecyparis pisifera
Cypress, smooth — Cupressus arizonica v glabra

Cypress, spurge — Euphorbia
Cypress, summer — Bassia scoparia f trichophylla

Cypress, swamp — Taxodium
Cypress, swamp — Taxodium distichum
Cypress, Swan River — Actinostrobus pyramidalis

Cypress vine — Ipomoea pennata
Cypress vine — Ipomoea quamoclit
Cypress, weeping Chinese — Cupressus funebris
Cypress, white — Chamaecyparis thyoides
Cyprus turpentine — Pistacia terebinthus
Da Qing — Baphicacanthus cusia
Da quing ye — Isatis tinctoria
Daffodil — Narcissus
Daffodil, Autumn — Sterbergia
Daffodil, bunch-flowered — Narcissus tazetta
Daffodil, hoop petticoat — Narcissus bulbocodium
Daffodil, hoop petticoat white — Narcissus cantabricus
Daffodil, Peruvian — Hymenocallis narcissiflora

Daffodil, polyanthus — Narcissus tazetta
Daffodil, Queen Anne's double — Narcissus 'Eystettensis'
Daffodil, sea — Pancratium maritimum
Daffodil, Tenby — Narcissus obvallaris
Daffodil, white-hoop petticoat — Narcissus cantabricus
Daffodil, wild — Narcissus pseudonarcissus

Dagger plant — Yucca aloifolia
Dagger Spanish — Yucca aloifolia
Dagger Spanish — Yucca gloriosa
Dahlia, climbing — Hidalgoa
Dahlia, mountain — Liparia splendens
Daily dew — Drosera
Daisy — Bellis
Daisy, African — Dimorphotheca
Daisy, African — Lonas inodora
Daisy, African blue-eyed — Arctotis venusta
Daisy, Barberton — Gerbera jamesonii
Daisy, beetle — Gorteria diffusa
Daisy, blue — Olearia ciliata
Daisy, bridal — Olearia microphylla
Daisy, bristle — Asteridea pulverulenta
Daisy, burr purple — Calotis cuneifolia
Daisy, burr tangled — Calotis erinacea
Daisy, burr woolly-headed — Calotis multicaulis

113

Common Name	Botanical Name
Daisy, burr yellow	Calotis lappulacea
Daisy bush	Heterolepis aliena
Daisy bush	Olearia
Daisy, butter	Verbesina encelioides
Daisy, carnation	Senecio gregorii
Daisy, climbing	Brachyscome latisquamea
Daisy, coastal dune	Olearia axillaris
Daisy, common	Bellis perennis
Daisy, cutleaf	Erigeron compositus
Daisy, Dahlberg	Thymophylla tenuiloba
Daisy, double	Bellis perennis
Daisy, edging yellow	Chrysocoma coma-aurea
Daisy, English	Bellis perennis
Daisy, fringed	Brachyscome ciliaris ssp ciliaris
Daisy , fringed	Olearia ciliata
Daisy, giant star	Inula gigantea
Daisy, globe	Globularia
Daisy, golden	Calendula
Daisy, Kingfisher	Felicia bergeriana
Daisy, lakeside	Tetraneuris acaulis
Daisy, Livingstone	Dorotheanthus
Daisy, Livingstone	Dorotheanthus bellidiformis
Daisy, Marborough rock	Pachystegia insignis
Daisy, Mexican mountain	Heterotheca mucronata
Daisy, Michaelmas	Aster novi-belgii
Daisy, Minnie	Minuria leptophylla
Daisy, Minuria woolly	Minuria denticulata
Daisy, moon alpine	Leucanthemopsis alpina
Daisy, mountain	Ixodia achillaeoides ssp achillaeoides
Daisy, mountain	Ixodia achillaeoides ssp alata
Daisy, mountain	Ixodia achillaeoides ssp arenicola
Daisy, mountain	Osmitopsis asteriscoides
Daisy, mountain orange	Helenium hoopesii
Daisy, Mt Atlas	Anacyclus depressus
Daisy, Mule's ear	Wyethia helenioides
Daisy, Namaqualand	Dimorphotheca sinuata
Daisy, Namaqualand white	Dimorphotheca pluvialis
Daisy, New Zealand	Celmisia
Daisy, ox-eye	Buphthalmum salicifolium
Daisy, ox-eye	Castalis tragus
Daisy, ox-eye	Leucanthemum vulgare
Daisy, painted	Chrysanthemum carinatum
Daisy, painted	Tanacetum coccineum
Daisy, paper	Psilostrophe tagetina
Daisy, paper desert	Leucochrysum stipitatum
Daisy, paper golden	Leucochrysum molle
Daisy, pimelea	Abeliophyllum
Daisy, pimelea	Olearia pimeleoides
Daisy, poached egg	Polycalymma stuartii
Daisy, rain	Dimorphotheca pluvialis
Daisy, rock	Brachyscome multifida
Daisy, Rottnest	Trachymene coerulea
Daisy, scented	Pterocaulon sphacelatum
Daisy, Shasta	Leucanthemum x superbum
Daisy, Silverton	Ixiochlamys cuneifolia
Daisy, star	Lindheimera
Daisy, star	Lindheimera texana
Daisy, Swan Rver	Brachyscome iberidifolia
Daisy, Tahoka	Machaeranthera tanacetifolia
Daisy, Transvaal	Gerbera jamesonii
Daisy, variable	Brachyscome ciliaris ssp ciliaris
Dakriet	Chondropetalum tectorum
Dalyeruk	Eucalyptus tetragona
Dalyongurd	Hakea victoriae
Damask flower	Hesperis matronalis
Damiana	Turnera diffusa
Dampiera, pouched	Dampiera sacculata
Damson	Prunus insititia
Damson, Gyro	Gyrocarpus americanus
Dandelion, cape	Arctotheca calendula
Dandelion, common	Taraxacum officinale
Dandelion, Montmogny	Taraxacum officinale
Dandelion, mountain	Agoseris grandiflora
Dandelion, pink	Crepis incana
Dandelion, prairie	Agoseris cuspidata
Dandjin	Hakea preissii
Danewort	Sambucus ebulus
Dang shen	Codonopsis pilosula
Dankobai	Lindera obtusiloba
Daphne, native (AU)	Pittosporum undulatum
Daphne, South African	Dais cotinifolia
Dasypogon, pineapple-leaved	Dasypogon bromeliifolius
Date, Chinese	Ziziphus jujuba
Date palm	Phoenix dactylifera
Date palm, Canary Island	Phoenix canariensis
Date palm, miniature	Phoenix roebelinii
Date palm, pygmy	Phoenix roebelinii
Dateplum	Diospyros lotus
Datil	Yucca baccata
Datura, Hindu	Datura metel
Daviesia, bookleaf	Daviesia cordata
Daviesia, grass	Daviesia longifolia
Dawn flower, blue	Ipomoea indica
Day flower	Commelina
Daylily	Hemerocallis
Daylily, fulvous	Hemerocallis fulva
Daylily, grass-leaved	Hemerocallis minor
Daylily, tawny	Hemerocallis fulva
Dead finish	Acacia tetragonophylla
Dead nettle	Lamium
Dead nettle, Pyrenean	Horminum pyrenaicum
Deadly nightshade	Atropa belladonna
Death Camas	Zigadenus venenosus
Deer bush	Ceanothus integerrimus
Deer weed	Lotus scoparius
Dekriet	Thamnochortus insignis
Deodar	Cedrus deodora
Desert biscuit root	Lomatium dissectum
Desert browse shrub	Atalaya hemiglauca
Desert candle	Eremurus
Desert marigold	Baileya multiradiata
Desert rose	Adenium
Desert rose	Alyogyne hakeifolia
Desert spoon	Dasylirion wheeleri
Desert tea	Ephedra viridis
Devil flower	Tacca chantrieri

Common-Botanical Names

Common	Botanical
Devil's apples	Mandragora officinarum
Devil's bit scabious	Succisa pratensis
Devil's claw	Harpagophytum procumbens
Devil's claw	Physoplexis comosa
Devil's claw, common	Proboscidea louisianica
Devil's club	Oplopanax horridus
Devil's fig	Argemone mexicana
Devil's horns	Dicerocaryum zangeubarium
Devil's pins	Hovea pungens
Devil's thorn	Dicerocaryum eriocarpum
Devil's tongue	Amorphophallus
Devil's tongue	Amorphophallus konjac
Devil's tongue	Sansevieria trifasciata
Devil's walking stick	Aralia spinosa
Devil-in-a-bush	Nigella
Devil-in-a-bush	Nigella damascena
Devils and angels	Arum maculatum
Dewdrop, golden	Duranta erecta
Dhak	Butea monosperma
Diamond flower	Ionopsidium acaule
Diamond maidenhair fern	Adiantum trapeziforme
Dickie's fern	Cystopteris dickieana
Dill	Anethum
Dill	Anethum graveolens
Dill, Indian	Anethum sowa
Dilya	Gastrolobium parviflorum
Dingle-dangle	Galanthus nivalis
Dingle-dangle tree	Euonymus planipes
Dingul Dingul	Eucalyptus guilfoylei
Dingul Dingul	Eucalyptus jacksonii
Diospyros, pink	Diospyros kirkii
Diplolaena, lesser	Diplolaena microcephala
Diplolaena, southern	Diplolaena dampieri
Disa, cluster red	Disa ferruginea
Disa, red	Disa uniflora
Disk plant	Calamus discolor
Ditaan	Damaeonorops mollis
Dittany	Dictamnus albus
Dittany, American	Cunila origanoides
Dittany, Cretan	Origanum dictamnus
Dittany, false	Ballota pseudodictaminus
Djiridjji	Macrozamia riedlei
Djuk	Exocarpos sparteus
Dock	Rumex
Dock, bloody	Rumex sanguineus
Dock, broadleaf	Rumex obtusifolius
Dock, pale	Rumex altimissus
Dock, prairie	Silphium
Dock, prairie	Silphium terebrinthinaceum
Dock, red-veined	Rumex sanguineus
Dock, softleaf	Rumex patientia
Dock, swamp	Rumex verticillatus
Dock, water great	Rumex hydrolapathum
Dock, yellow	Rumex crispus
Dockmackie	Viburnum acerifolium
Doddering dillies	Briza media
Dog violet, common	Viola riviniana
Dog violet, Western	Viola adunca
Dog's tooth violet	Erythronium
Dog's tooth violet	Erythronium dens-canis
Dog-hobble	Leucothoe catesbei
Dog-rose	Rosa canina
Dogwood	Cornus
Dogwood	Jacksonia scoparia
Dogwood	Rhamnus prinoides
Dogwood, American	Cornus stolonifera
Dogwood, common	Cornus sanguinea
Dogwood, common English	Cornus sanguinea
Dogwood, creeping	Cornus canadensis
Dogwood, eastern	Cornus florida
Dogwood, evergreen	Cornus capitata
Dogwood, flowering	Cornus florida rubra
Dogwood, flowering white	Cornus florida
Dogwood, giant	Cornus controversa
Dogwood, mountain	Cornus nuttallii
Dogwood, Pacific	Cornus controversa
Dogwood, Pacific	Cornus nuttallii
Dogwood, pagoda	Cornus alternifolia
Dogwood, red osier	Cornus stolonifera
Dogwood, red-barked	Cornus alba
Dogwood, silky	Cornus amomum
Dogwood, silky	Cornus amomum obliqua
Dogwood, Tartarian	Cornus alba
Dogwood, yellow	Pomaderris elliptica
Doll's eyes	Actaea alba
Doll's roses	Hermannia althaeifolia
Dombeya, autumn	Dombeya autumnalis
Dombeya, Natal	Dombeya cymosa
Dombeya, pink	Dombeya burgessiae
Dong Quai	Angelica sinensis
Donkey tail	Sedum morganianum
Donkieperske	Pentarrhinum insipidium
Doprium	Pappea capensis
Doringkaree	Rhus glauca
Douglas fir	Pseudotsuga menziesii
Douglas fir, blue	Pseudotsuga menziesii v glauca
Dove tree	Davidia
Dove tree	Davidia involucrata
Downy-rose, Sherard's	Rosa sherardii
Dragon lily, variegated	Dracaena massangeana
Dragon palm	Dracaena draco
Dragon tree	Dracaena draco
Dragon tree	Sesbania grandiflora
Dragon tree, flaming	Cordyline fruticosa
Dragon tree, large-leaved	Dracaena hookeriana
Dragon tree, Madagascar	Dracaena marginata
Dragon tree, white	Sesbania formosa
Dragon's head	Dracocephalum
Dragon's head, Siberian	Dracocephalum ruyschiana
Dragon's mouth	Horminum pyrenaicum
Dragon's teeth	Lotus maritimus
Dragonhead, false	Physostegia virginiana
Drop tree	Fuchsia magellanica
Drops of gold	Disporum hookeri
Dropseed, northern	Sporobolus heterolepis
Dropseed, prairie	Sporobolus heterolepis
Dropseed, rough	Sporobolus asper
Dropseed, sand	Sporobolus cryptandrus
Dropwort	Filipendula vulgaris
Drumsticks	Craspedia globosa
Drumsticks	Dasypogon bromeliifolius
Drumsticks, broad-leaved	Isopogon anemonifolius

Common	Botanical	Common	Botanical
Drumsticks, narrow-leaved	Isopogon anethifolius	Ebony	Bauhinia cattonii
Drumsticks, round-headed	Isopogon	Ebony	Diospyros ebenem
	sphaerocephalus	Ebony	Lysiphyllum carronnii
Drunkard's dream	Hatiora salicornioides	Ebony, mountain	Lysiphyllum hookeri
Dryandra, Albany	Dryandra serra	Ebony, Texas	Pithecellobium flexicaule
Dryandra, creeping	Dryandra calophylla	Ebony tree	Euclea pseudebenus
Dryandra, cut-leaf	Dryandra praemorsa	Ebony wood	Bauhinia variegata v
Dryandra, fern-leaf	Dryandra arctotidis		candida
Dryandra, fern-leaf	Dryandra pteridifolia	Eclipta	Eclipta alba
Dryandra, fish-bone	Dryandra preissii	Edelweiss	Leontopodium
Dryandra, golden	Dryandra nobilis	Edelweiss	Leontopodium alpinum
Dryandra, great	Dryandra nobilis	Edelweiss, Brazilian	Sinningia canescens
Dryandra, harsh	Dryandra armata	Edelweiss, New Zealand	Leucogenes
Dryandra, holly-leaf	Dryandra sessilis	Edelweiss, North Island	Leucogenes
Dryandra, Kamballup	Dryandra ionthocarpa		leontopodium
Dryandra, King	Dryandra proteoides	Eggs and bacon	Pultenaea procumbens
Dryandra, many-headed	Dryandra polycephala	Eglantine	Rosa rubiginosa
Dryandra, oak-leaved	Dryandra quercifolia	Egyptian star	Pentas lanceolata
Dryandra, prickly	Dryandra horrida	Elder	Sambucus
Dryandra, protea-like	Dryandra proteoides	Elder, American	Sambucus canadensis
Dryandra, shaggy	Dryandra speciosa	Elder, black	Sambucus nigra
Dryandra, showy	Dryandra formosa	Elder, box	Acer negundo
Dryandra, swordfish	Dryandra mucronulata	Elder, common	Sambucus nigra
Dryandra, tangled	Dryandra mucronulata	Elder, European	Sambucus nigra
Dryandra, tufted	Dryandra stuposa	Elder, golden	Sambucus nigra 'Aurea'
Dryandra, urchin	Dryandra praemorsa	Elder, ground	Aegopodium
Dryandra, wedge-leaved	Dryandra cuneata	Elder, red	Sambucus pubens
Dryandra, Yilgarn	Dryandra arborea	Elder, red-berried	Sambucus racemosa
Duck plant	Sutherlandia frutescens	Elder, yellow	Tecoma stans
Duck potato	Sagittaria latifolia	Elderberry	Sambucus nigra
Duckweed	Lemna minor	Elderberry, blue	Sambucus caerulea
Duckweed	Wolffia	Elderberry, sweet	Sambucus canadensis
Duckweed, least	Wolffia arrhiza	Elecampane	Inula helenium
Dudhi	Wrightia tinctoria	Elephant apple	Dillenia indica
Duinebastertaaibos	Allophylus natalensis	Elephant bush	Portulacaria afra
Duinekokoboom	Maytenus procumbens	Elephant creeper	Argyreia speciosa
Duingeelbos	Leucadendron coniferum	Elephant foot tree	Beaucarnea recurvata
Duke of Argyll's tea tree	Lycium barbarum	Elephant grass	Rytidosperma
Dulyumuk	Eucalyptus falcata		arundinacea
Dumb cane	Dieffenbachia	Elephant head	Pedicularis groenlandica
Dungwort	Helleborus foetidus	Elephant tree	Bursera microphylla
Dunwich buddle	Chrysanthemum	Elephant tree	Pachycormus discolor
	segetum	Elephant tree, Ombu	Phytolacca dioica
Durum wheat	Triticum durum	Elephant's ear	Enterolobium
Dusty miller	Lychnis coronaria		cyclocarpum
Dusty miller	Senecio cineraria	Elephant's ear	Hedera colchica 'Dentata'
Dutchman's breeches	Dicentra cucullaria	Elephant's ear	Philodendron
Dutchman's breeches	Dicentra spectablis		domesticum
Dutchman's pipe	Aristolochia	Elephant's ear, giant	Alocasia macrorrhiza
Dutchman's pipe	Aristolochia littoralis	Elephant's ear plant	Alocasia
Dutchman's pipe	Aristolochia macrophylla	Elephant's ears	Bergenia
Dwale	Atropa belladonna	Elephant's ears	Caladium
Dwarf snapdragon	Chaenorhinum	Elephant's foot	Beaucarnea gracilis
Dwed	Eucalyptus macarthurii	Elephant's foot	Beaucarnea recurvata
Dwoda	Eucalyptus loxophleba	Elephant's foot	Dioscorea elephantipes
	ssp loxophleba	Elephant's foot	Dioscorea sylvatica
Dwuda	Eucalyptus patens	Elephant's tusk	Proboscidea
Dyer's Rocket	Reseda luteola	Elephant-eared saxifrage	Bergenia
Early Nancy	Burchardia multiflora	Elephantwood	Bolusanthus speciosus
Earth chestnut	Bunium bulbocastanum	Elk horn	Platycerium superbum
Earth star	Cryptanthus	Elkhorn fern	Platycerium bifurcatum
Earth star, green	Cryptanthus acaulis	Elkhorn fern	Platycerium superbum
East African laburnum	Calpurnia aurea	Elkwood	Magnolia tripetala
Easter ledges	Persicaria bistorta	Ellangowan poison	Eremophila deserti
Eaton's firecracker	Penstemon eatonii	Elm	Ulmus
Eau-de-Cologne mint	Mentha x piperata f citrata	Elm, American Florida	Ulmus americana

Common-Botanical Names

Common name	Botanical name	Common name	Botanical name
Elm, American white	Ulmus americana	Evening primrose, desert	Oenothera deltoides
Elm, Camperdown	Ulmus glabra 'Camperdownii'	Evening primrose, white	Oenothera speciosa
Elm, Caucasian	Zelkova carpinifolia	Evening trumpet	Gelsemium sempervirens
Elm, Chinese	Ulmus parvifolia	Everglades palm	Acoelorraphe wrightii
Elm, Cornish	Ulmus minor 'Cornubiensis'	Everlasting	Antennaria
Elm, Cornish	Ulmus minor ssp angustifolia	Everlasting	Edmondia sesamoides
		Everlasting	Phaenocoma prolifera
Elm, Cornish golden	Ulmus minor 'Dicksonii'	Everlasting	Rhodanthe chlorocephala
Elm, Dickson's golden	Ulmus minor 'Dicksonii'		
Elm, Dutch	Ulmus x hollandica	Everlasting, alpine	Helichrysum splendidum
Elm, East Anglian	Ulmus minor	Everlasting, button	Helichrysum lepidophyllum
Elm, English	Ulmus procera		
Elm, European field	Ulmus minor	Everlasting, Cape	Syncarpha speciosissima
Elm, Exeter	Ulmus glabra 'Exoniensis'	Everlasting, Cape	Syncarpha vestita
		Everlasting, cluster golden	Rhodanthe humboltdtiana
Elm, Goodyer's	Ulmus minor ssp angustifolia		
		Everlasting, cluster pink	Schoenia cassiniana
Elm, Huntingdon	Ulmus x hollandica 'Vegeta'	Everlasting, clustered	Helichrysum semipapposum
Elm, Japanese	Ulmus japonica	Everlasting, common	Chrysocephalum
Elm, Jersey	Ulmus minor 'Sarniensis'	Everlasting, curling	Helichrysum lepidophyllum
Elm, Siberian	Ulmus pumila		
Elm, slippery	Ulmus rubra	Everlasting, gold dust	Erymophyllum ramosum ssp ramosum
Elm, small-leaved	Ulmus minor		
Elm, smooth-leaved	Ulmus minor	Everlasting, Lindley's	Lawrencella rosea
Elm, water	Ulmus americana	Everlasting, Mangles	Rhodanthe manglesii
Elm, Wheatley	Ulmus minor 'Sarniensis'	Everlasting pea	Lathyrus grandiflorus
Elm, Wych	Ulmus glabra	Everlasting pea	Lathyrus latifolius
Emerald creeper	Strongylodon macrobotrys	Everlasting, pink	Helichrysum adenocarpum
Emerald feather	Asparagus densiflorus Sprengeri Group	Everlasting, pink	Lawrencella davenportii
Emerald fern	Asparagus densiflorus Sprengeri Group	Everlasting, pink	Rhodanthe chlorocephala ssp rosea
Emerald ripple	Peperomia caperata	Everlasting, rock	Anemocarpa podolepidium
Empress tree	Paulownia tomentosa	Everlasting, satin	Helichrysum leucopsidium
Emu bush	Eremophila	Everlasting, scaly-leaved	Ozothamnus lepidophyllus
Emu bush	Eremophila longifolia	Everlasting, showy	Schoenia filicifolia
Emu bush, common	Eremophila glabra	Everlasting, silky white	Rhodanthe chlorocephala ssp splendida
Emu bush, silver	Eremophila scoparia		
Emu bush, spotted	Eremophila maculata	Everlasting, sticky	Lawrencella
Emu bush, spreading	Eremophila divaricata	Everlasting, strawberry	Syncarpha eximia
Emu bush, twiggy	Eremophila polyclada	Everlasting, sweet	Gnaphalium obtusifolium
Endive	Cichorium	Everlasting, tall	Leucochrysum albicans
Entada, tree	Entada abyssinica	Ewemack	Rosa canina
Epasote	Chenopodium	Ewwa-trewwa	Satyrium coriifolium
Epaulette tree	Pterostyrax hispida	Eyebright	Euphrasia officinalis
Epazote (Epasote)	Chenopodium ambrosioides	Ezo-yama-hagi	Lespedeza bicolor
		Fair maids of France	Ranunculus aconitifolius 'Flore Pleno'
Ephedra, blue	Ephedra nevadensis		
Ephedra, green	Ephedra viridis	Fair maids of France	Saxifraga granulata
Eryngo	Eryngium	Fair maids of Kent	Ranunculus aconitifolius 'Flore Pleno'
Eryngo, blue	Eryngium amethystinum		
Eryngo, silver	Eryngium spinalba	Fairies basins	Primula veris
Esh	Fraxinus excelsior	Fairy bells	Disporum
Eumong	Acacia stenophylla	Fairy duster	Calliandra eriophylla
Euonymus, Shakkalin	Euonymus planipes	Fairy foxglove	Erinus
Eurabbie	Eucalyptus bicostata	Fairy Lantern	Calochortus
Eurah	Eremophila bignoniiflora	Fairy moss	Azolla caroliniana
European silver fir	Abies alba	Fairy moss	Azolla filiculoides
Euryops, honey	Euryops virgineus	Fairy's thimbles	Campanula
Evening primrose	Oenothera		
Evening primrose	Oenothera biennis		
Evening primrose, beach	Oenothera cheiranthifolia		

Common-Botanical Names

Fairy-bells cochleariifolia

Fairy-bells Melasphaerula ramosa
Fairybell Dierama medium
Fairybells Disporum trachycarpum
Fairybells, Hooker's Disporum hookeri
Fairybells, Sierra Disporum trachycarpum
Falling stars Campanula isophylla
False indigo Baptisia
False saffron Carthamus tinctorius
False sago Cycas circinalis
Fame flower Talinum
Fame flower Talinum rugospermum
Fame flower, large Talinum calycinum
Fame flower, short Talinum parviflorum
Fan, European Chamaerops humilis
Fan flower, blue Goodenia scaevolina
Fan, Mediterranean Chamaerops humilis
Fan palm, dwarf Chamaerops
Fan palm, red Livistona mariae
Fan-flower, cushion Scaevola crassifolia
Fan-flower, fairy Scaevola aemula
Fan-leaf, northern Hakea brooksiana
Fan-leaf, northern Hakea brownii
Fan-leaf, southern Hakea baxteri
Fanwort Cabomba caroliniana
Farewell to spring Clarkia amoena
Farewell to summer Saponaria
Farges fir Abies fargesii
Fat hen Chenopodium bonus-
henricus

Fat pork tree Clusia major
Fatsia, Japanese Fatsia japonica
Feather climber Acridocarpus natalitius
Feather grass Stipa
Feather grass, giant Stipa gigantea
Feather, painted Vriesea carinata
Featherbush, broadleaf Aulax umbellata
Featherflower Verticordia plumosa
Featherflower, Forrest's Verticordia forrestii
Featherflower, painted Verticordia picta
Featherflower, Roe's Verticordia roei
Featherflower, scarlet Verticordia grandis
Featherflower, woolly Verticordia monadelpha
Featherfoil, American Hottonia inflata
Featherhead Phylica plumosa
Feathertop Pennisetum villosum
February fairmaids Galanthus nivalis
Felicia, dwarf Felicia dubia
Fennel Foeniculum
Fennel, dog Anthemis
Fennel, Florence Foeniculum dulce
Fennel, Florence Foeniculum vulgare v
azoricum
Fennel flower Nigella sativa
Fennel, giant Ferula
Fennel, giant anise Foeniculum vulgare
Fenugreek Trigonella foenum-
graecum
Fern Pteridium aquilinum
Fern, American wall Polypodium virginianum
Fern, Asparagus Asparagus densiflorus
Fern, Asparagus Asparagus setaceus
Fern, Australian Dicksonia antarctica
Fern, Bamboo Coniogramme japonica
Fern, Barbados maidenhair Adiantum tenerum
'Farleyense'

Fern, bear's paw Aglaomorpha
Fern, Beech Phegopteris
Fern, Beech Phegopteris connectilis
Fern, beech broad Phegopteris
hexagonoptera
Fern, berry bladder Cystopteris bulbifera
Fern, bird's nest Asplenium australasicum
Fern, bird's nest Asplenium nidus
Fern, bladder Cystopteris
Fern, blue Polypodium aureum
'Mandaianum'
Fern, Boston Nephrolepis exaltata
'Bostoniensis'
Fern, brittle bladder Cystopteris fragilis
Fern, buckler Dryopteris
Fern, buckler broad Dryopteris dilitata
Fern, buckler narrow Dryopteris carthusiana
Fern, button Pellaea rotundifolia
Fern, Byfield Bowenia serrulata
Fern, Byfield northern Bowenia spectabilis
Fern, cabbage Platycerium elephantotis
Fern, chain Woodwardia
Fern, chain American Woodwardia virginica
Fern, Christmas Polystichum
acrostichoides
Fern, cinnamon Osmunda cinnamomea
Fern, climbing Lygodium
Fern, crown Blechnum discolor
Fern, desert Lysiloma thornberi
Fern, Dickie's Cystopteris dickieana
Fern, elephant's ear Platycerium elephantotis
Fern, emerald Asparagus densiflorus
Sprengeri Group
Fern, English painted Athyrium otophorum
Fern, fancy Dryopteris intermedia
Fern, felt Pyrrosia
Fern, filmy Tunbridge Hymenophyllum
tunbrigense
Fern, fishtail Cyrtomium falcatum
Fern, flowering Osmunda regalis
Fern, fork Psilotum
Fern, foxtail Asparagus densiflorus
'Myersii'
Fern, glory Adiantum tenerum
'Farleyense'
Fern, goldback Pityrogramma
triangularis
Fern, golden male Dryopteris affinis
Fern, golden-scaled Dryopteris affinis
Fern, goldie's Dryopteris goldieana
Fern, hairy lip Cheilanthes tomentosa
Fern, hard Blechnum spicant
Fern, hard shield Polystichum aculeatum
Fern, hare's foot Davallia canariensis
Fern, hare's foot Polypodium aureum
Fern, hart's tongue Asplenium
scolopendrium
Fern, Hawaiian tree Cibotium glaucum
Fern, hen-and-chicken Asplenium bulbiferum
Fern, holly Cyrtomium
Fern, holly Polystichum
Fern, holly giant Polystichum munitum
Fern, holly large-leaved Cyrtomium
macrophyllum
Fern, interrupted Osmunda claytoniana
Fern, Japanese climbing Lygodium japonicum

Common-Botanical Names

Common	Botanical	Common	Botanical
Fern, Japanese felt	Pyrrosia lingua	Fern, tree black	Cyathea medullaris
Fern, Japanese holly	Cyrtomium falcatum	Fern, tree golden	Dicksonia fibrosa
Fern, Japanese painted	Athyrium niponicum	Fern, tree Norfolk Island	Cyathea brownii
Fern, Japanese shield	Dryopteris erythrosora	Fern, tree prickly	Cyathea leichhardtiana
Fern, Japanese tassel	Polystichum plyblepharum	Fern, tree rough-bark	Cyathea australis
		Fern, tree rough-barked	Cyathea cooperii
Fern, Korean rock	Polystichum tsussimense	Fern, tree soft	Dicksonia antarctica
		Fern, tree West Indian	Cyathea arborea
Fern, lace dwarf	Asparagus setaceus	Fern, tree woolly	Dicksonia antarctica
Fern, ladder	Nephrolepis cordifolia	Fern, Virginian chain	Woodwardia virginica
Fern, lady	Athyrium filix-femina	Fern, walking	Asplenium rhizophyllum
Fern, leather	Rumohra adiantiformis	Fern, walking	Camptosorus rhizophyllus
Fern, lip	Cheilanthes		
Fern, liquorice	Polypodium glycyrrhiza	Fern, water	Azolla caroliniana
Fern, maidenhair	Adiantum	Fern, water	Ceratopteris thalictroides
Fern, male	Dryopteris filix-mas	Fern, wood	Dryopteris atrata
Fern, man	Dicksonia antarctica	Fern, wood	Dryopteris dilatata
Fern, marsh	Thelypteris palustris	Fern, wood giant	Dryopteris goldiana
Fern, marsh buckler	Thelypteris palustris	Fern, wood Wallich's	Dryopteris wallichiana
Fern, mountain	Oreopteris limbosperma	Ferweelblom	Sparaxis villosa
Fern, mountain buckler	Oreopteris limbosperma	Fescue	Festuca
Fern, mountain wood	Oreopteris limbosperma	Fescue, amethyst	Festuca amethystina
Fern, Mrs. Frizell's lady	Athyrium filix-femina 'Frizelliae'	Fescue, Arizona	Festuca arizonica
		Fescue, blue	Festuca glauca
Fern, North American hay scented	Dennstaedtia punctiloba	Fescue, blue large	Festuca amethystina
Fern, oak	Gymnocarpian dryopteris	Fescue, creeping red	Festuca rubra
		Fescue, grey	Festuca glauca
Fern, ostrich	Matteuccia struthiopteris	Fescue, hard	Festuca longifolia
Fern, ostrich-feather	Matteuccia struthiopteris	Fescue, ice	Festuca glacialis
Fern palm	Cycas	Fescue, Idaho	Festuca idahoensis
Fern palm	Cycas circinalis	Fescue, nodding	Festuca obtusa
Fern, parsley	Cryptogramma crispa	Fescue, sheep	Festuca ovina
Fern, Queen Victoria's lady	Athyrium filix-femina Cruciatum Group 'Victoriae'	Fescue, tufted	Festuca amethystina
		Fetter bush	Leucothoe racemosa
Fern, rabbit's foot	Davallia solida v fejeensis	Fetterbush	Pieris floribunda
Fern, rabbit's foot	Polypodium aureum	Fetterbush, mountain	Pieris floribunda
Fern, rasp common	Doodia media	Fever tree	Acacia xanthophloia
Fern, resurrection	Polypodium polypodioides	Fever-berry, forest	Codiaeum sylvaticus
		Feverberry	Codiaeum megalobotrys
Fern, rockcap	Polypodium virginianum	Feverfew	Tanacetum parthenium
Fern, Royal	Osmunda regalis	Feverfew, golden	Tanacetum parthenium 'Aureum'
Fern, rusty back	Asplenium ceterach	Fiddleleaf	Philodendron bipennifolium
Fern, sago	Cyathes medullaris		
Fern, sensitive	Onoclea sensibilis	Fiddleneck	Phacelia tanacetifolia
Fern, shield	Dryopteris linearis	Fiddleneck, Bolander's	Phacelia bolanderi
Fern, shield	Polystichum	Field-rose	Rosa arvensis
Fern, shield marginal	Dryopteris marginalis	Fiery costus	Costus cuspidatus
Fern, shield prickly	Polystichum aculeatum	Fig	Ficus
Fern, shield soft	Polystichum setiferum	Fig, broom cluster	Ficus sur
Fern, shield spinulose	Dryopteris spinulosa	Fig, Cape	Ficus sur
Fern, shuttlecock	Matteuccia struthiopteris	Fig, cedar	Ficus superba v henneana
Fern, silver King	Cyathea dealbata		
Fern, silvery glade	Deparia acrosticoides	Fig, common	Ficus carica
Fern, spider	Pteris multifida	Fig, creeping	Ficus pumila
Fern squirrel's foot	Davallia mariesii	Fig, curtain	Ficus microcarpa
Fern, staghorn	Platycerium	Fig, fiddle-leaf	Ficus lyrata
Fern, sword	Nephrolepis	Fig, forest rare	Ficus craterostoma
Fern, sword	Nephrolepis cordifolia	Fig, giant-leaved	Ficus lutea
Fern, sword	Nephrolepis exaltata	Fig, India rubber	Ficus elastica
Fern, sword	Polystichum munitum	Fig, Indian	Ficus benghalensis
Fern, tatting	Athyrium fiix-femina 'Frizelliae'	Fig, Indian	Opuntia ficus-indica
		Fig, mistletoe	Ficus deltoidea
Fern, tongue	Pyrrosia lingua	Fig, Moreton bay	Ficus macrophylla
Fern, tree	Cyathea	Fig, Moreton bay small-leaf	Ficus platypoda
Fern, tree Australian	Cyathea australis	Fig, Natal	Ficus natalensis

Common-Botanical Names

Fig, Port Jackson — Ficus rubiginosa
Fig, rock African — Ficus glumosa
Fig, rock red-leaved — Ficus ingens
Fig, rusty — Ficus rubiginosa
Fig, sacred — Ficus religiosa
Fig, sandpaper — Ficus fraserii
Fig, spotted — Ficus virens
Fig, sycamore — Ficus sycamorus
Fig, Veld — Ficus burtt-davyi
Fig, weeping — Ficus benjamina
Fig, weeping Hill's — Ficus hillii
Fig, wild — Ficus palmeri
Fig, wild — Ficus thonningii
Fig, wild common — Ficus natalensis
Fig, wild common — Ficus thonningii
Fig, Wonderboom — Ficus cordata ssp salicifolia

Fighting cocks — Plantago lanceolata
Figwort — Scrophularia
Figwort, alpine — Scrophularia hoppei
Figwort, California — Scrophularia californica
Figwort, Cape — Phygelius capensis
Figwort, water — Scrophularia auriculata
Filbert — Corylus maxima
Fingernail plant — Neoregelia spectabilis
Finnochio — Foeniculum vulgare v dulce

Fir, alpine — Abies lasiocarpa
Fir, balsam — Abies balsamea
Fir, beautiful — Abies amabilis
Fir, bristlecone — Abies bracteata
Fir, California red — Abies magnifica
Fir, Caucasian — Abies nordmanniana
Fir, China — Cunninghamia lanceolata
Fir, Cilician — Abies cilicica
Fir, Coast Douglas — Pseudotsuga taxifolia v viridis
Fir, Colorado white — Abies cilicica
Fir, corkbark — Abies lasiocarpa v arizonica
Fir, Delavay — Abies delavayi
Fir, Douglas — Pseudotsuga menziesii
Fir, Douglas — Pseudotsuga menziesii f viridis
Fir, Douglas blue — Pseudotsuga menziesii v glauca
Fir, Douglas Rocky Mountains — Pseudotsuga menziesii v glauca
Fir, European silver — Abies alba
Fir, Faber's — Abies fabri
Fir, Farges — Abies fargesii
Fir, flaky — Abies squamata
Fir, Forrest — Abies forrestii
Fir, giant — Abies grandis
Fir, grand white — Abies grandis
Fir, Greek — Abies cephalonica
Fir, hedgehog — Abies pinsapo
Fir, Japanese — Abies firma
Fir, Korean — Abies koreana
Fir, Manchurian — Abies holophylla
Fir, Momi — Abies firma
Fir, Nikko — Abies homolepis
Fir, noble — Abies procera
Fir, Nordmann — Abies nordmanniana
Fir, Pacific silver — Abies amabilis
Fir, pindrow — Abies pindrow

Fir, Santa Lucia — Abies, bracteata
Fir, silver — Abies alba
Fir, Spanish — Abies pinsapo
Fir, Spanish blue — Abies pinsapo glauca
Fir, sub-alpine — Abies lasiocarpa
Fir, Veitch — Abies veitchii
Fir, Vejar — Abies vejarii
Fir, West Himalayan — Abies pindrow
Fir, white — Abies concolor
Fir, white — Abies concolor v lowiana
Fir, Yunnan — Abies georgei
Fire bush — Bassia scoparia f trichophylla
Fire bush, Chilean — Embothrium coccineum
Fire-leaf — Plantago lanceolata
Fire-on-the-mountain — Euphorbia cyathophora
Fire-weed — Plantago lanceolata
Firebush — Hymenodictyon floribundum
Firebush, common — Keraudrenia integrifolia
Firecracker, Brazilian — Manettia luteorubra
Firecracker, Californian — Dichelostemma ida-maia
Firecracker, Eaton's — Penstemon eatonii
Firecracker flower — Crossandra infundibuliformis
Firecracker, Mexican — Echeveria setosa
Firecracker plant — Russelia equisetiformis
Firecracker vine — Manettia cordifolia
Fireflower, smokey — Regelia velutina
Firesticks, Namaqua — Diospyros ramulosa
Firethorn — Pyracantha
Fireweed — Epilobium angustifolium
Firewheel — Gaillardia pulchella
Firewheel tree — Stenocarpus sinuatus
Firewheel tree, Australian — Stenocarpus sinuatus
Firewood — Eucalyptus botryoides
Fish-tail palm — Caryota
Fish-tail palm, Burmese — Caryota mitis
Fish-tail palm, clustered — Caryota mitis
Fish-tail palm, miniature — Chamaedorea microspadix
Fitweed — Eryngium foetidum
Five finger — Pseudopanax arboreus
Five fingers — Pseudopanax arboreus
Five fingers — Syngonium auritum
Five flavour vine — Schisandra chinensis
Five-spot — Nemophila maculata
Five-spot baby — Nemophila maculata
Fivecorner, pink — Styphelia triflora
Flag, blue — Iris versicolor
Flag, blue — Orthrosanthus multiflorus
Flag, butterfly — Diplarrhena moraea
Flag, common German — Iris germanica
Flag iris, hairy — Patersonia rudis
Flag iris, purple — Patersonia juncea
Flag, iris white — Diplarrhena moraea
Flag, Japanese — Iris ensata
Flag, Missouri — Iris missouriensis
Flag, morning — Orthrosanthus multiflorus
Flag, Myrtle — Acorus calamus 'Variegatus'
Flag, Siberian — Iris sibirica
Flag, soft — Typha angustifolia
Flag, Southern blue — Iris virginica

Common-Botanical Names

Common Name	Botanical Name	Common Name	Botanical Name
Flag, Spanish	Ipomoea lobata	Flax, perennial	Linum perenne
Flag, sweet	Acorus calamus	Flax, prairie	Linum lewisii
Flag, sweet	Calamus	Flax, yellow	Linum flavum
Flag, wall	Iris tectorum	Flax, yellow	Reinwardtia indica
Flag, western blue	Iris missouriensis	Fleabane	Erigeron
Flag, yellow	Iris pseudacorus	Fleabane, alpine	Erigeron alpinus
Flamboyant tree	Delonix regia	Fleabane, common	Pulicaria dysenterica
Flamboyant tree, yellow	Peltophorum pterocarpum	Fleabane, tufted	Erigeron caespitosus
		Fleawort	Plantago psyllium
Flame azalea	Rhododendron calendulaceum	Fleece vine, China	Fallopia baldschuanica
		Floating heart	Nymphoides
Flame bush	Templetonia retusa	Floating heart, yellow	Nymphoides peltata
Flame bush, Natal	Alberta magna	Floodway ephemereal	Rhodanthe charsleyae
Flame coral tree	Erythrina americana	Flora's paintbrush	Emilia coccinea
Flame creeper	Tropaeolum speciosum	Floradora	Stephanotis floribunda
Flame flower	Embothrium coccineum	Florida silver palm	Coccothrinax argentata
Flame of the forest	Butea monosperma	Florida swamp lily	Crinum americanum
Flame of the forest	Spathodea campanulata	Floripondio	Brugmansia x candida
Flame of the woods	Ixora coccinea	Floss flower	Ageratum
Flame pea, heart-leaved	Chorizema cordatum	Flower lawn	Wahlenbergia procumbens
Flame pea, holly	Chorizema ilicifolium		
Flame pea, prostrate	Chorizema rhombeum	Flower of Jove	Lychnis flos-jovis
Flame pea, showy	Chorizema reticulatum	Flower of Jupiter	Lychnis flos-jovis
Flame pea, yellow-eyed	Chorizema dicksonii	Flower of love	Lychnis flos-jovis
Flame tree	Brachychiton acerifolius	Flower of the west wind	Zephyranthes candida
Flame tree	Delonix regia	Flower-of-an-hour	Hibiscus trionum
Flame tree	Derris robusta	Flowering almond	Prunus triloba
Flame tree, African	Spathodea campanulata	Flowering currant, red	Ribes sanguineum
Flame tree, golden	Peltophorum pterocarpum	Flowering rush	Butomos
		Flowering tobacco	Nicotiana alata
Flame tree, Illawarra	Brachychiton acerifolius	Fluweeltjie	Sparaxis tricolor
Flame vine	Pyrostegia venusta	Fluwheelblom	Sparaxis bulbifera
Flame violet	Episcia cupreata	Flycatcher	Sarracenia alata
Flame, yellow	Peltophorum africanum	Fo-ti	Fallopia multiflora
Flameflower, swamp	Beaufortia sparsa	Foam bark tree	Jagera pseudorhus
Flames	Chasmanthe floribunda	Foam flower	Tiarella
Flames	Tritoniopsis caffra	Foam flower	Tiarella cordifolia
Flaming Katy	Kalanchoe blossfeldiana	Foam flower, Japanese	Tanakaea
Flaming sword	Vriesea splendens	Foam of May	Spiraea 'Arguta'
Flamingo flower	Anthurium	Forage plant	Ventilago viminalis
Flamingo flower	Anthurium andraeanum	Forest oak	Casuarina torulosa
Flamingo flower	Anthurium scherzerianum	Forget-me-not	Myosotis
		Forget-me-not, alpine	Eritrichium
Flamingo plant	Justicia carnea	Forget-me-not, alpine	Myosotis alpestris
Flannel bush	Fremontodendron	Forget-me-not, Cape	Anchusa capensis
Flannel flower	Actinotus helianthii	Forget-me-not, Chatham Island	Myosotidium hortensia
Flannel flower	Actinotus leucocephalus	Forget-me-not, Chinese	Cynoglossom amabile
Flannel flower	Actinotus superbus	Forget-me-not, creeping	Omphalodes verna
Flannel weed	Sidalcea cordifolia	Forget-me-not, field	Myosotis arvensis
Flask plant	Philodendron cannifolium	Forget-me-not, water	Myosotis scorpioides
		Forget-me-not-tree	Duranta repens
Flat root	Eucalyptus kitsoniana	Forsythia, white	Abeliophyllum
Flax	Linum	Fortnight lily	Dietes iridioides
Flax, alpine	Linum alpinum	Forythia, Korean	Forsythia ovata
Flax, blue	Heliophila coronopifolia	Fothergilla, dwarf	Fothergilla gardenii
Flax, blue	Linum lewisii	Fountain bush	Psoralea pinnata
Flax, blue	Linum perenne	Fountain flower	Ceropegia sandersonii
Flax, common	Linum usitatissimum	Fountain grass	Pennisetum alopecuroides
Flax, fibre	Linum usitatissimum		
Flax, flowering	Linum grandiflorum	Fountain grass	Pennisetum setaceum
Flax, golden	Linum flavum	Four corners	Grewia occidentalis
Flax, grooved yellow	Linum sulcatum	Four o' clock, desert	Mirabilis multiflora
Flax, holy	santolina rosmarinifolia	Four o' clock flower	Mirabilis jalapa
Flax, Lewis'	Linum lewisii	Fox and cubs	Pilosella aurantiaca
Flax, mountain	Phormium cookianum	Fox nuts	Euryale
Flax, New Zealand	Phormium tenax	Foxberry	Vaccinum vitis-idaea

Common-Botanical Names

Common	Botanical
Foxglove	Digitalis
Foxglove, Chinese	Rehmannia elata
Foxglove, common	Digitalis purpurea
Foxglove, fairy	Erinus
Foxglove, false purple	Agalinis purpurea
Foxglove, false purple	Gerardia purpurea
Foxglove, false slender	Gerardia tenuifolia
Foxglove, fern-leaved	Aureolaria pedicularia
Foxglove, Grecian	Digitalis lanata
Foxglove, Mexican	Tetranema roseum
Foxglove, purple	Digitalis purpurea
Foxglove, rusty	Digitalis ferruginea
Foxglove tree	Paulownia tomentosa
Foxglove, wild	Ceratotheca triloba
Foxglove, wild Oregon	Digitalis purpurea
Foxglove, woolly	Digitalis lanata
Foxglove, yellow	Digitalis lutea
Foxglove, yellow large	Digitalis grandiflora
Foxtail barley	Hordeum jubatum
Foxtail fern	Asparagus densiflorus 'Meyersii'
Foxtail, golden	Alopecurus pratensis 'Aureovariegatus'
Foxtail grass	Alopecurus
Foxtail grass, woolly	Alopecurus lanatus
Foxtail lily	Eremurus
Foxtail millet	Setaria italica
Foxtail, regal	Ptilotus nobilis
Foxtail, showy	Ptilotus exaltatus
Foxtail, swamp	Pennisetum alopecuroides
Frangipani	Plumeria
Frangipani, Australian	Hymenosporum flavum
Frangipani, common	Plumeria rubra
Frangipani, native (AU)	Hymenosporum
Frangipani, wild	Voacanga thouarsii
Frankincense	Boswellia thurifera
Frasera, clustered	Frasera fastigiata
Freckled face	Primula veris
Freckleface	Hypoestes phyllostachya
Freesia, wild	Freesia alba
French honeysuckle	Hedysarum coronarium
Friendship plant	Billbergia nutans
Friendship plant	Pilea involucrata
Friendship tree	Crassula ovata
Fringe cups	Tellima
Fringe lily	Thysanotus multiflorus
Fringe lily	Thysanotus patersonii
Fringe tree	Chionanthus
Fringe tree, Chinese	Chionanthus retusus
Fringe tree, white	Chionanthus virginicus
Fritillary	Fritillaria
Fritillary, black	Fritillaria biflora
Fritillary, rice-grain	Fritillaria affinis
Fritillary, scarlet	Fritillaria recurva
Fritillary, snake's head	Fritillaria meleagris
Fritillary, yellow	Fritillaria pudica
Frogbit	Hydrocharis
Frogbit	Hydrocharis morsus-ranae
Fruit salad bush	Acca sellowiana
Fruit salad plant	Monstera deliciosa
Frutang	Romulea flava
Fuchsia, Australian	Correa
Fuchsia, black	Fuchsia 'Gruss aus dem Bodethal'

Common	Botanical
Fuchsia bush, green	Eremophila serrulata
Fuchsia, Californian	Zauschneria
Fuchsia, creeping	Fuchsia procumbens
Fuchsia, desert	Eremophila gilesii
Fuchsia, harlequin	Eremophila duttonii
Fuchsia, lilac	Fritillaria arborescens
Fuchsia, limestone	Eremophila freelingii
Fuchsia, narrow-leaf	Eremophila alternifolia
Fuchsia, native (AU)	Eremophila maculata
Fuchsia, rock	Eremophila freelingii
Fuchsia, trailing	Fuchsia procumbens
Fuchsia, tree	Fuchsia arborescens
Fuchsia, tree	Fuchsia excorticata
Fuchsia, tree	Halleria lucida
Fuchsia, tree	Schotia brachypetala
Fuchsia, tree	Schotia latifolia
Fukanoki	Schefflera heptaphylla
Fumewort	Corydalis solida
Fumitory	Fumaria officinalis
Fumitory, yellow	Corydalis lutea
Funkia	Hosta
Furze	Ulex europaeus
Furze (fuzz, Fuzzen, Vuzzen)	Ulex
Fynblaarbruidsbos	Pavetta zeyheri
Galangal	Alpinia galanga
Gale, sweet	Myrica gale
Galingale	Cyperus longus
Galingale, American	Cyperus eragrostis
Galjoenblom	Lobelia valida
Gallberry	Ilex glabra
Gan cao	Glycyrrhiza uralensis
Gandergoose	Orchis morio
Gansgras	Cotula coronopifolia
Gansies	Conicosia pugioniformis
Gansies	Sutherlandia microphylla
Garcinia, granite	Garcinia buchananii
Garden mace	Achillea ageraatum
Gardener's gaiters (garters)	Phalaris arundinacea v picta 'Picta'
Gardenia, Australian	Randia fitzalanii
Gardenia, bell	Rothmannia globosa
Gardenia, common	Gardenia augusta
Gardenia, false	Randia sessilis
Gardenia, florist's	Gardenia augusta
Gardenia, horned	Gardenia cornuta
Gardenia, Natal	Gardenia cornuta
Gardenia, paper	Tabernaemontana divaricata
Gardenia, Transvaal large-leaved	Gardenia ternifolia ssp jovis-tonantis
Gardenia, white	Gardenia thunbergia
Gardenia, wild	Rothmannia capensis
Garget	Phytolacca americana
Garland flower	Daphne cneorum
Garland flower	Hedychium coronarium
Garlic	Allium sativum
Garlic, Canada	Allium canadense
Garlic, elephant	Allium ampeloprasum
Garlic, false	Nothoscordum
Garlic, golden	Allium moly
Garlic, Italian	Allium sativum ophioscordon
Garlic, mountain	Allium senescens
Garlic mustard	Alliaria petiolata
Garlic, Ramsom's wood	Allium ursinum
Garlic, rosy	Allium roseum

Common-Botanical Names

Common	Botanical
Garlic, serpent	Allium sativum ophioscordon
Garlic, wild	Allium canadense
Gas plant	Dictamnus
Gauje	Leucaena esculenta
Gaura, long-flowered	Gaura longiflora
Gayfeather	Liatris
Gayfeather, spike	Liatris spicata
Gayfeather, spotted	Liatris punctata
Gayfeather, thick spike	Liatris pycnostachya
Ge gen	Pueraria lobata
Gean	Prunus avium
Geebung	Persoonia virgata
Geebung, broad-leaf	Persoonia cornifolia
Geebung, broad-leaf	Persoonia laevis
Geebung, lance-leaf	Persoonia lanceolata
Geebung, narrow-leaf	Persoonia linearis
Geebung, pine-leaf	Persoonia pinifolia
Geebung, still-leaf	Persoonia laevis
Geekalossie	Ixia odorata
Geelberggranaat	Rhigozum obovatum
Geelbos	Leucadendron laureolum
Geelgousblom	Gazania lichtensteinii
Geelkalossie	Ixia maculata
Geelviooltjie	Ornithogalum multifolium
Geiger tree	Cordia sebestena
Gemsbok komkommer	Acanthosicyos naudinianus
Gemsboksuring	Anacampseros telephiastrum
Gemsbuck bean	Tylosema esculenta
Gentian	Gentiana
Gentian, Bavarian	Gentiana bavarica
Gentian, bottle	Gentiana andrewsii
Gentian, closed	Gentiana andrewsii
Gentian, cream	Gentiana flavida
Gentian, cross	Gentiana cruciata
Gentian, fringed	Gentianopsis crinita
Gentian, fringed smaller	Gentianopsis procera
Gentian, marsh	Gentiana pneumonanthe
Gentian, mountainbog	Gentiana calycosa
Gentian, pink	Gentiana tenuifolia
Gentian, prairie	Gentiana affinis
Gentian, prairie	Gentiana puberulenta
Gentian, short-leaved	Gentiana brachyphylla
Gentian, snow	Gentiana corymbifera
Gentian, Southern	Gentiana alpina
Gentian, spotted	Gentiana punctata
Gentian, spring	Gentiana verna
Gentian, star	Gentiana verna
Gentian, stiff	Gentiana quinquefolia
Gentian, Tibetan	Gentiana tibetica
Gentian, Triglav	Gentiana terglouensis
Gentian, trumpet	Gentiana acaulis
Gentian, trumpet	Gentiana clusii
Gentian, trumpet stemless	Gentiana clusii
Gentian, willow	Gentiana asclepiadea
Gentian, yellow	Gentiana lutea
Gentian, yellow great	Gentiana lutea
Geraldton wax	Chamelaucium uncinatum
Geranium, bedding	Pelargonium
Geranium, Buxton's variety (blue)	Geranium wallichianum 'Buxton's variety'
Geranium, Canary Island	Geranium canariense
Geranium, carpet	Geranium incanum
Geranium, jungle	Ixora coccinea
Geranium, peppermint scented	Pelargonium tomentosum
Geranium, rose	Pelargonium 'Graveolens' h
Geranium, scented	Pelargonium
Geranium, silver-leaf	Pelargonium 'Flower of Spring'
Geranium, sticky	Geranium viscosissimum
Geranium, strawberry	Saxifraga stolonifera 'Tricolor'
Geranium, sweet-scented	Pelargonium 'Graveolens' h
Geranium, western	Geranium oregonum
Geranium, wild	Geranium maculatum
Gerardia, slender	Gerardia tenuifolia
German sausage	Fallopia japonica
Germander	Teucrium x lucidrys
Germander, American	Teucrium canadense
Germander, Asian	Teucrium asiaticum
Germander, cat thyme	Teucrium marum
Germander, Caucasian	Teucrium hyrcanicum
Germander, grey	Teucrium racemosum ssp racemosum
Germander, shrubby	Teucrium fruticans
Germander, silver	Teucrium fruticans
Germander, speedwell	Veronica chamaedrys
Germander, sweet-scented	Teucrium x lucidrys
Germander, tree	Teucrium fruticans
Germander, wood	Teucrium scorodonia
Gewone giftou	Strophanthus speciosus
Gewone Haakdoring	Acacia caffra
Gewone kapokbossie	Eriocephalus ericoides
Gewone Kiepersol	Cussonia spicata
Gewone pendoring	Maytenus heterophylla
Gewone wildevy	Ficus thonningii
Gewonespeldekussing	Leucospermum cuneiforme
Ghokum	Carpobrotus edulis
Ghost plant	Artemisia
Ghost plant	Artemisia lactiflora
Ghost tree	Davidia
Ghost weed	Euphorbia marginata h
Ghwarrie, Natal	Euclea natalensis
Giant lily	Cardiocrinum
Giant maidenhair fern	Adiantum trapeziforme
Giant reed	Arundo donax
Giant Spaniard	Aciphylla scott-thompsonii
Gidgee	Acacia cambagei
Gidgee	Acacia pruinocarpa
Gidgee, Georgina	Acacia georginae
Gidyea	Acacia georginae
Gifolyf	Peddiea africana
Gifuintjie	Ferraria ferrariola
Gilia, globe	Gilia capitata
Gilia, scarlet	Ipomopsis aggregata
Gilia, showy blue	Gilia capitata
Gilja	Eucalyptus brachycalyx
Gillyflower	Erysimum cheiri
Gillyflower	Matthiola
Gillyflower	Matthiola incana
Gimlet	Eucalyptus salubris
Gimlet, bronze and silver	Eucalyptus salubris v

Common-Botanical Names

Common-Botanical Names

Common	Botanical
Golden pothos	chrysanthus Epipremnum
Golden rain	Laburnum
Golden rain tree	Koelreuteria paniculata
Golden rain tree, evergreen	Koelreuteria bipinnata
Golden root	Scutellaria baicalensis
Golden saxifrage	Chrysoplenium
Golden shower	Pyrostegia venusta
Golden shower (tree)	Cassia fistula
Golden Spaniard	Aciphylla aurea
Golden spray	Viminaria juncea
Golden stars	Bloomeria crocea
Golden Timothy	Setaria sphacelata
Golden tip	Goodia lotifolia
Golden top	Lamarckia aurea
Golden tower	Schizolobium parahybum
Golden tree	Grevillea pteridifolia
Golden trumpet	Allamanda cathartica
Golden trumpet tree	Tabebuia chrysotricha
Golden tuft	Aurinia saxatilis
Golden wonder	Senna didymobotrya
Golden-chalice vine	Solandra maxima
Goldeneye, bushy	Viguiera deltoidea
Goldeneye, showy	Viguiera multiflora
Goldenrod	Solidago
Goldenrod, Canada	Solidago canadensis
Goldenrod, Curtiss'	Solidago curtisii
Goldenrod, early	Solidago juncea
Goldenrod, early	Solidago pinetorum
Goldenrod, elm-leaved	Solidago ulmifolia
Goldenrod, false	Solidago sphacelata
Goldenrod, giant	Solidago gigantea
Goldenrod, grassleaf	Solidago graminifolia
Goldenrod, grey	Solidago nemoralis
Goldenrod, grey dwarf	Solidago nemoralis
Goldenrod, meadow	Solidago canadensis
Goldenrod, Missouri	Solidago missouriensis
Goldenrod, old field	Solidago nemoralis
Goldenrod, petioled	Solidago petiolaris
Goldenrod, Riddell's	Solidago riddellii
Goldenrod, rigid	Solidago rigida
Goldenrod, rough-leaved	Solidago rugosa
Goldenrod, seaside	Solidago sempervirens
Goldenrod, showy	Solidago speciosa
Goldenrod, stiff	Solidago rigida
Goldenrod, sweet	Solidago odora
Goldenrod, woodland	Solidago caesia
Goldenrod, zig zag	Solidago flexicaulis
Goldenseal	Hydrastis canadensis
Goldenseal, poor man's	Xanthorrhiza simplicissima
Goldenwave	Coreopsis lanceolata
Goldfish plant	Columnea gloriosa
Goldie's fern	Dryopteris goldieana
Goldilocks	Aster linosyris
Goldthread	Coptis trifolia
Goldy-locks	Helichrysum stoechas
Gollenweed	Galium aparine
Gonzui	Euscaphis japonica
Good for mother herb	Leonurus sibiricus
Good King Henry	Chenopodium bonus-henricus
Good luck plant	Oxalis tetraphylla
Good luck tree	Cordyline fruticosa
Goodenia, summer	Goodenia incana

Common	Botanical
Goodenia, wing-seeded	Goodenia pterigosperma
Goodenia, yellow-spiked	Goodenia stelligera
Gooramurra	Eremophila bignoniiflora
Gooseberry	Ribes uva-crispa v reclinatum
Gooseberry, Barbados	Pereskia aculeata
Gooseberry, coast black	Ribes divaricatum
Gooseberry, Siberian	Ribes latifolia
Goosebumps	Galium aparine
Goosefoot	Syngonium podophyllum
Goosefoot, desert	Chenopodium desertorum
Goosegrass	Galium aparine
Gooya	Owenia acidula
Gopher purge	Euphorbia
Gorgon plant	Euryale
Gorgon's head	Euphorbia gorgonis
Gorse	Ulex europaeus
Gorse, dwarf	Ulex gallii
Gorse, dwarf	Ulex minor
Gorse, Irish	Ulex europaeus 'Strictus'
Gorse, Spanish	Genista hispanica
Gorse, western	Ulex gallii
Gosling weed	Galium aparine
Gotu Kola	Centella asiatica
Gou qi zi	Lycium chinense
Gou-gi-zi	Lycium barbarum
Gourd, buffalo	Cucurbita foetidisima
Gourd, fig-leaved	Cucurbita ficifolia
Gourd, native	Trichosanthes cucumerina
Gourd, ornamental	Cucurbita pepo
Gourd, serpent	Trichosanthes cucumerina v anguina
Gourd, snake	Trichosanthes cucumerina v anguina
Gourd, snake Chinese	Trichosanthes kirilowii
Gousblom	Arctotis hirsuta
Gousblom	Arctotis venusta
Goutweed	Aegopodium podagraria
Goutweed variegated/ground elder	Aegopodium podagraria 'Variegatum'
Gramma, blue	Bouteloua gracilis
Gramma, hairy	Bouteloua hirsuta
Gramma, side-oats	Bouteloua curtipendula
Granadilla	Passiflora
Granadilla, giant	Passiflora quandrangularis
Granadilla, Montesa	Passiflora platyloba
Granadilla, purple	Passiflora edulis
Granadilla, red	Passiflora coccinea
Granadilla, sweet	Passiflora ligularis
Granadilla, yellow	Passiflora edulis
Granny's bonnet	Aquilegia vulgaris
Granny's nightcap	Aquilegia vulgaris
Grape, amur	Vitis amurensis
Grape, baboon	Rhoicissus digitata
Grape, Cape	Rhoicissus capensis
Grape hyacinth, feather	Muscari comosum 'Plumosum'
Grape ivy	Cissus rhombifolia
Grape ivy, miniature	Cissus striata
Grape, Oregon	Mahonia aquifolium
Grape, riverbank	Vitis riparia
Grape, tree	Cyphostemma juttae

Common-Botanical Names

Grape, Veldt — Cissus quadrangula
Grape vine — Vitis vinifera
Grape vine, wild — Cissus hypoglauca
Grape, wild — Rhoicissus tomentosa
Grape, wild — Vitis riparia
Grapplethorn — Harpagophytum procumbens

Grass, alkali — Puchinella distans
Grass, alpine meadow — Poa alpina
Grass, annual meadow — Poa annua
Grass, Bandicoot — Monachather paradoxa
Grass, barbed wire — Cymbopogon refractus
Grass, barcoo — Iseilema membranaeceum

Grass, basket — Oplismenus africanus
Grass, beach — Ammophila breviligulata
Grass, beak — Diarrhena americana
Grass, bear — Dasylirion
Grass, bear — Nolina
Grass, bear — Xerophyllum tenax
Grass, bear Sacahuista — Nolina microcarpa
Grass, bear Texas — Nolina texana
Grass, beard — Andropogon
Grass, beard annual — Polypogon monspeliensis

Grass, black-top — Enneapogon nigricans
Grass, blady — Imperata cylindrica
Grass, blown — Agrostis avenacea
Grass, blue — Poa
Grass, blue alpine — Poa alpina
Grass, blue Balkan — Sesleria heufleriana
Grass, blue big — Poa ampla
Grass, blue Canby — Poa canbyi
Grass, blue oat — Helictotrichon sempervirens

Grass, blue pine — Poa scabrella
Grass, blue Queensland — Dichanthium sericeum
Grass, blue sandberg — Poa sandbergii
Grass, blue silky — Dichanthium sericeum
Grass, blue-eyed — Sisyrinchium
Grass, blue-eyed — Sisyrinchium angustifolium

Grass, blue-eyed — Sisyrinchium campestre
Grass, blue-eyed — Sisyrinchium graminoides

Grass, bluejoint — Calamagrostis canadensis

Grass, bottlebrush — Hystrix patula
Grass, bottlebrush — Sitanion hystrix
Grass, Bowles' golden — Milium effusum 'Aureum'

Grass, box — Paspaladium constrictum

Grass boy — Xanthorrhoea gracilis
Grass, bristle — Setaria sphacelata
Grass, brome California — Bromus carinatus
Grass, brome Canada — Bromus pubescens
Grass, brome fringed — Bromus ciliatus
Grass, brome fringed — Bromus kalmii
Grass, brome hairy — Bromus ramosus
Grass, brome Kalm's — Bromus kalmii
Grass, brome prairie — Bromus kalmii
Grass, buffalo — Buchloe dactyloides
Grass, buffalo — Stenotaphrum secundatum

Grass, buffel — Cenchrus ciliaris

Grass, button — Dactyloctenium radulans
Grass, cane — Eragrostis australasica
Grass, cane sandhill — Zygochloa paradoxa
Grass, carpet — Axonopus affinis
Grass, cloud — Agrostis nebulosa
Grass, cloud — Aichryson x domestica 'Variegatum'
Grass, cord — Spartina pectinata
Grass, cotton — Eriophorum
Grass, cotton broad-leaved — Eriophorum latifolium
Grass, cotton common — Eriophorum angustifolium
Grass, couch — Cymbopogon dactylon
Grass, couch — Cynodon dactylon
Grass, crab — Pennisetum
Grass, creeping soft — Holcus mollis
Grass, Dallis — Paspaladium dilatum
Grass, desert Flinders — Yakirra australiensis
Grass, eel — Vallisneria spiralis
Grass, elephant — Rytidosperma arundinacea
Grass, esparto — Stipa tenacissima
Grass, eyelash pearl — Melica ciliata
Grass, feather — Stipa
Grass, feather giant — Stipa gigantea
Grass, feather reed — Calamagrostis x acutiflora
Grass, fish — Cabomba caroliniana
Grass, fountain — Pennisetum alopecuroides
Grass, fountain — Pennisetum setaceum
Grass, fountain Chinese — Pennisetum alopecuroides
Grass, foxtail — Alopecurus
Grass, foxtail — Setaria
Grass, foxtail hairy — Setaria italica
Grass, foxtail meadow — Alopecurus pratensis
Grass, frost — Spodiopogon sibiricus
Grass, Gamma — Tripsacum dactyloides
Grass, Gamma eastern — Tripsacum dactyloides
Grass, giant spear — Cyathochaeta clandestina
Grass, golden-eyed — Sisyrinchium californicum
Grass, grandmother — Elytrigia repens
Grass, green summer — Brachiaria miliiformis
Grass, hair — Aira
Grass, hair — Aira elegantissima
Grass, hair — Deschampsia
Grass, hair glaucous — Koeleria glauca
Grass, hair large blue — Koeleria glauca
Grass, hair tufted — Deschampsia cespitosa
Grass, hair wavy — Deschampsia flexuosa
Grass, hairy wood chess — Bromus purgans
Grass, hare's tail — Lagurus
Grass, Hunangemoho — Chionochloa conspicua
Grass, Indian — Sorghastrum nutans
Grass, June — Koeleria macrantha
Grass, June prairie — Koeleria macrantha
Grass, kangaroo — Themeda triandra
Grass, Kangaroo Albany — Evandra aristata
Grass, Kikuyu — Pennisetum clandestinum
Grass, Kunai — Imperata cylindrica
Grass, lawn Korean — Zoysia japonica
Grass, leg red — Bothriochloa macra
Grass, lemon — Cymbopogon citratus

126

Common-Botanical Names

Common name	Botanical name
Grass, lemon scented	Cymbopogon ambiguus
Grass, lens hairy	Paspaladium cilatifolium
Grass, love	Eragrostis
Grass, love Indian	Oryzopsis hymenoides
Grass, maiden	Miscanthus sinensis 'Gracillimus'
Grass, Manna	Glyceria australis
Grass, manna fowl	Glyceria striata
Grass, manna giant	Glyceria grandis
Grass, manna reed	Glyceria grandis
Grass, Marram	Amophila arenaria
Grass, marsh salt	Sporobolus virnicus
Grass, meadow	Poa
Grass, melic	Melica nitens
Grass, Mitchell barley	Astrebla pectinata
Grass, Mitchell curly	Astrebla lappacea
Grass, mondo black	Ophiopogon jaburan
Grass, moor	Sesleria
Grass, moor Balkan	Sesleria heufleriana
Grass, moor blue	Sesleria albicans
Grass, moor green	Sesleria heufleriana
Grass, moor nest	Sesleria nitida
Grass, mosquito	Bouteloua gracilis
Grass, Mulga	Thyridolepis mitchelliana
Grass, naked woollybutt	Eragrostis eriopoda
Grass, Natal	Melinis repens
Grass, needle	Stipa
Grass, needle green	Stipa spartea
Grass, needle purple	Stipa viridula
Grass, oat	Stipa pulchra
Grass, oat bulbous	Arrhenatherum
	Arrhenantherum elatius ssp bulbosum 'Variegatum'
Grass, oat curly	Danthonia spicata
Grass, oat false	Arrhenatherum elatius
Grass, oat Parry's	Danthonia parryi
Grass of Parnassus	Parnassia
Grass of Parnassus	Parnassia palustris
Grass, old-witch	Panicum capillare
Grass, orchard	Dactylis glomerata
Grass, palm	Setaria palmifolia
Grass, pampas	Cortaderia selloana
Grass, panic cotton	Digitaria brownii
Grass, panic Scribner's	Panicum scribnerianum
Grass, pheasant	Stipa arundinacea
Grass, pheasant's tail	Stipa arundinacea
Grass, pine	Calamagrostis rubescens
Grass, pitted blue	Bothriochloa decipiens
Grass, plains	Eragrostis lanipes
Grass, plume	Saccharum
Grass, plume giant	Saccharum giganteus
Grass, plume narrow	Saccharum strictus
Grass, plume shorthair	Dichelachne micrantha
Grass, plumed tussock	Chionochloa conspicua
Grass, porcupine	Stipa spartea
Grass, porcupine	Triodia irritans v laxispicata
Grass, quaking	Briza
Grass, quaking common	Briza media
Grass, quaking greater	Briza maxima
Grass, quaking lesser	Briza minor
Grass, rat's tail slender	Sporobolus creber
Grass, rattlesnake	Glyceria canadensis
Grass, rattlesnake large	Briza maxima
Grass, ravenna	Saccharum ravennae

Common name	Botanical name
Grass, reed	Calamagrostis
Grass, reed canary	Phalaris arundinacea
Grass, Rhodes	Chloris gayana
Grass, ribbon	Phalaris arundinacea
Grass, rice cut	Leersia oryzoides
Grass, rice Indian	Oryzopsis miliacea
Grass, rough meadow	Poa trivialis
Grass, ruby	Melinis repens
Grass, satin leafy	Muehlenbergia mexicana
Grass, scented	Cymbopogon
Grass, scented	Cymbopogon exaltatus
Grass, signal arm	Bouteloua gracilis
Grass, silk	Cymbopogon bombycinus
Grass, silk	Saccharum ravennae
Grass, silver	Corynephorus canescens
Grass, silver Amur	Miscanthus floridulus
Grass, silver banner	Miscanthus sacchariflorus
Grass, silver beard	Bothriochloa saccharoides
Grass, small Flinders	Iseilema membranaeceum
Grass, smilo	Oryzopsis miliacea
Grass, smooth	Poa pratensis
Grass, spangle	Chasmanthium latifolium
Grass, spear	Poa
Grass, spear	Stipa
Grass, spear	Stipa nitida
Grass, spear barbed	Stipa semibarbata
Grass, spear black	Heteropogon contortus
Grass, spear feather	Stipa elegantissima
Grass, sping early	Eriochloa pseudoacrotricha
Grass, squirrel tail	Hordeum jubatum
Grass, squirreltail	Sitanion hystrix
Grass, St. Augustine	Stenotaphrum secundatum
Grass, sweet	Hierochoe odorata
Grass, switch	Panicum virgatum
Grass, tape	Vallisneria spiralis
Grass, toothbrush	Lamarckia aurea
Grass tree	Richea
Grass tree, giant	Richea pandanifolia
Grass, trembling	Briza media
Grass, turf salt	Zoysia macrantha
Grass, tussock	Cortaderia
Grass, tussock	Deschampsia cespitosa
Grass, tussock	Poa labillardieri
Grass, tussock fine-leaf	Poa sieberiana
Grass, umbrella	Cyperus involucratus
Grass, umbrella	Digitaria divaricatissima
Grass, wallaby	Danthonia linkii v linkii
Grass, wallaby	Danthonia richardsonii
Grass, wallaby	Neurachne alopecuroides
Grass, wallaby bristly	Danthonia setacea
Grass, wallaby hill	Danthonia eriantha
Grass, wallaby ringed	Danthonia caespitosa
Grass, wallaby silver-top	Chionochloa pallida
Grass, Washington	Cabomba caroliniana
Grass, weaving	Xerophyllum tenax
Grass, wedge	Sphenopholis obtusata
Grass, weeping	Microlaena stipoides
Grass, wheat bluebunch	Agropyron spicatum

Common-Botanical Names

Common	Botanical	Common	Botanical
Grass, wheat common	Elymus scaber	Grevillea, white-plumed	Grevillea leucopteris
Grass, wheat Siberian	Elymus sibiricus	Grevillea, Wickham's	Grevillea wickhamii
Grass, wheat slender	Agropyron trachycalum	Grevillea, Wilson's	Grevillea wilsonii
Grass, wheat tall	Thyropyrum elongatum	Grevillea, woolly-cluster	Grevillea eriobotrya
Grass, wheat western	Agropyron smithii	Grevillea, woolly-flowered	Grevillea pilulifera
Grass, whitlow	Draba cunifolia	Grey Goddess palm	Brahea armata
Grass, whitlow yellow	Draba aizoides	Grey Nicker	Caesalpinia bonduc
Grass widow	Olsynium douglasii	Grindelia, Pacific	Grindelia stricta
Grass, widow	Sisyrinchium inflatum	Groenheide	Erica gilva
Grass, windarrie	Eragrostis lanipes	Groenhofiesuikerbos	Protea coronata
Grass, winderrie false	Eriachne aristidea	Groenkalossie	Ixia viridiflora
Grass, windmill	Chionochloa truncata	Groenviooltjie	Lachenalia contaminata
Grass, windmill curly	Enteropogon acicularis	Gromwell	Lithospermum officinale
Grass, windmill tall	Chionochloa ventricosa	Grootgeelbos	Leucadendron
Grass, witch	Panicum capillare		eucalyptifolium
Grass, wood	Sorghastrum		Carissa macrocarpa
	avenaceum	Grootnoemnoem	Senecio lautus
Grass, wood meadow	Poa nemoralis	Groudsel, variable	Aegopodium
Grass, wool	Scirpus cyperinus	Ground elder	Glechoma
Grass, woolly	Imperata cylindrica	Ground ivy	Glechoma hederacea
Grass, wooly foxtail	Alopecurus lanatus	Ground ivy, variegated	'Variegata'
Grass, yellow-eyed	Sisyrinchium		Astragalus crassicarpus
	californicum	Ground plum	Acotriche cordata
Grass, zebra	Miscanthus sinensis	Ground-berry, coast	Arachis hypogaea
	'Zebrinus'	Ground-nut	Apios americana
Grass, Zorro	Festuca megalura	Groundnut	Senecio triangularis
Grasstree, Australian	Xanthorrhoea australis	Groundsel, arrowleaf	Baccharis halimifolius
Grasstree, blackboy	Xanthorrhoea preissii	Groundsel, bush	Sinacalia tangutica
Grasstree, desert	Xanthorrhoea thorntonii	Groundsel, Chinese	Senecio anethifolius
Grasstree, spear	Xanthorrhoea resinosa	Groundsel, feathery	Senecio gregorii
Grassy bells	Edraianthus	Groundsel, fleshy	Ligularia dentata
Gravelroot	Eupatorium purpureum	Groundsel, golden	Senecio magnificus
Greek fir	Abies cephalonica	Groundsel, showy	Senecio viscosus
Greek mountain tea	Sideritis syriaca	Groundsel, sticky	Senecio platylepsis
Green and gold	Chrysogonum	Groundsel, toothed	Lapidarea margaretae
	virginianum	Group of stones	Brugmansia x candida
Green dragon	Arisaema dracontium	Guando	Cyamopsis
Green flower tree	Peddiea africana	Guar (gum)	tetragonobolus
Green osier	Cornus alternifolia		Euclea natalensis
Green thread	Thelesperma filifolia	Guarrie, Natal	Euclea undulata
Green-hair tree, wild	Parkinsonia africana	Guarrii, common	Euclea divinorum
Greenweed, dyer's	Genista tinctoria	Guarrii, magic	Euclea racemosa
Grevillea, bottlebrush	Grevillea paradoxa	Guarrii, sea	Psidium guajava
Grevillea, branching	Grevillea ramosissima	Guava	Ugni molinae
Grevillea, candle	Grevillea candelabroides	Guava, Chilean	Eupotamia laurina
Grevillea, desert	Grevillea juncifolia	Guava, native (AU)	Acca sellowiana
Grevillea, desert	Grevillea pterosperma	Guava, Pineapple	Psidium littorale v
Grevillea, fan	Grevillea ramosissima	Guava shrub, cherry	longipes
Grevillea, flame	Grevillea eriostachya		Psidium littorale v
Grevillea, fuchsia	Grevillea bipinnatifida	Guava, strawberry	longipes
Grevillea, golden	Grevillea pteridifolia		Psidium littorale v
Grevillea, grape	Grevillea bipinnatifida	Guava, strawberry yellow	lucidum
Grevillea, holly	Grevillea aquifolia	Guayiga	Zamia pumila
Grevillea, holly-leaf	Grevillea monticola	Guelder rose	Viburnum opulus
Grevillea, honeysuckle	Grevillea juncifolia	Guernsey lily	Cyrtanthus elatus
Grevillea, Mt. Brockman	Grevillea formosa	Guichenotia, large flowered	Guichenotia macrantha
Grevillea, oak-leaf	Grevillea quercifolia	Guinea flower	Hibbertia
Grevillea, orange	Grevillea eriostachya	Guinea flower, climbing	Hibbertia scandens
Grevillea, pine	Grevillea excelsior	Guinea flower, large	Hibbertia lasiopus
Grevillea, plumed red	Grevillea plurijuga	Gum	Eucalyptus
Grevillea, purple flowered	Grevillea pulchella	Gum, alpine cider	Eucalyptus archeri
Grevillea, rock	Grevillea heliosperma	Gum, alpine yellow	Eucalyptus subcrenulata
Grevillea, scarlet	Grevillea banksii forsteri	Gum, alpine yellow Tasmanian	Eucalyptus subcrenulata
Grevillea, silk pink	Grevillea petrophilioides	Gum, apple Argyle	Eucalyptus cinerea
Grevillea, spindly	Grevillea endlicherana	Gum, apple dwarf	Angophora hispida
Grevillea, sweet-scented	Grevillea pulchella	Gum, apple rough-barked	Angophora floribunda

Common-Botanical Names

Common name	Botanical name	Common name	Botanical name
Gum, apple smooth-barked	Angophora costata	Gum, grey	Eucalyptus canaliculata
Gum Arabic	Acacia arabica	Gum, grey	Eucalyptus major
Gum Arabic	Acacia senegal	Gum, grey	Eucalyptus punctata
Gum Arabic tree	Acacia nilotica	Gum, grey	Eucalyptus punctata v didyma
Gum bdellium	Commiphora africana		
Gum, black	Eucalyptus aggregata	Gum, Griffith's grey	Eucalyptus griffithsii
Gum, black	Nyssa sylvatica	Gum, gully	Eucalyptus smithii
Gum, blackbutt	Eucalyptus smithii	Gum, Hill Salmon	Eucalyptus tintinnans
Gum, Blakely's red	Eucalyptus blakelyi	Gum, Hillgrove	Eucalyptus michaeliana
Gum, blue	Eucalyptus globulus	Gum, honey white	Eucalyptus dealbata
Gum, blue	Eucalyptus leucoxylon	Gum, Kybean	Eucalyptus parvifolia
Gum, blue	Eucalyptus leucoxylon ssp megalocarpa	Gum, lemon flavoured	Eucalyptus woodwardii
		Gum, lemon-scented	Eucalyptus citriodora
Gum, blue Eyre Peninsular	Eucalyptus leucoxylon ssp petiolaris	Gum, Lindsay	Eucalyptus erythronema
		Gum, Maiden's	Eucalyptus globulus ssp maidenii
Gum, blue pink-flowered	Eucalyptus leucoxylon ssp pruinosa (rosea)	Gum, Maiden's	Eucalyptus maidenii
Gum, bog	Eucalyptus kitsoniana	Gum, Manna	Eucalyptus mannifera ssp maculosa
Gum, Bolly white	Neolitsea dealbata		
Gum, brittle	Eucalyptus mannifera ssp elliptica	Gum, Manna	Eucalyptus mannifera ssp mannifera
Gum, brittle	Eucalyptus mannifera ssp maculosa	Gum, Manna	Eucalyptus viminalis
		Gum, Manna Gippsland	Eucalyptus pryoriana
Gum, brittle	Eucalyptus mannifera ssp mannifera	Gum, Manna ribbon	Eucalyptus viminalis
Gum, broad-leaved	Eucalyptus camphora	Gum, marble	Eucalyptus gongylocarpa
Gum, broad-leaved ribbon	Eucalyptus dalrympleana	Gum, Melaleuca	Eucalyptus miniata
Gum, Brooker's	Eucalyptus brookerana	Gum, Mindanoa	Eucalyptus deglupta
Gum, brown	Eucalyptus brunnea	Gum, mitre	Eucalyptus coronata
Gum, Burdett's	Eucalyptus burdettiana	Gum, Mount Buffalo	Eucalyptus mitchelliana
Gum, cabbage	Eucalyptus amplifolia	Gum, Mount Manypeaks	Eucalyptus gongylocarpa
Gum, cabbage	Eucalyptus pauciflora	Gum, mountain	Eucalyptus dalrympleana
Gum, cabbage large-leaved	Eucalyptus grandiflora	Gum, mountain blue	Eucalyptus deanii
Gum, cabbage snow	Eucalyptus pauciflora	Gum, mountain grey	Eucalyptus cypellocarpa
Gum, candlebark	Eucalyptus rubida	Gum, mountain silver-leaved	Eucalyptus pulverulenta
Gum, caper tree	Eucalyptus praecox	Gum, mountain white	Eucalyptus dalrympleana ssp heptantha
Gum, Chinese	Liquidamber formosana	Gum, narrow-leaved red	Eucalyptus seeana
Gum, Chinese sweet	Liquidamber formosana	Gum, nodding	Eucalyptus nutans
Gum, cider	Eucalyptus gunnii	Gum, Omeo	Eucalyptus neglecta
Gum, Coolgardie	Eucalyptus torquata	Gum, orange	Eucalyptus bancroftii
Gum, coral	Eucalyptus torquata	Gum, oriental sweet	Liquidamber orientalis
Gum, cup	Eucalyptus cosmophylla	Gum, Paddy's River	Eucalyptus macarthurii
Gum, Deane's white	Eucalyptus deanii	Gum, Parramatta red	Eucalyptus parramattensis
Gum, desert	Eucalyptus gongylocarpa		
Gum, Die hardy	Eucalyptus formanii	Gum, pear red	Eucalyptus stoatei
Gum, Drummond's	Eucalyptus drummondii	Gum, pear scarlet	Eucalyptus stoatei
Gum, Duart	Eucalyptus gomphocephala	Gum, peppermint black	Eucalyptus amygdalina
		Gum, peppermint silver	Eucalyptus tasmanica
Gum, Dunn's white	Eucalyptus dunnii	Gum, peppermint white	Eucalyptus amygdalina
Gum, Dwyer's red	Eucalyptus dwyeri	Gum, pink	Eucalyptus fasciculosa
Gum, fiery	Eucalyptus phoenicia	Gum plant	Grindelia
Gum, firewood red	Eucalyptus camaldulensis	Gum plant, coast	Grindelia oregana
		Gum, Poplar	Eucalyptus alba
Gum, flooded	Eucalyptus grandis	Gum, Poplar	Eucalyptus bigalerita
Gum, flooded	Eucalyptus rudis	Gum, poplar	Eucalyptus platyphylla
Gum, flowering	Eucalyptus ficifolia	Gum, poplar	Eucalyptus populnea
Gum, fluted	Eucalyptus salubris	Gum, Port Lincoln	Eucalyptus lansdowneana ssp albopurpurea
Gum, forest red	Eucalyptus tereticornis		
Gum, Formosan	Liquidamber formosana		
Gum, fuchsia	Eucalyptus forestiana	Gum, powder bark	Eucalyptus lane poolei
Gum, ghost	Eucalyptus papuana	Gum, powdered	Eucalyptus pulverulenta
Gum, ghost Darling range	Eucalyptus laeliae	Gum, red	Ceratopetalum gummiferum
Gum, giant	Eucalyptus regnans		
Gum, golden	Eucalyptus eximia nana	Gum, red	Eucalyptus blakeyi
Gum, Gondwana	Eucalyptus georgei	Gum, red Bancroft's	Eucalyptus bancroftii
Gum, Grampians	Eucalyptus alpina	Gum, red Cape York	Eucalyptus brassiana

Common-Botanical Names

Gum, red Murray	Eucalyptus camaldulensis
Gum, red (scarlet)	Eucalyptus ficifolia
Gum, red spotted	Eucalyptus mannifera ssp maculosa
Gum, red tumbledown	Eucalyptus bancroftii
Gum, red-flowering	Eucalyptus ficifolia
Gum, ribbon	Eucalyptus viminalis
Gum, river red	Eucalyptus camaldulensis
Gum, river white	Eucalyptus radiata
Gum, rose	Eucalyptus grandis
Gum, rosebud	Eucalyptus erythrandra
Gum, round-leaved	Eucalyptus deanii
Gum, round-leaved snow	Eucalyptus perriniana
Gum, salmon	Eucalyptus salmonophloia
Gum, salmon northern	Eucalyptus bigalerita
Gum, salt	Eucalyptus salicola
Gum, salt river	Eucalyptus sargentii
Gum, scarlet	Eucalyptus phoenicia
Gum, scribbly	Eucalyptus haemastoma
Gum, scribbly	Eucalyptus racemosa
Gum, scribbly	Eucalyptus sclerophylla
Gum, scribbly	Eucalyptus signata
Gum, scribbly hard-leaved	Eucalyptus sclerophylla
Gum, scribbly inland	Eucalyptus rossii
Gum, scribbly white	Eucalyptus rossii
Gum, shining	Eucalyptus nitens
Gum, shiny barked	Eucalyptus pachycalyx
Gum, silver	Eucalyptus crenulata
Gum, silver dollar	Eucalyptus polyanthemos
Gum, silver heart-leaved	Eucalyptus cordata
Gum, small-fruited grey	Eucalyptus propinqua
Gum, small-leaved	Eucalyptus parvifolia
Gum, snappy	Eucalyptus leucophloia
Gum, snappy	Eucalyptus racemosa
Gum, snappy	Eucalyptus rossii
Gum, snappy tropical	Eucalyptus brevifolia
Gum, snow	Eucalyptus pauciflora
Gum, snow alpine	Eucalyptus pauciflora ssp debeuzevillei
Gum, snow alpine	Eucalyptus pauciflora ssp niphophila
Gum, snow cabbage	Eucalyptus pauciflora
Gum, snow cabbage	Eucalyptus pauciflora ssp pauciflora
Gum, snow dwarf	Eucalyptus gregsoniana
Gum, snow twisted	Eucalyptus pauciflora ssp niphophila
Gum, snow Wolgan	Eucalyptus gregsoniana
Gum, southern blue	Eucalyptus globulus ssp bicostata
Gum, spinning	Eucalyptus perriniana
Gum, spotted	Eucalyptus maculata
Gum, stoat	Eucalyptus stoatei
Gum, stocking	Eucalyptus kondinensis
Gum, Strickland's	Eucalyptus stricklandii
Gum, sugar	Eucalyptus cladocalyx
Gum, sugar dwarf	Eucalyptus cladocalyx nana
Gum, swamp	Eucalyptus rudis
Gum, swamp black	Eucalyptus ovata
Gum, swamp mountain	Eucalyptus camphora
Gum, sweet	Liquidamber styraciflua

Gum, sweet oriental	Liquidamber orientalis
Gum, Sydney blue	Eucalyptus saligna
Gum, Sydney red	Angophora costata
Gum, Tasmanian blue	Eucalyptus globulus
Gum, Tasmanian blue	Eucalyptus globulus ssp compacta
Gum, Tasmanian blue	Eucalyptus globulus ssp globulus
Gum, Tasmanian snow	Eucalyptus coccifera
Gum, Tasmanian yellow	Eucalyptus johnstonii
Gum, Tingiringi	Eucalyptus glaucescens
Gum, Tuart	Eucalyptus gomphocephala
Gum, tumbledown red	Eucalyptus dealbata
Gum, urn	Euacalyptus urnigera
Gum, urn-fruited	Eucalyptus urnigera
Gum, varnished	Eucalyptus vernicosa
Gum, Victorian blue	Eucalyptus globulus ssp bicostata
Gum, Victorian silver	Eucalyptus crenulata
Gum, water	Tristania neriifolia
Gum, water	Tristaniopsis laurina
Gum, water giant	Syzygium francisii
Gum, water small-leaved	Syzygium luehmanii
Gum, weeping	Eucalyptus pauciflora
Gum, weeping	Eucalyptus sepulcralis
Gum, white	Eucalyptus alba
Gum, white	Eucalyptus rossii
Gum, white	Eucalyptus viminalis
Gum, white	Eucalyptus wandoo
Gum, white Camden	Eucalyptus benthamii
Gum, white Dorrigo	Eucalyptus benthamii v dorrigoensis
Gum, white fine-leaved	Eucalyptus gullickii
Gum, white northern	Eucalyptus brevifolia
Gum, white Wallangarra	Eucalyptus sclerophylla
Gum, white Wallangarra	Eucalyptus scoparia
Gum, white western Qld	Eucalyptus argophloia
Gum, Woila	Eucalyptus olsenii
Gum, Woodward's	Eucalyptus woodwardii
Gum, yellow	Eucalyptus leucoxylon
Gum, yellow	Eucalyptus leucoxylon ssp leucoxylon
Gum, yellow	Eucalyptus leucoxylon ssp megalocarpa
Gum, yellow-flowering Goldfield's	Eucalyptus stricklandii
Gum, York	Eucalyptus loxophleba ssp loxophleba
Gumweed	Grindelia integrifolia
Gumweed, desert	Grindelia aphanactis
Gumweed, low	Grindelia nana
Gungurru	Eucalyptus caesia
Gungurru	Eucalyptus woodwardii
Gunyang	Solanum aviculare
Gutta-percha tree	Eucommia ulmoides
Gwarrie	Euclea lancea
Gwarrie	Euclea undulata
Gypsywort	Lycopus
Gypsywort	Lycopus europaeus
Haakdoring	Asparagus aethiopicus
Hackberry	Celtis
Hackberry, common	Celtis laevigata
Hackberry, common	Celtis occidentalis
Hackberry, Mississippi	Celtis laevigata
Hackberry, net-leaved	Celtis reticulata
Hackberry, sugar	Celtis laevigata

Common-Botanical Names

Common Name	Botanical Name
Hackberry, western	Celtis occidentalis
Hair grass	Aira
Hair grass	Deschampsia
Hair grass, grey	Corynephorus canescens
Hair grass, tufted	Deschampsia cespitosa
Hair grass, wavy	Deschampsia flexuosa
Hakea, ashy	Hakea cinerea
Hakea, beaked	Hakea rostrata
Hakea, bird-beak	Hakea orthorrynchia
Hakea, blue	Hakea lehmanniana
Hakea, bottlebrush	Hakea bucculenta
Hakea, broad-leaved	Hakea petiolaris
Hakea, bushy	Hakea sericea
Hakea, cauliflower	Hakea corymbosa
Hakea, Christmas	Hakea preissii
Hakea, coastal	Hakea clavata
Hakea, cricket ball	Hakea platysperma
Hakea, cup	Hakea cucullata
Hakea, curved-fruit	Hakea cyclocarpa
Hakea, dagger	Hakea teretifolia
Hakea, Echidna	Hakea erinacea
Hakea, elm-seed	Hakea cycloptera
Hakea, finger	Hakea dactyloides
Hakea, frog	Hakea nitida
Hakea, furrowed	Hakea sulcata
Hakea, furze	Hakea ulicina
Hakea, gorse	Hakea ulicina
Hakea, grass leak	Hakea francisiana
Hakea, grass-leaf	Hakea bucculenta
Hakea, grass-leaved	Hakea multilineata
Hakea, hairy	Hakea gibbosa
Hakea, harsh	Hakea prostrata
Hakea, holly-leaved	Hakea varia
Hakea, honey	Hakea suberea
Hakea, hood-leaved	Hakea cucullata
Hakea, lantern	Hakea victoriae
Hakea, Macrae's	Hakea macreana
Hakea, marble	Hakea incrassata
Hakea, mountain	Hakea lissosperma
Hakea, needle silver	Hakea leucoptera
Hakea, olive-leaved	Hakea oleifolia
Hakea, oval-leaved	Hakea elliptica
Hakea, peach	Hakea platysperma
Hakea, pincushion	Hakea laurina
Hakea, prickly	Hakea amplexicaulis
Hakea, red-beak	Hakea orthorrynchia
Hakea, ribbed	Hakea costata
Hakea, royal	Hakea victoriae
Hakea, scallop	Hakea cucullata
Hakea, sea-urchin	Hakea petiolaris
Hakea, shell	Hakea cucullata
Hakea, shell-leaved	Hakea conchifolia
Hakea, shining	Hakea nitida
Hakea, short winged	Hakea brachyptera
Hakea, silky	Hakea lissosperma
hakea, small fruit	Hakea macreana
Hakea, spike candle	Hakea ruscifolia
Hakea, spike pink	Hakea coriacea
Hakea, staghorn-leaved	Hakea ceratophylla
Hakea, sweet scented	Hakea suaveolens
Hakea, sweet-scented	Hakea florulenta
Hakea, thick-leaved	Hakea crassifolia
Hakea, tree	Hakea arborescens
Hakea, tree	Hakea eriantha
Hakea, two-leaf	Hakea trifurcata
Hakea, variable-leaved	Hakea varia
Hakea, wavy-leaved	Hakea undulata
Hakea, wedge-leaf	Hakea flabellifolia
Hakea, willow-leaved	Hakea salicifolia
Hakea, yellow	Hakea nodosa
Halse (Hezzel)	Corylus avellana
Hampshire weed	Fraxinus excelsior
Handkerchief tree	Davidia
Handkerchief tree, pocket	Davidia
Hangertjieheide	Erica diaphana
Hard fern	Blechnum
Hard fern	Blechnum spicant
Hard-heads	Plantago lanceolata
Hardepeer	Olinia ventosa
Hardhack	Spiraea douglasii
Hardheads	Centaurea
Hardheads	Centaurea nigra
Hardy age	Eupatorium rugosum
Hare's ears	Bupleurum rotundifolium
Hare's foot fern	Davallia canariensis
Hare's tail	Lagurus
Hare's tail	Lagurus ovatus
Harebell	Campanula rotundifolia
Harebell, California	Campanula prenanthoides
Harebell, Drakensberg	Dierama dracomontanum
Harebell, white	Wahlenbergia congesta
Harebells	Dierama
Harebells, small	Dierama medium
Harlequin flower	Sparaxis tricolor
Harpuisbos	Euryops linearis
Harry Lauder's walking stick	Corylus avellana 'Contorta'
Hart's tongue fern	Asplenium scolopendrium
Hat plant, Mexican	Kalanchoe daigremontiana
Hattie's pincushion	Astrantia
Haw, possum	Ilex decidua
Haw, yellow	Crataegus flava
Hawaiian tree fern	Cibotium
Hawk's beard	Crepis
Hawk's beard, pygmy	Crepis pygmaea
Hawkbit, rough	Leontodon hispidus
Hawkweed	Hieracium
Hawkweed, Canada	Hieracium canadense
Hawkweed, hairy	Hieracium longipilum
Hawkweed, hairy	Hieracium scabrum
Hawkweed, leafy	Hieracium umbellatum
Hawkweed, mouse-ear	Pilosella officinarum
Hawkweed, orange	Pilosella aurantiaca
Hawkweed, woolly	Hieracium lanatum
Hawthorn	Crataegus
Hawthorn, black	Crataegus douglasii
Hawthorn, Chinese	Photinia serrulata
Hawthorn, cockspur	Crataegus crus-galli
Hawthorn, common	Crataegus monogyna
Hawthorn, downy	Crataegus mollis
Hawthorn, Indian	Rhaphiolepis indica
Hawthorn, May	Crataegus laevigata
Hawthorn, May	Crataegus monogyna
Hawthorn, Midland	Crataegus laevigata
Hawthorn, Quick	Crataegus monogyna
Hawthorn, red	Crataegus columbiana
Hawthorn, Smith's	Crataegus smithii

Common-Botanical Names

Common	Botanical
Hawthorn, water	Aponogeton distachyos
Hawthorn, Yedda	Rhaphiolepis umbellata
Hazel	Corylus
Hazel, American	Corylus americana
Hazel, Chilean	Gevuina avellana
Hazel, common	Corylus avellana
Hazel, corkscrew	Corylus avellana 'Contorta'
Hazel, Turkish	Corylus colurna
Hazelnut	Corylus avellana
Hazelnut, beaked	Corylus cornuta v californica
Hazelnut, California	Corylus cornuta v californica
Hazelwort	Asarum europaeum
He (Ho)-shou-wu	Fallopia multiflora
Headache tree	Umbellularia californica
Heal all	Prunella
Heart leaf	Philodendron cordatum
Heart leaf	Philodendron scandens
Heart of flame	Bromelia balansae
Heart of Jesus	Caladium bicolor
Heart pea	Cardiospermum halicacabum
Heart seed	Cardiospermum
Heart vine	Ceropegia linearis ssp woodii
Heart-of-the-earth	Prunella vulgaris
Heartnut	Juglans ailanthifolia
Hearts on a string	Ceropegia linearis ssp woodii
Hearts-a-bustin'	Euonymus americanus
Hearts-and-honey vine	Ipomoea x multifida
Heartsease	Viola tricolor
Heartseed	Cardiospermum halicacabum
Heath	Erica
Heath, alpine	Erica carnea
Heath, Azores	Daboecia azorica
Heath, baby	Erica quadrangularis
Heath, beard	Leucopogon capitellatus
Heath, beard	Leucopogon nutans
Heath, beard	Leucopogon obovatus
Heath, beard	Leucopogon ovalifolius
Heath, beard	Leucopogon propinquus
Heath, beard	Leucopogon rubicundus
Heath, beard coast	Cyathodes parviflora
Heath, berry	Erica baccans
Heath, besom	Erica scoparia
Heath, blood-red	Erica cruenta
Heath, Blue Mountain	Phyllodoce caerulea
Heath, bridal	Erica baueri
Heath, button	Erica lateralis
Heath,Cantabrian	Daboecia cantabrica
Heath, chanelled	Erica canaliculata
Heath, common Australian	Epacris impressa
Heath, Cornish	Erica vagans
Heath, Corsican	Erica terminalis
Heath, cross-leaved	Erica tetralix
Heath, cup and saucer	Erica glauca v glauca
Heath, Darley Dale	Erica x darleyensis
Heath, Dorset	Erica ciliaris
Heath, erica	Erica cerintoides
Heath, fire	Erica cerinthoides
Heath, four sisters	Erica fastigiata
Heath, green	Erica gilva
Heath, hairy flowered	Erica hirtiflora
Heath, Irish	Erica erigena
Heath, Kappokkie	Erica peziza
Heath, Mackay's	Erica mackaiana
Heath, mealie	Erica patersonia
Heath, Mediterranean	Erica erigena
Heath, moss-leaved	Astroloma ciliatum
Heath, mountain red	Phyllodoce empetriformis
Heath, nine-pin	Erica mammosa
Heath, pin	Styphelia tenuiflora
Heath, pink	Leucopogon strictus
Heath, Portuguese	Erica lusitanica
Heath, Prince of Wales	Erica perspicua
Heath, rainbow	Erica versicolor
Heath, showy	Erica speciosa
Heath, signal red	Erica mammosa
Heath, Spanish	Erica australis
Heath, Spanish dwarf	Erica umbellata
Heath, Spanish tree	Erica australis
Heath, spike	Bruckenthalia spiculifolia
Heath, St. Dabeoc's	Daboecia cantabrica
Heath, tassel small	Erica coccinea
Heath, tree	Erica arborea
Heath, Veitch's	Erica x veitchii
Heath, wandering	Erica vagans
Heath, water	Erica caffra
Heath, water	Erica curviflora
Heath, Watson's	Erica x watsonii
Heath, white	Erica formosa
Heath, whorled	Erica manipuliflora
Heath, William's	Erica x williamsii
Heath, winter	Erica carnea
Heather	Calluna
Heather	Erica
Heather, bell	Erica cinerea
Heather, Cape	Erica
Heather, false	Cuphea hyssopifolia
Heather, golden	Cassinia leptophylla ssp fulvida
Heather, Scotch	Calluna vulgaris
Heather, Scots	Calluna vulgaris
Heather, silver	Cassinia leptophylla ssp vauvilliersii v albida
Hebe, disk-leaved	Hebe pinguifolia
Hedge garlic	Alliaria petiolata
Hedgehog fir	Abies pinsapo
Helen's flower	Helenium
Helen's flower	Helenium autumnale
Heliotrope	Heliotropium arborescens
Heliotrope, bushy	Heliotropium paniculatum
Heliotrope, garden	Valeriana
Heliotrope, winter	Petasites fragrans
Hellebore	Helleborus
Hellebore, Corsican	Helleborus argutifolius
Hellebore, false	Veratrum album
Hellebore, false black	Veratrum nigrum
Hellebore, false white	Veratrum album
Hellebore, fragrant	Helleborus odorus
Hellebore, green	Helleborus viridis
Hellebore, stinking	Helleborus foetidus
Helleborine	Epipactis
Helleborine, giant	Epipactis gigantea
Helmet flower	Aconitum napellus

Common-Botanical Names

Helmet flower	Scutellaria
Helmet flower	Sinningia cardinalis
Hemigenia, silky	Hemigenia sericea
Hemlock	Tsuga
Hemlock, Canada	Tsuga canadensis
Hemlock, Carolina	Tsuga caroliniana
Hemlock, eastern	Tsuga canadensis
Hemlock, mountain	Tsuga mertensiana
Hemlock, northern Japanese	Tsuga diversifolia
Hemlock, poison	Conium maculatum
Hemlock, southern Japanese	Tsuga sieboldii
Hemlock, water	Cicuta maculata
Hemlock, western	Tsuga heterophylla
Hemp, African	Sparrmannia africana
Hemp agrimony	Eupatorium cannabinum
Hemp, Bowstring	Sansevieria
Hemp, false	Datisca cannabina
Hemp, Indian	Apocynum
Hemp, Indian	Apocynum cannabinum
Hemp, Indian	Hibiscus cannabinus
Hemp, Queensland	Sida subspicata
Hempweed, climbing	Mikania scandens
Hen and chickens houseleek	Jovibarba sobolifera
Hen-and-chicken fern	Asplenium bulbiferum
Henbane	Hyoscyamus
Henbane, black	Hyoscyamus niger
Henbane, white	Hyoscyamus albus
Henna	Lawsonia inermis
Henna tree	Lawsonia
Hepatica, round-lobed	Hepatica americana
Hepatica, sharp-lobed	Hepatica acutiloba
Herald's trumpet	Beaumontia grandiflora
Herb Bennet	Geum urbanum
Herb Christopher	Actaea spicata
Herb of grace	Ruta graveolens
Herb Paris	Paris quadrifolia
Herb Robert	Geranium robertianum
Herberton	Leptospermum petersonii ssp lanceolatum
Hercules' club	Aralia spinosa
Heriff (hairiff)	Galium aparine
Heron's bill	Erodium
Heropito	Pseudowintera axillaris
Herringbone plant	Maranta leuconeura v erythroneura
Hesper palm	Brahea
Hesperaloe, giant	Hesperaloe parviflora
Heuningbossie	Crassula perfoliata v minor
Heuningheide	Erica curvirostris
Hiba	Thujopsis dolabrata
Hibiscus, beach	Hibiscus tiliaceus
Hibiscus, black-eyed Susan	Hibiscus diversifolius
Hibiscus, bush	Radyera farragei
Hibiscus, Cape	Hibiscus diversifolius
Hibiscus, Chinese	Hibiscus rosa-sinensis
Hibiscus, dark-eyed	Hibiscus caesius
Hibiscus, Hawaiian rose	Hibiscus rosa-sinensis
Hibiscus, native (AU)	Alyogyne huegelii
Hibiscus, Norfolk Island	Lagunaria
Hibiscus, purple	Alyogyne huegelii
Hibiscus, red	Hibiscus coccineus
Hibiscus, red-centred	Alyogyne hakeifolia
Hibiscus, satin	Alyogyne huegelii
Hibiscus, tree Chimanimani	Hibiscus burtt-davyi

Hibiscus, velvet	Melhania oblongifolia
Hibiscus, wild	Hibiscus lunarifolius
Hibiscus, wild	Hibiscus pedunculatus
Hibiscus, yellow	Hibiscus panduriformis
Hickory	Carya
Hickory, bitternut	Carya cordiformis
Hickory, kingnut	Carya laciniosa
Hickory, pignut	Carya glabra
Hickory, shagbark	Carya ovata
Hickory, shellbark	Carya laciniosa
Hickory, swamp	Carya cordiformis
Hickory, two-veined	Acacia binata
Hickory, two-veined	Acacia binervia
Hillock bush	Melaleuca hypericifolia
Himalayan maidenhair fern	Adiantum venustum
Hime-Iwa-tabako	Conandron ramondioides v nana
Hing	Ferula assa-foetida
Hissing tree	Parinari curatellifolia
Hobble bush	Viburnum lantanoides
Hobblebush, Japanese	Viburnum furcatum
Hognut	Carya glabra
Hogweed	Heracleum sphondylium
Hogweed, giant	Heracleum mantegazzianum
Hoja santa	Piper auritum
Hollin	Ilex aquifolium 'Flavescens'
Holly	Ilex
Holly, African	Ilex mitis
Holly, American	Ilex opaca
Holly, blue	Ilex x meserveae
Holly, box-leaved	Ilex crenata
Holly, California	Photinia arbutifolia
Holly, Chinese	Ilex cornuta
Holly, common	Ilex aquifolium
Holly, English	Ilex aquifolium
Holly fern, Japanese	Cyrtomium falcatum
Holly fern, large-leaved	Cyrtomium macrophyllum
Holly, hedgehog	Ilex aquifolium 'Ferox'
Holly, Highclere	Ilex x altaclerensis
Holly, Himalayan	Ilex dipyrena
Holly, horned	Ilex cornuta
Holly, Japanese	Ilex crenata
Holly, Kashi	Ilex chinensis
Holly, miniature	Malpighia coccigera
Holly, moonlight	Ilex aquifolium 'Flavescens'
Holly, mountain	Nemopanthus mucronatus
Holly, mountain	Olearia ilicifolia
Holly pea	Jacksonia scoparia
Holly, sea	Eryngium
Holly, sea	Eryngium maritimum
Holly, silver-margined	Ilex aquifolium 'Argentea Marginata'
Holly, Singapore	Malpighia coccigera
Holly, summer	Arctostaphylos diversifolia
Holly, tarajo	Ilex latifolia
Holly, Topel	Ilea x attenuata
Holly, water	Mahonia nervosa
Holly, West Indian	Leea guineensis
Hollyhock	Alcea
Hollyhock	Alcea rosea

Common-Botanical Names

Common	Botanical
Hollyhock, Antwerp	Alcea ficifolia
Hollyhock, Antwerp	Alcea fig-leaved
Hollyhock, Australian	Lavatera plebeia
Hollyhock, black	Alcea rosea 'Nigra'
Hollyhock, desert	Sphaeralcea ambigua
Hollyhock, figleaf	Alcaea ficifolia
Hollyhock, mountain	Sphaeralcea rivularis
Hollyhock, outhouse	Alcea rosea
Hollyhock, wild	Sphaeralcea
Holm	Ilex aquifolium 'Flavescens'
Honesty	Lunaria
Honesty	Lunaria annua
Honesty, perennial	Lunaria rediviva
Honey bush	Melianthus major
Honey flower	Lambertia formosa
Honey locust	Gleditsia triacanthos
Honey locust, thornless	Gleditsia triacanthos inermis
Honey pot, couch	Dryandra nivea
Honey pot, shining	Dryandra obtusa
Honey pot, tangled	Dryandra pteridifolia
Honey pot, yellow	Dryandra tridentata
Honey-balls	Cephalanthus occidentalis
Honeyberry	Celtis australis
Honeybush	Hakea lissocarpa
Honeyeater heaven	Grevillea hookeriana
Honeyplant	Ammi visnaga
Honeypot, tangled	Dryandra drummondii
Honeysuckle	Lonicera
Honeysuckle, Asian	Lonicera chamissoi
Honeysuckle, bush	Diervilla
Honeysuckle, bush mountain	Diervilla sessilifolia
Honeysuckle, Cape	Tecoma capensis
Honeysuckle, common	Lonicera periclymenum
Honeysuckle, coral	Lonicera sempervirens
Honeysuckle, coral yellow	Lonicera sempervirens sulphurea
Honeysuckle, early Dutch	Lonicera periclymenum 'Belgica'
Honeysuckle, Etruscan	Lonicera etrusca
Honeysuckle, fly	Lonicera xylosteum
Honeysuckle, French	Hedysarum coronarium
Honeysuckle, giant Burmese	Lonicera hildebrandiana
Honeysuckle, hairy	Lonicera hispidula v vacillens
Honeysuckle, Himalayan	Leycesteria formosa
Honeysuckle, Italian	Lonicera caprifolium
Honeysuckle, Japanese	Lonicera japonica
Honeysuckle, late Dutch	Lonicera periclymenum 'Serotina'
Honeysuckle, mock	Turraea obtusifolia
Honeysuckle, New Zealand	Knightia excelsa
Honeysuckle, red	Banksia serrata
Honeysuckle, Tartarian	Lonicera tatarica
Honeysuckle, tree	Banksia marginata
Honeysuckle, tree Australian	Banksia
Honeysuckle, tree small	Turraea obtusifolia
Honeysuckle, trumpet	Campsis radicans
Honeysuckle, trumpet	Lonicera sempervirens
Honeysuckle, trumpet orange	Lonicera ciliosa
Honeysuckle, trumpet scarlet	Lonicera x brownii
Honeysuckle, white	Banksia integrifolia
Honeywort	Cerinthe
Honeywort	Cerinthe major v purpurascens
Honeywort	Cryptotaenia canadensis
Hook thorn, common	Acacia caffra
Hoop pine	Araucaria cunninghamii
Hop	Humulus
Hop	Humulus lupulus
Hop bush, giant	Dodonaea viscosa
Hop bush, giant	Dodonaea viscosa v viscosa
Hop bush, horny	Dodonaea ceratocarpa
Hop bush, large-leaf	Dodonaea triquetra
Hop bush, lobe-leaved	Dodonaea lobulata
Hop bush, peach-scented	Dodonaea petiolaris
Hop bush, Perth	Dodonaea hackettiana
Hop bush, purple	Dodonaea viscosa v purpurea
Hop bush, stalked	Dodonaea peduncularis
Hop bush, sticky	Dodonaea viscosa
Hop bush, velvet	Dodonaea rupicola
Hop, common	Humulus lupulus
Hop, Japanese	Humulus japonicus
Hop tree	Ptelea trifoliata
Hop-headed barleria	Barleria lupulina
Hopbush, cork	Kallstroemeria platyptera
Hops, native (AU)	Dodonaea viscosa ssp cuneata
Horehound	Marrubium
Horehound	Marrubium vulgare
Horehound, black	Ballota nigra
Horehound, common water	Lycopus americanus
Horehound, Greek	Ballota acetabulosa
Horehound, pleated	Marrubium cyclenum
Horehound, silver	Marrubium incanum
Horehound, Spanish	Marrubium supinum
Horehound, stinking	Ballota nigra
Horehound, woolly	Marrubium incanum
Horlosies	Geranium incanum
Horn of plenty	Fedia cornucopiae
Hornbeam	Carpinus
Hornbeam, American	Carpinus caroliniana
Hornbeam, American hop	Ostrya virginiana
Hornbeam, common	Carpinus betulus
Hornbeam, European	Carpinus betulus
Hornbeam, hop	Ostrya carpinifolia
Hornbeam, hop Japanese	Ostrya japonica
Hornbeam, Japanese	Zelkova serrata
Horned poppy	Glaucium
Horned poppy, red	Glaucium corniculatum
Horned poppy, yellow	Glaucium flavum
Horned thorn	Acacia grandicornuta
Hornwort	Ceratophyllum
Hornwort	Ceratophyllum demersum
Horopito	Pseudowintera colorata
Horse chestnut	Aesculus
Horse chestnut	Aesculus hippocastanum
Horse chestnut, Chinese	Aesculus chinensis
Horse chestnut, Indian	Aesculus indica
Horse chestnut, Japanese	Aesculus turbinata
Horse chestnut, red	Aesculus x carnea
Horse chestnut, sunrise	Aesculus 'Erythroblastos'
Horse chestnut, sunrise	Aesculus x neglecta
Horsemint	Mentha longifolia
Horseradish	Armoracia rusticana

Common-Botanical Names

Horseradish tree	Moringa oleifera
Horseradish tree	Moringa pterygosperma
Horsetail	Equisetum arvense
Horsetail, scrubbing rushes	Equisetum arvense
Horsetail tree	Casuarina equisetifolia
Horseweed	Chenopodium sp
Horsewood	Clausena anisata
Hosta, white-backed	Hosta hypoleuca
Hot water plant	Achimenes
Hottentot bread	Dioscorea elephantipes
Hottentot fig	Carpobrotus edulis
Hound's tongue	Cynoglossum nervosum
Hound's tongue	Cynoglossum officinale
Hound's tongue, Himalayan	Cynoglossum nervosum
Hound's tooth	Cynoglossum
Houpara	Pseudopanax lessonii
Houseleek	Sempervivum
Houseleek, cobweb	Sempervivum arachnoideum
Houseleek, common	Sempervivum tectorum
Houseleek, roof	Sempervivum tectorum
Hovea, common	Hovea trisperma
Hovea, holly-leaved	Hovea chorizemifolia
Hovea, thorny	Hovea acanthoclada
Hovea, tree	Hovea elliptica
Huamuchil	Pithecellobium dulce
Huang Qi	Astragalus membranaceus
Huang-qin	Scutellaria baicalensis
Huckleberry	Gaylussacia
Huckleberry	Solanum burbankii
Huckleberry	Vaccinum myrtillus
Huckleberry, big	Vaccinum membranaceum
Huckleberry, black	Gaylussacia baccata
Huckleberry, evergreen	Vaccinum ovatum
Huckleberry, fool's	Menziesia ferruginea
Huckleberry, red	Vaccinum parvifolium
Huilboerboon	Schotia brachypetala
Huilboom	Peltophorum africanum
Huisache	Acacia farnesiana
Hulver	Ilex aquifolium 'Flavescens'
Humble plant	Mimosa pudica
Humbug apple	Schizomeria ovata
Hummingbird, vegetable	Sesbania grandiflora
Humming bird flower	Zauschneria californica
Huntsman's cup	Sarracenia purpurea
Hyacinth	Hyacinthus
Hyacinth, grape	Muscari
Hyacinth, Southern grape	Muscari neglectum
Hyacinth, summer	Galtonia candicans
Hyacinth, tassel	Muscari comosum
Hyacinth, tassel grape	Muscari comosum
Hyacinth, water	Eichhornia
Hyacinth, water	Eichhornia crassipes
Hyacinth, wild	Brodiaea douglasii
Hyacinth, wild	Camassia scilloides
Hyacinth, wild	Lachenalia contaminata
Hyacinth, wild narrow	Camassia angusta
Hydrangea, climbing	Decumaria barbara
Hydrangea, climbing	Hydrangea petiolaris
Hydrangea, common	Hydrangea macrophylla
Hydrangea, oak-leaved	Hydrangea quercifolia
Hydrangea vine, Japanese	Schizophragma hydrangeoides

Hypericum, marsh	Hypericum elodes
Hyssop	Hyssopus
Hyssop	Hyssopus officinalis
Hyssop, anise	Agastache foeniculum
Hyssop, camphor	Agastache sp
Hyssop, giant	Agastache urticifolia
Hyssop, giant purple	Agastache scrophularifolia
Hyssop, giant yellow	Agastache nepetoides
Hyssop, hedge	Gratiola officinalis
Hyssop, lemon	Bacopa caroliniana
Hyssop, Mexican	Agastache
Hyssop, Persian	Thymus capitata
Hyssop, water	Bacopa caroliniana
Iboza	Iboza riparia
Ibul	Oriana sylvicola
Ice plant	Dorotheanthus
Ice plant	Sedum spectabile
Iceplant, hardy	Delosperma cooperi
Ilang-ilang	Cananga odorata
Illawarra palm	Archontophoenix cunninghamiana
Illyari (Illyarrie)	Eucalyptus erythrocorys
Immortal	Asclepias asperula
Immortelle, golden	Waitzia nitida
Immortelle, orange	Waitzia acuminata v acuminata
Immortelle, pale	Rhodanthe citrina
Impala lily	Adenium
Incense cedar	Calocedrus
Incense cedar	Calocedrus decurrens
Incense plant	Calomeria
Incense plant	Calomeria amaranthoides
Incense rose	Rosa primula
Indarajou, Mitha	Wrightia tinctoria
Indian bean tree	Catalpa
Indian comb	Pachycereus pectin-aboriginum
Indian ginger	Alpinia calcarata
Indian laburnum	Cassia fistula
Indian laurel	Ficus microcarpa
Indian mast	Polyalthia longifolia v pendula
Indian paintbrush	Asclepias tuberosa
Indian physic	Gillenia trifoliata
Indian physic	Porteranthus trifoliatus
Indian poke	Veratrum viride
Indian rhododendron	Melastoma malabathricum
Indian root	Asclepias curassavica
Indian shot plant	Canna
Indian siris	Albizia lebbek
Indian spear	Chenopodium sp
Indigo	Indigofera tinctoria
Indigo, Australian	Indigofera australis
Indigo, bastard	Amorpha fruticosa
Indigo bush	Amorpha fruticosa
Indigo, Chinese	Indigofera decora
Indigo, Chinese	Indigofera kirilowii
Indigo, desert	Indigofera brevidens
Indigo, false	Amorpha fruticosa
Indigo, false	Baptisia australis
Indigo, false fragrant	Amorpha nana
Indigo, forest	Indigofera natalensis
Indigo, Kirilow	Indigofera kirilowii

Common-Botanical Names

Common	Botanical	Common	Botanical
Indigo plant	Swainsona galegifolia	Ironbark, broad-leaved	Eucalyptus fibrosa
Indigo, river	Indigofera frutescens	Ironbark, broad-leaved red	Eucalyptus fibrosa
Indigo, single leaf	Indigofera monophylla	Ironbark, drooping	Eucalyptus caleyi
Indigo, venda	Indigofera lyalli	Ironbark, grey	Eucalyptus paniculata
Indigo, white false	Baptisia lactea	Ironbark, grey	Eucalyptus siderophloia
Indigo wild	Baptisia	Ironbark, gum-topped	Eucalyptus decorticans
Indigo, wild blue	Baptisia australis	Ironbark, lemon-scented	Eucalyptus staeri
Indigo, wild cream	Baptisia bracteata	Ironbark, narrow-leaved	Eucalyptus crebra
Indigo, wild plains	Baptisia bracteata	Ironbark, narrow-leaved red	Eucalyptus crebra
Indigo, wild white	Baptisia alba	Ironbark, Queensland grey	Eucalyptus
Indigo, wild white	Baptisia lactea		drepanophylla
Indigo, wild yellow	Baptisia tinctoria	Ironbark, red	Eucalyptus sideroxylon
Indrajao	Wrightia tinctoria	Ironbark, red	Eucalyptus sideroxylon
Inkberry	Ilex glabra		ssp tricarpa
Innocence	Collinsia bicolor	Ironbark, red (pink) flowered	Eucalyptus sideroxylon
Inrygertjies	Crassula perfoliata v		rosea
	perfoliata		Acacia fasciculifera
Interrupted fern	Osmunda claytoniana	Ironbark, silver-leaved	Eucalyptus melanophloia
Inula, magnificient	Inula magnifica	Ironbark, silver-leaved Shirley's	Eucalyptus shirleyi
Inula, swordleaf	Inula ensifolia	Ironbark, Tasmanian	Eucalyptus sieberi
Inyanga, flat-top	Acacia abyssinica	Ironbark, white	Eucalyptus leucoxylon
Ipomoea, star	Ipomoea coccinea	Ironbark, white	Eucalyptus leucoxylon
Iris, African	Dietes iridoides		ssp leucoxylon
Iris, Alaska	Iris setosa	Ironbark, white	Eucalyptus sideroxylon
Iris, Arctic	Iris setosa	Ironbark, White's	Eucalyptus whitei
Iris, beachhead	Iris setosa	Ironbark, yellow	Eucalyptus melliodora
Iris, blue	Iris brevicaulis	Ironbox, black	Eucalyptus ravertiana
Iris, bristle-pointed	Iris setosa	Irongrass	Lomandra leucocephala
Iris, butterfly	Diplarrhena moraea		ssp robusta
Iris, cascade	Iris tenax	Ironweed	Vernonia
Iris, copper	Iris fulva	Ironweed, Arkansas	Vernonia arkansana
Iris, Dalmatian	Iris pallida	Ironweed, common	Vernonia fasciculata
Iris, dwarf	Iris cristata	Ironweed, great	Vernonia arkansana
Iris, dwarf-bearded	Iris pumila	Ironweed, Missouri	Vernonia missurica
Iris, English	Iris latifolia	Ironweed, New York	Vernonia noveboracensis
Iris, flag blue	Iris virginica shrevei	Ironwood	Acacia excelsa
Iris, flag slender blue	Iris prismatica	Ironwood	Erythrophleum
Iris, morning	Orthrosanthus		chlorostachys
	multiflorus	Ironwood	Ostrya virginiana
Iris, mourning	Iris susiana	Ironwood, black	Gliricidia sepium
Iris, native (AU)	Patersonia occidentalis	Ironwood, Catalina	Lyonothamnus
Iris, native slender (AU)	Patersonia umbrosa		floribundus
Iris, Oregon	Iris tenax	Ironwood, desert	Acacia estrophiolata
Iris, Rocky mountain	Iris missouriensis	Ironwood, desert	Olneya tesota
Iris, roof	Iris tectorum	Ironwood, fine-leaved	Chionanthus foveolatus
Iris, roof Japanese	Iris tectorum	Ironwood, lemon	Backhousia citriodora
Iris, Sahkalin	Iris maackii	Ironwood, mountain	Cercocarpus betuloides
Iris, Siberian	Iris sibirica	Ironwood, Persian	Parrotia persica
Iris, Spanish	Iris xiphium	Ironwood, white	Vepris lanceolata
Iris, stinking	Iris foetidissima	Isband	Peganum harmala
Iris, vernal	Iris verna	Isopogon, drumstick	Isopogon
Iris, wall	Iris tectorum		sphaerocephalus
Iris, widow	Hermodactylis tuberosus	Isopogon, showy	Isopogon cuneatus
Iris, wild	Iris versicolor	Isotome, rock	Isotoma petraea
Iris, wild blue	Iris virginica shrevei	Isotome, rock	Laurentia axillaris
Iris, wild yellow	Dietes bicolor	Isphaghula	Psyllium ovata
Iris, winter	Iris unguicularis	Ivory bells	Campanula alliariifolia
Iris, Yunnan	Iris delavayi	Ivory curl flower	Buckinghamia celsissima
Irishman, wild	Discaria toumatou	Ivy	Hedera
Iron martin	Laurophyllus capensis	Ivy, American	Parthenocissus
Ironbark	Eucalyptus		quinquefolia
Ironbark	Eucalyptus siderophloia	Ivy, Atlantic	Hedera hibernica
Ironbark, Beyer's	Eucalyptus beyeri	Ivy, bird's foot	Hedera helix 'Pedata'
Ironbark, black	Eucalyptus ravertiana	Ivy, broomrape	Orobanche hederae
Ironbark, blue-leaved	Eucalyptus fibrosa ssp	Ivy, Canary Island	Hedera canariensis
	nubila	Ivy, clustered	Hedera helix

Common-Botanical Names

Common name	Botanical name
	'Conglomerata' Hedera helix
Ivy, common	Hedera helix
Ivy, common English	Hedera helix
Ivy, English	Hedera helix
Ivy, German	Declairea odorata
Ivy, Irish	Hedera hibernica
Ivy, Japanese	Hedera rhombea
Ivy, Japanese	Parthenocissus tricuspidata
Ivy, Kennilworth	Cymbalaria muralis
Ivy, Nepal	Hedera nepalensis
Ivy, Nepalese	Hedera nepalensis
Ivy of Uruguay	Cissus striata
Ivy, Persian	Hedera colchica
Ivy, poet's	Hedera helix f poetarum
Ivy, purple-leaved	Hedera helix 'Atropurpurea'
Ivy, Swedish	Plectranthus australis
Ivy, Swedish	Plectranthus oertendahlii
Ivy, sweetheart	Hedera hibernica 'Deltoidea'
Ivy, tree	Schefflera heptaphylla
Ivy, tree	x Fatshedera lizei
Ixia, green	Ixia viridiflora
Ixora, red	Ixora coccinea
Jaarsalie	Aeollanthus suaveolaens
Jacaranda, yellow	Peltophorum dubium
Jacaranda, yellow	Tipuana tipu
Jack-behind-the-garden-gate	Viola tricolor
Jack-by-the-hedge	Alliaria petiolata
Jack-in-the-pulpit	Arisaema triphyllum
Jack-in-the-pulpit	Arum maculatum
Jack-jump-about	Angelica sylvestris
Jacob's coat	Acalypha wilkesiana
Jacob's ladder	Polemonium
Jacob's ladder	Polemonium caeruleum
Jacob's ladder	Polemonium reptans
Jacob's ladder, beautiful	Polemonium pulcherrimum
Jacob's ladder, Kashmir	Polemonium cashmerianum
Jacob's ladder, leafy	Polemonium foliossisimum
Jacob's ladder, showy	Polemonium pulcherrimum
Jacob's rod	Asphodeline
Jacob's staff	Fouquieria splendens
Jade plant	Crassula ovata
Jade tree	Crassula ovata
Jade vine	Strongylodon macrobotrys
Jakkalsbossie	Castalis tragus
Jakkalsbossie	Osteospermum pinnatum
Jam tree, inland	Acacia acuminata (narrow phyllodes)
Jamaican mint bush	Hedeoma
Japan pepper	Zanthoxylum piperitum
Japanese blood grass	Imperata cylindrica 'Rubra'
Japanese cedar	Cryptomeria
Japanese climbing fern	Lygodium japonicum
Japanese holly	Ardisia crispa
Japanese holly fern	Cyrtomium falcatum
Japanese painted fern	Athyrium niponicum
Japanese quince	Chaenomeles
Japanese rush	Acorus gramineus
Japanese Yew	Taxus cuspidata
Japonica	Chaenomeles japonica
Japweed	Fallopia japonica
Jarrah, blue-leaved	Eucalyptus marginata v thalassica
Jarrah (Djara)	Eucalyptus marginata
Jasmine	Jasminum
Jasmine, Arabian	Jasminum sambac
Jasmine, Cape	Gardenia augusta
Jasmine, Carolina	Gelsemium sempervirens
Jasmine, Chilean	Mandevilla laxa
Jasmine, coastal	Jasminum didyum ssp lineare
Jasmine, common	Jasminum officinale
Jasmine, crepe	Taberbnaemontana divaricata
Jasmine, desert	Jasminum didyum ssp lineare
Jasmine, false yellow	Gelsemium sempervirens
Jasmine, Italian	Solanum seaforthianum
Jasmine, Madagascar	Stephanotis floribunda
Jasmine, Maori	Parsonsia heterophylla
Jasmine, mock	Turraea obtusifolia
Jasmine, orange	Murraya paniculata
Jasmine, primrose	Jasminum mesneyi
Jasmine, Royal	Jasminum grandiflorum
Jasmine, Spanish	Jasminum grandiflorum
Jasmine, star	Trachelospermum jasminioides
Jasmine, West Indian	Plumeria alba
Jasmine, wild	Jasminum fruticans
Jasmine, winter	Jasminum nudiflorum
Jasmine, yellow	Jasminum humile
Jelly palm	Butia capitata
Jerusalem cross	Lychnis chalcedonica
Jerusalem oak	Chenopodium botrys
Jerusalem sage	Phlomis fruticosa
Jerusalem sage	Pulmonaria saccharata
Jerusalem thorn	Paliurus spina-christi
Jerusalem thorn	Parkinsonia aculeata
Jessamine	Jasminum
Jessamine, night-blooming	Cestrum nocturnum
Jessamine, night-scented	Cestrum nocturnum
Jessamine, orange	Murraya paniculata
Jessamine, willow-leaved	Cestrum parqui
Jesuit's nut	Trapa natans
Jew's mantle	Kerria
Jewel orchid	Goodyera
Jewels of Opar	Talinum paniculatum
Jewelweed, yellow	Impatiens pallida
Jie Geng	Platycodon grandiflora
Jimsonweed	Datura
Jimsonweed	Datura stramonium
Jing Jie	Nepeta tenuiflora
Jintipil	Erythrina vespertilio
Job's tears	Coix lacryma-jobi
Joe-pye weed	Eupatorium fistulosum
Joe-pye weed	Eupatorium purpureum ssp maculatum
Joe-pye weed, sweet	Eupatorium purpureum
Joe-pye-weed, purple	Eupatorium purpureum
Joe-pye-weed, spotted	Eupatorium purpureum ssp maculatum

Common-Botanical Names

Johnny buddle	Chrysanthemum segetum	Kaneelaandblom	Gladiolus liliaceus
Jointfir	Ephedra viridis	Kanferbos	Tarchonanthus c camphoratus
Jojoba	Simmondsia chinensis	Kangaroo paw	Anigozanthus
Jonquil, campernelle	Narcissus x odorus	Kangaroo paw, Albany	Anigozanthus flavidus
Jonquil, rush-leaved	Narcissus assoanus	Kangaroo paw, black	Macropidia fuliginosa
Jonquil, wild	Narcissus jonquila	Kangaroo paw, branching	Anigozanthus onycis
Joolta	Eucalyptus centralis	Kangaroo paw, dwarf	Anigozanthus gabrielae
Joshua tree	Yucca brevifolia	Kangaroo paw, golden	Anigozanthus pulcherrimus
Joyweed, lesser	Alternanthera denticulata		
Judas tree	Cercis siliquastrum	Kangaroo paw, green	Anigozanthus viridis
Jue-ming-zi	Cassia tora	Kangaroo paw, little	Anigozanthus bicolor
Jujube	Ziziphus mucronata ssp rhodesica	Kangaroo paw, Mangles	Anigozanthus manglesii
		Kangaroo paw, red	Anigozanthus rufus
Jujube, Chinese	Ziziphus jujuba	Kangaroo paw, red and green	Anigozanthus manglesii
Jujube, common	Ziziphus jujuba	Kangaroo paw, sand plain	Anigozanthus humilis
Jujube, Indian	Ziziphus mauritiana	Kangaroo paw, tall	Anigozanthus flavidus
Jumbie bean	Leucaena latisiliqua	Kangaroo paw, yellow	Anigozanthus flavidus
Jumping Jacks	Impatiens glandulifera	Kangaroo paw, yellow	Anigozanthus pulcherrimus
Juneberry	Amelanchier		
Juniper	Juniperus	Kangaroo tail	Xanthorrhoea australis
Juniper, African	Juniperus procera	Kangaroo thorn	Acacia paradoxa
Juniper, alligator	Juniperus deppeana	Kangaroo vine	Cissus antarctica
Juniper, alligator	Juniperus pachyphlaea	Kanji bush	Acacia pyrifolia
Juniper, Ashe	Juniperus ashei	Kankerblarebossie	Aptosimum spinescens
Juniper, Bonin Island	Juniperus procumbens	Kankerbos	Sutherlandia frutescens
Juniper, Chinese	Juniperus chinensis	Kanolpypie	Watsonia aletroides
Juniper, coffin	Juniperus recurva v coxii	Kanolpypie	Watsonia marginata
Juniper, common	Juniperus communis	Kanooka	Tristaniopsis laurina
Juniper, creeping	Juniperus horizontalis	Kansas feather	Liatris pycnostachya
Juniper, Dahurian	Juniperus davurica	Kantakari	Solanum xanthocarpum
Juniper, drooping	Juniperus recurva	Kantikari	Solanum xanthocaroum
Juniper, flaky	Jumiperus squamata	Kapiva, wild	Bulbine frutescens
Juniper, Formosan	Juniperus formosana	Kapok	Ceiba pentandra
Juniper, Himalayan weeping	Juniperus recurva	Kapok bush	Cochlospermum fraseri
Juniper, Phoenicean	Juniperus phoenicea	Kapok, native (AU)	Bombax
Juniper, Rocky Mountain	Juniperus scopulorum	Kapok, yellow	Cochlospermum fraseri
Juniper, Sargent	Juniperus sargentii	Kapokbossie	Aspalanthus nivea
Juniper, shore	Juniperus conferta	Kapokbossie	Eriocephalus africanus
Juniper, southern red	Juniperus silicicola	Kapur	Jacksonia sternbergiana
Juniper, Syrian	Juniperus drupacea	Karaka	Corynocarpus laevigatus
Juniper, temple	Juniperus rigida	Karee	Rhus lancea
Juniper, weeping Mexican	Juniperus flaccida	Karee, bitter	Rhus marlothii
Jupiter's beard	Centranthus ruber	Karee, thorny	Rhus glauca
Jupiter's distaff	Salvia glutinosa	Karee, white	Rhus pendulina
Justicia, red	Megaskepasma erythrochlamys	Karkeicotyledon	Tylecodon cacaloides
		Karlya	Chorizema cordatum
Kaapse klapperpeul	Crotalaria capensis	Karo	Pittosporum crassifolium
Kaapse Vaderlandswilg	Combretum caffrum	Karoo gold	Rhigozum obovatum
Kaffir bean	Schotia afra	Karoo sage	Buddleja glomerata
Kaffir bread	Encephalartos caffer	Karookruisbessie	Grewia robusta
Kaffir fig	Carpobrotus edulis	Karoosalie	Buddleja glomerata
Kaiwhiria	Parsonsia heterophylla	Karri	Eucalyptus diversicolor
Kakaho	Cortaderia fulvida	Karri blue bush	Hovea elliptica
Kale, flowering	Brassica	Karri tree	Paulownia tomentosa
Kale, sea	Crambe maritima	Karroo bluebush	Diospyros lycioides ssp lycioides
Kalkoentjie	Gladiolus alatus		
Kalkoentjie	Gladiolus alatus v alatus	Karroobloubos	Diospyros lycioides ssp lycioides
Kalmoes, star-flowered	Alepidea natalensis		
Kalossie	Ixia conferta v ochroleuca	Karum tree	Pongamia pinnata
Kalwerbossie	Dissotis canescens	Kassod tree (Cassod)	Senna siamea
Kalyang	Acacia microbotrya	Katbosdoring	Asparagus virgatus
Kamahi	Weinmannia racemosa	Katbossie	Stachys aethiopica
Kamarere	Eucalyptus deglupta	Katdoring	Protasparagus retrofractus
Kambro	Fockea edulis		
Kana-mugura	Humulus japonicus	Katdoring	Protasparagus subulatus

Common-Botanical Names

Common	Botanical	Common	Botanical
Katmia, bladder	Hibiscus trionum	Klapperbossie	Triaspis hypericoides
Katsterbos	Stoebe alopecuroides	Klein-den-suikerbos	Protea aristata
Katstert	Hebenstreitia dentata	Kleinkamperfoelie-boom	Turraea obtusifolia
Katsura tree	Cercidiphyllum japonicum	Kleinplakkie	Adromischus sphenophyllus
Kauri pine	Agathis	Klimop	Convolvulus capensis
Kauri pine	Agathis australis	Klipdagga	Leonotis ocymifolia
Kauri, Queensland	Agathis robusta	Klokkieskatjiepiering	Rothmannia globosa
Kava kava root	Piper methysticum	Knapweed	Centaurea
Kawaka	Libocedrus plumosa	Knapweed, greater	Centaurea scabiosa
Keaki	Zelkova serrata	Knapweed, greater golden	Centaurea macrocephala
Keck	Heracleum sphondylium	Knapweed, lesser	Centaurea nigra
Kei-appel	Dovyalis caffra	Knapweed, plume	Centaurea uniflora v nervosa
Keibaakhout	Greyia flanaganii	Knob thorn	Acacia nigrescens
Keidjngund	Eucalyptus doratoxylon	Knobweed, small	Zanthoxylum capense
Kenaf	Hibiscus cannabinus	Knopiesheide	Erica lateralis
Kenikir	Cosmos sulphureus	Knotgrass	Polygonum aviculare
Kennedia, Cape Arid	Kennedia beckxiana	Knotweed	Persicaria
Kennedia, desert	Kennedia prorepens	Knotweed, dyer's	Polygonum tinctorium
Kentia, northern	Gromophyllum ramsayi	Knotweed, Japanese	Fallopia japonica
Kentucky coffee tree	Gymnocladus dioica	Kodjeningara	Verticordia nitens
Ker-ker	Erica imbricata	Kodjet	Hakea laurina
Ker-ker	Erica sparsa	Kohuhu	Pittosporum tenuifolium
Kerosene bush	Ozothamnus ledifolius	Kokerboom	Aloe dichotoma
Kerse	Protea aurea ssp aurea	Kokerbos	Tylecodon wallichii (Cotyledon)
Kerse	Protea aurea ssp potbergensis	Kolomikta vine	Actinidia kolomikta
Keurboom	Virgilia oroboides	Koma	Patersonia occidentalis
Keurtjie	Podalyria calyptrata	Kondil	Allocasuarina fraseriana
Keurtjie	Polygala fruticosa	Kooboo berry	Cassine aethiopica
Khat (Qat)	Catha edulis	Kooigoed	Helichrysum petiolare
Khella	Ammi visnaga	Koonjerung	Morinda citrifolia
Khus-Khus	Vetiveria zizanioides	Korean fir	Abies koreana
Kiaat	Pterocarpus angolensis	Korentebos	Rhus tomentosa
Kidney vetch	Anthyllis vulneraria	Koringblom	Scabiosa africana
Kiepersol, mountain	Cussonia paniculata	Koringblommetjie	Ixia flexuosa
Kikuba-kuwagata	Veronica schmidtiana v nana	Koringblommetjie	Ixia polystachya
		Koringblommetjie	Scabiosa incisa
Killi	Porophyllum ruderale	Korokio	Corokia buddlejoides
Kilmarnock willow	Salix caprea 'Kilmarnock'	Korokio	Corokia cotoneaster
King Billy pine	Athrotaxis selaginoides	Kotukutuku	Fuchsia excorticata
King palm	Archontophoenix	Kougoed	Sceletium tortuosum
King protea	Protea cynaroides	Koweda	Viminaria juncea
King William pine	Athrotaxis selaginoides	Kowhai	Sophora microphylla
King's crown	Justicia carnea	Kowhai	Sophora tetraptera
King's mantle	Thunbergia erecta	Kraanvoelblom	Strelitzia reginae
King's spear	Asphodeline lutea	Krauss' spikemoss	Selaginella kraussiana
King's spear	Eremurus	Krimpsiektebos	Cotyledon cuneata
Kingcup	Caltha	Kris plant	Alocasia sanderiana
Kingcup	Caltha palustris	Kruidjie-roer-my nie	Melianthus comosus
Kingfisher daisy	Felicia	Kruidjie-roer-my nie	Melianthus villosus
Kinnikinnick	Arctostaphylos uva-ursi	Kruisbessie	Grewia occidentalis
Kinnikinnik	Cornus suecia	Kruisement	Mentha longifolia ssp wissii
Kiss-me-over-the-garden-gate	Persicaria orientale	Kudjid	Hypocalymma angustifolium
Kiss-me-quick	Brunfelsia latifolia		
Kiss-me-quick	Brunfelsia pauciflora 'Floribunda'		
Kiss-me-quick	Viola tricolor	Kudjong	Acacia saligna
Kisses	Galium aparine	Kudu berry	Pseudolachnostylis maprouneifolia
Kittentails	Wulfenia bullii		
Kiwano	Cucumis metaliferus	Kudzu vine	Pueraria lobata
Kiwi bush	Allocasuarina muelleriana	Kugai-so	Veronica sibirica
		Kuli	Casuarina obesa
Kiwi fruit	Actinidia deliciosa	Kullingal	Eucalyptus pruinosa
Klaaslouwbos	Athanasia crithmifolia	Kulurda	Eucalyptus rudis
Klapperbos	Nymania capensis	Kumquat	Fortunella

Common-Botanical Names

Common	Botanical
Kumquat, round	Fortunella japonica
Kuni-bush	Rhus glauca
Kunzea, granite	Kunzea pulchella
Kunzea, scarlet	Kunzea baxteri
Kunzea, violet	Kunzea parvifolia
Kunzea, yellow	Kunzea ericifolia
Kurara	Acacia tetragonophylla
Kurrajong	Brachychiton
Kurrajong	Brachychiton discolor
Kurrajong	Brachychiton gregorii
Kurrajong	Brachychiton populneus
Kurrajong, Darwin	Brachychiton paradoxum
Kurrajong, desert	Brachychiton gregorii
Kurrajong, desert northern	Brachychiton acuminatus
Kurrajong, flame	Brachychiton acerifolius
Kurrajong, little	Brachychiton bidwillii
Kurrajong, northern	Brachychiton diversifolius
Kurrajong, white	Brachychiton discolor
Kurulbardang	Anigozanthus viridis
Kurulbrang	Anigozanthus manglesii
Kurup	Billardiera lehmanniana
Kusamaki	Podocarpus macrophyllus
Kuthmi(n)thi	Withania somnifera
Kwakiutl	Lomatium nudicaule
Kwararl	Eucalyptus angulosa
Kwidjard	Melaleuca uncinata
Kwoakol	Eucalyptus gardneri
Kwowdjard	Calothamnus quadrifidus
Kwowl	Allocasuarina huegeliana
Kyo-Chiku	Dendrocalamus giganteus
Labrador tea	Ledum groenlandicum
Laburnum , common	Laburnum anagyroides
Laburnum, Dalmatian	Petteria ramentacea
Laburnum, East African	Calpurnia aurea
Laburnum, evergreen	Piptanthus nepalensis
Laburnum, Indian	Cassia fistula
Laburnum, Natal	Calpurnia aurea
Laburnum, Nepal	Piptanthus nepalensis
Laburnum, Scotch	Laburnum alpinum
Laburnum, Voss's	Laburnum x watereri
Laburnum, wild	Calpurnia aurea ssp aurea
Lace bark	Hoheria populnea
Lace flower	Episcia dianthiflora
Lace flower	Trachymene oleracea
Lace flower, blue	Trachymene coerulea
Lace plant	Aponogeton madagascariensis
Lace vine, silver	Fallopia baldschuanica
Lacebark tree	Brachychiton discolor
Laceflower	Ammi majus
Lad's love	Artemisia abrotanum
Lad's love	Artemisia absinthium
Ladies fingers	Anthyllis vulneraria
Ladies' tresses, nodding	Spiranthes cernua
Lady fern	Athyrium
Lady fern	Athyrium filix-femina
Lady of the night	Brunfelsia americana
Lady of the night	Cestrum nocturnum
Lady palm	Rhapis
Lady's bedstraw	Galium vernum
Lady's eardrops	Fuchsia magellanica v molinae
Lady's mantle	Alchemilla
Lady's mantle	Alchemilla vulgaris
Lady's mantle, alpine	Alchemilla alpina
Lady's slipper orchid	Cypripedium
Lady's slipper orchid	Cypripedium calceolus
Lady's slipper orchid, showy	Cypripedium reginae
Lady's smock	Cardamine pratensis
Ladybell	Adenophora confusa
Ladybell, bush	Adenophora potaninii
Ladybell, common	Adenophora liliifolia
Lakpypie	Watsonia meriana
Lamb's ears	Stachys byzantina
Lamb's ears, woolly	Stachys byzantina
Lamb's lugs	Stachys byzantina
Lamb's quarters	Chenopodium album
Lamb's quarters	Chenopodium giganteum 'Magentaspreen'
Lamb's tail	Physopsis lachnostachya
Lamb's tails	Lachnostachys eriobotrya
Lamb's tails	Stachys byzantina
Lamb's tails (catkins)	Corylus avellana
Lamb's tongue	Plantago media
Lamb's tongues	Stachys byzantina
Lance-pod, broad	Lonchocarpus eriocalyx
Lancewood	Acacia crassicarpa
Lancewood	Acacia doratoxylon
Lancewood	Acacia shirleyi
Lancewood	Pseudopanax crassifolius
Lancewood, toothed	Pseudopanax ferox
Lantern, Japanese	Hibiscus schizopetalus
Lantern, Japanese	Physalis alkekengi
Lantern plant	Physalis alkekengi
Lantern tree	Crinodendron hookerianum
Larch	Larix
Larch, Dunkeld	Larix x marschlinsii
Larch, European	Larix decidua
Larch, golden	Pseudolarix amabilis
Larch, hybrid	Larix x marschlinsii
Larch, Japanese	Larix kaempferi
Larch, Siberian	Larix sibirica
Larch, sub-alpine	Larix lyallii
Larch, Western	Larix occidentalis
Lardy balls (fruit)	Symphoricarpos albus
Larkspur	Consolida
Larkspur, Chinese	Delphinium grandiflorum
Larkspur, giant	Consolida ajacis Imperial Series
Larkspur, Menzies'	Delphinium menziesii
Larkspur, mountain tall	Delphinium glaucum
Larkspur, prairie	Delphinium virescens
Larkspur, rocket	Consolida ajacis
Larkspur, scarlet	Delphinium cardinale
Larkspur, upland	Delphinium nuttallianum
Larkspur, western tall	Delphinium occidentale
Larkspur, wild	Delphinium nuttallianum
Latan palm	Latania
Lattice leaf plant	Aponogeton madagascariensis
Laudanum	Cistus ladanifer
Laurel	Magnolia grandiflora
Laurel	Prunus laurocerasus

Common-Botanical Names

Common	Botanical	Common	Botanical
Laurel	Prunus lusitanica	Leadwort	Plumbago
Laurel, Alexandrian	Danae racemosa	Leadwort, Cape	Plumbago auriculata
Laurel, bay	Laurus nobilis	Leadwort, scarlet	Plumbago indica
Laurel, Brisbane	Pittosporum revolutum	Leatherleaf	Chamaedaphne
Laurel, California	Umbellularia californica		calyculata
Laurel, cherry	Prunus laurocerasus	Leatherwood	Cyrilla racemiflora
Laurel, Chilean	Laurelia sempervirens	Leatherwood	Dirca
Laurel, common	Prunus laurocerasus	Leatherwood	Eucryphia lucida
Laurel, diamond-leaved	Pittosporum	Lebombotrosblaar	Terminalia
	rhombifolium		phanerophlebia
Laurel, eastern bog	Kalmia polifolia	Ledum, marsh	Ledum palustre
Laurel, glossy	Cryptocarya laevigata	Leek, blue-tongue	Allium karataviense
Laurel, Grecian	Laurus nobilis	Leek, native (AU)	Bulbine frutescens
Laurel, Indian	Ficus microcarpa	Leek, rose	Allium canadense
Laurel, mountain	Kalmia latifolia	Leek, roundheaded	Allium sphaerocephalon
Laurel, Portugal	Prunus lusitanica	Leek, sand	Allium scorodoprasum
Laurel, red-haired	Cryptocarya glaucescens		rotundum
Laurel, rusty	Cryptocarya	Leek, wild	Allium tricoccum
	mackinnoniana	Leeubekkie	Nemesia strumosa
Laurel, sheep	Kalmia angustifolia	Lemoenbos	Psychotria capensis
Laurel, Sierra	Leucothoe davisiae	Lemoendoring	Cassinopsis ilicifolia
Laurel, spotted	Aucuba japonica	Lemon	Citrus limon
Laurel, spurge	Daphne laureola	Lemon bush	Psychotria capensis
Laurel, Tasmanian	Anopterus glandulosus	Lemon fluff	Centaurea macrocephala
Laurel, Texas mountain	Sophora secundiflora	Lemon grass	Cymbopogon
Laurel, Western	Kalmia microphylla	Lemon grass, East Indian	Cymbopogon flexuosus
Laurelwood	Calophyllum inophyllum	Lemon grass, West Indian	Cymbopogon citratus
Laurustinus	Viburnum tinus	Lemon ironwood	Backhousia citriodora
Lavandin	Lavandula x intermedia	Lemon verbena	Aloysia triphylla
Lavatera, tree	Lavatera thuringiaca	Lemon vine	Pereskia aculeata
Lavender	Lavandula angustifolia	Lemonade berry	Rhus integrifolia
Lavender, Canary Island	Lavandula canariensis	Lemonade tree	Adansonia digitata
Lavender, cotton	Santolina	Lemonwood	Pittosporum eugenioides
	chamaecyparissus	Lenten rose	Helleborus orientalis
Lavender, desert	Hyptis emory	Lentil	Lens esculenta
Lavender, English	Lavandula angustifolia	Leopard flower	Belamcanda chinensis
Lavender, English	Lavandula x intermedia	Leopard lily	Belamcanda chinensis
Lavender, fern	Lavandula pinnata	Leopard plant	Ligularia
Lavender, fernleaf	Lavandula multifida	Leopard tree	Caesalpinia ferrea
Lavender, French	Lavandula stoechas	Leopard tree, broad-leaved	Flindersia collina
Lavender, French green	Lavandula dentata	Leopard wood	Flindersia maculosa
Lavender, French grey	Lavandula dentata v	Leopard's bane	Arnica montana
	candicans	Leopard's bane	Doronicum
Lavender, lace	Lavandula multifida	Lepelhout	Cassine peragua
Lavender, lemon-scented	Lavandula pedunculata	Leschenaultia, blue	Leschenaultia biloba
Lavender, lemon-scented	Lavandula viridis	Leschenaultia, free-flowering	Leschenaultia floribunda
Lavender, pinate leaved	Lavandula canariensis	Leschenaultia, (tall) red	Leschenaultia formosa
Lavender, sea	Limonium latifolium	Leschenaultia, wreath	Leschenaultia macrantha
Lavender, sea	Limonium peregrinum	Lettuce, prairie	Lactuca ludoviciana
Lavender, Spanish	Lavandula stoechas	Lettuce, rough white	Prenanthes aspera
Lavender, Spanish	Lavandula stoechas ssp	Lettuce, water	Pistia
	lusitanica	Lettuce, water	Pistia stratiotes
Lavender, Spanish	Lavandula stoechas ssp	Lettuce, wild	Lactuca canadensis
	pedunculata	Lettuce, wild	Lactuca virosa
Lavender, spike	Lavandula latifolia	Lettuce, wild	Mimulus guttatus
Lavender, sweet	Lavandula angustifolia	Lettuce, woodland	Lactuca floridana
Lavender, sweet	Lavandula heterophylla	Leyland Cypress	x Cupressocyparis
Lavender, toothed	Lavandula dentata		leylandii
Lavender tree	Heteropyxis natalensis	Lian qiao	Forsythia suspensa
Lavender, woolly	Lavandula lanata	Liana	Semele
Lavender, yellow	Lavandula viridis	Lidbossie	Peucedanum capense
Laventelboom	Heteropyxis natalensis	Life-of-man	Aralia racemosa
Lawson Cypress	Chamaecyparis	Lightwood	Acacia implexa
	lawsoniana	Ligiri	Idesia polycarpa
Lead plant	Amorpha canescens	Lignum, climbing	Muehlenbeckia adpressa
Leadwood	Combretum imberbe	Lignum, flowering	Eremophila polyclada

Common-Botanical Names

Common	Botanical
Lilac	Syringa
Lilac, California	Ceanothus
Lilac, common	Syringa vulgaris
Lilac, French	Galega officinalis
Lilac, Himalayan	Syringa emodi
Lilac, japanese	Syringa reticulata
Lilac, Korean early	Syringa oblata
Lilac, lake	Syringa villosa
Lilac, New Zealand	Hebe hulkeana
Lilac, Peking	Syringa reticulata ssp pekinensis
Lilac, Persian	Melia azedarach
Lilac, Persian	Syringa x persica
Lilac, Rouen	Syringa x chinensis
Lilac, St. Vincent	Solanum seaforthianum
Lilac vine	Hardenbergia violacea
Lilac, wild	Ceanothus sanguineus
Lilly pilly	Acmena smithii
Lilly Pilly, blue	Syzygium oleosum
Lilly Pilly, weeping	Waterhousia floribunda
Lily	Lilium
Lily, African blue	Agapanthus
Lily, Amazon	Eucharis grandiflora
Lily, American trout	Erythronium revolutum
Lily, American Turkscap	Lilium superbum
Lily, Arum	Zantedeschia
Lily, Aspanalado	Hippeastrum vittatum
Lily, Atamasco	Zephyranthes atamasco
Lily, August	Hosta plantaginea
Lily, Avalanche	Erythronium montanum
Lily, Aztec	Sprekelia formosissima
Lily, belladonna	Amaryllis belladonna
Lily, Bermuda	Lilium longiflorum
Lily, blackberry	Belamcanda chinensis
Lily, blood	Haemanthus
Lily, blood	Scadoxus
Lily, blue-grass	Agrosticrinum scabrum
Lily, blue-grass	Aphyllanthes monspeliensis
Lily, bush	Clivia miniata
Lily, Canada	Lilium canadense
Lily, Canadian	Lilium canadense
Lily, checker	Fritillaria affinis
Lily, checkered	Fritillaria meleagris
Lily, chocolate	Dichopogon strictus
Lily, climbing	Littonia modesta
Lily, cobra	Darlingtonia californica
Lily, cobra yellow-flowered	Arisaema flavum
Lily, Columbia	Lilium columbianum
Lily, corn	Clintonia borealis
Lily, corn	Ixia
Lily, Cunjevoi	Alocasia macrorhiza
Lily, desert	Hesperocallis undulata
Lily, Dobo	Cyrtanthus brachyscyphus
Lily, dwarf ginger	Kaempferia roscoeana
Lily, Easter	Lilium longiflorum
Lily, fawn	Erythronium grandiflorum
Lily, fire	Cyrtanthus
Lily, fire	Cyrtanthus contractus
Lily, fire	Lilium bulbiferum v croceum
Lily, fire yellow	Cyrtanthus breviflorus
Lily, flame	Gloriosa superba
Lily, flax	Dianella caerulea
Lily, flax	Dianella revoluta
Lily, flax blue	Dianella brevipedunculata
Lily, flax spreading	Dianella revoluta
Lily, Florida swamp	Crinum americanum
Lily, forest	Veltheimia bracteata
Lily, fortnight	Dietes bicolor
Lily, foxtail	Eremurus
Lily, fringed	Thysanotus multiflorus
Lily, garland	Hedychium
Lily, giant	Cardiocrinum
Lily, giant pineapple	Eucomis pallidiflora
Lily, ginger	Alpinia
Lily, ginger	Hedychium
Lily, ginger white	Hedychium coronarium
Lily, glacier yellow	Erythronium grandiflorum
Lily, Glehn's	Cardiocrinum glehnii
Lily, globe	Calochortus albus
Lily, gloden	Bulbine frutescens
Lily, glory	Gloriosa superba
Lily, golden spider	Lycoris aurea
Lily, golden-rayed	Lilium auratum
Lily, golden-rayed of Japan	Lilium auratum
Lily, Guernsey	Nerine sarniensis
Lily, Gumbo	Oenothera caespitosa
Lily, Gymea	Doryanthes excelsa
Lily, hooded	Johnsonia lupulina
Lily, Ifafa	Cyrtanthus mackenii
Lily, impala	Adenium
Lily, Jaburan	Ophiopogon jaburan
Lily, Jacobean	Sprekelia formosissima
Lily, Japanese pond	Nuphar japonica
Lily, Josephine's	Brunsvigia josephinae
Lily, Kaffir	Schizostylis
Lily, Kamchatka	Fritillaria camschatcensis
Lily, Lady Washington	Lilium washingtonianum
Lily, lantern Chinese	Sandersonia aurantiaca
Lily, Lent	Narcissus pseudonarcissus
Lily, leopard	Belamcanda chinensis
Lily, leopard	Dieffenbachia
Lily, leopard	Lilium pardalinum
Lily, Loddon	Leucojum aestivum
Lily, lotus water	Nelumbo nucifera
Lily, Madonna	Lilium candidum
Lily, Manipur	Lilium mackliniae
Lily, Martagon	Lilium martagon
Lily, May	Maianthemum
Lily, meadow	Lilium canadense
Lily, Mediterranean	Pancratium maritimum
Lily, Mexican	Hippeastrum reginae
Lily, morning star	Lilium concolor
Lily, Mount Cook	Ranunculus lyallii
Lily, Mt. Hood	Lilium washingtonianum
Lily, Nankeen	Lilium x testaceum
Lily, nodding	Lilium cernuum
Lily of the Nile	Agapanthus
Lily of the valley tree	Clethra arborea
Lily, orange	Lilium bulbiferum
Lily, orange	Stenomesson aurantiacum
Lily, Oregon	Lilium columbianum
Lily, painted wood	Trillium undulatum
Lily, panther	Lilium pardalinum
Lily, paradise	Paradisea

142

Common-Botanical Names

Common	Botanical	Common	Botanical
Lily, Paroo	Dianella caerulea	Lily, voodoo	Sauromatum venosum
Lily, Paroo	Dianella caerulea v protensa	Lily, water	Nymphaea
		Lily, water yellow	Nuphar lutea
Lily, peace	Spathiphyllum wallisii	Lily, waterwhite	Nymphaea alba
Lily, peacock	Kaempferia roscoeana	Lily, wild yellow	Lilium canadense
Lily, perennial	Agapanthus praecox ssp orientalis	Lily, wire slender	Laxmannia gracilis
		Lily, wood	Trillium
Lily, Peruvian	Alstroemeria	Lily, yellow pond	Nuphar lutea
Lily, pineapple	Eucomis	Lily-of-the-valley	Convallaria
Lily, pink porcelain	Alpinia zerumbet	Lily-of-the-valley, flame	Maianthemum bifolium
Lily, plantain	Hosta	Lily-of-the-valley, star-flowered	Smilacina stellata
Lily, poker	Kniphofia	Lily-of-the-valley, wild	Pyrola rotundifolia
Lily, prairie	Lilium philadelphicum	Lime	Tilia
Lily, purple	Dichopogon capillipes	Lime, American	Tilia americana
Lily, pyjama	Crinum macowanii	Lime, broad-leaved	Tilia platyphyllos
Lily, Pyrenean	Lilium pyrenaicum	Lime, Caucasian	Tilia x euchlora
Lily, Queen	Curcuma petiolata	Lime, common	Tilia x europaea
Lily, Queen	Phaedranassa	Lime, Crimean	Tilia x euchlora
Lily, rain	Zephyranthes candida	Lime, European white	Tilia tomentosa
Lily, rain	Zephyranthes grandiflora	Lime, Japanese	Tilia japonica
Lily, red and green	Stenomesson rauii	Lime, large-leaved	Tilia platyphyllos
Lily, red spider	Lycoris radiata	Lime, Mongolian	Tilia mongolica
Lily, Regal	Lilium regale	Lime, pendulous silver	Tilia 'Petiolaris'
Lily, resurrection	Kaempferia rotunda	Lime, red-twigged	Tilia platyphyllos 'Rubra'
Lily, resurrection	Lycoris squamigera	Lime, silver	Tilia tomentosa
Lily, Rienga	Arthropodium cirratum	Lime, small-leaved	Tilia cordata
Lily, river scarlet	Hesperantha coccinea	Limestone polypody	Gymnocarpium robertianum
Lily, rock	Arthropodium cirratum		
Lily, rush	Johnsonia lupulina	Linden	Tilia
Lily, sacred	Nelumbo nucifera	Linden, little-leaf	Tilia cordata
Lily, Sakhalin	Cardiocrinum glehnii	Linden tree	Tilia cordata
Lily, salt	Crinum pedunculatum	Ling	Calluna
Lily, Scarborough	Cyrtanthus elatus	Ling	Calluna vulgaris
Lily, sea	Pancratium	Lingaro	Elaeagnus philippinensis
Lily, sego big pod	Calochortus eurycarpus	Liniment plant	Comesperma virgatum
Lily, Shasta	Lilium washingtonianum	Linseed	Linum usitatissimum
Lily, slender yellow	Xyris lanata	Lion's ear	Leonotis ocymifolia
Lily, Snowdon	Lloydia serotina	Lion's ear, white	Leonotis ocymifolia v alba
Lily, spear	Doryanthes		
Lily, spear globe	Doryanthes excelsa	Lion's foot	Prenanthes alba
Lily, spear Palmer	Doryanthes palmerii	Lip fern	Cheilanthes
Lily, spider	Hymenocallis	Lip fern, hairy	Cheilanthes tomentosa
Lily, St. Bernard's	Anthericum liliago	Lipstick palm	Cyrtostachys lakka
Lily, St. Bruno's	Paradisea liliastrum	Lipstick tree	Bixa orellana
Lily, St. Joseph's	Hippeastrum vittatum	Lipstick vine	Aeschynanthus radicans
Lily, storm pink	Zephyranthes grandiflora	Liquorice	Glycyrrhiza
Lily, swamp	Crinum pedunculatum	Liquorice	Glycyrrhiza glabra
Lily, swamp	Lilium superbum	Liquorice, Chinese	Glycyrrhiza uralensis
Lily, Taiwan	Lilium formosanum	Liquorice, false	Abrus precatorius
Lily, tiger	Lilium lancifolium	Liquorice, Roman	Glycyrrhiza echinata
Lily, tiger orange	Lilium columbianum	Liquorice, Russian	Glycyrrhiza echinata
Lily, toad	Tricyrtis	Liquorice, wild	Glycyrrhiza lepidota
Lily, torch African	Kniphofia	Little pickles	Othonna capensis
Lily tree	Magnolia denudata	Little-men-in-a-boat	Androcymbium melanthioides f striatum
Lily, trout	Erythronium		
Lily, trout white	Erythronium albidum	Liverberry	Streptopus roseus
Lily, trumpet white	Lilium longiflorum	Liverwort	Hepatica
Lily turf	Liriope	Liverwort	Hepatica acutiloba
Lily turf	Ophiopogon	Living baseball	Euphorbia obesa
Lily, turf blue	Liriope muscari	Living granite	Pleiospilos
Lily, turf white	Ophiopogon jaburan	Living rock	Ariocarpus
Lily, Turkscap	Lilium michiganense	Living rock	Pleiospilos bolusii
Lily, Turkscap common	Lilium martagon	Living stones	Lithops
Lily, Turkscap scarlet	Lilium chalcedonicum	Livingstone daisy	Dorotheanthus
Lily, Turkscap yellow	Lilium pyrenaicum	Lizard plant	Tetrastigma voinierianum
Lily vine, Easter	Beaumontia grandiflora	Lizard tail	Anemopsis californica

Common-Botanical Names

Common	Botanical
Lizard tail	Crassula muscosa
Lizard's tail	Saururus cernuus
Lobelia, gold	Lobelia lutea
Lobelia, great blue	Lobelia siphilitica
Lobelia, red	Lobelia cardinalis
Lobelia, sandplain	Lobelia tenuior
Lobelia, scarlet	Lobelia splendens
Lobelia, spiked pale	Lobelia spicata
Lobelia, swamp	Lobelia paludosa
Lobelia, tufted	Lobelia rhombifolia
Lobelia, water	Lobelia dortmanna
Lobelia, wing-seeded	Lobelia heterophylla
Lobster claw	Clianthus puniceus
Lobster claw	Vriesea carinata
Lobster claws	Heliconia
Lobster flower	Plectranthus neochilus
Loco weed, showy	Oxytropis lambertii
Loco weed, silky	Oxytropis sericea
Locust	Robinia pseudoacacia
Locust, black	Robinia pseudoacacia
Locust, bristly	Robinia hispida
Locust, Caspian	Gleditsia caspica
Locust, honey	Gleditsia triacanthos
Locust, New Mexico	Robinia neomexicana
Locust tree	Ceratonia siliqua
Lollipop plant	Pachystachys lutea
Lolly bush	Clerodendrum floribundum
Lomatia, forest	Lomatia fraseri
Lomatia, long-leaf	Lomatia myricoides
Lomatia, river	Lomatia myricoides
Lomatia, silky	Lomatia fraseri
Lomatium, fern-leaved	Lomatium dissectum
Lomatium, large-fruited	Lomatium macrocarpum
Lomatium, nine-leaf	Lomatium triternatum
Lomatium, pestle	Lomatium nudicaule
Lomboy blanco	Jatropha cinerea
London plane	Platanus x hispanica
London pride	Saxifraga x urbium
Long tails	Ptilotus polystachyus
Loofah, dishcloth	Luffa cylindrica
Loofah (luffa)	Luffa aegyptica
Looking glass plant	Coprosma repens
Loosestrife	Lysimachia
Loosestrife	Lythrum
Loosestrife, Fraser's	Lysimachia fraseri
Loosestrife, garden	Lysimachia punctata
Loosestrife, gooseneck	Lysimachia clethroides
Loosestrife, prairie	Lysimachia quadriflora
Loosestrife, purple	Lythrum salicaria
Loosestrife, swamp	Decodon verticillatus
Loosestrife, winged	Lythrum alatum
Loosestrife, yellow	Lysimachia vulgaris
Loosestrife, yellow large	Lysimachia punctata
Loquat	Eriobotrya japonica
Loquat, bronze	Eriobotrya deflexa
Loquat, green	Eriobotrya japonica
Lord Anson's blue pea	Lathyrus nervosus
Lords and Ladies	Arum
Lords and Ladies	Arum maculatum
Lote tree	Celtis australis
Lotus	Nelumbo
Lotus, American	Nelumbo lutea
Lotus, blue	Nymphaea caerulea
Lotus, sacred	Nelumbo nucifera
Lousewort	Pedicularis bracteosa
Lousewort, leafy	Pedicularis foliosa
Lovage	Levisticum officinalis
Lovage, black	Smyrnium olusatrum
Lovage, Hulten's	Ligusticum hultenii
Love flower	Agapanthus
Love flower	Leucochrysum albicans
Love grass	Eragrostis
Love grass, paddock	Eragrostis leptostachya
Love grass, purple	Eragrostis spectabilis
Love grass, sand	Eragrostis trichodes
Love grass, weeping	Eragrostis curvula
Love in a mist	Passiflora foetida
Love leaves	Arctium sp
Love tree	Cercis siliquastrum
Love-in-a-mist	Nigella damascena
Love-in-a-puff	Cardiospermum halicacabum
Love-in-idleness	Viola tricolor
Love-in-vain	Viola tricolor
Love-lies-bleeding	Amaranthus caudatus
Love-lies-bleeding, green	Amaranthus viridis
Lucerne	Medicago sativa
Luisiesboom	Leucospermum grandiflorum
Luisiesbos	Leucospermum cuneiforme
Lungwort	Pulmonaria
Lunumidella	Melia composita
Lupin, Alaska	Lupinus nootkatensis
Lupin, broad-leaf	Lupinus latifolius
Lupin, Carolina	Thermopsis villosa
Lupin (e)	Lupinus
Lupin, false	Thermopsis lupinoides
Lupin, pine	Lupinus albicaulis
Lupin, sickle-keeled	Lupinus albicaulis
Lupin, silky	Lupinus sericeus
Lupin, silvery	Lupinus argenteus
Lupin, spurred	Lupinus laxiflorus
Lupin, tree yellow	Lupinus arboreus
Lupin, white	Lupinus albus
Lupin, yellow	Lupinus luteus
Lupine, Arroyo	Lupinus succulentus
Lupine, Carolina	Thermopsis villosa
Lupine, false	Thermopsis villosa
Lupine, golden	Linaria densiflorus
Lupine, many leaved	Lupinus polyphyllus
Lupine, sky	Lupinus nanus
Lupine, southern	Thermopsis villosa
Lupine, succulent	Lupinus succulentus
Lupine, wild	Lupinus perennis
Lyonia, rusty	Lyonia ferruginea
Lyre flower	Dicentra spectabiis
Maagpynbossie	Pelargonium betulinum
Macadamia nut	Macadamia integrifolia
Macadamia, nut rough shell	Macadamia teraphylla
Macassar oil tree	Cananga odorata
Macaw fat palm	Elaeis guineensis
Mace, sweet	Tagetes lucida
Macquarie vine	Muehlenbergia adpressa
Macqui	Aristotelia chilensis
Madagascar periwinkle	Catharanthus
Madar	Calotropis gigantea
Madder	Rubia tinctorium
Madder, Indian	Rubia cordifolia
Madeira vine	Anredera cordifolia
Madeliefiebos	Heterolepis aliena

Common-Botanical Names

Madre	Gliricidia sepium	Maize	Zea mays
Madrono (Madrona(e))	Arbutus menziesii	Maize, ornamental	Zea mays
Madrono, Pacific	Arbutus menziesii	Makaka	Plagianthus divaricatus
Madswort	Lobularia	Malard	Eucalyptus astringens
Magnolia, Fraser	Magnolia fraseri	Male-fern	Dryopteris filix-mas
Magnolia, great-leaved	Magnolia macrophylla	Mallee	Eucalyptus glaucescens
Magnolia, Japanese big-leaf	Magnolia hypoleuca	Mallee	Eucalyptus
Magnolia, Loebner	Magnolia x loebneri		lansdowneana
Magnolia, Oayama	Magnolia sieboldii	Mallee, Alexander river	Eucalyptus micranthera
Magnolia, saucer	Magnolia x soulangeana	Mallee, apple	Eucalyptus bupestium
Magnolia, southern	Magnolia grandiflora	Mallee, ash Faulconbridge	Eucalyptus burgessiana
Magnolia, star	Magnolia stellata	Mallee, ash Kybean	Eucalyptus kybeanensis
Magnolia, sweetbay	Magnolia virginiana	Mallee, Ash narrow-leaved	Eucalyptus apiculata
Magnolia, umbrella	Magnolia tripetala	Mallee, ash yellow-top	Eucalyptus
Magnolia vine	Schisandra chinensis		luehmanniana
Magnolia, willow-leaved	Magnolia salicifolia	Mallee, baker's	Eucalyptus bakerii
Mahoe	Hibiscus tiliaceus	Mallee, Barren mountain	Eucalyptus approximans
Mahoe	Melicytus ramiflorus	Mallee, bell-fruited	Eucalyptus preissiana
Mahoe	Thespesia populnea	Mallee, black-stemmed	Eucalyptus arachnaea
Mahoe-wao	Melicytus lanceolatus	Mallee, Blackbutt	Eucalyptus
Mahogany	Swietenia mahogani		zopherophloia
Mahogany, Blue Mountains	Eucalyptus notabilis	Mallee, blue	Eucalyptus frutecitorum
Mahogany, broad-leaved white	Eucalyptus umbra	Mallee, blue	Eucalyptus gamophylla
Mahogany, broad-leaved white	Eucalyptus umbra ssp	Mallee, blue	Eucalyptus oxymitra
	umbra	Mallee, blue desert	Eucalyptus gamophylla
Mahogany, Ceylon	Melia composita	Mallee, blue flower	Halgania cyanea
Mahogany, Dundas	Eucalyptus brockwayi	Mallee, blue-leaved	Eucalyptus cyanophylla
Mahogany, large-fruited	Eucalyptus pellita	Mallee, blue-leaved	Eucalyptus polybracteata
Mahogany, large-fruited red	Eucalyptus pellita	Mallee, bog	Eucalyptus kitsoniana
Mahogany, mountain	Cercocarpus montanus	Mallee, book	Eucalyptus kruseana
Mahogany, mountain birch-leaf	Cercocarpus betuloidess	Mallee, book-leaf	Eucalyptus kruseana
Mahogany, mountain curl-leaf	Cercocarpus ledifolius	Mallee, Boorabbin	Eucalyptus platycorys
Mahogany, narrow-leaved white	Eucalyptus tenuipes	Mallee, Boranup	Eucalyptus calcicola
Mahogany, red	Eucalyptus resinifera	Mallee, Box	Eucalyptus porosa
Mahogany, red	Khaya nyasica	Mallee, box crimson	Eucalyptus
Mahogany, southern	Eucalyptus botryoides		lansdowneana
Mahogany, swamp	Eucalyptus robusta	Mallee, Boyagin	Eucalyptus exilis
Mahogany, white	Eucalyptus acmenioides	Mallee, breakaway	Eucalyptus redacta
Mahogany, white	Eucalyptus tenuipes	Mallee, bull	Eucalyptus behriana
Maiden pink	Dianthus deltoides	Mallee, Burdett	Eucalyptus burdettiana
Maiden's tears	Silene uniflora	Mallee, Burracoppin	Eucalyptus
Maiden's wreath	Francoa ramosa		burracoppinensis
Maidenhair fern	Adiantum	Mallee, bushy	Eucalyptus dumosa
Maidenhair fern	Adiantum aethiopicum	Mallee, cap-fruited	Eucalyptus dielsii
Maidenhair fern	Adiantum pedatum	Mallee, capped	Eucalyptus pileata
Maidenhair fern, Aleutian	Adiantum aleuticum	Mallee, clay	Eucalyptus recondita
Maidenhair fern, Australian	Adiantum formosum	Mallee, coarse-flowered	Eucalyptus grossa
Maidenhair fern, Barbados	Adiantum tenerum	Mallee, coarse-leaved	Eucalyptus grossa
	'Farleyense'	Mallee, coastal dune	Eucalyptus foecunda
Maidenhair fern, brittle	Adiantum tenerum	Mallee, coastal white	Eucalyptus diversifolia
Maidenhair fern, delta	Adiantum raddianum	Mallee, Congoo	Eucalyptus dumosa
Maidenhair fern, dwarf	Adiantum aleuticum v	Mallee, crowned	Eucalyptus coronata
	subpumilum	Mallee, Cue York	Eucalyptus striaticalyx
Maidenhair fern, giant	Adiantum formosum	Mallee, curly	Eucalyptus gillii
Maidenhair fern, northern	Adiantum aleuticum	Mallee, dainty	Eucalyptus websteriana
Maidenhair fern, northern	Adiantum pedatum		ssp norsemanica
Maidenhair fern, rough	Adiantum hispidulum	Mallee, desert	Eucalyptus macrocarpa
Maidenhair fern, silver dollar	Adiantum peruvianum	Mallee, desert	Eucalyptus orbifolia
Maidenhair fern, tassel	Adiantum raddianum	Mallee, Desmond	Eucalyptus
	'Grandiceps'		desmondensis
Maidenhair fern, trailing	Adiantum caudatum	Mallee, disc-leaf	Eucalyptus orbifolia
Maidenhair fern, true	Adiantum capillus-	Mallee, Dongara	Eucalyptus obtusiflora
	veneris	Mallee, dune red	Eucalyptus pimpiniana
Maidenhair tree	Ginkgo biloba	Mallee, Ettrema	Eucalyptus sturgissiana
Maikoa	Brugmansia	Mallee, Ewart's	Eucalyptus ewartiana
Maiten	Maytenus boaria	Mallee, Fink river	Eucalyptus sessilis

Common-Botanical Names

Mallee, fluted horn — Eucalyptus stowardii
Mallee, forest — Eucalyptus aspersa
Mallee, four-winged — Eucalyptus tetraptera
Mallee, giant — Eucalyptus oleosa v oleosa
Mallee, giant blue — Eucalyptus oleosa v glauca
Mallee, Gippsland — Eucalyptus kitsoniana
Mallee, glossy-leaved — Eucalyptus oleosa
Mallee, Goldfields — Eucalyptus flavida
Mallee, gooseberry — Eucalyptus calycogona
Mallee, green — Eucalyptus viridis
Mallee, grey — Eucalyptus morrisii
Mallee, heart-leaf — Eucalyptus websteriana ssp norsemanica
Mallee, hook-leaved — Eucalyptus uncinata
Mallee, Hopetown — Eucalyptus leptocalyx
Mallee, iron bark — Eucalyptus incrassata
Mallee, Kalgan Plains — Eucalyptus pachyloma
Mallee, Kamarooka — Eucalyptus froggattii
Mallee, Kangaroo Island — Eucalyptus anceps
Mallee, Kangaroo Island — Eucalyptus lansdowneana ssp albopurpurea
Mallee, Kangaroo Island narrow-leaved — Eucalyptus cneorifolia
Mallee, Kingscote — Eucalyptus rugosa
Mallee, Kingsmill's — Eucalyptus kingsmillii
Mallee, Kopi — Eucalyptus striaticalyx
Mallee, Kruse's — Eucalyptus kruseana
Mallee, large fruited — Eucalyptus youngiana
Mallee, large-leaved spotted — Eucalyptus henryii
Mallee, laterite — Eucalyptus lateritica
Mallee, Lerp — Eucalyptus incrassata
Mallee, long-leaf — Eucalyptus macranda
Mallee, Mann Ranges — Eucalyptus mannensis
Mallee, many-flowered — Eucalyptus cooperiana
Mallee, Merrit — Eucalyptus floctoniae
Mallee, Mount Day — Eucalyptus incerata
Mallee, Mt. Gillen — Eucalyptus gillenii
Mallee, narrow-leaved — Eucalyptus angustissima
Mallee, narrow-leaved red — Eucalyptus floctoniae
Mallee, narrow-leaved red — Eucalyptus foecunda
Mallee, narrow-leaved red — Eucalyptus leptophylla
Mallee, Nundroo — Eucalyptus calcareana
Mallee, oil — Eucalyptus kochii
Mallee, oily — Eucalyptus oleosa
Mallee, Ooldea — Eucalyptus pyriformis
Mallee, Ooldea — Eucalyptus youngiana
Mallee, open-fruited — Eucalyptus annulata
Mallee, pear-fruited — Eucalyptus pyriformis
Mallee, Pimpin — Eucalyptus pimpiniana
Mallee pine — Callitris preissii ssp verrucosa
Mallee, Plunkett — Eucalyptus curtisii
Mallee, Pokolbin — Eucalyptus pumila
Mallee, Port Jackson — Eucalyptus obtusiflora
Mallee, Port Lincoln — Eucalyptus conglobata
Mallee, purple-flowered — Eucalyptus lansdowneana ssp lansdowneana
Mallee, purple-leaved — Eucalyptus pluricaulis ssp pluricaulis
Mallee, purple-leaved — Eucalyptus pluricaulis ssp porphyrea
Mallee, Quorn — Eucalyptus porosa
Mallee, Ravensthorpe — Eucalyptus pileata

Mallee, red — Eucalyptus calycogona
Mallee, red — Eucalyptus socialis
Mallee, red bud — Eucalyptus pachyphylla
Mallee, red-flowered — Eucalyptus erythronema v marginata
Mallee, ribbon-barked — Eucalyptus sheathiana
Mallee, ridge-fruited — Eucalyptus angulosa
Mallee, rose — Eucalyptus rhodantha
Mallee, rough-fruited — Eucalyptus coronata
Mallee, round-leaf — Eucalyptus orbifolia
Mallee, salt blue — Eucalyptus rigens
Mallee, salt green — Eucalyptus famelica
Mallee, salt lake — Eucalyptus halophila
Mallee, sand Goldfield's — Eucalyptus eremophila
Mallee, sand tall — Eucalyptus eremophila
Mallee, sand tall pink-flowering — Eucalyptus eremophila
Mallee, sandplain — Eucalyptus ebbanoensis
Mallee, sandplain northern — Eucalyptus gillii
Mallee, sharp-capped — Eucalyptus oxymitra
Mallee, silver — Eucalyptus crucis ssp crucis
Mallee, silver — Eucalyptus gillii
Mallee, slender — Eucalyptus decurva
Mallee, small — Eucalyptus albida
Mallee, small — Eucalyptus porosa
Mallee, soap — Eucalyptus diversifolia
Mallee, southern cross silver — Eucalyptus crucis ssp crucis
Mallee, spearwood — Eucalyptus doratoxylon
Mallee, square-fruited — Eucalyptus calycogona
Mallee, square-fruited — Eucalyptus tetraptera
Mallee, stiff leaved — Eucalyptus rigidula
Mallee, Sturt creek — Eucalyptus odontocarpa
Mallee, summer red — Eucalyptus socialis
Mallee, Tammin — Eucalyptus leptopoda
Mallee, thick-leaved — Eucalyptus pachyphylla
Mallee, Victoria desert — Eucalyptus concinna
Mallee, Victoria Spring — Eucalyptus trivalvis
Mallee, white — Eucalyptus anceps
Mallee, white — Eucalyptus cylindriflora
Mallee, white — Eucalyptus dumosa
Mallee, white — Eucalyptus erythronema
Mallee, white — Eucalyptus gracilis
Mallee, white-leaved — Eucalyptus albida
Mallee, woodline — Eucalyptus cylindrocarpa
Mallee, Woolbernup — Eucalyptus acies
Mallee, Yallata — Eucalyptus yalatensis
Mallee, Yate — Eucalyptus lehmannii
Mallee, yellow — Eucalyptus incrassata
Mallee, yellow hardy — Eucalyptus macranda
Mallee, Yumbarra — Eucalyptus yumbarrana
Mallee, Yuna — Eucalyptus jucunda
Mallet, Balladonia — Eucalyptus balladoniensis
Mallet, blue — Eucalyptus gardneri
Mallet, brown — Eucalyptus astringens
Mallet, fuchsia — Eucalyptus forestiana
Mallet, Newby's — Eucalyptus newbeyi
Mallet, Pallinup — Eucalyptus melanophitra
Mallet, salt river — Eucalyptus sargentii
Mallet, silver — Eucalyptus argyphea
Mallet, silver — Eucalyptus falcata
Mallet, Steedman's — Eucalyptus steedmannii
Mallet, swamp — Eucalyptus spathulata
Mallet, white — Eucalyptus falcata
Mallet, Yate — Eucalyptus sporadica

Common-Botanical Names

Mallow	Lavatera	Manzanita, eastwood	Arctostaphylos
Mallow	Malva		glandulosa
Mallow, annual	Malope	Manzanita, greenleaf	Arctostaphylos patula
Mallow, annual	Malope trifida	Manzanita, Parry	Arctostaphylos
Mallow, common	Malva sylvestris		manzanita
Mallow, country	Sida cordifolia	Manzanita, pine-mat	Arctostaphylos
Mallow, desert	Malva fastigiata		nevadensis
Mallow, dwarf	Malva neglecta	Manzanita, pine-nut	Arctostaphylos
Mallow, false	Sphaeralcea		nevadensis
Mallow, flood	Lavatera plebeia	Manzanita, Stanford	Arctostaphylos
Mallow, glade	Napea dioica		stanfordiana
Mallow, globe	Sphaeralcea	Manzanita, white leaf	Arctostaphylos viscida
Mallow, globe Munro's	Sphaeralcea munroana	Maple	Acer
Mallow, globe orange	Sphaeralcea munroana	Maple, amur	Acer tataricum ssp
Mallow, Hollyhock	Malva alcea		ginnala
Mallow, Indian	Abutilon	Maple, Ash-leaved	Acer negundo
Mallow, Kankakee	Sphaeralcea remota	Maple, big-leaf	Acer macrophyllum
Mallow, Kashmir tall	Lavatera cachemiriana	Maple, big-toothed	Acer saccharum ssp
Mallow, marsh salt	Kosteletzkya virginicus		grandidentatum
Mallow, musk	Malva moschata	Maple, broad-leaf	Acer macrophyllum
Mallow, musk white	Malva moschata v alba	Maple, canyon	Acer saccharum ssp
Mallow, poppy	Callirhoe		grandidentatum
Mallow, prairie	Sphaeralcea coccinea	Maple, Cappadocian	Acer cappadocicum
Mallow, prairie white	Sidalcea candida	Maple, Caucasian	Acer cappadocicum
Mallow, rose	Hibiscus lasiocarpus	Maple cherry	Sorbus torminalis
Mallow, rose common	Hibiscus moscheutos	Maple, coral-bark	Acer palmatum 'Sengo-
Mallow, rose confederate	Hibiscus mutabilis		kaku'
Mallow, rose great	Hibiscus grandiflorus	Maple, Eagle's claw	Acer platanoides
Mallow, rose hairy	Hibiscus lasiocarpus		'Laciniatum'
Mallow, rose scarlet	Hibiscus militaris	Maple, field	Acer campestre
Mallow, rose swamp	Hibiscus moscheutos	Maple, flowering	Abutilon
Mallow, seashore	Kosteletzkya	Maple, full-moon	Acer japonicum
Mallow, sleepy	Malvaviscus	Maple, Greek	Acer heldreichii ssp
Mallow, tree	Lavatera arborea		trautvetteri
Mallow, tree Cornish	Lavatera arborea	Maple, Hawthorn	Acer crataegifolium
Mallow, Venice	Hibiscus trionum	Maple, hedge	Acer campestre
Mallow, wax	Malvaviscus arboreus	Maple, Her's	Acer davidii v grosseri
Maltese cross	Lychnis chalcedonica	Maple, Hornbeam	Acer carpinifolium
Malu creeper	Bauhinia vahlii	Maple, Italian	Acer opalus
Mamaku	Cyathea medullaris	Maple, Japanese	Acer japonicum
Mamane	Sophora chrysophylla	Maple, Japanese	Acer palmatum
Mammoth tree of California	Sequoiadendron	Maple, Korean	Acer
	giganteum		pseudosieboldianum
Man fern	Dicksonia antarctica	Maple, Lobel's	Acer lobelii
Mandarin	Citrus reticulata	Maple, Manchurian	Acer mandshuricum
Mandarin's hat plant	Holmskioldia sanguinea	Maple, Montpellier	Acer monpessulanum
Mandrake	Mandragora	Maple, mountain	Acer spicatum
Mandrake, American	Podophyllum peltatum	Maple, Nikko	Acer maximowiczianum
Mandrake, Autumn	Mandragora autumnalis	Maple, Norway	Acer platanoides
Mandrake, common	Mandragora officinarum	Maple, oblong leaf	Acer oblongum
Mandrake, European	Mandragora officinarum	Maple, Oregon	Acer macrophyllum
Mangard	Acacia acuminata	Maple, painted	Acer truncatum v mono
Mango	Mangifera indica	Maple, paper-bark	Acer griseum
Mangosteen, Malayan	Garcinia buchananii	Maple, parlour	Abutilon
Mangosteen, yellow	Randia fitzalanii	Maple, Pere David's	Acer davidii
Manioc	Manihot esculenta	Maple, Queensland	Flindersia brayleyana
Manketti tree	Schinziophyton	Maple, red	Acer rubrum
	rautenenii	Maple, red bud	Acer heldreichii ssp
Manuka	Leptospermum		trautvetteri
	scoparium	Maple, redleaf	Acer palmatum
Manuka	Leptospermum		atropurpureum
	scoparium roseum	Maple, rock	Acer saccharum
Manzanita	Arbutus	Maple, Rocky Mountain	Acer glabrum
Manzanita	Arctostaphylos	Maple, rough-barked	Acer triflorum
Manzanita, bigberry	Arctostaphylos glauca	Maple, scarlet	Acer rubrum
Manzanita, dune	Arctostaphylos pumila	Maple, Shantung	Acer truncatum

Common-Botanical Names

Maple, silver	Acer saccharinum	Marjoram, mastic	Thymus mastichiana
Maple, snake-bark	Acer capillipes	Marjoram, pot	Origanum onites
Maple, snake-bark	Acer davidii	Marjoram, small-leaved	Origanum microphylla
Maple, snake-bark	Acer pensylvanicum	Marjoram, Spanish	Thymus mastichiana
Maple, snake-bark	Acer rufinerve	Marjoram, sweet	Origanum majorana
Maple, striped	Acer pensylvanicum	Marjoram, wild	Origanum vulgare
Maple, sugar	Acer saccharum	Marjoram, wild golden	Origanum vulgare
Maple, swamp	Acer rubrum		'Aureum'
Maple, Tatarian	Acer tataricum	Marlberry	Ardisia japonica
Maple, threadleaf	Acer palmatum	Marlock, Bald Island	Eucalyptus
	atropurpureum		conferruminata
	dissectum group	Marlock, Bald Island	Eucalyptus lehmannii
Maple, three-toothed	Acer buergerianum	Marlock, black	Eucalyptus redunca
Maple, trident	Acer buergerianum	Marlock, long-flowered	Eucalyptus macarthurii
Maple, vine	Acer circinatum	Marlock, long-flowered	Eucalyptus macranda
Mar(r)i, pink-flowered	Eucalyptus calophylla	Marlock, silver	Eucalyptus tetragona
	rosea	Marmalade bush	Streptosolen jamesonii
Mar(r)i, white	Eucalyptus calophylla	Maro	Callitris preissii
Maracuja de refresco	Passiflora alata	Marpoo	Acacia ligulata
Marama nut	Tylosema esculenta	Marri, mountain	Eucalyptus
Maravilla	Mirabilis multiflora		haematoxylon
Marbled rainbow plant	Billbergia Fantasia Group	Marsh andromeda	Andromeda polifolia
Marbleseed	Onosmodium mollis	Marsh felwort	Swertia perennis
Mardja	Haemodorum	Marsh mallow	Althaea officinalis
	paniculatum	Marsh marigold	Caltha
Mardja	Haemodorum spicatum	Marsh marigold	Caltha palustris
Mare's fart	Senecio jacobaea	Marsh marigold, giant	Caltha palustris v
Marguerite	Argyranthemum		palustris
Marguerite	Leucanthemum vulgare	Marsh orchid	Dactylorhiza
Marguerite, blue	Felicia amelloides	Marsh orchid, robust	Dactylorhiza elata
Marguerite, golden	Anthemis tinctoria	Marsh pink	Sabatia angularis
	'Kelwayi'	Marula	Sclerocarya birrea ssp
Marigold	Arctotis acaulis		caffra
Marigold	Calendula	Marvel of Peru	Mirabilis jalapa
Marigold	Ursinia anthemoides	Mary 's taper	Galanthus nivalis
Marigold, African	Tagetes African Group	Mascarena	Hyophorbe
Marigold, Afro-French	Tagetes Afro-French	Mask flower	Alonsoa
	Group	Masterwort	Astrantia
Marigold, Aztec	Tagetes erecta	Masterwort	Peucedanum ostrutium
Marigold, corn	Chrysanthemum	Masterwort, great	Astrantia major
	segetum	Masterwort, lesser	Astrantia minor
Marigold, desert	Baileya multiradiata	Mastic, Chinese	Pistacia chinensis
Marigold, English	Calendula	Mastic tree	Pistacia lentiscus
Marigold, French	Tagetes French Group	Mastic tree, Peruvian	Schinus molle
Marigold, gold	Chrysanthemum	Mat rush	Lomandra
	segetum	Mat rush	Lomandra hastilis
Marigold, hens-and-chickens	Calendula officinalis	Mat rush	Lomandra purpurea
	'Prolifera'	Mat rush, pale	Lomandra glauca
Marigold, Himalayan	Tagetes lunulata	Mat rush, spiny-headed	Lomandra longifolia
Marigold, marsh	Caltha	Matacabra	Ipomoea carnea
Marigold, Mexican	Tagetes minuta	Matagallo	Phlomis purpurea
Marigold, nematocidal	Tagetes minuta	Matchweed	Gutierrezia
Marigold, pot	Calendula	Maten	Maytenus boaria
Marigold, Signet Group	Tagetes	Matilija poppy	Romneya
Marigold, vining	Tagetes lacera	Matrimony vine	Lycium barbarum
Mariola	Solanum hindsianum	Matrimony vine, Chinese	Lycium chinense
Mariposa tulip	Calochortus	Mauto	Lysiloma divaricata
Mariposa, yellow	Calochortus luteus	May	Crataegus laevigata
Marjoram	Origanum	May apple	Podophyllum peltatum
Marjoram, common	Origanum vulgare	May apple, Himalayan	Podophyllum
Marjoram, compact	Origanum vulgare		hexandrum
	'Compactum'	May pops	Passiflora incarnata
Marjoram, French	Origanum onites	May, swamp	Leptospermum
Marjoram, golden	Origanum majorana		liversidgei
	'Aurea'	May, wild	Baeckia virgata
Marjoram, hop	Origanum dictamnus	Mayali	Banksia dentata

Common-Botanical Names

Common	Botanical	Common	Botanical
Mayflower	Epigaea repens	Mexican creeper	Antigonon leptopus
Mayflower, Canada	Maianthemum canadense	Mexican fern palm	Dioon edule
		Mexican firecracker	Echeveria setosa
Mayten tree	Maytenus boaria	Mexican flame bush	Calliandra tweedii
Maytenus, willow	Maytenus bachmannii	Mexican flame leaf	Euphorbia pulcherrima
Mayweed	Matricaria	Mexican flame vine	Senecio confusus
Meadow beauty	Rhexia virginica	Mexican foxglove	Tetranema roseum
Meadow foam	Limnanthes douglasii	Mexican giant	Pachycereus pringlei
Meadow rue	Thalictrum	Mexican grass plant	Dasylirion longissimum
Meadow rue	Thalictrum polyganum	Mexican hat, red	Ratibida columnifera (red form)
Meadow rue, early	Thalictrum dioicum		
Meadow rue, lesser	Thalictrum minus	Mexican horncone	Ceratozamia mexicana
Meadow rue, purple	Thalictrum dasycarpum	Mexican orange blossom	Choisya
Meadow rue, tall	Thalictrum revolutum	Mexican sunflower	Tithonia
Meadow rue, waxy	Thalictrum revolutum	Mexican tea	Chenopodium ambrosioides
Meadow rue, yellow	Thalictrum flavum		
Meadow saffron	Cochicum autumnale	Mexican tulip poppy	Hunnemannia fumariifolia
Meadowsweet	Filipendula ulmaria		
Meadowsweet	Spiraea alba	Mexican violet	Tetranema roseum
Meadowsweet, pink	Spiraea alba rosea	Mezereon	Daphne mezereum
Mealy Bundy	Eucalyptus nortonii	Miami mist	Phacelia purshii
Medick	Medicago	Michaelmas daisy	Aster novi-belgii
Medick, black	Medicago lupulina	Mickey mouse plant	Ochna serrulata
Medick, tree	Medicago arborea	Midgen berry	Austromyrtus dulcis
Medlar	Mespilus germanica	Midsummer men	Rhodiola rosea
Medlar, Bronvaux	+Crataegomespilus dardarii	Mielieheide	Erica patersonia
		Mignonette	Reseda
Medlar, false	Sophora chamaemespilus	Mignonette, common	Reseda odorata
		Mignonette tree	Lawsonia
Medlar, Japanese	Eriobotrya japonica	Mignonette tree	Lawsonia inermis
Medlar, wild	Vangueria infausta	Mignonette vine	Anredera cordifolia
Medlar, wild forest	Vangueria esculenta	Mignonette, wild	Reseda lutea
Medusa's head	Euphorbia caput-medusae	Migum	Eucalyptus leucophloia
		Mile-a-minute climber	Stictocardia beraviensis
Mee Mee	Myoporum tenuifolium	Mile-a-minute plant	Fallopia baldschuanica
Melaleuca, tangling	Melaleuca cardiophylla	Milfoil	Achillea millefolium
Melic(k)	Melica	Milfoil	Myriophyllum
Melic(k), Siberian	Melica altissima	Milfoil, diamond	Myriophyllum aquaticum
Melic, silky spike	Melica ciliata	Milfoil, dwarf	Achillea nana
Melick, mountain	Melica nutans	Milfoil, water whorled	Myriophyllum v erticillatum
Melick, wood	Melica nutans		
Melilot	Melilotus officinalis	Milfoil, Western	Myriophyllum hippuroides
Melilot, common	Melilotus officinalis		
Melilot, ribbed	Melilotus officinalis	Miljee	Acacia oswaldii
Melilot, white	Melilotus alba	Milk bush	Gomphocarpus fruticosus
Melissa, Turkish	Dracocephalum moldavica		
		Milk maidens	Primula veris
Melon, wild	Citrullus lanatus	Milkmaids	Burchardia
Meloncillo	Passiflora suberosa	Milkvetch, Canadian	Astragalus canadensis
Merrybells	Uvularia	Milkvetch, Chinese	Astragalus chinensis
Merrybells, great	Uvularia grandiflora	Milkvetch, Chinese	Astragalus membranaceus
Merrybells, large	Uvularia grandiflora		
Mescal bean tree	Sophora secundiflora	Milkvetch, cicer	Astragalus cicer
Mescal button	Lophophora williamsii	Milkvetch, Mogollon	Astragalus lentiginosus
Mesquite	Prosopis juliflora	Milkvetch, Platte	Astragalus plattensis
Mesquite, Chilean	Prosopis glandulosa	Milkvetch, Portuguese	Astragalus lusitanicus
Mesquite, screwbean	Prosopis pubescens	Milkweed	Asclepias
Messmate	Eucalyptus obliqua	Milkweed	Euphorbia
Messmate, Gympie	Eucalyptus cloeziana	Milkweed	Xysmalobium undulata
Messmate, red	Eucalyptus resinifera	Milkweed, climbing	Funastrum crispum
Messmate, swamp	Eucalyptus robusta	Milkweed, common	Asclepias syriaca
Messmate, yellow	Eucalyptus cloeziana	Milkweed, prairie	Asclepias sullivantii
Messmate, yellow	Eucalyptus exserta	Milkweed, purple	Asclepias purpurascens
Metake	Pseudosasa japonica	Milkweed, sand	Asclepias amplexicaulis
Mexican blood flower	Distictis buccinatoria	Milkweed, short green	Asclepias viridiflora
Mexican bush sage	Salvia leucantha	Milkweed, spider	Asclepias viridis

Common-Botanical Names

Common	Botanical
Milkweed, swamp	Asclepias incarnata
Milkweed, tall green	Asclepias hirtella
Milkweed, whorled	Asclepias verticillata
Milkwood, white	Sideroxylon inerme
Milkwort	Polygala
Milkwort	Polygala calcarea
Milkwort, blue-spike	Comesperma calymega
Millet	Panicum miliaceum
Millet, dragon's claw	Eleusine coracana
Millet, finger	Eleusine coracana
Millet, golden wood	Milium effusum 'Aureum'
Millet, Italian	Setaria italica
Millet, native (AU)	Panicum decompositum
Millet, wood	Milium effusum
Mimicry plant	Cheiridopsis peculiaris
Mimicry plant	Pleiospilos bolusii
Mimidi	Xanthorrhoea gracilis
Mimosa	Acacia dealbata
Mimosa	Albizia julibrissin
Mimosa bush	Acacia formesiana
Mimosa, florists	Acacia decurrens
Mimosa, Texas	Acacia gregii
Mind your own business	Soleirolia soleirolii
Mindiyed	Melaleuca nesophila
Mineritchi	Acacia cyperophylla
Mingerhout	Breonadia salicina
Miniature holly	Malpighia coccigera
Miniritchie	Acacia grasbyi
Miniritchie, sweet-scented	Acacia trachycarpa
Mint	Mentha
Mint, apple	Mentha suaveolens
Mint, Austrian	Mentha x gracilis
Mint, Bowles'	Mentha x villosa f alopecuroides
Mint bush	Elsholtzia stauntonii
Mint bush	Prostanthera
Mint bush, alpine	Prostanthera cuneata
Mint bush, Australian	Prostanthera
Mint bush, Costa Rican	Satureja viminea
Mint bush, oval-leaved	Prostanthera ovalifolia
Mint bush, round-leaved	Prostanthera rotundifolia
Mint bush, snowy	Prostanthera nivea
Mint bush, striped	Prostanthera striatiflora
Mint, candy	Mentha x piperata
Mint, Chinese	Mentha haplocalyx
Mint, chocolate	Mentha x piperata
Mint, Corsican	Mentha requienii
Mint, coyote	Monardella odoratissima
Mint, Egyptian	Mentha nilaca
Mint, English	Mentha spicata cvs
Mint, field	Mentha arvensis
Mint, Florida	Micromeria
Mint, Florida	Micromeria brownii
Mint, ginger	Mentha x gracilis 'Variegata'
Mint, green pea mint	Mentha spicata
Mint, horse	Mentha longifolia
Mint, horse	Monarda punctata
Mint, horse common	Pycnanthemum tenuifolium
Mint, Jamaican	Micromeria viminea
Mint, Korean	Agastache rugosa
Mint, lemon	Monarda citriodora
Mint, mountain	Micromeria thymifolia
Mint, mountain	Pycnanthemum incanum

Common	Botanical
Mint, mountain	Pycnanthemum pilosum
Mint, mountain	Pycnanthemum virginianum
Mint, mountain common	Pycnanthemum tenuifolium
Mint, mountain hairy	Pycnanthemum pilosum
Mint, mountain hoary	Pycnanthemum pycnanthemoides
Mint, peppermint	Mentha x piperata
Mint, pineapple	Mentha suaveolens 'Variegata'
Mint, Roman	Micromeria sp
Mint shrub	Elsholtzia
Mint shrub	Elshotzia stauntonii
Mint, spearmint	Mentha spicata
Mint, squaw	Hedeoma pulegioides
Mint, stone	Cunila origanoides
Mint, Vietnamese	Mentha x gracilis
Mint, water	Mentha aquatica
Mint, wild	Mentha longifolia ssp capensis
Mint, wild	Mentha longifolia ssp wissii
Mint-balm	Elsholtzia stauntonii
Mintbush, Jamaican	Hedeoma viminea
Mintleaf	Plectranthus madagascariensis
Mired	Eucalyptus celastroides
Mirret	Eucalyptus celastroides
Mirror orchid	Ophrys vernixia
Miss Wilmott's ghost	Eryngium giganteum
Mission bells	Fritillaria affinis
Mistflower	Eupatorium coelestinum
Mistflower	Eupatorium rugosum
Mistletoe	Viscum album
Mitrewort	Mitella
Moccasin flower	Cypripedium acaule
Mock orange	Philadelphus
Mock orange	Philadelphus coronarius
Mock orange	Styrax americanus
Mock orange, Australian	Pittosporum undulatum
Mock orange, Japanese	Pittosporum tobira
Moer, karee	Trichodiadema stellatum
Moidj	Eucalyptus occidentalis
Moit	Eucalyptus decipiens
Moitch	Eucalyptus rudis
Mole plant	Euphorbia lathyris
Mole's spectacles	Craterostigma wilmsii
Monarch of the East	Sauromatum venosum
Monarch of the Veldt	Arctotis fastuosa
Monarda, Bradbury's	Monarda bradburniana
Money tree	Crassula ovata
Money wort	Lysimachia
Moneywort	Lysimachia nummularia
Moneywort, golden	Lysimachia nummularia 'Aurea'
Monkey cup	Nepenthes
Monkey flower	Mimulus
Monkey flower	Mimulus guttatus
Monkey flower, allegheny	Mimulus ringens
Monkey flower, orange	Mimulus aurantiacus
Monkey flower, red	Mimulus lewisii
Monkey flower, red	Mimulus puniceus
Monkey flower, scarlet	Mimulus cardinalis
Monkey flower, square-stemmed	Mimulus ringens

Common-Botanical Names

Monkey flower, winged	Mimulus alatus	Mosquito plant	Azolla filiculoides
Monkey flower, yellow	Mimulus aurantiacus	Moss, locust	Robinia hispida
Monkey musk	Mimulus laurantiacus	Moss rose	Portulaca
Monkey nut	Hicksbeachia pinnatifolia	Moss, Spanish	Tillandsia usneoides
Monkey plant	Ruellia makoyana	Moss, water	Fontinalis antipyretica
Monkey pod	Enterolobium cyclocarpum	Mosse;baaikalkoentjie	Tritonia crocata
		Moth orchid	Phalaenopsis
Monkey pod	Senna petersiana	Mother of pearl plant	Graptopetalum paraguayense
Monkey puzzle	Araucaria araucana		
Monkey rope	Secamone alpini	Mother of thousands	Cymbalaria muralis
Monkey thorn, black	Acacia burkei	Mother of thousands	Saxifraga stolonifera 'Tricolor'
Monkey-bread tree	Adansonia digitata		
Monkshood	Aconitum	Mother of thousands	Soleirolia soleirolii
Monkshood, English	Aconitum napellus	Mother of thyme	Acinos arvensis
Monkshood, yellow	Aconitum anthora	Mother-in-law's cushion	Echinocactus grusonii
Montbretia	Crocosmia	Mother-in-law's seat	Echinocactus grusonii
Moon flower	Stellaria holostea	Mother-in-law's tongue	Dieffenbachia
Moon trefoil	Medicago arborea	Mother-in-law's tongue	Sansevieria trifasciata
Moonah	Melaleuca lanceolata	Motherum-bung	Acacia cheelii
Moonflower	Ipomoea alba	Motherumbah	Acacia cheelii
Moonseed	Menispermum	Motherwort	Leonurus cardiaca
Moonseed, Canada	Menispermum canadense	Motherwort, Siberian	Leonurus sibiricus
		Mottlecah	Eucalyptus macrocarpa
Moonseed, Canadian	Menispermum canadense	Mottlecah, rose	Eucalyptus macrocarpa
		Mottlecah, small-leaved	Eucalyptus macrocarpa
Moonstones	Pachyphytum oviferum	Mountain ash, American	Sorbus aucuparia
Moonwort	Botrychium lunaria	Mountain ash, cascade	Sorbus scopulina
Moor-King	Pedicularis sceptrum-carolinum	Mountain ash, European	Sorbus aucuparia
		Mountain ash, Korean	Sorbus alnifolia
Moort, coastal	Eucalyptus platypus v heterophylla	Mountain ash, showy	Sorbus decora
		Mountain ash, Sitka	Sorbus sitchensis
Moort, red-flowered	Eucalyptus nutans	Mountain balm	Calamintha officinalis
Moort, round-leaved	Eucalyptus platypus v platypus	Mountain berry, pink	Cyathodes parviflora
		Mountain devil	Lambertia formosa
Moort, thicket	Eucalyptus platypus ssp congregata	Mountain ebony	Bauhinia variegata
		Mountain fringe	Adlumia fungosa
Mop, woolly pink	Isopogon baxteri	Mountain mint, slender	Pycnanthemum tenuifolium
Mopane	Colophospermum mopane		
		Mountain pepper	Drimys lanceolata
Mopani, false large	Guibourtia coleosperma	Mountain phlox	Linanthus grandiflorus
Moradilla	Conyza carminifolia	Mountain pine	Pinus mugo sspuncinata
Moreton Bay pine	Araucaria cunninghamii	Mountain pine, dwarf	Pinus mugo
Moril	Eucalyptus longicornis	Mountain pride	Penstemon newberryi
Mormon tea	Ephedra nevadensis	Mountain rocket	Bellendena montana
Mormon tea	Ephedra viridis	Mountain rose	Protea nana
Morning glory	Ipomoea	Mountain sanicle	Astrantia major
Morning glory, beach	Ipomoea brasiliensis	Mountain sow thistle	Cicerbita alpina
Morning glory, bush	Convolvulus	Mountain tassel	Soldanella montana
Morning glory, bush	Ipomoea leptophylla	Mountain thistle	Acanthus montanus
Morning glory, common	Ipomoea purpurea	Mountain tobacco	Arnica montana
Morning glory, goats foot	Ipomoea pes-caprae	Mourning widow	Geranium phaeum
Morning glory, Mexican	Rivea corymbosa	Mouse plant	Arisarum proboscideum
Morning glory, poison	Ipomoea muelleri	Mouse-ear, alpine	Cerastium alpinum
Morning glory, red	Ipomoea coccinea	Mousewood	Acer pensylvanicum
Morning glory, rock	Ipomoea costata	Moutan	Paeonia suffruticosa
Morning glory, silver	Argyreia splendens	Mrs. Frizell's lady fern	Athyrium filix-femina 'Frizelliae'
Morning glory, star	Ipomoea coccinea		
Morning glory, tangled	Polymeria ambigua	Mrs. Robb's bonnet	Euphorbia amygdaloides v robbiae
Morning glory, yellow	Merremia tuberosa		
Morrel, black	Eucalyptus melanoxylon	Msasa	Brachystegia spiciformis
Morrell, red	Eucalyptus longicornis	Mudelka	Eucalyptus macrocarpa
Morrison	Verticordia nitens	Mudja	Nuytsia floribunda
Mortina	Vaccinum floribundum	Mugga	Eucalyptus sideroxylon
Moses-in-the-cradle	Tradescantia spathacea	Muggar	Artemisia vulgaris
Mosquito bills	Dodecatheon hendersonii	Mugwort	Artemisia
		Mugwort	Artemisia vulgaris

Common-Botanical Names

Mugwort, Western	Artemisia ludoviciana
Mugwort, white	Artemisia lactiflora
Muhly, spike	Muhlenbergia wrightii
Muisdoring	Acacia hebeclada ssp hebeclada
Muishondblaar	Plectranthus australis
Muishondblaar	Plectranthus fruticosus
Mulberry	Morus
Mulberry, black	Morus nigra
Mulberry, French	Callicarpa americana
Mulberry, paper	Broussonetia papyrifera
Mulberry, red	Morus rubra
Mulberry, Russian	Morus alba
Mulberry, white	Morus alba
Mule's ears	Wyethia angustifolia
Mulga, broad-leaved	Acacia craspedocarpa
Mulga, grey	Acacia brachybotra
Mulga, Hop	Acacia craspedocarpa
Mulga, large-podded	Acacia aneura v macrocarpa
Mulga, narrow-leaf	Acacia ramulosa
Mulga, red	Acacia cyperophylla
Mulga, silver	Acacia argyrophylla
Mulga, slender	Acacia tenuissima
Mulga, turpentine	Acacia brachystachya
Mulga, umbrella	Acacia brachystachya
Mulga, Wanderry	Acacia linophylla
Mulga, weeping	Acacia paraneura
Mulga wood	Acacia aneura
Mulla mulla, common	Ptilotus polystachyus
Mulla mulla, ear-leaved	Ptilotus auriculifolius
Mulla mulla, green	Ptilotus macrocephalus
Mulla mulla, hairy	Ptilotus helipteroides
Mulla mulla, mat	Ptilotus axillaris
Mulla mulla, pink	Ptilotus exaltatus
Mulla mulla, purple	Ptilotus exaltatus
Mulla mulla, shrubby	Ptilotus obovatus
Mulla mulla, silver	Ptilotus obovatus
Mulla mulla, tall	Ptilotus exaltatus
Mulla mulla, weeping	Ptilotus carlostachyus
Mullein	Verbascum
Mullein, common	Verbascum thapsus
Mullein, dark	Verbascum nigrum
Mullein, great	Verbascum thapsus
Mullein, Greek	Verbascum olympicum
Mullein, large-flowered	Verbascum densiflorum
Mullein, moth	Verbascum blattaria
Mullein, nettle-leaved	Verbascum chaixii
Mullein, Olympic	Verbascum olympicum
Mullein pinks	Lychnis coronaria
Mullein, purple	Verbascum phoeniceum
Mullein, Turkish	Verbascum bombyciferum
Mullein, white	Verbascum lychnitis
Mullein, woolly	Verbascum phlomoides
Mullimbimby marvel	Macadamia ternifolia
Munjerenje	Albizia adianthifolia
Murd	Eucalyptus platypus v platypus
Murray pine	Callitris columellaris
Murray pine	Callitris preissii ssp murrayensis
Musk	Mimulus
Musk cucumber	Sicana odorifera
Musk flower	Mimulus moschatus
Musk, yellow	Mimulus luteus

Mustard, Mithridate	Thlaspi arvense
Mustard, treacle	Thlaspi arvense
Muzzlewood	Eucalyptus stellulata
Myall, coast	Acacia binervia
Myall, coast	Acacia glaucescens
Myall, fragrant	Acacia stenophylla
Myall, weeping	Acacia pendula
Myall, western	Acacia papyrocarpa
Myallie (Mallalie)	Eucalyptus eudesmoides ssp eudesmoides
Myriad leaf	Myriophyllum verticillatum
Myrobalan	Phyllanthus emblica
Myrobalan	Prunus cerasifera
Myrrh	Commiphora myrrha
Myrrh, garden	Myrrhis odorata
Myrtle	Myrtus
Myrtle, apple fine-leaf	Angophora bakeri
Myrtle, bog	Myrica gale
Myrtle, camphor	Baeckea camphorosmae
Myrtle, Cape	Myrsine africana
Myrtle, common	Myrtus communis
Myrtle, drooping	Melaleuca armillaris
Myrtle, fringe	Calytrix tetragona
Myrtle, German	Myrtus communis ssp tarentina
Myrtle, Greek	Myrtus communis
Myrtle, grey	Backhousia myrtifolia
Myrtle, heath	Thryptomene
Myrtle, honey	Melaleuca radula
Myrtle, honey bracelet	Melaleuca armillaris
Myrtle, honey broom	Melaleuca uncinata
Myrtle, honey chenille	Melaleuca huegelii
Myrtle, honey cork-bark	Melaleuca suberosa
Myrtle, honey creamy	Melaleuca acuminata
Myrtle, honey creekline	Melaleuca hamulosa
Myrtle, honey cross-leaved	Melaleuca decussata
Myrtle, honey dainty	Melaleuca tenella
Myrtle, honey desert	Melaleuca glomerata
Myrtle, honey feather	Melaleuca thymifolia
Myrtle, honey glowing	Melaleuca urceolaris
Myrtle, honey graceful	Melaleuca radula
Myrtle, honey granite	Melaleuca elliptica
Myrtle, honey green	Melaleuca diosmifolia
Myrtle, honey grey	Melaleuca incana
Myrtle, honey heart-leaf	Melaleuca cordata
Myrtle, honey hidden	Melaleuca undulata
Myrtle, honey hillock	Melaleuca hypericifolia
Myrtle, honey inland	Melaleuca pauperifolia
Myrtle, honey lemon	Melaleuca densa
Myrtle, honey limestone	Melaleuca quadrifaria
Myrtle, honey Mallee	Melaleuca brevifolia
Myrtle, honey Mallee	Melaleuca neglecta
Myrtle, honey marsh	Melaleuca teretifolia
Myrtle, honey mauve	Melaleuca glaberrima
Myrtle, honey pretty	Melaleuca tricophylla
Myrtle, honey pungent	Melaleuca leiocarpa
Myrtle, honey purple	Melaleuca violacea
Myrtle, honey rosy	Melaleuca diosmatifolia
Myrtle, honey rough	Melaleuca scabra (tall)
Myrtle, honey rough	Melaleuca scabra v tuberculata
Myrtle, honey salt lake	Melaleuca thyoides
Myrtle, honey sand	Melaleuca striata
Myrtle, honey scarlet	Melaleuca fulgens
Myrtle, honey scented	Melaleuca acuminata

Common-Botanical Names

Common name	Botanical name
Myrtle, honey silky	Melaleuca holosericea
Myrtle, honey slender	Melaleuca gibbosa
Myrtle, honey Steedman's	Melaleuca steedmannii
Myrtle, honey swamp	Melaleuca squamea
Myrtle, honey thyme	Melaleuca thymifolia
Myrtle, honey violet	Melaleuca violacea
Myrtle, honey violet	Melaleuca wilsonii
Myrtle, honey wiry	Melaleuca filifolia
Myrtle, honey wiry	Melaleuca nematophylla
Myrtle, iridescent	Melaleuca scabra
Myrtle, juniper	Agonis juniperina
Myrtle, lemon-scented	Backhousia citriodora
Myrtle, lemon-scented	Darwinia citriodora
Myrtle, mattress	Melaleuca biconvexa
Myrtle, mini purple	Melaleuca spathulata dw
Myrtle, peppermint	Agonis flexuosa
Myrtle, pink	Metrosideros queenslandica
Myrtle, pompom purple	Melaleuca conothamnoides
Myrtle, pompom yellow	Melaleuca megacephala
Myrtle, pretty pink	Kunzea pauciflora
Myrtle, prickly	Rhapithamnus spinosus
Myrtle, purple	Melaleuca spathulata
Myrtle, snow	Calytrix alpestris
Myrtle, spiny	Melaleuca pungens
Myrtle, Swan River	Hypocalymma angustifolium
Myrtle, Swan River	Hypocalymma robustum
Myrtle, wattle rock	Melaleuca citrina
Myrtle, wattle sand	Melaleuca thymoides
Myrtle, wax southern	Myrica cerifera
Myrtle, western tea	Melaleuca nesophila
Myrtle, white	Hypocalymma angustifolium
Myrtle, willow	Agonis flexuosa
Myrtleberry	Ugni molinae
Nainga	Eucalyptus phoenicia
Naked ladies	Colchicum
Namib tsamma	Citrullus ecirrhosus
Nana-berry	Rhus dentata
Nannyberry	Viburnum lentago
Napuka	Hebe speciosa
Naranjilla	Solanum quitoense
Nardoo, common	Marsilea drummondii
Narukalja	Hakea francisiana
Nasturtium	Tropaeolum majus
Nasturtium, flame	Tropaeolum
Nasturtium, garden	Tropaeolum majus
Natal grass	Melinis repens
Natal ivy	Ficus natalensis
Natal ivy	Senecio macroglossus
Natal palm	Carissa macrocarpa
Natal plane	Ochna natalita
Natalkatjiepiering	Gardenia cornuta
Natalse geelkeur	Calpurnia aurea ssp aurea
Navajo tea, showy	Thelesperma filifolia
Navelwort	Omphalodes
Navelwort	Umbilicus rupestris
Navelwort, Venus'	Omphalodes linifolia
Nawashiro-gumi	Elaeagnus pungens
Ndea	Sarcocephalus xanthoxylon
Nealie	Acacia loderi
Nealie	Acacia rigens
Nealie, dwarf	Acacia wilhelmiana
Nectarine	Prunus persica v nectarina
Nedik	Bossiaea aquifolium
Needle and thread	Stipa comata
Needle bush	Azima tetracantha
Needlebark	Eucalyptus planchoniana
Needlebush	Hakea gilbertii
Needlebush	Hakea sericea
Needlebush, bag	Hakea recurva
Needles and corks	Hakea obliqua
Needlewood	Hakea leucoptera
Needlewood, willow	Hakea macreana
Neem	Melia azedarach
Neem tree	Azadarichta indica
Nelia	Acacia loderi
Nentabos	Kalanchoe rotundifolia
Nerve plant	Fittonia
Net bush	Calothamnus
Net bush, cliff	Calothamnus rupestris
Net bush, common	Calothamnus quadrifolia
Net bush, crimson	Calothamnus quadrifidus
Net bush, granite	Calothamnus rupestris
Net bush, hairy	Calothamnus quadrifidus
Net bush, rough	Calothamnus asper
Net bush, silky	Calothamnus villosus
Net bush, woolly	Calothamnus villosus
Net-leaf, painted	Fittonia verschaffeltii
Nettle, flame	Solenostemon
Nettle, flame	Solenostemon scutellarioides
Nettle, hedge	Stachys
Nettle, mid-eastern	Urtica pilulifera
Nettle, painted	Solenostemon
Nettle, painted	Solenostemon scutellarioides
Nettle, purple stingless	Lamium purpureum
Nettle, smooth hedge	Stachys tenuifolia
Nettle, stinging annual	Urtica urens
Nettle, stinging perennial	Urtica dioica
Nettle tree	Celtis
Nettle tree, southern	Celtis australis
Nettle, wood	Laportea canadensis
Neverfail	Eragrostis setifolia
New Caledonian pine	Araucaria columnaris
New England aster	Aster novae-angliae
New Guinea creeper	Mucuna bennettii
New Jersey tea	Ceanothus americanus
New York aster	Aster novi-belgii
New Zealand Burr	Acaena
New Zealand daisy	Celmisia
New Zealand flax	Phormium tenax
Ngaio	Myoporum laetum
Ngbaka	Sarcocephalus xanthoxylon
Ngow	Melaleuca elliptica
Ngural	Myoporum platycarpum
Ngyamingyaming	Rhodanthe manglesii
Nightshade, black	Solanum nigrum
Nightshade, deadly	Atropa belladonna
Nightshade, Indian	Solanum khasianum
Nightshade, rock	Solanum petrophilum
Nightshade, soda apple	Solanum aculeatissimum
Nightshade, Thargomindah	Solanum sturtianum
Nightshade, yellow-berried	Solanum xanthocarpum

Common-Botanical Names

Common	Botanical	Common	Botanical
Nikko fir	Abies homolepis	Oak, evergreen	Quercus ilex
Nine bark	Physocarpus malvaceus	Oak fern	Gymnopcarpium dryopteris
Nine bark	Physocarpus opulifolius		
Nine bark, prairie	Physocarpus opulifolius	Oak, forest	Quercus torulosa
Nineawn, purple head	Enneapogon oblongus	Oak, Hill's	Quercus ellipsoidalis
Ninebark	Physocarpus opulifolius	Oak, holly	Quercus ilex
Nipple fig	Ficus watkinsiana	Oak, Holm	Quercus ilex
Nipple fruit	Solanum mammosum	Oak, Hungarian	Quercus frainetto
Nirre	Nothofagus antarctica	Oak, Indian	Barringtonia acutangular
Nitre bush	Nitraria billardierei	Oak, Kermes	Quercus coccifera
Noble bamboo	Himalayacalamus falconeri	Oak, Korean	Quercus acutissima
		Oak, Lebanon	Quercus libani
Noble fir	Abies procera	Oak, live Californian	Quercus agrifolia
Nodding onion	Allium cernuum	Oak, live coast	Quercus agrifolia
Noni fruit	Morinda citrifolia	Oak, Lucombe	Quercus x lucombeana 'William Lucombe'
Nonsuch	Medicago lupulina		
Noon-flower	Disphyma clavellatum	Oak, Lusitanian	Quercus lusitanica
Noon-flower, rounded	Disphyma crassifolium	Oak, Mirbeck's	Quercus canariensis
Nordmann fir	Abies nordmammiana	Oak, mountain silver	Brachylaena rotundata
Norfolk Island pine	Araucaria heterophylla	Oak, Northern pin	Quercus ellipsoidalis
Norse fire plant	Columnea 'Stavanger'	Oak, Oregon	Quercus garryana
Northern bangalow palm	Archontophoenix alexandrae	Oak, oriental white	Quercus aliena
		Oak, pedunculate	Quercus robur
Norway spruce	Picea abies	Oak, pine	Quercus palustris
Notsung	Halleria lucida	Oak, Pontine	Quercus pontica
November shower	Cassia multijuga	Oak, red	Quercus borealis
Nui xi	Achyranthes bidentata	Oak, red	Quercus rubra
Numnum	Carissa macrocarpa	Oak, river salt	Casuarina obesa
Nutmeg	Myristica fragrans	Oak, sawtooth	Quercus acutissima
Nutmeg bush	Iboza riparia	Oak, scarlet	Quercus coccinea
Nutmeg flower	Nigella sativa	Oak, sessile	Quercus petraea
Nutmeg tree, California	Torreya californica	Oak, she	Casuarina
Nutmeg yew	Torreya	Oak, she black	Casuarina cristata
Nutwood	Terminalia arostrata	Oak, she black	Casuarina pauper
Nuxia, forest	Nuxia floribunda	Oak, she black	Casuarina suberosa
Nyala tree	Xanthocercis zambesiaca	Oak, she coastal	Casuarina equisetifolia
Nymoo	Myoporum acuminatum	Oak, she coastal	Casuarina equisetifolia ssp incana
Oak	Quercus		
Oak, Algerian	Quercus lusitanica mirbeckii	Oak, she inland	Casuarina pauper
		Oak, she river	Casuarina cunninghamia
Oak, American white	Quercus alba	Oak, she swamp	Casuarina glauca
Oak, Armenian	Quercus pontica	Oak, she weeping	Casuarina equisetifolia
Oak, Bartram's	Quercus x heterophylla	Oak, she western Australia	Casuarina obesa
Oak, basket	Quercus montana	Oak, shingle	Casuarina equisetifolia ssp incana
Oak, black	Quercus velutina		
Oak, black Californian	Quercus kelloggii	Oak, shingle	Quercus imbricaria
Oak, black Jack	Quercus marilandica	Oak, silky	Grevillea robusta
Oak, blue	Quercus douglasii	Oak, silky brown	Darlingia darlingiana
Oak, bootlace	Hakea lorea	Oak, silky Darwin	Grevillea pteridifolia
Oak, bull grey	Casuarina glauca	Oak, silky dwarf	Grevillea banksii alba
Oak, bur	Quercus macrocarpa	Oak, silky northern	Cardwellia sublimis
Oak, canyon	Quercus chrysolepis	Oak, silky Queensland	Grevillea robusta
Oak, Caucasian	Quercus macranthera	Oak, silky red	Grevillea banksii forsteri
Oak, chestnut-leaved	Quercus castaneifolia	Oak, silky rose	Darlingia ferruginea
Oak, chinkapin	Quercus muehlenbergii	Oak, silky rose	Placospermum coriaceum
Oak, column	Quercus robur fastigiata		
Oak, common	Quercus robur	Oak, silky spotted	Buckinghamia celsissima
Oak, cork	Quercus suber	Oak, southern	Quercus virginiana
Oak, cork bark	Hakea lorea	Oak, swamp	Casuarina glauca
Oak, daimio	Quercus dentata	Oak, swamp white	Quercus bicolor
Oak, desert	Acacia coriacea	Oak, tanbark	Lithocarpus densiflorus
Oak, Durmast	Quercus petraea	Oak, Turkey	Quercus cerris
Oak, Engelmann	Quercus engelmannii	Oak, valley	Quercus lobata
Oak, English	Quercus pyrenaica	Oak, water	Quercus nigra
Oak, English	Quercus robur	Oak, white	Quercus alba
Oak, evergreen	Quercus engelmannii	Oak, wild silver	Brachylaena discolor v

Common-Botanical Names

Common Name	Botanical Name
	discolor
Oak, willow	Quercus phellos
Oakmoss	Evernia purpuracea
Oat	Avena sativa
Oat grass	Arrhenatherum
Oat grass, bulbous	Arrhenatherum elatius ssp bulbosum 'Variegatum'
Oat, wild	Avena fatua
Oatgrass	Helictotrichon
Oats, flat	Chasmanthium latifolium
Oats, golden	Stipa gigantea
Oats, river	Chasmanthium latifolium
Oats, river small	Chasmanthium laxum
Oats, sea	Chasmanthium latifolium
Obblyonkers (fruit)	Aesculus hippocastanum
Obedient plant	Physostegia
Obedient plant	Physostegia virginiana
Obedient plant, showy	Physostegia virginiana speciosa
Ocean spray	Holodiscus discolor
Ocean spray, grand	Holodiscus dumosus
Oconee bells	Shortia galacifolia
Ocote	Gochnatia arborescens
Ocotillo	Fouquieria splendens
Oil bush	Geijera linearifolia
Oil palm	Elaeis
Oil palm, African	Elaeis guineensis
Oil tree, Karum	Pongamia pinnata
Oil tree, Macassar	Cananga odorata
Oil tree, Poona (Ponga)	Pongamia pinnata
Ojo de Pajarito	Rhynchosia pyramidalis
Olapa	Cheirodendron trigynum
Old man	Artemisia abrotanum
Old man	Artemisia absinthium
Old man	Atriplex nummularia
Old man of the Andes	Oreocereus celsianus
Old man of the Andes	Oreocereus trollii
Old man's beard	Clematis
Old man's beard	Clematis aristata
Old man's beard	Clematis vitalba
Old woman	Artemisia stelleriana
Old-man-live-forever	Pelargonium cotyledonis
Oleander	Nerium
Oleander, yellow	Thevetia peruviana
Oleaster	Elaeagnus angustifolia
Olienhout	Olea africana
Olinia, mountain	Olinia emarginata
Olive	Olea
Olive	Olea europaea
Olive, autumn	Elaeagnus umbellata
Olive berry, red inland	Cassine australis v angustifolia
Olive, fragrant	Osmanthus fragrans
Olive, Russian	Elaeagnus angustifolia
Olive, sand	Dodonaea angustifolia
Olive, wild	Olea africana
Ololiuqui	Rivea corymbosa
Onion	Allium
Onion, cliff	Allium stellatum
Onion couch	Arrhenatherum elatius ssp bulbosum 'Variegatum'
Onion, giant	Allium giganteum
Onion, Japanese bunching	Allium fistulosum
Onion, nodding	Allium cernuum
Onion, ornamental	Allium
Onion, prairie	Allium stellatum
Onion, prairie	Allium textile
Onion, sea	Ornithogalum caudatum
Onion, sea	Urginea maritima
Onion, Turkistan	Allium karataviense
Onion, Welsh	Allium fistulosum
Onion, wild	Allium cernuum
Oondooroo	Solanum simile
Ooragmandee	Eucalyptus oraria
Oorlosieblom	Galaxia ovata
Opera flower	Gardenia thunbergia
Orach(e)	Atriplex
Orange ball tree	Buddleja globosa
Orange blossom, Mexican	Choisya ternata
Orange Champaca	Michelia champaca
Orange, Japanese bitter	Poncirus trifoliata
Orange, Japanese mock	Pittosporum tobira
Orange, mock	Philadelphus
Orange, mock Australian	Pittosporum undulatum
Orange, monkey black	Strychnos madagascariensis
Orange, monkey corky-bark	Strychnos cocculoides
Orange, native (AU)	Capparis mitchellii
Orange, osage	Maclura pomifera
Orange, Panama	x Citrofortunella
Orange, Panama	x Citrofortunella microcarpa
Orange, Seville	Citrus aurantium
Orange, spiny	Strychnos spinosa
Orange, spiny-leaved	Strychnos pungens
Orange, sweet	Citrus sinensis 'Washington'
Orange, trifoliate	Poncirus trifoliata
Orchid, bee	Ophrys apifera
Orchid, bee sombre	Ophrys fusca
Orchid, butterfly	Orchis papilionacea
Orchid, clown	Rossioglossum grande
Orchid, common spotted	Dactylorhiza fuchsii
Orchid, cradle	Anguloa clowesii
Orchid, crucifix	Epidendrum ibaguense
Orchid, dancing doll	Oncidium flexuosum
Orchid, golden chain	Dendrochilum
Orchid, green-veined	Orchis morio
Orchid, heath-spotted	Dactylorhiza maculata
Orchid, jewel	Goodyera
Orchid, lady's slipper	Cypripedium calceolus
Orchid, lady's slipper showy	Cypripedium reginae
Orchid, lady's slipper white	Cypripedium montanum
Orchid, lady's slipper yellow	Cypripedium calceolus
Orchid, lizard	Himantoglossum hircinum
Orchid, marsh	Dactylorhiza
Orchid, marsh robust	Dactylorhiza elata
Orchid, marsh southern	Dactylorhiza praetermissa
Orchid, military	Orchis militaris
Orchid, mirror	Ophrys vernixia
Orchid, moth	Phalaenopsis
Orchid, pansy	Miltoniopsis
Orchid, poor man's	Schizanthus pinnatus
Orchid, purple early	Orchis mascula
Orchid, pyramidal	Anacamptis pyramidalis
Orchid, red beak	Lyperanthus nigricans
Orchid, red cactus	Nopalxochia ackermannii
Orchid, sawfly	Ophrys tenthredinifera

Common-Botanical Names

Orchid, scorpion
Orchid, shower
Orchid, slipper
Orchid, spider
Orchid, spider early
Orchid, spider late
Orchid, spotted
Orchid, star of Bethlehem
Orchid, stream
Orchid, sun
Orchid, swan
Orchid, tiger
Orchid tree
Orchid tree
Orchid tree, white

Orchid, tulip
Oregano
Oregano, Greek
Oregano, Mexican
Oregano, Mexican bush
Oregano, seedless
Oregon grape
Oregon grape, Burmese
Oregon grape, cascade
Oregon grape, creeping
Oregon grape, highbush
Oregon grape, holly-leaf

Oregon grape, lowbush
Oregon grape, shining
Orkor
Oroznz
Orpine
Orpine, stone
Orris

Osage orange
Osha del campo
Osha root
Osier, common
Osier, purple
Osmaronia
Oso berry
Ostrich fern
Oswego tea
Ouhout
Our Lord's candle
Outeniekwageelhout
Owl's eyes
Ox eye
Ox-eye daisy
Ox-eye, willowleaf

Ox-eye, yellow

Oxford weed
Oxknee
Oxknee, Sichuan
Oxlip
Oyster plant
Oyster plant
Pacific fir
Paddle-pod, smooth-leaved
Paddle-pod, velvet-leaved
Paddy's pride

Arachnis
Congea tomentosa
Paphiopedilum
Brassia lawrenceana
Ophrys sphegodes
Ophrys holserica
Dactylorhiza
Angraecum sesquipedale
Epipactis gigantea
Thelymitra benthamiana
Cynoches
Rossioglossum grande
Amherstia nobilis
Bauhinia variegata
Bauhinia variegata v candida
Anguloa
Origanum vulgare
Origanum heracleoticum
Lippia graveolens
Poliomintha longiflora
Origanum viride
Mahonia aquifolium
Mahonia lomarifolia
Mahonia nervosa
Mahonia repens
Mahonia aquifolium
Mahonia japonica Bealei Group
Mahonia repens
Mahonia nervosa
Acacia harpophylla
Lippia dulcis
Sedum telephium
Sedum rupestre
Iris x germanica florentina
Maclura pomifera
Angelica pinnata
Ligusticum porteri
Salix viminalis
Salix purpurea
Oemleria
Oemleria cerasiformis
Matteuccia struthiopteris
Monarda didyma
Leucosidea sericea
Yucca whipplei
Podocarpus falcatus
Huernia zebrina
Heliopsis
Leucanthemum vulgare
Buphthalmum salicifolium
Buphthalmum salicifolium
Cymbalaria muralis
Achyranthes bidentata
Cyathula officinalis
Primula elatior
Mertensia maritima
Tragopogon pratensis
Abies amabilis
Hippocratea parviflora
Hippocratea buchananii
Hedera colchica 'Sulphur

Paeony
Pagoda flower

Pagoda tree
Pagoda tree, Japanese
Paintbrush
Paintbrush, common red
Paintbrush, harsh
Paintbrush, Indian
Paintbrush, Indian
Paintbrush, Royal
Paintbrush, scarlet
Paintbrush, scarlet
Paintbrush, split leaf
Painted cup, downy
Painted drop tongue
Painted lady
Painted lady

Painted leaf
Painted net leaf
Painted nettle

Painted tongue
Palas
Pale blue trumpets
Palga
Pallinup Gold

Palm, African oil
Palm, Alexander

Palm, Alexander
Palm, Areca
Palm, Assai
Palm, Atherton
Palm, bamboo
Palm, bamboo
Palm, banga

Palm, bangalow

Palm, Barbel
Palm, Betel nut
Palm, Bismarck
Palm, black
Palm, bottle
Palm, bottle
Palm, broom
Palm, buccaneer
Palm, Buriti
Palm, butterfly
Palm, cabbage
Palm, cabbage Australian
Palm, cabbage Central Australian
Palm, cabbage New Zealand
Palm, cane golden
Palm, cane ivory
Palm, cardboard
Palm, cat

Palm, champagne
Palm, Chestnut
Palm, Chilean wine
Palm, Christmas

Heart'
Paeonia
Clerodendrum paniculatum
Plumeria
Sophora japonica
Haemanthus albiflos
Castilleja miniata
Castilleja hispida
Castilleja coccinea
Castilleja integra
Scadoxus puniceus
Castilleja miniata
Crassula falcata
Castilleja rhexifolia
Castilleja sessiliflora
Aglaonema crispum
Gladiolus carneus
Gompholobium scabrum
Euphorbia cyathophora
Fittonia
Solenostemon scutellarioides
Salpiglossis
Butea monosperma
Ipomopsis longiflora
Xanthorrhoea preissii
Acacia declinata (prostrate)
Elais guineensis
Archontophoenix alexandrae
Ptychosperma elegans
Dypsis lutescens
Euterpe edulis
Laccospadix austalasiaca
Chamaedorea seifrizii
Rhapis excelsa
Archontophoenix alexandrae
Archontophoenix cunninghamia
Acanthophoenix rubra
Areca catechu
Bismarckia nobilis
Normanbya normanbyi
Beaucarnea recurvata
Hyophorbe lagenicaulis
Thrinax parviflora
Pseudophoenix sargentii
Trithrinax acanthocoma
Dypsis lutescens
Cordyline
Livistona australis
Livistona mariae
Cordyline australis
Dypsis lutescens
Pinanga kuhlii
Zamia furfuracea
Chamaedorea cataractarum
Hyophorbe lagenicaulis
Dioon edule
Jubaea chilensis
Veitchia merrillii

Common-Botanical Names

Palm, Chusan	Trachycarpus fortunei	Palm, Guadalupe	Brahea armata
Palm, cluster featherleaf	Hydruastele wendlandiana	Palm, Guadalupe	Brahea edulis
		Palm, hat Puerto Rican	Sabal causarium
Palm, cluster small	Ptychosperma macarthurii	Palm, hesper	Brahea
		Palm, hesper blue	Brahea armata
Palm, coquito	Jubaea chilensis	Palm, hesper San Jose	Brahea brandegeei
Palm, cotton	Washingtonia robusta	Palm, honey	Jubaea chilensis
Palm, cotton American	Washingtonia filifera	Palm, hurricane	Ptychosperma
Palm, Coyure	Aiphanes caryotifolia		macarthurii
Palm, curly	Howea belmoreana	Palm, Illawarra	Archontophoenix
Palm, date	Phoenix dactylifera		cunninghamia
Palm, date Canary Island	Phoenix canariensis	Palm, ivy Australian	Schefflera actinophylla
Palm, date Ceylon	Phoenix pusilla	Palm, jaggery	Caryota urens
Palm, date cliff	Phoenix rupicola	Palm, jelly	Butia capitata
Palm, date dwarf	Phoenix acaulis	Palm, Joannis	Veitchia joannis
Palm, date dwarf Formosan	Phoenix hanceana	Palm, Jucara	Euterpe edulis
Palm, date Mangrove	Phoenix paludosa	Palm, Kentia	Howea forsteriana
Palm, date miniature	Phoenix roebelinii	Palm, Kermadec Nikau	Rhopalostylis
Palm, date pygmy	Phoenix roebelinii		cheesemanii
Palm, date Senegal	Phoenix reclinata	Palm, key	Thrinax morrisii
Palm, date silver	Phoenix sylvestris	Palm, King	Archontophoenix
Palm, date wild	Phoenix reclinata	Palm, lady	Rhapis
Palm, doum	Hyphaene coriacea	Palm, lady China	Rhaphis excelsa
Palm, Elala	Hyphaene petersiana	Palm, lady slender	Rhapis excelsa
Palm, Elala dwarf	Hyphaene coriacea	Palm, Latan	Latania
Palm, everglades	Acoelorraphe wrightii	Palm, Latan blue	Latania loddigesii
Palm, fan	Livistona	Palm, Latan golden	Latania verschaffelti
Palm, fan	Serenoa repens	Palm, Latan red	Latania borbonica
Palm, fan Australian	Licuala ramsayi	Palm, Licuala spiny	Licuala spinosa
Palm, fan Australian	Livistona australis	Palm, lipstick	Cyrtostachys lakka
Palm, fan blue	Brahea armata	Palm, Macarthur	Ptychosperma
Palm, fan blue	Erythea armata		macarthurii
Palm, fan California	Washingtonia filifera	Palm, Macaw	Acrocomia aculeata
Palm, fan Chinese	Livistona chinensis	Palm, Macaw fat	Elais guineensis
Palm, fan desert	Washingtonia filifera	Palm, Madagascar	Pachypodium lamerei
Palm, fan dwarf	Chamaerops	Palm, majestic	Ravanea rivularis
Palm, fan dwarf	Livistona muelleri	Palm, Manila	Veitchia merrillii
Palm, fan Fiji	Pritchardia pacifica	Palm, metallic	Chamaedorea tenella
Palm, fan Mexican	Washingtonia robusta	Palm, Mexican dwarf	Chamaedorea atrovirens
Palm, fan millstream	Livistona alfredii	Palm, mini bamboo Honduran	Chamaedorea seifrizii
Palm, fan miniature	Rhapis excelsa	Palm, mountain mist	Laccospadix austalasiaca
Palm, fan Mission Beach	Licuala ramsayi	Palm, needle	Rhapidophyllum
Palm, fan red	Livistona mariae	Palm, needle	Yucca filamentosa
Palm, fan ruffled	Licuala grandis	Palm, Nibung	Oncosperma tigillarium
Palm, feather duster	Rhopalostylis sapida	Palm, Nikau	Rhopalostylis sapida
Palm, feather golden	Dypsis lutescens	Palm, Norfolk Island	Rhopalostylis baueri
Palm, feather leaf	Aiphanes erosa	Palm, northern bungalow	Archontophoenix
Palm, fern	Cycas circinalis		alexandrae
Palm, fern Mexican	Dioon edule	Palm, nut	Cycas media
Palm, fish-tail	Caryota	Palm, oil	Elais
Palm, fish-tail	Caryota cummingii	Palm, palmetto	Sabal palmetto
Palm, fish-tail	Caryota rumphiana	Palm, palmyra	Borassus flabellifer
Palm, fish-tail Burmese	Caryota mitis	Palm, panama hat	Carludovica palmat
Palm, fish-tail Chinese	Caryota ochlandra	Palm, Paradise	Howea forsteriana
Palm, fish-tail clustered	Caryota mitis	Palm, parlour	Chamaedorea elegans
Palm, fish-tail dwarf	Arenga caudata	Palm, peach	Bactris gasipaes
Palm, fish-tail miniature	Chamaedorea metallica	Palm, petticoat	Copernicia macroglossa
Palm, fish-tail solitaire	Caryota urens	Palm, petticoat	Washingtonia filifera
Palm, footstool	Livistona rotundifolia	Palm, piccabean	Archontophoenix
Palm, fountain Chinese	Livistona chinensis		cunninghamiana
Palm, fountain Gippsland	Livistona australis	Palm, porcupine	Rhapidophyllum hystrix
Palm, foxtail	Wodyetia bifurcata	Palm, Princess	Dictyosperma
Palm, gingerbread	Hyphaene thebaica	Palm, Princess	Dictyosperma album v
Palm, grey	Ptychosperma macarthurii		rubrum
		Palm, purple	Pinanga insignis
Palm, grey goddess	Brahea armata	Palm, Queen	Syagrus romanzoffiana

Common-Botanical Names

Common	Botanical
Palm, Rattan	Calamus
Palm, reed	Chamaedorea seifrizii
Palm, reed	Rhaphis humilis
Palm, reed	Rhapis excelsa
Palm, royal	Roystonea
Palm, royal Caribbean	Roystonea oleracea
Palm, royal Cuban	Roystonea regia
Palm, royal Florida	Roystonea elata
Palm, royal South America	Roystonea oleracea
Palm, ruffle	Aiphanes
Palm, Sagasi	Heterospathe elata
Palm, sago	Caryota urens
Palm, sago Japanese	Cycas revoluta
Palm, sago Queen	Cycas circinalis
Palm, sand	Livistona humilis
Palm, saw	Acoelorraphe
Palm, saw cabbage	Acoelorraphe wrightii
Palm, saw silver	Acoelorraphe wrightii
Palm, screw	Pandanus
Palm, sealing wax	Cyrtostachys lakka
Palm, sentry	Howea
Palm, silver Florida	Coccothrinax argentata
Palm, silver Hispaniolan	Coccothrinax argentea
Palm, snake	Amorphophallus konjac
Palm, solitaire	Ptychosperma elegans
Palm, spindle	Hyophorbe verschaffeltii
Palm, spine	Aiphanes caryotifolia
Palm, spiny club	Bactris
Palm, spiny fibre	Trithrinax acanthocoma
Palm Springs daisy	Cladanthus
Palm, stilt	Iriartea gigantea
Palm, sugar	Arenga
Palm, sugar	Arenga pinnata
Palm, sugar dwarf	Arenga engleri
Palm, sunshine	Veitchia macdanielsii
Palm, Syragus	Lytocaryum weddellianum
Palm, talipot	Corypha umbraculifera
Palm, Tamy's	Pinanga maculata
Palm, Taraw	Livistona saribus
Palm, teddy	Phoenix sylvestris
Palm, thatch	Coccothrinax
Palm, thatch	Thrinax parviflora
Palm, thatch leaf	Howea
Palm, thread	Washingtonia robusta
Palm, Thurston	Pritchardia thurstonii
Palm, tiger	Pinanga maculata
Palm, toddy	Borassus flabellifer
Palm, toddy	Caryota urens
Palm, Traveller's	Ravenala madagascariensis
Palm, tree cabbage	Livistona australis
Palm, triangle	Dypsis decaryi
Palm, umbrella	Hedyscepe
Palm, Virgin's	Dioon edule
Palm, walking stick	Linospadix monostachya
Palm, Wanga	Pigafetta filaris
Palm, wax	Copernicia
Palm, Weddell	Lytocaryum weddellianum
Palm, Wedding	Lytocaryum weddellianum
Palm, weeping cabbage	Livistona decipiens
Palm, windmill	Trachycarpus fortunei
Palm, window pane	Reinhardtia gracilis
Palm, wine	Borassus flabellifer
Palm, wine	Butia capitata
Palm, wine	Caryota urens
Palm, Yatay	Butia yatay
Palm, yellow	Dypsis lutescens
Palm, Zamia	Cycas media
Palm, Zamia	Macrozamia communis
Palm, Zamia	Macrozamia fraseri
Palm, Zamia	Macrozamia lucida
Palm, Zamia	Macrozamia riedlei
Palm, Zamia	Macrozamia spiralis
Palma	Yucca faxoniana
Palma barreta	Yucca carnerosana
Palmarosa	Cymbopogon
Palmarosa	Cymbopogon marinii motia
Palmetto	Sabal
Palmetto, blue	Rhapidophyllum hystrix
Palmetto, cabbage	Sabal palmetto
Palmetto, common blue	Sabal palmetto
Palmetto, dwarf	Sabal minor
Palmetto, Hispaniolan-	Sabal umbraculifera
Palmetto, saw	Serenoa
Palmetto, scrub	Sabal minor
Palmetto, scrub	Serenoa repens
Palmetto, Texas	Sabal mexicana
Palmito de campo	Syagrus flexuosa
Palmyra palm	Borassus flabellifer
Palo blanco	Lysiloma candida
Palo brea	Cercidium praecox
Palo chino	Pithecellobium mexicanum
Palo escopeta	Albizia occidentalis
Palo San Juan	Forchammeria watsonii
Palo verde, blue	Cercidium floridum
Palo verde, foothills	Cercidium microphyllum
Palo zorrillo	Cassia emarginata
Pambati boom	Anastrabe integerrima
Pambati tree	Anastrabe integerrima
Pampas grass	Cortaderia
Pampas grass	Cortaderia selloana
Panama hat palm	Carludovica palmata
Panamiga	Pilea involucrata
Panda plant	Kalanchoe tomentosa
Panda plant	Philodendron bipennifolium
Panda plant	Philodendron bipinnatafidum
Pandani tree	Richea pandanifolia
Pandanus, dwarf	Pandanus montana
Panic, hairy	Panicum effusum
Pansy	Viola x wittrochiana
Pansy, field	Viola arvensis
Pansy, mountain	Viola lutea
Pansy orchid	Miltoniopsis
Pansy, wild	Viola tricolor
Papache	Randia megacarpa
Papalo	Porophyllum ruderale ssp macrocephalum
Papaloquelite	Porophyllum ruderale ssp macrocephalum
Papaya	Carica papaya
Paper bark maple	Acer griseum
Paper bush	Edgeworthia
Paper mulberry	Broussonetia papyrifera
Paper reed	Cyperus papyrus
Paperbark	Melaleuca

Common-Botanical Names

Common	Botanical
Paperbark	Melaleuca nervosa
Paperbark, broad-leaved	Melaleuca leucadendron
Paperbark, broad-leaved	Melaleuca viridiflora
Paperbark, broad-leaved	Melaleuca viridiflora v rubriflora
Paperbark, creekline	Melaleuca rhaphiophylla
Paperbark, flax-leaved	Melaleuca linariifolia
Paperbark, freshwater	Melaleuca preissiana
Paperbark, grey	Melaleuca dealbata
Paperbark, inland	Melaleuca glomerata
Paperbark, Kangaroo Island	Melaleuca halmaturorum
Paperbark, pink	Melaleuca diosmatifolia
Paperbark, prickly	Melaleuca styphelioides
Paperbark, prickly-leaved	Melaleuca nodosa
Paperbark, saltwater	Melaleuca cuticularis
Paperbark, scented	Melaleuca squarrosa
Paperbark, silvery	Melaleuca argentea
Paperbark, swamp	Melaleuca ericifolia
Paperbark, swamp	Melaleuca rhaphiophylla
Paperbark, swamp dwarf	Melaleuca ericifolia nana
Paperbark, swamp (S.AU)	Melaleuca halmaturorum
Paperbark thorn	Acacia siebierana v woodii
Paperbark tree	Melaleuca viridiformis v rubriflora
Paperbark, weeping	Melaleuca leucadendron
Paperbark, white	Melaleuca cuticularis
Paperflower	Psilostrophe tagetina
Papierblom	Limonium purpuratum
Paprika	Capsicum annuum
Papyrus	Cyperus papyrus
Para cress	Spilanthes acmella
Parachute plant	Ceropegia sandersonii
Paradise flower	Solanum wenlandii
Paradise lily	Paradisea
Paraiso	Melia composita
Parapara	Pisonia umbellifera
Parasol tree	Polyscias fulva
Parasol tree, Chinese	Firmiana simplex
Parilla, yellow	Menispermum canadense
Parlour palm	Chamaedorea elegans
Parrot bush	Dryandra sessilis
Parrot leaf	Alternanthera ficoidea
Parrot plant	Crotalaria cunninghamii
Parrot, tree	Schotia brachypetala
Parrot's beak	Clianthus puniceus
Parrot's beak	Lothus berthelotii
Parrot's bill	Clianthus puniceus
Parrot's feather	Myriophyllum acquaticum
Parrot's flower	Heliconia psittacorum
Parrot's plantain	Heliconia psittacorum
Parrot-pea, prickly	Dillwynia juniperina
Parrot-pea, showy	Dillwynia sericea
Parrot-pea, silky	Dillwynia uncinata
Parsley	Petroselinum
Parsley	Petroselinum crispum
Parsley celery, wild	Lomatium californicum
Parsley, cow	Anthriscus sylvestris
Parsley, desert barestem	Lomatium dissectum
Parsley, desert big-seeded	Lomatium macrocarpum
Parsley, French	Petroselinum crispum v neapolitanum
Parsley, Hamburg	Petroselinum crispum v tuberosum
Parsley, Italian	Petroselinum crispum v neapolitanum
Parsley, mountain fern-leaf	Lomatium dissectum
Parsley, prairie	Polytaenia nuttallii
Parsley tree	Heteromorpha trifoliata
Parsley, wild	Lomatia silaifolia
Parsnip, buck	Lomatium triternatum
Parsnip, cow	Heracleum maximum
Parsnip, cow	Heracleum sphondylium
Parsnip, cow giant	Heracleum mantegazzianum
Parsnip, meadow	Thaspium trifoliatum
Parsnip, pestle	Lomatium nudicaule
Parsnip, wild	Pastinaca sativa
Parson-in-the-pulpit	Arum maculatum
Partridge berry	Gaultheria procumbens
Partridge berry	Mitchella repens
Partridge pea	Cassia fasciculata
Pasque flower	Pulsatilla vulgaris
Pasque flower, alpine	Pulsatilla alpina
Pasque flower, Eastern	Pulsatilla patens
Passion flower	Passiflora
Passion flower, annual	Passiflora gracilis
Passion flower, banana	Passiflora mollissima
Passion flower, blue	Passiflora caerulea
Passion flower, common	Passiflora caerulea
Passion flower, cream	Passiflora ampullacea
Passion flower, goat-scented	Passiflora foetida
Passion flower, lilac	Passiflora zamorana
Passion flower, native (AU)	Passiflora cinnarbarina
Passion flower, native (US)	Passiflora incarnata
Passion flower, orange	Passiflora aurantia
Passion flower, red	Passiflora cinnarbarina
Passion flower, red	Passiflora coccinea
Passion flower, red	Passiflora racemosa
Passion flower, red banana	Passiflora antioquiensis
Passion flower, tree	Passiflora lindeniana
Passion flower, vine-leaved	Passiflora vitifolia
Passion flower, winged-stem	Passiflora alata
Passion fruit	Passiflora edulis
Passion fruit, black	Passiflora edulis
Patchouli	Pogostemon cablin
Pato de gallo	Geranium canariense
Patrybos	Leucospermum truncatulum
Patterson's poison	Tephrosia rosea
Pau d'arco	Tabebuia impetiginosa
Paulownia, Royal	Paulownia fortunei
Pawpaw	Asimina triloba
Paws	Conostylis setigera
Pea, Ashburton	Swainsona macullochiana
Pea, Australian	Lablab purpureus
Pea, ballon	Sutherlandia frutescens
Pea, beach	Lathyrus maritimus
Pea, blue	Clitoria ternatea
Pea, bright yellow	Gompholobium polymorphum
Pea, broken hill	Swainsona fissimontana
Pea, Broughton	Swainsona procumbens
Pea, bush	Pultenaea procumbens
Pea bush, pink	Tephrosia grandiflora
Pea, butterfly	Clitoria ternatea
Pea, chickling	Lathyrus sativus
Pea, cluster orange	Gompholobium preissii
Pea, cluster yellow	Gompholobium

Common-Botanical Names

Common	Botanical
	capitatum
Pea, coral	Hardenbergia
Pea, coral	Kennedia
Pea, coral purple	Hardenbergia violacea
Pea, dainty	Gompholobium venustum
Pea, Dampier	Swainsona pterostylis
Pea, darling	Swainsona galegifolia
Pea, darling	Swainsona greyana ssp greyana
Pea, darling	Swainsona murrayana
Pea, darling creeping	Swainsona viridis
Pea, darling downy	Swainsona swainsonioides
Pea, darling orange	Swainsona stipularis
Pea, darling slender	Swainsona murrayana
Pea, darling woolly	Swainsona burkittii
Pea, earth-nut	Lathyrus tuberosus
Pea, everlasting	Lathyrus grandiflorus
Pea, everlasting	Lathyrus latifolius
Pea, everlasting narrow-leaved	Lathyrus sylvestris
Pea, everlasting Persian	Lathyrus rotundifolius
Pea, flat	Platylobium formosum
Pea, glory	Clianthus formosus
Pea, glory	Clianthus puniceus
Pea, glory golden	Gompholobium latifolium
Pea, golden	Aotus ericoides
Pea, King	Swainsona kingii
Pea, Lord Anson's blue	Lathyrus nervosus
Pea, marsh	Lathyrus palustris
Pea, partridge	Chamaecrista fasciculata
Pea, perennial	Lathyrus grandiflorus
Pea, perennial	Lathyrus latifolius
Pea, perennial	Lathyrus sylvestris
Pea, pidgeon	Cajanus cajan
Pea, pretty	Gompholobium venustum
Pea, prickle mauve	Mirbelia dilatata
Pea, prickly bush	Mirbelia pungens
Pea, prostrate	Aotus diffusa
Pea, purple	Hovea acutifolia
Pea, rattle	Daviesia oppositifolia
Pea, Rosary	Abrus precatorius
Pea, salt lake	Swainsona cyclocarpa
Pea, scurfy	Psoralea tenuiflora
Pea, sea	Lathyrus maritimus
Pea, sensitive	Chamaecrista fasciculata
Pea, shamrock	Parochetus africana
Pea shrub, Russian	Caragana frutex
Pea shrub, Siberian	Caragana arborescens
Pea, soft mauve	Gompholobium villosum
Pea, spring	Lathyrus vernus
Pea, Sturt's desert	Clianthus formosus
Pea, Sturt's desert pink	Swainsona pubescens
Pea, Swan River	Brachysema celsianum
Pea, sweet	Lathyrus odoratus
Pea, Tangier scarlet	Lathyrus tingitanus
Pea, thorny	Daviesia horrida
Pea tree	Caragana arborescens
Pea tree, Siberian	Caragana arborescens
Pea, two-flowered	Lathyrus grandiflorus
Pea, wedge broad	Gompholobium latifolium
Pea, wedge Wallum	Gompholobium virgatum
Pea, wild	Lathyrus sylvestris
Pea, wild	Pisum sativum
Pea, wreath	Leptosema chambersii
Pea, zig-zag	Daviesia flexuosa
Peaberry	Thrinax
Peabush, yellow	Sesbania cannabima
Peach	Prunus persica
Peach, African	Kiggelaria africana
Peach, David's	Prunus davidiana
Peach, Indian	Oemleria cerasiformis
Peach, native (AU)	Santalum acuminatum
Peach, nemaguard	Prunus persica
Peach palm	Bactris gasipaes
Peach, Pere David's	Prunus davidiana
Peach, rainforest	Cochlospermum vitifolium
Peach, wild	Kiggelaria africana
Peacock flower	Delonix regia
Peacock flower	Homeria elegans
Peacock flower	Moraea villosa
Peacock flower	Tigridia
Peacock flower	Tigridia pavonia
Peacock lily	Kaempferia roscoeana
Peacock plant	Calathea makoyana
Peanut	Arachis hypogaea
Pear	Pyrus
Pear, Callery	Pyrus calleryana
Pear, common	Pyrus communis
Pear, Djandin	Xylomelum occidentale
Pear, Harbin	Pyrus ussuriensis
Pear, hard	Olinia ventosa
Pear, native (AU)	Cynanchum floribundum
Pear, native (AU)	Xylomelum pyriformis
Pear, sand	Pyrus pyrifolia
Pear, sand plain	Xylomelum
Pear, sand plain	Xylomelum angustifolium
Pear, sandplain woody	Xylomelum angustifolium
Pear, white	Apodytes dimidiata ssp dimidiata
Pear, wild	Dombeya rotundifolia
Pear, wild forest	Dombeya tiliacea
Pear, wild pink	Dombeya burgessiae
Pear, wild silver	Dombeya pulchra
Pear, woody	Xylomelum angustifolium
Pear, woody	Xylomelum occidentale
Pear, woody eastern	Xylomelum pyriformis
Pear, woody western	Xylomelum occidentale
Pearl berry	Margyricarpus pinnatus
Pearl bush	Exochorda
Pearl everlasting	Anaphalis
Pearlwort	Sagina
Pearlwort, heath	Sagina subulata
Pebble bush	Stylobasium spathulatum
Pecan, northern	Carya illinoensis
Pecan nut tree	Carya pecan
Peepul	Ficus religiosa
Pelargonium, lemon-scented	Pelargonium citronellum
Pelargonium, lemon-scented	Pelargonium crispum
Pelargonium, pheasant's foot	Pelargonium glutinosum
Pelargonium, rose-scented	Pelargonium capitatum
Pelican flower	Aristolochia grandiflora
Pelican's beak	Lotus berthelotii

Common-Botanical Names

Common	Botanical	Common	Botanical
Pennant flower	Chasmanthe floribunda	Pepper tree, Brazilian	Schinus terebinthifolius
Penny-cress, alpine	Thlaspi alpinum	Pepper tree, Peruvian	Schinus molle
Penny-cress, field	Thlaspi arvense	Pepper, white	Piper nigrum
Penny-cress, round-leaved	Thlaspi rotundifolium	Pepper-tree, Californian	Schinus molle
Pennyroyal, alpine	Teucrium montanum	Peppercress, shrubby	Lepidium leptopetalum
Pennyroyal, American	Hedeoma pulegioides	Pepperflower	Diplopeltis huegelii
Pennyroyal, English	Mentha pulegium	Pepperflower, hairy	Diplopeltis eriocarpa
Pennyroyal, Hart's	Mentha cervina	Peppergrass	Lepidium ruderale
Pennyroyal, mountain thyme	Hedeoma pulegioides	Peppermint	Mentha x piperata
Pennywort	Cymbalaria muralis	Peppermint, black	Eucalyptus novangelica
Pennywort	Hydrocotyle	Peppermint, broad-leaved	Eucalyptus dives
Pennywort	Umbilicus rupestris	Peppermint, fine-leaved	Eucalyptus nicholii
Penstemon, beardlip	Penstemon barbatus	Peppermint, grey	Eucalyptus radiata
Penstemon, blue	Penstemon procerus	Peppermint, Mount Wellington	Eucalyptus coccifera
Penstemon, Blue Mountain	Penstemon venustus	Peppermint, narrow-leaved	Eucalyptus radiata ssp radiata
Penstemon, cascade	Penstemon serrulatus		
Penstemon, dark blue	Penstemon cyaneus	Peppermint, narrow-leaved	Eucalyptus radiata ssp robertsonii
Penstemon, foothill	Penstemon heterophyllus		
		Peppermint, narrow-leaved black	Eucalyptus nicholii
Penstemon, gilia	Penstemon ambiguus	Peppermint, New England	Eucalyptus novangelica
Penstemon, glandular	Penstemon glandulosus	Peppermint, Queensland	Eucalyptus exserta
Penstemon, globe	Penstemon globosus	Peppermint, Risdon	Eucalyptus risdonii
Penstemon, ground runner	Penstemon procerus	Peppermint, Risdon	Eucalyptus silver
Penstemon, high desert	Penstemon thurberi	Peppermint, river	Eucalyptus elata
Penstemon, large purple	Penstemon cobaea	Peppermint, shining	Eucalyptus nitida
Penstemon, little-flowered	Penstemon procerus	Peppermint, shiny-leaved	Eucalyptus nitida
Penstemon, lovely	Penstemon venustus	Peppermint, silver	Eucalyptus novangelica
Penstemon, narrow-leaved	Penstemon angustifolius	Peppermint, silver	Eucalyptus risdonii
Penstemon, Palmer's	Penstemon palmeri	Peppermint, silver	Eucalyptus tenuiramis
Penstemon, pine-leaf	Penstemon pinifolius	Peppermint, small-leaved	Eucalyptus nicholii
Penstemon, rock	Penstemon rupicola	Peppermint, Smithton	Eucalyptus nitida
Penstemon, rock hot	Penstemon deustus	Peppermint, swamp	Eucalyptus rodwayi
Penstemon, Rocky Mountain	Penstemon strictus	Peppermint, Sydney	Eucalyptus piperata
Penstemon, Rydberg's	Penstemon rydbergii	Peppermint tree	Agonis flexuosa
Penstemon, sand-dune	Penstemon acuminatus	Peppermint, urn-fruited	Eucalyptus piperita ssp urceolaris
Penstemon, shining	Penstemon nitidus		
Penstemon, shrubby	Penstemon fruticosus	Peppermint, urn-fruited	Eucalyptus urceolaris
Penstemon, smooth	Penstemon nitidus	Peppermint, wattle-leaved	Eucalyptus acaciiformis
Penstemon, taper-leaved	Penstemon attenuatus	Peppermint, white	Eucalyptus linearis
Penstemon, Wasatch	Penstemon cyananthus	Peppermint, white	Eucalyptus pulchella
Penstemon, Whipple's	Penstemon whippleanus	Peppermint, willow	Eucalyptus elata
Penstemon, whorled	Penstemon triphyllus	Peppermint, willow	Eucalyptus nichollii
Penstemon, Wilcox's	Penstemon wilcoxii	Pepperwort	Lepidium ruderale
Peony	Paeonia	Pepperwort	Marsilea
Peony, Himalayan	Paeonia emodi	Perennial pea	Lathyrus sylvestris
Peony, Majorcan	Paeonia cambessedesii	Periwinkle	Vinca
Peony, wild	Paeonia brownii	Periwinkle, greater	Vinca major
Peperomia, Cupid	Peperomia scandens	Periwinkle, lesser	Vinca minor
Peperomia, felted	Peperomia incana	Periwinkle, Madagascar	Catharanthus roseus
Peperomia, flowering	Peperomia fraseri	Periwinkle, rose	Catharanthus roseus
Peperomia, ivy-leaf	Peperomia griseoargentea	Persdrolpeer	Dombeya burgessiae
		Persian lilac	Melia azederach
Peperomia, prayer	Peperomia dolabriformis	Persian shield	Strobilanthes dyerianus
Peperomia, silverleaf	Peperomia griseoargentea	Persian violet	Exacum affine
		Persimmon	Diospyros virginiana
Peperomia, sweetheart	Pepeomia marmorata	Persimmon, Chinese	Diospyros kaki
Peperomia, watermelon	Peperomia argyreia	Persimmon, Japanese	Diospyros kaki
Peperomia, wax privet	Peperomia glabella	Peruvian lily	Alstroemeria
Pepper and salt	Eriostemon spicatus	Petrophile, granite	Petrophile biloba
Pepper, black	Piper nigrum	Petrophile, prickly	Petrophile serruriae
Pepper face	Peperomia obtusifolia	Petrophile, scented	Petrophile longifolia
Pepper, mountain	Drimys lanceolata	Petticoat palm	Copernicia macroglossa
Pepper, ornamental	Capsicum annuum	Petunia, hairy	Ruellia humilis
Pepper tree	Pseudowintera axillaris	Petunia, wild	Ruellia caroliniana
Pepper tree	Pseudowintera colorata	Petunia, wild	Ruellia humilis
Pepper tree	Schinus molle	Peyote	Lophophora

Common-Botanical Names

Common	Botanical	Common	Botanical
Phacelia, fringe purple	Phacelia sericea	Pinang	Areca catechu
Phacelia, fringed	Phacelia purshii	Pinati	Erythrina vespertilio
Phacelia, silky	Phacelia sericea	Pincushion	Leucospermum
Phanera	Bauhinia corymbosa	Pincushion	Scabiosa africana
Pheasant berry	Leycesteria	Pincushion, Albertinia	Leucospermum muirii
Pheasant's eye	Adonis annua	Pincushion, Bolus'	Leucospermum bolusii
Pheasant's eye	Narcissus poeticus	Pincushion, Catherine's	Leucospermum
Pheasant's eye, old	Narcissus poeticus v		catherinae
	recurvus	Pincushion, elegant	Leucospermum tottum
Philippine violet	Barleria cristata	Pincushion flower	Scabiosa
Philodendron, black gold	Philodendron	Pincushion, fountain grey-leaf	Leucospermum
	melanochrysum		grandiflorum
Philodendron, blushing	Philodendron	Pincushion, Mosselbay	Leucospermum praecox
	erubescens	Pincushion, ornamental	Leucospermum
Philodendron, red-leaf	Philodendron		cordifolium
	erubescens	Pincushion, Oudtshoorn	Leucospermum
Philodendron, tree	Philodendron		erubescens
	bipinnatifidum	Pincushion, Outeniqua	Leucospermum glabrum
Philodendron, velour	Philodendron	Pincushion, rose	Mammillaria
	melanochrysum		zeilmanniana
Phlox, annual	Phlox drummondii	Pincushion, silverleaf-wheel	Leucospermum
Phlox, blue wild	Phlox divaricata		formosum
Phlox, Carolina	Phlox carolina	Pincushion, tree	Leucospermum
Phlox, creeping	Phlox stolonifera		conocarpodendron ssp
Phlox, downy	Phlox pilosa		viridum
Phlox, hairy	Phlox amoena	Pincushion, tufted	Leucospermum
Phlox, marsh	Phlox glaberrima		oleifolium
Phlox, meadow	Phlox maculata	Pincushion, wart-stemmed	Leucospermum
Phlox, moss	Phlox subulata		cuneiforme
Phlox, mountain	Linanthus grandiflorus	Pindak	Calothamnus
Phlox, night	Zaluzianskya katherinae		sanguineus
Phlox, Ozark	Phlox pilosa v ozarkana	Pine, Aleppo	Pinus halepensis
Phlox, perennial	Phlox paniculata	Pine, Aleppo	Pinus koraiensis
Phlox, prairie	Phlox pilosa	Pine, ancient	Pinus longaeva
Phlox, sand	Phlox bifida	Pine, Apache	Pinus engelmannii
Phlox, Santa Fe	Phlox nana	Pine, Armand	Pinus armandii
Phlox, sticky	Phlox viscida	Pine, Arolla	Pinus cembra
Phlox, thick-leaf	Phlox carolina	Pine, Australian	Casuarina
Physic nut	Jatropha curcas	Pine, Austrian	Pinus nigra
Piara	Banksia attenuata	Pine, beach	Pinus contorta
Piccabeen palm	Archontophoenix	Pine, Benguet	Pinus khasya
	cunninghamiana	Pine, Bhutan	Pinus wallichiana
Pick-a-back-plant	Tolmiea	Pine, big-cone	Pinus coulteri
Pickerel weed	Pontederia	Pine, Bishop	Pinus muricata
Pickerel weed	Pontederia cordata	Pine, black	Pinus jeffreyi
Pied Piper bush	Dichrostachys spicata	Pine, black	Pinus nigra
Pienk keurboom	Virgilia divaricata	Pine, blue	Pinus wallichiana
Pig's ears	Cotyledon spp	Pine, Bosnian	Pinus heldreichii v
Pigeon berry	Duranta erecta		leucodermis
Pigeon berry	Phytolacca americana	Pine, bristlecone	Pinus aristata
Pigeonwood	Trema orientalis	Pine, bristlecone	Pinus longaeva aristata
Pigface, coastal	Carpobrotus	Pine, brown	Podocarpus elatus
	glaucescens	Pine, Bunya	Araucaria bidwillii
Pigface, Sturt's	Gunniopsis quadrifida	Pine, Calabrian	Pinus halepensis v brutia
Piggy back plant	Tolmiea menziesii	Pine, Canary Island	Pinus canariensis
Pignut	Carya glabra	Pine, Canton	Pinus massoniana
Pikake	Jasminum sambac	Pine, celery top	Phyllocladus
Pilewort	Ranunculus ficaria	Pine, Chilean	Araucaria araucana
Pilot plant	Silphium laciniatum	Pine, Chinese red	Pinus tabuliformis
Pilot weed	Silphium laciniatum	Pine, Chinese white	Pinus armandii
Pimpernel	Anagallis	Pine, Chir	Pinus roxburghii
Pimpernel, scarlet	Anagallis arvensis	Pine, cluster	Pinus pinaster
Pimpernel, yellow	Taenidia integerrima	Pine, Cook	Araucaria columnaris
Pin bush	Acacia burkittii	Pine, Corsican	Pinus nigra ssp laricio
Pin cushion, blue	Brunonia australis	Pine, Coulter	Pinus coulteri
Pin cushions	Brunonia australis	Pine, cowtail	Cephalotaxus

Common-Botanical Names

Common	Botanical
Pine, Cuban	harringtoniana Pinus caribaea v bahamensis
Pine, Cuban	Pinus caribaea v caribaea
Pine, Cuban	Pinus caribaea v hondurensis
Pine, cypress	Callitris canescens
Pine, cypress	Callitris roei
Pine, cypress scrub	Callitris preissii ssp verrucosa
Pine, David's	Pinus armandii
Pine, digger	Pinus sabiniana
Pine, dwarf	Pinus mugo
Pine, eastern white	Pinus strobus
Pine, European black	Pinus nigra
Pine, Formosa	Pinus taiwanensis
Pine, foxtail	Pinus balfouriana
Pine, giant	Pinus lambertiana
Pine, Himalayan blue	Pinus wallichiana
Pine, Himalayan east	Pinus khasya
Pine, Himalayan white	Pinus wallichiana
Pine, Holford	Pinus x holfordiana
Pine, hoop	Araucaria cunninghamii
Pine, Illawarra	Callitris muelleri
Pine, Jack	Pinus banksiana
Pine, Japanese black	Pinus thunbergii
Pine, Japanese red	Pinus densiflora
Pine, Japanese umbrella	Sciadopitys verticillata
Pine, Japanese white	Pinus parviflora
Pine, Jeffrey	Pinus jeffreyi
Pine, Jelecote	Pinus patula
Pine, Jerusalem	Pinus halepensis
Pine, Kauri	Agathis australis
Pine, King William	Arthrotaxis selaginoides
Pine, knobcone	Pinus attenuata
Pine, Korean	Pinus koraiensis
Pine, lacebark	Pinus bungeana
Pine, Leichardt	Nauclea orientalis
Pine, limber	Pinus flexilis
Pine, Loblolly	Pinus taeda
Pine, lodgepole	Pinus contorta
Pine, lodgepole	Pinus contorta v latifolia
Pine, long-leaf	Pinus palustris
Pine, Macedonian	Pinus peuce
Pine, maritime	Pinus pinaster
Pine, Mexican rough-barked	Pinus montezumae
Pine, Mexican weeping	Pinus patula
Pine, Mexican white	Pinus ayacahuite
Pine, Monterey	Pinus radiata
Pine, Montezuma	Pinus montezumae
Pine, Moreton Bay	Araucaria columnaris
Pine, mountain	Pinus mugo
Pine, mountain dwarf	Pinus mugo
Pine, mountain Swiss	Pinus mugo
Pine, mountain Swiss dwarf	Pinus mugo ssp pumilio
Pine, Norfolk Island	Araucaria heterophylla
Pine, northern pitch	Pinus rigida
Pine nut	Pinus pinea
Pine, Oyster	Callitris rhomboidea
Pine, Oyster Bay	Callitris rhomboidea
Pine, pencil	Cupressus sempervirens 'Stricta'
Pine, Pinyon (Pinon)	Pinus edulis
Pine, pitch	Pinus rigida
Pine, plum Australian	Podocarpus elatus
Pine, plum Australian	Podocarpus elatus
Pine, plum Illawarra	Podocarpus elatus
Pine, Ponderosa	Pinus ponderosa
Pine, Port Jackson	Callitris rhomboidea
Pine, Port Jackson	Callitris roei
Pine, Prince's	Chimaphila
Pine, red	Pinus resinosa
Pine, Rottnest Island	Callitris preissii
Pine, sandhill	Callitris preissii ssp verrucosa
Pine, Scots	Pinus sylvestris
Pine, screw Veitch's	Pandanus veitchii
Pine, scrub	Pinus virginiana
Pine, shore	Pinus contorta
Pine, short-leaf	Pinus echinata
Pine, Siberian dwarf	Pinus pumila
Pine, silver	Pinus monticola
Pine, slash	Pinus elliottii
Pine, Southern pitch	Pinus palustris
Pine, stone	Pinus pinea
Pine, stone dwarf	Pinus pumila
Pine, stone Italian	Pinus pinea
Pine, sugar	Pinus lambertiana
Pine, Swiss stone	Pinus cembra
Pine, Tasman celery	Phyllocladus aspleniifolius
Pine, Tasmanian Cypress	Callitris oblonga
Pine, Torrey	Pinus torreyana
Pine, umbrella	Pinus pinea
Pine, Virginia	Pinus virginiana
Pine, western white	Pinus monticola
Pine, western yellow	Pinus ponderosa
Pine, Weymouth	Pinus strobus
Pine, white	Pinus strobus
Pine, white bark	Pinus albicaulis
Pine, Yunnan	Pinus yunnanensis
Pineapple	Ananas
Pineapple flower	Eucomis
Pineapple flower, giant	Eucomis pallidiflora
Pineapple guava	Acca sellowiana
Pineapple lily	Eucomis
Pineapple, red	Ananas bracteatus
Pineapple shrub	Calycanthus floridus
Pineapple, wild	Ananas bracteatus
Pinedrops	Pterospora andromeda
Pingurl (Pingle)	Dryandra carduacea
Pink	Dianthus
Pink, alpine	Dianthus alpinus
Pink, amur	Dianthus amurensis
Pink and white shower	Cassia nodosa
Pink candles	Ptilotus rotundifolius
Pink, Carolina	Silene carolina
Pink, Carthusian	Dianthus carthusianorum
Pink, Cheddar	Dianthus gratianopolitanus
Pink, Chinese	Dianthus chinensis
Pink, clove	Dianthus caryophyllus
Pink, clusterhead	Dianthus carthusianorum
Pink, cottage	Dianthus plumarius
Pink, Deptford	Dianthus armeria
Pink, fire	Silene virginica
Pink Geraldton wax	Chamaelaucium uncinatum
Pink, Indian	Dianthus chinensis
Pink, Indian	Spigelia marilandica

Common-Botanical Names

Common	Botanical	Common	Botanical
Pink, Japanese	Dianthus chinensis	Plantain, rose	Plantago major
Pink, maiden	Dianthus deltoides		'Rosularis'
Pink mink	Protea neriifolia	Plantain, water	Alisma plantago-aquatica
Pink pokers	Grevillea petrophilioides	Plantain, woolly	Plantago purshii
Pink pokers	Psylliostachys suworowii	Pleurisy root	Asclepias tuberosa
Pink porcelain lily	Alpinia zerumbet	Plough breaker	Erythrina zeyheri
Pink, rainbow	Dianthus chinensis	Plover's eggs	Adromischus festivus
Pink, sand	Dianthus arenarius	Pluimbossie	Clematopsis scabiosifolia
Pink shower	Cassia grandis	Pluisbossie	Lopholaena coriifolia
Pink shower	Cassia javanica	Plum	Prunus domestica
Pink stars	Crowea angustifolia	Plum, American	Prunus americana
Pink, superb	Dianthus superbus	Plum, Assyrian	Cordia myxa
Pink, swamp	Helonias bullata	Plum, billygoat	Terminalia ferdinandiana
Pinon, Mexican	Pinus cembroides	Plum, Burdekin	Pleiogynium cerasiferum
Pinon, one-needled	Pinus monophylla	Plum, Burdekin	Pleiogynium timorense
Pinon, Rocky Mountain	Pinus edulis	Plum, cherry	Prunus cerasifera
Pinon, single-leaf	Pinus monophylla	Plum, date	Diospyros lotus
Pinwheel	Aeonium haworthii	Plum, Davidson's	Davidsonia pruriens
Pinyuru	Eremophila cuneifolia	Plum, green	Buchanania obovata
Pipsissewa	Chimaphila umbellata	Plum, Indian	Oemleria cerasiformis
Pistachio	Pistacia	Plum, Java	Syzygium cuminii
Pistachio, Chinese	Pistacia chinensis	Plum, Kaffir	Harpephyllum caffrum
Pistol bush	Justicia adhatadoides	Plum, monkey hard-leaved	Diospyros scabrida v
Pistoolbos	Justicia adhatadoides		cordata
Pitaya	Cereus uruguayanus	Plum, Natal	Carissa macrocarpa
Pitch apple	Clusia major	Plum, Oregon	Oemleria cerasiformis
Pitcher , hooded	Sarracenia minor	Plum, sand	Prunus besseyi
Pitcher plant	Nepenthes	Plum, sugared-almond	Pachyphytum oviferum
Pitcher plant	Sarracenia	Plum, tulip	Pleiogynium timorense
Pitcher plant, common	Sarracenia purpurea	Plum, wild	Harpephyllum caffrum
Pitcher plant, tropical	Nepenthes	Plum, wild	Prunus americana
Pitcher plant, yellow	Sarracenia flava	Plum yew	Cephalotaxus
Pittosporum, Cape	Pittosporum viridiflorum	Plum yew	Cephalotaxus
Pittosporum, Japanese	Pittosporum tobira		harringtoniana
Pittosporum, narrow-leaved	Pittosporum	Plum yew	Prumnopitys andina
	phillyreoides	Plum yew, Chinese	Cephalotaxus fortunei
Pittosporum, Queensland	Pittosporum	Plum yew, fortune	Cephalotaxus fortunei
	rhombifolium	Plum-fruited yew	Prumnopitys andina
Pittosporum, sweet	Pittosporum undulatum	Plume plant	Calomeria
Pittosporum, weeping	Pittosporum		amaranthoides
	phillyreoides	Plume poppy	Macleaya
Pittosporum, yellow	Pittosporum revolutum	Plume poppy	Macleaya cordata
Pixie mops	Petrophile linearis	Plume thistle	Cirsium
Pixie mops, southern	Petrophile teretifolia	Plumed tussock grass	Chionochloa
Plakkie	Cotyledon orbiculata	Plush plant	Echeveria pulvinata
Plakkie	Cotyledon orbiculata v	Poached egg plant	Limnanthes
	orbiculata	Poached egg plant	Limnanthes douglasii
Plakkies	Crassula ovata	Poached eggs	Myriocephalus stuartii
Plane	Platanus	Podalyria, fragrant	Podalyria calyptrata
Plane, London	Platanus x hispanica	Podalyria, silky	Podalyria sericea
Plane, Oriental	Platanus x orientalis	Podocarp, Tasmanian	Podocarpus alpinus
Plantain	Musa	Podocarp, Tasmanian	Prumnopitys alpinus
Plantain, Chinese	Plantago asiatica	Podocarp, willowleaf	Podocarpus salignus
Plantain, French	Musa acuminata 'Dwarf	Podolepis, showy	Podolepis jaceoides
	Cavendish'	Poet's daffodil	Narcissus poeticus
Plantain, great	Plantago major	Poet's narcissus	Narcissus poeticus
Plantain, hoary	Plantago media	Pohutakawa	Metrosideros
Plantain, Indian great	Cacalia muhlenbergii	Pohutakawa, common	Metrosideros excelsus
Plantain, Indian pale	Cacalia atriplicifolia	Poinciana, yellow	Peltophorum
Plantain, Indian prairie	Cacalia tuberosa		pterocarpum
Plantain, Indian sweet	Cacalia suaveolens	Poincinia	Delonix regia
Plantain lily	Hosta	Poincinia, royal	Delonix regia
Plantain, mud	Alisma subcordatum	Poinsettia	Euphorbia pulcherrima
Plantain, narrow-leaved	Plantago lanceolata	Poinsettia, annual	Euphorbia cyathophora
Plantain, ribwort	Plantago lanceolata	Poinsettia, desert	Euphorbia cyathophora
Plantain, Robin's	Erigeron pulchellus	Poinsettia, wild	Euphorbia cyathophora

Common-Botanical Names

Common	Botanical
Poison arrow plant	Acokanthera oblongifolia
Poison, Box	Gastrolobium parviflorum
Poison bulb	Crinum asiaticum
Poison, crinkle-leaved	Gastrolobium villosum
Poison, kite-leaf	Gastrolobium laytonii
Poison, lamb	Isotropis cuneifolia
Poison, narrow-leaved	Gastrolobium stenophyllum
Poison, net-leaf	Gastrolobium racemosum
Poison, prickly	Gastrolobium spinosum
Poison rope, common	Strophanthus speciosus
Poison, woodbridge	Isotoma hypocrateriformis
Poison, York road	Gastrolobium calycinum
Poke	Phytolacca americana
Poke, Tibetan	Phytolacca acinosa
Poke, Tibetan	Phytolacca thibetica
Pokeberry	Phytolacca
Pokeroot	Phytolacca americana
Pokeroot, domestic	Phytolacca americana
Pokers, pink	Grevillea petrophilioides
Pokers, red	Hakea bucculenta
Pokeweed	Phytolacca americana
Pokeweed, Virginian	Phytolacca americana
Polar plant	Silphium laciniatum
Policeman's helmet	Impatiens glandulifera
Polka dot plant	Hypoestes
Polvillo, Guayacan	Tabebuia serratifolia
Polyanthus	Primula Polyanthus Group
Polypody	Polypodium
Polypody	Polypodium vulgare
Polypody, common	Polypodium vulgare
Pomegranate	Punica
Pomegranate	Punica granatum
Pomegranate, African	Burchellia bubalina
Pomegranate, dwarf	Punica granatum v nana
Pomegranate, native (AU)	Balaustion pulcherrimum
Pomegranate, wild	Burchellia bubalina
Pomme de liane zombie	Passiflora rubra
Pompoms, white	Rhodanthe sterilescens
Pompon tree	Dais cotinifolia
Pond lily, yellow	Nuphar advena
Pondil	Kunzea ericifolia
Pondweed	Elodea
Pondweed	Potamogeton
Pondweed, curled	Potamogeton crispus
Pondweed, shining	Potamogeton lucens
Pony, common	Paeonia officinalis
Pony tail	Beaucarnea recurvata
Pony tail, desert	Beaucarnea stricta
Pony tail, ruby red	Beaucarnea guatemalensis
Poontoo	Scaevola spinescens
Poor man's orchid	Impatiens glandulifera
Poor man's orchid	Schizanthus
Poor man's weather glass	Anagallis arvensis
Poot	Eucalyptus longicornis
Popcorn bush	Senna didymobotrya
Popinac, white	Leucaena latisiliqua
Poplar	Populus
Poplar, balsam	Populus balsamifera
Poplar, Berlin	Populus x berolinensis
Poplar, black	Populus nigra
Poplar, Canadian	Populus x canadensis
Poplar, Chinese necklace	Populus lasiocarpa
Poplar, desert	Codonocarpus cotinifolius
Poplar, grey	Populus x canescens
Poplar, Lombardy	Populus nigra v italica
Poplar, necklace	Populus deltoides
Poplar, Ontario	Populus x candicans
Poplar, water	Populus nigra
Poplar, Western balsam	Populus trichocarpa
Poplar, white	Populus alba
Poppy	Papaver
Poppy, alpine	Papaver alpinum
Poppy, Arctic	Papaver nudicaule
Poppy, Arctic	Papaver radicatum
Poppy, blue	Eustoma grandiflorum
Poppy, blue	Meconopsis
Poppy, California	Eschscholzia californica
Poppy, California tufted	Eschscholzia caespitosa
Poppy, Californian	Romneya
Poppy, corn	Papaver rhoeas
Poppy, feathered	Papaver laciniatum
Poppy, field	Papaver rhoeas
Poppy, Flanders	Papaver rhoeas
Poppy, harebell	Meconopsis quintuplinervia
Poppy, Himalayan blue	Meconopsis betonicifolia
Poppy, Himalayan blue	Meconopsis grandis
Poppy, Icelandic	Papaver nudicaule
Poppy, ladybird	Papaver commutatum
Poppy, lampshade	Meconopsis integrifolia
Poppy, long-headed	Papaver dubium
Poppy mallow	Callirhoe
Poppy mallow, clustered	Callirhoe triangulata
Poppy mallow, prairie	Callirhoe involucrata
Poppy, Opium	Papaver somniferum
Poppy, oriental	Papaver orientale
Poppy, prickly-headed long	Papaver argemone
Poppy, satin	Meconopsis nepaulensis
Poppy, Shirley	Papaver rhoeas
Poppy, Tibetan	Meconopsis horridula
Poppy, Tibetan blue	Meconopsis betonicifolia
Poppy, Tibetan yellow	Dicranostigma lactucoides
Poppy, tulip	Papaver glaucum
Poppy, water	Hydrocleys nymphoides
Poppy, Welsh	Meconopsis cambrica
Poppy, wild	Papaver aculeatum
Poppy, wind	Stylidium macranthum
Porcupine plant	Melicytus alpinus
Poroporo	Solanum aviculare
Poroporo	Solanum laciniatum
Port St. John's creeper	Podranea ricasoliana
Portia oil nut	Thespesia populnea
Portia tree	Thespesia populnea
Portland sago	Arum maculatum
Possum haw	Viburnum acerifolium
Possumwood	Diospyros virginiana
Posybush	Dais cotinifolia
Pot marigold	Calendula
Potato bush	Operculina brownii
Potato bush, blue	Solanum rantonnetii
Potato bush, spiny	Solanum ferosissimum
Potato creeper	Solanum seaforthianum
Potato, sweet native (AU)	Ipomoea costata
Potato tree	Solanum macranthum

Common-Botanical Names

Common Name	Botanical Name
Potato tree, Chilean	Solanum crispum
Potato vine	Solanum jasminioides
Potato vine	Solanum wendlandii
Poublom	Homeria elegans
Pouch flower	Calceolaria
Poui, pink	Tabebuia rosea
Poui, yellow	Tabebuia serratifolia
Poverty bush	Acacia translucens
Poverty bush	Eremophila foliosissima
Powder-puff, pink/red	Calliandra haematocephala
Powder-puff tree	Calliandra
Powderbark Wandoo	Eucalyptus accedens
Prairie colver	Dalea candidum
Prairie dock	Parthenium integrifolium
Prairie smoke	Geum triflorum
Prairie star	Lithophragma
Prairie tea	Potentilla rupestris
Prayer plant	Maranta
Pretty Betsy	Centranthus
Prickle ear	Acanthostachys
Prickly Moses	Acacia brownii
Prickly Moses	Acacia formesiana
Prickly Moses	Acacia ulicifolia
Prickly Moses	Acacia verticillata
Prickly Moses, dainty	Acacia pulchella v goadbyi
Prickly Moses, Tasmanian	Acacia riceana
Prickly Moses, western	Acacia pulchella
Prickly Moses, western	Acacia pulchella v glaberrima
Prickly pear	Opuntia compressa
Prickly pear, brittle	Opuntia fragilis
Prickly pear, eastern	Opuntia compressa
Prickly pear, Engelmann	Opuntia ficus-indica
Prickly pear, fragile	Opuntia fragilis
Prickly pear, plains	Opuntia polycantha
Prickly poppy	Argemone
Prickly poppy	Argemone mexicana
Pricklybark	Eucalyptus todtiana
Pride of Bolivia	Tipuana tipu
Pride of Burma	Amherstia nobilis
Pride of India	Koelreuteria
Pride of India	Lagerstroemeria flos reginae
Pride of India	Lagerstroemeria speciosa
Pride of India	Melia azedarach
Pride of Madeira	Echium candicans
Pride of Table Mountain	Disa uniflora
Pride-of-de-kaap	Bauhinia galpinii
Pride-of-the-Cape	Bauhinia galpinii
Primavera	Cybistax donnell-smithii
Primrose	Primula
Primrose	Primula vulgaris
Primrose, alpine red	Primula erythra
Primrose, alpine sticky	Primula viscosa
Primrose, bird's eye	Primula farinosa
Primrose, Cape	Streptocarpus
Primrose, evening	Oenothera caespitosa
Primrose, evening common	Oenothera biennis
Primrose, evening desert	Oenothera deltoides
Primrose, fairy	Primula malacoides
Primrose, Japanese	Primua japonica
Primrose, New Mexico	Oenothera berlandieri
Primrose, Piedmont	Primula pedemontana
Primrose, sand	Oenothera rhombipetala
Primrose, showy	Oenothera speciosa
Primula, drumstick	Primula denticulata
Prince of Wales' feathers	Celosia spicata
Prince's feather	Amaranthus cruentus
Prince's feather	Amaranthus hypochondriacus
Prince's feather	Persicaria orientale
Prince's pine	Chimaphila
Princess feather	Persicaria orientale
Princess palm	Dictyosperma
Princess tree	Paulownia tomentosa
Prinsepia, cherry	Prinsepia sinensis
Privet	Ligustrum
Privet, amur	Ligustrum amurense
Privet, Chinese	Ligustrum lucidum
Privet, common	Ligustrum vulgare
Privet, desert	Peperomia obtusifolia Magnoliifolia Group
Privet, Japanese	Ligustrum japonicum
Proboscis flower	Proboscidea
Propeller bush	Dodonaea truncatiales
Propeller plant	Crassula perfoliata v minor
Propeller plant, airplane	Crassula falcata
Prophet flower	Arnebia pulchra
Protea, blackbeard	Protea lepidocarpodendron
Protea, Bot River	Protea compacta
Protea, bredasdorp	Protea neriifolia
Protea, bredasdorp	Protea susannae
Protea, broadleaf	Protea eximia
Protea, Burchell's	Protea burchellii
Protea, doll's	Dicoma anomala
Protea, doll's	Dicoma zeyheri
Protea, forest	Protea mundii
Protea, giant	Protea cynaroides
Protea, green	Protea coronata
Protea, Hotentot's Holland	Protea lacticolor
Protea, king	Protea cynaroides
Protea, Ladismith	Protea aristata
Protea, oleanderleaf	Protea neriifolia
Protea, peach	Protea grandiceps
Protea, pincushion	Leucospermum cordifolium
Protea, Potberg	Protea aurea ssp potbergensis
Protea, Queen	Protea magnifica
Protea, red	Protea grandiceps
Protea, shuttlecock	Protea aurea ssp aurea
Protea, small green	Protea scolymocephala
Protea, Transvaal	Protea rubropilosa
Protea, waterlily	Protea aurea
Protea, waterlily	Protea punctata
Protea, woolly giant	Protea magnifica
Protea, woolly-bearded	Protea magnifica
Pry	Tilia cordata
Psoralea, large-bracted	Psoralea cuspidata
Psoralea, tall	Psoralea pustulata
Psychotria, mountain	Psychotria zombamontana
Psyllium, blond	Plantago ovata
Psyllium, Indian	Plantago ovata
Pua keni keni	Fagraea berterana
Puawhanganga	Clematis paniculata
Puccoon, red	Sanguinaria

Common-Botanical Names

Pudding pipe-tree — Cassia fistula
Pudjak — Dryandra sessilis
Pudjarn — Dryandra nivea
Puffed wheat — Briza maxima
Puka — Mertya sinclairii
Pulgarla — Banksia grandis
Pulidj (Bullich) — Eucalyptus megacarpa
Pulsatilla, Chinese — Pulsatilla chinensis
Pulsatilla, wild — Pulsatilla patens
Pumpkin bark — Eucalyptus pachycalyx
Puncturevine — Tribulus terrestris
Pungul — Eucalyptus transcontinentalis
Pungura — Banksia littoralis
Puno — Beaufortia squarrosa
Purple bell vine — Rhodochiton
Purple moor grass — Molinia caerulea
Purple toothwort — Lathraea clandestina
Purple waffle plant — Hemigraphis 'Exotica'
Purple wreath — Petrea volubilis
Purslane — Claytonia
Purslane — Portulaca
Purslane, Siberian — Claytonia sibirica
Purslane, tree — Atriplex halimus
Pussy ears — Cyanotis somaliensis
Pussy ears — Kalanchoe tomentosa
Pussy tails — Ptilotus exaltatus
Pussy-toes — Antennaria
Pussy-toes — Antennaria plantaginifolia
Pussy-toes, rosy — Antennaria microphylla
Pussycats tails — Ptilotus clementii
Puyenak — Hovea pungens
Puzzle bush — Ehretia rigida
Pygmy bamboo — Pleioblastus pygmaeus
Pyjama lily — Crinum macowanii
Pyramid tree, Queensland — Lagunaria patersonii
Pyramidal bugle — Ajuga pyramidalis
Pyrethrum — Tanacetum
Pyrethrum — Tanacetum coccineum
Pyrethrum, Dalmatian — Tanacetum cinerariaefolium
Pyrola, pink — Pyrola asarifolia
Pyrola, white-vein — Pyrola picta
Qing-guo — Artemisia annua
Qua(n)dong, sweet — Santalum acuminatum
Quadong — Santalum acuminatum
Quailbush — Atriplex lentiformis
Quaking grass — Briza
Quaking grass, common — Briza media
Quaking grass, greater — Briza maxima
Quaking grass, lesser — Briza minor
Qualupbell — Pimelea physodes
Quamash — Camassia
Quamash — Camassia quamash
Quandong, blue — Elaeocarpus grandis
Quandong, white — Elaeocarpus foveolatus
Quassia — Picrasma quassioides
Quater — Vinca major
Queen Anne's double daffodil — Narcissus 'Eystettensis'
Queen Anne's jonquil — Narcissus jonquilla 'Flore Pleno'
Queen Anne's lace — Daucus carota
Queen Anne's thimbles — Gilia capitata
Queen lily — Curcuma petiolata
Queen lily — Phaedranassa
Queen of the night — Hylocereus undatus

Queen of the night — Selenicereus grandiflorus
Queen of the prairie — Filipendula rubra
Queen Victoria's lady fern — Athyrium filix-femina Cruciatum Group
Queen's tears — Billbergia nutans
Queen's wreath — Antigonon
Queen's wreath — Petrea volubilis
Queencup — Clintonia uniflora
Queensland lacebark — Brachychiton discolor
Queensland nut — Macadamia integrifolia
Queensland pyramidal tree — Lagunaria patersonii
Queensland umbrella tree — Schefflera actinophylla
Quickthorn — Crataegus monogyna
Quillquina — Porophyllum ruderale
Quince — Cydonia
Quince, common — Cydonia oblonga
Quince, flowering — Chaenomeles
Quince, Japanese — Chaenomeles
Quince, Japanese — Chaenomeles japonica
Quince, Mauele's — Chaenomeles japonica
Quinine berry — Petalostigma pubescens
Quinine brush — Purshia tridentata
Quinine bush — Garrya elliptica
Quinine bush — Garrya fremontii
Quinine tree — Rauvolfia caffra
Quinine, wild — Parthenium integrifolium
Quinoa — Chenopodium quinoa
Quito orange — Solanum quitoense
Quiver tree — Aloe dichotoma
Quoll's paw — Anigozanthus humilis
Quoll's paw, Albany — Anigozanthus preissii
Rabbit tracks — Maranta leuconeura v kerchoveana
Rabbit's foot fern — Davallia solida v fejeenis
Rabbitbrush, low — Chrysothamnus viscidiflorus
Rabbitbrush, rubber — Chrysothamnus nauseosus
Radiator plant — Peperomia maculosa
Radish plant — Phytolacca americana
Raffia — Raphia
Ragged robin — Lychnis flos-cuculi
Ragwort — Senecio jacobaea
Ragwort, Leopard's bane — Senecio doronicum
Ragwort, London — Senecio x subnebrodensis
Ragwort, Oxford — Senecio squalidus
Ragwort, prairie — Senecio plattensis
Rain flower — Zephyranthes
Rain tree — Lonchocarpus cappassa
Rain tree — Samanea saman
Rain tree, monkey pod — Samanea saman
Rainbow star — Cryptanthus bromelioides
Raisin, climbing — Grewia caffra
Raisin, rough-leaved — Grewia flavescens v flavescens
Raisin tree — Hovenia dulcis
Raisin tree, Japanese — Hovenia dulcis
Rampion — Campanula rapunculus
Rampion, horned — Phyteuma scheuzeri
Rampion, Pyrenean — Phyteuma charmelii
Rampion, spiked — Phyteuma spicatum
Ranger — Corylus avellana
Rangiora — Brachyglottis repanda
Rangoon creeper — Quisqualis indica

Common-Botanical Names

Rankals
Rankplatboontjie
Rankrosyntjie
Ranktolbos
Rankvygies
Ranting widow
Rape
Raripila, red
Raspberry, black-cap
Raspberry, evergreen
Raspberry, flowering
Raspberry jam wood
Raspberry, Mysore black
Raspberry, red
Raspwort, glandular

Rat's tail cactus
Rata
Rata
Rata
Rata, northern
Ratama
Rattan cane
Rattle, hay
Rattle, yellow
Rattle-pod
Rattle-pod
Rattle-pod, Cape
Rattlebox
Rattlebox
Rattlebox
Rattlesnake master
Rattlesnake root
Rau ngo
Rau om
Rau rum
Rauli (Raoul)
Rauvolfia
Ray flower, coastal
Ray flower, grey
Red berry tree
Red cole
Red flame ivy
Red hot poker
Red hot poker, dwarf

Red hot poker tree
Red ink plant
Red mountain spinach
Red Orache
Red root
Red root
Red root
Red toothbrushes
Red tree
Red-hot cat's tail
Red-hot poker
Red-ink plant
Redbird flower

Redbud
Redbud, California
Redbud, Chinese
Redbud, eastern
Redbud, western
Redheart

Hippia frutescens
Dalbergia obovata
Grewia caffra
Diospyros simii
Cephalophyllum alstonii
Epilobium angustifolium
Brassica napus
Mentha x smithiana
Rubus leucodermis
Rubus laciniatus
Rubus odoratus
Acacia acuminata
Rubus niveus
Rubus idaeus
Haloragodendron
glandulosum
Aporocactus
Metrosideros
Metrosideros excelsa
Metrosideros robustus
Metrosideros robusta
Parkinsonia aculeata
Calamus rotang
Rhinanthus minor
Rhinanthus minor
Crotalaria medicaginea
Crotalaria novae-hollandii
Crotalaria capensis
Crotalaria
Crotalaria sagittalis
Ludwigia alternifolia
Eryngium yuccifolium
Prenanthes racemosa
Limnophila aromatica
Limnophila aromatica
Persicaria odorata
Nothofagus alpina
Rauvolfia serpentina
Anthocercis littorea
Anthocercis littorea
Allophylus natalensis
Armoracia rusticana
Hemigraphis alternata
Kniphofia
Kniphofia triangularis ssp
triangularis
Erythrina abyssinica
Phytolacca americana
Atriplex hortensis
Atriplex hortensis
Ceanothus americanus
Ceanothus ovatus
Ceanothus velutinus
Grevillea hookeriana
Peperomia metallica
Acalypha hispida
Arum maculatum
Phytolacca americana
Pedilanthus
tithymaloides 'Variegata'
Cercis canadensis
Cercis occidentalis
Cercis chinensis
Cercis canadensis
Cercis occidentalis
Eucalyptus decipiens

Redroot
Redwing
Redwood

Redwood, Californian
Redwood, coastal
Redwood, dawn

Redwood, giant

Redwood, Sierra

Reed
Reed, common
Reed, giant
Reed grass
Reed, Norfolk
Reed palm
Reed, paper
Reed, thatching

Reed, thatching
Reed, wood stout
Reedmace
Reedmace, narrow-leaved
Regelia, Barrens
Regelia, large
Rengarenga
Resin bush
Resin tree, Cape east
Resin tree, Namaqua
Restharrow
Restharrow, common
Restharrow, large
Restharrow, round-leaved
Restharrow, shrubby
Restharrow, spiny
Resurrection lily
Resurrection plant

Resurrection plant
Reuseomsambeet
Rewa rewa
Rheumatism root
Rhododendron, Fortune's
Rhododendron, Himalayan tree

Rhododendron, Pacific

Rhubarb
Rhubarb, Asian
Rhubarb, butcher's
Rhubarb, Chinese
Rhubarb, Sally
Rhubarb, Tartarian
Rhubarb, Turkey
Rhubarb, wild
Rhus, furry
Rhus, red currant
Rhynco
Ribbon bush
Ribbon plant
Ribbon wood, marsh
Ribbonwood
Ribgrass
Rice

Wackendorfia thyrsiflora
Pterolobium stellatum
Eucalyptus
transcontinentalis
Sequoia sempervirens
Sequoia sempervirens
Metasequoia
glyptostroboides
Sequoiadendron
giganteum
Sequoiadendron
giganteum
Phragmites
Phragmites australis
Arundo donax
Calamagrostis
Phragmites australis
Chamaedorea seifrizii
Cyperus papyrus
Chondropetalum
tectorum
Thamnochortus insignis
Cinna arundinacea
Typha
Typha angustifolia
Regelia velutina
Regelia megacephala
Arthropodium cirratum
Euryops tenuissimus
Ozoroa mucronata
Ozoroa dispar
Ononis
Ononis repens
Ononis natrix
Ononis rotundifolia
Ononis fruticosa
Ononis spinosa
Kaempferia rotunda
Myrothamnus
flabellifolius
Selaginella lepidophylla
Milletia sutherlandii
Knightia excelsa
Jeffersonia diphylla
Rhododendron fortunei
Rhododendron
arboreum
Rhododendron
macrophyllum
Rheum
Rheum australe
Petasites hybridus
Rheum palmatum
Fallopia japonica
Rheum tataricum
Rheum palmatum
Petasites hybridus
Rhus tomentosa
Rhus chirindensis
Rhynchosia minima
Hypoestes aristata
Dracaena sanderiana
Plagianthus divaricatus
Hoheria sexstylosa
Plantago lanceolata
Oryza

Common-Botanical Names

Common	Botanical
Rice, annual wild	Zizania aquatica
Rice, Canada wild	Zizania aquatica
Rice, Canadian wild	Zizania aquatica
Rice flower	Ozothamnus diosmifolium
Rice flower	Pimelea
Rice flower, pink	Pimelea ferruginea
Rice flower, smooth	Pimelea glauca
Rice flower, white	Pimelea floribunda
Rice, millet	Oryzopsis miliacea
Rice, petty	Chenopodium quinoa
Rice root	Fritillaria affinis
Rice root, northern	Fritillaria camschatcensis
Rice, water	Zizania aquatica
Rice, wild	Zizania
Rice-paper plant	Tetrapanax papyrifer
Rimu	Dacrydium cupressinum
Ringwood tree	Maerua schinzii
River bells	Phygelius capensis
River pumpkin	Gunnera perpensa
Rivierals	Matricaria nigellifolia
Rivierharpuisbos	Euryops virgineus
Riviertolbos	Leucadendron salicifolium
Riviervaderlandswilg	Combretum erythrophyllum
Rivierverfbos	Indigofera frutescens
Roast-beef plant	Iris foetidissima
Robin redbreast	Melaleuca lateritia
Robin-run-the-hedge	Galium aparine
Roble	Nothofagus obliqua
Rocambole	Allium sativum ophioscordon
Rock bells	Aquilegia canadensis
Rock brake, purple	Pellaea atropurpurea
Rock cress	Arabis
Rock cress	Aubrieta
Rock cress, purple	Aubrieta deltoidea
Rock cress, wall	Arabis caucasica 'Compacta'
Rock daisy	Brachyscome multifida
Rock fringe	Epilobium obcordatum
Rock harlequin	Corydalis sempervirens
Rock jasmine	Androsace
Rock purslane	Calandrinia umbellata
Rock rose	Cistus
Rock rose	Helianthemum
Rock rose	Helianthemum nummularium
Rock rose, Montpellier	Cistus monspeliensis
Rock rose, white	Helianthemum appeninum
Rock spiraea	Petrophytum
Rock spray	Cotoneaster acutifolius
Rockcap fern	Polypodium virginianum
Rocket, Dame's	Hesperis matronalis
Rocket, sweet	Hesperis matronalis
Rocket, yellow	Barbarea vulgaris
Roebuck berry	Rubus saxatilis
Rolvarkie	Aptosimum spinescens
Rooi-ertjie	Tephrosia grandiflora
Rooiberglalie	Cyrtanthus huttonii
Rooibostee	Aspalanthus linearis
Rooiels	Cunonia capensis
Rooigeeltulp	Homeria comptonii
Rooikanol	Wachendorfia thyrsiflora
Rooikeur	Hypocalyptus coluteoides
Rooiklossieheide	Erica mammosa
Rooikweper	Cryptocarya glaucescens
Rooipypie	Gladiolus priorii
Rooipypie	Tritoniopsis caffra
Rooistompie	Brunia stokoei
Rooistompie	Mimetes cucullatus
Rooisuikerkan	Protea grandiceps
Rooiwortel	Bulbine latifolia
Rooiwortel	Dilatris corymbosa
Root beer plant	Piper auritum
Rosal de la pasion	Passiflora arida v cerralbensis
Rosary vine	Ceropegia linearis ssp woodii
Rose, Apothecary's	Rosa gallica v officinalis
Rose apple	Syzygium moorei
Rose, Austrian briar	Rosa foetida
Rose, Austrian copper	Rosa foetida 'Bicolor'
Rose, Austrian yellow	Rosa foetida
Rose, baldhip	Rosa gymnocarpa
Rose, Bansian	Rosa banksiae
Rose bay	Nerium oleander
Rose, burnet	Rosa pimpinellifolia
Rose, burr	Rosa roxburghii
Rose, Camellia	Rosa laevigata
Rose, Cherokee	Rosa laevigata
Rose, Chestnut	Rosa roxburghii
Rose, Chickasaw	Rosa bracteata
Rose, China old blush	Rosa x odorata 'Pallida'
Rose, China Parson's pink	Rosa x odorata 'Pallida'
Rose, China Slater's crimson	Rosa x odorata 'Semperflorens'
Rose, Chinquapin	Rosa roxburghii
Rose cockade	Leucadendron tinctum
Rose, crested moss	Rosa x centifolia 'Cristata'
Rose, damask	Rosa damascena
Rose, damask autumn	Rosa damascena v semperflorens
Rose, damask crimson	Rosa gallica v officinalis
Rose, damask painted	Rosa 'Leda'
Rose, desert	Adenium
Rose, desert	Gossypium australe
Rose, desert Sturt's	Gossypium sturtianum
Rose, Dowerin	Eucalyptus pyriformis
Rose, Eglantine	Rosa rubiginosa
Rose, father Hugo's	Rosa xanthina f hugonis
Rose, Fortune's double yellow	Rosa x odorata 'Pseudindica'
Rose, four seasons	Rosa damascena v semperflorens
Rose, French	Rosa gallica
Rose, great white	Rosa x alba 'Alba Maxima'
Rose, green	Rosa x odorata 'Viridiflora'
Rose, hedgehog	Rosa rugosa
Rose, Himalayan musk	Rosa brunonii
Rose, Illinois	Rosa setigera
Rose, incense	Rosa primula
Rose, Jacobite	Rosa 'Alba Maxima'
Rose, Japanese	Rosa rugosa
Rose, lenten	Helleborus orientalis
Rose, Macartney	Rosa bracteata
Rose, memorial	Rosa wichurana

Common-Botanical Names

Common	Botanical
Rose, moss red	Rosa 'Henri Martin'
Rose, mundi	Rosa gallica 'Versicolor'
Rose, musk	Rosa moschata
Rose, myrrh scented	Rosa 'Splendens'
Rose, Nootka	Rosa nutkana
Rose of Castille	Rosa damascena v semperflorens
Rose of China	Hibiscus rosa-sinensis
Rose of Jericho	Selaginella lepidophylla
Rose of Sharon	Hibiscus syriacus
Rose of Sharon	Hypericum calycinum
Rose of the West	Eucalyptus macrocarpa
Rose, old black	Rosa 'Nuits de Young'
Rose, old glory	Rosa 'Gloire de Dijon'
Rose, pasture	Rosa arkansana
Rose, Persian yellow	Rosa foetida 'Persiana'
Rose, Portland	Rosa 'Portlandica'
Rose, prickly	Rosa acicularis
Rose, Provins	Rosa gallica v officinalis
Rose, Ramanas	Rosa rugosa
Rose, red of Lancaster	Rosa gallica v officinalis
Rose, red-leaf	Rosa rubrifolia
Rose, Redwood	Rosa gymnocarpa
Rose, riverine	Gossypium robinsonii
Rose, rugosa	Rosa rugosa
Rose, Sacramento	Rosa stellata v mirifica
Rose, Scotch	Rosa pimpinellifolia
Rose, Scots	Rosa pimpinellifolia
Rose, snowbush	Rosa 'Dupontii'
Rose, swamp	Rosa palustris
Rose, sweet briar	Rosa rubiginosa
Rose, thornless	Rosa 'Zephirine Drouhin'
Rose, velvet double	Rosa 'Tuscany Superb'
Rose, white of York	Rosa x alba 'Alba Maxima'
Rose, wild early	Rosa blanda
Rose, winged thorn	Rosa sericea ssp omeiensis f pteracantha
Rose, wood	Merremia tuberosa
Rose, Woods'	Rosa woodsii
Rosebay, East Indian	Tabernaemontana divaricata
Rosebay, white	Epilobium angustifolium f album
Rosebay, willow herb	Epilobium angustifolium
Roselle, Jamaica	Hibiscus sabdariffa
Rosemary	Rosmarinus
Rosemary	Rosmarinus officinalis
Rosemary, Australian	Westringia fruticosa
Rosemary, coast	Westringia fruticosa
Rosemary, Cumberland	Conradina verticillata
Rosemary, pine-scented	Rosmarinus angustifolia
Rosemary, wild	Dampiera rosmarinifolia
Rosemary, wild	Eriocephalus africanus
Roseroot	Rhodiola rosea
Rosewood	Acacia binervia
Rosewood	Acacia fasciculifera
Rosewood	Acacia rhodoxylon
Rosewood	Dysoxylum fraserianum
Rosewood	Pterocarpus marsupium
Rosewood, Arizona	Vaquelina californica
Rosewood, Brazilian	Tipuana tipu
Rosewood, Burmese	Pterocarpus indicus
Rosewood, hairy	Dysoxylum rufum
Rosewood of India	Dalbergia latifolia
Rosewood, western	Heterodendron
Rosin weed	oleifolium
Rosin weed	Silphium dentatum
Rosinweed	Silphium integrifolium
Rothmannia, small-flowered	Grindelia
Rotsdrolpeer	Rothmannia globosa
Rotsessenhout	Dombeya autumnalis
Rotssuikerbos	Ekebergia pterophylla
Rotstolbos	Protea venusta
	Leucadendron strobilinium
Rowan	Sorbus aucuparia
Rowan, Hubei	Sorbus hupehensis
Rowan, Hupeh	Sorbus hupehensis
Rowan, Sargent's	Sorbus sargentiana
Rowan, snowberry	Sorbus commixta
Royal palm	Roystonea
Rubber plant	Ficus elastica
Rubber plant, baby	Peperomia clusiifolia
Rubber rabbit bush	Chryothamnus nauseosus
Rubber tree, hardy	Eucommia ulmoides
Rubber tree, India	Ficus elastica
Rubber vine	Cryptostegia grandiflora
Rue	Ruta
Rue, African	Peganum harmala
Rue, common	Ruta graveolens
Rue, fringed	Ruta chalapensis
Rue, goat's	Tephrosia virginiana
Rue, mid-eastern	Ruta chalapensis
Rue, Syrian	Peganum harmala
Rue, wall	Asplenium ruta-muraria
Ruffle palm	Aiphanes
Ruikpypie	Freesia alba
Running postman	Kennedia prostrata
Rupturewort	Herniaria glabra
Rush	Juncus
Rush, club bristle	Scirpus setaceus
Rush, common	Juncus effusus
Rush, cord	Restio gracilis
Rush, cord fringed	Restio fimbriatus
Rush, corkscrew	Juncus effusus 'Spiralis'
Rush, dwarf	Juncus ensifolius
Rush, Egyptian paper	Cyperus papyrus
Rush, flowering	Butomus
Rush, inland	Juncus interior
Rush, jointed	Juncus articulatus
Rush, knotted	Juncus nodosus
Rush, needle-spike	Eleocharis acicularis
Rush, pale	Juncus pallida
Rush, path	Juncus tenuis
Rush, plume	Restio tetraphyllus
Rush, scouring	Equisetum hyemale
Rush, short-fruited	Juncus brachycarpus
Rush, soft	Juncus effusus
Rush, spike	Eleocharis acicularis
Rush, stout	Juncus nodatus
Rush, sword-leaved	Juncus ensifolius
Rush, tassel	Restio tetraphyllus ssp meiostachys
Rush, Torrey's	Juncus torreyi
Rush, two-flowered	Juncus biflorus
Russian vine	Fallopia baldschuanica
Rusty back fern	Asplenium ceterach
Rusty jacket	Eucalyptus peltata
Rusty leaf	Menziesia ferruginea
Rusty pods	Hovea longifolia

Common-Botanical Names

Common	Botanical
Rye, lyme	Elymus
Rye, wild	Elymus
Rye, wild blue	Elymus hispidus
Rye, wild Canadian	Elymus canadensis
Rye, wild riverbank	Elymus riparius
Rye, wild silky	Elymus villosus
Rye, wild Virginian	Elymus virginicus
Sacaton, alkali	Sporobolus airoides
Sacaton, giant	Sporobolus wrightii
Sacred bamboo	Nandina domestica
Sacred flower of the Incas	Cantua buxifolia
Sadadhatura	Datura metel
Safflower	Carthamus
Safflower	Carthamus tinctorius
Saffron	Crocus sativus
Saffron thistle	Carthamus tinctorius
Sage	Salvia
Sage, Autumn	Salvia greggii
Sage, blue	Eranthemum pulchellum
Sage, blue	Salvia azurea
Sage, blue	Salvia clevelandii
Sage, blue wild	Salvia aurita
Sage, bog	Salvia uliginosa
Sage, brown	Salvia africana-lutea
Sage brush, California	Artemisia california
Sage brush, sand	Artemisia filifolia
Sage, California white	Salvia apiana
Sage, candelabra	Salvia clevelandii
Sage, clary silver	Salvia argentea
Sage, Cleveland	Salvia clevelandii
Sage, coastal	Salvia scabra
Sage, common	Salvia officinalis
Sage, creeping	Salvia pratensis
Sage, Ethiopian	Salvia aethiopsis
Sage, fine-leaved	Salvia namaensis
Sage, fringed	Artemisia frigida
Sage, garden	Salvia officinalis
Sage, gentian	Salvia cacaliifolia
Sage, golden	Salvia africana-lutea
Sage, hummingbird	Salvia leucantha
Sage, hummingbird Texas	Salvia coccinea
Sage, Jerusalem	Phlomis fruticosa
Sage, Jerusalem	Pulmonaria saccharata
Sage, Jim	Salvia clevelandii
Sage, lavender-scented	Salvia lavandulifolia
Sage, linden-leaved	Salvia tiliifolia
Sage, Louisiana	Artemisia ludoviciana
Sage, lyre-leaved	Salvia lyrata
Sage, mealy	Salvia farinacea
Sage, mealycup	Salvia farinacea
Sage, Mediterranean	Salvia aethiopsis
Sage, mid-eastern	Salvia fruticosa
Sage, pineapple	Salvia elegans
Sage, pitcher	Salvia azurea
Sage, prairie	Artemisia ludoviciana
Sage, purple	Salvia officinalis 'Purpurascens'
Sage, red	Salvia militorrhiza
Sage, red-veined	Salvia haematodes
Sage, red-veined	Salvia pratensis
Sage, Russian	Perovskia atriplicifolia
Sage, sacred	Salvia apiana
Sage, sand	Artemisia filifolia
Sage, scarlet	Salvia coccinea
Sage, scarlet	Salvia splendens
Sage, silver	Seriphidium canum
Sage, silvery downy	Salvia chamaedryoides
Sage, Spanish	Salvia lavandulifolia
Sage, vervain	Salvia verbenaca
Sage, white	Salvia apiana
Sage, wild blue	Salvia azurea
Sage, yellow	Lantana camara
Sage, Zapotec	Salvia divinorum
Sagebrush	Artemisia
Sagebrush	Seriphidium tridentatum
Sagebrush, basin	Seriphidium tridentatum
Sago, Australian	Macrozamia communis
Sago palm	Cycas
Sago palm	Cycas circinalis
Sago palm, Japanese	Cycas revoluta
Saguaro	Carnegiea gigantea
Sailor's caps	Dodecatheon hendersonii
Sainfoin	Onobrychis viciifolia
Sainfoin, alpine	Hedysarum obscurum
Salad burnet	Poterium sanguisorba
Salad burnet	Sanguisorba minor ssp muricata
Salal	Gaultheria shallon
Salieblaarbloubos	Diospyros lycioides ssp geurkei
Sallee, white	Eucalyptus pauciflora
Sallies	Salix
Sallow thorn	Hippophae rhamnoides
Sally, broad-leaved	Eucalyptus camphora
Sally, little	Eucalyptus moorei nana
Salmon-berry	Rubus spectabilis
Salt bush, annual	Atriplex holocarpa
Salt bush, annual	Atriplex semilunaris
Salt bush, Australian	Atriplex semibaccata
Salt bush, bladder	Atriplex vesicaria
Salt bush, blue	Atriplex glauca
Salt bush, coast	Atriplex isatidea
Salt bush, creeping	Atriplex semibaccata
Salt bush, diamond	Atriplex semibaccata
Salt bush, dwarf	Atriplex codonocarpa
Salt bush, fan	Atriplex angulata
Salt bush, four-winged	Atriplex canescens
Salt bush, Gardner's	Atriplex gardneri
Salt bush, giant	Atriplex nummularia
Salt bush, grey	Atriplex cinerea
Salt bush, marsh	Atriplex paludosa
Salt bush, Nuttall's	Atriplex nuttallii
Salt bush, pop	Atriplex holocarpa
Salt bush, river	Atriplex amnicola
Salt bush, shadscale	Atriplex confertifolia
Salt bush, silver	Atriplex bunburyana
Salt bush, spiny	Atriplex confertifolia
Salt bush, wavy-leaf	Atriplex undulata
Salt tree	Halimodendron halodendron
Saltbush, ruby	Enchylaena tomentosa
Salvia, black	Salvia mellifera
Salvia, grape-scented	Salvia mellissifolia
Salvia, Himalayan	Salvia moorcroftiana
Salvia, Moorcroft's	Salvia moorcroftiana
Salwood, brown	Acacia aulacocarpa
Samphire	Crithium maritimum
Samphire	Halosarcia pergranulata
San Jose hesper palm	Brahea brandegeei
San Pedro cactus	Trichocereus pachanoi
Sand dollar cactus	Astrophytum asterias

Common-Botanical Names

Common	Botanical
Sand myrtle	Leiophyllum buxifolium
Sandalwood, fragrant	Santalum spicatum
Sandalwood, Indian white	Santalum album
Sandalwood, northern	Santalum lanceolatum
Sandalwood, red	Adenanthera pavonina
Sandbush, yellow	Leucadendron coniferum
Sandcherry, eastern	Prunus pumila
Sandflower	Ammobium alatum
Sandpaperbush	Kissenia capensis
Sandpypie	Gladiolus gracilis
Sandpypie	Gladiolus gracilis v latifolius
Sandui	Veltheimia bracteata
Sandvygie	Dorotheanthus rourkei
Sandwort	Arenaria
Sandwort	Minuartia
Sandwort, Corsican	Arenaria balearica
Sandwort, mountain	Arenaria montana
Sandwort, pink	Arenaria purpurascens
Sandwort, stiff	Arenaria stricta
Sandwort, vernal	Minuartia verna
Sansalie	Salvia africana-lutea
Santa Lucia fir	Abies bracteata
Santolina, green	Santolina rosmarinifolia ssp rosmarinifolia
Santolina, grey	Santolina incana
Santonica	Artemisia chamaemifolia
Sapodilla	Manilkara zapota
Sapphire berry	Symplocos paniculatus
Sapphire flower	Browallia speciosa
Sarana, black	Fritillaria camschatcensis
Sarawag	Pinanga insignis
Sarpghanda	Rauvolfia serpentina
Sarsaparilla, American	Aralia nudicaulis
Sarsaparilla, wild	Aralia nudicaulis
Sarsparilla	Hardenbergia comptonia
Sarsparilla, Australian	Hardenbergia violacea
Sassafras, Australian	Atherosperma moschatum
Sassafras, Tasmanian	Atherosperma
Satin flower	Clarkia amoena
Satin flower	Lunaria
Satin flower	Sisyrinchium
Satin flower	Stellaria holostea
Satin flower, New Zealand	Libertia grandiflora
Satinash, rose	Syzygium crebrinerve
Satinwood	Phebalium
Satinwood	Phebalium squameum
Satinwood, tulip	Rhodosphaera rhodanthema
Satsuma	Citrus unshiu
Saucer berry, grey-leaved	Cordia sinensis
Sauchan	Salix
Saugh	Salix
Sausage tree	Kigelia
Sausage tree	Kigelia africana
Savin	Juniperus sabina
Savory	Satureja
Savory, lemon	Satureja biflora
Savory, ornamental	Calamintha grandiflora
Savory, summer	Satureja hortensis
Savory, winter	Satureja montana
Savory, winter creeping	Satureja montana ssp illyrica
Savory, winter pygmy	Satureja montana 'Nana'
Saw cabbage palm	Acoelorraphe wrightii
Saw palm	Acoelorraphe
Saw-wort, alpine	Serratula tinctoria
Saxifrage	Saxifraga
Saxifrage, blue	Saxifraga caesia
Saxifrage, burnet	Pimpinella saxifraga
Saxifrage, livelong	Saxifraga paniculata
Saxifrage, meadow	Saxifraga granulata
Saxifrage, mountain yellow	Saxifraga aizoides
Saxifrage, purple	Saxifraga oppositifolia
Saxifrage, purple mountain	Saxifraga oppositifolia
Saxifrage, Pyrenean	Saxifraga longifolia
Saxifrage, starry	Saxifraga stellaris
Saxifrage, swamp	Saxifraga pensylvanica
Scabious, alpine	Cephalaria alpina
Scabious, field	Knautia arvensis
Scabious, giant	Cephalaria gigantea
Scabious, sheep's bit	Jasione laevis
Scabious, shepherd's	Jasione laevis
Scabious, shining	Scabiosa lucida
Scabious, small	Scabiosa columbaria
Scabious, sweet	Scabiosa atropurpurea
Scabious, wild	Scabiosa incisa
Scabious, yellow	Cephalaria gigantea
Scallops	Hakea cucullata
Scarborough lily	Cyrtanthus elatus
Scarlet ball cactus	Parodia haselbergii
Scarlet bugler	Penstemon barbatus
Scarlet plume	Euphorbia fulgens
Scarlet runner	Kennedia prostrata
Scarlet trompetilla	Bouvardia ternifolia
Scarlet trumpets	Ipomopsis aggregata
Scented bark	Eucalyptus aromaphloia
Scoke	Phytolacca americana
Scoly	Protea scolymocephala
Scorpion orchid	Arachnis
Scorpion senna	Coronilla varia
Scorpion weed	Phacelia
Scotch thistle	Onopordum acanthium
Scots flame flower	Tropaeolum speciosum
Scots pine	Pinus sylvestris
Scotsman's rattle	Amblygonocarpus andongensis
Scottish bluebell	Campanula rotundifolia
Scrambled eggs	Goodenia pinnatifida
Scrambled eggtree	Cassia surattensis
Screw pine	Pandanus
Scurvygrass	Cochlearia officinalis
Sea buckthorn	Hippophae rhamnoides
Sea fennel	Crithium maritimum
Sea holly	Eryngium
Sea holly	Eryngium maritimum
Sea holly, flat	Eryngium planum
Sea holly, giant	Eryngium giganteum
Sea kale	Crambe maritima
Sea lavender	Limonium
Sea myrtle	Baccharis halimifolia
Sea onion	Ornithogalum longibracteatum
Sea pink	Armeria
Sea poppy	Glaucium
Sea spurry	Spergularia media
Sea urchin	Astrophytum asterias
Sea urchin cactus	Astrophytum asterias
Sea-heath, bristly	Flindersia xanthoxyla
Sea-heath, bristly	Frankenia serpyllifolia
Sea-heath, clustered	Frankenia connata

Common-Botanical Names

Common	Botanical
Sealing wax palm	Cyrtostachys lakka
Seaside grape	Cocoloba uvifera
Sedge	Carex
Sedge, awl-fruited	Carex stipata
Sedge, beaked long	Carex sprengelii
Sedge, bottlebrush	Carex comosa
Sedge, Bowles' golden	Carex elata 'Aurea'
Sedge, broom woolly	Andropogon glomeratus
Sedge, Bush's	Carex bushii
Sedge, Buxbaum's	Carex buxbaumii
Sedge, crested	Carex cristatella
Sedge, crowsfoot	Carex crus-corvi
Sedge, Davis'	Carex davisii
Sedge, drooping	Carex pendula
Sedge, fen	Cladium mariscus
Sedge, fescue	Carex festucacea
Sedge, fox	Carex vulpinoidea
Sedge, foxtail	Carex alopecoidea
Sedge, Frank's	Carex frankii
Sedge, fringed	Carex crinita
Sedge, hairy green	Carex hirsutella
Sedge, heavy	Carex gravida
Sedge, high meadow	Carex pensylvanica
Sedge, hook	Uncinia
Sedge, hop	Carex lupilina
Sedge, lake	Carex lacustris
Sedge, leatherleaf	Carex buchananii
Sedge, mace	Carex grayi
Sedge, Mead's	Carex meadii
Sedge, meadow	Carex granularis
Sedge, Muhlenberg's	Carex muhlenbergii
Sedge, necklace	Carex projecta
Sedge, oval spreading	Carex normalis
Sedge, palm branch	Carex muskingumensis
Sedge, pendulous	Carex pendula
Sedge, Pennsylvania	Carex pensylvanica
Sedge, pointed broom	Carex scoparia
Sedge, pond greater	Carex riparia
Sedge, porcupine	Carex hystricina
Sedge, prairie	Carex bicknellii
Sedge, prairie	Carex prairea
Sedge, redhead	Gahnia subaequiglumis
Sedge, round-headed	Carex molesta
Sedge, sallow	Carex lurida
Sedge, sand	Carex muhlenbergii
Sedge, saw	Gahnia aspera
Sedge, saw red-fruit	Gahnia sieberiana
Sedge, saw slender	Gahnia microstachya
Sedge, saw tall	Gahnia clarkei
Sedge, seersucker	Carex plantaginea
Sedge, semaphore	Mesomelaena teragona
Sedge, short	Carex brevior
Sedge, Short's	Carex shortiana
Sedge, slough	Carex obnupta
Sedge, spiny	Cyperus gymnocaulos
Sedge, squarrose	Carex squarrosa
Sedge, sword spreading	Lepidosperma effusum
Sedge, tall	Carex appressa
Sedge, Texas	Carex texensis
Sedge, Tollway	Carex praegracilis
Sedge, trembling	Restio tremulus
Sedge, Tuckerman's	Carex tuckermanii
Sedge, tufted	Carex elata
Sedge, tussock	Carex stricta
Sedge, variegated russet	Carex saxatilis 'Ski Run'
Sedge, weeping	Carex pendula
Sedge, wood straight-styled	Carex radiata
Sedge, woolly	Carex lanuginosa
Sedge, yellow-fruited	Carex annectens
Sedgc, ycllow-fruited	Carex annectens xanthocarpa
Sedge-rush	Ecdeiocolea monostachya
Seedbox	Ludwigia alternifolia
Sego lily	Calochortus macrocarpus
Sego lily	Calochortus nitidus
Sego lily, big pod	Calochortus nitidus
Sego lily, Nuttall's	Calochortus nuttallii
Self-heal	Prunella
Self-heal	Prunella vulgaris
Self-heal, large	Prunella grandiflora
Seminole bread	Zamia pumila
Sendai-hagi	Thermopsis lupinoides
Seneca	Polygala
Senita	Pachycereus schottii
Senna, American	Cassia marilandica
Senna, bladder	Colutea arborescens
Senna, Chinese	Cassia tora
Senna, dainty	Senna glutinosa ssp luerssenii
Senna, feathery	Senna artemisioides
Senna, Maryland	Cassia marilandica
Senna, pepper-leaf	Cassia barclayana
Senna, wild	Cassia hebecarpa
Sensitive fern	Onoclea sensibilis
Sensitive plant	Mimosa pudica
Sentry palm	Howea
September bells	Rothmannia globosa
Sequoia, giant	Sequoiadendron giganteum
Sermountain	Laserpitium siler
Service tree	Sorbus domestica
Service tree of Fontainebleu	Sorbus latifolia
Service-tree, wild	Sorbus torminalis
Serviceberry, alleghany	Amelanchier laevis
Serviceberry, running	Amelanchier stolonifera
Serviceberry, sand	Amelanchier sanguinea
Serviceberry, Saskatoon	Amelanchier alnifolia
Sesame	Sesamum indicum
Sesame, wild	Sesamum triphyllum
Sevenbark	Hydrangea arborescens
Sewejaartjie	Syncarpha variegata
Sewejaartjie	Syncarpha vestita
Sha yuan	Astragalus chinensis
Shadbush	Amelanchier
Shadbush	Amelanchier canadensis
Shallon	Gaultheria shallon
Shamrock	Oxalis
Shamrock	Trifolium repens
Shamrock pea	Parochetus africana
Shamrock pea	Parochetus communis
Shasta daisy	Leucanthemum x superbum
Shaving brush plant	Haemanthus albiflos
Shaving brush tree	Bombax ellipticum
She-gan	Belamcanda chinensis
She-oak	Allocasuarina fraseriana
She-oak	Casuarina
She-oak, bead	Allocasuarina monilifera
She-oak, black	Allocasuarina littoralis
She-oak, coast	Allocasuarina stricta

Common-Botanical Names

She-oak, desert — Allocasuarina decaisneana
She-oak, drooping — Allocasuarina verticillata
She-oak, dwarf — Allocasuarina pusilla
She-oak, forest — Allocasuarina torulosa
She-oak, granite — Allocasuarina huegeliana
She-oak, horned — Allocasuarina thuyoides
She-oak, Karri — Allocasuarina decussata
She-oak, pencil — Allocasuarina erecta
She-oak, pine — Allocasuarina pinaster
She-oak, ridge — Allocasuarina distyla
She-oak, rose — Allocasuarina torulosa
She-oak, shrubby — Allocasuarina campestris
She-oak, slaty — Allocasuarina muelleriana

She-oak, stunted — Allocasuarina nana
She-oak, swamp — Allocasuarina paludosa
Sheep bush — Geijera linearifolia
Sheep laurl — Kalmia angustifolia
Sheep's bit — Jasione
Sheep's ears — Helichrysum appendiculatum

Sheepberry — Viburnum lentago
Shell flower — Alpinia zerumbet
Shell flower — Chelone
Shell flower — Moluccella laevis
Shell flower — Pistia
Shell flower, Mexican — Tigridia pavonia
Shell ginger — Alpinia zerumbet
Shepherd's needle — Scandix pecten-veneris
Shepherd's purse — Capsella bursa-pastoris
Shepherd's tree — Boscia albitrunca
Shepherd's tree, broad-leaved — Boscia mossambicensis
Shepherd's tree, smelly — Boscia foetida
Shield fern — Polystichum
Shingle plant — Monstera acuminata
Shingle plant — Rhaphidophora celatocaulis

Shining bark — Prunus potaninii
Shinleaf — Pyrola
Shinleaf, white — Pyrola secunda
Shock-headed Peter — Clematopsis stanleyi
Shojobakama — Heloniopsis orientalis
Shoo-fly — Nicandra
Shooting star — Thymophylla tenuiloba
Shooting stars — Dodecatheon
Shooting stars — Dodecatheon pulchellum
Shooting stars, amethyst — Dodecatheon amethystinum

Shooting stars, midland — Dodecatheon meadia
Shooting stars, tall — Dodecatheon jeffreyi
Short bobs — Plantago lanceolata
Shower orchid — Congea tomentosa
Shrimp plant — Justicia brandegeana
Shrub verbena — Lantana
Shrub veronica — Hebe
Shrubby hare's ears — Bupleurum fruticosum
Shrubby plumbago — Ceratostigma
Shui-sa — Metasequoia glyptostroboides

Shungiku — Chrysanthemum
Shungiku — Chrysanthemum coronarium

Shuttlecock fern — Matteuccia struthiopteris
Sickle plant — Crassula falcata
Sickle thorn — Asparagus falcatus

Sida, narrow-leaf — Sida filiformis
Sida, rock — Sida petrophila
Sida, spiked — Sida subspicata
Sidebells — Pyrola secunda
Silk cotton tree — Bombax
Silk cotton tree, red — Bombax ceiba
Silk cotton tree, white — Ceiba pentandra
Silk tassel bush — Garrya
Silk tassel bush — Garyya elliptica
Silk tassel tree — Garrya elliptica
Silk tree — Albizia julibrissin
Silk tree, floss — Chorisia
Silk tree, Persian — Albizia julibrissin
Silk vine — Periploca graeca
Silkgrass — Heterotheca graminifolia
Silkweed — Asclepias
Silkweed — Asclepias syriaca
Silkweed, purple — Asclepias purpurascens
Silky heads — Cymbopogon obtectus
Silver beard grass — Bothriochloa saccharoides

Silver bell — Halesia
Silver bell, Carolina — Halesia carolina
Silver berry — Elaeagnus commutata
Silver bush — Ptilotus obovatus
Silver chain — Dendrochilum glumaceum

Silver cushion — Leucophyta brownii
Silver dollar tree — Eucalyptus cinerea
Silver fir — Abies
Silver heart — Peperomia marmorata
Silver inch plant — Tradescantia zebrina
Silver jade plant — Crassula arborescens
Silver King — Artemisia
Silver mound — Artemisia
Silver mound — Artemisia schmidtiana
Silver net-leaf — Fittonia albivensis Argyroneura Group
Silver net-leaf — Fittonia albivensis Verschaffeltii Group

Silver nugget — Pachypodium leali
Silver Princess — Eucalyptus caesia ssp magna
Silver Queen — Artemisia
Silver rod — Asphodelus ramosus
Silver saw palm — Acoelorraphe wrightii
Silver tails — Ptilotus obovatus
Silver Top — Eucalyptus nitens
Silver torch — Cleistocactus strausii
Silver tree — Leucadendron argenteum

Silver tree — Pilea involucrata
Silver vase plant — Aechmea fasciata
Silver vine — Actinidia polygama
Silver vine — Scindapus pictum 'Argyraeus'
Silverbush — Sophora tomentosa
Silwerboom — Leucadendron argenteum

Simpler's joy — Verbena hastata
Singapore holly — Malpighia coccigera
Sinicuiche (Sinkuiche) — Heimia
Siris tree — Albizia lebbek
Sirpad hakadurim — Urtica pilulifera
Skaamblom — Protea nana
Skeweblaar taaibos — Rhus pyroides

Common-Botanical Names

Common	Botanical	Common	Botanical
Skilpadbessie	Nylandtia spinosa	Snakeroot, seneca	Polygala seneca
Skilpadbos	Crassula muscosa	Snakeroot, white	Eupatorium rugosum
Skullcap	Scutellaria lateriflora	Snakeroot, wild	Eupatorium rugosum
Skullcap, alpine	Scutellaria alpina	Snakewood	Acacia xiphophylla
Skullcap, Baikal	Scutellaria baicalensis	Snapdragon	Antirrhinum
Skullcap, mad dog	Scutellaria lateriflora	Snapdragon, Sicilian	Antirrhinum siculum
Skullcap, marsh	Scutellaria epibiifolia	Snapdragon, twining	Asarina
Skunk cabbage	Dracontium foetidum	Snapdragon, wild	Penstemon palmeri
Skunk cabbage	Lysichiton	Snapweed	Impatiens
Skunk cabbage, yellow	Lysichiton americanus	Sneezeweed	Helenium autumnale
Skuweblaarrosyntjie	Grewia flavescens v flavescens	Sneezeweed, orange	Helenium hoopesii
		Sneezewood	Ptaeroxylon obliquum
Sky flower	Duranta repens	Sneezewort	Achillea ptarmica
Sky plant	Tillandsia ionantha	Snottygobble	Persoonia elliptica
Skyrocket	Ipomopsis aggregata	Snow brake	Pteris ensiformis
Slangappelbos	Solanum tomentosum	Snow bush	Breynia disticha
Slangbessie	Lycium ferocissimum	Snow creeper	Porana paniculata
Slangkop	Urginea sanguinea	Snow flakes, summer	Goodenia scapigera
Slangkop, Natal	Urginea macrocentra	Snow in summer	Cerastium tomentosum
Slanguintjie	Dipcadi ciliare	Snow in summer	Euphorbia marginata
Slipper flower	Calceolaria	Snow in summer	Melaleuca linariifolia
Slipper orchid	Pathiopedilum	Snow in summer	Ozothamnus thyrsoideus
Slipperwort	Calceolaria	Snow in the jungle	Porana paniculata
Sloe blackthorn	Prunus spinosa	Snow on the mountain	Euphorbia marginata
Slymstok	Bulbine praemorsa	Snow piercer	Galanthus nivalis
Smallweed	Calamagrostis	Snow poppy	Eomecon
Smartweed, cultivated	Polygonum hydropiper 'Fastigiatum'	Snow Queen	Eucalyptus victrix
		Snow-in-summer	Cerastium tomentosum
Smoke bush	Cotinus	Snowball bush	Viburnum macrocephalum
Smoke bush	Cotinus coggygria		
Smoke tree, American	Cotinus obovatus	Snowball bush, Japanese	Viburnum plicatum
Smokebush	Conospermum	Snowball, pincushion	Mammillaria candida
Smokebush, blue	Conospermum caeruleum	Snowball, pink	Dombeya x cayeuxii
Smokebush, blue pale	Conospermum amoenum	Snowball tree	Viburnum opulus 'Roseum'
Smokebush, fluffy	Conospermum incurvum	Snowbell	Soldanella
Smokebush, plume	Conospermum incurvum	Snowbell	Styrax
Smokebush, slender	Conospermum huegelii	Snowbell, alpine	Soldanella alpina
Smokebush, tall	Conospermum triplinervium v minor	Snowbell, American	Styrax americanus
Smokebush, tree	Conospermum triplinervium	Snowbell, dwarf	Soldanella pusilla
Smokebush, white	Conospermum distichum	Snowbell, fragrant	Styrax obassia
Smokebush, white	Conospermum incurvum	Snowbell, Japanese	Styrax japonicus
Smokegrass	Conospermum stoechadis	Snowbell, least	Soldanella minima
		Snowberry	Gaultheria hispida
Snail bean	Vigna caracalla	Snowberry	Symphoricarpos
Snail flower	Vigna caracalla	Snowberry	Symphoricarpos albus v laevigatus
Snake bean	Swartzia madagascariensis	Snowberry, common	Symphoricarpos albus
		Snowberry, creeping	Symphoricarpos mollis
Snake bush	Justicia adhatodoides	Snowberry, mountain	Symphoricarpos oreophilus
Snake palm	Amorphophallus		
Snake palm	Amorphophallus konjac	Snowbush	Ceanothus cordulatus
Snake plant	Sansevieria trifasciata	Snowbush rose	Rosa 'Dupontii'
Snake root	Persicaria bistorta	Snowdon lily	Lloydia serotina
Snake vine	Hibbertia scandens	Snowdrop	Galanthus
Snake's head fritillary	Fritillaria meleagris	Snowdrop	Galanthus nivalis
Snake's head iris	Hermodactylus	Snowdrop, autumn	Galanthus reginae-olgae
Snake's meat	Arum maculatum	Snowdrop, Cape	Crassula saxifraga
Snakebush	Hemiandra pungens	Snowdrop, common	Galanthus nivalis
Snakeroot	Polygala	Snowdrop, common double	Galanthus nivalis 'Flore Pleno'
		Snowdrop tree	Halesia
		Snowflake	Leucojum
		Snowflake, autumn	Leucojum autumnale
		Snowflake, spring	Leucojum vernum
		Snowflake, summer	Leucojum aestivum

Common-Botanical Names

Common	Botanical
Snowflake tree	Trevesia palmata
Snowflakes	Leucojum aestivum
Snowflakes, summer	Agonis hypericifolia
Snowy Mespilus	Amelanchier
Soap bush	Manochlamys albicans
Soap tree	Alphitonia excelsa
Soap tree	Gymnocladus chinensis
Soapbark	Quillaja saponaria
Soapberry, Western	Sapindus drummondii
Soapweed, small	Yucca glauca
Soapwood	Yucca glauca
Soapwort	Saponaria
Soapwort, Calabrian	Saponaria calabrica
Soapwort, rock	Saponaria ocymoides
Soapwort, yellow	Saponaria lutea
Soetharpuisbos	Euryops lateriflorus
Soft tree fern	Dicksonia antarctica
Soldaat	Kniphofia
Soldier in a sentry box	Arum maculatum
Soldiers and sailors	Plantago lanceolata
Soldiers and sailors	Pulmonaria officinalis
Solitaire palm	Ptychosperma elegans
Solomon's plume	Smilacina racemosa
Solomon's plume, starry	Smilacina stellata
Solomon's seal	Polygonatum
Solomon's seal	Polygonatum biflorum
Solomon's seal, anguled	Polygonatum odoratum
Solomon's seal, common	Polygonatum x hybridum
Solomon's seal, false	Smilacina
Solomon's seal, great	Polygonatum biflorum
Solomon's seal, lesser	Polygonatum odoratum
Solomon's seal, whorled	Polygonatum verticillatum
Sonerila, pearly	Sonerila margaritacea 'Argentea'
Sorghum	Sorghum vulgare
Sorrel	Oxalis
Sorrel, climbing	Rumex sagittatus
Sorrel, garden	Rumex acetosa
Sorrel, mountain	Oxyria
Sorrel, sheep	Rumex acetosella
Sorrel tree	Oxydendron arboreum
Sorrel tree	Oxydendrum
Sorrel, wood	Oxalis acetosella
Sorrel, wood violet	Oxalis tetraphylla
Sorrel, wood violet	Oxalis violacea
Sosatieplant	Crassula perfoliata v perfoliata
Sotol	Dasylirion wheeleri
Sotol, narrow-leaf	Dasylirion longissimum
Sotol, Texas	Dasylirion texanum
Sour berry	Rhus integrifolia
Sour dock	Rumex acetosa
Sourberry, dune	Dovyalis rotundifolia
Soursop	Annona muricata
Sourwood	Oxydendron arboreum
Sourwood	Oxydendrum
South African sagewood	Buddleja salviifolia
South African Wisteria	Bolusanthus
Southern beech	Nothofagus
Southern cross	Xanthosia rotundifolia
Southernwood	Artemisia abrotanum
Southernwood, camphor	Artemisia alba
Sow thistle	Cicerbita
Sowbread	Cyclamen
Spade leaf	Philodendron
	domesticum
Spangle grass	Chasmanthium latifolium
Spaniard, giant	Aciphylla scott-thomsonii
Spanish bluebell	Hyacinthoides hispanica
Spanish broom	Spartium junceum
Spanish dagger	Yucca gloriosa
Spanish gorse	Genista hispanica
Spanish shawl	Heterocentron elegans
Spantou	Sarcostemma viminale
Spatterdock	Nuphar
Spatterdock, American	Nuphar advena
Spear grass	Stipa
Spear lily	Doryanthes
Speargrass	Aciphylla
Spearmint	Mentha spicata
Spearwood bush	Pandorea pandorana
Spearwood tree	Pandorea doratoxylon
Spearwort, greater	Ranunculus lingua
Spearwort, lesser	Ranunculus flammula
Speedwell	Veronica
Speedwell, common	Veronica officinalis
Speedwell, digger	Parahebe perfoliata
Speedwell, garden	Veronica longifolia
Speedwell, Germander	Veronica chamaedrys
Speedwell, prostrate	Veronica prostrata
Speedwell, rock	Veronica fruticans
Speedwell, silver	Veronica spicata ssp incana
Speedwell, spiked	Veronica spicata
Speldedoring	Azima tetracantha
Speldekussing	Leucospermum cordifolium
Speldekussing	Leucospermum erubescens
Speldekussing	Leucospermum oleifolium
Spelt	Triticum aestivum
Spice bush	Lindera
Spiceberry	Ardisia crenata
Spicebush	Calycanthus
Spicebush, Western	Calycanthus occidentalis
Spider flower	Cleome
Spider flower	Grevillea
Spider flower, Brazilian	Tibouchina urvilleana
Spider flower, comb	Grevillea huegelii
Spider flower, sandhill	Grevillea stenobotrya
Spider lily	Hymenocallis
Spider lily	Tradescantia
Spider orchid	Brassia lawrenceana
Spider orchid, early	Ophrys sphegodes
Spider orchid, late	Ophrys holoserica
Spider plant	Anthericum
Spider plant	Chlorophytum comosum
Spider plant	Cleome hassleriana
Spiderwort	Tradescantia
Spiderwort, blue	Commelina coelestis
Spiderwort, common	Tradescantia virginiana
Spiderwort, hairy	Tradescantia hirsuticaulis
Spiderwort, mountain	Lloydia serotina
Spiderwort, Ohio	Tradescantia ohioensis
Spiderwort, prairie	Tradescantia bracteata
Spiderwort, western	Tradescantia occidentalis
Spignel	Meum athamanticum
Spike heath	Bruckenthalia spiculifolia
Spike, red	Cephalophyllum alstonii

Common Name	Botanical Name
Spike-thorn, common	Maytenus heterophylla
Spiked star of Bethlehem	Ornithogalum pyrenaicum
Spikemoss, Krauss'	Selaginella kraussiana
Spikenard	Aralia californica
Spikenard, American	Aralia racemosa
Spikenard, false	Smilacina racemosa
Spinach, red mountain	Atriplex hortensis 'Rubra'
Spinach, sea	Tetragonia decumbens
Spindle, Japanese	Euonymus japonicus
Spindle tree	Euonymus
Spindle tree, European	Euonymus europaeus
Spindle, winged	Euonymus alatus
Spine palm	Aiphanes caryotifolia
Spinifex, buck	Triodia mitchellii
Spinifex, hairy	Spinifex sericeus
Spinifex, hard	Triodia wiseana
Spinifex, limestone	Triodia wiseana
Spinifex, soft	Triodia pungens
Spiny club palm	Bactris
Spiraea, blue mist	Caryopteris
Spiraea, cliff	Holodiscus dumosus
Spiral bud	Knautia arvensis aff
Spiral ginger	Costus malortieanus
Spirea, Douglas	Spiraea douglasii
Spirea, false	Sorbaria
Spirea, false Ural	Sorbaria sorbifolia
Spirea, shiny-leaf	Spiraea betulifolia
Spirea, sub-alpine	Spiraea densiflora
Spleenwort	Asplenium
Spleenwort, black	Asplenium adiantum-nigrum
Spleenwort, ebony	Asplenium platyneuron
Spleenwort, maidenhair	Asplenium trichomanes
Spleenwort, mother	Asplenium bulbiferum
Spleenwort, shining	Asplenium oblongifolium
Spotted dog	Pulmonaria officinalis
Spotted laurel	Aucuba japonica
Spotted orchid	Dactylorhiza
Spotted orchid, heath	Dactylorhiza maculata
Spring beauty	Claytonia
Spring bell	Olsynium douglasii
Spring gold	Lomatium utriculatum
Spruce	Picea
Spruce, black	Picea mariana
Spruce, Black Hills	Picea glauca densata
Spruce, blue	Picea pungens f glauca
Spruce, Brewer's weeping	Picea breweriana
Spruce, Caucasian	Picea orientalis
Spruce, Chinese	Picea asperata
Spruce, Colorado	Picea pungens
Spruce, Colorado blue	Picea pungens f glauca
Spruce, common	Picea abies
Spruce, dragon	Picea asperata
Spruce, Engelman	Picea engelmannii
Spruce, Himalayan	Picea morinda
Spruce, Himalayan	Picea smithiana
Spruce, Hondo	Picea jezoensis ssp hondoensis
Spruce, Lijiang (Likian)	Picea likiangensis
Spruce, Morinda	Picea smithiana
Spruce, mountain	Picea engelmannii
Spruce, Norway	Picea excelsa
Spruce, oriental	Picea orientalis
Spruce, purple-cone	Picea purpurea
Spruce, sargent	Picea brachytyla
Spruce, Serbian	Picea omorika
Spruce, Sitka	Picea sitchensis
Spruce, Taiwan	Picea morrisonicola
Spruce tree	Pinus glabra
Spruce, west Himalayan	Picea smithiana
Spruce, white	Picea glauca
Spruce, Wilson's	Picea wilsonii
Spruce, Yeddo	Picea jezoensis
Spurge	Euphorbia
Spurge, allegheny	Pachysandra procumbens
Spurge, blue	Euphorbia myrsinites
Spurge, caper	Euphorbia lathyris
Spurge, cushion	Euphorbia polychroma
Spurge, Cypress	Euphorbia cyparissias
Spurge, flowering	Euphorbia corollata
Spurge, gopher	Euphorbia lathyris
Spurge, hairy	Euphorbia pilosa
Spurge, honey	Euphorbia meloformis
Spurge, marsh	Euphorbia palustris
Spurge, Mediterranean large	Euphorbia characias
Spurge, wood	Euphorbia amygdaloides
Spyridium, blushing	Spyridium rotundifolium
Squaw bush	Rhus trilobata
Squaw carpet	Ceanothus prostratus
Squaw vine	Mitchella repens
Squawroot	Trillium erectum
Squeaker apple	Schizomeria ovata
Squill, alpine	Scilla bifolia
Squill, blue	Chamaescilla corymbosa
Squill, blue	Chamaescilla corymbosa v latifolia
Squill, blue	Scilla natalensis
Squill, curly-leaved	Chamaescilla spiralis
Squill, sea	Urginea maritima
Squill, Siberian	Scilla siberica
Squill, striped	Puschkinia scilloides
Squirrel's foot fern	Davallia mariesii
Squitch	Elytrigia repens
St. Augustine grass	Stenotaphrum secundatum
St. Barbara's herb	Barbarea
St. Bernard's lily	Anthericum liliago
St. Catherine's lace	Eriogonum
St. Catherine's lace	Eriogonum giganteum
St. Dabeoc's heath	Daboecia
St. James' wort	Senecio jacobaea
St. John's bread	Ceratonia siliqua
St. John's wort	Hypericum
St. John's wort	Hypericum balearicum
St. John's wort, dotted	Hypericum punctatum
St. John's wort, giant	Hypericum pyramidatum
St. John's wort, great	Hypericum pyramidatum
St. John's wort, Kalm	Hypericum kalmianum
St. John's wort, perforate	Hypericum perforatum
St. John's wort, spotted	Hypericum punctatum
St. John's wort, square-stemmed	Hypericum tetrapterum
St. Martin's flower	Alstroemeria Ligtu Hybrids
St. Patrick's cabbage	Saxifraga x urbium
St. Thomas' tree	Bauhinia monandra
Stace, Tatarian	Goniolimon tataricum
Staff tree	Celastrus scandens
Staff vine	Celastrus
Staff vine	Celastrus orbiculatus
Stagger-bush	Lyonia mariana

Common-Botanical Names

Common	Botanical	Common	Botanical
Staggerwort	Senecio jacobaea	Stinkblaarsuikerbos	Protea susannae
Staghorn fern	Platycerium	Stinking Benjamin	Trillium erectum
Staghorn fern	Platycerium superbum	Stinking Gladwyn	Iris foetidissima
Staghorn fern, common	Platycerium bifurcatum	Stinking nightshade	Hyoscyamus niger
Staghorn, South American	Platycerium bifurcatum	Stinking Willie	Senecio jacobaea
Stammerwort	Senecio jacobaea	Stinkkruid	Pentzia grandiflora
Star, blue	Amsonia tabernaemontana	Stinkwood tree, white	Celtis africana
		Stinky pops	Impatiens glandulifera
Star, blue Texas	Amsonia illustris	Stitchwort, greater	Stellaria holostea
Star, blue willow	Amsonia tabernaemontana	Stock	Matthiola
		Stock	Matthiola incana
Star cluster	Pentas lanceolata	Stock, Brompton	Matthiola
Star cluster, Egyptian	Pentas lanceolata	Stock, East Lothian	Matthiola
Star daisy	Lindheimera	Stock, night-scented	Mattgiola longipetala ssp bicornis
Star daisy	Lindheimera texana		
Star flower	Eriostemon	Stock, Virginian	Malcomia maritima
Star flower	Hypoxis	Stokes' Aster	Stokesia
Star flower	Stapelia orbea	Stompies	Brunia albiflora
Star flower, pink	Trianthema turgidifolia	Stompstertbobbejaantjie	Babiana stricta
Star glory	Ipomoea quamoclit	Stone cress	Aethionema
Star grass, yellow	Hypoxis hirsuta	Stone cress, Persian	Aethionema grandiflorum
Star jasmine	Trachelospermum		
Star of Bethlehem	Hypoxis argentea	Stone mint	Cunila origanoides
Star of Bethlehem	Ornithogalum	Stone plant	Lithops
Star of Bethlehem	Ornithogalum umbellatum	Stone plants	Pleiospilos
		Stonecrop	Sedum
Star of Bethlehem, drooping	Ornithogalum nutans	Stonecrop	Sedum ternatum
Star of Persia	Allium cristophii	Stonecrop, biting	Sedum acre
Star of the veldt	Dimorphotheca sinuata	Stonecrop, common	Sedum acre
Star thistle	Centaurea	Stonecrop, ditch	Penthorum sedoides
Star-chestnut, African	Sterculia africana	Stonecrop, hairy	Sedum villosum
Star-chestnut, large-leaved	Sterculia quinqueloba	Stonecrop, reflexed	Sedum rupestre
Star-of-Bethlehem	Campanula isophylla	Stonecrop, rock	Sedum rupestre
Starfish cactus	Orbea variegata	Stonecrop, wall-pepper	Sedum acre
Starfish flower	Stapelia gettleffii	Stonecrop, widow's-cross	Sedum pulchellum
Starfish plant	Cryptanthus	Stoneroot	Collinsonia canadensis
Starflower	Calytrix	Stork's bill	Erodium
Starflower	Grewia oppositifolia	Strandblommetjie	Senecio elegans
Starflower	Mentzelia	Strandpatat	Ipomoea brasiliensis
Starflower	Scabiosa stellata	Strandroos	Limonium purpuratum
Starflower, northern	Calytrix exstipulata	Strawberry	Fragaria
Starflower, purple	Calytrix leschenaultii	Strawberry blite	Chenopodium foliosum
Starflower, summer	Calytrix flavescens	Strawberry bush	Calycanthus floridus
Starfruit	Damasonium	Strawberry, Indian	Duchesnea indica
Starwort, false	Boltonia	Strawberry, mock	Duchesnea indica
Statice	Limonium	Strawberry sticks	Chenopodium virgatum
Statice	Limonium sinuatum	Strawberry tree	Arbutus
Statice, pink	Psylliostachys suworowii	Strawberry tree	Arbutus unedo
Stekelsalie	Pycnostachys reticulata	Strawberry tree, Grecian	Arbutus andrachne
Steppe tree	Haloxylon persicum	Strawberry, wild	Fragaria vesca
Stevia	Stevia rebaudiana	Strawberry, wild	Fragaria virginiana
Stick-a-back	Galium aparine	Strawflower	Bracteantha bracteata
Stickleback	Galium aparine	Strawflower	Rhodanthe
Sticklebacks	Arctium sp	Strawflower, white	Bracteantha macrantha
Sticky bobs	Arctium sp		
Sticky bobs	Galium aparine	Strelitzia, white	Strelitzia alba
Sticky buds	Galium aparine	Strelitzia, yellow	Strelitzia reginae 'Mandela's Gold'
Sticky grass	Galium aparine		
Sticky Jack	Arctium sp	String of beads	Senecio rowleyanus
Sticky weed	Galium aparine	String of hearts	Ceropegia linearis ssp woodii
Sticky William	Galium aparine		
Sticky Willy	Arctium sp	String of pearls	Monilaria pisiformis
Sticky Willy	Galium aparine	Stringybark, blue-leaved	Eucalyptus agglomerata
Stink pod	Scoliopus bigelovii	Stringybark, brown	Eucalyptus baxteri
Stinkaalwyn	Kniphofia	Stringybark, brown	Eucalyptus capitellata
Stinkblaarsuikerbos	Protea roupelliae	Stringybark, Camfield's	Eucalyptus camfieldii

Common-Botanical Names

Stringybark, Capertree	Eucalyptus macrorrhyncha ssp cannonii
Stringybark, Darwin	Eucalyptus tetrodonta
Stringybark, Grampian	Eucalyptus alpina
Stringybark, gum-top	Eucalyptus delegatensis
Stringybark, Mckie's	Eucalyptus mckieana
Stringybark, mealy	Eucalyptus cephalocarpa
Stringybark, messmate	Eucalyptus obliqua
Stringybark, narrow-leaved	Eucalyptus oblonga
Stringybark, New England	Eucalyptus caliginosa
Stringybark, Planchon's	Eucalyptus planchoniana
Stringybark, privet-leaved	Eucalyptus ligustrina
Stringybark, Queensland white	Eucalyptus nigra
Stringybark, Queensland white	Eucalyptus tindaliae
Stringybark, red	Eucalyptus macrorrhyncha ssp macrorrhyncha
Stringybark, silver	Eucalyptus cephalocarpa
Stringybark, silver top	Eucalyptus laevopinea
Stringybark, swamp	Eucalyptus conglomerata
Stringybark, thin-leaved	Eucalyptus eugenioides
Stringybark, white	Eucalyptus globoidea
Stringybark, yellow	Eucalyptus muelleriana
Stringybark, Youman's	Eucalyptus youmanii
Striped inch plant	Callisia elegans
Striped torch	Guzmania monostachya
Stroggle	Elytrigia repens
Stuartiana	Eucalyptus bridgesiana
Stud thorn	Dicerocaryum senecioides
Sturt's desert pea	Clianthus formosus
Stylewort	Levenhookia chippendalei
Stylewort, midget	Levenhookia pusilla
Succory, wild	Cichorium intybus
Sugar bush	Rhus ovata
Sugar-almond plant	Pachyphytum oviferum
Sugarberry	Celtis occidentalis
Sugarbowls	Clematis hirsutissima
Sugarbush	Protea
Sugarbush, broadleaf	Protea eximia
Sugarbush, Cape	Protea repens
Sugarbush, real	Protea repens
Sugarbush, red	Protea grandiceps
Sugarbush, silver	Protea roupelliae
Sugarbush, stinkleaf	Protea susannae
Sugarleaf	Cistus salvifolius
Sugarwood	Myoporum platycarpum
Suikerbos	Protea burchellii
Suikerbos	Protea repens
Suikerkannetjie	Gladiolus saccatus
Sulphur flower	Eriogonum gracilipes
Sulphur flower	Eriogonum umbellatum
Sumac(h)	Rhus
Sumach, African	Rhus lancea
Sumach, Cape	Colpoon compressum
Sumach, dwarf	Rhus copallina
Sumach, evergreen	Rhus virens ssp choriophylla
Sumach, fragrant	Rhus aromatica
Sumach, laurel	Rhus laurina
Sumach, Mearn	Rhus virens ssp choriophylla
Sumach, scarlet	Rhus glabra
Sumach, skunkbush	Rhus trilobata

Sumach, smooth	Rhus glabra
Sumach, stag horn's	Rhus typhina
Sumach, velvet	Rhus typhina
Summer holly	Arctostaphylos diversifolia
Summer-sweet	Clethra
Sun plant	Portulaca
Sun rose	Cistus
Sun rose	Helianthemum
Sundew	Drosera
Sundew	Drosera rotundifolia
Sundew, Cape	Drosera capensis
Sundew, climbing	Drosera macrantha ssp macrantha
Sundew, climbing	Drosera peltata
Sundew, forked	Drosera binata
Sundew, leafy	Drosera stolonifera
Sundew, long-leaved	Drosera intermedia
Sundew, pale	Drosera peltata
Sundew, pink rainbow	Drosera menziesii
Sundew, red ink	Drosera erythrorhiza
Sundew, red leaved	Drosera bulbosa ssp bulbosa
Sundew, scarlet	Drosera glanduligera
Sundew, scented	Drosera whittakeri
Sundrop, common	Oenothera fruticosa ssp glauca
Sundrop, Ozark	Oenothera missouriensis
Sundrops	Oenothera
Sundrops	Oenothera fruticosa
Sunflower	Helianthus
Sunflower, alpine	Tatraneuris grandiflora
Sunflower, annual	Helianthus annuus
Sunflower, bush	Encelia californica
Sunflower, cucumber-leaved	Helianthus debilis ssp cucumerifolius
Sunflower, downy	Helianthus mollis
Sunflower, early	Heliopsis helianthoides
Sunflower, false	Heliopsis
Sunflower, hairy	Helianthus tomentosus
Sunflower, little	Helianthella uniflora
Sunflower, Maximilian's	Helianthus maximilianii
Sunflower, Mexican	Tithonia
Sunflower, Mexican	Tithonia rotundifolia
Sunflower, narrow-leaved	Helianthus angustifolius
Sunflower, narrow-leaved	Helianthus simulans
Sunflower, Oregon	Balsamorhiza sagittata
Sunflower, ox-eye	Heliopsis helianthoides
Sunflower, paper	Schoenia macivorii
Sunflower, prairie	Helianthus rigidus
Sunflower, rough	Helianthus hirsutus
Sunflower, saw-tooth	Helianthus grosseserratus
Sunflower, showy	Helianthus laetiflorus
Sunflower, silverleaf	Helianthus argophyllus
Sunflower, thin-leaved	Helianthus decapetalus
Sunflower, western	Helianthus occidentalis
Sunflower, willow-leaved	Helianthus salicifolius
Sunflower, wood hairy	Helianthus atrorubens
Sunflower, woodland	Helianthus divaricatus
Sunflower, woodland	Helianthus strumosus
Sunflower, woolly	Eriophyllum lanatum
Sunray, bright	Hyalosperma cotula
Sunray, brilliant	Rhodanthe polygalifolia
Sunray, charming	Hyalosperma glutinosum ssp venustum

Common-Botanical Names

Common	Botanical
Sunray, fine-leaf	Hyalosperma praecox
Sunray, flowery	Rhodanthe floribunda
Sunray, glandular	Leucochrysum fitzgibbonii
Sunray, hoary	Leucochrysum molle
Sunray, Mayweed	Hyalosperma cotula
Sunray, pink	Rhodanthe manglesii
Sunray, sand	Leucochrysum stipitatum
Sunray, slender	Erymophyllum ramosum ssp tenellum
Sunray, slender	Rhodanthe stricta
Sunray, soft	Leucochrysum molle
Sunray, western	Rhodanthe chlorocephala ssp chlorocephala
Sunray, white	Rhodanthe floribunda
Sunray, woolly	Leucochrysum stipitatum
Supplejack	Ventilago viminalis
Sussex weed	Quercus robur
Suurberg Kussingbos	Oldenburgia arbuscula
Suurkanol	Chasmanthe floribunda
Suurkanolpypie	Chasmanthe aethiopica
Swallow-wort	Asclepias curassavica
Swamp bottlebrush	Beaufortia sparsa
Swamp cypress	Taxodium
Swamp pink	Helonias bullata
Swamp root	Anemopsis californica
Swan flower	Aristolochia grandiflora
Swan orchid	Cycnoches
Swan plant	Gomphocarpus physocarpus
Swan river daisy	Brachyscome iberidifolia
Swan river pea	Brachysema celsianum
Swartbas	Diospyros whyteana
Swartteebossie	Vernonia mespilifolia
Swartturk	Bulbinella nutans
Swedish ivy	Plectranthus australis
Sweet Alice	Lobularia
Sweet Alison	Lobularia
Sweet Alyssum	Lobularia
Sweet Annie	Artemisia annua
Sweet cicely	Myrrhis odorata
Sweet cicely	Osmorhiza claytoni
Sweet corn	Zea mays
Sweet cup	Passiflora maliformis
Sweet herb	Stevia
Sweet herb of Paraguay	Stevia rebaudiana
Sweet Nancy	Achillea ageratum
Sweet pea	Lathyrus odoratus
Sweet pepper bush	Clethra
Sweet pepper bush	Clethra alnifolia
Sweet rocket	Hesperis matronalis
Sweet shade	Calycanthus floridus
Sweet shade	Hymenosporum flavum
Sweet sop	Annona squamosa
Sweet sultan	Amberboa
Sweet sultan	Amberboa moschata
Sweet tea	Osmanthus fragrans
Sweet thorn	Acacia karroo
Sweet William	Dianthus barbatus
Sweet William, wild	Phlox divaricata
Sweet woodruff	Galium odoratum
Sweet-briar	Rosa rubiginosa
Sweet-hearts	Galium aparine
Sweetbells	Leucothoe racemosa
Sweetcup	Annona squamosa
Sweetgrass	Hierochloe odorata
Sweetheart plant	Philodendron scandens
Sweetpea bush, silver	Podalyria calyptrata
Sweetroot	Osmorhiza occidentalis
Sweetshrub, common	Calycanthus floridus
Sweetspire	Itea virginica
Sweetwood	Glycyrrhiza
Swiss chard	Beta vulgaris ssp cicla
Swiss cheese plant	Monstera deliciosa
Switch grass	Panicum virgatum
Sybossie	Senecio coronatus
Sycamore	Acer pseudoplatanus
Sycamore, American	Platanus occidentalis
Sycamore, Arizona	Platanus wrightii
Sycamore, California	Platanus racemosa
Synaphea, granite	Synaphea acutiloba
Syringa	Philadelphus lewisii
Syringa, mountain	Kirkia wilmsii
Syringa, red	Burkea africana
Syringa, white	Kirkia acuminata
Taaibos	Rhus burchellii
Taaibos, blunt-leaved	Rhus rehmanniana v glabrata
Tacamahac	Populus balsamifera
Tagasaste	Chamaecytisus palmensis
Taginaste roja	Echium wildpretii
Tail flower	Anthurium
Talipot palm	Corypha umbraculifera
Tallerack	Eucalyptus tetragona
Tallow tree, Chinese	Sapium sebiferum
Tallow wood	Eucalyptus microcorys
Tallow wood	Pittosporum bicolor
Tallow wood, bastard	Eucalyptus planchoniana
Tamarillo	Cyphomandra
Tamarind	Tamarindus indica
Tamarind, Indies	Vangueria edulis
Tamarind, Manila	Inga edulis
Tamarind, native (AU)	Diploglottis cunninghamii
Tamarind, rose	Arytera divaricata
Tamarind, wild	Diploglottis diphyllostegia
Tamarisk	Tamarix
Tamma	Allocasuarina corniculata
Tampala	Amaranthus tricolor
Tan shen	Salvia militorrhiza
Tanbark oak	Lithocarpus
Tanekaha	Phyllocladus trichomanoides
Tangerine	Citrus reticulata
Tanguru	Olearia albida
Tansy	Tanacetum vulgare
Tansy, fernleaf	Tanacetum vulgare 'Crispum'
Tansy, Hulten's	Tanacetum hultenii
Tansy, Indian	Tanacetum huronense
Tansy leaf	Phacelia tanacetifolia
Tansy, silver	Tanacetum niveum
Tansy, wild	Hippia frutescens
Tansy-leaved thorn	Crataegus tanacetifolia
Tar bush	Eremophila glabra
Tara vine	Actinidia arguta
Tarata	Pittosporum eugenioides

Common-Botanical Names

Common name	Botanical name
Tarenna, mountain	Tarenna zimbabwensis
Taro	Colocasia esculenta
Taro, blue	Xanthosma violaceum
Taro, giant	Alocasia macrorhiza
Tarragon, Mexican	Tagetes lucida
Tarragon, Russian	Artemisia dracunculus
Tartar bread plant	Crambe tatarica
Tarweed	Grindelia
Tarweed	Madia elegans
Tasmanian cedar	Athrotaxis
Tasmanian cedar	Athrotaxis x laxifolia
Tasmanian cypress pine	Callitris oblonga
Tasmanian laurel	Anopterus glandulosus
Tassel berry	Antidesma venosum
Tassel bush	Garrya
Tassel flower	Amaranthus caudatus
Tassel flower	Emilia
Tassel flower	Leucopogon verticillatus
Tassel hyacinth	Muscari comosum 'Plumosum'
Tassel plant	Leucopogon verticillatus
Tassel-white	Itea virginica
Tatting fern	Athyrium filix-femina 'Frizelliae'
Tea	Camellia sinensis
Tea, California	Psoralea physodes
Tea plant, common	Camellia sinensis
Tea tree	Leptospermum
Tea tree	Melaleuca alternifolia
Tea tree, black	Melaleuca lanceolata
Tea tree, broad-leaved	Melaleuca viridiflora
Tea tree, creeping	Leptospermum rupestre
Tea tree, green	Leptospermum coriaceum
Tea tree, heath	Leptospermum mysinoides
Tea tree, large-flowered	Leptospermum grandiflorum
Tea tree, lemon	Leptospermum petersonii
Tea tree, lemon-scented	Leptospermum petersonii
Tea tree, mountain	Leptospermum grandifolium
Tea tree, myrtle	Leptospermum myrtifolium
Tea tree, New Zealand	Leptospermum scoparium
Tea tree, northern	Leptospermum brachyandrum
Tea tree, olive	Leptospermum liversidgei
Tea tree, peach blossom	Leptospermum spinescens
Tea tree, peach blossom	Leptospermum squarrosum
Tea tree, pink	Leptospermum erubescens
Tea tree, pink	Leptospermum squarrosum
Tea tree, pink fairy	Leptospermum epacridoideum
Tea tree, prickly	Leptospermum juniperinum
Tea tree, river	Leptospermum obovatum
Tea tree, round-leaf	Leptospermum rotundifolium
Tea tree, sheen copper	Leptospermum nitidum
Tea tree, shining	Leptospermum nitidum
Tea tree, silky	Leptospermum lanigerum
Tea tree, silky	Leptospermum mysinoides
Tea tree, spiny	Leptospermum spinescens
Tea tree, Tantoon	Leptospermum flavescens
Tea tree, Tantoon	Leptospermum polygalifolium
Tea tree, Victorian	Leptospermum laevigatum
Tea tree, woolly	Leptospermum lanigerum
Tea-berry	Gaultheria procumbens
Tea-oil plant	Camellia oleifera
Teak	Flindersia australis
Teak	Tectona grandis
Teak, Rhodesian	Baikiaea plurijuga
Teak, round-leaved	Pterocarpus rotundifolius
Tearthumb, arrow-leaved	Polygonum sagittatum
Teasel	Dipsacus
Teasel, Fuller's	Dipsacus sativus
Teasel, wild	Dipsacus fullonum
Tecoma, pink	Tabebuia rosea
Teddy bear plant	Cyanotis kewensis
Teddy bear vine	Cyanotis kewensis
Teerertjie	Bolusafra bituminosa
Teff	Eragrostis tef
Telegraph plant	Desmodium gyrans
Tellon, Hawaiian	Passiflora edulis
Temple bells	Smithiana
Temple tree	Polyalthia longifolia v pendula
Templetonia, red	Templetonia retusa
Templetonia, tropic	Templetonia hookeri
Teosinte	Zea mexicana
Terebinth	Pistacia terebinthus
Terminalia, Burrup	Terminalia supranitifolia
Terminalia, Kalahari sand	Terminalia brachystemma
Terminalia, large-leaved	Terminalia mollis
Terminalia, zig-zag	Terminalia stuhlmannii
Termite plant	Jatropha curcas
Texan bluebell	Eustoma
Texas bluebonnet	Lupinus texensis
Texas mountain laurel	Sophora secundiflora
Texas plume	Ipomopsis rubra
Texas ranger	Leucophyllum frutescens
Thatch, brittle	Thrinax morrisii
Thatch, Buffalo	Thrinax morrisii
Thatch palm	Coccothrinax
Thatch palm	Thrinax
Thatch palm	Thrinax parviflora
Thatch, silver	Coccothrinax fragrans
The golden Wattle of Australia	Acacia pycnantha
The hog	Heracleum mantegazzianum
Thermopsis, mountain	Thermopsis montana
Thermopsis, western	Thermopsis montana
Thimbleberry	Rubus odoratus
Thimbleberry	Rubus parviflorus

Common-Botanical Names

Common	Botanical
Thimbleweed	Anemone virginiana
Thimblweed, prairie	Anemone cylindrica
Thistle, alpine	Carlina acaulis
Thistle, Blessed	Cnicus benedictus
Thistle, Carline	Carlina
Thistle, Carline stemless	Carlina acaulis
Thistle, cotton	Onopordum
Thistle, globe	Echinops
Thistle, globe blue	Echinops ritro
Thistle, golden	Centaurea macrocephala
Thistle, ivory	Ptilostemon afer
Thistle, milk	Silybum marianum
Thistle, milk silver	Silybum eburneum
Thistle, mountain	Acanthus montanus
Thistle, mountain sow	Cicerbita alpina
Thistle, musk	Carduus nutans
Thistle, nodding	Carduus nutans
Thistle, prickle	Dryandra carduacea
Thistle, Scotch	Onopordum
Thistle, Scotch	Onopordum acanthium
Thistle, silver	Carlina acaulis
Thistle, sow blue	Cicerbita alpina
Thistle, St. Mary's	Silybum marianum
Thistles, cabbage	Cirsium oleraceum
Thistles, Hill's	Cirsium hillii
Thistles, melancholy	Cirsium heterophyllum
Thistles, plumed	Cirsium
Thistles, Siberian	Cirsium oleraceum
Thorn	Crataegus
Thorn apple	Datura stramonium
Thorn pear	Scolopia zeyheri
Thorny rope	Dalbergia armata
Thorow-wax	Bupleurum
Thorow-wax	Bupleurum rotundifolium
Thousand mothers	Tolmiea menziesii
Three-men-in-a-boat	Tradescantia spathacea
Thrift	Armeria
Thrift, pinkball	Armeria pseudarmeria
Thrift, sea	Armeria maritima
Throatwort, blue	Trachelium caeruleum
Thuja, Chinese	Thuja orientalis
Thuja, Korean	Thuja koraiensis
Thyme	Thymus
Thyme, Basil	Acinos arvensis
Thyme, camphor	Thymus camphorata
Thyme, caraway	Thymus herba-barona
Thyme, creeping	Thymus glabrescens
Thyme, creeping	Thymus serpyllum
Thyme, curly water	Lagarosiphon
Thyme, garden	Thymus vulgaris
Thyme, hop-headed	Thymbra capitata
Thyme, lemon-scented	Thymus x citriodorus
Thyme, mother of	Acinos arvensis
Thyme, mother of	Thymus pulegioides
Thyme, sauce	Thymus zygis
Thyme, tufted	Thymus caespititus
Thyme, water curly	Legarosiphon
Thyme, wild large	Thymus pulegioides
Ti plant	Cordyline fruticosa
Ti tree	Cordyline fruticosa
Ti tree	Leptospermum
Ti tree, coastal	Leptospermum laevigatum
Ti tree, oil	Melaleuca alternifolia
Ti tree, Rottnest	Melaleuca lanceolata ssp occidentalis
Ti-tree, fine	Agonis parviceps
Tian hua fen	Trichosanthes kirilowii
Tick, beggar nodding	Bidens cernua
Tick bush	Kunzea ambigua
Tick trefoil, hoary	Desmodium canescens
Tick trefoil, Illinois	Desmodium illinoense
Tick trefoil, pointed-leaf	Desmodium glutinasum
Tick trefoil, sessile-leaf	Desmodium sessilifolium
Tick trefoil, showy	Desmodium canadense
Tickseed	Coreopsis
Tickseed, purple-stemmed	Bidens connata
Tickseed, sunflower	Bidens coronata
Tiddly winks	Exacum affine
Tidy tips	Layia platyglossa
Tiger flower	Tigridia
Tiger flower	Tigridia pavonia
Tiger jaws	Faucaria
Tiger orchid	Rossioglossum grande
Tiger-snake vine	Kennedia nigricans
Timor	Hibiscus tiliaceus
Timothy grass	Phleum pratense
Tineo	Weinmannia trichosperma
Tingle, red	Eucalyptus jacksonii
Tingle, yellow	Eucalyptus guilfoylei
Tinsel bush	Cyanostegia angustifolia
Tipa tree	Tipuana tipu
Tipu tree	Tipuana tipu
Tisty tosty	Primula veris
Tittle-me-fancy	Viola tricolor
Tjienkerientjee	Ornithogalum thyrsoides
Tjuta	Eucalyptus centralis
Toad cactus	Orbea variegata (Stapelia)
Toad lily	Tricyrtis
Toad plant, giant	Stapelia gigantea
Toad-shade	Trillium sessile
Toadflax	Linaria
Toadflax	Linaria vulgaris
Toadflax, alpine	Linaria alpina
Toadflax, Dalmatian	Linaria genistifolia v dalmatica
Toadflax, ivy-leaved	Cymbalaria muralis
Toadflax, purple	Linaria purpurea
Toadflax, purple-net	Linaria reticulata
Toadflax, three birds	Linaria triornithophora
Toatoa	Haloragis erecta 'Wellington Bronze'
Tobacco brush	Ceanothus velutinus
Tobacco, flowering	Nicotiana alata
Tobacco, flowering	Nicotiana sylvestris
Tobacco, Hopi	Nicotiana rustica
Tobacco, Huichol	Nicotiana lansdorfii
Tobacco, Indian	Lobelia inflata
Tobacco plant	Nicotiana
Tobacco, sacred	Nicotiana rustica
Tobacco, smoking	Nicotiana tobacum
Tobacco, tree	Nicotiana glauca
Tobacco, tree yellow	Nicotiana glauca
Tobacco, wild	Nicotiana rustica
Tobacco, wild	Silene undulata
Tobacco, wild Aztec	Nicotiana rustica
Toddy palm	Borassus flabellifer
Toe toe	Cortaderia fulvida
Tokoonja	Morinda citrifolia

Common-Botanical Names

Tolbos | Leucadendron sessile
Toloache | Datura inoxia
Tomatillo | Physalis
Tomatillo | Physalis ixocarpa
Tomato, strawberry | Physalis peruviana
Tomato, wild | Solanum phlomoides
Tongue fern | Pyrrosia
Toog tree | Bischofia javanica
Toothache berry | Chironia baccifera
Toothache plant | Spilanthes acmella
Toothbrush grass | Lamarckia aurea
Toothpick plant | Ammi visnaga
Toothwort | Cardamine heptaphylla
Toothwort | Dentaria laciniata
Toothwort | Lathraea clandestina
Torch ginger | Etlingera elatior
Torch ginger | Phaeomeria magnifica
Torch lily | Kniphofia
Torch plant | Aloe aristata
Torchwood | Balanites maughamii
Torchwood, simple-thorned | Balanites aegyptica
Tormentil | Potentilla erecta
Tornillo | Prosopis pubescens
Torote, Colorado | Bursera filicifolia
Tortoise plant | Dioscorea elephantipes
Totara, alpine | Podocarpus nivalis
Totem poles | Melaleuca decussata
Touch-me-not, Burton's | Impatiens burtonii
Touch-me-not, spotted | Impatiens capensis
Tower mustard | Arabis glabra
Tower of jewels | Echium wildpretii
Toyon | Heteromeles arbutifolia
Trailing velvet plant | Ruellia makoyana
Transvaal kaffirboom | Erythrina lysistemon
Transvaalbergsuikerbos | Protea rubropilosa
Transvaalliguster | Galpinia transvaalica
Transvaalse Baakhout | Greyia radlkoferi
Transvaaltaaibos | Rhus transvaalensis
Traveller's joy | Clematis
Traveller's joy | Clematis brachiata
Traveller's joy | Clematis vitalba
Traveller's tree | Ravenala
Travelling sailor | Cymbalaria muralis
Treasure flower | Gazania rigens
Tree buchu | Empleureum unicapsulare
Tree cabbage | Brassica oleracea Tronchuda Group
Tree fern | Cyathea
Tree fern, black | Cyathea medullaris
Tree fern, Brazilian | Schizolobium parahybum
Tree fuchsia | Halleria lucida
Tree heath | Erica arborea
Tree ivy | x Fatshedera lizei
Tree lucerne | Chamaecytisus palmensis
Tree lucerne, false | Chamaecytisus proliferus
Tree mallow | Lavatera
Tree of heaven | Ailanthus altissima
Tree paeony | Paeonia suffruticosa
Tree poppy | Dendromecon
Tree poppy | Romneya
Tree spinach | Chenopodium giganteum 'Magentaspreen'

Tree tomato | Cyphomandra
Tree tomato, Ecuadorian | Cyphomandra betacea
Tree wisteria | Bolusanthus speciosus
Trefoil, bird's foot | Lotus corniculatus
Trefoil, bird's foot greater | Lotus uliginosus
Trefoil, red | Trifolium rubens
Trefoil, red flowered | Lotus cruentus
Trefoil, sweet | Trigonella caerulea
Trembling grass | Briza media
Trigger plant | Stylidium graminifolium
Trigger plant, grass | Stylidium graminifolium
Trigger plant, Queen | Stylidium affine
Trillium, large-flowered | Trillium grandiflorum
Trillium, painted | Trillium undulatum
Trillium, snow | Trillium nivale
Trinity flower | Trillium
Trout lily | Erythronium
Trout lily | Erythronium revolutum v smithii
Trout lily, American | Erythronium revolutum
True love | Paris quadrifolia
Trumpet bush | Tecoma stans
Trumpet bush, yellow | Tecoma stans
Trumpet creeper | Campsis radicans
Trumpet creeper, Chinese | Campsis grandiflora
Trumpet creeper, common | Campsis radicans
Trumpet flower | Bignonia capreolata
Trumpet flower | Campsis
Trumpet flower, velvet | Salpiglossis sinuata
Trumpet gentian | Gentiana acaulis
Trumpet tree, Argentine | Tabebuia avellandae
Trumpet tree, golden | Tabebuia chrysantha
Trumpet tree, pink | Tabebuia rosea
Trumpet tree, rosy | Tabebuia rosea
Trumpet tree, silver | Tabebuia argentea
Trumpet vine | Campsis
Trumpet vine, blue | Thunbergia grandiflora
Trumpet vine, Chinese | Campsis grandiflora
Trumpet vine, pink | Podranea ricasoliana
Trumpets | Sarracenia flava
Tsamma | Citrullus lanatus
Tsuri-fune-so | Impatiens glandulifera
Tuberose | Polianthes tuberosa
Tuckeroo | Alphitonia excelsa
Tuckeroo | Cupaniopsis anacardioides
Tulip | Tulipa
Tulip, Cape | Homeria comptonii
Tulip gentian | Eustoma grandiflorum
Tulip, golden globe | Calochorus amablis
Tulip, horned | Tulipa acuminata
Tulip, lady | Tulipa clusiana
Tulip Orchid | Anguloa
Tulip tree | Liriodendron
Tulip tree | Liriodendron tulipifera
Tulip tree, African | Spathodea campanulata
Tulip tree, chinese | Liriodendron chinense
Tulip, water-lily | Tulipa kaufmanniana
Tulipwood | Harpullia pendula
Tulp | Homeria elegans
Tulp, apricot | Homeria ochroleuca
Tulsi | Ocimum tenuiflorum
Tumbling Ted | Saponaria ocymoides
Tung oil tree | Aleurites fordii
Tunic flower | Petrorhagia saxifraga
Tupelo | Nyssa

Common-Botanical Names

Common name	Botanical name	Common name	Botanical name
Tupelo, black	Nyssa sylvatica	Unicorn plant, common	Proboscidea louisianica
Tupelo, Chinese	Nyssa sinensis	Unicorn root	Alectris farinosa
Tupelo, water	Nyssa aquatica	Upright bugle	Ajuga genevensis
Turk's cap cactus	Melocactus	Urn plant	Aechmea fasciata
Turkey berry	Canthium inerme	Uva ursi	Arctostaphylos uva-ursi
Turkey bush	Calytrix exstipulata	Vaaltolbos	Leucadendron conicum
Turkey bush	Eremophila deserti	Valerian	Centranthus
Turkey bush, green	Eremophila gilesii	Valerian	Valeriana
Turkey gobbler	Hakea rostrata	Valerian, cat's	Valerianella officinalis
Turmeric	Curcuma domestica	Valerian, common	Valeriana officinalis
Turnip, prairie	Psoralea esculenta	Valerian, Greek	Polemonium caeruleum
Turpentine tree	Pistacia terebinthus	Valerian, mountain	Valeriana montana
Turpentine tree	Syncarpia glomulifera	Valerian, red	Centranthus ruber
Turquoise berry	Drymophila cyanocarpa	Valerian, wild	Plectritis congesta
Turtlehead	Chelone	Vanilla	Vanilla planifolia
Turtlehead	Chelone obliqua	Vanilla grass	Anthoxanthum odoratum
Turtlehead, Balmone	Chelone glabra		
Turtlehead, pink	Chelone lyonii	Vanilla lily, pale	Arthropodium milleflorum
Turtlehead, white	Chelone glabra		
Tussock grass	Cortaderia	Vanilla lily, vanilla	Arthropodium capillipes
Tussock grass	Deschampsia cespitosa	Vanstadens scepter	Paranomus reflexus
Tutsan	Hypericum androsaemum	Vap ca	Houttuynia cordata
		Variegated ginger	Alpinia vittata
Twin leaf	Jeffersonia	Varkslaai	Conicosia pugioniformis
Twin-flower	Linnaea	Varnish tree	Rhus verniciflua
Twin-flower Knawel	Scleranthus biflorus	Vase plant	Aechmea fasciata
Twin-stem, yellow	Flaveria australasica	Veegeetmynietjie	Anchusa capensis
Twinberry, black	Lonicera involucrata	Vegetable sheep	Haastia
Twinberry, red	Lonicera utahensis	Vegetable sheep	Haastia pulvinaris
Twinleaf, climbing	Zygophyllum eremaeum	Veitch fir	Abies veitchii
Twinleaf, shrubby	Zygophyllum aurantiacum	Vejar fir	Abies vejarii
		Velcro plant	Arctium sp
Twinspur, upturned	Diascia anastrepta	Veldvy	Ficus burtt-davyi
Twirly bush	Persoonia tortifolia	Velvet bean	Pseudarthria hookeri
Twisted stalk	Streptopus amplexifolius	Velvet bells	Bartsia alpina
Twitch	Elytrigia repens	Velvet bent	Agrostis canina
Uiltjie	Moraea villosa	Velvet bush, drooping	Lasiopetalum schulzenii
Ulmo	Eucryphia cordifolia	Velvet bush, Helena	Lasiopetalum behrii
Umbinza	Halleria lucida	Velvet bush, pink	Lasiopetalum behrii
Umbrella Arum	Amorphophallus konjac	Velvet bush, slender	Lasiopetalum baueri
Umbrella bush	Acacia oswaldii	Velvet plant	Gynura aurantiaca
Umbrella bush	Melaleuca cardiophylla	Velvet plant, purple	Gynura aurantiaca
Umbrella grass	Cyperus involucratus	Velvet plant, Royal	Gynura aurantiaca
Umbrella leaf	Diphylleia cymosa	Velvet rose	Aeonium canariense
Umbrella palm	Hedyscepe	Vendaverfbos	Indigofera lyalli
Umbrella plant	Cyperus involucratus	Venetian sumach	Cotinus coggygria
Umbrella plant	Darmera peltata	Venus' basin	Dipsacus fullonum
Umbrella plant, yellow	Eriogonum flavum	Venus fly trap	Dionaea
Umbrella thorn, bastard	Acacia luderitzii v luderitzii	Venus fly trap	Dionaea muscipula
		Venus' lokking glass	Triodanis perfoliata
Umbrella tree	Magnolia macrophylla	Venus' looking glass	Legousia speculum-veneris
Umbrella tree	Magnolia tripetala		
Umbrella tree	Polyscias murrayi	Verbena, anise	Lippia alba
Umbrella tree	Schefflera actinophylla	Verbena, lemon	Aloysia triphylla
Umbrella tree, Australian dwarf	Schefflera arboricola	Verbena, prairie	Verbena bipinnatifida
Umbrella tree, Queensland	Schefflera actinophylla	Verbena, sand snowball	Abronia fragrans
Umdoni	Syzygium cordatum	Verbena, sand yellow	Abronia latifolia
Umhluhluwe	Dalbergia armata	Verbine, tall	Psoralea australasica
umPhisamakhasa	Galpinia transvaalica	Vernal grass, sweet	Anthoxanthum odoratum
Umsenya	Erythrophleum africanum		
		Vernonia, tree	Vernonia amygdalina
Umzimbeet	Milletia grandis	Vervain	Verbena officinalis
Umzimbeet, giant	Milletia sutherlandii	Vervain, blue	Verbena hastata
Unicorn, false	Chamaelirium luteum	Vervain, Brazilian	Verbena bonariensis
Unicorn plant	Proboscidea	Vervain, Dakota	Verbena bipinnatifida
Unicorn plant	Proboscidea louisianica	Vervain, hoary	Verbena stricta

Common-Botanical Names

Common	Botanical
Vervain, moss	Verbena tenuisecta
Vervain, white	Verbena urticifolia
Vetch	Hippocrepis
Vetch, bitter	Lathyrus linifolius v montanus
Vetch, bladder	Swainsona colutoides
Vetch, common	Vicia sativa
Vetch, hairy	Vicia villosa
Vetch, horseshoe	Hippocrepis
Vetch, large	Vicia gigantea
Vetch, sweet northern	Hedysarum boreale
Vetch, sweet western	Hedysarum occidentale
Vetch, tufted	Vicia cracca
Vetch, wood	Vicia sylvatica
Vetchling, common	Lathyrus pratensis
Vetchling, meadow	Lathyrus pratensis
Vetchling, spring	Lathyrus vernus
Vetchling, tuberous	Lathyrus tuberosus
Veterbos	Crassula muscosa
Vetiver grass	Vetiveria zizanioides
Vetkousie	Carpanthea pomeridiana
Viburnum, maple-leaved	Viburnum acerifolium
Viburnum, mousewood	Viburnum edule
Viburnum, sweet	Viburnum odoratissimum
Viburnum, withered	Viburnum cassinoides
Vicious hairy Mary	Calamus radicales
Vicks plant	Plectranthus purpuratus
Vine	Vitis
Vine, bean red	Kennedia rubicunda
Vine reed, Mauritania	Ampelodesmos mauritanica
Vine, tiger-snake	Kennedia nigricans
Vine-bower, Italian	Clematis viticella
Viola	Viola cornuta
Violet	Viola
Violet, African	Saintpaulia
Violet, arrowleaf	Viola sagittata
Violet, Australian	Viola hederacea
Violet, bird's foot	Viola pedata
Violet, Canada	Viola canadensis
Violet, common blue	Viola soraria
Violet, cream	Viola striata
Violet, crow-foot	Viola pedata
Violet, dog	Viola canina
Violet, dog	Viola conspersa
Violet, downy yellow	Viola pubescens
Violet, early blue	Viola palmata
Violet, English	Viola odorata
Violet, finger-leaved	Viola pinnata
Violet, garden	Viola odorata
Violet, Great Basin	Viola beckwithii
Violet, great-spurred	Viola selkirkii
Violet, heath	Viola canina
Violet, hooked-spur	Viola adunca
Violet, horned	Viola cornuta
Violet, ivy-leaved	Viola hederacea
Violet, Karoo	Aptosimum procumbens
Violet, Labrador	Viola labradorica
Violet, larkspur	Viola pedatifida
Violet, native (AU)	Hybanthus calycinus
Violet, native (AU)	Viola betonicifolia
Violet, Persian	Exacum affine
Violet, prairie purple	Viola pedatifida
Violet, purple	Viola betonicifolia
Violet, Selkirk's	Viola selkirkii
Violet, shrub	Hybanthus floribundus
Violet, shrub	Hybanthus floribundus ssp adpressus
Violet, sister	Viola soraria
Violet, stream	Viola glabella
Violet, sweet	Viola odorata
Violet, trailing	Viola hederacea
Violet tree, wild	Securidaca longepedunculata
Violet, twin-flowered	Viola bicolor
Violet, twin-flowered	Viola biflora
Violet, water	Hottonia palustris
Violet, wild	Swainsona microcalyx
Violet, wood	Viola riviniana
Violet, woodland	Viola reichenbachiana
Violet, woolly blue	Viola soraria
Violet, yellow	Viola eriocarpa
Violet-twining snapdragon	Maurandella antirrhiniflora
Viper's bugloss	Echium vulgare
Virgin's bower	Clematis
Virgin's bower	Clematis virginiana
Virginia creeper	Parthenocissus
Virginia creeper	Parthenocissus quinquefolia
Virginia creeper, Chinese	Parthenocissus henryana
Virginian stock	Malcomia maritima
Vitex	Vitex negundo heterophylla
Vlam-van-die-vlakte	Bauhinia galpinii
Vleiblommetjie	Micranthus alopecuroides
Vleiknoppiesbos	Berzelia lanuginosa
Voelneskatstert	Bulbinella elegans
Vomitweed	Lobelia inflata
Voorlopertjie	Gladiolus recurvus
Vriesea, giant	Vriesea imperialis
Vuurpyl	Kniphofia
Waaibossie	Trachyandra divaricata
Wahoo	Euonymus atropurpurea
Wait-a-minute-bush	Mimosa biuncifera
Wait-a-while	Acacia colletioides
Wait-a-while	Calamus moti
Wake robin	Trillium
Wake robin, white	Trillium grandiflorum
Walking fern	Asplenium rhizophyllum
Walking-stick palm	Linospadix
Wall plant, Roman	Erinus alpinus
Wall-spray	Cotoneaster horizontalis
Wallaby paw	Anigozanthus gabrielae
Wallflower	Erysimum
Wallflower	Erysimum cheiri
Wallflower, Siberian	Erysimum x allionii
Wallflower, western	Erysimum asperum
Wallflower, western	Erysimum capitatum
Wallich's wood fern	Dryopteris wallichiana
Wallowa	Acacia calamifolia
Walnut	Juglans
Walnut, black	Juglans nigra
Walnut, californian	Juglans Californica
Walnut, Carpathian	Juglans regia
Walnut, Chinese	Juglans cathayensis
Walnut, common	Juglans regia
Walnut, desert	Owenia reticulata
Walnut, English	Juglans regia
Walnut, Japanese	Juglans ailanthifolia

Common-Botanical Names

Walnut, little — Juglans microcarpa
Walnut, Manchurian — Juglans mandschurica
Walnut, native (AU) — Endiandra palmerstonii
Walnut, Texan — Juglans microcarpa
Wamboom — Protea nitida
Wampi — Clausena lansium
Wandering Jew — Tradescantia fluminensis
Wandering Jew — Tradescantia zebrina
Wandflower — Dierama
Wandflower — Galax
Wandoo, desert — Eucalyptus nigrifunda
Wandoo, granite Mallee — Eucalyptus livida
Wandoo, inland — Eucalyptus capillosa ssp capillosa
Wandoo, mallee — Eucalyptus capillosa ssp polyclada
Wandoo, salmon bark — Eucalyptus lane poolei
Wang bu liu xing — Vaccaria
Wapatoo — Sagittaria latifolia
Waratah — Telopea
Waratah, braidwood — Telopea mongaensis
Waratah, common — Telopea speciosissima
Waratah, Gippsland — Telopea oreades
Waratah, Monga — Telopea mongaensis
Waratah, N.S.W. — Telopea speciosissima
Waratah, Sydney — Telopea speciosissima
Waratah, Tasmanian — Telopea truncata
Waratah, tree — Oreocallis wickhamii
Waratah, Victorian — Telopea oreades
Waratah, white of Tasmania — Agastachys odorata
Warnga — Santalum acuminatum
Washington thorn — Crataegus phaenopyrum
Water archer — Sagittaria sagittifolia
Water arum — Calla
Water avens — Geum rivale
Water clover — Marsilea
Water clover — Marsilea quadrifolia
Water dragon — Saururus cernuus
Water fern — Azolla
Water figwort — Scrophularia auriculata
Water fringe — Nymphoides peltata
Water gladiolus — Butomus
Water hawthorn — Aponogeton distachyos
Water hyacinth — Eichhornia crassipes
Water lily — Nympaea
Water lily, Australian — Nymphaea gigantea
Water lily, blue — Nymphaea nouchali v caerulea
Water lily, Cape blue — Nymphaea capensis
Water lily, Egyptian — Nymphaea lotus
Water lily, fringed — Nymphoides peltata
Water lily, white — Nymphaea alba
Water lily, yellow — Nymphaea mexicana
Water mint — Mentha aquatica
Water plantain — Alisma
Water plantain, floating — Luronium natans
Water plantain, great — Alisma plantago-aquatica
Water poppy — Hydrocleys nymphoides
Water purslane — Ludwigia palustris
Water snowflake — Nymphoides indica
Water soldier — Stratiotes aloides
Water squirt — Angelica sylvestris
Water starwort — Callitriche
Water trumpet — Cryptocoryne
Water vine — Cissus hypoglauca
Water violet — Hottonia palustris

Water wisteria — Hygrophila difformis
Waterbessie — Syzygium cordatum
Waterbossie — Erica curviflora
Waterdissel — Senecio glastifolius
Waterheide — Erica caffra
Waterleaf, broad-leaved — Hydrophyllum canadense
Waterleaf, Virginia — Hydrophyllum virginianum
Watermelon plant — Peperomia argyreia
Watermelon tree — Syzygium moorei
Waterpepper — Polygonum hydropiper 'Fastigiatum'
Waterwitels — Brachylaena neriifolia
Waterwitsuikerbos — Protea punctata
Wattle — Acacia
Wattle, arid — Acacia arida
Wattle, autumn-flowered — Acacia luteola
Wattle, awl — Acacia subulata
Wattle, Baratta — Acacia barattensis
Wattle, barbed-wire — Acacia baxteri
Wattle, Barrier range — Acacia beckleri
Wattle, bent-leaf — Acacia flexifolia
Wattle, bipinnate — Acacia trachyphloia
Wattle, black — Acacia mabellae
Wattle, black — Acacia mearnsii
Wattle, black — Callicoma
Wattle, black Darwin — Acacia auriculiformis
Wattle, boomerang — Acacia amoena
Wattle, bower — Acacia cognata
Wattle, box-leaf — Acacia buxifolia
Wattle, bramble — Acacia victoriae
Wattle, Broome Pindan — Acacia eriopoda
Wattle, candelabra — Acacia holosericea
Wattle, Cape — Paraserianthes lophantha
Wattle, Cape Leeuwin — Paraserianthes lophantha
Wattle, cedar — Acacia elata
Wattle, clay — Acacia glaucoptera
Wattle, club-leaf — Acacia hemignosta
Wattle, coast west — Acacia truncata
Wattle, coast western — Acacia cyclops
Wattle, coastal — Acacia cochlearis
Wattle, coastal — Acacia sophorae
Wattle, coastal dune — Acacia littorea
Wattle, Coonavittra — Acacia jennerae
Wattle, Cootamundra — Acacia baileyana
Wattle, corkwood — Acacia bidwillii
Wattle, crested — Paraserianthes lophantha
Wattle, crowded leaf — Acacia conferta
Wattle, curry — Acacia spondylophylla
Wattle, dagger — Acacia shirleyi
Wattle, Deane's — Acacia deanii
Wattle, desert — Acacia dictyophleba
Wattle, desert — Acacia eremaea
Wattle, desert hardy — Acacia coriacea
Wattle, drooping — Acacia difformis
Wattle, Drummond's — Acacia drummondii
Wattle, Drummond's — Acacia drummondii ssp candolleana
Wattle, Drummond's — Acacia drummondii ssp drummondii
Wattle, Drummond's — Acacia drummondii ssp elegans
Wattle, dwellingup — Acacia laterriticola
Wattle, ear-leaf — Acacia auriculiformis
Wattle, ear-pod — Acacia auriculiformis

186

Common-Botanical Names

Wattle, early black	Acacia decurrens
Wattle, elegant	Acacia victoriae
Wattle, elephant ear	Acacia dunnii
Wattle, fat-leaved	Acacia pinguifolia
Wattle, fern-leaf	Acacia filicifolia
Wattle, Fitzroy	Acacia ancistrocarpa
Wattle, flat	Acacia glaucoptera
Wattle, flat-stemmed	Acacia complanata
Wattle, flax-leaved	Acacia linifolia
Wattle, Flinders range	Acacia iteaphylla
Wattle, fringed	Acacia fimbriata
Wattle, frost	Acacia frigescens
Wattle, frosty	Acacia pruinosa
Wattle, ghost	Acacia platycarpa
Wattle, Gladstone	Acacia wattsiana
Wattle, glory	Acacia glaucocarpa
Wattle, gold	Acacia baileyana
Wattle, gold dust	Acacia acinacea
Wattle, golden	Acacia pycnantha
Wattle, golden Brisbane	Acacia fimbriata
Wattle, golden dwarf	Acacia drummondii ssp drummondii
Wattle, golden gravel	Acacia guinetii
Wattle, golden miniature	Acacia drummondii ssp affinis
Wattle, golden rain	Acacia prominens
Wattle, golden Sydney	Acacia longifolia
Wattle, golden western	Acacia decora
Wattle, golden wreath	Acacia saligna
Wattle, Gosford	Acacia prominens
Wattle, gossamer	Acacia floribunda
Wattle, graceful	Acacia decora
Wattle, green	Acacia decurrens
Wattle, green	Acacia irrorata ssp irrorata
Wattle, green Sydney	Acacia parramattensis
Wattle, hairy	Acacia vestita
Wattle, hairy leaved	Acacia pruinosa
Wattle, Hakea	Acacia hakeoides
Wattle, half-moon	Acacia cultriformis
Wattle, Halls creek	Acacia cowleana
Wattle, hard-leaf	Acacia sclerophylla
Wattle, Harrow	Acacia acanthoclada
Wattle, heath	Acacia ulicifolia v brownii
Wattle, hedge	Acacia paradoxa
Wattle, hickory	Acacia aulacocarpa
Wattle, hickory	Acacia falciformis
Wattle, hickory	Acacia implexa
Wattle, hickory	Acacia penninervis
Wattle, hickory mountain	Acacia obliquinervia
Wattle, hindmarsh	Acacia trineura
Wattle, honey-scented	Acacia melleodora
Wattle, hook-leaf	Acacia curvata
Wattle, hop	Acacia stricta
Wattle, hop-leaved	Acacia dodonaeifolia
Wattle, jam	Acacia acuminata
Wattle, Jibberding	Acacia jibberdingensis
Wattle, juniper	Acacia ulicifolia
Wattle, Karri	Acacia pentadenia
Wattle, knife-leaf	Acacia cultriformis
Wattle, Kybean	Acacia kybeanensis
Wattle, large leafy	Acacia binervata
Wattle, leafless	Acacia wildenowiana
Wattle, lime-sand	Acacia lasiocarpa
Wattle, limestone	Acacia sclerosperma
Wattle, limestone	Acacia tysonii

Wattle, long pod	Acacia elongata
Wattle, Mabel's	Acacia mabellae
Wattle, Maiden's	Acacia maidenii
Wattle, Mallee	Acacia montana
Wattle, Manna	Acacia microbotrya
Wattle, Manna	Acacia microcarpa
Wattle, mist	Acacia wilhelmiana
Wattle, Mitta	Acacia dawsonii
Wattle, Mount Morgan	Acacia podalyriifolia
Wattle, Mudgee	Acacia spectabilis
Wattle, myrtle	Acacia myrtifolia
Wattle, myrtle grey	Acacia celastrifolia
Wattle, mystery	Acacia difformis
Wattle, needle	Acacia havilandii
Wattle, needle bush	Acacia rigens
Wattle, notable	Acacia notabilis
Wattle, oleander	Acacia neriifolia
Wattle, Ongerup	Acacia redolens
Wattle, Ovens	Acacia pravissima
Wattle, Padjang	Acacia lasiocarpa
Wattle, perfume	Acacia farnesiana
Wattle, perfumed	Acacia nervosa
Wattle, Pilbara prostrate	Acacia gregorii
Wattle, Pindan	Acacia tumida
Wattle, Porongorup	Acacia leioderma
Wattle, Port Lincoln	Acacia iteaphylla
Wattle, prickly	Acacia nyssophylla
Wattle, prickly	Acacia victoriae
Wattle, prickly swamp	Acacia hastulata
Wattle, Queen	Acacia decurrens
Wattle, Queensland	Acacia podalyriifolia
Wattle, Queensland silver	Acacia podalyriifolia
Wattle, raspberry jam	Acacia acuminata
Wattle, red	Acacia silvestris
Wattle, red stem	Acacia rubida
Wattle, Rice's	Acacia riceana
Wattle, river	Acacia cognata
Wattle, rock	Acacia rupicola
Wattle, rock leafless	Acacia aphylla
Wattle, rough	Acacia aspera
Wattle, round-leaf	Acacia rotundifolia
Wattle, round-leaf	Acacia uncinata
Wattle, rush-leaved	Acacia juncifolia
Wattle, sallow	Acacia longifolia
Wattle, sallow	Acacia sophorae
Wattle, salt	Acacia ampliceps
Wattle, salt gully	Acacia patagiata
Wattle, sand plain	Acacia murrayana
Wattle, sand western	Acacia prainii
Wattle, sandhill	Acacia burkittii
Wattle, sandhill	Acacia ligulata
Wattle, sandpaper	Acacia denticulosa
Wattle, scented Musa	Acacia dictyoneura
Wattle, scorpion	Acacia cincinnata
Wattle, silky	Acacia acradenia
Wattle, silver	Acacia dealbata
Wattle, silver	Acacia neriifolia
Wattle, silver	Acacia retinodes
Wattle, silver	Acacia rivalis
Wattle, silver Bodalla	Acacia silvestris
Wattle, silver old	Acacia podalyriifolia
Wattle, silver western	Acacia decora
Wattle, silver western	Acacia glaucocarpa
Wattle, silver-grey	Acacia steedmanii
Wattle, silver-stemmed	Acacia parvipinnula
Wattle, Sim's	Acacia simsii

Common-Botanical Names

Common name	Botanical name
Wattle, smooth-leaved	Acacia leiophylla
Wattle, Snowy River	Acacia boormanii
Wattle, spike	Acacia oxycedrus
Wattle, spiky	Acacia maitlandii
Wattle, spiniflex	Acacia coolgardiensis aff
Wattle, spiny	Acacia erinacea
Wattle, spreading	Acacia genistifolia
Wattle, spur-wing	Acacia triptera
Wattle, sticky	Acacia dodonaeifolia
Wattle, sticky	Acacia howittii
Wattle, sticky	Acacia viscidula
Wattle, sticky-leaved	Acacia ixiophylla
Wattle, straight-podded	Acacia orthocarpa
Wattle, streaked	Acacia lineata
Wattle, stringybark	Acacia linearifolia
Wattle, summer rain	Acacia fauntleroyi
Wattle, summer-scented	Acacia triptycha
Wattle, sunshine	Acacia terminalis
Wattle, swamp	Acacia elongata
Wattle, swamp	Acacia retinodes
Wattle, swamp	Paraserianthes lophantha
Wattle, sweet	Acacia farnesiana
Wattle, sweet-scented	Acacia suaveolens
Wattle, sword	Acacia gladiiformis
Wattle, Sydney golden	Albizia longifolia
Wattle, Tallebung	Acacia menzelii
Wattle, tan	Acacia hemiteles
Wattle, Tanumbirini	Acacia tanumbirinensis
Wattle, thorn	Acacia continua
Wattle, toothed	Acacia dentifera
Wattle, Townsville	Acacia leptostachya
Wattle, turpentine	Acacia lysiphloia
Wattle, two nerved	Acacia binervata
Wattle, two-nerved	Acacia bivenosa
Wattle, umbrella	Acacia oswaldii
Wattle, vanilla	Acacia redolens
Wattle, varnish	Acacia verniciflua
Wattle, veined	Acacia urophylla
Wattle, veined fine	Acacia venulosa
Wattle, velvety	Acacia mollifolia
Wattle, Wallangarra	Acacia adunca
Wattle, Wanderrie	Acacia kempeana
Wattle, weeping	Acacia saligna
Wattle, weeping	Acacia uncinata
Wattle, weeping	Peltophorum africanum
Wattle, western black	Acacia hakeoides
Wattle, Whirrakee	Acacia williamsonii
Wattle, whispery	Acacia merinthophora
Wattle, white	Acacia neriifolia
Wattle, white flowered	Acacia gilbertii
Wattle, white sallow	Acacia floribunda
Wattle, willow	Acacia saliciformis
Wattle, willow-leaf	Acacia iteaphylla
Wattle, Wilyurwur	Acacia lasiocalyx
Wattle, winged	Acacia alata
Wattle, wiry	Acacia falcata
Wattle, Woogenellup	Acacia browniana v intermedia
Wattle, woolly	Acacia lanigera
Wattle, Wyalong	Acacia cardiophylla
Wattle, yellowdine	Acacia rossei
Wattle, zig zag	Acacia macradenia
Wax flower	Cerinthe
Wax flower	Hoya
Wax flower	Jamesia
Wax flower	Stephanotis floribunda
Wax flower, long-leaved	Eriostemon myoporoides
Wax flower, pink	Eriostemon australasius
Wax palm	Copernicia
Wax plant	Hoya carnosa
Wax privet	Peperomia glabella
Wax tree	Rhus succedanea
Wax vine	Senecio macroglossus
Wax-flower, Ravensthorpe	Chamelaucium megalopetalum
Wax-work	Celastrus scandens
Waxberry	Gaultheria hispida
Waxflower	Eriostemon
Waxflower, esperance	Chamaelaucium megalopetalum
Waxflower, Philippine	Etlingera elatior
Wayfaring tree	Viburnum lantana
Weasel's snout	Antirrhinum orontium
Weddell palm	Lytocaryum weddellianum
Wedding bells	Dierama
Wedding bush	Ricinocarpus tuberculatus
Wedding bush, large	Ricinocarpus tuberculatus
Wedding-cake tree	Cornus controversa 'Variegata'
Weed, caustic	Euphorbia drummondii
Weeskindertjies	Nemesia versicolor
Welcome home husband, however drunk you may be	Sempervivum tectorum
Weld	Reseda luteola
Wellingtonia	Sequoiadendron giganteum
West Indian holly	Leea guineensis
Western Golden Pennants	Glischrocaryon aureum
Western laurel	Kalmia microphylla
Whauwhaupaku	Pseudopanax arborescens
Wheel of fire	Stenocarpus sinuatus
Whin	Ulex europaeus
Whinberry	Vaccinum myrtillus
Whinny luck	Ulex
Whipcord, trailing	Hebe epacridea
White alder	Clethra
White fir	Abies concolor
White forsythia	Abeliophyllum
White paint brush	Haemanthus albiflos
White sails	Spathiphyllum wallisii
White Sally	Eucalyptus pauciflora
White velvet	Tradescantia sillamontana
Whitebeam	Sorbus aria
Whitebeam, Swedish	Sorbus intermedia
Whitewood	Atalaya hemiglauca
Whitewood, large pod	Eucalyptus leucoxylon ssp macrocarpa
Whitey wood	Acradenia frankliniae
Whitey-wood	Melicytus ramiflorus
Whitlow grass	Draba
Whitlow grass, yellow	Draba aizoides
Whitlow-wort	Paronychia
Whorlflower	Morina longifolia
Whortleberry	Vaccinum
Whortleberry	Vaccinum myrtillus
Whortleberry, Caucasian	Vaccinum arctostaphylos

Common-Botanical Names

Whortleberry, grouse	Vaccinum scoparium
Whortleberry, red	Vaccinum parvifolium
Wickens	Elytrigia repens
Widow maker	Fraxinus excelsior
Widow's teas	Commelina
Wilarak	Santalum spicatum
Wild Dagga	Leonotis ocymifolia
Wild date	Yucca baccata
Wild Irishman	Discaria toumatou
Wild okra	Viola soraria
Wild pride of India	Galpinia transvaalica
Wild Spaniard	Aciphylla colensoi
Wild water lemon	Passiflora foetida
Wilde kastaaing	Calodendron capense
Wilde-als	Artemisia afra
Wildedadelboom	Phoenix reclinata
Wildedatal (wildewortel)	Sansevieria hyacinthoides
Wildegranaat	Burchellia bubalina
Wildekatjiepiering	Rothmannia capensis
Wildekopieva	Bulbine narcissifolia
Wildemalva	Pelargonium cucullatum
Wildemispel	Vangueria infausta
Wildepampoen	Radyera urens
Wildeperske	Kiggelaria africana
Wildepiesang	Strelitzia nicolai
Wildepieterseliebos	Heteromorpha trifoliata
Wildestokroos	Hibiscus ludwigii
Wildestokroos	Hibiscus pedunculatus
Wildeui	Allium dregeanum
Wilga	Geijera parviflora
Willow	Salix
Willow, Australian	Geijera parviflora
Willow, bay	Salix pentandra
Willow, beaked	Salix bebbiana
Willow, black	Salix gracilistyla 'Melanostachys'
Willow, black	Salix nigra
Willow broom	Viminaria juncea
Willow, bush	Combretum collinum
Willow, bush Cape	Combretum caffrum
Willow, bush forest	Combretum krausii
Willow, bush oleaster	Combretum elaeagnoides
Willow, bush river	Combretum erythrophyllum
Willow, bush sand	Combretum engleri
Willow, bush savanna	Combretum celastroides
Willow, bush thicket	Combretum padoides
Willow, bush velvet	Combretum molle
Willow, coyote	Salix exigua
Willow, crack	Salix fragilis
Willow, creeping	Salix repens
Willow, creeping golden	Salix x sepulcralis
Willow, cricket-bat	Salix alba v caerulea
Willow, desert	Chilopsis linearis
Willow, desert	Pittosporum phillyreoides
Willow, dragon's claw	Salix babylonica v pekinensis 'Tortuosa'
Willow, dwarf	Salix herbacea
Willow, gentian	Gentiana asclepiadea
Willow, goat	Salix caprea
Willow, golden	Salix alba ssp vitellina
Willow, heart-leaved	Salix discolor
Willow herb	Epilobium

Willow herb, alpine	Epilobium dodonaei
Willow herb, northern	Epilobium glandulosum
Willow herb, small-flowered	Epilobium parviflorum
Willow, hoary	Salix elaeagnos
Willow, least	Salix herbacea
Willow moss	Fontinalis antipyretica
Willow, mountain	Salix arbuscula
Willow, Murchison	Acacia decurrens
Willow, musk	Salix aegyptiaca
Willow, native (AU)	Acacia stenophylla
Willow, net-veined	Salix reticulata
Willow peppermint	Agonis flexuosa
Willow peppermint, white	Agonis flexuosa
Willow, pussy	Salix caprea
Willow, pussy	Salix discolor
Willow shrub, prairie	Salix humilis
Willow, silver	Salix alba v sericea
Willow, Swiss	Salix helvetica
Willow, thyme-leaved	Salix serpyllifolia
Willow, violet	Salix daphnoides
Willow, weeping	Salix babylonica
Willow, weeping golden	Salix x sepulcralis v chrysocoma
Willow, white	Salix alba
Willow, woolly	Salix lanata
Willy lily	Arum maculatum
Windflower	Anemone
Windflower	Anemone nemerosa
Windflower	Anemone virginiana
Windflower, snowdrop	Anemone sylvestris
Wine cups	Babiana rubrocyanea
Wine palm	Borassus flabellifer
Wine-cup, lacquered	Aechmea 'Foster's Favourite'
Wineberry	Rubus phoenicolasius
Winecups	Callirhoe involucrata
Winecups	Geissorhiza radians
Winecups, cowboy's	Callirhoe involucrata
Wing nut	Pterocarya
Wing nut, Caucasian	Pterocarya fraxinifolia
Wing nut, Chinese	Pterocarya stenoptera
Wing nut, Japanese	Pterocarya rhoifolia
Winged everlasting	Ammobium
Winged everlasting	Ammobium alatum
Wingstem	Verbesina alternifolia
Winter aconite	Eranthis
Winter bells	Blancoa canescens
Winter's bark	Drimys winteri
Winterberry	Ilex verticillata
Winterberry, smooth	Ilex laevigata
Winterfat	Ceratoides lanata
Wintergreen	Gaultheria procumbens
Wintergreen	Pyrola
Wintergreen, Oregon	Gaultheria fragrantissima
Wintergreen, round-leaf	Pyrola rotundifolia
Wintergreen, serrated	Pyrola secunda
Wintersweet	Chimonanthus
Wintersweet	Chimonanthus praecox
Wintersweet, African	Acokanthera oblongifolia
Wire-netting bush	Corokia cotoneaster
Wirewood	Acacia coriacea
Wirilda	Acacia retinodes
Wishbone flower	Torenia
Wistaria	Wisteria
Wistaria, American	Wisteria frutescens
Wisteria, Chinese	Wisteria sinensis

Common-Botanical Names

Common	Botanical
Wisteria, climber wild	Hardenbergia comptonia
Wisteria, Japanese	Wisteria floribunda
Wisteria, native (AU)	Hardenbergia comptonia
Wisteria, silky	Wisteria brachybotrys
Wisteria, silky	Wisteria venusta
Wisteria, South African	Bolusanthus
Wisteria, tree	Pongamia pinnata
Wisteria tree	Sesbania tripetii
Wisteria tree, scarlet	Sesbania grandiflora
Wit Klipdagga	Leonotis ocymifolia v alba
Wit Tamarak	Albuca maxima
Witch grass	Panicum capillare
Witch hazel	Hamamelis
Witch hazel, Chinese	Hamamelis mollis
Witch hazel, Japanese	Hamamelis japonica
Witch hazel, Ozark	Hamamelis vernalis
Witch hazel, Persian	Parrotia persica
Witch hazel, Virginian	Hamamelis virginiana
Witchetty bush	Acacia kempeana
Witchweed, yellow	Alectra sessiliflora
Witgousblom	Arctotis venusta
Witheide	Erica formosa
Without	Ilex mitis
Withy	Salix
Witkaree	Rhus pendulina
Witkatjiepiering	Gardenia thunbergia
Witolienhout	Buddleja saligna
Witpeer	Apodytes dimidiata ssp dimidiata
Witsewejaartjie	Helichrysum grandiflorum
Witskollie	Protea scolymocephala
Witstinkhout	Celtis africana
Witsuikerbos	Protea lacticolor
Witsuikerbos	Protea mundii
Witysterhout	Vepris lanceolata
Wldroosmaryn	Eriocephalus africanus
Woad	Isatis tinctoria
Woad, Chinese	Baphicacanthus cusia
Woad, waxen	Genista sagittalis
Woad, waxen	Genista tinctoria
Wodi	Agonis juniperina
Wolfberry	Lycium exsertum
Wolfberry, Chinese	Lycium barbarum
Wolfberry, Chinese	Lycium chinense
Wolfsbane	Aconitum lycoctonum
Wolfsbane	Aconitum lycoctonum ssp lycoctonum
Wolly tree fern	Dicksonia antarctica
Woman's tongue	Albizia lebbek
Wombat berry	Eustrephus
Wonder tree	Idesia polycarpa
Wondu	Eucalyptus wandoo
Wonga wonga vine	Pandorea pandorana
Wonidj	Callistachys lanceolata
Wonil	Agonis flexuosa
Wood betony	Stachys officinalis
Wood lily	Trillium
Wood lily, dwarf white	Trillium nivale
Wood lily, painted	Trillium undulatum
Wood mint, downy	Blephilia ciliata
Wood mint, hairy	Blephilia hirsuta
Wood rose, Hawaiian	Merremia tuberosa
Wood sage	Teucrium scorodonia
Wood violet	Viola riviniana
Woodbine	Lonicera periclymenum
Woodbine	Parthenocissus thunbergii
Wooden pear, wing-leaved	Schrebera alata
Wooden rose	Merremia tuberosa
Woodland star	Lithophragma
Woodrose, Baby Hawaiian	Argyreia nervosa
Woodruff	Asperula
Woodruff, sweet	Galium odoratum
Woodrush	Luzula
Woodrush, greater	Luzula sylvatica
Woodrush, snowy	Luzula nivea
Woodsage	Teucrium scorodonia
Woodsia, alpine	Woodsia alpina
Woodsia, holly-fern	Woodsia polystichoides
Woodsia, rusty	Woodsia ilvensis
Woolly morning glory	Argyreia nervosa
Woollybutt	Eucalyptus delegatensis
Woollybutt	Eucalyptus longifolia
Woollybutt, Camden	Eucalyptus macarthurii
Woollybutt, Darwin	Eucalyptus miniata
Woollybutt, Tenterfield	Eucalyptus banksii
Worcestorberry	Ribes divaricatum
Wormseed	Chenopodium
Wormseed	Chenopodium ambrosioides
Wormwood	Artemisia
Wormwood	Artemisia absinthium
Wormwood, African	Artemisia afra
Wormwood, beach	Artemisia stellerana
Wormwood, cassia	Senna artemisoides
Wormwood, Chinese	Artemisia apiacea
Wormwood, fringed	Artemisia frigida
Wormwood, glacier	Artemisia glacialis
Wormwood, Roman	Artemisia pontica
Wormwood, sweet	Artemisia annua
Wormwood, tree	Artemisia arborescens
Wort seed	Vaccaria
Woundwort	Stachys
Woundwort, downy	Stachys germanica
Woundwort, hedge	Stachys sylvatica
Woundwort, Mediterranean	Stachys cretica
Wrinklewort, grey	Rutidosis helichrysoides
Wu-wei-zi	Schisandra chinensis
Wullies	Salix
Wurak	Eucalyptus salmonophloia
Wyethia white	Wyethia helenioides (helianthoides)
Yabu-myoga	Polla japonica
Yam, hop	Dioscorea hastifolia
Yam, mountain	Dioscorea japonica
Yam, ornamental	Dioscorea discolor
Yam, wild	Dioscorea dregeana
Yam, wild	Dioscorea villosa
Yanchep bell	Diplolaena angustifolia
Yanchep rose	Diplolaena
Yanchep rose	Diplolaena angustifolia
Yandee	Eucalyptus loxophleba ssp loxophleba
Yandee, Mallee northern	Eucalyptus loxophleba ssp lissophloia
Yandee, Mallee southern	Eucalyptus loxophleba ssp gratiae
Yanga bush	Maireana brevifolia
Yanquapin	Nelumbo lutea

Common-Botanical Names

Common	Botanical
Yapunyah	Eucalyptus ochrophloia
Yapunyah, mountain	Eucalyptus thozettiana
Yardarlba	Eucalyptus youngiana
Yarran	Acacia aneura
Yarran	Acacia burrowii
Yarri	Eucalyptus patens
Yarrow	Achillea
Yarrow, broad-leaved	Achillea macrophylla
Yarrow, fern-leaved	Achillea filipendulina
Yarrow, florist's	Achillea ageratifolia
Yarrow, golden	Eriophyllum
Yarrow, mace	Achillea ageratum
Yarrow, woolly	Achillea tomentosa 'Aurea'
Yate	Eucalyptus cornuta
Yate, bushy	Eucalyptus conferruminata
Yate, bushy	Eucalyptus lehmannii
Yate, flat-topped	Eucalyptus occidentalis
Yate, inland Mallee	Eucalyptus occidentalis v stenantha
Yate, pretty	Eucalyptus talyuberlup
Yate, swamp	Eucalyptus occidentalis
Yate, warted	Eucalyptus megacornuta
Yautia	Zanthosma
Yeid	Eucalyptus cornuta
Yellow bells	Geleznowia verrucosa
Yellow bells	Tecoma stans
Yellow buttons	Chrysocephalum
Yellow candle	Asphodeline lutea
Yellow palm	Chrysalidocarpus
Yellow pond lily	Nuphar
Yellow root	Xanthorrhiza simplicissima
Yellow tails	Ptilotus nobilis
Yellow top	Senecio gregorii
Yellow tops	Senecio jacobaea
Yellow wood	Cladrastis lutea
Yellowjacket, inland	Eucalyptus signata
Yellowjacket, large-fruited	Eucalyptus watsoniana
Yellowroot	Xanthorhixa simplicissima
Yellowwood, Breede river	Podocarpus elongatus
Yellowwood, Henkell's	Podocarpus henkelii
Yellowwood, Outeniqua	Podocarpus falcatus
Yellowwood, true	Podocarpus latifolius
Yerba buena	Satureja douglasii
Yerba del lobo	Helenium hoopesii
Yerba mansa	Anemopsis californica
Yerba mate	Ilex paraguariensis
Yerba santa	Eriodictyon californicum
Yertchuk	Eucalyptus consideniana
Yesterday, today and tomorrow	Brunfelsia calycina v floribunda
Yew	Taxus
Yew	Taxus baccata
Yew, Californian	Taxus brevifolia
Yew, Chinese	Taxus chinensis
Yew, Japanese	Podocarpus macrophyllus
Yew, Japanese	Taxus cuspidata
Yew, Pacific	Taxus brevifolia
Yew, Prince Albert's	Celosia spicata
Yew, southern	Podocarpus macrophyllus
Yi-mu-cao	Leonurus sibiricus
Yieh-hsia-hung	Emilia coccinea
Ylang-ylang	Cananga odorata
Yorkshire fog	Holcus lanatus
Yorrell	Eucalyptus gracilis
Youth-on-age	Tolmiea
Yuca	Merremia aurea
Yucca, banana	Yucca baccata
Yucca, beaked	Yucca rostrata
Yucca, blue	Yucca rigida
Yucca, blue	Yucca rostrata
Yucca, broad-leaf	Yucca baccata
Yucca, dwarf blue	Yucca glauca
Yucca, giant	Yucca elephantipes
Yucca, hoary	Yucca schottii
Yucca, Kanab	Yucca kanabensis
Yucca, Mohave	Yucca schidigera
Yucca, mountain	Yucca schottii
Yucca, narrow-leaf	Yucca glauca v gurneyi
Yucca, plains	Yucca glauca
Yucca, soaptree	Yucca elata
Yucca, spineless	Yucca elephantipes
Yucca, Torrey	Yucca torreyi
Yucca, Trans-Pecos	Yucca thompsoniana
Yucca, twisted leaf	Yucca rupicola
Yulan	Magnolia denudata
Zabala fruit	Lardizabala biternata
Zamia	Macrozamia miquelii
Zamia palm	Cycas circinalis
Zarandaja	Lablab purpureus
Zebra grass	Miscanthus 'Zebrinus'
Zebra plant	Aphelandra squarrosa
Zebra plant	Calathea zebrina
Zebra plant	Cryptanthus zonatus
Zebrawood	Dalbergia melanoxylon
Zelkova, Japanese	Zelkova serrata
Zelkova, sawleaf	Zelkova serrata
Zephyr flower	Zephyranthes candida
Zhi zi	Gardenia augusta
Zi Su Ye	Perilla frutescens
Zig-zag vine	Melodorum leichhardtii
Zimbabwe creeper	Podranea ricasoliana
Zinnia, creeping	Sanvitalia
Zinnia, creeping	Sanvitalia procumbens
Zinnia, Mexican	Zinnia haageana
Zuta levana	Micromeria fruticosa
Zygadene	Zigadenus venosus

Family Names

Family Names

Abelia	Caprifoliaceae	Agarista	Ericaceae
Abeliophyllum	Oleaceae	Agastache	Lamiaceae
Abelmoschus	Malvaceae	Agathis	Araucariaceae
Abies	Pinaceae	Agathosma	Rutaceae
Abromeitiella	Bromeliaceae	Agave	Agavaceae
Abrotanella	Asteraceae	Ageratum	Asteraceae
Abrus	Papilionaceae	Aglaomorpha	Polypodiaceae
Abutilon	Malvaceae	Aglaonema	Araceae
Acacia	Mimosaceae	Agonis	Myrtaceae
Acaena	Rosaceae	Agrimonia	Rosaceae
Acalypha	Euphorbiaceae	Agropyron	Poaceae
Acanthocalycium	Cactaceae	Agrostemma	Caryophyllaceae
Acanthocarpus	Xanthorrhoeaceae	Agrostis	Poaceae
Acantholimon	Plumbaginaceae	Agrostocrinum	Phormiaceae
Acantholobivia	Cactaceae	Aichryson	Crassulaceae
Acanthophoenix	Arecaceae/Palmae	Ailanthus	Simaroubaceae
Acanthosicyos	Cucurbitaceae	Ainsliaea	Asteraceae
Acanthostachys	Bromeliaceae	Aiphanes	Arecaceae
Acanthus	Acanthaceae	Aira	Poaceae
Acca	Myrtaceae	Aizoon	Aizoaceae
Acer	Aceraceae	Ajania	Asteraceae
Achillea	Asteraceae	Ajuga	Lamiaceae
Achimenes	Gesneriaceae	Akebia	Lardizabalaceae
Achlys	Berberidaceae	Alangium	Alangiaceae
Acinos	Lamiaceae	Alberta	Rubiaceae
Aciphylla	Apiaceae	Albizia	Mimosaceae
Acmena	Myrtaceae	Albuca	Hyacinthaceae
Acnistus	Solanaceae	Alcea	Malvaceae
Acoelorrhaphe	Arecaceae	Alchemilla	Rosaceae
Acokanthera	Apocynaceae	Alectra	Scrophulariaceae
Aconitum	Ranunculaceae	Alectryon	Sapindaceae
Acorus	Araceae	Alepidea	Apiaceae
Acradenia	Rutaceae	Aletris	Melanthiaceae
Acridocarpus	Malpighiaceae	Aleurites	Euphorbiaceae
Acrolophia	Orchidaceae	Alisma	Alismataceae
Acrotriche	Epacridaceae	Alkanna	Boraginaceae
Actaea	Ranunculaceae	Allagoptera	Arecaceae
Actinella	Asteraceae	Allamanda	Apocynaceae
Actinidia	Actinidiaceae	Allardia	Asteraceae
Actinostrobus	Cupressaceae	Alliaria	Brassicaceae
Actinotus	Apiaceae	Allium	Alliaceae
Ada	Orchidaceae	Allocasuarina	Casuarinaceae
Adansonia	Bombacaceae	Allophyllus	Sapindaceae
Adenia	Passifloraceae	Alluaudia	Didiereaceae
Adenium	Apocynaceae	Alnus	Betulaceae
Adenocarpus	Papilionaceae	Alocasia	Araceae
Adenophora	Campanulaceae	Aloe	Aloeaceae
Adenostyles	Asteraceae	Aloinopsis	Aizoaceae
Adiantum	Adiantaceae	Alonsoa	Scrophulariaceae
Adlumia	Papaveraceae	Alopecurus	Poaceae
Adonis	Ranunculaceae	Alophia	Iridaceae
Adoxa	Adoxaceae	Aloysia	Verbenaceae
Adromischus	Crassulaceae	Alphitonia	Rhamnaceae
Aechmea	Bromeliaceae	Alpinia	Zingiberaceae
Aegle	Rutaceae	Alstroemeria	Alstroemeriaceae
Aegopodium	Apiaceae	Alternanthera	Amaranthaceae
Aeonium	Crassulaceae	Althaea	Malvaceae
Aerangis	Orchidaceae	Altingia	Hamamelidaceae
Aerides	Orchidaceae	Alyogyne	Malvaceae
Aeschynanthus	Gesneriaceae	Alysicarpus	Fabaceae
Aesculus	Hippocastanaceae	Alyssoides	Brassicaceae
Aethionema	Brassicaceae	Alyssum	Brassicaceae
Aetoxicon	Aetoxicaceae	Alyxia	Apocynaceae
Afrocarpus	Podocarpaceae	Amaranthus	Amaranthaceae
Agapanthus	Alliaceae	Amaryllis	Amaryllidaceae
Agapetes	Ericaceae	Amberboa	Asteraceae

Family Names

Genus	Family	Genus	Family
Ambrosia	Asteraceae	Anthocleista	Loganiaceae
Ambrosinia	Araceae	Antholyza	Iridaceae
Amelanchier	Rosaceae	Anthotium	Goodeniaceae
Amellus	Asteraceae	Anthoxanthum	Poaceae
Amesiella	Orchidaceae	Anthriscus	Apiaceae
Amethystea	Lamiaceae	Anthurium	Araceae
Amherstia	Caesalpiniaceae	Anthyllis	Papilionaceae
Amianthum	Melianthaceae	Antidesma	Euphorbiaceae
Amicia	Papilionaceae	Antigonon	Polygonaceae
Ammi	Apiaceae	Antimima	Aizoaceae
Ammobium	Asteraceae	Antirrhinum	Scrophulariaceae
Ammocharis	Amaryllidaceae	Aotus	Fabaceae
Ammophila	Poaceae	Apatesia *	Mesembryanthaceae
Amomum	Zingiberaceae	Aphanes	Rosaceae
Amomyrtus	Myrtaceae	Aphelandra	Acanthaceae
Amorpha	Papilionaceae	Aphyllanthes	Aphyllanthaceae
Amorphophallus	Araceae	Apios	Papilionaceae
Ampelodesmos	Poaceae	Apium	Apiaceae
Ampelopsis	Vitaceae	Apocynum	Apocynaceae
Amsonia	Apocynaceae	Apodytes	Icacinaceae
Anacampseros	Portulaceae	Aponogeton	Aponogetonaceae
Anacamptis	Orchidaceae	Aporocactus	Cactaceae
Anacardium	Anarcardiaceae	Aptenia	Aizoaceae
Anacyclus	Asteraceae	Aptosimum	Scrophulariaceae
Anagallis	Primulaceae	Aquilegia	Ranunculaceae
Ananas	Bromeliaceae	Arabis	Brassicaceae
Anapalina	Iridaceae	Arachis	Papilionaceae
Anaphalis	Asteraceae	Arachniodes	Dryopteridaceae
Anarrhinum	Scrophulariaceae	Arachnis	Orchidaceae
Anchusa	Boraginaceae	Araeococcus	Bromeliaceae
Andersonia	Epacridaceae	Araiostegia	Davalliaceae
Androcymbium	Colchicaceae	Aralia	Araliaceae
Andromeda	Ericaceae	Araucaria	Araucariaceae
Andropogon	Poaceae	Araujia	Asclepiadaceae
Androsace	Primulaceae	Arbutus	Ericaceae
Andryala	Asteraceae	Archontophoenix	Arecaceae
Anemarrhena	Asphodelaceae	Arctanthemum	Asteraceae
Anemathele	Poaceae	Arctium	Asteraceae
Anemia	Schizaeaceae	Arctopus	Apiaceae
Anemocarpa	Asteraceae	Arctostaphylos	Ericaceae
Anemone	Ranunculaceae	Arctotheca	Asteraceae
Anemonella	Ranunculaceae	Arctotis	Asteraceae
Anemonopsis	Ranunculaceae	Ardisia	Myrsinaceae
Anemopaegma	Bignoniaceae	Areca	Arecaceae
Anemopsis	Saururaceae	Arenaria	Caryophyllaceae
Anethum	Apiaceae	Arenga	Arecaceae
Angelica	Apiaceae	Arequipa	Cactaceae
Angelonia	Scrophulariaceae	Argemone	Papaveraceae
Angianthus	Asteraceae	Argylia	Bignoniaceae
Angophora	Myrtaceae	Argyranthemum	Asteraceae
Angraecum	Orchidaceae	Argyreia	Convolvulaceae
Anguloa	Orchidaceae	Argyroderma	Aizoaceae
Anigozanthus	Haemodoraceae	Ariocarpus	Cactaceae
Anisacanthus	Acanthaceae	Arisaema	Araceae
Anisodontea	Malvaceae	Arisarum	Araceae
Anisotome	Apiaceae	Aristea	Iridaceae
Annona	Annonaceae	Aristida	Poaceae
Anoda	Malvaceae	Aristolochia	Aristolochiaceae
Anomatheca	Iridaceae	Aristotelia	Elaeocarpaceae
Anopterus	Escalloniaceae	Armatocereus	Cactaceae
Anredera	Basellaceae	Armeria	Plumbaginaceae
Ansellia	Orchidaceae	Armoracia	Brassicaceae
Antennaria	Asteraceae	Arnebia	Boraginaceae
Anthemis	Asteraceae	Arnica	Asteraceae
Anthericum	Anthericaceae	Aronia	Rosaceae
Anthocercis	Solanaceae	Arrabidaea	Bignoniaceae

Family Names

Arrhenatherum	Poaceae	Azolla	Azollaceae
Arrojadoa	Cactaceae	Azorella	Apiaceae
Artemisia	Asteraceae	Azorina	Campanulaceae
Arthrocereus	Cactaceae	Aztekium	Cactaceae
Arthropodium	Anthericaceae	Azureocereus	Cactaceae
Arum	Araceae	Babiana	Iridaceae
Aruncus	Rosaceae	Baccharis	Asteraceae
Arundinaria	Poaceae-Bambusoideae	Backhousia	Myrtaceae
Arundo	Poaceae	Bactris	Arecaceae
Arytera	Sapindaceae	Baeckea	Myrtaceae
Asarina	Scrophulariaceae	Baeometra	Colchicaceae
Asarum	Aristolochiaceae	Bahia	Asteraceae
Asclepias	Asclepiadaceae	Baileya	Asteraceae
Ascocentrum	Orchidaceae	Baillonia	Verbenaceae
Asimina	Annonaceae	Balanites	Balanitaceae
Askidiosperma	Restionaceae	Balaustion	Myrtaceae
Asparagus	Asparagaceae	Balbisia	Geraniaceae
Asperula	Rubiaceae	Baldellia	Alismataceae
Asphodeline	Asphodelaceae	Ballota	Lamiaceae
Asphodelus	Asphodelaceae	Balsamorhiza	Asteraceae
Aspidistra	Convallariaceae	Bambusa	Poaceae-Bambusoiseae
Asplenium	Aspleniaceae	Banisteriopsis	Malpighiaceae
Astartea	Myrtaceae	Banksia	Proteaceae
Astelia	Asteliaceae	Baptisia	Papilionaceae
Aster	Asteraceae	Barbarea	Brassicaceae
Asteranthera	Gesneriaceae	Barkeria	Orchidaceae
Asteridea	Asteraceae	Barleria	Acanthaceae
Asteriscus	Asteraceae	Barnardiella	Iridaceae
Asteromoea	Asteraceae	Bartsia	Scrophulariaceae
Asteromyrtus	Asteraceae	Bashania	Poaceae-Bambusoideae
Astilbe	Saxifragaceae	Bassia	Chenopodiaceae
Astilboides	Saxifragaceae	Basutica	Thymelaeaceae
Astragalus	Papilionaceae	Bauera	Cunoniaceae
Astranthium	Asteraceae	Bauhinia	Papilionaceae
Astrantia	Apiaceae	Baumea	Cyperaceae
Astrebla	Poaceae	Beaucarnea	Agavaceae
Astroloma	Epacridaceae	Beaufortia	Myrtaceae
Astrophytum	Cactaceae	Beaumontia	Apocynaceae
Asyneuma	Campanulaceae	Beccariophoenix	Arecaceae
Asystasia	Acanthaceae	Becium	Lamiaceae
Atalaya	Sapindaceae	Beckmannia	Poaceae
Athamanta	Apiaceae	Bedfordia	Asteraceae
Atherosperma	Monimiaceae	Begonia	Begoniaceae
Athrotaxis	Taxodiaceae	Belamcanda	Iridaceae
Athyrium	Athyriaceae	Bellardia *	Scrophulariaceae
Atractylodes	Asteraceae	Bellevalia	Hyacinthaceae
Atraphaxis	Polygonaceae	Bellida	Asteraceae
Atriplex	Chenopodiaceae	Bellis	Asteraceae
Atropa	Solanaceae	Bellium	Asteraceae
Atropanthe	Solanaceae	Bensoniella	Saxifragaceae
Atylosia	Fabaceae	Berardia *	Asteraceae
Aubrieta	Brassicaceae	Berberidopsis	Flacourtiaceae
Aucuba	Cornaceae	Berberis	Berberidaceae
Augea	Zygophyllaceae	Berchemia	Rhamnaceae
Aulax	Protaceae	Bergenia	Saxifragaceae
Aurinia	Brassicaceae	Bergerocactus	Cactaceae
Austrocactus	Cactaceae	Berkheya	Asteraceae
Austrocedrus	Cupressaceae	Berlandiera	Asteraceae
Austrocephalocereus	Cactaceae	Bertolonia	Melastomataceae
Austrocylindropuntia	Cactaceae	Berula	Apiaceae
Austromyrtus	Myrtaceae	Berzelia	Bruniaceae
Avena	Poaceae	Beschorneria	Agavaceae
Averrhoa	Geraniaceae	Bessera	Alliaceae
Aylostera	Cactaceae	Besseya	Scrophulariaceae
Azanza	Malvaceae	Beta	Chenopodiaceae
Azara	Flacourtiaceae	Betula	Betulaceae

Family Names

Biarum	Araceae	Bridelia	Euphorbiaceae
Bidens	Asteraceae	Briggsia	Gesneriaceae
Bignonia	Bignoniaceae	Brimeura	Hyacinthaceae
Billardiera	Pittosporaceae	Briza	Poaceae
Billbergia	Bromeliaceae	Brocchonia	Bromeliaceae
Biscutella	Brassicaceae	Brodiaea	Alliaceae
Bismarckia	Arecaceae	Bromelia	Bromeliaceae
Bixa	Bixaceae	Bromus	Poaceae
Blackstonia	Gentianaceae	Broughtonia	Orchidaceae
Blaeria	Ericaceae	Broussonetia	Moraceae
Blandfordia	Blandfordiaceae	Browallia	Solanaceae
Blechnum	Blechnaceae	Brownea	Caesalpiniaceae
Bletilla	Orchidaceae	Browningia	Cactaceae
Bloomeria	Alliaceae	Bruckenthalia	Ericaceae
Blossfeldia	Cactaceae	Brugmansia	Solanaceae
Bobartia	Iridaceae	Brunfelsia	Solanaceae
Bocconia	Papaveraceae	Brunia	Bruniaceae
Boehmeria	Urticaceae	Brunnera	Boraginaceae
Boenninghausenia	Rutaceae	Brunonia	Goodeniaceae
Boisduvalia	Onagraceae	Brunsvigia	Amaryllidaceae
Bolax	Apiaceae	Bryanthus	Ericaceae
Bolbitis	Lomaripsidaceae	Bryonia	Cucurbitaceae
Bolivicereus	Cactaceae	Bryum	Sphagnaceae
Boltonia	Asteraceae	Buchanania	Anacardiaceae
Bolusanthus	Papilionaceae	Buchloe	Poaceae
Bomarea	Alstroemeriaceae	Buckinghamia	Proteaceae
Bombax	Bombaceae	Buddleja	Buddlejaceae
Bonatea	Orchidaceae	Buglossoides	Boraginaceae
Bongardia	Berberidaceae	Buiningia	Cactaceae
Boophane	Amaryllidaceae	Bulbine	Asphodelaceae
Borago	Boraginaceae	Bulbinella	Asphodelaceae
Borassus	Arecaceae	Bulbocodium	Colchicaceae
Borinda	Poaceae	Bulbophyllum	Orchidaceae
Bornmuellera	Brassicaceae	Bunium	Apiaceae
Boronia	Rutaceae	Buphthalmum	Asteraceae
Boscia	Capparaceae	Bupleurum	Apiaceae
Bossiaea	Papilionaceae	Burchardia	Colchicaceae
Bothriochloa	Poaceae	Burchellia	Rubiaceae
Bougainvillea	Nyctaginaceae	Bursaria	Pittosporaceae
Boussingaultia	Basellaceae	Bursera	Pittosporaceae
Bouteloua	Poaceae	Butea	Papilionaceae
Bouvardia	Rubiaceae	Butia	Arecaceae
Bowenia	Boweniaceae	Butomus	Butomaceae
Bowiea	Hyacinthaceae	Buttonia	Scrophulariaceae
Bowkeria	Scrophulariaceae	Buxus	Buxaceae
Boykinia	Saxifragaceae	Cabomba	Cabombaceae
Brabejum	Proteaceae	Cacalia	Asteraceae
Brachiaria	Poaceae	Caesalpinia	Caesalpiniaceae
Brachycalycium	Cactaceae	Caiophora	Loasaceae
Brachychiton	Sterculiaceae	Caladenia	Orchidaceae
Brachyglottis	Asteraceae	Caladium	Araceae
Brachylaena	Asteraceae	Calamagrostis	Poaceae
Brachypodium	Asteraceae	Calamintha	Lamiaceae
Brachyscome	Asteraceae	Calamovilea	Poaceae
Brachysema	Papilionaceae	Calamus	Arecaceae
Brachystachyum	Poaceae-Bambusoideae	Calandrinia	Portulacaceae
Brachystelma	Asclepiadaceae	Calanthe	Orchidaceae
Bracteantha	Asteraceae	Calathea	Marantaceae
Brahea	Arecaceae	Calceolaria	Scrophulariaceae
Brassavola	Orchidaceae	Caldcluvia	Cunoniaceae
Brassia	Orchidaceae	Calendula	Asteraceae
Brassica	Brassicaceae	Calibanus	Agavaceae
Brassiophoenix	Arecaceae	Calla	Araceae
Bravoa	Agavaceae	Calliandra	Mimosaceae
Braya	Brassicaceae	Callianthemum	Ranunculaceae
Breynia	Euphorbiaceae	Callicarpa	Verbenaceae

Family Names

Callicoma	Cunoniaceae
Calliergon	Sphagnaceae
Callirhoe	Malvaceae
Callisia	Commelinaceae
Callistemon	Myrtaceae
Callistephus	Asteraceae
Callitriche	Callitrichaceae
Callitris	Cupressaceae
Calluna	Ericaceae
Calocedrus	Cupressaceae
Calocephalus	Asteraceae
Calochone	Rubiaceae
Calochortus	Liliaceae
Calodendrum	Rutaceae
Calomeria	Asteraceae
Calophaca	Papilionaceae
Calophyllum*	Clusiaceae
Calopogon	Orchidaceae
Calopsis	Restionaceae
Caloptris	Asclepiadaceae
Caloscordum	Alliaceae
Calothamnus	Myrtaceae
Calotis	Asteraceae
Calpurnia	Papilionaceae
Caltha	Ranunculaceae
Calycanthus	Calycanthaceae
Calydorea	Iridaceae
Calymmanthium	Cactaceae
Calypso	Orchidaceae
Calyptridium	Portulacaceae
Calystegia	Convolvulaceae
Calytrix	Myrtaceae
Camassia	Hyacinthaceae
Camellia	Theaceae
Campanula	Campanulaceae
Campanula xSymphyandra	Campanulaceae
Camphorosma	Chenopodiaceae
Campsis	Bignoniaceae
Camptotheca	Nyssaceae
Campylotropis	Papilionaceae
Cananga	Annonaceae
Canarina	Campanulaceae
Canistrum	Bromeliaceae
Canna	Cannaceae
Cannomois	Restionaceae
Canthium	Rubiaceae
Cantua	Polemoniaceae
Capparis	Capparaceae
Capsicum	Solanaceae
Caragana	Papilionaceae
Caralluma	Asclepiadaceae
Cardamine	Brassicaceae
Cardiandra	Hydrangeaceae
Cardiocrinum	Liliaceae
Cardiospermum	Sapindaceae
Carduncellus	Asteraceae
Carduus	Asteraceae
Carex	Cyperaceae
Carica	Caricaceae
Carissa	Apocynaceae
Carlina	Asteraceae
Carludovica	Cyclanthaceae
Carmichaelia	Papilionaceae
Carnegiea	Cactaceae
Carpanthea	Aizoaceae
Carpentaria	Arecaceae

Carpenteria	Hydrangeaceae
Carpinus	Corylaceae
Carpobrotus	Aizoaceae
Carpodetus	Escalloniaceae
Carruanthus	Aizoaceae
Carthamus	Asteraceae
Carum	Apiaceae
Carya	Juglandaceae
Caryopteris	Verbenaceae
Caryota	Arecaceae
Cassia	Caesalpiniaceae
Cassine	Celastraceae
Cassinia	Asteraceae
Cassinia x Helichrysum	Asteraceae
Cassiope	Ericaceae
Cassytha	Lauraceae
Castalis	Asteraceae
Castanea	Fagaceae
Castanopsis	Fagaceae
Castanospermum	Papilionaceae
Castellanosia	Cactaceae
Castilleja *	Scrophulariaceae
Casuarina	Casuarinaceae
Catalpa	Bignoniaceae
Catananche	Asteraceae
Catapodium	Poaceae
Catasetum	Orchidaceae
Catha	Celastraceae
Catharanthus	Apocynaceae
Catophractes	Bignoniaceae
Catopsis	Bromeliaceae
Cattleya	Orchidaceae
Caulophyllum	Berberidaceae
Cautleya	Zingiberaceae
Cavendishia	Ericaceae
Cayratia	Vitaceae
Ceanothus	Rhamnaceae
Cedrela	Meliaceae
Cedronella	Lamiaceae
Cedrus	Pinaceae
Ceiba	Bombaceae
Celastrus	Celastraceae
Celmisia	Asteraceae
Celosia	Amaranthaceae
Celtis	Ulmaceae
Cenia	Asteraceae
Cenolophium	Apiaceae
Centaurea	Asteraceae
Centaurium	Gentianaceae
Centella	Apiaceae
Centradenia	Melastomataceae
Centranthus	Valerianaceae
Cephalanthera	Orchidaceae
Cephalanthus	Rubiaceae
Cephalaria	Dipsacaceae
Cephalipterum	Asteraceae
Cephalocereus	Cactaceae
Cephalocleistocactus	Cactaceae
Cephalophyllum	Aizoaceae
Cephalotaxus	Cephalotaxaceae
Cephalotus	Cephalotaceae
Ceraria	Portulaceae
Cerastium	Caryophyllaceae
Ceratonia	Caesalpiniaceae
Ceratopetalum	Cunoniaceae
Ceratophyllum	Ceratophyllaceae

Family Names

Ceratostigma	Plumbaginaceae
Ceratotheca	Pedaliaceae
Ceratozamia	Zamiaceae
Cercidiphyllum	Cercidiphyllaceae
Cercis	Caesalpiniaceae
Cercocarpus	Rosaceae
Cereus	Cactaceae
Cerinthe	Boraginaceae
Ceropegia	Asclepiadaceae
Ceroxylon	Arecaceae
Cestrum	Solanaceae
Chaenactis	Asteraceae
Chaenomeles	Rosaceae
Chaenorhinum	Scrophulariaceae
Chaerophyllum	Apiaceae
Chaetacanthus	Acanthaceae
Chamaebatiaria	Rosaceae
Chamaecrista	Caesalpiniaceae
Chamaecyparis	Cupressaceae
Chamaecytisus	Papilionaceae
Chamaedaphne	Ericaceae
Chamaedorea	Arecaceae
Chamaelirium	Melanthiaceae
Chamaemelum	Asteraceae
Chamaerops	Arecaceae
Chamaescilla	Anthericaceae
Chambeyronia	Arecaceae
Chamelaucium	Myrtaceae
Chasmanthe	Iridaceae
Chasmanthium	Poaceae
Cheilanthes	Adiantaceae
Cheiranthera	Pittosporaceae
Cheiridopsis	Aizoaceae
Chelidonium	Papaveraceae
Chelone	Scrophulariaceae
Chelonopsis	Lamiaceae
Chenopodium	Chenopodiaceae
Chenorhinum	Scrophulariaceae
Chevreulia	Asteraceae
Chiastophyllum	Crassulaceae
Chiliotrichum	Asteraceae
Chilopsis	Bignoniaceae
Chimaphila	Pyrolaceae
Chimonanthus	Calycanthaceae
Chimonobambusa	Poaceae-Bambusoideae
Chionanthus	Oleaceae
Chionochloa	Poaceae
Chionodoxa	Hyacinthaceae
Chionographis	Liliaceae
Chionohebe	Scrophulariaceae
Chirita	Gesneriaceae
Chironia	Gentianaceae
Chlidanthus	Amaryllidaceae
Chloranthus	Chloranthaceae
Chlorophytum	Anthericaceae
Choisya	Rutaceae
Chondropetalum	Restionaceae
Chondrosum	Poaceae
Chordospartium	Papilionaceae
Chorilaena	Rutacaceae
Chorisia	Bombacaceae
Chorizandra*	Cyperaceae
Chorizema	Papilionaceae
Chrysalidocarpus	Arecaceae
Chrysanthemoides	Asteraceae
Chrysanthemum	Asteraceae

Chrysocephalum	Asteraceae
Chrysocoma	Asteraceae
Chrysogonum	Asteraceae
Chrysolepis	Fagaceae
Chrysopogon	Poaceae
Chrysopsis	Asteraceae
Chrysosplenium	Saxifragaceae
Chrysothamnus	Asteraceae
Chrysothemis	Gesneriaceae
Chuniophoenix	Arecaceae
Chuquiraga	Asteraceae
Chusquea	Poaceae
Cibotium	Dicksoniaceae
Cicerbita	Asteraceae
Cichorium	Asteraceae
Cicuta	Apiacaeae
Cimicifuga	Ranunculaceae
Cineraria	Asteraceae
Cinnamomum	Lauraceae
Cionura	Asclepiadaceae
Cipocereus	Cactaceae
Circaea	Onagraceae
Cirsium	Asteraceae
Cissus	Vitaceae
Cistus	Cistaceae
Citharexylum	Verbenaceae
Citronella	Icacinaceae
Citrullus	Cucurbitaceae
Citrus	Rutaceae
Cladanthus	Asteraceae
Cladium	Cyperaceae
Cladothamnus	Ericaceae
Cladrastis	Papilionaceae
Clarkia	Onagraceae
Clausena	Rutaceae
Clavinodum	Poaceae-Bambusoideae
Claytonia	Portulacaceae
Cleistocactus	Cactaceae
Clematis	Ranunculaceae
Clematopsis	Ranunculaceae
Cleome	Capparaceae
Cleretum	Aizoaceae
Clerodendrum	Verbenaceae
Clethra	Clethraceae
Cleyera	Theaceae
Clianthus	Papilionaceae
Cliffortia	Rosaceae
Clinopodium	Lamiaceae
Clintonia	Convallariaceae
Clitoria	Papilionaceae
Clivia	Amaryllidaceae
Clusia	Clusiaceae
Clytostoma	Bignoniaceae
Cneorum	Cneoraceae
Cnicus	Asteraceae
Cobaea	Cobaeaceae
Coccinea	Cucurbitaceae
Coccoloba	Polygonaceae
Coccothrinax	Arecaceae
Cocculus	Menispermaceae
Cochlearia	Brassicaceae
Cochlioda	Orchidaceae
Cochlospermum	Bixaceae
Cocos	Arecaceae
Coddia	Rubiaceae
Codiaeum	Euphorbiaceae

Family Names

Codonanthe	Gesneriaceae
Codonocarpus *	Phytolaccaceae
Codonopsis	Campanulaceae
Coelia	Orchidaceae
Coelogyne	Orchidaceae
Coffea	Rubiaceae
Coix	Poaceae
Colchicum	Colchicaceae
Coleonema	Rutaceae
Colletia	Rhamnaceae
Collinsia	Scrophulariaceae
Collinsonia	Lamiaceae
Collomia	Polemoniaceae
Collospermum	Asteliaceae
Colobanthus	Caryophyllaceae
Colocasia	Araceae
Colpias	Scrophulariaceae
Colpoon	Santalaceae
Colquhounia	Lamiaceae
Columnea	Gesneriaceae
Colutea	Papilionaceae
Coluteocarpus	Brassicaceae
Colvillea	Caesalpiniaceae
Combretum	Combretaceae
Comesperma*	Polygalaceae
Commelina	Commelinaceae
Commiphora	Burseraceae
Comptonia	Myricaceae
Conandron	Gesneriaceae
Conanthera	Tecophilaeaceae
Congea	Verbenaceae
Conicosia	Aizoaceae
Coniogramme	Adiantaceae
Conioselinum	Apiaceae
Conium	Apiaceae
Conocephalum	Conocephalaceae
Conophytum	Aizoaceae
Conopodium	Apiaceae
Conospermum	Proteaceae
Conostomium	Rubiaceae
Conostylis	Haemodoraceae
Conothamnus	Myrtaceae
Conradina	Lamiaceae
Consolida	Ranunculaceae
Convallaria	Convallariaceae
Convolvulus	Convolvulaceae
Coopernookia	Goodeniaceae
Copernicia	Arecaceae
Copiapoa	Cactaceae
Coprosma	Rubiaceae
Coptis	Ranunculaceae
Corallocarpus	Cucurbitaceae
Corallospartium	Papilionaceae
Corchorus*	Tiliaceae
Cordia	Boraginaceae
Cordyline	Agavaceae
Coreopsis	Asteraceae
Corethrogyne	Asteraceae
Coriandrum	Apiaceae
Coriaria	Coriariaceae
Coris	Primulaceae
Cornus	Cornaceae
Corokia	Escalloniaceae
Coronilla	Papilionaceae
Correa	Rutaceae
Corryocactus	Cactaceae
Cortaderia	Poaceae
Cortusa	Primulaceae
Corybas	Orchidaceae
Corydalis	Papaveraceae
Corylopsis	Hamamelidaceae
Corylus	Corylaceae
Corymbium	Asteraceae
Corynanthera	Myrtaceae
Corynephorus	Poaceae
Corynocarpus	Corynocarpaceae
Corypha	Arecaceae
Coryphantha	Cactaceae
Cosmos	Asteraceae
Costus	Zingiberaceae
Cotinus	Anacardiaceae
Cotoneaster	Rosaceae
Cotula	Asteraceae
Cotyledon	Crassulaceae
Cowania	Rosaceae
Craibodendron	Ericaceae
Crambe	Brassicaceae
Craspedia	Asteraceae
Crassula	Crassulaceae
+ Crataegomespilus	Rosaceae
Crataegus	Rosaceae
Craterostigma	Scrophulariaceae
Crawfurdia	Gentianaceae
Cremanthodium	Asteraceae
Crepis	Asteraceae
Crinodendron	Elaeocarpaceae
Crinum	Amaryllidaceae
Crithmum	Apiaceae
Crocosmia	Iridaceae
Crocus	Iridaceae
Crossandra	Acanthaceae
Crotalaria	Papilionaceae
Crowea	Rutaceae
Crucianella	Rubiaceae
Cruciata	Rubiaceae
Cryptandra	Rhamnaceae
Cryptantha	Boraginaceae
Cryptanthus	Bromeliaceae
Cryptocarya	Lauraceae
Cryptocoryne	Araceae
Cryptogramma	Cryptogrammaceae
Cryptomeria	Taxodiaceae
Cryptostegia	Asclepiadaceae
Cryptotaenia	Apiaceae
Ctenanthe	Marantaceae
Ctenium	Poaceae
Cucubalus	Caryophyllaceae
Cucumis	Cucurbitaceae
Cucurbita	Cucurbitaceae
Cudrania	Moraceae
Cuminum	Apiaceae
Cunila	Lamiaceae
Cunninghamia	Taxodiaceae
Cunonia	Cunoniaceae
Cupaniopsis	Sapindaceae
Cuphea	Lythraceae
Cupressus	Cupressaceae
Curcuma	Zingiberaceae
Curtisia	Cornaceae
Cussonia	Araliaceae
Cyananthus	Campanulaceae
Cyanella	Tecophilaeaceae

Family Names

Genus	Family	Genus	Family
Cyanostegia*	Chloanthaceae	Davallia	Davalliaceae
Cyanotis	Commelinaceae	Davidia	Davidiaceae
Cyathea	Cyatheaceae	Daviesia	Papilionaceae
Cyathochaeta*	Cyperaceae	Debregeasia	Urticaceae
Cyathodes	Epacridaceae	Decaisnea	Lardizabalaceae
Cybestetes	Amaryllidaceae	Decarya	Didiereaceae
Cybistax	Bignoniaceae	Decodonn	Lythraceae
Cycas	Cycadaceae	Decumaria	Saxifragaceae
Cyclamen	Primulaceae	Degenia	Brassicaceae
Cyclanthera	Cucurbitaceae	Deinanthe	Hydrangeaceae
Cyclosorus	Thelypteridaceae	Delairea	Asteraceae
Cycnoches	Orchidaceae	Delonix	Caesalpiniaceae
Cydista	Bignoniaceae	Delosperma	Aizoaceae
Cydonia	Rosaceae	Delphinium	Ranunculaceae
Cylindrophyllum	Aizoaceae	Dendranthema	Asteraceae
Cymbalaria	Scrophulariaceae	Dendrobium	Orchidaceae
Cymbidium	Orchidaceae	Dendrocalamus	Poaceae
Cymbopogon	Poaceae	Dendrochilum	Orchidaceae
Cymophyllus	Cyperaceae	Dendromecon	Papaveraceae
Cymopterus	Apiaceae	Dendroseris	Asteraceae
Cynanchum	Asclepiadaceae	Denmoza	Cactaceae
Cynara	Asteraceae	Dennstaedtia	Dennstaedtiaceae
Cynoglossum	Boraginaceae	Dentaria	Brassicaceae
Cynosurus	Poaceae	Dermatobotrys	Scrophulariaceae
Cypella	Iridaceae	Derris	Papilionaceae
Cyperus	Cyperaceae	Deschampsia	Poaceae
Cyphanthera	Solanaceae	Desfontainia	Loganiaceae
Cyphia	Lobeliaceae	Desmanthus	Mimosaceae
Cyphomandra	Solanaceae	Desmazeria	Poaceae
Cyphostemma	Vitaceae	Desmodium	Papilionaceae
Cypripedium	Orchidaceae	Desmoschoenus	Cyperaceae
Cyrilla	Cyrillaceae	Deutzia	Hydrangeaceae
Cyrtanthus	Amaryllidaceae	Dianella	Phormiaceae
Cyrtomium	Aspidiaceae	Dianthus	Caryophyllaceae
Cyrtosperma	Araceae	Diapensia	Diapensiaceae
Cyrtostachys	Arecaceae	Diarrhena	Poaceae
Cyrtostylis	Orchidaceae	Diascia	Scrophulariaceae
Cysticapnos *	Fumariaceae	Dicentra	Papaveraceae
Cystopteris	Athyriaceae	Dicerocaryum	Pedaliaceae
Cytisus	Papilionaceae	Dichanthium	Poaceae
Daboecia	Ericaceae	Dichelostemma	Alliaceae
Dacrycarpus	Podocarpaceae	Dichopogon	Anthericaceae
Dacrydium	Podocarpaceae	Dichorisandra	Commelinaceae
Dactylis	Poaceae	Dichotomanthes	Rosaceae
Dactyloctenium	Poaceae	Dichroa	Hydrangeaceae
Dactylopsis	Aizoaceae	Dichromena	Cyperaceae
Dactylorhiza	Orchidaceae	Dichrostachys	Mimosaceae
Dahlia	Asteraceae	Dicksonia	Dicksoniaceae
Dais	Thymelaeaceae	Dicliptera	Acanthaceae
Dalea	Papilionaceae	Dicoma	Asteraceae
Damasonium	Alismataceae	Dicranostigma	Papaveraceae
Dampiera	Goodeniaceae	Dicrastylis*	Chloanthaceae
Danae	Ruscaceae	Dictamnus	Rutaceae
Daphne	Thymelaeaceae	Dictymochlaena	Aspidiaceae
Daphniphyllum	Daphniphyllaceae	Dictyolimon	Plumbaginaceae
Darlingtonia	Sarraceniaceae	Dictyosperma	Arecaceae
Darmera	Saxifragaceae	Didelta	Asteraceae
Darwinia	Myrtaceae	Didymaotus	Aizoaceae
Dasispermum	Apiaceae	Didymochlaena	Dryopteridaceae
Dasylirion	Dracaenaceae	Didymosperma	Arecaceae
Dasyphyllum	Asteraceae	Dieffenbachia	Araceae
Dasypogon	Dasypogonaceae	Dierama	Iridaceae
Dasypyrum	Poaceae	Diervilla	Caprifoliaceae
Datisca	Datiscaceae	Dietes	Iridaceae
Datura	Solanaceae	Digitalis	Scrophulariaceae
Daucus	Apiaceae	Dilatris	Haemodoraceae

Family Names

Dillenia	Dilleniaceae	Drimys	Winteraceae
Dillwynia	Papilionaceae	Drosanthemum	Aizoaceae
Dimorphotheca	Asteraceae	Drosera	Droseraceae
Dinteranthus	Aizoaceae	Dryandra	Proteaceae
Dionaea	Droseraceae	Dryas	Rosaceae
Dionysia	Primulaceae	Drynaria	Polypodiaceae
Dioon	Zamiaceae	Dryopteris	Aspidiaceae
Dioscorea	Dioscoreaceae	Drypis	Caryophyllaceae
Diosma	Rutaceae	Duchesnea	Rosaceae
Diosphaera	Campanulaceae	Dudleya	Crassulaceae
Diospyros	Ebenaceae	Dumortiera	Weisnerellaceae
Dipcadi	Hyacinthaceae	Dunalia	Solanaceae
Dipelta	Caprifoliaceae	Duranta	Verbenaceae
Diphylleia	Berberidaceae	Duvalia	Asclepiadaceae
Diplarrhena	Iridaceae	Duvernoia	Acanthaceae
Diplazium	Athyriaceae	Dyckia	Bromeliaceae
Diplolaena	Rutaceae	Dyerophytum	Plumbaginaceae
Diplopeltis	Sapindaceae	Dymondia	Asteraceae
Diplotaxis	Brassicaceae	Dypsis	Arecaceae
Dipogon	Papilionaceae	Dyschoriste	Acanthaceae
Dipsacus	Dipsacaceae	Dysphania	Chenopodiaceae
Dipteronia	Aceraceae	Ebenus	Papilionaceae
Dirca	Thymeleaceae	Ebracteola	Aizoaceae
Disa	Orchidaceae	Ecballium	Cucurbitaceae
Disanthus	Hamamelidaceae	Eccremocarpus	Bignoniaceae
Discaria	Rhamnaceae	Ecdeiocolea*	Restionaceae
Dischisma	Selaginaceae	Echeveria	Crassulaceae
Discocactus	Cactaceae	Echidnopsis	Asclepiadaceae
Diselma	Cupressaceae	Echinacea	Asteraceae
Disocactus	Cactaceae	Echinacea	Asteraceae
Disphyma	Aizoaceae	Echinocactus	Cactaceae
Disporopsis	Convallariaceae	Echinocereus	Cactaceae
Disporum	Convallariaceae	Echinops	Asteraceae
Dissotis	Melastomataceae	Echinopsis	Cactaceae
Distictis	Bignoniaceae	Echium	Boraginaceae
Distylium	Hamamelidaceae	Edgeworthia	Thymelaeaceae
Diuris	Orchidaceae	Edithcolea	Asclepiadaceae
Dobinea	Podoaceae	Edmondia	Asteraceae
Docynia	Rosaceae	Edraianthus	Campanulaceae
Dodecadenia	Lauraceae	Egeria	Hydrocharitaceae
Dodecatheon	Primulaceae	Ehretia	Boraginaceae
Dodonaea	Sapindaceae	Ehrharta	Poaceae
Dolichos	Papilionaceae	Eichhornia	Pontederiaceae
Dolichothrix	Asteraceae	Ekebergia	Meliaceae
Dombeya	Sterculiaceae	Elaeagnus	Elaeagnaceae
Doodia	Blechnaceae	Elaeis	Arecaceae
Doronicum	Asteraceae	Elaeocarpus	Elaeocarpaceae
Dorotheanthus	Aizoaceae	Elatostema	Urticaceae
Dorstenia	Moraceae	Elegia	Restionaceae
Doryanthes	Doryanthaceae	Eleocharis	Cyperaceae
Doryopteris	Sinopteridaceae	Elephantopus	Asteraceae
Douglasia	Primulaceae	Elettaria	Zingiberaceae
Dovea	Restionaceae	Eleusine	Poaceae
Dovyalis	Flacourtiaceae	Eleutherococcus	Araliaceae
Draba	Brassicaceae	Elingamita	Myrsinaceae
Dracaena	Dracaenaceae	Elisena	Amaryllidaceae
Dracocephalum	Lamiaceae	Elliottia	Ericaceae
Dracophilus	Aizoaceae	Ellisiophyllum	Scrophulariaceae
Dracophyllum	Epacridaceae	Elmera	Saxifragaceae
Dracula	Orchidaceae	Elodea	Hydrocharitaceae
Dracunculus	Araceae	Elsholtzia	Lamiaceae
Drapetes	Thymelaeaceae	Elymus	Poaceae
Dregea	Asclepiadaceae	Elytropus	Apocynaceae
Drepanostachyum	Poaceae-Bambusoideae	Embothrium	Proteaceae
Drimia	Hyacinthaceae	Emilia	Asteraceae
Drimiopsis	Hyacinthaceae	Eminium	Araceae

Family Names

Genus	Family	Genus	Family
Emmenopterys	Rubiaceae	Eucharidium *	Onagraceae
Empetrum	Empetraceae	Eucharis	Amaryllidaceae
Empleurum	Rutaceae	Euclea	Ebenaceae
Enceliopsis	Asteraceae	Eucodonia	Gesneriaceae
Encephalartos	Zamiaceae	Eucomis	Hyacinthaceae
Enchylaena	Chenopodiaceae	Eucommia	Eucommiaceae
Encyclia	Orchidaceae	Eucrosia	Amaryllidaceae
Engelmannia	Asteraceae	Eucryphia	Eucryphiaceae
Enkianthus	Ericaceae	Eugenia	Myrtaceae
Enneapogon	Poaceae	Eulophia	Orchidaceae
Ensete	Musaceae	Eulychnia	Cactaceae
Entandrophragma	Meliaceae	Eumorphia	Asteraceae
Entelea	Tiliaceae	Euodia	Rutaceae
Eomatucana	Cactaceae	Euonymus	Celastraceae
Eomecon	Papaveraceae	Eupatorium	Asteraceae
Epacris	Epacridaceae	Euphorbia	Euphorbiaceae
Ephedra	Ephedraceae	Euptelea	Eupteleaceae
Epidendrum	Orchidaceae	Eurya	Theaceae
Epigaea	Ericaceae	Euryale	Nymphaeaceae
Epilobium	Onagraceae	Euryops	Asteraceae
Epimedium	Berberidaceae	Euscaphis *	Staphyleaceae
Epipactis	Orchidaceae	Eustepha	Amaryllidaceae
Epiphyllum	Cactaceae	Eustoma	Gentianaceae
Epipremnum	Araceae	Eustrephus	Philesiaceae
Episcia	Gesneriaceae	Euterpe	Arecaceae
Epithelantha	Cactaceae	Evandra	Cyperaceae
Equisetum	Equisetaceae	Evodia *	Rutaceae
Eragrostis	Poaceae	Evolvulus	Convolvulaceae
Eranthemum	Acanthaceae	Ewartia	Asteraceae
Eranthis	Ranunculaceae	Exacum	Gentianaceae
Ercilla	Phytolaccaceae	Exocarpos*	Santalaceae
Eremaea	Myrtaceae	Exochorda	Rosaceae
Eremophila	Myoporaceae	Fabiana	Solanaceae
Eremurus	Asphodelaceae	Fagopyrum	Polygonaceae
Eria	Orchidaceae	Fagus	Fagaceae
Eriachne	Poaceae	Fallopia	Polygonaceae
Erica	Ericaceae	Fallugia	Rosaceae
Erigeron	Asteraceae	Farfugium	Asteraceae
Erinacea	Papilionaceae	Fargesia	Poaceae
Erinus	Scrophulariaceae	Farsetia	Commeliaceae
Eriobotrya	Rosaceae	Fascicularia	Bromeliaceae
Eriocephalus	Asteraceae	Fatsia	Araliaceae
Eriogonum	Polygonaceae	Faucaria	Aizoaceae
Eriophorum	Cyperaceae	Faurea	Proteaceae
Eriophyllum	Asteraceae	Fedia	Valerianaceae
Eriosermum	Eriospermaceae	Felicia	Asteraceae
Eriostemon	Rutaceae	Fendlera	Hydrangeaceae
Eriosyce	Cactaceae	Fenestraria	Aizoaceae
Eritrichium	Boraginaceae	Feretia	Rubiaceae
Erodium	Geraniaceae	Ferocactus	Cactaceae
Eruca	Brassicaceae	Ferraria	Iridaceae
Erymophyllum	Asteraceae	Ferreyranthus	Asteraceae
Eryngium	Apiaceae	Ferula	Apiaceae
Erysimum	Brassicaceae	Festuca	Poaceae
Erythea	Arecaceae	Fibigia	Brassicaceae
Erythrina	Papilionaceae	Ficus	Moraceae
Erythronium	Liliaceae	Filipendula	Rosaceae
Erythrophleum	Caesalpiniaceae	Fingerhuthia	Poaceae
Erythrophysa	Sapindaceae	Firmiana	Sterculiaceae
Escallonia	Escalloniaceae	Fittonia	Acanthaceae
Eschscholzia	Papaveraceae	Fitzroya	Cupressaceae
Escobaria	Cactaceae	Flaveria	Asteraceae
Espostoa	Cactaceae	Flindersia	Rutaceae
Etlingera	Zingiberaceae	Fockea	Asclepiadaceae
Euanthe	Orchidaceae	Foeniculum	Apiaceae
Eucalyptus	Myrtaceae	Fokienia	Cupressaceae

Family Names

Fontanesia	Oleaceae	Gilia	Polemoniaceae
Fontinalis	Sphagnaceae	Gillenia	Rosaceae
Forestiera	Oleaceae	Ginkgo	Ginkgoaceae
Forsythia	Oleaceae	Gladiolus	Iridaceae
Fortunearia	Hamamelidaceae	Glandularia	Verbenaceae
Fortunella	Rutaceae	Glaucidium	Glaucidiaceae
Fothergilla	Hamamelidaceae	Glaucium	Papaveraceae
Fouquieria	Fouquieriaceae	Glaux	Primulaceae
Fragaria	Rosaceae	Glechoma	Lamiaceae
Frailea	Cactaceae	Gleditsia	Caesalpiniaceae
Francoa	Saxifragaceae	Glischrocaryon	Haloragaceae
Frankenia	Frankeniaceae	Globba	Zingiberaceae
Franklinia	Theaceae	Globularia	Globulariaceae
Frasera	Gentianaceae	Gloriosa	Colchicaceae
Fraxinus	Oleaceae	Glottiphyllum	Aizoaceae
Freesia	Iridaceae	Gloxinia	Gesneriaceae
Fremontodendron	Sterculiaceae	Glumicalyx	Scrophulariaceae
Freylinia	Scrophulariaceae	Glyceria	Poaceae
Fritillaria	Liliaceae	Glycyrrhiza	Papilionaceae
Fuchsia	Onagraceae	Glyptostrobus	Taxodiaceae
Fumana	Cistaceae	Gmelina	Verbenaceae
Fumaria	Papaveraceae	Gnaphalium	Asteraceae
Furcraea	Agavaceae	Gomphocarpus	Asclepiadaceae
Gagea	Liliaceae	Gompholobium	Papilionaceae
Gahnia	Cyperaceae	Gomphostigma	Buddlejaceae
Gaillardia	Asteraceae	Gomphrena	Amaranthaceae
Galactites	Asteraceae	Goniolimon	Plumbaginaceae
Galanthus	Amaryllidaceae	Goodenia	Goodeniaceae
Galax	Diapensiaceae	Goodia	Papilionaceae
Galaxia	Iridaceae	Goodyera	Orchidaceae
Galega	Papilionaceae	Gordonia	Theaceae
Galeopsis	Lamiaceae	Gorteria	Asteraceae
Galium	Rubiaceae	Gossypium	Malvaceae
Galpinia	Malpighiaceae	Graptopetalum	Crassulaceae
Galtonia	Hyacinthaceae	Graptophyllum	Acanthaceae
Gamochaeta	Asteraceae	Gratiola	Scrophulariaceae
Garcinia	Clusiaceae	Greenovia	Crassulaceae
Gardenia	Rubiaceae	Grevillea	Proteaceae
Garrya	Garryaceae	Grewia	Tiliaceae
Gasteria	Aloeaceae	Greyia	Greyiaceae
Gastrolobium	Papilionaceae	Grielium	Rosaceae
Gaultheria	Ericaceae	Grindelia	Asteraceae
Gaura	Onagraceae	Griselinia	Cornaceae
Gaussia	Arecaceae	Gueldenstaedtia	Papilionaceae
Gaylussacia	Ericaceae	Guichenotia	Sterculiaceae
Gazania	Asteraceae	Gundelia	Asteraceae
Geijera	Rutaceae	Gunnera	Gunneraceae
Geissorhiza	Iridaceae	Gunniopsis	Aizoaceae
Gelasine	Iridaceae	Gutierrezia	Asteraceae
Geleznowia	Rutaceae	Guzmania	Bromeliaceae
Gelidocalamus	Poaceae-Bambusoideae	Gymnadenia	Orchidaceae
Gelsemium	Loganiaceae	Gymnocalycium	Cactaceae
Genista	Papilionaceae	Gymnocarpium	Thelypteridaceae
Gennaria	Orchidaceae	Gymnocladus	Caesalpiniaceae
Gentiana	Gentianaceae	Gymnopteris	Adiantaceae
Gentianella	Gentianaceae	Gymnospermum	Berberidaceae
Gentianopsis	Gentianaceae	Gynandriris	Iridaceae
Geogenanthus	Commelinaceae	Gynerium	Poaceae
Geranium	Geraniaceae	Gynura	Asteraceae
Gerbera	Asteraceae	Gypsophila	Caryophyllaceae
Gesneria	Gesneriaceae	Gyrocarpus*	Gyrocarpaceae
Geum	Rosaceae	Gyrostemon*	Gyrostemonaceae
Gevuina	Proteaceae	Haageocereus	Cactaceae
Gibasis	Commelinaceae	Haastia	Asteraceae
Gibbaeum	Aizoaceae	Habenaria	Orchidaceae
Gigaspermum	Gigaspermaceae	Haberlea	Gesneriaceae

Family Names

Hablitzia	Chenopodiaceae
Habranthus	Amaryllidaceae
Hacquetia	Apiaceae
Haemadorum*	Haemadoraceae
Haemanthus	Amaryllidaceae
Hakea	Proteaceae
Hakonechloa	Poaceae
Halenia	Gentianaceae
Halesia	Styracaceae
Halgania	Boraginaceae
Halimione	Chenopodiaceae
Halimium	Cistaceae
Halimodendron	Papilionaceae
Halleria	Scrophulariaceae
Halocarpus	Podocapaceae
Haloragis	Haloragaceae
Haloragodendron	Haloragaceae
Halosarcia	Chenopodiaceae
Hamamelis	Hamamelidaceae
Hanabusaya	Campanulaceae
Hannonia	Amaryllidaceae
Haplocarpha	Asteraceae
Haplopappus	Asteraceae
Hardenbergia	Papilionaceae
Harpagophytum	Pedalliaceae
Harpephyllum	Anarcardiaceae
Harrisia	Cactaceae
Hatiora	Cactaceae
Haworthia	Aloeaceae
Hebe	Scrophulariaceae
Hebenstreitia	Scrophulariaceae
Hechtia	Bromeliaceae
Hectorella	Hectorellaceae
Hedeoma	Lamiaceae
Hedera	Araliaceae
Hedychium	Zingiberaceae
Hedyotis	Rubiaceae
Hedysarum	Papilionaceae
Hedyscepe	Arecaceae
Heimia	Lythraceae
Helenium	Asteraceae
Heliamphora	Sarraceniaceae
Helianthella	Asteraceae
Helianthemum	Cistaceae
Helianthus	Asteraceae
Helichrysum	Asteraceae
Helicodiceros	Araceae
Heliconia	Musaceae
Helictotrichon	Poaceae
Helinus	Rhamnaceae
Heliocereus	Cactaceae
Heliophila	Brassicaceae
Heliopsis	Asteraceae
Heliotropium	Boraginaceae
Helipterum	Asteraceae
Helleborus	Ranunculaceae
Helonias	Melanthiaceae
Heloniopsis	Melanthiaceae
Helwingia	Helwingiaceae
Hemerocallis	Hemerocallidaceae
Hemiandra	Lamiaceae
Hemigenia	Lamiaceae
Hemigraphis	Acanthaceae
Hemimeris	Scrophulariaceae
Hemionitis	Adiantaceae
Hemiphragma	Scrophulariaceae

Hemitelia *	Cyathaceae
Hemizygia	Lamiaceae
Hepatica	Ranunculaceae
Heptacodium	Caprifoliaceae
Heracleum	Apiaceae
Herbertia	Iridaceae
Hereroa	Aizoaceae
Hermannia	Sterculiaceae
Hermas	Apiaceae
Hermodactylus	Iridaceae
Herniaria	Caryophyllaceae
Herpolirion	Anthericaceae
Hesperaloe	Agavaceae
Hesperantha	Iridaceae
Hesperis	Brassicaceae
Hesperochiron	Hydrophyllaceae
Heterocentron	Melastomataceae
Heterodendron*	Sapindaceae
Heterolepis	Asteraceae
Heteromorpha	Apiaceae
Heteropapppus	Asteraceae
Heteropyxis	Myrtaceae
Heterotheca	Asteraceae
Heuchera	Saxifragaceae
Hexaglottis	Iridaceae
Hibbertia	Dilleniaceae
Hibiscus	Malvaceae
Hieracium	Asteraceae
Hierochloe	Poaceae
Himalayacalamus	Poaceae
Hippeastrum	Amaryllidaceae
Hippia	Asteraceae
Hippocratea	Celastraceae
Hippocrepis	Papilionaceae
Hippolytia	Asteraceae
Hippophae	Elaeagnaceae
Hippuris	Hippuridaceae
Hirpicium	Asteraceae
Histiopteris	Dennstaedtiaceae
Hohenbergia	Bromeliaceae
Hohenbergiopsis	Bromeliaceae
Hoheria	Malvaceae
Holboellia	Lardizabalaceae
Holcus	Poaceae
Holmskioldia	Verbenaceae
Holodiscus	Rosaceae
Holothrix	Orchidaceae
Homalocephala	Cactaceae
Homalocladium	Polygonaceae
Homalotheca	Asteraceae
Homeria	Iridaceae
Homogyne	Asteraceae
Hoodia	Asclepiadaceae
Hookeria	Hookeriaceae
Hordeum	Poaceae
Horkelia	Rosaceae
Horminum	Lamiaceae
Hosta	Hostaceae
Hottonia	Primulaceae
Houstonia	Rubiaceae
Houttuynia	Saururaceae
Hovea	Papilionaceae
Hovenia	Rhamnaceae
Howea	Arecaceae
Hoya	Asclepiadaceae
Huernia	Asclepiadaceae

Family Names

Hugueninia	Brassicaceae	Isolepis	Cyperaceae
Humata	Davalliaceae	Isoplexis	Scrophulariaceae
Humulus	Cannabaceae	Isopogon	Proteaceae
Hunnemannia	Papaveraceae	Isopyrum	Ranunculaceae
Huntleya	Orchidaceae	Isotoma	Campanulaceae
Hyacinthella	Hyacinthaceae	Isotropis*	Papilionaceae
Hyacinthoides	Hyacinthaceae	Itea	Escalloniaceae
Hyacinthus	Hyacinthaceae	Itoa	Flacourtiaceae
Hyalosperma	Asteraceae	Ivesia	Rosaceae
Hybanthus	Violaceae	Ixia	Iridaceae
Hydrangea	Hydrangeaceae	Ixiochlamys	Asteraceae
Hydrastis	Ranunculaceae	Ixiolirion	Amaryllidaceae
Hydrocharis	Hydrocharitaceae	Ixora	Rubiaceae
Hydrocleys	Limnocharitaceae	Jaborosa	Solanaceae
Hydrocotyle	Apiaceae	Jacaranda	Bignoniaceae
Hydrophyllum	Hydrophyllaceae	Jacksonia*	Papilionaceae
Hygrophila	Acanthaceae	Jacobinia	Acanthaceae
Hylocereus	Cactaceae	Jacquemontia	Convolvulaceae
Hylomecon	Papaveraceae	Jamesbrittenia	Scrophulariaceae
Hymenanthera	Violaceae	Jamesia	Hydrangeaceae
Hymenocallis	Amaryllidaceae	Jancaea	Gesneriaceae
Hymenocardia	Euphorbiaceae	Jasione	Campanulaceae
Hymenodictyon	Rubiaceae	Jasminum	Oleaceae
Hymenogyne	Aizoaceae	Jatropha	Euphorbiaceae
Hymenolepis	Asteraceae	Jeffersonia	Berberidaceae
Hymenosporum	Pittosporaceae	Johannesteijsmannia	Arecaceae
Hymenoxys	Asteraceae	Johnsonia	Anthericaceae
Hyophorbe	Arecaceae	Jovellana	Scrophulariaceae
Hyoscyamus	Solanaceae	Jovibarba	Crassulaceae
Hypericum	Clusiaceae	Juania	Arecaceae
Hypertelis	Aizoaceae	Juanulloa	Solanaceae
Hyphaene	Arecaceae	Jubaea	Arecaceae
Hypocalymma	Myrtaceae	Juglans	Juglandaceae
Hypochaeris	Asteraceae	Juncus	Juncaceae
Hypoestes	Acanthaceae	Junellia	Verbenaceae
Hypolepis	Hypolepidaceae	Juniperus	Cupressaceae
Hypoxis	Hypoxidaceae	Jurinea	Asteraceae
Hypoxis x Rhodohypoxis	Hypoxidaceae	Justicia	Acanthaceae
Hypsela	Campanulaceae	Juttadinteria	Aizoaceae
Hypseocharis	Oxalidaceae	Kadsura	Schisandraceae
Hyssopus	Lamiaceae	Kaempferia	Zingiberaceae
Hystrix	Poaceae	Kalanchoe	Crassulaceae
Iberis	Brassicaceae	Kalimeris	Asteraceae
Ibervillea	Cucurbitaceae	Kallstroemia	Zygophyllaceae
Idesia	Flacourtiaceae	Kalmia	Ericaceae
Ilex	Aquifoliaceae	Kalmiopsis	Ericaceae
Illicium	Illiciaceae	Kalopanax	Araliaceae
Ilysanthes	Scrophulariaceae	Karomia	Verbenaceae
Impatiens	Balsaminaceae	Keckiella	Scrophulariaceae
Imperata	Poaceae	Kelseya	Rosaceae
Incarvillea	Bignoniaceae	Kennedia	Papilionaceae
Indigofera	Papilionaceae	Kentia	Arecaceae
Indocalamus	Poaceae	Keraudrenia	Sterculiaceae
Inula	Asteraceae	Kernera	Brassicaceae
Inulanthera	Asteraceae	Kerria	Rosaceae
Iochroma	Solanaceae	Khadia	Aizoaceae
Ionopsidium	Brassicaceae	Khaya	Meliaceae
Ipheion	Alliaceae	Kickxia	Scrophulariaceae
Ipomoea	Convolvulaceae	Kigelia	Bignoniaceae
Ipomopsis	Polemoniaceae	Kiggelaria	Flacourtiaceae
Iresine	Amaranthaceae	Kirengeshoma	Hydrangeaceae
Iris	Iridaceae	Kirkia	Simaroubaceae
Isatis	Brassicaceae	Kissenia	Loasaceae
Ischyrolepis	Restionaceae	Kitaibela	Malvaceae
Iseilema	Poaceae	Kleinia	Asteraceae
Islaya	Cactaceae	Knautia	Dipsacaceae

Family Names

Knightia	Proteaceae
Kniphofia	Asphodelaceae
Knowltonia	Ranunculaceae
Kobresia	Cyperaceae
Koeleria	Poaceae
Koellikeria	Gesneriaceae
Koelreuteria	Sapindaceae
Kohleria	Gesneriaceae
Kolkwitzia	Caprifoliaceae
Kosteletzkya	Malvaceae
Kummerowia	Papilionaceae
Kunzea	Myrtaceae
Labichea	Caesalpiniaceae
Lablab	Caesalpiniaceae
+ Laburnocytisus	Papilionaceae
Laburnum	Papilionaceae
Laccospadix	Arecaceae
Lachenalia	Hyacinthaceae
Lachnanthes	Haemodoraceae
Lachnospermum	Asteraceae
Lachnostachys*	Chloanthaceae
Lachnostilyis	Euphorbiaceae
Lactuca	Asteraceae
Laelia	Orchiadaceae
Lagarosiphon	Hydrocharitaceae
Lagarostrobos	Podocarpaceae
Lagenophora	Asteraceae
Lagerstroemia	Lythraceae
Lagunaria	Malvaceae
Lagurus	Poaceae
Lallemantia	Lamiaceae
Lamarchea	Myrtaceae
Lamarckia	Poaceae
Lambertia	Proteaceae
Lamium	Lamiaceae
Lampranthus	Aizoaceae
Lanaria	Haemodoraceae
Lantana	Verbenaceae
Lapageria	Philesiaceae
Lapeirousia	Iridaceae
Lapidarea	Aizoaceae
Lapiedra	Amaryllidaceae
Lapsana	Asteraceae
Lardizabala	Lardizabalaceae
Larix	Pinaceae
Larrea	Zygophyllaceae
Laser	Apiaceae
Laserpitium	Apiaceae
Lasiopetalum	Sterculiaceae
Lasiospermum	Asteraceae
Lasthenia *	Asteraceae
Latania	Arecaceae
Lathraea	Scrophulariaceae
Lathyrus	Papilionaceae
Laurelia	Monimiaceae
Laurentia	Campanulaceae
Laurophyllus	Anacardiaceae
Laurus	Lauraceae
Lavandula	Lamiaceae
Lavatera	Malvaceae
Lawrencella	Asteraceae
Lawrencia	Malvaceae
Lawsonia	Lythraceae
Laxmannia*	Anthericaceae
Layia	Asteraceae
Ledebouria	Hyacinthaceae

Ledum	Ericaceae
Leea	Leeaceae
Legousia	Campanulaceae
Leibnitzia	Asteraceae
Leiophyllum	Ericaceae
Leipoldtia	Aizoaceae
Lemboglossum	Orchidaceae
Lemna	Lemnaceae
Lenophyllum	Crassulaceae
Lens	Papilionaceae
Leonotis	Lamiaceae
Leontice	Berberidaceae
Leontodon	Asteraceae
Leontopodium	Asteraceae
Leonurus	Lamiaceae
Leopoldia	Hyacinthaceae
Lepechinia	Lamiaceae
Lepidium	Brassicaceae
Lepidosperma	Cyperaceae
Lepidothamnus	Podocarpaceae
Lepidozamia	Zamiaceae
Leptarrhena	Saxifragaceae
Leptinella	Asteraceae
Leptodactyon	Polemoniaceae
Leptomeria*	Santalaceae
Leptopteris	Osmundaceae
Leptosema	Papilionaceae
Leptosiphon *	Polemoniaceae
Leptospermum	Myrtaceae
Leschenaultia	Goodeniaceae
Lespedeza	Papilionaceae
Lesquerella	Brassicaceae
Leucadendron	Proteaceae
Leucaena	Mimosaceae
Leucanthemella	Asteraceae
Leucanthemopsis	Asteraceae
Leucanthemum	Asteraceae
Leucas *	Lamiaceae
Leuchtenbergia	Cactaceae
Leucochrysum	Asteraceae
Leucocoryne	Alliaceae
Leucogenes	Asteraceae
Leucojum	Amaryllidaceae
Leucophyta	Asteraceae
Leucopogon	Epacridaceae
Leucosceptrum	Lamiaceae
Leucosidea	Rosaceae
Leucospermum	Proteaceae
Leucothoe	Ericaceae
Leuzea	Asteraceae
Levenhookia	Stylidaceae
Levisticum	Apiaceae
Lewisia	Portulacaceae
Leycesteria	Caprifoliaceae
Leymus	Poaceae
Leyssera	Asteraceae
Lhotskya	Myrtaceae
Liatris	Asteraceae
Libertia	Iridaceae
Libocedrus	Cupressaceae
Licuala	Arecaceae
Ligularia	Asteraceae
Ligusticum	Apiaceae
Ligustrum	Oleaceae
Lilaeopsis	Apiaceae
Lilium	Liliaceae

Family Names

Limnanthes	Limnanthaceae	Lycianthes	Solanaceae
Limnocharis	Limnocharitaceae	Lycium	Solanaceae
Limnophila	Scrophulariaceae	Lycopersicon	Solanaceae
Limonium	Plumbaginaceae	Lycopodium	Lycopodiaceae
Linanthus	Polemoniaceae	Lycopus	Lamiaceae
Linaria	Scrophulariaceae	Lycoris	Amaryllidaceae
Lindelofia	Boraginaceae	Lygeum	Poaceae
Lindera	Lauraceae	Lygodium	Schizaeaceae
Lindheimera	Asteraceae	Lyonia	Ericaceae
Linnaea	Caprifoliaceae	Lyonothamnus	Rosaceae
Linospadix	Arecaceae	Lyperanthus	Orchidaceae
Linum	Linaceae	Lyperia	Scrophulariaceae
Liparis	Orchidaceae	Lysichiton	Araceae
Lippia	Verbenaceae	Lysimachia	Primulaceae
Liquidambar	Hamamelidaceae	Lysinema	Epacridaceae
Liriodendron	Magnoliaceae	Lysionotus	Gesneriaceae
Liriope	Convallariaceae	Lysiphyllum	Caesalpiniaceae
Listera	Orchidaceae	Lythrum	Lythraceae
Lithocarpus	Fagaceae	Lytocaryum	Arecaceae
Lithodora	Boraginaceae	Maackia	Papilionaceae
Lithophragma	Saxifragaceae	Macaranga	Euphorbiaceae
Lithops	Aizoaceae	Macfadyena	Bignoniaceae
Lithospermum	Boraginaceae	Machaeranthera	Asteraceae
Litsea	Lauraceae	Mackaya	Acanthaceae
Littonia	Colchicaceae	Macleania	Ericaceae
Littorella	Plantaginaceae	Macleaya	Papaveraceae
Livistona	Arecaceae	Maclura	Moraceae
Lloydia	Liliaceae	Macropidia	Haemodoraceae
Loasa	Loasaceae	Macropiper	Piperaceae
Lobelia	Campanulaceae	Macrozamia	Zamiaceae
Lobelia x Pratia	Campanulaceae	Madia	Asteraceae
Lobivia	Cactaceae	Maerua	Capparaceae
Lobostemon	Boraginaceae	Maesa	Myrsinaceae
Lobularia	Brassicaceae	Magnolia	Magnoliaceae
Lodoicea	Arecaceae	Mahonia	Berberidaceae
Loeselia	Polemoniaceae	Maianthemum	Convallariaceae
Logania	Loganiaceae	Maihuenia	Cactaceae
Loiseleuria	Ericaceae	Maireana	Chenopodiaceae
Lomandra	Xanthorrhoeaceae	Malcomia	Brassicaceae
Lomatia	Proteaceae	Malephora	Aizoaceae
Lomatium	Apiaceae	Malleostemon	Myrtaceae
Lomatogonium	Gentianaceae	Mallotus	Euphorbiaceae
Lomatophyllum	Aloeaceae	Malope	Malvaceae
Lonas	Asteraceae	Malpighia	Malpighiaceae
Lonicera	Caprifoliaceae	Malus	Rosaceae
Lopezia	Onagraceae	Malva	Malvaceae
Lopholaena	Asteraceae	Malvastrum	Malvaceae
Lophomyrtus	Myrtaceae	Malvaviscus	Malvaceae
Lophophora	Cactaceae	Mammillaria	Cactaceae
Lophosoria	Lophosoriaceae	Mandevilla	Apocynaceae
Lophospermum	Scrophulariaceae	Mandragora	Solanaceae
Lophostemon	Myrtaceae	Manettia	Ribiaceae
Loropetalum	Hamamelidaceae	Mangifera	Anacardiaceae
Lotus	Papilionaceae	Manglietia	Magnoliaceae
Loxostylis	Anacardiaceae	Manihot	Euphorbiaceae
Luculia	Rubiaceae	Manochlamys	Chenopodiaceae
Ludwigia	Onagraceae	Mansoa	Bignoniaceae
Luetkea	Rosaceae	Manulea	Scrophulariaceae
Luffa	Cucurbitaceae	Maranta	Marantaceae
Luma	Myrtaceae	Marchantia	Marchantiaceae
Lunaria	Brassicaceae	Margyricarpus	Rosaceae
Lupinus	Papilionaceae	Markhamia	Bignoniaceae
Luzula	Juncaceae	Marlothistella	Aizoaceae
Luzuriaga	Philesiaceae	Marrubium	Lamiaceae
Lycaste	Orchidaceae	Marsdenia	Asclepiadaceae
Lychnis	Caryophyllaceae	Marshallia	Asteraceae

Family Names

Marsilea	Marsileaceae
Mascagnia	Malpighiaceae
Masdevallia	Orchidaceae
Massonia	Hyacinthaceae
Matelea	Asclepiadaceae
Matricaria	Asteraceae
Matteuccia	Aspidiaceae
Matthiola	Brassicaceae
Maughaniella	Aizoaceae
Maurandella	Scrophulariaceae
Maurandya	Scrophulariaceae
Maxillaria	Orchidaceae
Maytenus	Celastraceae
Mazus	Scrophulariaceae
Meconopsis	Papaveraceae
Medemia	Arecaceae
Medeola	Convallariaceae
Medicago	Papilionaceae
Medinilla	Melastomataceae
Meehania	Lamiaceae
Megacarpaea	Brassicaceae
Megacodon	Gentianaceae
Megaskepasma	Acanthaceae
Melaleuca	Myrtaceae
Melampodium	Asteraceae
Melanoselinum	Apiaceae
Melanthium	Melanthiaceae
Melasphaerula	Iridaceae
Melastoma	Melastomataceae
Melhania	Sterculiaceae
Melia	Meliaceae
Melianthus	Melianthaceae
Melica	Poaceae
Melicope	Rutaceae
Melicytus	Violaceae
Melilotus	Papilionaceae
Melinis	Poaceae
Meliosma	Meliosmaceae
Melissa	Lamiaceae
Melittis	Lamiaceae
Melocactus	Cactaceae
Menispermum	Menispermaceae
Menodora	Oleaceae
Mentha	Lamiaceae
Mentzelia	Loasaceae
Menyanthes	Menyanthaceae
Menziesia	Ericaceae
Mercurialis	Euphorbiaceae
Merendera	Colchicaceae
Merremia	Convolvulaceae
Mertensia	Boraginaceae
Merxmuellera	Poaceae
Meryta	Araliaceae
Mesembryanthemum	Aizoaceae
Mesomelaena	Cyperaceae
Mespilus	Rosaceae
Metalasia	Asteraceae
Metarungia	Acanthaceae
Metasequoia	Taxodiaceae
Metrodiseros	Myrtaceae
Meum	Apiaceae
Mibora	Poaceae
Michauxia	Campanulaceae
Michelia	Magnoliaceae
Micranthus	Iridaceae
Microbiota	Cupressaceae

Microcachrys	Podocarpaceae
Microglossa	Asteraceae
Microlepia	Dennstaedtiaceae
Microloma	Asclepiadacee
Micromeria	Lamiaceae
Microseris	Asteraceae
Microsorum	Polypodiaceae
Microstrobos	Podocarpaceae
Mikania	Asteraceae
Milium	Poaceae
Milla	Alliaceae
Millettia	Papilionaceae
Milligania	Asteliaceae
Miltonia	Orchidaceae
Miltoniopsis	Orchidaceae
Mimetes	Proteaceae
Mimosa	Mimosaceae
Mimulus	Scrophulariaceae
Minuartia	Caryophyllaceae
Minuria	Asteraceae
Mirabilis	Nyctaginaceae
Mirbelia	Papilionaceae
Miscanthus	Poaceae
Misopates	Scrophulariaceae
Mitchella	Rubiaceae
Mitella	Saxifragaceae
Mitraria	Gesneriaceae
Mitrasacme	Loganiaceae
Mitriostigma	Rubiaceae
Modiolastrum	Malvaceae
Moekringia	Caryophyllaceae
Molinia	Poaceae
Molopospermum	Apiaceae
Moltkia	Boraginaceae
Moluccella	Lamiaceae
Momordica	Cucurbitaceae
Monachather	Poaceae
Monadenia	Orchidaceae
Monadenium	Euphorbiaceae
Monanthes	Crassulaceae
Monarda	Lamiaceae
Monardella	Lamiaceae
Monilaria	Aizoaceae
Monopsis	Campanulaceae
Monotoca	Epacridaceae
Monsonia	Gerianaceae
Monstera	Araceae
Montia	Portulacaceae
Montinia	Montiniaceae
Moraea	Iridaceae
Morgania	Scrophulariaceae
Moricandia	Brassicaceae
Morina	Morinaceae
Morinda	Rubiaceae
Moringa	Moringaceae
Morisia	Brassicaceae
Morus	Moraceae
Mucuna	Papilionaceae
Muehlenbeckia	Polygonaceae
Muhlenbergia	Poaceae
Mukdenia	Saxifragaceae
Mukia	Cucurbitaceae
Mundulea	Papilionaceae
Murbeckiella	Brassicaceae
Murdannia	Commelinaceae
Murraya	Rutaceae

Family Names

Musa	Musaceae	Neurachne	Poaceae
Muscari	Hyacinthaceae	Neviusia	Rosaceae
Muscarimia	Hyacinthaceae	Newcastelia *	Chloanthaceae
Mussaenda	Rubiaceae	Nicandra	Solanaceae
Musschia	Campanulaceae	Nicotiana	Solanaceae
Mutisia	Asteraceae	Nidorella	Asteraceae
Myoporum	Myoporaceae	Nidularium	Bromeliaceae
Myosotidium	Boraginaceae	Nierembergia	Solanaceae
Myosotis	Boraginaceae	Nigella	Ranunculaceae
Myosurus	Ranunculaceae	Niphaea	Gesneriaceae
Myrceugenia	Myrtaceae	Nipponanthemum	Asteraceae
Myrianthus	Moraceae	Nitraria *	Zygophyllaceae
Myrica	Myricaceae	Nivenia	Iridaceae
Myricaria	Tamaricaceae	Nolana	Nolanaceae
Myriocephalus	Asteraceae	Nolina	Dracaenaceae
Myriophyllum	Haloragaceae	Nomocharis	Liliaceae
Myrothamnus	Myrothamnaceae	Nonea	Boraginaceae
Myrrhis	Apiaceae	Nopalxochia	Cactaceae
Myrsine	Myrsinaceae	Notelaea	Oleaceae
Myrsiphyllum	Asparagaceae	Nothofagus	Fagaceae
Myrteola	Myrtaceae	Notholirion	Liliaceae
Myrtillocactus	Cactaceae	Nothoscordum	Alliaceae
Myrtus	Myrtaceae	Notobuxus	Buxaceae
Mystropetalon	Balanophoraceae	Notospartium	Papilionaceae
Naiocrene	Portulacaceae	Nototriche	Malvaceae
Namaquanthus	Aizoaceae	Nuphar	Nymphaeaceae
Nandina	Berberidaceae	Nuxia	Buddlejaceae
Nannorrhops	Arecaceae	Nuytsia *	Loranthaceae
Narcissus	Amaryllidaceae	Nylandtia	Polygalaceae
Nardophyllum	Asteraceae	Nymania	Meliaceae
Nardostachys	Valerianaceae	Nymphaea	Nymphaeaceae
Narthecium	Melanthiaceae	Nymphoides	Menyanthaceae
Nassauvia	Asteraceae	Nyssa	Nyssaceae
Nassella	Poaceae	Obregonia	Cactaceae
Nasturtium	Brassicaceae	Ochagavia	Bromeliaceae
Nauclea	Rubiaceae	Ochna	Ochnaceae
Nautilocalyx	Gesneriaceae	Ocimum	Lamiaceae
Nebelia	Bruniaceae	Odontoglossum	Orchidaceae
Nectaroscordum	Alliaceae	Odontonema	Acanthaceae
Neillia	Rosaceae	Odontophorus	Aizoaceae
Nelumbo	Nymphaeaceae	Oemleria	Rosaceae
Nemastylis	Iridaceae	Oenanthe	Apiaceae
Nematanthus	Gesneriaceae	Oenothera	Onagraceae
Nemcia *	Papilionaceae	Olax *	Olacaceae
Nemesia	Scrophulariaceae	Olea	Oleaceae
Nemopanthus	Aquifoliaceae	Olearia	Asteraceae
Nemophila	Hydrophyllaceae	Oligostachyum	Poaceae
Neobakeria	Hyacinthaceae	Olsynium	Iridaceae
Neobuxbaumia	Cactaceae	Omphalodes	Boraginaceae
Neochilenia	Cactaceae	Omphalogramma	Primulaceae
Neodypsis	Arecaceae	Oncidium	Orchidaceae
Neolitsea	Lauraceae	Oncoba	Flacourtiaceae
Neolloydia	Cactaceae	Oncosiphon	Asteraceae
Neomarica	Iridaceae	Onixotis	Colchicaceae
Neopaxia	Portulacaceae	Onobrychis	Papilionaceae
Neoporteria	Cactaceae	Onoclea	Aspidiaceae
Neoregelia	Bromeliaceae	Ononis	Papilionaceae
Neottianthe	Orchidaceae	Onopordum	Asteraceae
Nepenthes	Nepenthaceae	Onoseris	Asteraceae
Nepeta	Lamiaceae	Onosma	Boraginaceae
Nephrolepis	Oleandraceae	Onychium	Adiantaceae
Nephrophyllidium	Menyanthaceae	Oophytum	Aizoaceae
Neptunia *	Papilionaceae	Opercularia	Rubiaceae
Nerine	Amaryllidaceae	Operculina	Convolvulaceae
Nerium	Apocynaceae	Ophiopogon	Convallariaceae
Nertera	Rubiaceae	Ophrys	Orchidaceae

Family Names

Ophthalmophyllum	Aizoaceae	Paesia	Hypolepidaceae
Opithandra	Gesneriaceae	Palisota	Commelinaceae
Oplismenus	Poaceae	Paliurus	Rhamnaceae
Opuntia	Cactaceae	Pallenis	Asteraceae
Orbea	Asclepiadaceae	Pamianthe	Amaryllidaceae
Orbeopsis	Asclepiadaceae	Panax	Araliaceae
Orchis	Orchidaceae	Pancratium	Amaryllidaceae
Oreobolus	Cyperaceae	Pandanus	Pandanaceae
Oreocereus	Cactaceae	Pandorea	Bignoniaceae
Oreopanax	Araliaceae	Panicum	Poaceae
Oreopteris	Thelypteridaceae	Papaver	Papaveraceae
Origanum	Lamiaceae	Paphiopedilum	Orchidaceae
Orixa	Rutaceae	Pappea	Sapindaceae
Orlaya	Apiaceae	Paradisea	Asphodelaceae
Ornithogalum	Hyacinthaceae	Parahebe	Scrophulariaceae
Ornithoglossum	Colchicaceae	Parajubaea	Arecaceae
Ornithophora	Orchidaceae	Paranomus	Proteaceae
Orontium	Araceae	Paraquilegia	Ranunculaceae
Orostachys	Crassulaceae	Paraserianthes	Mimosaceae
Oroya	Cactaceae	Pardanthopsis	Iridaceae
Orphium	Gentianaceae	Pardoglossum	Boraginaceae
Ortegocactus	Cactaceae	Parietaria	Urticaceae
Orthophytum	Bromeliaceae	Parinari	Chrysobalanaceae
Orthosiphon	Lamiaceae	Paris	Trilliaceae
Orthrosanthus	Iridaceae	Parkinsonia	Caesalpiniaceae
Orychophragmus	Brassicaceae	Parnassia	Parnassiaceae
Oryza	Poaceae	Parochetus	Papilionaceae
Oryzopsis	Poaceae	Parodia	Cactaceae
Osbeckia	Melastomataceae	Paronychia	Illecebraceae
Oscularia	Aizoaceae	Parrotia	Hamamelidaceae
Osmanthus	Oleaceae	Parrotiopsis	Hamamelidaceae
Osmitopsis	Asteraceae	Parrya	Brassicaceae
Osmunda	Osmundaceae	Parsonsia	Apocynaceae
Ostecarpum	Chenopodiaceae	Parthenium	Asteraceae
Osteomeles	Rosaceae	Parthenocissus	Vitaceae
Osteospermum	Asteraceae	Pasithea	Asphodelaceae
Ostrowskia	Campanulaceae	Paspalum	Poaceae
Ostrya	Corylaceae	Passerina	Thymelaceae
Otacanthus	Scrophulariaceae	Passiflora	Passifloraceae
Otanthus	Asteraceae	Pastinaca	Apiaceae
Othonna	Asteraceae	Patersonia	Iridaceae
Ourisia	Scrophulariaceae	Patrinia	Valerianaceae
Owenia	Meliaceae	Paulownia	Scrophulariaceae
Oxalis	Oxalidaceae	Pavetta	Rubiaceae
Oxera	Verbenaceae	Pavonia	Malvaceae
Oxydendrum	Ericaceae	Paxistima	Celastraceae
Oxylobium	Papilionaceae	Pecteilis	Orchidaceae
Oxypetalum	Asclepiadaceae	Pedicularis	Scrophulariaceae
Oxyria	Polygonaceae	Pedilanthus	Euphorbiaceae
Oxytropis	Papilionaceae	Pediocactus	Cactaceae
Ozoroa	Anacardiaceae	Peganum	Zygophyllaceae
Ozothamnus	Asteraceae	Pelargonium	Geraniaceae
Pachycarpus	Asclepediaceae	Pellaea	Sinopteridaceae
Pachycereus	Cactaceae	Peltandra	Araceae
Pachycormus	Anacardiaceae	Peltaria	Brassicaceae
Pachycymbium	Asclepiadaceae	Peltoboykinia	Saxifragaceae
Pachylaena	Asteraceae	Peltophorum	Caesalpiniaceae
Pachyphragma	Brassicaceae	Penaea	Penaeaceae
Pachyphytum	Crassulaceae	Peniocereus	Cactaceae
Pachypodium	Apocynaceae	Pennantia	Icacinaceae
Pachysandra	Buxaceae	Pennisetum	Poaceae
Pachystachys	Acanthaceae	Penstemon	Scrophulariaceae
Packera	Asteraceae	Pentachondra	Epacridaceae
Paederia	Rubiaceae	Pentaglottis	Boraginaceae
Paederota	Scrophulariaceae	Pentalinon	Apocynaceae
Paeonia	Paeoniaceae	Pentapeltis	Apiaceae

Family Names

Pentarrhinum	Asclepiadaceae	Phygelius	Scrophulariaceae
Pentas	Rubiaceae	Phyla	Verbenaceae
Pentaschistis	Poaceae	Phylica	Rhamnaceae
Peperomia	Piperaceae	Phyllanthus	Euphorbiaceae
Pereskia	Cactaceae	Phyllocladus	Phyllocladaceae
Pereskiopsis	Cactaceae	Phyllodoce	Ericaceae
Perezia	Asteraceae	Phyllostachys	Poaceae
Pergularia	Asclepiadaceae	Phyllota *	Papilionaceae
Pericallis	Asteraceae	Phymatocarpus	Myrtaceae
Pericalymma	Myrtaceae	Phymosia	Malvaceae
Perilla	Lamiaceae	Physalis	Solanaceae
Periploca	Asclepiadaceae	Physaria	Brassicaceae
Peristrophe	Acanthaceae	Physocarpus	Rosaceae
Perovskia	Lamiaceae	Physochlaina	Solanaceae
Perrottetia	Celastraceae	Physoplexis	Campanulaceae
Persea	Lauraceae	Physopsis	Chloanthaceae
Persicaria	Polygonaceae	Physostegia	Lamiaceae
Persoonia	Proteaceae	Phyteuma	Campanulaceae
Petalostigma	Euphorbiaceae	Phytolacca	Phytolaccaceae
Petalostylis *	Papilionaceae	Piaranthus *	Asclepiadaceae
Petasites	Asteraceae	Picairnia	Bromeliaceae
Petrea	Verbenaceae	Picea	Pinaceae
Petrocallis	Brassicaceae	Picrasma	Simaroubaceae
Petrocoptis	Caryophyllaceae	Picris	Asteraceae
Petrocosmea	Gesneriaceae	Picrorhiza	Scrophulariaceae
Petromarula	Campanulaceae	Pieris	Ericaceae
Petrophile	Proteaceae	Pilea	Urticaceae
Petrophytum	Rosaceae	Pileostegia	Hydrangeaceae
Petrorhagia	Caryophyllaceae	Pilocereus	Cactaceae
Petroselinum	Apiaceae	Pilosella	Asteraceae
Petteriia	Papilionaceae	Pilularia	Marsileaceae
Petunia	Solanaceae	Pimelea	Thymelaeaceae
Peucedanum	Apiaceae	Pimenta	Myrtaceae
Peumus	Monimiaceae	Pimpinella	Apiaceae
Phacelia	Hydrophyllaceae	Pinanga	Arecaceae
Phaedranassa	Amaryllidaceae	Pinellia	Araceae
Phaenocoma	Asteraceae	Pinguicula	Lentibulariaceae
Phaenosperma	Poaceae	Pinus	Pinaceae
Phagnalon	Asteraceae	Piper	Piperaceae
Phaiophleps	Iridaceae	Piptanthus	Papilionaceae
Phaius	Orchidaceae	Pisonia	Nyctaginaceae
Phalaenopsis	Orchidaceae	Pistacia	Anacardiaceae
Phalaris	Poaceae	Pistia	Araceae
Phalocallis	Iridaceae	Pisum	Papilionaceae
Phanerophlebia	Dryopteridaceae	Pittosporum	Pittosporaceae
Pharnaceum	Aizoaceae	Pityrodia	Chloanthaceae
Phaseolus	Papilionaceae	Pityrogramma	Hemionitidaceae
Phebalium	Rutaceae	Plagianthus	Malvaceae
Phegopteris	Thelypteridaceae	Plagiomnium	Sphagnaceae
Phellocalyx	Rubiaceae	Planera	Ulmaceae
Phellodendron	Rutaceae	Plantago	Plantaginaceae
Philadelphus	Hydrangeaceae	Platanthera	Orchidaceae
Philesia	Philesiaceae	Platanus	Platanaceae
Phillyrea	Oleaceae	Platycarya	Juglandaceae
Philodendron	Araceae	Platycerium	Polypodiaceae
Phleum	Poaceae	Platycladus	Cupressaceae
Phlomis	Lamiaceae	Platycodon	Campanulaceae
Phlox	Polemoniaceae	Platysace	Apiaceae
Phoebe	Lauraceae	Platystemon	Papaveraceae
Phoenicaulis	Brassicaceae	Plecostachys	Asteraceae
Phoenix	Arecaceae	Plectocolea	Jungermanniaceae
Phormium	Phormiaceae	Plectrachne	Poaceae
Photinia	Rosaceae	Plectranthus	Lamiaceae
Phragmipedium	Orchidaceae	Pleioblastus	Poaceae
Phragmites	Poaceae	Pleiogynium	Anacardiaceae
Phuopsis	Rubiaceae	Pleione	Orchidaceae

Family Names

Pleiospilos	Aizoaceae	Prunella	Lamiaceae
Pleurochaete	Sphagnaceae	Prunus	Rosaceae
Pleurospermum	Apiaceae	Pseuderanthemum	Acanthaceae
Pleurothallis	Orchidaceae	Pseudocydonia	Rosaceae
Plexipus	Verbenaceae	Pseudofumaria	Papaveraceae
Plumbago	Plumbaginaceae	Pseudolachnostylis	Euphorbiaceae
Plumeria	Apocynaceae	Pseudolarix	Pinaceae
Plygala	Polygalaceae	Pseudomertensia	Boraginaceae
Poa	Poaceae	Pseudopanax	Araliaceae
Podalyria	Papilionaceae	Pseudophegopteris	Thelypteridaceae
Podanthus	Asteraceae	Pseudophoenix	Arecaceae
Podocarpus	Podocarpaceae	Pseudosasa	Poaceae-Bambusoideae
Podolepis	Asteraceae	Pseudosbeckia	Melastomataceae
Podophyllum	Berberidaceae	Pseudotsuga	Pinaceae
Podranea	Bignoniaceae	Pseudowintera	Winteraceae
Pogonatherum	Poaceae	Psidium	Myrtaceae
Pogonia	Orchidaceae	Psilostrophe	Asteraceae
Pogostemon	Lamiaceae	Psilotum	Psilotaceae
Polemonium	Polemoniaceae	Psoralea	Papilionaceae
Polianthes	Agavaceae	Psychopsis	Orchidaceae
Poliomintha	Lamiaceae	Psychotria	Rubiaceae
Poliothyrsis	Flacourtiaceae	Psylliostachys	Plumbaginaceae
Pollia	Commelinaceae	Ptaeroxylon	Ptaeroxylaceae
Polyacaymmia	Asteraceae	Ptelea	Rutaceae
Polyalthia	Annonaceae	Pteleopsis	Combretaceae
Polyanthus	Primulaceae	Pteridium	Hypolepidaceae
Polygala	Polygalaceae	Pteridophyllum	Papaveraceae
Polygonatum	Convallariaceae	Pteris	Pteridaceae
Polygonum	Polygonaceae	Pterocactus	Cactaceae
Polylepis	Rosaceae	Pterocarya	Juglandaceae
Polymeria	Convolvulaceae	Pterocaulon	Asteraceae
Polymnia	Asteraceae	Pteroceltis	Ulmaceae
Polypodium	Polypodiaceae	Pterocephalus	Dipsacaceae
Polypogon	Poaceae	Pterochaeta	Asteraceae
Polyscias	Araliaceae	Pterodiscus	Pedaliaceae
Polystichum	Aspidiaceae	Pteronia	Asteraceae
Polyxena	Hyacinthaceae	Pteropogon	Asteraceae
Pomaderris	Rhamnaceae	Pterostylis	Orchidaceae
Poncirus	Rutaceae	Pterostyrax	Styracaceae
Ponerorchis	Orchidaceae	Ptilimnium	Apiaceae
Pongamia	Papilionaceae	Ptilostemon	Asteraceae
Pontederia	Pontederiaceae	Ptilotrichium	Brassicaceae
Populus	Salicaceae	Ptilotus	Amaranthaceae
Porana	Convolvulaceae	Ptychosperma	Arecaceae
Portea	Bromeliaceae	Pueraria	Papilionaceae
Portulaca	Portulacaceae	Pulicaria	Asteraceae
Portulacaria	Portulaceae	Pulmonaria	Boraginaceae
Posoqueria	Rubiaceae	Pulsatilla	Ranunculaceae
Potamogeton	Potamogetonaceae	Pultenaea	Papilionaceae
Potentilla	Rosaceae	Punica	Punicaceae
Pratia	Campanulaceae	Purshia	Rosaceae
Prenia	Aizoaceae	Puschkinia	Hyacinthaceae
Preslia	Lamiaceae	Putoria	Rubiaceae
Primula	Primulaceae	Putterlickia	Celastraceae
Prinsepia	Rosaceae	Puya	Bromeliaceae
Printzia	Asteraceae	Pycnanthemum	Lamiaceae
Prismatocarpus	Campanulaceae	Pycnostachys	Lamiaceae
Pritchardia	Arecaceae	Pyracantha	Rosaceae
Pritzelago	Brassicaceae	Pyracomeles	Rosaceae
Proboscidea	Pedaliaceae	Pyrethropsis	Asteraceae
Promenaea	Orchidaceae	Pyrethrum	Asteraceae
Pronaya	Pittosporaceae	Pyrocydonia	Rosaceae
Prosopis	Mimosaceae	Pyrola	Ericaceae
Prostanthera	Lamiaceae	Pyrostegia	Bignoniaceae
Protea	Proteaceae	Pyrrocoma	Asteraceae
Prumnopitys	Podocarpaceae	Pyrrosia	Polypodiaceae

Family Names

Pyrus	Rosaceae
Quaqua	Asclepiadaceae
Quercus	Fagaceae
Quesnelia	Bromeliaceae
Quillaja	Rosaceae
Quiongzhuea	Poaceae-Bambusoideae
Quisqualis	Combretaceae
Rabdosiella	Lamiaceae
Rabiea	Aizoaceae
Racopilum	Sphagnaceae
Radermacheria	Bignoniaceae
Radyera	Malvaceae
Ramonda	Gesneriaceae
Ranunculus	Ranunculaceae
Ranzania	Berberidaceae
Raoulia	Asteraceae
Raphanus	Brassicaceae
Raphia	Myrsinaceae *
Raphiolepis *	Rosaceae
Ratibida	Asteraceae
Rauvolfia	Apocynaceae
Ravenala	Musaceae
Ravenea	Arecaceae
Rebutia	Cactaceae
Reevesia	Sterculiaceae
Regelia	Myrtaceae
Rehderodendron	Styraceae
Rehmannia	Scrophulariaceae
Reineckea	Convallariaceae
Reinwardtia	Linaceae
Relhania	Asteraceae
Reseda	Resedaceae
Restio	Restionaceae
Retama	Papilionaceae
Rhabdothamnus	Gesneriaceae
Rhadamanthus	Hyacinthaceae
Rhagodia	Chenopodiaceae
Rhamnus	Rhamnaceae
Rhaphidophora	Araceae
Rhaphithamnus	Verbenaceae
Rhapidophyllum	Arecaceae
Rhapiolepis	Rosaceae
Rhapis	Arecaceae
Rhaponticum	Asteraceae
Rhazya	Apocynaceae
Rheum	Polygonaceae
Rhexia	Melastomataceae
Rhigozum	Bignoniaceae
Rhinanthus	Scrophulariaceae
Rhinephyllum	Aizoaceae
Rhipsalis	Cactaceae
Rhodanthe	Asteraceae
Rhodanthemum	Asteraceae
Rhodiola	Crassulaceae
Rhodochiton	Scrophulariaceae
Rhodocoma	Restionaceae
Rhododendron	Ericaceae
Rhodohypoxis	Hypoxidaceae
Rhodohypoxis x Hypoxis	Hypoxidaceae
Rhodomyrtus	Myrtaceae
Rhodophiala	Amaryllidaceae
Rhodothamnus	Ericaceae
Rhodotypos	Rosaceae
Rhoicissus	Vitaceae
Rhombophyllum	Aizoaceae
Rhopaloblaste	Arecaceae

Rhopalostylis	Arecaceae
Rhus	Anacardiaceae
Rhynchosia *	Papilionaceae
Rhynchostylis	Orchidaceae
Ribes	Grossulariaceae
Richea	Epacridaceae
Ricinus	Euphorbiaceae
Rigidella	Iridaceae
Rivina	Phytolaccaceae
Robinia	Papilionaceae
Rodentiophila	Cactaceae
Rodgersia	Saxifragaceae
Rodriguezia	Orchidaceae
Roella	Campanulaceae
Rogeria	Pedaliaceae
Rohdea	Convallariaceae
Romanzoffia	Hydrophyllaceae
Romneya	Papaveraceae
Romulea	Iridaceae
Rondeletia	Rubiaceae
Rorippa	Brassicaceae
Rosa	Rosaceae
Roscoea	Zingiberaceae
Rosmarinus	Lamiaceae
Rossioglossum	Orchidaceae
Rostrinucula	Lamiaceae
Rosularia	Crassulaceae
Rothmannia	Rubiaceae
Roystonea	Arecaceae
Rubia	Rubiaceae
Rubus	Rosaceae
Rudbeckia	Asteraceae
Ruellia	Acanthaceae
Rulingia	Sterculiaceae
Rumex	Polygonaceae
Rumohra	Davalliaceae
Rupicapnos	Papaveraceae
Ruschia	Aizoaceae
Ruscus	Ruscaceae
Ruspolia	Acanthaceae
Russelia	Scrophulariaceae
Ruta	Rutaceae
Rutidosis	Asteraceae
Ruttya	Acanthaceae
Rytidosperma	Poaceae
Sabal	Arecaceae
Saccharum	Poaceae
Sadleria	Blechnaceae
Sageretia	Rhamnaceae
Sagina	Caryophyllaceae
Sagittaria	Alismataceae
Saintpaulia	Gesneriaceae
Salix	Salicaceae
Salpiglossis	Solanaceae
Salvia	Lamiaceae
Salvinia	Salviniaceae
Sambucus	Caprifoliaceae
Samolus	Primulaceae
Sanchezia	Acanthaceae
Sandersonia	Colchicaceae
Sanguinaria	Papaveraceae
Sanguisorba	Rosaceae
Sanicula	Apiaceae
Saniella	Hypoxidaceae
Sansevieria	Dracaenaceae
Santalum *	Santalaceae

Family Names

Santolina	Asteraceae	Scoliopus	Trilliaceae
Sanvitalia	Asteraceae	Scolopia	Flacourtiaceae
Sapindus	Sapindaceae	Scopolia	Solanaceae
Sapium	Euphorbiaceae	Scorzonera	Asteraceae
Saponaria	Caryophyllaceae	Scrophularia	Scrophulariaceae
Sarcocapnos	Papaveraceae	Scutellaria	Lamiaceae
Sarcocaulon	Geraniaceae	Scutia	Rhamnaceae
Sarcococca	Buxaceae	Sebaea	Gentianaceae
Sarcopoterium	Rosaeae	Secamone	Asclepiadaceae
Sarcostemma	Asclepiadaeae	Securidaca	Polygalaceae
Saritaea	Bignoniaceae	Securinega	Euphorbiaceae
Sarmienta	Gesneriaceae	Sedum	Crassulaceae
Sarracenia	Sarraceniaceae	Selaginella	Selaginellaceae
Sasa	Poaceae-Bambusoideae	Selago	Selaginellaceae
Sasaella	Poaceae-Bambusoideae	Selenicereus	Cactaceae
Sasamorpha	Poaceae	Selinum	Apiaceae
Sassafras	Lauraceae	Selliera	Goodeniaceae
Satureja	Lamiaceae	Semele	Ruscaceae
Satyrium	Orchidaceae	Semiaquilegia	Ranunculaceae
Saurauia	Actinidiaceae	Semiarundinaria	Poaceae-Bambusoideae
Sauromatum	Araceae	Semnanthe	Aizoaceae
Saururus	Saururaceae	Sempervivum	Crassulaceae
Saussurea	Asteraceae	Senecio	Asteraceae
Saxegothaea	Podocarpaceae	Senna	Caesalpiniaceae
Saxifraga	Saxifragaceae	Sequoia	Taxodiaceae
Scabiosa	Dipsacaceae	Sequoiadendron	Taxodiaceae
Scadoxus	Amaryllidaceae	Serapias	Orchidaceae
Scaevola	Goodeniaceae	Serenoa	Arecaceae
Scandix	Apiaceae	Sericanthe	Rubiaceae
Sceletium	Aizoaceae	Seriphidium	Asteraceae
Schefflera	Araliaceae	Serissa	Rubiaceae
Schima	Theaceae	Serratula	Asteraceae
Schinus	Anacardiaceae	Serruria	Proteaceae
Schinziophyton	Euphorbiaceae	Sesamum	Pedaliaceae
Schisandra	Schisandraceae	Sesbania	Papilionaceae
Schistostega	Sphagnaceae	Seseli	Apiaceae
Schivereckia	Brassicaceae	Sesleria	Poaceae
Schizachryium	Poaceae	Setaria	Poaceae
Schizanthus	Solanaceae	Severinia	Rutaceae
Schizochilus	Orchidaceae	Shepherdia	Elaeagnaceae
Schizolobium	Papilionaceae	Sherardia	Rubiaceae
Schizopetalon	Brassicaceae	Shibataea	Poaceae-Bambusoideae
Schizophragma	Hydrangeaceae	Shortia	Diapensiaceae
Schizostachyum	Poaceae-Bambusoideae	Sibbaldia	Rosaceae
Schizostylis	Iridaceae	Sibbaldiopsis	Rosaceae
Schkuhria *	Asteraceae	Sibiraea	Rosaceae
Schlumbergera	Cactaceae	Sicana *	Cucurbitaceae
Schoenia	Asteraceae	Sida	Malvaceae
Schoenoplectus	Cyoeraceae	Sidalcea	Malvaceae
Schoenus	Cyperaceae	Sideritis	Lamiaceae
Scholtzia	Myrtaceae	Sideroxylon	Sapotaceae
Schomburgkia	Orchidaceae	Siegfriedia	Rhamnaceae
Schotia	Caesalpiniaceae	Sieversia	Rosaceae
Schrebera	Oleaceae	Silaum	Apiaceae
Schwantesia	Aizoaceae	Silene	Caryophyllaceae
Sciadopitys	Sciadopityaceae	Silphium	Asteraceae
Scilla	Hyacinthaceae	Silybum	Asteraceae
Scindapus	Araceae	Simmondsia	Simmondsiaceae
Scirpoides	Poaceae	Sinacalia	Asteraceae
Scirpus	Cyperaceae	Sinapsis	Brassicaceae
Scleranthus	Caryophyllaceae	Sinarundinaria	Poaceae-Bambusoideae
Sclerocactus	Cactaceae	Sinningia	Gesneriaceae
Sclerocarya	Anacardiaceae	Sinobambusa	Poaceae-Bambusoideae
Sclerochiton	Acanthaceae	Sinocalycanthus	Calycanthaceae
Sclerolaena	Chenopodiaceae	Sinofranchetia	Lardizabalaceae
Sclerostegia	Chenopodiaceae	Sinojackia	Styracaceae

Family Names

Sinowilsonia	Hamamelidaceae	Stackhousia *	Stackhousiaceae
Siphonochilus	Zingiberaceae	Staehelina	Asteraceae
Sisymbrium	Brassicaceae	Stangeria	Stangeriaceae
Sisyndite	Zygophyllaceae	Stanhopea	Orchidaceae
Sisyrinchium	Iridaceae	Stanleya	Brassicaceae
Sium	Apiaceae	Stapelia	Asclepiadaceae
Skimmia	Rutaceae	Stapelianthus	Asclepiadaceae
Smelowskia	Brassicaceae	Stapeliopsis	Asclepiadaceae
Smilacina	Convallariaceae	Staphylea	Staphyleaceae
Smilax	Smilacaceae	Stauntonia	Lardizabalaceae
Smithiantha	Gesneriaceae	Steganotaenia	Apiaceae
Smyrnium	Apiaceae	Stegnogramma	Thelypteridaceae
Sobralia	Orchidaceae	Steirodiscus	Asteraceae
Socratea	Arecaceae	Stellaria	Caryophyllaceae
Solandra	Solanaceae	Stemodia	Scrophulariaceae
Solanum	Solanaceae	Stenanthium	Melanthiaceae
Soldanella	Primulaceae	Stenocactus	Cactaceae
Soleirolia	Urticaceae	Stenocarpus	Proteaceae
Solenomelus	Iridaceae	Stenocereus	Cactaceae
Solenopsis	Campanulaceae	Stenochlaena	Blechnaceae
Solenostemon	Lamiaceae	Stenoglottis	Orchidaceae
Solidago	Asteraceae	Stenomesson	Amaryllidaceae
Sollya	Pittosporaceae	Stenopetalum	Brassicaceae
Sonchus	Asteraceae	Stenotaphrum	Poaceae
Sonerila	Melastomataceae	Stenotus	Asteraceae
Sophora	Papilionaceae	Stephanandra	Rosaceae
Sophronitis	Orchidaceae	Stephania	Menispermaceae
Sopubia	Scrophulariaceae	Stephanocereus	Cactaceae
Sorbaria	Rosaceae	Stephanotis	Asclepiadaceae
Sorbus	Rosaceae	Stereospermum	Bignoniaceae
Sorghastrum	Poaceae	Sternbergia	Amaryllidaceae
Sorghum	Poaceae	Stevia	Asteraceae
Sparaxis	Iridaceae	Stewartia	Theaceae
Sparganium	Sparganiaceae	Stictocardia	Convolvulaceae
Sparrmannia	Tiliaceae	Stigmaphyllon	Malpighiaceae
Spartina	Poaceae	Stipa	Poaceae
Spartium	Papilionaceae	Stirlinia	Proteaceae
Spathantheum	Araceae	Stoebe	Asteraceae
Spathicarpa	Araceae	Stokesia	Asteraceae
Spathiphyllum	Araceae	Stomatium	Aizoaceae
Spathodea	Bignoniaceae	Stratiotes	Hydrocharitaceae
Speirantha	Convallariaceae	Strelitzia	Musaceae
Spergularia	Caryophyllaceae	Streptocarpus	Gesneriaceae
Sphaeralcea	Malvaceae	Streptoglossa	Asteraceae
Sphaerolobium *	Papilionaceae	Streptolirion	Commelinaceae
Sphaeromeria	Asteraceae	Streptopus	Convallariaceae
Sphagnum	Sphagnaceae	Streptosolen	Solanaceae
Sphalmanthus	Aizoaceae	Strobilanthes	Acanthaceae
Sphedamnocarpus	Malphigiaceae	Stromanthe	Marantaceae
Sphenotoma	Epacridaceae	Strombocactus	Cactaceae
Spigelia	Loganiaceae	Strongylodon	Papilionaceae
Spilanthes	Asteraceae	Strophanthus	Apocynaceae
Spiloxene	Hypoxidaceae	Struthiopteris	Blechnaceae
Spinacia	Chenopodiaceae	Strychnos	Loganiaceae
Spiraea	Rosaceae	Stylidium	Stylidiaceae
Spiranthes	Orchidaceae	Stylobasium *	Surianaceae
Spirodela	Lemnaceae	Stylomecon	Papaveraceae
Spodiopogon	Poaceae	Stylophorum	Papaveraceae
Sporobolus	Poaceae	Styphelia	Epacridaceae
Spraguea	Portulacaceae	Styrax	Styraceae
Sprekelia	Amaryllidaceae	Succisa	Dipsacaceae
Spyridium	Rhamnaceae	Sutera	Scrophulariaceae
Staberoha	Restionaceae	Sutherlandia	Papilionaceae
Stachys	Lamiaceae	Swainsona	Papilionaceae
Stachytarpheta	Verbenaceae	Swertia	Gentianaceae
Stachyurus	Stachyuraceae	Swietenia *	Meliaceae

Family Names

Syagrus	Arecaceae	Tetraselago	Selaginaceae
Sycopsis	Hamamelidaceae	Tetrastigma	Vitaceae
Symphoricarpos	Caprifoliaceae	Tetratheca	Tremendraceae
Symphyandra	Campanulaceae	Teucridium	Lamiaceae
Symphytum	Boraginaceae	Teucrium	Lamiaceae
Symplocarpus	Araceae	Thalia	Marantaceae
Symplocos	Symplocaceae	Thalictrum	Ranunculaceae
Synadenium	Euphorbiaceae	Thamnocalamus	Poaceae-Bambusoideae
Synaphea	Proteaceae	Thamnochortus	Restionaceae
Syncarpha	Asteraceae	Thapsia	Apiaceae
Syncarpia	Myrtaceae	Thelesperma	Asteraceae
Syneilesis	Asteraceae	Thelocactus	Cactaceae
Syngonium	Araceae	Thelymitra	Orchidaceae
Synthyris	Scrophulariaceae	Thelypteris	Thelypteridaceae
Syringa	Oleaceae	Themeda	Poaceae
Syringodea	Iridaceae	Thereianthus	Iridaceae
Syzygium	Myrtaceae	Thermopsis	Papilionaceae
Tabebuia	Bignoniaceae	Thespesia	Malvaeae
Tabernaemontana	Apocynaceae	Thevetia	Apocynaceae
Tacca	Taccaceae	Thladiantha	Cucurbitaceae
Tagetes	Asteraceae	Thlaspi	Brassicaceae
Taiwania	Taxodiaceae	Thomasia	Sterculiaceae
Talbotia	Velloziaceae	Thorncroftia	Lamiaceae
Talinum	Portulaceae	Threlkeldia	Chenopodiaceae
Tamarindus	Caesalpiniaceae	Thrinax	Arecaceae
Tamarix	Tamaricaceae	Thryptomene	Myrtaceae
Tamus	Dioscoreaceae	Thuja	Cupressaceae
Tanacetum	Asteraceae	Thujopsis	Cupressaceae
Tanakaea	Saxifragaceae	Thunbergia	Acanthaceae
Tanquana	Aizoaceae	Thymophylla	Asteraceae
Tapeinochilos	Zingiberaceae	Thymus	Lamiaceae
Tapiscia	Staphyleaceae	Thysanotus	Anthericaceae
Tarasa	Malvaceae	Tiarella	Saxifragaceae
Taraxacum	Asteraceae	Tibouchina	Melastomataceae
Tarchonanthus	Asteraceae	Tigridia	Iridaceae
Tarenna	Rubiaceae	Tilia	Tiliaceae
Taxodium	Taxodiaceae	Tillandsia	Bromeliaceae
Taxus	Taxaceae	Tinantia	Commelinaceae
Tecoma	Bignoniaceae	Tinnea	Lamiaceae
Tecomanthe	Bignoniaceae	Tipuana	Papilionaceae
Tecophilaea	Tecophilaeaceae	Titanopsis	Aizoaceae
Tectaria	Dryopteridaceae	Tithonia	Asteraceae
Tecticornia *	Chenopdiaceae	Tittmannia	Bruniaceae
Tectona *	Verbenaceae	Todea	Osmundaceae
Telanthophora	Asteraceae	Tofieldia	Melanthiaceae
Telekia	Asteraceae	Tolmieia	Saxifragaceae
Tellima	Saxifragaceae	Tolpis	Asteraceae
Telopea	Proteaceae	Tonestus	Asteraceae
Teloxys *	Chenopodiaceae	Toona	Meliaceae
Templetonia	Papilionaceae	Torenia	Scrophulariaceae
Tephroseris	Asteraceae	Torreya	Taxaceae
Tephrosia	Papilionaceae	Tortula	Sphagnaceae
Terminalia	Combretaceae	Townsendia	Asteraceae
Ternstroemia	Theaceae	Trachelium	Campanulaceae
Tersonia *	Gyrostemonaceae	Trachelospermum	Apocynaceae
Testudinaria	Dioscoreaceae	Trachyandra	Asphodelaceae
Tetracentron	Tetracentraceae	Trachycarpus	Arecaceae
Tetraclinis	Cupressaceae	Trachymene	Apiaceae
Tetradenia	Lamiaceae	Trachystemon	Boraginaceae
Tetradium	Rutaceae	Tradescantia	Commelinaceae
Tetragonia	Aizoaceae	Tragopogon	Asteraceae
Tetragonolobus	Papilionaceae	Trapa	Trapaceae
Tetranema	Scrophulariaceae	Trema	Ulmaceae
Tetraneuris	Asteraceae	Trevesia	Araliaceae
Tetrapanax	Araliaceae	Trianthema	Aizoaceae
Tetrarrhena	Poaceae	Triaspis	Malphigiaceae

Family Names

Tribonanthes *	Amaryllidaceae
Tribulus *	Zygophyllaceae
Trichocaulon	Asclepiadaceae
Trichocereus	Cactaceae
Trichocolea	Trichocoleaceae
Trichodendron	Trichidendraceae
Trichodesma	Boraginaceae
Trichodiadema	Aizoaceae
Tricholaena *	Poaceae
Trichopetalum	Anthericaceae
Trichophorum	Cyperaceae
Trichosanthes	Cucurbitaceae
Trichostema	Lamiaceae
Tricoryne	Anthericaceae
Tricyrtis	Convallariaceae
Tridens	Poaceae
Trientalis	Primulaceae
Trifolium	Papilionaceae
Trigonella	Papilionaceae
Trigonotis	Boraginaceae
Trillium	Trilliaceae
Trinia	Apiaceae
Triodia	Poaceae
Triosteum	Caprifoliaceae
Tripetaleia	Ericaceae
Tripleurospermum	Asteraceae
Tripogandra	Commelinaceae
Tripteris	Asteraceae
Tripterococcus *	Stackhousiaceae
Tripterospermum	Gentianaceae
Tripterygium	Celastraceae
Trisetum	Poaceae
Tristagma	Alliaceae
Tristania	Myrtaceae
Tristaniopsis	Myrtaceae
Tristellateia	Malpighiaceae
Triteleia	Alliaceae
Trithrinax	Arecaceae
Triticum	Poaceae
Tritonia	Iridaceae
Tritoniopsis	Iridaceae
Triumfetta	Tiliaceae
Trochetiopsis	Sterculiaceae
Trochocarpa	Epacridaceae
Trollius	Ranunculaceae
Tromotriche	Asclepiadaceae
Tropaeolum	Tropaeolaceae
Trymalium	Rhamnaceae
Tsuga	Pinaceae
Tsusiophyllum	Ericaceae
Tuberaria	Cistaceae
Tulbaghia	Alliaceae
Tulipa	Liliaceae
Turbina	Convolvulaceae
Turnera	Turneraceae
Turraea *	Meliaceae
Tussilago	Asteraceae
Tutcheria	Theaceae
Tweedia	Asclepiadaceae
Tylecodon	Crassulaceae
Tylophora	Asclepiadaceae
Typha	Typhaceae
Uebelmannia	Cactaceae
Ugni	Myrtaceae
Ulex	Papilionaceae
Ulmus	Ulmaceae

Umbellularia	Lauraceae
Umbilicus	Crassulaceae
Uncinia	Cyperaceae
Ungnadia	Sapindaceae
Uniola	Poaceae
Urceolina	Amaryllidaceae
Urginea	Hyacinthaceae
Urodon *	Papilionaceae
Urospermum	Asteraceae
Ursinia	Asteraceae
Urtica	Urticaceae
Utricularia	Lentibulariaceae
Uvularia	Convallariaceae
Vaccaria	Caryophyllaceae
Vaccinum	Ericaceae
Vagaria	Amaryllidaceae
Valeriana	Valerianaceae
Valerianella	Valerianaceae
Vallea	Elaeocarpaceae
Vallota	Amaryllidaceae
Vancouveria	Berberidaceae
Vandia	Orchidaceae
Vanheerdia	Aizoaceae
Vania	Brassicaceae
Veitchia	Arecaceae
Vella	Brassicaceae
Velleia	Goodeniaceae
Vellozia	Velloziaceae
Veltheimia	Hyacinthaceae
Ventilago	Rhamnaceae
Vepris	Rutaceae
Veratrum	Melanthiaceae
Verbascum	Scrophulariaceae
Verbena	Verbenaceae
Verbesina	Asteraceae
Vernonia	Asteraceae
Veronica	Scrophulariaceae
Veronicastrum	Scrophulariaceae
Verticordia	Myrtaceae
Vestia	Solanaceae
Vetivera	Poaceae
Viburnum	Caprifoliaceae
Vicia	Papilionaceae
Victoria	Nymphaeaceae
Vigna	Papilionaceae
Viguiera	Asteraceae
Villadia	Crassulaceae
Villarsia *	Menyanthaceae
Viminaria	Papilionaceae
Vinca	Apocynaceae
Vincetoxicum	Asclepiadaceae
Viola	Violaceae
Virgilia	Papilionaceae
Viscaria	Caryophyllaceae
Vitaliana	Primulaceae
Vitex	Verbenaceae
Vitis	Vitaceae
Vittadinia	Asteraceae
Voacanga	Apocynaceae
Vriesea	Bromeliaceae
Wachendorfia	Haemodoraceae
Wahlenbergia	Campanulaceae
Waitzia	Asteraceae
Waldsteinia	Rosaceae
Wallichia	Arecaceae
Wasabia	Brassicaceae

Family Names

Washingtonia	Arecaceae
Watsonia	Iridaceae
Weberocereus	Cactaceae
Wedelia	Asteraccac
Wehlia	Myrtaceae
Weigela	Caprifoliaceae
Weinmannia	Cunoniaceae
Weldenia	Commelinaceae
Welwitschia	Welwitschiaceae
Westringia	Lamiaceae
Wettinia	Arecaceae
Whiteheadia	Liliaceae
Widdringtonia	Cupressaceae
Wigandia	Hydrophyllaceae
Wikstroemia	Thymelaeaceae
Willdeknowia	Restionaceae
Wisteria	Papilionaceae
Withania	Solanaceae
Wittrockia	Bromeliaceae
Wittsteinia	Alseuosmiaceae
Wodyetia	Arecaceae
Wolffia	Lemnaceae
Woodsia	Aspidiaceae
Woodwardia	Blechnaceae
Worsleya	Amaryllidaceae
Wulfenia	Scrophulariaceae
Wurmbea	Colchicaceae
Wyethia	Asteraceae
x Achicodonia	Gesneriaceae
x Achimenantha	Gesneriaceae
x Aliceara	Orchidaceae
x Amarcrinum	Amaryllidaceae
x Amarygia	Amaryllidaceae
x Angulocaste	Orchidaceae
x Aporoheliocereus	Cactaceae
x Ascocenda	Orchidaceae
x Brassocattleya	Orchidaceae
x Brassolaelio-Cattleya	Orchidaceae
x Brigandra	Gesneriaceae
x Brunscrinum	Amaryllidaceae
x Carmispartium	Papilionaceae
x Chionoscilla	Hyacinthaceae
x Citrofortunella	Rutaceae
x Citroncirus	Rutaceae
x Codonatanthus	Gesneriaceae
x Crataemespilus	Rosaceae
x Cryptbergia	Bromeliaceae
x Cupressocyparis	Cupressaceae
x Dactyloglossum	Orchidaceae
x Fatshedera	Araliaceae
x Halimiocistus	Cistaceae
x Heppimenes	Gesneriaceae
x Heucherella	Saxifragaceae
x Hibanobambusa	Poaceae-Bambusoideae
x Kalmiothamnus	Ericaceae
x Laeliocattleya	Orchidaceae
x Ledodendron	Ericaceae
x Leucoraoulia	Asteraceae
x Lycene	Caryophyllaceae
x Mahoberberis	Berberidaceae
x Niphimenes	Gesneriaceae
x Odontioda	Orchidaceae
x Odontocidium	Orchidaceae
x Odontonia	Orchidaceae
x Osmarea	Oleaceae
x Pachyveria	Crassulaceae

x Pardacanda	Iridaceae
x Philageria	Philesiaceae
x Phylliopsis	Ericaceae
x Phyllothamnus	Ericaceae
x Potinara	Orchidaceae
x Ruttyruspolia	Acanthaceae
x Smithicodonia	Gesneriaceae
x Solidaster	Asteraceae
x Sophrolaelio-Cattleya	Orchidaceae
x Sycoparrotia	Hamamelidaceae
x Wilsonara	Orchidaceae
Xanthoceras	Sapindaceae
Xanthophthalmum	Asteraceae
Xanthorrhiza	Ranunculaceae
Xanthorrhoea	Xanthorrhoeaceae
Xanthosia	Apiaceae
Xanthosoma	Araceae
Xanthostemon	Myrtaceae
Xeranthemum	Asteraceae
Xerodraba	Brassicaceae
Xeronema	Phormiaceae
Xerophyllum	Melanthiaceae
Xerophyta	Velloziaceae
Ximenia	Olacaceae
Xylomelum	Proteaceae
Xylosma	Flacourtiaceae
Xyris	Xyridaceae
Xysmalobium	Asclepiadaceae
Yakirra	Poaceae
Ypsilandra	Liliaceae
Yucca	Agavaceae
Yushania	Poaceae-Bambusoideae
Zaluzianskya	Scrophulariaceae
Zamia	Zamiaceae
Zamioculcas	Araceae
Zantedeschia	Araceae
Zanthoxylum	Rutaceae
Zauschneria	Onagraceae
Zea	Poaceae
Zehneria	Cucurbitaceae
Zelkova	Ulmaceae
Zenobia	Ericaceae
Zephyranthes	Amaryllidaceae
Ziera	Rutaceae
Zigadenus	Melanthiaceae
Zingiber	Zingiberaceae
Zinnia	Asteraceae
Zizania	Poaceae
Zizia	Apiaceae
Ziziphus	Rhamnaceae
Zygochloa	Poaceae
Zygopetalum	Orchidaceae
Zygophyllum	Zygophyllaceae

Vegetables, Herbs and Fruit

Vegetables, Herbs and Fruit

Agrimony	Agrimonia eupatoria	Bean, tepary	Phaseolus acutifolius
Agrimony, Chinese	Agrimonia pilosa	Bean, Yard Long	See Bean, Asparagus
Agrimony, Hemp	Eupatorium cannabinum	Beetberry	Chenopodium foliosum
Ajwain	Carum copticum	Beetroot	Beta vulgaris
Alexanders	Smyrnium olusatrum	Belladonna	Atropa belladonna
Alfalfa	Medicago sativa	Bergamot, Lemon	Monarda citriodora
Alkanet	Anchusa foeniculum	Bergamot, Sweet	Monarda didyma
Allheal	Prunella vulgaris	Bergamot, Wild	Monarda fistulosa
Allspice	Pimenta dioica	Betony	Stachys officinalis
Almond	Prunus dulcis	Blackberry	Rubus villosus
Aloe Vera	Aloe vera	Blackberry	Rubus fruticosus
Amaranth	Amaranthus sp	Blackcurrant	Ribes nigrum
Amaranth, leaf	Amaranthus gangeticus	Blueberry	Vaccinum corymbosum
Anchusa	Anchusa italica	Borage	Borago officinalis
Angelica	Angelica archangelica	Boysenberry	Rubus sp
Anise	Pimpinella anisum	Broccoli, Chinese	Brassica oleracea v
Anise Hyssop	Agastache foeniculum		alboglabra
Apple	Malus domesticus	Broccoli, green	See Calabrese
Apple, crab	Malus	Broccoli, heading	Brassica oleracea
Apricot	Prunus armeiaca		Botrytis Group
Arnica, American	Arnica chamissonis	Broccoli, purple sprouting	Brassica oleracea Italica
Arnica, European	Arnica montana		Group
Artichoke, Chinese	Stachys affinis	Broccoli, white flowering	See Broccoli, Chinese
Artichoke, Globe	Cynara scolymus	Brocoletto	See Choy sum
Artichoke, Japanese	See Artichoke, Chinese	Brussel sprouts	Brassica oleracea
Artichoke, Jerusalem	Helianthus tubersosus		Gemmifera Group
Arugula	See Rocket, Salad	Buckwheat	Fagopyrum
Ashwagandha	Withania somnifera	Bullace	Prunus insititia
Asparagus	Asparagus officinalis	Burdock, greater	Arctium lappa
Asparagus Pea	Tetragonolobus	Burdock, lesser	Arctium minus
	purpureus	Burnet, salad	Sanguisorba minor
Aubergine	Solanum melongena	Butterfly weed	See Pleurisy root
Australian Cress	See Toothache Plant	Cabbage	Brassica oleracea
Avocado	Persea		Capitata Group
Balm, Lemon	Melissa officinalis	Cabbage, Chinese	Brassica rapa v
Balm of Gilead	Cedronella canariensis		pekinensis
Balsam	Impatiens balsamina	Cabbage, Chinese headed	Brassica rapa v
Banana	Musa		pekinensis
Barley	Hordeum vulgare	Cabbage, mustard	See Pak choi
Basella	Basella sp	Cabbage, napa	See Cabbage, Chinese
Basil	Ocimum basilicum	Cabbage, ornamental	Brassica oleracea Capita
Basil, Bush	Ocimum basilicum		Group
	minimum	Cabbage, white Chinese	See Pak choi
Basil, Camphor	Ocimum	Calabrese	Brassica oleraceae Italica
	kilimandscharicum		Group
Basil, East Indian	Ocimum gratissimum	Calamint	Calamintha grandiflora
Basil, Lemon/Lime	Ocimum americanum	Calomondin	x Citrofortunella
Basil, Mammoth/Sweet/Anise/Cinnamon	Ocimum basilicum	Camas	Camassia quamash
Basil, Sacred, Holy	Ocimum tenuiflorum	Canna, edible	Canna edulis
Basil Thyme	Acinos thymoides	Cape gooseberry	Physalis peruviana
Basil, Wild	Clinopodium vulgare	Caper Bush	Capparis spinosa inermis
Bay, Laurel	Laurus nobilis	Carambola	Averrhoa carambola
Bean, Adzuki	Phaseolus angularis	Caraway	Carum carvi
Bean, Asparagus	Vigna sesquipedalis	Cardamom	Elettaria cardamum
Bean, Broad	Vicia faba	Cardoon	Cynara cardunculus
Bean, cluster	Tetragonolobus	Carob	Ceratonia siliqua
Bean, Fava	See Bean, Broad	Carrot	Daucus carota
Bean, French	Phaseolus vulgaris	Catnip	Nepeta cataria
Bean, gyar	Tetragonolobus	Catnip, lemon	Nepeta cataria 'Citriodora'
Bean, Hyacinth	See Bean, Lablab	Cauliflower	Brassica oleracea
Bean, Kidney	Phaseolus vulgaris		Botrytis Group
Bean, Lablab	Lablab purpureus	Celeriac	Apium graveolens v
Bean, lima	Phaseolus lunatus		rapaceum
Bean, Runner	Phaseolus coccineus	Celery	Apium graveolens v
Bean, Snap	Phaseolus vulgaris		dulce
Bean, soya	Glycine max	Celery, Turnip Rooted	See Celeriac

Vegetables, Herbs and Fruit

Celtuce	See Lettuce, Stem	Damson	Prunus insititia
Celtuce	See Lettuce, stem	Dandelion	Taraxacum officinale
Chamomile, German	Matricaria recutita	Date	Phoenix dactylifera
Chamomile, Roman	Chamaemelum nobile	Dill	Anethum graveolens
Chard	Beta vulgaris	Dong quai	Angelica polymorpha
Chard, Swiss	Beta vulgaris Cicla Group		sinensis
Cherry	Prunus spp	Dropwort	Filipendula vulgaris
Cherry, ground	Physalis pruinosa	Earth chestnut	Bunium bulbocastanum
Chervil	Anthriscus cerefolium	Eggplant	See Aubergine
Chestnut	Castanea	Elderberry	Sambucus
Chia	Salvia columbariae	Elecampane	Inula helenium
Chick pea	Cicer arietinum	Endive	Cichorium endivia
Chicory	Cichorium intybus	Epazote	Chenopodium
Chicory, Catalogna	Cichorium intybus		ambrosioides
Chinese Chives	Allium tuberosum	Escarole	See Endive
Chives	Allium schoenoprasum	Eucalyptus, lemon	Eucalyptus citriodora
Chop Suey Greens	See Chrysanthemum	Eucalyptus, peppermint	Eucalyptus radiata
	greens	Evening primrose	Oenothera biennis
Choy Sum	Brassica rapa v	Fat hen	Chenopodium album
	parachinensis and ssp	Feldsalat	See Corn Salad
Choy Sum, purple flowered	See Choy sum	Fennel, common	Foeniculum vulgare
Chrysanthemum Greens	Chrysanthemum	Fennel, Florence	Foeniculum vulgare
	coronarium	Fennel, sweet	Foeniculum dulce
Citron	Citrus medica	Fenugreek	Trigonella foenum-
Citronella Grass	Cymbopogon nardus		graecum
Claytonia	See Purslane, Winter	Feverfew	Tanacetum parthenium
Clover	Trifolium spp	Fig	Ficus carica
Clover, sweet	Melilotus officinalis	Figwort	Scrophularia nodosa
Coconut	Cocos nucifera	Filbert	Corylus maxima
Coltsfoot	Tussilago farfara	Flax	Linum usitatissimum
Comfrey	Symphytum officinale	Foo	Momordica charantia
Comfrey, Russian	Symphytum x	Foxglove, purple	Digitalis purpurea
	uplandicum	Foxglove, woolly	Digitalis lanata
	Echinacea	Frankinscense	Boswellia thurifera
Coneflower, Purple	Coriandrum sativum	Gai Laan	See Broccoli, Chinese
Coriander	Zea mays	Garbanzo	Cicer arietinum
Corn	Zea mexicana	Garland chrysanthemum	See Chrysanthemum
Corn	Sorghum bicolor		greens
Corn, broom	Zea mays	Garlic chives	See Chinese chives
Corn, dent	Zea mays	Garlic, elephant	Allium ampeloprasum
Corn, flint	Zea mays	Garlic, Ramsoms	See Garlic, Wild
Corn, flour	Zea mays	Garlic, wild	Allium ursinum
Corn, pop	Valerianella locusta	Gayfeather	Liatris spicata
Corn Salad	Zea mays	Germander	Teucrium x lucidrys
Corn, sweet	Cucurbita pepo	Gherkin	Cucumis sativus
Courgette	Vigna unguiculata ssp	Ginger, wild	Asarum canadense
Cowpea	unguiculata	Ginseng, American	Panax quinquefolius
	Vaccinum	Ginseng, Asiatic	Panax ginseng
Cranberry	See Cress, Land	Ginseng, Siberian	Eleutherococcus
Cress, American Land	See Cress, Land		senticosus
Cress, Belle Isle	See Cress, Land	Goat's rue	Galega officinalis
Cress, Early Winter	Lepidium sativum	Goldeseal	Hydrastis canadensis
Cress, Garden	See Rocket, Salad	Good King Henry	Chenopodium bonus-
Cress, Italian	Barbarea verna/		henricus
Cress, Land	B.praecox	Gooseberry	Ribes uva-crispa v
Cress, Pepper	See Cress, Garden		reclinatum
Cress, Upland	See Cress, Land	Gourd	Lagenaria siceria
Crown Vetch	Coronilla varia	Gourd, bitter	Momordica charantia
Cucumber	Cucumis sativus	Granadilla	Passiflora
Cucumber, African horned	Cucumis metuliferus	Grape	Vitis
Cucumber, Armenian	Cucumis melo Flexuosus	Grapefruit	Citrus x paradisi
	Group	Groundnut, American	Apios americana
Cumin	Cuminum cyminum	Guava	Psidium guajava
Cumin, Black	Nigella sativa	Gypsywort	Lycopus europeus
Curd herb	See Trefoil, sweet	Hazelnut	Corylus
Daikon	See Radish	Heartsease	Viola tricolor

Vegetables, Herbs and Fruit

Hemlock	Conium maculatum	Mandarin	Citrus reticulata
Henbane	Hyoscyamus niger	Mandrake, European	Mandragora officinarum
Herb Robert	Geranium robertianum	Mangel	Beta vulgaris
Horseradish	Armoracia rusticana	Mango	Mangifera indica
Horseradish, Japanese	Wasabia japonica	Marguerite, golden	Anthemis tinctoria
Huauzontli	Chenopodium berlandieri	Marigold	Tagetes spp
Huckleberry	Solanum burbankii	Marigold, African	Tagetes erecta
Hyssop	Hyssopus officinalis	Marigold, English	See Marigold, Pot
Iceplant	Dorotheanthus spp	Marigold, French	Tagetes patula
Indian greens	See Mustard greens	Marigold, Mexican	Tagetes minuta
Indian lettuce	See Purslane, Winter	Marigold, pot	Calendula officinalis
Indian mustard	See Mustard greens	Marigold, sweet	Tagetes lucida
Indian spinach	Basella	Marjorum	Origanum sp
Japanese greens	See Chrysanthemum greens	Marrow	Cucurbita pepo
		Marshmallow	Althaea officinalis
Japanese parsley	See Mitsuba	Mashua	Tropaolum tuberosum
Jicama	Pachyrrhizus tuberosus	Medlar	Mespilus germanica
Jujube	Ziziphus jujuba	Melhukie	Corchorus olitorius
Jupiter's beard	See Valerian, red	Melon	Cucumis melo
Kailan	See Broccoli, Chinese	Melon, bitter	Momordica charantia
Kale, Chinese	See Broccoli, Chinese	Melon, pickling	Cucumis melo
Kale, curled	Brassica oleracea Acephala Group		Conomom Group
		Mercury	See Good King Henry
Kale, ornamental	Brassica oleracea Acephala Group	Mibuna greens	Brassica spp
		Milfoil	See Yarrow
Kiwano	Cucumis metuliferus	Miner's lettuce	See Purslane, Winter
Kiwi	Actinidia deliciosa	Mint	Mentha sp
Kohl Rabi	Brassica oleracea Gongylodes Group	Mint, apple	Mentha suaveolens
		Mint, Korean	Agastache rugosa
Komatsuna	Brassica rapa Perviridis Group	Mint, menthol	Mentha spicata
		Mint, mountain	Pycnanthemum pilosum
Kumquat	Fortunella margarita	Mint, peppermint	Mentha x piperata
Kyona	See Mizuna Greens	Mint, spearmint	Mentha spicata
Lady's bedstraw	Galium verum	Mint, water	Mentha aquatica
Lady's mantle	Alchemilla vulgaris	Mistletoe	Viscum album
Lamb's lettuce	See Corn Salad	Mitsuba	Cryptotaenia japonica
Lamb's quarters	See Fat Hen	Mizuna Greens	Brassica rapa v japonica
Lavender	Lavandula sp	Mooli	See Radish
Leek	Allium porrum	Mother of thyme	See Thyme, wild
Lemon	Citrus limon	Motherwort	Leonurus cardiaca
Lemongrass	Cymbopogon citratus	Mountain Spinach	See Orach
Lemongrass, East Indian	Cymbopogon flexuosus	Mugwort	Artemisia vulgaris
Lentils	Lens esculenta	Mulberry	Morus
Lettuce	Lactuca sativa	Mulberry	Morus nigra
Lettuce, asparagus	See Lettuce, Stem	Mustard, Abyssinian	See Texsel greens
Lettuce, Chinese	See Lettuce, Stem	Mustard, black	Brassica nigra
Lettuce, stem	Lactuca sativa v angustana	Mustard, brown	See Mustard, Oriental
		Mustard, Ethiopian	See Texsel greens
Licorice	Glycyrrhiza glabra	Mustard greens	Brassica juncea
Lime	Citrus aurantiifolia	Mustard, leaf	See Mustard greens
Lime	Tilia x europaea	Mustard, Oriental	Brassica juncea
Linden	Tilia x europaea	Mustard, potherb	See Mizuna Greens
Loganberry	Ribes	Mustard spinach	See Komatsuna
Loquat	Eriobotrya japonica	Mustard, white	Sinapsis alba
Lovage	Levisticum officinale	Myrrh	Myrrhis
Lucerne	See Alfalfa	Nectarine	Prunus persica v nectarina
Lungwort	Pulmonaria officinalis		
Mache	See Corn Salad	Nettle, stinging	Urtica dioica
Madder	Rubia cordifolia	Nussli	See Corn Salad
Maidenhair tree	Ginkgo biloba	Nut, cob	Corylus avellana
Malabar spinach	Basella spp	Nut, filbert	Corylus maxima
Mallow, common	Malva sylvestris	Nutmeg	Myristica fragrans
Mallow, curled	Malva verticillata 'Crispa'	Oca	Oxalis tuberosa
Mallow, musk	Malva moschata	Okra	Abelmoschus esculentus
Mallow, tree	Malva sylvestris ssp mauritanica	Onion, bulb	Allium cepa
		Onion, bulb-bearing	See Onion, tree

Vegetables, Herbs and Fruit

Common name	Botanical name
Onion, bunching	See Onion, salad
Onion, Egyptian	See Onion, tree
Onion, everlasting	See Allium perutile
Onion, multiplier	See Shallot
Onion, Oriental bunching	Allium fistulosum
Onion, pickling	Allium cepa
Onion, salad	Allium fistulosum
Onion, scallions	See Onion, Salad
Onion, spring	See Onion, salad
Onion, tree	Allium cepa Proliferum Group
Onion, Welsh	Allium fistulosum
Orach	Atriplex hortensis
Orange	Citrus
Oregano, golden	Origanum vulgare 'Aureum'
Oregano, Greek	Origanum vulgare ssp hirtum
Oregano, showy	Origanum vulgare cv
Oregano, wild	Origanum vulgare
Orris	Iris x germanica florentina
Oxlip	Primula elatior
Oyster plant	See Salsify
Pak choi	Brassica rapa Chinensis Group
Pak choi, flowering	See Choy sum
Pak choi, rosette	Brassica rapa v rosularis
Parsley	Petroselinum crispum
Parsley, Hamburg	Petroselinum crispum v tuberosum
Parsnip	Pastinaca sativa
Passion fruit	Passiflora spp
Patchouli	Patchouli cablin
Paw paw	Carica papaya
Pe-tsai	see Cabbage, Chinese headed
Pea	Pisum sativum
Pea shoots	Pisum sativum
Pea, tuberous	Lathyrus sativus
Peach	Prunus persica
Peanut	Arachis hypogaea
Pear	Pyrus communis
Pear, Asian	Pyrus pyrifolia
Pear, balsam	Momordica charantia
Peas, edible pod	See Peas, mangetout
Peas, mangetout	Pisum sativum v macrocarpon
Peas, snow	See Peas, Mangetout
Peas, sugar	See Peas, Mangetout
Pecan	Carya
Pennyroyal	Mentha pulegium
Pepino	Solanum muricatum
Pepper, black	Piper nigrum
Pepper, capsicum	See Pepper, Sweet
Pepper, Sweet	Capsicum annuum Grossum Group
Perilla	Perilla frutescens
Periwinkle	Vinca major
Periwinkle, Madagascar	Catharanthus roseus
Pimpernel	Anagallis arvensis
Pine nut	Pinus pinea
Plantain	Plantago coronopus
Pleurisy root	Asclepia tuberosa
Plum	Prunus domestica
Pokeroot	Phytolacca americana
Pomegranate	Punica granatum
Poppy, corn	Papaver rhoeas
Poppy, opium	Papaver somniferum
Potato	Solanum tuberosum
Pummelo	Citrus maxima
Pumpkin	Cucurbita maxima
Pumpkin	Cucurbita spp
Purple medick	See Alfalfa
Purslane, summer	Portulaca oleracea
Purslane, winter	Claytonia perfoliata
Pyrethrum	Tanacetum cinearifolium
Pyrethrum, painted daisy	Tanacetum coccineum
Queen Anne's Lace	Daucus carota
Quince	Cydonia
Quinoa	Chenopodium quinoa
Radicchio	Cichorium intybus
Radish	Raphanus sativus
Rampion	Campanula rapunculus
Rape, salad	Brassica napus
Raspberry	Rubus idaeus
Rauwolfia	Rauvolfia serpentina
Redcurrant	Ribes rubrum
Rhubarb	Rheum sp
Rice	Oryza sativa
Rocambole	Allium scorodoprasum
Rocket, salad	Eruca sativa
Rocket, sweet	Hesperis matronalis
Rocket, Turkish	Bunias orientalis
Rose, dog	Rosa canina
Rose, sweet briar	Rosa rubiginosa
Rose, wild	Rosa canina
Rosemary, common	Rosmarinum officinalis
Rye	Secale cereale
Safflower	Carthamus tinctorius
Saffron	Crocus sativus
Sage, blue	Salvia clevlandii
Sage, Chinese	Salvia militorrhiza
Sage, clary	Salvia sclarea
Sage, common	Salvia officinalis
Sage, Greek	Salvia fruticosa
Sage, Painted	Salvia viridis
Sage, pineapple	Salvia elegans
Sage, red	Salvia militorrhiza
Sage, Russian	Perovskia atriplicifolia
Salsify	Tragopogon porrifolius
Sand leek	See Rocambole
Sassafras	Sassafras albidum
Satsuma	Citrus unshiu
Savory, Summer	Satureja hortensis
Savory, Winter	Satureja montana
Scorzonera	Scorzonera hispanica
Scorzonera, French	Scorzonera picroides
Seakale	Crambe maritima
Senna, bladder	Colutea arborescens
Senposai Hybrids	Brassica Hybrids
Sesame	Sesamum indicum
Shallot	Allium cepa Aggregatum Group
Shepherd's purse	Capsella bursa-pastoris
Shiso	See Perilla
Shungiku	See Chrysanthmum greens
Skirret	Sium sisarum
Skullcap	Scutellaria lateriflora
Soapwort	Saponaria officinalis
Sorghum	Sorghum bicolor

Vegetables, Herbs and Fruit

Sorrel	Rumex acetosa	Viper's grass	See Scorzonera
Sorrel, buckler-leaved	Rumex scutatus	Vitex	Vitex negundo
Sorrel, French	Rumex scutatus	heterophylla	
Spinach	Spinacia oleracea	Walnut	Juglans
Spinach, beet	Beta vulgaris ssp cicla	Watercress	Nasturtium officinale
Spinach, Chinese	See Amaranth	Watermelon	Citrullus lanatus
Spinach, perpetual	See Spinach, Beet	Wheat	Triticum vulgare
Squash	Cucurbita spp	Whitecurrant	Ribes rubrum
St. John's wort	Hypericum perforatum	Willow herb	Epilobium parviflorum
Strawberry	Fragaria vesca	Witch hazel	Hamamelis vorginiana
Strawberry spinach	Chenopodium capitatum	Woad	Isatis tinctoria
Sunflower	Helianthus annuus	Woad, Chinese	Bapthicacanthus cusia
Swamp root	See Yerba buena	Wolfberry, Chinese	Lycium barbarum
Swede	Brassica napa	Wong bok	See Cabbage, Chinese
Sweet cicely	Myrrhis odorata		headed
Swiss chard	See Spinach, Beet	Woodruff, dyer's	Asperula tinctoria
Tamarind	Tamarindus indica	Woodruff, sweet	Galium odoratum
Tangerine	Citrus reticulata	Woodsage	Teucrium scorodonia
Tansy	Tanacetum vulgare	Wormwood, African	Artemisia afra
Tansy, curly	Tanacetum vulgare 'Crispum'	Wormwood, beach	Artemisia stelleriana
		Wormwood, Chinese	Artemisia apiacea
Tansy, fernleaf	Tanacetum vulgare 'Crispum'	Wormwood, Roman	Artemisia pontica
		Wormwood, sweet	Artemisia annua
Tarragon	Artemisia dracunculus	Wormwood, tree	Artemisia arborescens
Tarragon, Mexican	See Marigold, sweet	Yacon	Polyamia sonchifolia
Tatsoi (Tasai)	See Pak choi, rosette	Yam, wild	Dioscorea villosa
Tea	Camellia sinensis	Yarrow	Achillea millefolium
Tea tree	Melaleuca alternifolia	Yarrow, red	Achillea millefolium 'Reine Cerise'
Teff	Eragrostis tef		
Texsel greens	Brassica carinata	Yarrow, sneezewort	Achillea ptarmica
Thistle, blessed	Cnicus benedictus	Yarrow, woolly	Achillea tomentosa 'Aurea'
Thistle, milk	Silybum marianum		
Thistle, silver	Carlina acaulis	Yarrow, yellow	Achillea filipendula 'Cloth of Gold'
Thyme	Thymus sp		
Thyme, caraway	Thymus herba-barona	Yerba buena	Anemopsis californica
Thyme, creeping	Thymus polytrichus	Yerba mate	Ilex paraguayensis
Thyme, English	Thymus vulgaris	Yerba santa	Eriodictyom californicum
Thyme, German	Thymus vulgaris	Zucchini	See Courgette
Thyme, lavender	Thymus thracicus		
Thyme, Portuguese	Thymus carnosus		
Thyme, wild	Thymus serpyllum		
Thyme, winter	Thymus vulgaris		
Thyme, woolly	Thymus pseudolanuginosus		
Tiger nut	Cyperus esculentus		
Tomatillo	Physalis ixocarpa		
Tomato	Lycopersicum lycopersicum		
Toothache plant	Spilanthes acmella		
Tormentil	Potentilla tormentilla		
Tree tomato	Cyphomandra betacea		
Trefoil, sweet	Trigonella caerulea		
Turmeric	Curcuma domestica		
Turnip	Brassica campestris Rapifera Group		
Ugli	Citrus x tangelo 'Ugli'		
Valerian	Valerianella officinalis		
Valerian, red	Centranthus ruber		
Vanilla grass	Anthoxanthum odoratum		
Vegetable oyster	See Salsify		
Velvet bean	Mucuna spp		
Verbena, lemon	Aloysia triphylla		
Vervain	Verbena officinalis		
Vetiver grass	Vetiveria zizanioides		
Violet, sweet	Viola odorata		

Latin Terms

Latin Terms

Latin	Meaning
acaulis	stemless
acerus	hornless
acetosellus	slightly acid
achillea	after Achilles
acris	acrid
aculeatus	prickly
aculeatus	thorny
aculeolatus	with small prickles
adamantinus	Diamond Lake, Oregon
adenophyllus	hairy leaves
adpressus	lying flat
adulterinus	adulterous, easily hybridizes
aegypticus	Egypt
aequinoctialus	at the equinox
aeruginosus	rusty brown
aesculifolius	almond-like
aestivalis	summer
aethiopicus	African
aetnensis	from Mt. Etna
afer	Africa, northern
afghanicus	Afghanistan
africanus	Africa
agetus	wonderful
aggregatus	clustered together
ailanthus	reaching heaven
ailanthus	touching the sky
ajacis	Ajax
alatus	winged
alba	white
albescens	turning white
albicans	becoming white
albicans	off white
albidus	whitish
albomaculatus	spotted white
albopictus	painted white
albovariegatus	variegated white
aleppicus	Aleppo, Syria
aleuticus	Aleutian
algidus	cold
algidus	mountainous
allium	garlic
alpestris	of mountains
alpicolus	of high mountains
alpinus	alpine
alpinus	growing in mountains
alternatus	alternate
altilis	nutritious
amaranticolor	purple
americanus	American
amethystinus	violet
amicorum	Friendly Isles, Tonga
amygdalinus	almond-like
andromeda	Ethiopian Princess
angularis	angular
annulatus	ringed
annuus	annual
anosmus	without scent
anthracinus	coal-black
antipodus	Antipodes
antipyreticus	against fire
aphyllus	without leaves
apius	bee-like
aquaticus	in water
aquatilis	underwater
aquilus	blackish brown
arabicus	Arabia
arboreus	tree-like
arctotis	bear's ear
arcturus	bear's tail
argenteus	silver(y)
aridus	dry places
armatus	thorny
armatus	armed
aromaticus	aromatic
arundinaceus	reed-like
arvensis	of ploughed fields
ascendens	ascending
asiaticus	Asia
asper	rough
assurgens	ascending
astictus	unspotted
astictus	perfect
atropurpureus	dark purple
atrovirens	deep green
aurantiacus	orange
aureus	golden
australiensis	Austalia
australis	southern
austriacus	Austria
autumnalis	autumn
azureus	sky blue
azureus	azure
baldensis	from Mt. Baldo
barbatus	bearded
beccabunger	stream blocker
bellus	beautiful
betonicifolius	betony-leaved
biennis	biennial
bifidus	deeply cleft leaves
bifoliatus	bifoliate
bifoliatus	two leaflets
blepharophyllus	fringed
bombycinus	silky
bonariensis	Buenos Aires
bonduc	hazelnut
borealis	northern
botryoides	like a bunch of grapes
brumalis	winter flowering
brunneus	deep brown
bryoides	moss-like
bupthalmoides	ox-eyed
cacumenus	of mountain tops
cadmicus	metallic-looking
caerulescens	bluish
caeruleus	blue
caeruleus	dark blue
caesius	lavender
caespitosus	tufted
caespitosus	dense clumps
calcaratus	horned
calceolatus	slipper-shaped
californicus	California
callistus	very beautiful
camara	arched
campanulatus	bell-shaped
campestre	of open fields
campestre	of pasture
canarius	canary yellow
capillipes	slender stalked
capreus	goat-like
capriolatus	with tendrils

Latin Terms

caricius	carex-like	croceus	saffron
carneus	flesh-coloured	crocus	saffron
carpaticus	from the Carpathian mountains	crucifer	cruciform
		crucifer	crossed
cashmerianus	Kashmir	crus-galli	cock's spur
castus	unspotted	cupreus	coppery
castus	pure	cyaneus	Prussian blue
cataris	cat-like	dalmaticus	Dalmatia
caudatus	tailed	damascenus	Damascus
causticus	caustic	dealbatus	whitened
cauticolus	of cliffs	dealbatus	white-powdered
cenisia	Mt.Cenis	debilis	weak, feeble
centralis	central	debilis	debilitated
ceraceus	waxy	decandrus	ten-stamened
cernuus	drooping	deciduus	deciduous
cernuus	nodding	deciduus	loses leaves every year
ceterach	fern	decipiens	deceptive
chamae-	prostrate	declinatus	downward curving
chasmanthus	open flowers	decolorans	discolouring
cheilanthus	lipped flowers	decolorans	staining
chinensis	China	decumbens	decumbent with upturned tips
chirophyllus	hand-shaped		
chlorus	yellowish green	decumbens	reclining
chryseus	golden yellow	deflexus	turned sharply downwards
chrysoleucus	gold and white		
cibarius	edible	deformis	malformed
cicerbita	chick pea	deformis	deformed
ciliaris	fringed with hairs	delphicus	Delphi, Greece
cinerascens	becoming ash grey	demersus	submerged
cinereus	ash grey	demersus	underwater
cinnabarinus	vermillion	dens-canis	dog's tooth
cinnamomeus	cinnamon	dentatus	toothed
citrinus	lemon yellow	deodarus	Deodar State, India
citrinus	citrus	depressus	pressed down flatwards
citrodorus	lemon-scented	dianthus	flower of Jove
cocciferus	berry bearing	dianthus	flower of Zeus
coccineus	scarlet	dianthus	divine flower
cochlearis	spoon-shaped	diaphanus	diaphanous
codonopsis	bell	diaphanus	transparent
coerulescens	bluish	dichromus	two-coloured
coeruleus	blue	difformis	misshapen
colombius	dove-like	diffusus	spreading
colubrinus	snake-like	digitalis	fingered
columnaris	columnar	digitalis	digit-like
columnaris	pillar-like	digitalis	thimble
communis	growing in company	digraphis	lined with two colours
comosus	tufts of flowers	diphyllus	two-leaved
concolor	evenly coloured	divionensis	Dijon, France
concolor	uniformly coloured	dryophyllus	oak-leaved
conjunctus	joined together	dulcis	sweet
conspersus	scattered	dumetorum	of thickets
conspersus	speckled	dumetorum	of bushes
constrictus	erect	dumnoniensis	Devon
constrictus	dense	dunensis	of sand dunes
contortus	contorted	eboracensis	York, England
contortus	twisted	edulis	edible
convolutus	rolled up	elatus	tall
corallinus	coral pink	elegantissima	very elegant
coralloides	coral pink	elephantipes	elephants' foot
cordatus	heart-shaped	ellipticus	elliptical
coriaceus	leathery	elodes	of boggy ground
cornubiensis	Cornwall	elodes	of marshes
cornutus	horned	emarginatus	notched at the top
corydalis	lark	emeticus	emetic
crispus	curled	emodensis	from Mt. Emodus
crista-galli	cock's comb	ensatus	sword-shaped

Latin Terms

epigeios	of dry places	fuscatus	brownish
epihydrus	floating	fuscus	brown
epihydrus	on the surface of water	galbinus	greenish yellow
epiteius	annual	gallicus	France
equinus	of horses	garganicus	from Mt. Gargano
equisetum	of horses	gelidae	frozen, cold (of water)
erectus	upright	genavensis	Geneva
erectus	erect	generalis	usual, normal
ericetorum	of heathland	georgianus	Georgia, USA
eriophorus	woolly	georgicus	Georgia, formerly USSR
erubescens	turning red	germanicus	Germany
esculentus	tasty	giganteus	gigantic
esculentus	edible	giluus	dull yellow
estriatus	without stripes	glaber	smooth
euchlorus	fresh green	glaber	glabrous
europeus	Europe	glabratus	becoming smooth
exaltus	very tall	glacialis	of icy habitats
excelsior	very tall	glaucus	glaucous green
exoniensis	Exeter, England	glaucus	sea green
fallax	false	glaucus	whitish bloom
farinosus	white powdered	globosus	round
farleyensis	Farley Hill Gardens, Barbados	globosus	globe-shaped
		globularis	ball-shaped
fastigiatus	with upright branches	glomeratus	collected together
fecundus	fruitful	gracilis	slender
felosmus	foul-smelling	gracilis	graceful
fennicus	Finnland	gradifolius	large-leaved
feris	wild	graecus	Greece
ferox	very prickly	gramineus	grass-like
ferrugineus	rust red	grammatus	with raised lines
ferrugineus	rusty brown	grandiflorus	large-flowered
ferulaceus	fennel-like	grandis	showy
ficifolia	fig-leaved	grandis	large
fimbriatus	fringed	grandis	big
flabellatus	fan-shaped	gratianopolitanus	Grenoble, France
flammeus	flame red	graveolens	strong smelling
flaveolus	yellowish	griseus	grey
flavescens	turning yellow	griseus	pearly grey
flavovirens	yellowish green	grossularia	gooseberry
flavus	bright yellow	hastatus	arrow-shaped
flexuosus	wavy	hederaceus	ivy-like
flore-pleno	double-flowers	hedys	sweet
floribundus	free-flowering	hedys	pleasant smelling
flos cuculi	cuckoo-flowered	helenium	Helen of Troy
fluitans	floating	hellenicus	Greece
fluminensis	in running water	helodes	of marshes
fluvialis	in rivers	helodes	of boggy ground
fluvialis	in streams	helveticus	Switzerland
foetidus	stinking	helvolus	light yellowish brown
foetidus	foetid	helvus	pale honey coloured
foliossisimum	leafy	hesleris	evening
formicarius	ant-like	hexandrus	six-stamened
fragrans	fragrant	himalaicus	from the Himalayas
fragrantissimus	very fragrant	himalayense	Himalayas
fraxineus	ash-like	himalayensis	from the Himalayas
fresnoensis	Fresno County, California	hircinus	smelling of goats
frigidus	of cold habitats	hirsutissimus	very hairy
frutescens	shrubby	hirsutus	hairy
fucatus	painted	hispanicus	Spain
fucatus	dyed	hispidus	bristly
fulgens	shining	hispidus	stiff hairs
fulgineus	sooty	hollandicus	Holland
fulginosus	sooty	hollandicus	Netherlands
fulvus	tawny yellow	horizontalis	horizontal
fulvus	reddish yellow	horminoides	clary-like
furcatus	forked	humilis	low-growing

Latin Terms

hungaricus	Hungary	lanatus	woolly
hybernalis	winter	lanceolatus	narrow-leaved
hybernus	winter	landra	radish
hydro	water	lanuginosus	soft hairs
hyemalis	winter	latebrosus	of shady, dark places
hylaeus	of woods	lateritius	brick red
hylophilus	of woods	laurifolius	laurel-leaved
hyperboreus	far north	lazicus	Lazistan
hystrix	of porcupines	lentiginosus	freckled
ianthus	violet	lentiginosus	mottled
ibericus	Iberia	leodensis	Liege, Belgium
icterinus	yellowed	leonotis	lion's ear
icterinus	jaundiced	leontodon	lion's tooth
idaeus	from Mt.Ida	leonurus	lion's tail
igneus	flame red	lepidotus	scurfy
illinitus	smudged	lepidotus	scaly
illustris	illustrious, brilliant	lilacinus	lilac
illyricus	Illyria	liliaceus	lily-like
imbricatus	overlapping	limaeus	of stagnant wtaer
immersus	immersed	limensis	Lima, Peru
immersus	underwater	limnophilus	of marshes
incanus	hoary grey	limosus	of muddy places
incarnatus	flesh pink	linearis	narrow
incisus	deeply cut	linearis	linear
indicus	India	litoralis	of the sea shore
inebrians	inebriating	lividus	lead colour
inebrians	intoxicating	lividus	grey
inodorus	without smell	lividus	greyish blue
inscriptus	with script-like markings	lochmius	of thickets
insignis	significant	lochmius	of coppices
insignis	striking	lophanthus	crested flowers
insignis	remarkable	lucidus	lucid
insipidus	insipid	lucidus	shining
insubricus	from Insubria, the Lapontine Alps	lucorus	of woods
		luridus	dirty yellow
insubricus	southern Switzerland	lusitanicus	Portugal
insularis	growing on islands	lutarius	of muddy places
intactus	un-opened	luteolus	yellowish
inundatus	of places where flooding occurs	lutescens	pale yellow
		lutescens	turning yellow
involucratus	surrounded by bracts	lutetianus	Paris, France
iodes	violet-like	luteus	yellow
ioensis	Iowa	lychnis	lamp
iridescens	iridescent	macellus	rather meagre
irrigatus	of wet places	macer	meagre
irrigatus	of flooded places	macilentus	thin
irritans	irritable	macrophylla	broad-leaved
irritans	discomforting	maculatus	blotched
islandicus	Iceland	maculatus	spotted
italicus	Italy	magnificus	magnificent
jasminoides	jasmine-like	magnus	large
juanensis	Genoa	magnus	great
kewensis	Kew Gardens	majalis	May flowering
koreanus	Korea	majesticus	majestic
labiatus	lip-shaped	major	bigger
laciniatus	slashed	major	larger
laciniatus	jagged	major	major
laciniatus	cut-leaf	margaritus	pearly
lactescens	becoming milky white	marginata	edged
lacteus	milky white	marinus	marine
lacteus	exuding milky sap	marinus	by the sea
lactiflora	milky	marinus	of the sea
lacustris	of lakes	maritimus	by the sea (shore)
lacustris	of ponds	marmoratus	mottled
laevigatus	smooth	marmoratus	marbled
laevigatus	polished	massiliensis	Marseilles, France

Latin Terms

matritenensis	Madrid, Spain	novae-angliae	New England
maximus	largest	novae-zelandiae	New Zealand
medicago	a type of grass	novi-belgii	New York, USA
mediopictus	striped down the middle	nummularis	round
medius	medium	nuphar	lily
medius	middle-sized	nutans	nodding
meridianus	noon	nyssa	water nymph
meridianus	midday	obesus	fat
meridionalis	midday	obesus	succulent
meridionalis	noon	occelatus	eye-like
metallicus	metallic	occidentalis	western
micans	glittering	oceanicus	near the sea
miniatus	red-lead red	ochraeus	ochre
minimus	smallest	ochroleucus	yellowish white
minor	small	ochroleucus	buff
minutissimus	very small	odoratus	fragrant
minutissimus	minute	odorus	fragrant
minutissimus	tiny	oenothera	ass-catcher
mirabilis	extraordinary	olidus	stinking
mirabilis	wonderful	olympicus	from Mt. Olympus
mirabilis	remarkable	omeiensis	from Mt. Omei
mixtus	mixed	oporinus	of autumn
modestus	modest	oporinus	of late summer
moldavicus	Moldavia	orarius	of the shoreline
monstrosus	monstrous	oreophilus	mountain loving
monstrosus	abnormal	oresbius	growing on mountains
montanus	of mountains	orientalis	eastern
mortuiflumis	stagnant water	ostruthius	purplish
mucosus	slimy	paeonia	from Paeon, physician
mucronatus	sharp tipped		changed into a flower
muralis	growing on walls	paganus	from the country
murinus	mouse-like	paliurus	Christ-thorn
murinus	mouse-lgrey	pallescens	becoming pale
mutabilis	changeable	palmatus	palmate
myosotis	mouse ear	palmatus	palm-shaped
myosurus	mouse tail	palustris	of marshy ground
nanellus	very dwarf	pandorea	Pandora
nanus	dwarf	papilio	butterfly-flowered
napellus	turnip-like	papyraceus	papery
narcissus	youth in Greek	pardulinus	spotted like a leopard
	mythology	parnassicus	from Mt. Parnassus
natans	floating underwater	parvius	small
natans	swimming	parvulus	very small
nauseosus	nauseating	passifora	passion flower
neapolitanus	Naples, Italy	pastoralis	in pastures
nemoralis	of woods	patens	spreading
neomontanus	Neuberg, Germany	pavonicus	peacock blue
nepalensis	Nepal	pavonius	peacock blue
nervosus	ribbed	pedicularis	of lice
nesophilus	growing on islands	peltatus	staked from the middle
niger	black	pendulus	handing
nigrescens	black	pendulus	pendulous
nigricans	blackish	peninsularis	of a peninsular
nigropunctatus	spotted black	pensylvanicus	Pennsylvania
niloticus	Nile Valley	perennis	perennial
nitens	shining	perennis	flowering more than one
nitidus	glossy		season
nivalis	snow white	permixtus	confusing
nivalis	growing where there is	perpusillus	very small
	snow	persicarius	peach-like
niveus	snow white	persicifolia	peach-leaved
nobilis	notable	persicus	Persia
nobilis	worthy	peruvianus	Peru
noctiflorus	night-flowering	pes-caprae	goat's foot
non-scriptus	un-marked	petiolaris	having a leaf stalk
notatus	spotted	petunia	tobacco

Latin Terms

Term	Meaning
phoenicius	Phoenician red dye
phyllus	pertaining to leaves
pictus	painted
pilosus	long soft hairs
pineus	pine-like
pinnatus	pinnate
pinnatus	leaflets on either side of the leaf stalk
pleniflorus	double flowers
plumbeus	lead grey
plumosus	feathery
pluvialis	of rainy places
polemonium	after King Polemon
poly	many-headed
polygyrus	twining
pomaceus	apple-like
pomeridianus	afternoon
ponderosus	heavy
ponderosus	large
porcinus	of pigs
porophilus	of soft stony ground
porphyreus	warm red
potamophilis	river-loving
praealtus	very tall
praecox	very early
praevernus	early season
prasinus	leek green
pratensis	of meadows
pratericolus	of meadows
pratericolus	of grassy places
prenans	drooping
primuloides	primula-like
procerus	very tall
profusus	profuse
profusus	very abundant
prostratus	prostrate
protea	Sea-god Proteus
pruhonicus	Pruhonice
prunella	treatment for quinsy
pubescens	downy
pullus	raven black
pullus	pitch black
pumilus	dwarf
pumilus	small
punctatus	dotted
pungens	pointed
pungens	pungent
puniceus	carmine red
puniceus	purple-red
purpureus	purple
pusillus	very small
pygmaeus	dwarf
pygmaeus	pygmy
pyrenaeus	Pyrenees
pyrenaicus	from the Pyrenees
quercifolius	oak-leaved
quisqualis	who?
quisqualis	what?
quitensis	Quito, Ecuador
racemosus	many-branched
racemosus	in a raceme
radiatus	radiating
radiosus	many-rayed
ramontioides	ramonda-like
ravenala	traveller's tree
ravus	greyish

Term	Meaning
reclinatus	reclined
rectus	erect
rectus	upright
recurvus	recurved
reflexus	bent back
reflexus	reflexed
repens	creeping
reptans	creeping
reticulatus	netted
reticulatus	veined
revolutus	rolled backwards
rhaeticus	Rhaetium Alps
rhaponticus	Black Sea
ringens	two-lipped
riparius	of banks
riparius	of rivers
rivalis	by brooks
rivalis	by streams
robustus	robust
robustus	strong-growing
roseus	rosy pink
rosmarinifolius	rosemary like leaves
rosularis	with rosettes
rotundatus	round
rotundatus	rotund
rotundifolius	round
rubellus	reddish
rubens	red
ruber	red
rubescens	turning red
rubicundus	rubicund
rubicundus	ruddy
rubiginosus	rusty-red
rudis	wild
rudis	of rough areas
rufescens	turning red
rufinus	red
rufus	red
rugosus	wrinkled
rupicola	growing amongst rocks
rupifragus	growing in crevices or cracks
ruralis	of the country
russatus	russet red
rutilans	bright red
sabatius	Savona, Italy
sabulosus	growing on sand
saccharinus	sweet
saccharinus	sugary
salicifolius	willow-leaved
sanguineus	blood-red
sanguineus	sanguine
sassafras	saxifrage
sauro	lizard-like
saxatilis	growing on rocks
scaber	rough
scandens	climbing
scandens	ascending
scarlatinus	scarlet
scarlatinus	bright red
scopulorum	growing on rock faces
scopulorum	growing on cliffs
scoticus	Scotland
scriptus	marked with script-like lines
sculptus	sculpted

Latin Terms

sculptus	carved
scutellatus	shield-shaped
seclusus	hidden
segetalis	of cornfields
sempervirens	always green
sempervirens	ever green
serotinus	late season
sessile	without stems
siliceus	growing on sand
silvaticus	of woods
silvaticus	of the wild
silvicola	of woods
simplex	simple
sinensis	China
singularis	singular
singularis	distinct
singularis	unusual
solaris	of sunny places
solstitialis	midsummer
sordidus	sordid
sordidus	dirty-looking
spadiceus	chestnut brown
spadiceus	date brown
speciosa	showy
sphaerocephalus	round-headed
spicata	spiked
stamineus	with prominent stamens
stellatus	star-shaped
stevenagensis	Stevenage, England
stoloniferus	creeping
stramineus	straw-coloured
striatus	marked with long lines
suaveolens	sweet-smelling
subcaeruleus	slightly blue
subcanus	slightly grey
submersus	submerged
succulentus	succulent
succulentus	juicy
sudeticus	Sudentenland
suecius	Sweden
sulphureus	sulphur
sulphureus	pale yellow
supinus	supine
supinus	flat
suspendus	suspended
suspendus	hanging down
sylvestris	of woods
Symphytum	comfrey
syriacus	Syria
syringilfolius	lilac-like leaves
tardus	late
tauricus	Crimea
tenacissimus	strong
tenuis	thin
tenuis	slender
testaceus	brick-coloured
thalassicus	marine
thalassicus	in the sea
thermalis	of warm springs
thibetianus	Tibet
tigrinus	of tigers
tinctoria	dye
tomentosus	thickly haired
tortilis	twisted
tortuosus	meandering
trimestris	maturing in three months

triplinervis	three-ribbed
tristis	sad appearance
tristis	dull
trivalis	common
trivalis	wayside
tuberosus	with tubers
tubiformis	trumpet-shaped
tulipa	turban
uliginosus	of marshes
umbellatus	umbelled
urceolatus	pitcher-shaped
urginea	Algerian tribe
Uruguayensis	Uruguay
vaccinus	of cows
variegatus	variegated
velox	quick growing
veris	spring
vermiculatus	of worms
vernalis	spring
verticalis	vertical
vespertinus	evening-flowering
vestalis	white
vialis	wayside
vicinus	neighbouring
vinaceus	wine red
vindobonensis	Vienna, Austria
vinicolor	wine red
vinosus	wine red
violaceus	violet
violescens	with violet colouring
violescens	turning violet
virens	green
virescens	light green
virginalis	virginal white
virginianus	Virginia
virginicus	Virgin Islands
virgultorum	of thickets
viridescens	becoming green
viridifuscus	greenish brown
viridior	greener
viridis	green
viridissimus	very green
viridulus	greenish
viscidus	sticky
vitellinus	egg-yolk yellow
vitis-ideae	vine of Mount Ida, Greece
vulgare	common
warleyensis	Warley Place, Essex, England
wisleyensis	Wisley Gardens, England
xanthinus	yellow
xanthospilus	spotted yellow
xerophilus	of dry places
yucca	cassava
zaleucus	very white
zalil	delphinium

Horticultural Dictionary

Horticultural Dictionary

+ Denotes a graft hybrid.

abortive imperfectly developed, failure to produce seed.

acaulescent Stemless, or short stem below ground. Botanical term acaulis.

accelerator substance added to compost heap to speed decomposition.

accent plant individual eye-catching plant.

acclimatization adaptation of plant to changes in climate or site.

accrescent increasing in size with age.

achene Dry, one-sided fruit that does not split.

acid soil Has a pH lower than 7.

actinomorphic A flower that is radially symmetrical.

activator see accelerator.

acute Tapering to a point, usually of leaves.

adpressed Flatly pressed back, leaf lying flat against a stem.

adventitious Growing in an unusual place.

adventitious roots Grow directly from a stem or leaf.

adventive Exotic plant, briefly established but unable to survive for long.

aerate Supplying oxygen to the soil by digging.

aerator Tool used to aerate.

aerial roots Roots growing from a stem, above ground level.

air layering A method of propagation. A cut is made in the stem, wrapped in damp moss, sealed in a plastic.

algae Flowerless plants of simple structure.

alkaline soil With a pH higher than 7.

alkaloid A bitter-tasting plant compound containing nitrogen, defends plants against predators.

allelopathy The release of chemicals by a plant to inhibit the growth of other plants in its immediate vicinity.

alpine A small plant suitable for growing in a rock garden. Look out for the botanical term alpinus.

alpine house An unheated greenhouse designed for alpines.

alternate Occurring singly on alternate sides of the stem, of leaves. Look for the botanical term alternatus.

alternate host A host upon which a plant disease lives for part of its life, finding another host to complete its cycle.

amendment Organic or mineral material added to the soil to improve or condition.

anaerobe An organism that can live without oxygen.

angiosperms The flowering plants, the largest group in the plant world, with around 250,000 species. Contain their seeds in an ovary.

annual A plant which germinates, grows, flowers, sets seed and dies normally in one season. The botanical term annuus.

annual ring The ring of wood developed in each growing season in trees seen on a cross-section of the trunk.

anther The terminal part of a stamen, producing pollen.

anthesis The opening of a flower ready for pollination.

anthracnose A soilborne fungal disease.

antitranspirant Sprayed on stems and leaves of plants to reduce water loss.

anvil pruning shears Hand pruners.

apex Tip or growing point .

apical bud A bud at the tip of a stem.

apical dominance The tendency of the main stem to grow upwards without bushy growth.

apical meristem When the cells at the tip of the stem divide and expand, the stem length extends.

aquatic Plants growing submerged in water with roots in soil.

arborescent Branching, like a tree.

arboretum A collection of trees.

arboriculture The art of growing and cultivating trees.

arborising Pruning an overgrown shrub into a treelike specimen with one or sometimes two trunks.

arborist One who cares for and maintains trees.

arbour A shady resting place in a garden.

archegonium The female reproductive organ of a fern or moss.

areole The pit on a cactus stem or pad from which the flower or spine develops.

aril An extra, often coloured, coat or appendage to a seed.

armyworm A grass eating caterpillar.

Horticultural Dictionary

aroid A plant with small flowers crowded into the spadix, surrounded by a spathe.

asexual Methods of propagation excluding seed.

attenuated Long and tapering, usually of leaves.

auxin A hormone which controls plant growth.

awn A bristle-like projection, mostly on grass seeds.

axil The junction between a stem and a leaf.

axis The central stalk of a compound leaf or flower cluster, the main stem of a plant.

bacillus A genus of biological insecticides which are usually non-toxic.

backbulb An old pseudobulb on an orchid which can be used for propagation.

backcross A plant derived from a cross between a hybrid and one of its parents.

backfill Returning soil to the planting hole once the plant is in position.

bare-root Lifted out of the ground when dormant .

bark The tough covering of woody trunks.

basal break A new shoot which emerges from the base of a plant.

basal leaf A new leaf which emerges at the base of an herbaceous plant.

beard Hairs found on the lower petals of bearded iris.

bed An isolated flower or vegetable plot.

bedding out Filling in a bed with a mass of identical flowers.

bedding plant A fast-growing plant used to create a mass, short-term display.

bee plant Attracting bees and yields pollen and nectar.

bell jar A glass, bell-shaped jar used as a modern cloche to protect plants.

beneficial insect Controls harmful pests, improves the soil or pollinates plants.

berry A fleshy fruit with one to many seeds developed from a single ovary.

biennial A plant which germinates in the first year and grows foliage, producing flowers, setting seed and dying in the second.

bifurcate Forked or divided, as of branches.

binomial The two-name system of plant naming. The first part is the genus, the second the species.

biological control Uses predators and parasites to control pests.

biota The combined flora and fauna of a region.

bisexual Having both stamens and pistils in the same flower.

black spot A fungal disease of roses, causing unsightly black spots on leaves.

blade Broad flat part of a leaf.

bleeding The sap exuded by some plants when cut.

bloom A plant in flower. Also a whitish powdery or waxy coating on some fruits or plant parts.

blossom end rot Often affects tomatoes.

bog An area of soft, naturally waterlogged land.

bog garden A landscaped natural or artificial bog kept damp.

bole Trunk of a tree from the ground to the lowest branch.

bolting Prematurely seeding.

bonemeal A natural high-phosphorous fertilizer made from crushed and powdered animal bones. Stimulates root growth.

bonsai The Japanese art of pruning and shaping trees and shrubs.

border Usually a long, narrow garden bed, backed by shrubs, walls etc.

borer Grubs or larvae which bore into trees.

botanic(al) garden Primarily an institution for research in the field of botany, horticulture.

botanical A natural insecticide.

botanical Latin The universal language of the plant world.

botanize To collect plants for study

botany The science and study of plants.

botrytis A fungus which forms grey mouldy patches.

bottom heat Heat applied to the bottom of propagating beds to speed or aid germination of seeds or the rooting of cuttings.

bottom watering Watering into a tray and letting the water soak up from the bottom of pots to wet soil.

bough A branch of a tree.

bower A shady resting place in a garden.

bract A special modified leaf at

Horticultural Dictionary

bramble — the base of a flower or inflorescence. Shrubs such as blackberry or raspberry with prickly or thorny stems.

branch — A secondary woody stem or limb growing from the main trunk or stem.

branch collar — The swelling where a branch joins the trunk of a tree.

broad-leaved evergreen — Evergreen trees, shrubs which are not conifers.

broadcast — To sow seeds evenly but not in rows.

bromeliad — Epiphytic plant.

bud — A young, undeveloped leaf, flower, shoot.

bud union — The place on the stem of a plant where the scion or bud is joined to the rootstock or trunk.

bulb — A storage organ, usually formed underground.

bulbil — A small bulb-like organ found in the axil of a leaf.

bulblet — A small bulb produced at the base of a larger bulb.

bur — Rough or prickly husk or covering of a seed ,fruit.

bush — A many-branched small shrub with no distinct main stem.

bypass pruning shears — Pruners which cut with a scissor-like action.

caliche — Hard deposit of white limestone which some times underlies alkaline soils in arid climates.

callus — The corklike tissue developed to cover wounds in the bark of trees or shrubs.

calyx — The outer part of a flower, with the petals in bud.

cambium — A layer of cells which divide to produce new tissue in plant stems.

cane — A long, woody pliable stem.

canker — A sunken area on woody stems or twigs.

canopy — The uppermost layer in wood or forest, formed by the crown of trees.

capillary matting — Mats which retain moisture to water plants.

capillary water — Moisture held in the tiny spaces between soil particles.

capitate — Forming a dense compact head of flowers.

capsule — A dry seedpod which splits open when ripe.

carnivorous plant — A plant which captures and digests insects.

carpel — The female reproductive organs of a flower - ovary, stigma and style.

carpet bedding — a mass planting of low, mostly foliage patterns.

catkin — A cluster of small, petalless, flowers.

caudex — The stem base of a woody plant .

caulescent — Having an obvious stem usually above ground.

cauline — Usually of leaves growing on a stem.

cedar-apple rust — A fungal disease which affects juniper, apple and crab apple.

cell — The basic structural unit of an organaism.

cell pack — A container which keeps roots separate.

cellulose — Main constituent of the cell walls in most plants.

centripetal — Developing or progressing inward toward the centre or axis.

chaff — Thin, dry bracts or scales borne among the small individual flowers of the daisy family. Also, those enclosing mature grains of wheat and other cereal plants.

chelate — A chemical compound to treat plants suffering from chlorosis

chinch bug — A destructive insect whose tiny larvae suck the sap from grasses.

chloroblast — The cellular body containing chlorophyll for photosynthesis.

chlorophyll — The green pigment in plant leaves which captures light and uses its energy to manufacture food in the process of photosynthesis.

chlorosis — Deficiency of iron or magnesium, leaves turn pale or yellowish.

cilium — One of the hairs along the margin or edge of a leaf.

cladode — A stem with the function, appearance of a leaf.

clay soil — Soil of small particles, with a large capacity for holding water.

cleistogamous — The development of seed from an un-opened, self-pollinated flower.

climate zones — Devised in US/ Canada to represent different climatic conditions for hardiness of plants.

climber — A plant which uses tendrils, twining stems,

Horticultural Dictionary

adhesive rootlets or other means of support to climb.

cloche A protective structure of glass or plastic.

clone A group of genetically identical plants vegetatively propagated from a single parent.

clubroot A disease which affects members of the cabbage family. Stunts plants.

codling moth An insect whose larvae feeds inside apples.

cold compost Compost decomposing at air temperature.

cold frame A low, bottemless structure used to shelter small plants.

collar A bottomless band placed around certain plants at soil level to protect from cutworms.

column The fused structure of the union of the pistils and stamen in orchids, or the stamens of mallows.

companion planting Growing plants together which help one another.

complete fertiliser One which supplies nitrogen, phosphorous and potassium.

complete flower Has normal flower parts i.e. sepals, petals, stamens and pistil.

composite The daisy family.

compost Decomposed organic matter. A fertiliser and soil conditioner.

compost material Includes small quantities of grass, dead plants, twigs and vegetable kitchen waste.

compost tea The liquid drained from compost .Can be diluted and used as a fertiliser.

compound leaf A leaf with two or more leaflets branching off a single petiole (stalk).

cone Seed-bearer of conifers.

conifer A tree or shrub, usually evergreen, with needlelike leaves.

coniferous Of or relating to conifers.

contact insecticide A chemical which kills on contact. It does not have to be ingested.

container gardening Growing in containers.

container grown Raised in a pot which is removed before planting.

container plant A plant which stays in a pot for its entire life.

contorted Twisted spirally.

controlled-release fertiliser A synthetic fertiliser, often in coated capsules, which release nutrients over a period of time.

coppice A thicket or grove of small trees and shrubs. Periodic cutting, pruning almost to ground level.

cordon A tree or shrub, especially fruit, pruned and trained to grow on a support as a single rope-like stem.

cork The nonliving, water resistant outer tissue of bark.

cork cambium A layer of cells in the stem of woody plants which produce the outer bark.

cork cambium Produces the outer bark which protects woody stems and roots.

corm A solid, bulb-like underground storage organ. Roots at the base.

cormel A small corm, produced and nourished at the base of a mature one.

cormlet A small corm, produced and nourished at the base of a mature one.

Cornell mix Cornell University soilless potting mixture.

corolla The part of a flower formed by the petals.

corona A crown-like structure on some corollas.

cortex Layer of cells in the roots and stems inside the epidermis of herbaceous plants

corymb A flat-topped cluster of flowers which begin blooming at the edge and proceed towards the centre. Inner flower stalks are shorter than the outer.

cotyledon Seed leaves. A food-storage organ in seeds. Monocots have one cotyledon, dicots two.

cover crop A quick-growing crop used to cover exposed ground, prevent erosion, and retard leaching.

creeper Prostrate,trailing plant.

crenulate Minuteley scalloped.

crisped Wavy edged.

crop rotation The planting of different species in rotation to reduce the risk of disease.

cross-pollination Transfer of pollen from a flower on one plant to that on a different plant.

crotch Where a main branch of a tree joins the trunk.

crown 1. Where root and stem meet. 2. The part of a tree or shrub above the level of the lowest branch.

Horticultural Dictionary

Term	Definition
crown gall	A bacterial disease.
culm	A stem, especially of grasses, usually hollow, except at the nodes.
cultivar	Plant variety propagated vegetatively. Cultivar names are shown in single quotation marks.
cultivate	To scratch or dig up the surface of the soil.
cultivator	A pronged tool for soil cultivation.
cushion plant	A tight, ball-like mass of stems with clusters.
cuticle	Waxy surface reducing water loss from leaves.
cutting	A section of a plant for propagation.
cutworm	A smooth, wormlike moth larva that feeds near the soil.
cyme	A branched flower cluster in which each growing point results in a flower.
cytology	The scientific study of cells
damping off	Fungal disease which attacks seedlings.
dappled shade	The shade provided by trees whose branches and leaves allow some sunlight to pass through.
day length	The number of hours from sunrise to sunset.
day length sensitive	Flowering, dormancy or growth patterns affected by daylight.
day neutral	Flowering not affected by the length of the day.
dead heading	Removing old flowers encouraging new buds . Prevents seed forming.
deciduous	Trees or shrubs which drop their leaves yearly.
declinate	Bent downward or forward.
decumbent	Lying on the ground with growing tips turned upward.
deflexed	Bent or turned abruptly downward at a sharp angle.
defoliant	A chemical which causes leaves to be shed.
dehiscence	The naturally occurring opening of a seedpod to release seeds, or of an anther to release pollen.
dendroid	Tree-like in form not size.
dendrology	Botanical study of trees.
dense	Thick, compact, crowded
dentate	Toothed. Dentatus.
denticulate	Fine toothed.
determinate	Terminal growth stopped by the production of a flower and fruit cluster.
diatomaceous earth	An abrasive powder.
dibber	A pointed tool for planting seedlings.
dichotomous	Forking into two equal branches at the growing point.
dicot	Short for dicotyledon.
dicotyledon	Having two cotyledons in the seed and usually a netlike pattern of veins on the leaf blades and flower parts in groups of four or five.
dieback	Death of a plant's stems.
diffuse	Of a loose, open habit.
dimorphic	A species which exists in two distinct forms, can be on the same plant as in the young and the mature foliage of English ivy.
dioecious	Male and female flowers on separate plants.
direct seeding	Sowing seeds directly in the ground where they are to flower.
disbudding	Removing most of the immature buds from a plant to boost the size of the remaining ones.
disc	The centre of the flowers of the daisy family.
dissected	A leaf whose blade is divided into many slender segments, the clefts not reaching the midrib.
diurnal	A flower which only opens during daytime.
division	A means of propagation by separating a clump into pieces.
dormancy	Reduced activity.
dorsal sepal	Uppermost 'petal' of a flower, in orchids.
double digging	A method of cultivation to two spade depths.
double-flowered	More than the usual number of petals.
downy mildew	A disease cause by fungi and spread by windblown spores.
drainage	Movement of water down through the soil.
dried blood	Natural fertiliser.
drift	A group of plants.
drill	A narrow trench for planting seeds.
drill hoe	A hoe with a triangular blade, used to make the trench for planting seeds.
drip feed	A system of pipes, hoses or emitters which deliver a slow trickle of water and fertiliser onto the soil.
drip irrigation	Similar to drip feed, only carries water.
drip line	An imaginary line on the

soil around a tree, mirrors the circumference of the branches above.

drooping Pendent or hanging.

drupe A fleshy, one-seeded fruit that does not split.

drupelets Small drupes, such as those on raspberries, held together by almost invisible hairs.

dry wall A stone wall constructed without mortar.

dry well A hole filled with rocks and gravel, to absorb water which would otherwise flood the area.

Dutch hoe A hoe with a flat blade that works by being pushed away from the user.

dwarf Shorter and or slower growing than the normal.

echinate Bearing stiff, prickly hairs.

ecology 1. The scientific study of the relationships between plants, animals and the environment.
2. The study of the detrimental effects of man on the environment.

ecosystem A community of plants, animals and their environment, with a view toward prevention through conservation.

edging A shallow physical barrier to define a border.

edging plant A neat, low-growing plant planted next to the turf or a path.

edible landscape Growing edible plants.

embryo The rudimentary plant contained within a seed.

encarsia wasp A beneficial wasp.

endemic Having a natural distribution within a geographic area.

entire Leaves which have a smooth edge with no teeth or lobes.

ephemeral A plant which flowers for a very short time.

epiphyte A plant which attaches itself to another plant for support. Not parasites.

ericaceous The heath family.

espalier A shrub or tree which has been trained to grow flat against a wall or support.

ethnobotany The scientific study of plant lore and agricultural customs of traditional societies.

ethylene Gaseous plant hormone which promotes stem thickening and the development of flowers

etiolated in some species. Describes the condition of a plant grown in darkness or low light.

everblooming Of roses which flower over a long period.

evergreen A plant which retains its leaves for more than one annual cycle of growth. The term sempervirens.

everlasting A plant whose flowers can be dried successfully.

exfoliating Bark which peels.

exotic A plant which is native to one part of the world but has been introduced elsewhere.

exposure The intensity, duration and variation in sun, wind and temperature, typical of a particular site.

eye 1. A bud on a cutting, tuber or tuberous root.
2. A dark spot at the centre of a flower.

f1 hybrid A first-generation offsping of two plants of closely related species or strains. Seed from these plants do not breed true.

f2 hybrid A cross between two f1 hybrids.

falcate Sickle-shaped. Falcatus.

fall The drooping lower petal of the flowers of irises and related plants.

family A group of plants defined by characteristics of flowers and fruit.

farina A powdery deposit naturally occuring on some leaves and flowers.

fasciation An abnormal widening and flattening of a stem, typically of a flower stalk.

fastigiate Branches turning upward and close to the trunk.

feeder roots A dense network of slender branching roots which spread close to the surface of the soil and absorb nutrients.

felted Covered with short, dense hairs.

female A plant having only pistillate flowers.

fern A non-flowering plant reproducing by spores, not seeds, has fronds instead of leaves.

fertile 1. Soil which has a ready supply of nutrients.
2. Seed with an embryo to become a new plant.

fertiliser A substance which contains one or more of

Horticultural Dictionary

the nutrients required for plant growth.

fibril A root hair.

fibrous roots Fine root hairs.

filament The slender stalk which supports the pollen-bearing anther.

filiform Long and thin, threadlike.

fimbriate Fringed, as the edge of a frilly petal or leaf.

fire blight A bacterial disease which causes sudden browning

firm To press down the soil after planting.

first true leaves Having the appearance of the species.

fistulose Hollow and tubular, as the leaf of a scallion or a bamboo culm.

flask-grown A plant grown by micropropagation.

flat A shallow tray for starting seeds, holding or carrying cell packs or pots.

flea beetle A tiny dark beetle which feeds on seedlings.

flesh Pulpy, normally edible part of fruit, vegetable.

flocculate To cause soil to form clumps or masses.

flora All kinds of plants.

floret A small flower.

floriculture The raising of flowers.

floriferous Having flowers, often many flowers.

florilegium A collection of flowers, a book on plants.

flower The reproductive organ of most garden plants.

flower head An inflorescence which appears to be a single flower. Made up of a dense cluster of florets.

flush A sudden burst of bloom.

foliage plant Grown mainly for leaves.

foliar feeding Applying a liquid fertiliser to leaves.

follicle A dry, single-chambered fruit, splits along only one seam to release its seed.

forb A broad-leaved herbaceous plant which grows alongside grasses.

forcing Artificially changing light and temperature to accelerate growth.

fork The point at which two branches divide.

form A subdivision of a variety, differing in one characteristic. The botanical term forma.

formal garden A garden in regular geometric patterns with defined paths and pruned and clipped hedges.

friable Loose, crumbly and easily worked soil texture.

frond The leaflike part of a fern, the leaf of a palm.

frost pocket A low-lying place where late and early frosts are more likely than in surrounding areas.

frost-free Tender plants which need to be kept under conditions where frost is not likely to affect them.

fruit The mature or ripened ovary of a flower, containing one or more seeds. E.g. a berry or nut.

fruit fly Tiny flies which lay eggs on fruit, causing rot.

fruiting body Spore-producing organ found in fungi, mosses.

fruticose Shrubby. The botanical term frutescens.

full shade Shade of mature trees.

full sun A location which receives a minimum of six hours direct sun each day in the growing season.

fungicide A compound which inhibits the growth of fungal organisms.

fungus Plants which lack chlorophyll and feed on organic matter.

furcate Forked.

furrow A narrow trench made by spade, hoe or plough.

fusarium wilt Soilborne fungal disease.

gall An abnormal growth on a plant.

gamete A sex cell, either sperm or egg, capable of fusing with another gamete of the opposite sex to form a fertilised egg.

gazebo A roofed, open-sided garden structure.

genera Plural of genus

generic Of or relating to a genus.

genus A group of plant species with similarities in flower form and often in general appearance, growth habit and cultural needs.

germination Initial sprouting of seed.

gibberellin A plant hormone which can be artificially applied to affect the formation of flowers and size of fruit.

gill A finlike structure on the underside of the cap of a mushroom.

girdle To remove or damage the bark around a trunk in a complete ring, causing death to the tree.

girdling root A root which has coiled

glabrous around the inside of a pot. Smooth, having no hairs. Look out for the botanical term glaber.

glade An open space in a wood.

glasshouse Greenhouse.

glaucous Covered with a bluish, greyish,or whitish waxy coating or bloom, easily brushed off.The botanical term glaucus.

globose Spherical. The botanical term globosus.

glochid A barbed bristle or hair, usually found on cactus.

grade 1. The slope on a piece of ground. 2. To smooth or level a ground.

graft union The place on the stem of a plant where the scion or bud is joined to the rootstock or trunk.

grafting A method of propagation involving the artificial union of two plants.

granular fertiliser Dry, pelleted fertiliser which can be mixed into the soil or spread over the surface of a garden bed.

green manure A quick-growing crop which is cut down and dug in to the soil to decompose and provide nutrients and humus.

grey mould see botrytis

ground cover A continuous low mass of foliage.

growing medium Potting soil or other material in which a container plant is grown.

growing on Caring for a seedling or rooted cutting which has been transplanted.

growing point The tip of a stem where new growth occurs.

growing season Average number of days from the last spring frost to the first of autumn.

growth regulator Chemical to alter the natural growth of plants.

growth retardant A chemical used to reduce plant size.

growth ring The ring of wood developed in each growing season,clearly seen on a cross-section of a tree trunk.

grub The larva of many kinds of beetles.

grub out To clear an area of roots and stumps.

guano Bird droppings which make excellent manure.

gymnosperms One of the two largest groups of plants in the plant kingdom. Form their seeds in the open spaces of cones.

gypsum A mineral, calcium sulphate, adds calcium to the soil to improve texture. Of particular use on clay soils. Does not affect pH.

gypsy moth A type of silk moth which feeds on the leaves of hardwood trees.

ha-ha A deep ditch.

habit The characteristic form or shape of a plant.

habitat The area or type of environment in which a plant or an ecological community normally lives or occurs.

half shade Receiving alternating sun and shade.

half-hardy Plants which can tolerate a slight frost.

half-ripened Current year's wood on a plant still in active growth.

halophyte A plant tolerant of a large amount of salt in the soil.

hardening off The gradual exposure of a plant raised under shelter to cold, heat, sun and wind.

hardiness A plant's ability to withstand cold or frost.

hardiness zones A system used in the USA and Canada to denote hardiness.

hardpan A layer of compacted subsoil which often prevents the penetration of water or of roots.

hardscape The permanent features in a garden.

hardwood That produced by broad-leaved flowering trees or shrubs.

hardwood cutting A cutting of the previous season's growth taken from a dormant tree or shrub.

hardy A term used to describe a plant which is capable of surviving freezing temperatures.

hay Dried stems of grass and other herbaceous plants.

heart rot Decay of internal plant tissue, most commonly in root vegetable or trees.

heartwood The dead wood at the centre of a trunk or branch of a tree.

heath Open land covered with scrub or low plants.

heaving The uprooting of newly planted or shallow-rooted specimens in

Horticultural Dictionary

heavy soil — winter, due to frost. Clay soil.

heel cutting — A cutting made from a side shoot with part of the main stem attached.

heeling in — Temporary storage by covering a plant's roots with soil.

heirloom — Generally a cultivar of a flowering plant or vegetable in cultivation for at least 50 years.

herb — Plant grown for medicinal or culinary purposes.

herbaceous — A plant which naturally dies down at the end of the growing season.

herbaceous border — A perennial border.

herbal — A book describing plants.

herbarium — An institution housing a collection of dried plants for scientific study.

herbicide — A chemical to kill plants.

hilum — The scar on a seed coat marking the place where it was attached to the ovary in development.

hip — The closed and ripened firm or fleshy fruit of a rose containing seeds.

holdfast — An aerial root on the stems of vines which enable them to climb by attaching themselves.

honeydew — The sweet, sticky substance secreted by aphids and other sap-sucking insects.

horizon — Layer within a soil profile.

horticulture — The cultivation of plants for ornament or food.

hose-in-hose — A form of flower which appears to have another growing from its centre.

host — Plant supporting a parasite.

hot cap — An individual cone-shaped cover to protect new plants.

hotbed — An enclosed bed of soil heated with fermenting manure, or a heated cable, used to germinate seeds or protect seed lings or tender plants.

hothouse — A heated greenhouse.

humus — Organic matter, partially decomposed plant material, animal remains.

hybrid — A plant resulting from the cross between two parents which belong to different varieties, cultivars, species or, rarely genera.

hybrid vigour — Hybrids which grow stonger than parents.

hydroponics — Growing plants with their roots immersed in containers of a nutrient solution other than soil.

hypertufa — A man-made imitation of lightweight tufa rock.

ikebana — Japanese formal flower arrangement.

imbricate — Describes leaves or petals which overlap.

immortelle — Everlasting.

inbred seed — Seed of a bisexual plant pollinating itself.

incise — To make a cut in a leaf or stem before grafting.

indefinite — Flower with numerous petals, or inflorescense with numerous florets.

indehiscent — Fruits which do not split open to release seeds or anthers which do not open to discharge pollen.

indeterminate — Stems which can grow after flowering starts.

indigenous — Native to an area.

indumentum — Coating of hairs on under side of some leaves.

infertile — Soils lacking in nutrients.

inflorescence — Clusters of flowers.

infundibular — Funnel-shaped.

inorganic fertiliser — A chemical product, mineral or synthetic which provides nutrients for plant growth.

insecticidal soap — An insecticidal spray.

insecticide — Kills insects.

insectivorous — Plants which trap and digest insects.

integument — The coating of an ovule which becomes the skin of a seed.

Inter species hybrid — Indicated by x between the species.

inter-nodal cutting — One taken from the stem between nodes.

intercropping — Planting rows of fast-maturing plants between rows of slower-growers.

intergeneric cross — A hybrid cross between plants of two different genera.

internode — The section of stem between two adjacent nodes.

interplant — To combine plants with different flowering times or growth habits.

interrupted — An inflorescence which has flowers unevenly distributed along the axis, with conspicuous gaps.

interspecific cross — A hybrid between two species.

intraspecific cross — A hybrid between plants of the same species.

Horticultural Dictionary

invasive — An aggressive plant.

involucre — Whorls of small leaves or bracts, arranged directly underneath a flower.

iron — A nutrient needed to make chlorophyll.

iron chelate — Useful for adding to soils deficient in iron.

irregular flower — A flower with petals which are not uniform in size or shape.

island bed — An isolated flower or vegetable plot, visible from all sides.

Japanese beetle — A destructive beetle which eats the roots of grass and other plants.

John Innes compost — Potting soils developed by the John Innes Horticultural Institute.

June drop — The normal early dropping of some immature fruits of apple and other trees.

juvenile foliage — Distinct form of young foliage unlike the adult foliage of the same plant.

K — Chemical symbol for potassium.

keel — A sharp ridge or rib on the underside of a petal, leaf or other plant part.

keiki — An orchid plantlet developing on a node on the stem or cane.

key — A winged seed.

kitchen garden — A plot or garden planted with vegetables and herbs used in cooking. May also include flowers.

knot garden — A formal bed in an intricate pattern.

labellum — Lip.

labiate — Flower parts arranged into two lips.

lacewing — A beneficial insect .

lanceolate — Lance-like, longer than wide, usually refers to leaves. Hence the botanical lanceolatus.

lateral — Attached to or at the side, a bud in the axil of a leaf.

lax — A term which describes the loose or floppy habit of some plants.

layering — A method of propagation. A stem is fastened down to the ground and partially covered with soil.

leaching — The loss of nutrients when they are carried through the soil by water.

leader — The central, upward-growing stem of a single-trunked tree.

leaf cutting — A means of propagating certain tropical plants.

leaf hopper — Any of numerous insects suck juices from plants.

leaf margin — The edge of a leaf.

leaf miner — Small flies and moths whose larvae tunnel through and feed on leaf tissue.

leaf mould — Partially decayed or composted leaves.

leaf roller — Moths.Larvae make nests of rolled leaves.

leaf scar — The mark left on a stem or twig after leaf fall.

leaf spot — Fungal or bacterial diseases which result in spots of various colours on leaves.

leaflet — A subdivision of a compound leaf.

leggy — Tall stalks or shoots with sparse foliage.

legume — The pea family.

lenticel — A breathing pore in the young bark of a woody stem.

lichen — A composite organism formed by the symbiotic association of a fungus and an alga.

light shade — An area receiving full shade for a few hours during the hottest part of the day, or sun and shade throughout the day.

light soil — Sandy soil which dries out rapidly.

ligneous — Woody. Look out for the botanical term lignosus.

lignin — The compound which binds fibres and strengthens the cell wall of plants, giving stiffness to stems and stalks.

limb — A main branch of a tree or shrub.

limbing up — Removing the lower limbs of large trees.

lime, limestone — A mineral compound used to rectify soil acidity and to supply calcium.

limestone — Calcium carbonate

Linnaean system — The binomial naming of plants in Latin.

lip — A lobe of two or more perianth segments.

lithophyte — A plant which grows on rock and derives its nourishment chiefly from the atmosphere.

loam — Soil with moderate amounts of sand, silt and clay.

lobe — A segment of a cleft leaf or petal.

lobed — A leaf whose margin is

Horticultural Dictionary

loess — Wind-deposited, very fine rich soils.

long-day plant — A plant whose flowering is triggered by long hours of light.

loppers — Pruners.

lopping shears — Long-handled pruners with easy-reach for pruning tree branches.

macronutrients — Major elements needed for plant growth.

male — A plant having only staminate flowers.

manure tea — A solution made by soaking manure in water used as a liquid fertiliser.

margin — Edge, border of a leaf.

marginal plant — A plant growing on the edge of water.

marsh — Soft, wet, low-lying land.

mass planting — Filling an area with one or a few kinds of plants spaced closely together.

meadow garden — A mixed planting of wildflowers and grasses.

mealybug — A sucking insect.

medium — Potting soil or other material in which a container plant is grown.

medulla — Pith, the soft tissue at the centre of young shoots and roots.

mericlone — An exact copy of a plant made by meristem propagation.

meristem — An area of actively dividing cells found at the tips of shoots and roots in the cambium.

microclimate — Local conditions which affect plant growth.

micronutrients — Essential elements needed for plant growth in very small quantities.

micropropagation — Making new plants with laboratory techniques, using tiny pieces of the parent plant.

midrib — The central rib or vein of a leaf or leaflet.

mildew — Fungal growth on plants.

monocarpic — A plant which flowers and fruits once then dies.

monocot — Short for monocotyledon

monocotyledon — A plant with one cotyledon, usually with parallel-veined leaves and flower parts arranged in groups of three.

monoecious — Having separate male and female flowers on the same plant.

monopodial — One of two forms of orchid vegetative growth, divided into broad, round segments.

morphology — The study of the form and structure of plants and animals.

mosaic virus — A disease resulting in shrivelled, marked leaves.

moss — Small, flowerless, nonvascular plants.

mowing strip — A flat, level edging between a flower bed and the lawn.

mulch — A layer of organic matter spread over soil to inhibit water loss.

multiflora — Roses or petunias which produce small clusters of flowers.

mutant — Accidental variation in a plant, e.g double flowers, variegated leaves.

mycology — The study of fungi.

mycorrhiza — The association between mycelium and the roots of certain plants.

N — The chemical symbol for nitrogen

naked — Unprotected by scales, lacking a perianth, without leaves.

native — A plant which grows naturally in an area.

naturalised — Establish as if in the wild.

necrosis — The death of plant tissue in small patches in response to disease.

nectar — A sweet substance secreted by some flowers to attract pollinators.

nectary — Gland containing nectar.

neem — A non-toxic botanical insecticide.

nematode — A microscopic roundworm in the soil.

neutral soil — Neither acid nor alkaline, has a pH of 7.

new wood — Stems or branches produced during the current growing season.

nitrogen — One of the main nutrients for plant growth.

nitrogen-fixing bacteria — Live in nodules on roots of the legume family.

no-dig gardening — Spreading mulch on beds and leaving to smother weeds. Plant through the mulch.

nocturnal — Having flowers which open at night.

node — A place on a stem where leaves or branches are attached.

nodule — A small swelling on the roots of some plants

a single vegetative shoot growing continually upward, no branching.

Horticultural Dictionary

which contain bacteria able to absorb nitrogen from the air around roots.

non-selective herbicide A chemical to kill a wide range of plants.

NPK The chemical symbols of the nutrients nitrogen, phosphorous and potassium which make up a complete fertiliser.

nucleus The part of the cell which contains chromosomes.

nursery A place where young plants are propagated.

nursery bed A bed used to grow seedlings or transplants.

nut A large, hard, one-seeded fruit.

nutrients Elements needed for plant growth.

oblate Spherical but slightly flattened at the top and bottom.

obtuse Blunt or rounded tip.

occlusion 1. The closing up of a tree wound by the formation of a callus.
2. The plugging of the xylem by fungi, causing the plant to wilt.

offset A short, lateral shoot arising near the base of a plant and readily producing new roots.

old wood Stems or branches produced one or more years before the current growing season.

open-pollinated Varieties which result from natural pollination.

opposite Describes leaves which are arranged in pairs along a stem or shoot.

orangery A heated glasshouse for growing citrus fruits.

organic Any material which contains carbon compounds and is derived from living or once-living plants or animals.

organic fertiliser An animal or plant product or by-product.

organic gardening Growing plants without the use of chemicals.

organic matter Plant ,animal residues.

organism A living plant, animal, fungus or bacterium.

orientation Direction with regard to points of a compass.

ornamental A plant cultivated for its showy appearance.

ornamental grass Allowed to grow to maturity.

ovary The ovule-bearing part of a pistil which develops into a fruit.

ovate Oval, with the broader end at the base.

overpotting Growing a plant in a pot which is too large for its root system. Results in root growth.

overseeding Sowing seed where other plants are growing.

ovule A group of cells within the ovary which develop into a seed after fertilisation.

oxalic acid A bitter tasting compound in the leaves of some plants.

oxygenator A submerged aquatic plant which releases oxygen into the water.

P The chemical symbol for phosphorous.

palmate Having veins or leaflets arranged like the fingers on a hand, radiating out from the centre point.

pan A shallow, free-draining pot used for alpines or bulbs.

panicle A loose, open, branching cluster of flowers which bloom from the centre or bottom towards the edges or top.

papilla A pimple-like projection on the surface of a petal or leaf.

parasite A plant which lives off a host.

part shade An area in which plants receive alternating sun and shade.

part sun An area in which plants receive alternating sun and shade.

parterre A geometric pattern of ornamental beds separated by paths.

parthenocarpic Describes a plant which can develop fruit without fertilisation.

pathogen An organism whch causes disease.

patio An outdoor paved area.

pea gravel Round, pea-sized gravel used for paths.

peat moss Partially decomposed mosses and sedges taken from boggy areas to improve garden soil.Found in potting compost - a cause for environmental concern.

peat pot A pot for seed sowing, decomposes naturally.

pectin A substance in a cell wall which binds cells.

pedicel — The stalk of an individual flower in an inflorescence or cluster.

peduncle — The stalk of a solitary flower.

pelleted seed — Coated seed.

peltate — Having the stalk attached away from the margin of a leaf, often in the centre. Look out for the botanical term peltatus.

pendent — Drooping, hanging. Look for the botanical term pendulus.

perennial — A plant which lives for a number of years, usually flowering each year.

perfect flower — One which has both male and female parts.

perfoliate — Describes a leaf or pair of leaves which encircle a stem. Thus the botanical term perfoliatus.

pergola — A structure of columns and overhead trellis for climbers.

perianth — All the sepals and petals of a flower.

perianth segment — A portion of the perianth, resembling a petal and referred to as a tepal.

perlite — A lightweight substance which lacks nutrients, used for rooting cuttings and added to soilless potting mixes.

permaculture — Agricultural system based on perennial plants.

perpetual — A plant in bloom more or less continuously.

persistent — 1. Lasting past maturity without falling off. 2. A pesticide which remains effective for a long time after application.

pest — Any insect or creature which damages plants.

pesticide — Any compound used to kill pests.

petal — A flower part.

petaloid — Petal-like.

petiole — Leaf stalk.

pH — A measure of the hydrogen ion content of a substance, showing the acidity or alkalinity of soil.

pH scale — Ranges from pH0 to pH14 to denote acidity or alkalinity.

phenology — The scientific study of periodic biological phenomena.

pheromone — A chemical released by an animal to communicate with others of the same species.

phloem — The food-conducting tissue of plants.

phosphorous — An essential nutrient necessary for plant growth. Responsible for root growth in particular.

photoperiod — The number of hours from sunrise to sunset.

photoperiodism — The response of plants to the length of the day, with regard to flowering.

photosynthesis — Chlorophyll, the green pigment in leaves, takes energy from the light and transforms it into sugars needed for the plant.

phototropism — The tendency of shoots and leaves to grow toward the light.

phyllode — A flattened leaf stalk, functions as and resembles a leaf.

phylum — The first level of division in the plant kingdom.

phytochrome — A pigment in plants which senses daylength and plays a role in controlling flowering, dormancy and seed germination.

phytogeography — The study of the distribution of plants.

pileus — The cap of a mushroom or toadstool.

pinching, pinch out — Removing the top or central growing point to promote development of side shoots.

pinetum — An arboretum or collection of conifers.

pinna — Primary division of a pinnate leaf.

pinnate — Feather-like, with regard to leaves, fronds in two rows on either side of a central stalk.

pip — An offset or individual rootstock of a plant used for propagation.

pistil — The complete female organ of reproduction in flowers.

pith — The soft, sponge-like tissue in the centre of young stems and stalks.

planlet — A tiny plant produced on the leaves of some plants.

plant — Any multicellular organsim in the plant kingdom.

plant lice — Aphids.

plant lights — Specialised lights under which to grow seedlings.

pleaching — A method of pruning and

Horticultural Dictionary

plug A seedling or cutting grown in a plastic tray to minimise root disturbance.

plunge 1. To bury a pot in soil outdoors upto its rim. 2. To water a potted plant by immersing in water until the moisture rises to the surface of the soil.

pod A dry one-celled fruit with thicker walls than a capsule.

pollard To cut back to the main branches of a tree to restrict growth.

pollen Minute grains containing the male germ cells, produced in the anthers of flowers.

pollination The transfer of pollen from stamens to pistils.

pollinator Any agent which transfers pollen.

polyandrous Having a large, indefinite number of stamens.

polygamous Bearing both unisexual and perfect flowers on the same or different plants.

pompon A compact, round-headed flower.

postemergent weedkiller A herbicide which acts on weeds after they have sprouted.

pot-bound A plant with roots confined in a small pot.

potager A French-style vegetable garden, incorporating flowers.

potash Potassium.

potassium One of the essential nutrients for plant growth. Important in the development of flowers and fruits.

potting on Transplanting a plant into the next size pot.

potting up Transplanting seedlings or rooted cuttings from a seed tray into individual pots or containers.

powdery mildew A fungal disease with whitish or greyish residue on leaves.

prairie A habitat of perennial grasses and forbs.

praying mantis A large predatory insect which eats other insects.

precocious Flowering before the appearance of leaves.

predator An insect which preys on another which eat plants.

preemergent weedkiller A herbicide applied before a plant emerges or sprouts, preventing weed seeds from germinating.

pressure treated wood Wood protected against fungi.

pricking out Transplanting seedlings .

prickle A small weak spine which grows from a plant's bark.

primary growth Elongation of the stem or stalk.

primary nutrients Nitrogen, phosphorous and potassium.

procumbent Prostrate, lying on the ground. The botanical term procumbens.

prop root A root acting as a prop or support, originating on the stem.

propagate To produce new plants.

propagule A naturally occurring portion of a plant, except seeds, from which a new plant may develop.

prostrate Lying on the ground, creeping.The botanical term prostratus.

prune To cut back, to keep the plant in good shape, maintain vigour or spur new growth.

pruning saw A saw with a long, narrow cutting blade.

pruning shear Hand held for removing small twigs, stems, branches.

pseudobulb Found on the base of orchids.

pubescent Hairy or downy. Look out for the botanical term pubescens.

pyrethrin A natural contact insecticide.

pyriform pear shaped. Look out for the botanical term pyrifomis.

quicklime Calcium oxide

quilled Having a petal shape like that of a quill pen.

raceme A long inflorescence with individual flowers borne on short, unbranched side stalks off a larger central stalk.

rachis The central axis of a compound leaf or frond to which the leaflets are attached.

radial Spine at the perimeter of an ariole on a cactus.

radicle The primary root of a plant, developed in a seedling, the embryonic root.

rain gauge A device for measuring

Horticultural Dictionary

raised bed — A garden bed built up higher than the surrounding soil.

ray — A flat marginal floret.

receptacle — Expanded tip of a flower stalk or axis which bears floral organs, group of flowers in a head.

recurved — Curved downward or backward, of petals, leaves or hairs. Look for the botanical term recurvatus.

reflexed — Curved downward or backward, of petals, leaves or hairs. Look out for the botanical term reflexus.

regular flower — A flower with petals and sepals arranged around the centre like the spokes of a wheel.

remontant — A plant which flowers more than once a year.

renewal pruning — A method to revive some old, overgrown shrubs by cutting down to the ground in early spring.

repeat bloomer — A plant which flowers more than once a year.

repellent — A substance which is sprayed near plants to ward off animals.

resin — Secretion from conifers.

resistant — A plant immune to a particular disease.

respiration — Oxygen taken up by the plant and carbon dioxide given off.

resting period — A period of suspended growth or dormancy.

retaining wall — A wall constructed to hold back soil.

reticulate — Netlike or weblike, often refers to leaves. Look out for the botanical term reticulatus.

revert — A plant which changes back to its original state.

rhizome — An underground stem acting as a storage organ.

rib — The main vein or prominent ridge or vein of a leaf or other plant organ.

riddle — A large-meshed sieve.

rock garden — A landscape created with rocks and alpines.

rogue — 1. A plant different to typical members of its species.

rogue out — To weed out inferior plants.

root — The underground portion of a plant which anchors the amount of rainfall. it and absorbs water and nutrients from the soil.

root ball — The roots and soil of a plant.

root crops — Plants whose edible portion is the root.

root cutting — A piece of root used for propagation.

root hairs — The invisible hairs on tip ends of the root through which the plant absorbs water and dissolved nutrients.

root pruning — Cutting back the roots of trees .

root rot — Fungal diseases which attack plants.

root run — The area in the soil taken up by the roots of a plant.

root-bound — A term used to describe a plant left too long in a container with roots subsequently tangled and densely crowded.

rooting hormone — An auxin which stimulates cuttings to produce roots.

rootstock — A well-rooted plant, used in grafting.

rose — A nozzle on a hose or watering can.

rosette — A low flat cluster of leaves.

rotenone — A natural contact insecticide which is toxic to both humans and animals.

runner — A slender shoot growing along the ground and used for propagation.

rust — Fungal disease causing rusty-looking spots on leaves and stems.

sabadilla — A natural contact insecticide in high doses toxic to bees.

samara — A dry winged seed.

sand — The worn grains of rock, one of the largest minerals which form the basis of soil.

sandy soil — Soil with large particles which drains quickly.

sap — The fluid in plants.

sapling — A young tree.

saprophyte — A plant , without chlorophyll, which feeds on dead or decaying organic matter.

sapwood — The layer of wood in a tree between the heartwood and the bark, through which nutrients and water pass.

sawfly — A wasp-like insect whose larvae feed on the foliage

Horticultural Dictionary

scab and fruit of many plants. Fungal diseases which cause rough raised spots on leaves and fruit.

scaffolding Limiting the number of branches, especially on fruit trees.

scald A superficial discoloration on some plants caused by sudden exposure to intense sunlight.

scale 1. A small, often dry, leaf or bract. 2. A small sucking insect. 3. Part of a conifer cone.

scandent A climbing plant without tendrils. Look out for the botanical term scandens.

scape A flower stalk which grows directly from the base of a plant.

scarify To scratch or nick the hard coating of a seed.

scion A detached shoot of a woody plant, containing two or more buds, used in grafting.

sclerification The hardening of cells by the formation of a secondary wall and the deposit of lignin, woodiness.

sclerosis The hardening of cells by the formation of a secondary wall and the deposit of lignin, woodiness.

scorch A browning of leaves.

scree A mixture of gravel, sand and small stones for growing alpine plants.

scrub Stunted trees, shrubs.

scurfy Covered with tiny, broad scales.

scythe Implement for cutting long grass.

secateurs Handheld pruners.

secondary growth Growth resulting in the thickening of the stem, stalk or root produced by cell division in the vascular cambium.

secondary nutrients Needed in small quantities.

sedge A grass-like plant.

seed A fertilised, ripened ovule containing a fruit.

seed bank An organisation which preserves old varieties.

seed head Holds the ripe seeds.

seed leaf The first leaf (or pair) produced by the embryo of the seed

plant.seedling A young plant raised from seed.

seep hose Hose with perforations to allow water to soak into the ground.

selection The best plants for propagation purposes.

selective herbicide A chemical to kill selective plants.

selective weedkiller A herbicide which kills some plants only.

self-branching Plants which do not need pinching out, but produce side shoots of their own accord.

self-pollination The transfer of pollen from one flower to the same or other flowers on the same plant.

self-seed A plant which seeds itself with no help.

selfing Manually pollinating a flower by placing its pollen on its own stigma.

semi-evergreen Retaining at least some foliage throughout winter.

semi-hardwood cutting Taken from new growth of a woody plant after the stems have partially matured.

sepal Flower part, arranged in a ring outside the petals. Collectively, they make up the calyx.

serrate Having sharp, forward-pointing teeth on the margin, usually of leaves. Look out for the botanical term serratus.

sessile Stalkless, attached directly to the main stem. Look out for the botanical term sessilis.

set A small bulb instead of seed, of onions.

shear To prune, cutting back all stems.

sheath An organ surrounding the base of a stalk.

shoot A stem above ground, which bears leaves.

short-day plant A plant which flowers when days grow short.

short-lived perennial One which only lives for a few years, although they often self-seed.

shredder A machine to chop material for composting.

shrub A woody plant with several stems, usually shorter than a tree.

shy-flowering Reluctant to flower.

silt Soil with medium sized particles, larger than clay, smaller than sand.

simple leaf A leaf with only one blade, not divided into leaflets.

slaked lime Calcium hydroxide

Horticultural Dictionary

slip — A cutting taken for grafting or rooting.

slow-release fertiliser — A natural fertiliser releasing nutrients gradually.

sludge — An organic fertiliser from dried processed sewage.

sod — A section of grass-covered surface soil.

soft-stemmed — Opposite of woody-stemmed.

softwood cutting — A cutting taken from young, soft tips or stems of herbaceous and woody plants.

soil — The thin layer of weathered rock particles and organic matter, containing water and tiny air spaces, provides support and nutrients for plant growth.

soil horizon — The layers in the uppercrust of the earth- topsoil, subsoil etc.

soil profile — The layers or horizons of soil.

soil sample — Several trowels of soil mixed together.

soil test — A way of measuring the pH and nutrients of soil.

soilless gardening — Growing plants with their roots immersed in containers of a nutrient solution other than soil.

soilless mix — A medium which contains no soil.

solarisation — A non-toxic method of killing weeds and insect pests by covering the ground with layers of clear plastic.

solitary — Borne singly or alone, not in clusters.

soluble fertiliser — A powdered synthetic fertiliser used mixed with water.

sooty mildew — A fungus which leaves dusty, grey spots on the leaves and stems.

sour soil — Extremely acid soil.

spadix — A fleshy, club-like spike bearing minute flowers, usually enclosed in a sheath-like spathe.

spathe — A leaf-like bract which encloses a flower cluster or spadix.

species — A group of individual plants which share the same characteristics and interbreed freely. The second part of the binomial system.

specific epithet — The second word in the binomial system, designating the species.

specimen plant — A plant conspicuously placed to show off its ornamental value.

sphagnum — A type of moss.

spike — An elongated flower cluster with individual flowers borne on very short stalks or attached directly to the main stem. Look out for the botanical term spicatus.

spine — A sharp, stiff projection. Look out for the botanical tern spinosus.

spit — A spadeful of soil.

sporangium — Spore-producing body.

spore — The microscopic means of reproduction of some flowerless plants.

sport — A plant showing a natural mutation with different characteristics to the parent.Can be used to propagate a new plant.

spreader — A device for spreading fertiliser or seeds evenly.

spreading plant — A plant whose branches grow fairly horizontally.

sprig — An ornamental small branch.

sprout — 1. The first shoot from a seed. 2. To begin to grow.

spur — 1. A tubular elongation of the petals or sepals. 2. A short, specialised fruit-bearing branch on apple and other trees.

squamous — Scaly. Look out for the botanical term squamatus.

stalk — The stem of any organ.

stamen — The male reproductive organ of a flower, including anther and filament.

staminate — Male, having stamens.

standard — 1. A plant trained to grow a round, bushy head of branches with just one single upright stem of a certain length. 2. A full-size fruit tree. 3. The erect central petals of for example irises.

stem — The main axis of a plant.

stem cutting — A cutting taken from the stem, not its tip or apex.

sterile — 1. A flower without any functional sexual parts. 2. A plant unable to produce seed. 3. Soil heated to a high temperature to kill weed seed and pathogens. 4. A growing medium

Horticultural Dictionary

stigma — containing no pathogens. The receptive apex of the pistil of a flower, where pollen is deposited.

stipe — Stalk of a fern frond.

stipule — A small scale or leaf-like appendage. Look out for the botanical term stipularis.

stolon — A horizontally spreading or arching stem, usually above ground, which roots at its tip to produce a new plant. Look out for the botanical term stoloniferus.

stomata — Pores on a plant's leaves.

stop — To remove growing point to control size.

stratify — Expose seeds to the cold.

strike — To send out roots, of cuttings.

style — The elongated part of a pistil between the stigma and the ovary.

subsoil — The mineral soil of decomposed rocks, without any humus, which lies directly beneath the topsoil.

subspecies — A naturally occurring geographical variant of a species.

substrate — 1. An underlying layer, referring to soil. 2. A medium used for growing plants especially in laboratory exeriments.

succession planting — Planting repeatedly for a continuous supply.

succulent — A plant with thick, fleshy leaves or stems which can store water. Look out for the botanical term succulentus.

sucker — A shoot arising from an underground bud on the roots or rootstock of a plant. Remove from parent plant.

suckering — The tendency of a plant to develop suckers.

sunken garden — The lowest part of a garden landscaped on different levels.

superphosphate — A high-phosphate fertiliser for planting.

surfactant — A soap-like compound added to liquid to increase its wetting properties.

sustainable agriculture — A system of gardening or farming without damage to the soil.

swamp — Seasonally flooded land.

sweet soil — Llimy or alkaline.

symbiosis — A relationship between two different organisms, with mutual benefit.

systemic insecticide — One which is absorbed into the tissues of the plant, repels or kills most pests feeding upon it.

tamping — Gently pressing down the soil on top of seeds or around roots.

tannin — A substance found in leaves and bark of some plants which protects against insects and fungi.

taproot — A long tapering root with little or no side growth.

taxonomy — The classification of organisms in an ordered system which indicates natural relationships.

tender — A plant which cannot withstand frost or very cold temperatures.

tender perennial — A perennial which will not survive winter without protection in cold areas.

tendril — A modified stem used by the plant to give support by clinging.

tentacle — A sensitive hair or filament on a carnivorous plant.

tepals — Sepals and petals which are similar in size, shape and colour.

terminal — Borne at the tip of a stem or shoot. Look out for the botanical term terminalis.

terrarium — A transparent container with a cover in which plants are grown in soil.

terrestrial — Of the earth, grown in the ground. Look out for the botanical term terrestris.

tetraploid — Having twice the number of chromosomes.

thatch — An impenetrable mat occuring on lawns.

thicket — A dense area of scrubby undergrowth, small trees and shrubs.

thimble pot — A small flowerpot.

thin soil — Shallow soil, poor in nutrient and or humus.

thinning — Pulling out seedlings to give space to the ones which remain.

thinning out — Pruning at the base of a branch or stem, to thin the plant.

thorn — A sharp outgrowth on a stem.

thrips — A tiny insect which feeds on leaves, flowers, buds and stems.

Horticultural Dictionary

throat — On flowers with partially or fully fused petals, the place where the corolla lobes lead into the tube.

thug — Invasive plant .

thumb pot — A pot slightly larger than a thimble.

till — To prepare land for growing, to cultivate.

tilth — A fine, crumbly soil texture.

timed-release fertiliser — A synthetic fertiliser, often in coated capsules, which release nutrients over a period of time.

timed-release insecticide — One encapsulated in tiny particles which break down gradually over a period of time.

tip cutting — A soft wood or semi-hardwood cutting made from the tip of a shoot.

tired soil — Soil exhausted by crops, lacking nutrients.

tissue culture — A laboratory technique of propagating new plants from tiny portions of the parent plant.

toothed — A leaf whose margin is shallowly divided into tooth-like segments. Look out for the botanical term dentatus.

top-dress — 1. Applying compost or soil conditioner without turning it into the soil. 2. Spreading of fresh soil over a newly seeded patch of lawn. 3. Removing the top layer of soil and adding a fresh layer of compost to a container plant.

topiary — The art of shaping and pruning a tree or shrub into a desired shape.

topping — Pruning most of the crown of a tree.

topsoil — Soil with humus and mineral elements.

trace elements — Essential elements needed for plant growth in very small quantities.

trailing — A plant whose stems trail along the ground.

transpiration — The normal loss of water through a plant's leaves.

transplant — Moving a seedling or plant to a permanent site.

tree — A perennial woody plant with usually one main trunk and a distinct crown.

tree wrap — Protects a young tree.

trellis — Ornamental slat fencing.

trickle irrigation — See drip irrigation.

trifoliate — Having leaves in groups of three. Look out for the botanical term trifoliatus, and the genus Trifolium.

tropism — A reaction to an external stimulus, such as light.

trough — Stone sinks for alpines.

true — Seedlings which bear the characteristics of the parent plant when raised from seed.

truss — A compact cluster of flowers.

tuber — A swollen underground storage system, modified from a root or rhizome, with buds where new shoots and roots develop after a dormant period. Look out for the botanical term tuberosus.

tubercle — A small tuber.

tufted — Growing in tufts or dense clusters.

tunic — A loose membranous outer covering of a bulb or corm which should remain intact.

turion — 1. A bud on a rhizome. 2. An overwintering bud found on water plants.

tussock — A grass-covered mound.

twining vine — Climbs by wrapping its stem around a support.

umbel — 1. A flower cluster in which the individual flower stalks emerge from the same point on the stem, like the ribs of an umbrella.

underbrush, undergrowth — Low-growing plants in a forest or woodland.

understory — The smaller trees under large specimens in a woodland or forest.

union — The place on the stem of a plant where the scion or bud is joined to the rootstock or trunk.

unisexual flower — A flower bearing only stamens or pistils, but not both.

upright — With vertical or semi-vertical main branches.

variegated — Leaves of two colours.

variety — Plants which differ consistently from the typical form of the species, occurring naturally. Indicated by the word varietas.

vascular bundle — A strand of tissue containing both the xylem and the phloem in the young stems, leaves

Horticultural Dictionary

vascular cambium Responsible for the thickening or increase in girth of a stem.

vascular plant A plant containing food-conducting tissues (the phloem) and water-conducting tissues (the xylem).

vegetation The plants in an area or region.

vegetative bud Contains a leaf or a shoot but not a flower.

vegetative propagation The production of new plants by means other than seed.

vein One of the vascular bundles or ribs which form the branching framework of conductive and supportive tissue in a leaf, flower or fruit.

velamen The water-absorbing tissue on the outside of an epiphyte's roots.

venation The arrangement of veins usually on a leaf.

vermiculite A micaceous, lightweight substance used in some soilless mixtures and to top dress seeds.

vernalisation Exposure to weeks of cold temperatures.

verticillium Soilborne fungal disease

viability Capacity to germinate.

vigour Strong, healthy growth.

viridescence The process by which variegated leaves revert to green.

virys A disease organism.

viviparous Bearing plantlets on the leaves, stems or flowers.

volunteer A plant which grows from self-sown seed.

Wardian case An airtight enclosed glass case to transport plants over great distances.

water garden Any ornamental container containing water and aquatic plants.

weed An undesirable plant.

weeping Drooping branches.

weevil Beetle pests which feed on leaves leaving notches, larvae feed on roots causing death. Active at night.

wetting agent A soap-like compound added to liquid to increase its wetting properties.

whip A young, unbranched shoot of a woody plant, the first year's growth from a graft or bud.

whitefly A tiny, mothlike insect or flowers of a plant. which feeds upon sap.

whorl A group of three or more leaves or shoots which emerge from a single node.

wildflower A plant, usually native, which grows wild in a region.

wilt A plant disease caused by bacteria or fungi.

wind-pollinated Pollen carried by the wind.

windbreak One or more rows of closely spaced trees or hedges positioned to shelter plants against the force of the wind.

windfall Ripe or near-ripe fruit which falls to the ground.

window box An outdoor container for windows and ledges.

wing A thin, flat extension found at the margin of a seed or leafstalk, or along a stem.

wireworm A shiny grub which feeds on many vegetable crops and gladiolus corms.

wood The secondary xylem or tough inner core of a tree, shrub or perennial vine.

woody perennial A plant which lives more than a year, has hard rather than fleshy stems and bears buds which survive above the ground in winter.

woody stemmed A woody, fibrous stem.

woolly adelgid A mealy-bug which attacks hemlock trees.

wort An Old English name for plant, occurs in many common names.

x The sign used to denote a hybrid plant derived from the crossing of two or more botanically distinct plants.

xeriscape A water-conserving landscape.

xylem The water-conducting tissue of plants.

Zen garden A minimalist style of Japanese gardening.

zygomorphic Describes an irregular flower with bilateral symmetry.